Modern Jewish Thinkers:
From Mendelssohn to Rosenzweig

Emunot: Jewish Philosophy and Kabbalah

ACADEMIC
STUDIES
PRESS

Modern Jewish Thinkers:
From Mendelssohn to Rosenzweig

Gershon Greenberg

Academic Studies Press

2011

Library of Congress Cataloging-in-Publication Data

Greenberg, Gershon.
 Modern Jewish thinkers : from Mendelssohn to Rosenzweig / Gershon
Greenberg.
     p. cm. -- (Emunot : Jewish philosophy and Kabbalah)
 Includes bibliographical references and index.
 ISBN 978-1-936235-31-5 (hardback) -- ISBN 978-1-936235-46-9 (pbk.) 1.
Jewish philosophy. I. Title.
 B5800.G74 2011
 181'.06--dc22
                        2010054450

Cover: *Lavater and Lessing visit Moses Mendelssohn*. Painting by Moritz Daniel Oppenheim, 1856. The Magnes Collection of Jewish Art and Life.

Layout by Adell Medovoy

Published by Academic Studies Press in 2011
28 Montfern Avenue
Brighton, MA 02135, USA
press@academicstudiespress.com
www.academicstudiespress.com

In loving memory of my father
Morris Greenberg
1897 - 1969

The most insightful and foresightful, generous and warm human being I have known. His life-long affection for Jewish religious thought is ever-present in my mind and heart.

TABLE OF CONTENTS

[Quantity]; [Note on Time, Space and Matter]; [Discrete and Continuous Quantity]; [Mathematics and Geometry]; [Numerical Quantity]; [Logic, Nature and Spirit]; [Finite and Infinite]

PREFACE

This volume proposes to reshape the way in which Jewish thinkers of the modern era have been studied in the English-speaking world. It covers the period from the emancipation of around 1800 to the interwar years of the twentieth century, offering an incentive to correct existing scholarship by providing English translations for the first time (excepting Mendelssohn and Rosenzweig) of texts which are often referred to but rarely read. The book is structured around the five points of departure which emerged from the uncharted territory of Jewish life and culture that opened up following societal changes at the end of the eighteenth and beginning of the nineteenth centuries. Lengthy portions of the texts are translated here, to enable the reader to immerse him- or herself in the various authors' content and style. The volume does not include texts of the major, well-known thinkers from the interwar period and following, as these are readily available in English. They also require a volume of their own.

After an introductory statement about the emancipation and its aftermath with regard to Jewish thought, I proceed in terms of five rubrics: dialectical truth, intellection and developing consciousness; revelation; history; and universal morality. There are individual introductions to each respective text, which describe the life and thought of the author and the relationship of the text to the respective rubric.

Acknowledgment

This work was conceived years ago, during a chance encounter with Emil Fackenheim in the Old City of Jerusalem and a subsequent drive together from Hanover, New Hampshire to Burlington, Vermont; and then after discussions with Neal Kozodoy in New York. The intention has been both to bring to light the world of nineteenth-century European Jewish thought, which had been eclipsed by historical events, and to provide a needed impetus to the scholarship and teaching of the inclusive history of modern Jewish thought by translating lengthy and substantial texts into English. As I selected and translated the materials it became clear that in order to reflect their proper place in the history of Jewish thought, I needed to revise the classical portrayals of that history.

My teacher Eugen Kullmann, the greatest historian of western religious thought that I have known and will ever know, opened the window to European Jewish thought for me. He also provided essential insights and corrections for my translations of the Hebrew texts included in this volume. Jacob Taubes opened the window further. The intellectual community in Israel has been a lifeline for my scholarship. I am grateful to my students at Hebrew, Tel Aviv, Bar-Ilan, and Haifa universities for bringing life to my research. My teachers and colleagues in Israel have nourished my very scholarly existence over the years. First and foremost, Eliezer Schweid. Also Nathan Rotenstreich, Avi Ravitzky, Yosef Ben-Shelomoh, Moshe Davis, Dan Michman, Dov Schwartz, Ya'akov Dekel, and Uriel Barak. I finalized the work in the conducive atmosphere of the Institute for Advanced Studies at Hebrew University. In America, Paul Mendes-Flohr and David Sorkin provided impetus, and Barbara Ellen Galli provided inspiration, at crucial moments of the process.

The Hebraica Section at the Library of Congress has been my scholarly home in Washington, D.C. My ever-faithful and reliable secretary Debbie Flores did the typing, and Michal Michelson the copy editing; I am grateful to both. Most appropriately, it was Raphael Jospe, a scholar instilled with the spirit of Fackenheim's world, who shepherded the work into publication.

Lastly (and first of all), I have been blessed throughout the arduous process of this work, which experienced no small number of setbacks, with the presence in my soul of my beloved wife Erika and our son Ariel Moisheleh.

Gershon Greenberg

0. INTRODUCTION

0.1. THE OPENING OF UNCHARTED TERRITORY

Important changes took place at the end of the eighteenth and beginning of the nineteenth century, both within Jewish society and outside it. A new environment was created which provided a receptive context in which new Jewish thought could emerge. A territory opened up in a neutral space between the autonomous, Halakhically-structured Jewish society which had existed until then and the Christian world, in which new streams of thought developed. As the territory was unsettled and undefined, *de novo* thinking and pluralistic development were possible.

0.1.1. Changes From The Outside

The emergence of national entities in Western Europe, a phenomenon traceable to the after-effects of the Thirty Years War (1618-1648), occurred in tandem with the deconstruction of the Jewish community (*Kehillah*). The Jewish community had previously governed its own affairs according to *Halakhah*, the ideological premises of which provided a common body of knowledge and values, along with societal cohesion and identity. The newly-emergent national entities encroached upon that community, extracting judicial and civil function from the Halakhic framework and unsettling its autonomous character. From the perspective of the Jewish community, this deconstruction meant dispersal in terms of economic life, along geographic and demographic lines, and by societal affiliation. It also meant the beginning of the acquisition of equal rights with other segments of the population, and absorption into the national entity. In Germany, this emancipation began with Napoleon's dismantling the political framework of the Holy Roman Empire in Central Europe, and his reorganizing of the German states (1806). In France, Napoleon convened an Assembly of Notables (1806). While intended to rectify the "unwise generosity" of granting equal rights to Jews that had occurred in 1790-1791, the Assembly ultimately provided the means by which Halakhic ideology and the social cohesiveness resulting from it were reconciled with centralized, secular French national authority.[1]

The historian Yehezkel Kaufmann holds that assimilation (or absorption) associated with emancipation was inner-driven and that it was already underway before the historic period of emancipation began. As the process unfolded, assimilation would also be generated by emancipation. In fact, the desire to unify Jewish society with elements of the surrounding culture reached a new level at the end of the eighteenth century. While diaspora Jewry had always been influenced within itself by foreign culture, Kaufmann wrote, something inevitable for any exiled people, in this instance Jews wanted to participate together with non-Jews in the same society and identify points of unity with the outside world. For example, for many Jews redemption did not mean ingathering in the Land of Israel, but settling into their respective lands of exile and joining together with those of the formerly other society; the opportunity to do so was now a welcome prospect available to them.[2] Ben Zion Dinur and Eliezer Schweid qualify Kaufmann's analysis, pointing out that some of those who sought emancipation and equal rights resisted social togetherness or compromising the distinctiveness of the Jewish community.[3]

Whatever the cause-effect sequence, David Sorkin wrote, emancipation and assimilation involved "reciprocally dependent processes," representing "inseparable halves of a *quid pro quo*, the two clauses of a complex contract.... [E]mancipation was what the states were to grant, assimilation what the Jews were to give in return." An ideology of emancipation existed, Sorkin explains, to guide the change from autonomous to non-autonomous status. The 1800 years of Jewish ex-

---

1   On this sequence of events see Jacob Katz, *Tradition and Crisis* (Glencoe: Free Press, 1961): 247; Gerson D. Cohen, "German Jewry as a Mirror of Modernity," *Leo Baeck Institute Yearbook* 20 (1975): ix-xxxi; and David Sorkin, *Transformation of German Jewry, 1780-1840* (Detroit: Wayne State University Press, 1987), 41-62, 79-80. See further Katz, "The Term 'Jewish Emancipation': Its Origin and Historical Impact," in *Studies in Nineteenth Century Jewish Intellectual History*, ed. Alexander Altmann (Cambridge: Harvard University Press, 1964), 1-26; and *Jewish Emancipation and Self-Emancipation* (Philadelphia: Jewish Publication Society, 1986); and Caesar Seligmann, *Geshichte der jüdischen Reformbewegung: Von Mendelssohn bis zur Gegenwart* (FaM: J. Kauffmann Verlag, 1922).

2   Yehezkel Kaufmann, "Hitmotetut Ha'yahas Ha'yeshenah," in *Golah Ve'nekhar*, vol. 2, book 1 (Tel Aviv: 1960/61),1-2.

3   Eliezer Schweid, *Toledot Ha'hagut Ha'yehudit Be'et Ha'hadashah: Ha'meah Ha'tesha Esrei* (Erets Yisrael: Ha'kibuts Ha'meuhad, 1978), 12.

istence prior to emancipation were essentially years of suffering and persecution. The new absolute state provided an opportunity to correct the deformities of Jews and Judaism that had resulted from previous historical circumstances by applying the enlightenment ideal of universal humanity to the political arena. Simultaneously, Jewish culture was to exemplify moral individualism and tolerance through its inclusion in the broader culture. In exchange for the inalienable right for the Jewish people to perfect itself according to its own tradition and to concurrently acquire civil rights, Judaism's culture and ideas were to be regenerated through occupational restructuring, religious return, and moral rehabilitation. In exchange for emancipation, Jews were to contribute to the welfare of the whole.[4]

0.1.2. Changes From Within

Meanwhile, changes were independently underway within the Jewish religion itself. The movement known as "*Musar*" sought to reverse a perceived intellectual decay that had in its adherents' view been caused by casuistic Talmudism among Ashkenazi Jews; it did so by instilling moralistic values, piety, and fear of God into the Halakhic world. The Jewish enlightenment movement (*Haskalah*) sought to replace perceived prejudice and superstition with ethical ideas. Moses Mendelssohn, for example, spoke of a "poisoning breath of hypocrisy and superstition," emanating from this world and complained that there were individuals, acquainted or half-acquainted with rabbinic literature, who were disseminating misconceptions drawn from old volumes that were outside the ken of any rational Jew.[5] Shemuel Feiner describes how the perceived failings of Ashkenazi rabbinical culture aroused *Maskilim* (advocates of *Haskalah*) to strive for rationalism, humanism, and science in their writings so as to counteract ignorance, religious enthusiasm, and kabbalistic fantasies. The *Maskilim* emphasized moral rehabilitation and *Bildung*—the harmony of culture and innate individual character and development which formed the educational ideal of the German enlightenment. They envisioned the Jew as a rational and moral

---

4   Sorkin, "Emancipation and Assimilation—Two Concepts and Their Application to German-Jewish History," *LBIY* 35 (1990): 18; and *Transformation of German Jewry*, 86-99.
5   Moses Mendelssohn, *Gesammelte Schriften: Jubiläumsausgabe*, vol. 4 (Stuttgart: F. Frommann), 9-10.

being, a citizen who placed his skills at the disposal of society and the state.[6] Jacob Katz wrote that the *Maskilim* sought to expose Jews to moral ideas through participation in the ongoing social and cultural integration that was transferring the community's social goals to a non-Jewish *milieu*.[7]

These externally and internally generated transformations opened up a new social space, boundaried by the Christian society of the absolute state on one end, and the traditional Jewish society undergoing change on the other. In it, Jews integrated into the general culture and gained equal rights, non-Jewish political attitudes were refashioned, Jews redefined themselves, and the idea of "Jewish character" underwent restructuring and re-education. The space had a probationary air, however, and Jews suffered setbacks in achieving these goals. Following the 1815 Congress of Vienna, Jews lost improvements in their political status that had been made under the German confederation (1780-1815). Additionally, along with the economic advances in the Prussian north, avenues of religious and educational regeneration were closed off—one restriction was that Jews were not allowed to teach at universities. In the south, while there were reforms in education and religious affairs that increased the number of equal rights that Jews enjoyed in these realms, further restrictions were imposed on places of residence and marriage.[8] Katz wrote that an overarching disjunction existed between realized political emancipation and unrealized social and cultural emancipation. From the non-Jewish side, nationalists and romanticists resisted social and cultural emancipation. From the Jewish, there was resistance to inter-marriage, certain professions, and to the process of the dissolution of the Jewish community as such.[9]

There was also, however, an atmosphere of hope. In Germany, the Jewish ideologues sought the creation of a coherent German-Jewish culture, which was in keeping with the ideal of *Bildung* and was ground-

---

6   Shemuel Feiner, *The Jewish Enlightenment* (Philadelphia: University of Pennsylvania, 2002), 80, 92. Sorkin identifies *Bildung* as a process of self-development on the basis of a form that was an inherent part of the individual, the development of which was innate. *Transformation of German Jewry*, 15.

7   Katz, *Tradition and Crisis*, 251.

8   Sorkin, *Transformation of German Jewry*, 86-99.

9   Katz, "Profile of Emancipated Jewry," in *Out of the Ghetto: The Social Background of Jewish Emancipation, 1770-1870* (Syracuse: Syracuse University Press, 1973), 191-219

ed in rationalism. Integration into an age of toleration was the goal; love of fellow man and universal morality did not have to preclude particularized forms of collective life with their own specific character and moral model.[10] Katz wrote that a neutral social *milieu* began to emerge in Germany at this time. In it, rationalists of different religious backgrounds formulated moral positions addressing universal values. Jews, who were moving away from their community, with its separate historical existence, and from their own distinct nationalistic identity, which included yearning for homeland, tradition, and the Yiddish and Hebrew languages, encountered non-Jews similarly moving away from identification with distinctive elements of Christianity. The two groups shared a common commitment to rationality, utilitarian ethics, and individuality. From rational law, they learned together that every person had the right to unlimited independence. From rationalist philosophy, they ascertained that the individual was authorized to act on the basis of reason alone, and to remove restraints which were imposed by cultural and religious tradition. From utilitarian ethics, they espoused the correlation between the good and the useful.[11]

0.2. *WISSENSCHAFT* AND HISTORICISM

The corridor which opened up between the formerly demarcated areas of Jewish and non-Jewish societies provided fertile ground for both the scientific study of Judaism (*Wissenschaft des Judentums*) and Jewish thought. Ismar Elbogen distinguishes pre-emancipation Judaic-centered learning, which was a self-sufficient entity divorced from the rest of the world, from post-emancipation *Wissenschaft*, which bridged traditional polity with the surrounding environment and explored connections and interactions between Jewish and non-Jewish cultures. Pre-emancipation learning was tied to the belief in an inviolable tradition, with a metaphysical basis and grounded upon authoritative representatives. *Wissenschaft*, on the other hand, subjected Jewish learning to free and neutral critical analysis; to objective classification and evaluation; and to universal scholarly discourse and conceptual standards.[12] While *Wissenschaft* was itself enabled by emancipation, it also

---

10   Sorkin, *Transformation of German Jewry*, 94-104.
11   Katz, "The Emergence of the Neutral Society," in *Tradition and Crisis*, 245-259.
12   Ismar Elbogen, "A Century of *Wissenschaft des Judentums*," in *Studies in Jewish Thought:*

in its turn enhanced the emancipation process. Its proponents shed light on Jewish history and literature, changing the image of the Jews in ways which offered support for their new social status. For example, through the study of ancient texts in their originally pure form, Leopold Zunz (1794-1866) hoped to erode prejudices about Jewish antiquity. By separating what he deemed to be essence out of evanescence in Israel's legacy, he aspired to identify a form of Judaism that could be aligned with emancipation.[13]

The first proponents of *Wissenschaft* were historians. According to Karl Löwith, by the mid-nineteenth century, Christian theology had become the history of dogma, economics had been replaced by naturalistic philosophy of history, philosophy had changed into the history of philosophy, and biology had become the Darwinian history of evolution. Overall, the permanent, absolute, and universal truths of an earlier era, subjected to time and the historical process, were perceived in a manner aligned with the *Zeitgeist* of the times.[14] Judaism, according to Nahum N. Glatzer, saw the development of "lower historicism," which probed the roots of religious observance as a way to reform synagogue ritual, and "higher historicism," which looked for points of contact between the people of Israel and the world over the generations, in order to clarify the nature of contemporary integration.[15] Nathan Rotenstreich points to the dialectical character of the *Wissenschaft*-historicism relationship: *Wissenschaft* cultivated historical consciousness, while historical consciousness nourished *Wissenschaft*.[16] Concerning the emancipation-historicism tie, Ismar Schorsch observes that historians sought to resolve dilemmas of Jewish identity created by the emancipation process by means of a

---

An Anthology of German Jewish Scholarship, ed. Alfred Jospe (Detroit: Wayne State, 1981), 26-37.

13 Sorkin, *Transformation of German Jewry*, 134-136; Ismar Schorsch, "The Emergence of Historical Consciousness," *LBIY*: 416; Schorsch, "Ideology and History in the Age of Emancipation," in Heinrich Graetz, *The Structure of Jewish History and Other Essays*, ed. Schorsch (New York: Jewish Theological Seminary of America, 1955), 9-40.

14 Karl Löwith, "Die Dynamik der Geschichte und Historicismus," *Eranos Jahrbuch*, vol. 21 (1952): 229-230.

15 Nahum N. Glatzer, "The Beginnings of Modern Jewish Studies," in *Studies in Nineteenth Century Jewish Intellectual History*, ed. Alexander Altmann (Cambridge: Harvard University Press, 1964), 27-46.

16 Nathan Rotenstreich, "Kelaster Panim," in *Ha'mahshavah Ha'yehudit Be'et Ha'hadashah* (Tel Aviv: Am Oved, 1966), 9-16.

proper reading of the past, and by drawing from historical documenta-
tion to align Judaism with its new legal status.[17] There were three salient
historical approaches taken by scholars. That of Isaak Marcus Jost focused on positive interrelations between respective national surround-
ings in order to justify present governmental openness to Jews living
under emancipation, and that represented by Abraham Geiger focused
on the inner history of Israel's unique religious genius, which needed to
be preserved amid current changes. The existence of this quality meant
that no particular phase of Israel's religious development was binding
on any other—such that Israel was naturally open to the new stage of
emancipation. The third, that represented by Heinrich Graetz, brought
these two approaches together. Considered from without, Israel's history
of interrelations was one of suffering. Considered from within, the national soul had developed a rich religious culture. Taken together, the
two meant that Israel's national self-identity was demonstrably strong
enough to persist amid the great transition of the present.[18]

0.3. JEWISH THOUGHT

The mediating space of this historical era gave rise to new philosophical
thought. With the Halakhists' hold on the community loosened, Judaism fell into the hands of the historians. In turn, the discipline of history
facilitated self-conscious reflection about religious belief as well as identification and systematizing by philosophers (see Katz).[19] The sources of
ancient Judaism, which the historians converted into western categories in order to advance emancipation ideology, eased the way towards
the philosophical discussion of doctrine. The availability of objective
standards for study (*Wissenschaft*) meant that the divisive issue of the
relationship between philosophy and theology could now be grappled
with.[20] The philosophical past itself belonged to the sources that *Wis-*

---

17   Ismar Schorsch, "Ideology and History in the Age of Emancipation," in Graetz, 1-62.
18   Michael A. Meyer, "The Emergence of Modern Historiography Among Jewish *Maskilim*,"
in *Essays in Jewish Historiography*, ed. Ada Rapoport-Alpert (Atlanta: Scholars Press, 1991),
160-175. On this topic, see also Shemuel Feiner, *Haskalah and History: The Emergence of a
Modern Jewish Historical Consciousness* (Oxford: Littman Library, 2002).
19   Katz, "Profile of Emancipated Jewry," in *Out of the Ghetto*, 212; "Jewry and Judaism in
the Nineteenth Century," in *Jewish Emancipation and Self-Emancipation*, 11, 13-14.
20   Glatzer, "The Beginning of Modern Jewish Studies," in *Studies in Nineteenth Century
Jewish Intellectual History* (Cambridge, MA: Harvard University Press, 1964), 27-45. Ismar
Schorsch, "Historical Consciousness in Modern Judaism," *LBIY* 28 (1983): 413-38.

senschaft had made available to historical consciousness—notably that of medieval Jewish philosophy.[21]

0.3.1. Beyond the Autonomous Community

The new philosophical thought differed radically from its predecessor. In the autonomous Jewish community, the realia of Jewish life (laws, education, language, and social fabric) were aligned to belief and thought, so much so that tangible activities of daily life and religious consciousness evoked one another as interchanging concentric circles. When this autonomous structure was dismantled, consciousness and realia gravitated towards two separate spheres (in Christianity, ecclesiastical values remained instilled in national entities at this time). In the newly emancipated Jewish world, consciousness took its perspective from points outside the permitted sphere once ruled exclusively by the Halakhic community. At the same time, many of the realia (in-group marriage, occupations, trans-national Jewish ties) remained behind an invisible line that still separated the former autonomous structure from the non-Jewish world. Pursuit of philosophy during this period functioned as a way of objectifying the realia by means of religious consciousness.

Diverse historians attribute the emergence of the Jewish philosophical texts of the period to efforts to resolve the bifurcation between the two arenas. Max Wiener wrote that modern Jewish philosophical thought developed out of a midpoint between the challenge of absorbing the outside culture and the desire to hold fast to the ancestral heritage of Israel.[22] Julius Guttmann locates emerging Jewish thought between the unchanging essence of Judaism on the one side, and historical process and changing traditions on the other.[23] Jacob Katz, in a related vein, wrote that the new philosophy was born at the interstice between plunging into the outside world and endeavoring to remain part of a distinctive entity; between the hope of amalgamating with surrounding nations and the desire to defend three thousand years of Jewish history; and finally, between the turmoil of transition and the establishment of

---

21   See Amos Funkenstein, *Perceptions of Jewish History* (Berkeley: University of California Press, 1993), 234-235.
22   Max Wiener, "Moses Mendelssohn and the Religious Forms of Judaism in the Nineteenth Century," in *Studies in Jewish Thought* (Detroit: Wayne State, 1981), 404-416.
23   Julius Guttmann, "Die Idee der religiösen Gemeinschaft im Judentum," in *Zum 60 jährigen Bestehen der Hochschule für die Wissenschaft des Judentums in Berlin* (Berlin, 1932).

traditional ideological moorings so as to maintain the community.[24] Michael A. Meyer speaks of the philosophical reflections as an attempt to maintain the old faith among cultured Jews by making that faith intellectually viable.[25]

The mediating area gave rise to a series of essential questions: What was the relationship between the old Judaism of the autonomous community and its remnants, and the new Judaism which was in the process of integration into formerly non-Jewish territory? How could the formerly particularized society be reconciled to a society of shared, universal values? In what way did traditionalism and the liberalism of modern society correlate? What was the connection between faith and rationalism; a-historical values and historical development; statutory religion and morality-in-itself? Finally, what were Judaism's intrinsic values and historical truths, and what would be the meaning of all this for the future?

0.3.2. De Novo *Points of Departure*

Emerging philosophical thought struck roots in the unsettled ground between the formerly autonomous Jewish community and the non-Jewish world. It created starting points, new driving concepts, to cope with the questions which emerged from the new territory. Within the autonomous community, the concentric spheres of thought and the realia were grounded in, and centered around, *Torah*-revelation. When thought and realia separated, however, *Torah*-revelation lost its centrality. Left to their own resources, some thinkers found a basis by focusing on a particular principle, while others found it in a focal element of the emancipation-*Haskalah* universe. Thus, Mendelssohn, Reggio, and Krokhmal rooted themselves in the principle of dialectical logic, and applied it to revelation and philosophical reason. Maimon, Formstecher, and Samuel Hirsch (who also relied on the principle of active religiosity) were committed to rationalism in terms of intellection and developing consciousness. Steinheim and Rosenzweig grounded their systems in revelation, while Ascher and Einhorn based their systems

---

24   Katz, "Profile of Emancipated Jewry," in *Out of the Ghetto*, 208.
25   Meyer, "Reform Jewish Thinkers and Their German Intellectual Context," in *The Jewish Response to German Culture*, eds. Jehuda Reinharz and Walter Schatzberg (Hanover and London: University Press of New England, 1985), 64-84.

on historical events (Einhorn also relied on the principle of central-ization). Finally, Luzzatto, Lazarus, and Cohen lay their foundation in universal morality. The *de novo*, pluralistic situation, however, meant there would be little interaction between one thinker and another. Max Wiener observes that the respective systems had little influence on one another, and that they were like "erratically dispersed, unconnected blocks, representing only the last stage of the process by which external ideas affected Jewish thought."[26]

0.3.3. Shared Characteristics

Despite this pluralism, the emerging sets of departure points and the respective bodies of thought or systems which developed around them were all disposed towards issues of Jewish identity, religious relativ-ism, and historicity. With individual ties to the community disintegrat-ing, the philosophers stepped up to define and promote consciousness of Jewish identity. Upon the dissolution of the autonomous commu-nity and dispersal into the wider world, tradition no longer provided ideological mooring. Was there still such a thing as Jewish identity? Should there be, or should Judaism accept the fact that the "river" it had always been had now run into the "sea"?[27] In the medieval period, Rotenstreich observes, encounters with Christianity and Islam induced Jewish thinkers to define the absolute content of Judaism. In the mod-ern period, there was a question as to whether Judaism, now seen as belonging to historical process, had any absolute value at all. It was left to the philosophers to determine whether in fact there existed any such enduring identity.[28] With regard to Germany in particular, the context for Jewish identity had shifted from the static categories of Jew *vis-à-vis* German, or Jew *vis-à-vis* Christian, to the context of the German-Jewish subculture, which was in flux.[29] The de-ghettoization of Juda-ism, both geographically and intellectually, reopened the fundamental question of Jewish identity.[30]

---

26   Wiener, "Moses Mendelssohn and the Religious Form of Judaism in the Nineteenth Century," in *Studies in Jewish Thought*, 405-416.

27   Katz, "Profile of Emancipated Jewry," in *Out of the Ghetto*, 191-222.

28   Rotenstreich, "Kelaster Panim," in *Ha'mahshavah Ha'yehudit Be'et Ha'hadashah* (Tel Aviv: Am Oved, 1966), 9-16.

29   Sorkin, "Introduction," in *Transformation of German Jewry*, 6.

30   Meyer, "Reform Jewish Thinkers and Their German Intellectual Context."

A second common trait of the era's thought was that of relativism. According to Guttmann, *Wissenschaft*'s rational assertions and theories of knowledge eclipsed the metaphysical bases for the philosophy of religion that had been accepted by medieval Jewish philosophers. With *Wissenschaft*, the departure point for philosophical religious deliberation shifted from a cosmically structured absolute reality that was independent of human consciousness into (non-absolute) human consciousness itself. Philosophical deliberation moved from probing the *Vorstellungen* (representative images) and *Lehre* (teachings) of historical Judaism as the one true and absolute religion, to probing Judaism's function within universal religious consciousness—and Judaism's *Vorstellungen* as they related to universal postulates. For example, while medieval Jewish philosophers had interpreted *Torah*'s philosophical meaning within the boundaries of *Torah*'s absolute truth, the modern thinker Hermann Cohen drew the absolute reality of truth to the boundaries of human consciousness. Even the most radical of the medieval Jewish philosophers had accepted revelational authority as a self-evident presupposition; modern philosophers did not.[31] No single religion was absolute, and none of them exhausted all of human consciousness. For modern thinkers, all religions were valid modes of the human consciousness which shaped religion. For the medieval mind only one religion, whether Judaism, Christianity, or Islam, could be metaphysically true—the other two were not. As Judaism encountered other religions in the modern world, religious thinkers drew comparisons—and moved Judaism from an absolute to a relative status.[32]

Philosophical thought emerged within the contexts of *Wissenschaft* and historicism. Accordingly, the respective systems recognized the reality and significance of historical process. Nineteenth-century thinkers did not regard Jewish law and doctrine as unique or outside histori-

---

31   Guttmann, *Religion und Wissenschaft im mittelalterlichen und in modernen Denken* (Berlin: Philo, 1923): 63-64, 72; *Die Philosophie des Judentums*, 259, 346. Translated as *Philosophies of Judaism: The History of Jewish Philosophy from Biblical Times to Franz Rosenzweig*, introduction by R. J. Zwi Werblowsky, translation by David W. Silverman (New York: Holt, Rinehart and Winston, 1964): 244-45, 353). See also Leo Strauss, "The Conflict of Ancients and Moderns and the Philosophy of Judaism: Comments on Julius Guttmann's *Philosophies of Judaism*," in Strauss, *Philosophy and Law: Essays Toward the Understanding of Maimonides and His Predecessors*, trans. Fred Baumann (Philadelphia: JPS, 1987), 33-40.

32   Rotenstreich, "Kelaster Panim," in *Ha'mahshavah Ha'yehudit*, 9-16.

cal time, but rather as subject to historical development.[33] Whereas medieval philosophical systems had separated beliefs and opinions out of the historical process as fixed, definitive doctrines, the Judaism of *Wissenschaft*-committed philosophers belonged to history. While religion for the former had a-temporal grounding, post-emancipation thinkers situated religion in humanity, which functioned according to historical time. These thinkers probed the relationship between Judaism's permanent essence and the changes it had undergone in history. They asked whether Judaism should accept its relative position in world history or annul itself; whether Judaism should adopt universal standards of measurement or remove itself from history's stage. If Judaism was a historical phenomenon, did it have an end as well as a beginning? Had it actualized its potential, and become consequently irrelevant to current historical reality?[34] Schweid contrasts medieval thinkers, for whom the generations collapsed into a single, trans-historical entity, with modern thinkers, for whom past divided off from the present, and who evaluated the past according to the present. While there had been historicist strains before (e.g., Yehudah Halevi), modern historicism was a matter of objective critical analysis—and not of subjective, trusting self-testimony.[35] Schorsch observes that in the modern period, time was infused into Jewish consciousness, such that what had been eternal verities now belonged to the realm of change.[36]

0.4. BARUKH SPINOZA (1632-1677): FORERUNNER

The development of Jewish philosophical thought in the wake of the emancipation was anticipated in several ways by Barukh Spinoza. Spinoza was born into a family of Portuguese *Anusim* (forced converts) who had returned to Judaism. As portrayed by Schweid, when some converts returned they found refuge in Halakhic structures; others, having been liberated from the oppressiveness of the Catholic church, resisted Halakhic authority. Spinoza positioned himself between the *Kehillah* (with

---

33   Katz, "Jewry and Judaism in the Nineteenth Century," in *Jewish Emancipation and Self-Emancipation*, 13.

34   Rotenstreich, "Kelaster Panim," in *Ha'mahshavah Ha'yehudit*, 9-16.

35   Schweid, *Toledot Ha'hagut Ha'yehudit Be'et Ha'hadashah: Ha'meah Ha'tesha Esrei* (Erets Yisrael: Ha'kibuts Ha'meuhad, 1978), 19-20.

36   Schorsch, "The Emergence of Historical Consciousness in Modern Judaism," *LBIY* 27 (1983): 413-438.

its rabbinic walls) and the Christian church, in the public arena of universal modern culture, grounding himself in philosophy and identifying himself as an individual state-citizen. His thought did not fall under the category of the history of Jewish philosophy—except for the very fact that his position in the universal area was itself a position representative of Jewish thought, with its internalized humanistic culture and enlightenment principles. Schweid evokes the metaphor of a single photograph—where other Jewish thinkers made up the positive to Spinoza's negative.

Spinoza's position as forerunner is also illumined by comparing him with Moses Ben Maimon (Rambam). For Rambam, God was outside man. Human understanding was limited to creation, and for the intellect to reach God it had to include revelation and faith. For Spinoza, God was of nature, through which the human intellect could understand God. These two thinkers agreed that the human purpose was to acquire complete knowledge of the truth, and that this itself was intellectual love of God, who in essence was eternal truth. For Rambam, this knowledge was found in the *Torah*, which synthesized with philosophy; faith and knowledge, *Torah* and intellect were one and the same. For Spinoza, truth lay in philosophy; knowing eternal truths replaced divine self-revelation. Indeed, while prophetic revelation taught moral obedience, it was not philosophical truth, and the biblical text, which was addressed to an enslaved and isolated people, was not applicable to individuals in a free society.

As a pure philosopher and free individual citizen of a universalistic environment, Spinoza anticipated the perspective of the post-emancipation modern Jewish philosophical thinker. He turned away from the church or *Kehillah* as state, and to a secular, democratic state which cultivated individualistic free thought. When it came to a choice between the *Torah*-grounded *Kehillah* and non-Jewish culture with a Christian universalist ingredient, he chose the latter. From his trans-religious perspective of philosophical truth, he viewed Judaism and Christianity as equally religious. He also related to Judaism on historical terms. The *Torah* of Moses was a product of, and appropriate to, its time, and as such was not appropriate to the present. As post-emancipation thinkers would divide between the *Kehillah* of the past and the emancipated present, and confront the new realities with historical consciousness, Spinoza divided the *Kehillah* off from his present secular context; between the individual as an organic part of the *Kehillah* who stood before God and depended upon Him and the individual of the present, part of an all-inclusive Nature that was identified with the infinite God.[37]

0.5. SCHOLARSHIP ON MODERN JEWISH PHILOSOPHICAL THOUGHT

The study of the history of Jewish philosophical thought in modern times began with Simon Bernfeld in 1897, continued within the disciplines of Hebrew literature (Joseph Klausner and Yeruham Fishel Lachover) as a subject for intellectual history and the history of philosophy, and reached a peak in the 1930s with Max Wiener, Julius Guttmann, Hans-Joachim Schoeps, Alfred Lewkowitz, and Leo Strauss in Germany, and Samuel Hugo Bergman in Palestine. Yitshak Heinemann and Nathan Rotenstreich published their work in the 1940s, Jacob Agus did so in 1954; the work of Arthur A. Cohen, Ya'akov Fleischmann, and Mosheh Schwarcz appeared in the 1960s and that of Emil Fackenheim and Eliezer Schweid in the 1970s.[38]

---

37 Schweid, "Spinoza's and Mendelssohn's Contributions to the Modern Approach to the Bible," in *The Philosophy of the Bible: As Foundation of Jewish Culture*, trans. Leonard Levin (Boston: Academic Studies Press, 2008), 7-8; "Ha'etgar Ha'iyuni Shel Ha'et He'hadashah: Haguto Shel Barukh Shpinoza Be'yahasah Le'yahadut," in *Toledot Ha'hagut Ha'yehudit Be'et Ha'hadashah: Ha'meah Ha'tesha Esrei* (Erets Yisrael: Ha'kibuts Ha'me'uhad, 1978), 28-62; "Shpinoza Veha'yahadut," in *Ha'yehudi Ha'boded Veha'yahadut* (Tel Aviv: Am Oved, 1974): 115-153.

38 Simon Bernfeld, *Da'at Elohim* (Warsaw: Schuldberg, 1897), Joseph Klausner, *Toledot Ha'sifrut Ha'ivrit Ha'hadashah* (Jerusalem: Ha'shiloah, 1930-1950); Yeruham Fishel Lachover, *Toledot Ha'sifrut Ha'ivrit Ha'hadashah* (Tel Aviv: Devir, 1928-1931); Wiener, *Jüdische Religion im Zeitalter der Emanzipation* (Berlin: Philo, 1933); Julius Guttmann, *Die Philosophie des Judentums* (Munich: Reinhardt, 1933) and *Religion und Wissenschaft im mittelalterlichen und in modernen Denken* (Berlin: Philo, 1922); Alfred Lewkowitz, *Das Judentum und die geistigen Strömungen des 19. Jahrhundert* (Breslau: Marcus, 1935); Hans-Joachim Schoeps, *Geschichte der jüdischen Religionsphilosophie in der Neuzeit*, vol. 1 (Berlin: Vortrupp, 1935); Schoeps, *Jüdischer Glaube in diese Zeit* (Berlin: Vortrupp, 1934); Leo Strauss, *Philosophie und Gesetz* (Berlin: Schocken, 1935); Samuel Hugo Bergman, *Hogei Ha'dor* (Jerusalem: Magnes, 1984); Jacob B. Agus, *Guideposts in Modern Judaism: An Analysis of Current Trends in Jewish Thought* (New York: Bloch, 1954); Yitshak Heinemann, *Ta'amei Ha'mitsvot Be'sifrut Yisrael* (Jerusalem: Jewish Agency, 1942); Rotenstreich, *Ha'mahshavah Ha'yehudit Be'et Ha'hadashah* (Tel Aviv: Am Oved, 1945-46), 9-20; Ya'akov Fleischmann, *Be'ayat Ha'natsrut Be'mahshavah Ha'yehudit Mi'mendelson ad Rozentsvayg* (Jerusalem: Magnes, 1964); Mosheh Schwarcz, *Safah, Mitos, Omanut* (Jerusalem: Schocken, 1966); Arthur A. Cohen, *The Natural and Supernatural Jew* (New York: Pantheon, 1962); Eliezer Schweid, *Toledot Ha'hagut Ha'yehudit: Ha'meah Ha'tesha Esrei; Ha'yehudi*

The data which was chosen for analysis varied from historian to historian. Guttmann and Agus focused on dominant personalities. Bernfeld, Wiener, and Schweid explored intellectual and social streams of development and Lewkowitz and Fackenheim probed encounters between Jewish and non-Jewish philosophical thought. Schoeps and Cohen dwelled on central Jewish religious-philosophical ideas; and Heinemann, Fleischmann and Schwarcz considered the way in which central ideas developed historically. Rotenstreich presented the material he researched systematically in terms of religious-philosophical issues.

The Jewish philosophers that these figures selected for analysis varied as well. Nahman Krokhmal, Steinheim, Samuel Hirsch and Salomon Formstecher were treated by all. Francolm, Avraham Krokhmal, Hurwitz, Benamozegh, and Lazarus were treated only by one or two. None of the studies included American Jewish thinkers, such as David Einhorn, Meir Rabinowitz, or Emil Hirsch. Some included nationalistic philosophers while others did not. Guttmann presumed a comprehensive linear development while Heinemann, Rotenstreich and Schweid structured the inquiry according to distinct frameworks of deliberation.[39]

The overall approaches of these thinkers differed. Simon Bernfeld presented religious philosophies as responses to cultural development—with the observation that sometimes a religious philosophy could provide only a morphine-like "cure" for cultural problems and consequently leave the patient even sicker after its effect wore off. The responses to cultural development synthesized *Torah* and intellect (i.e., revelation lent itself to reflection while reflection provided form to the divine word) and developed in linear fashion. Guttmann contrasted modern

---

Ha'boded Veha'yahadut (Tel Aviv: Am Oved, 1974); and Fackenheim, *Encounters Between Judaism and Modern Philosophy* (New York: Schocken, 1973).

On the respective methodologies see Esther Seidel, *Jüdische Philosophie in nichtjüdischer und jüdischer Philosophiegeschichtsschreibung* (FaM: Lang, 1984); and "Jewish Philosophy and Jewish Thought," in *La Storia Della Filosofia Ebraica*, ed. Irene Kajon (Milan: CEDAM, 1993), 509-524.

39   Isaac Ascher Francolm, *Das rationale Judentum* (Breslau: In Commission bei M. Friedländer, 1840); Avraham Krokhmal, *Da'at Elohim Ba'arets* (Lemberg: M. Volf, 1863); Philipp Lazarus Hurwitz, *Torat Hashem Temimah: Religion und Judentum. Vernunft und Glaube in gegenseitiger Beziehung und Beleuchtung* (Berlin: n.p., 1832); Elia Benamozegh, *Dio* (Livorno: Tip. Di F. Vigo, 1877); *Israel et L'humanité* (Paris: A. Michel, 1961); Meir Rabinowitz, *Ha'mahanayim* (New York: Brodi Printing, 1888); and Emil A. Hirsch, in *The Reform Advocate, passim*, published in Chicago.

with pre-modern Jewish philosophical developments: Hellenistic Jewish philosophy was absorbed into the non-Jewish realm and medieval thought absorbed non-Jewish realities into itself while Jewish philosophy developed both from within and outside of Judaism. Rotenstreich aligned philosophical personalities with various aspects of modernity: re-evaluation of medieval culture; assimilation into the Christian world; transition from Jewish culture's absolute status to cultural pluralism; change from the domination of eternal revelation to the historical development of religion; experiencing the impact of communal changes on spiritual imperatives; and moving from abstract thought to social structure as the foundation for spiritual values. Schweid dealt with systematic philosophers as well as with Jewish thinkers who expressed philosophy in a variety of forms—including scientific research, belles lettres, and lyric poetry. He also characterized modern Jewish philosophy as a collective response to foreign ideas rather than the product of internal urges, and he drew a categorical division between Jewish philosophers or thinkers concerned with the essence of Judaism and those concerned with Jewishness and national survival.

As Meyer observes, Rotenstreich, writing during World War II, reflected a new preoccupation with history which would increasingly characterize Jewish theological thought in the years following the war. His approach was thematic, and he endeavored to classify thinkers—those who subordinated religion to ethics (Mendelssohn, Hermann Cohen), those who gave precedence to metaphysics (Samuel Hirsch, Salomon Formstecher, Krokhmal), and those whose grounding was the shattering force of revelation (Steinheim, Rosenzweig). For Schweid, modern Jewish thought was a struggle with problems which were first raised by Spinoza. In contrast to Lewkowitz and Rotenstreich, Schweid de-emphasized Kant, Hegel, and Schelling, and was less interested in abstract theological issues than in reflections upon Jewish existence.[40]

---

40   Meyer, "Recent Historiography on the Jewish Religion," *LBIY* 35 (1996): 3-16.

0.6. GLOSSARY OF TRANSLATED GERMAN TERMS

die Anordnung or die Verordnung = ordinance (*Hoq*)

die Anschauung = perception

aufgehoben = annulled and/or affirmed and/or sublimated; *aufheben* = sublimates and/or affirms and/or negates; *die Aufhebung* = affirmation and/or negation and/or sublimation

der Begriff = concept or notion; *begreifen* = grasp/conceptualize

die Bestimmung = regulation

der Einfall = notion

erkennen = know; *das Erkennen* = knowing or knowledge; *die Erkenntnis* = knowledge or wisdom; *die Erkenntnislehre* = doctrines of knowledge

die Erscheinung = appearance or phenomenon

der Geist = mind/spirit or spirit; *geistigen* = spiritual or intellectual

der Gedanke = idea, thinking, thought

die Gesetzgebung or das Gesetz = legislation or law; *die Gesetzlichkeit* = legality

die Gesinnung = mindset

die Gestalt = shape; *die Gestaltung* = construction

die Glaubenslehre = doctrine of faith/belief; *der Glaube* = faith/belief

der Grund = ground; *der Grundbegriff* = basic concept; *die Grundlehre* = basic doctrine; *der Grundsatz* = principle; *die Grundlage* = premise; *der Grundgedanke* = theme

die Handlung = activity

der Lehrbegriff = doctrines; *der Lehrgehalt* = instructional context; *der Lehrsatz* = teachings; *die Lehrmeinung* = tenet or dogma; *die Lehre* = doctrine

das Prinzip = principle

das Recht = law or legislation

die Satzung or das Grundgesetz = statute or ordinance

das Sein or das Dasein = existence

sittliche or ethische = ethical; *die Sittenlehre* = ethical doctrine; *die Sittlichkeit* = morality; *moralisch* = moral; *die Moralität* = morality; *die Moral* = morals

der Stamm = stock

strenge = absolutely, strictly

der Urheber = originator

die Verfassung = system or system of government
das Verhalten = relationship
die Vorschrift = prescription
die Vorstellung = representative or mental image; representation, imagination
das Wesen = essence or being
die Willkühr = freedom, discretion; *willkührlich* = capriciously
der Widerspruch = antithesis
das Wissen = knowledge, wisdom, awareness; *Weisheit* = wisdom
die Wissenschaft = scientific study or science

Chapter One

THE DIALECTICAL TRUTH

1.0. INTRODUCTORY STATEMENT: BETWEEN REASON AND REVEALED TRUTH: MENDELSSOHN, REGGIO, KROKHMAL

One starting point for the systems of thought which emerged from the uncharted territory between the formerly boundaried areas of Jewish and non-Jewish societies was the dialectical principle, according to which religious and philosophical truths belonged to a synthetic unity. Moses Mendelssohn's dialectical structure surfaced as he retreated from the polarities of modern rationalism and traditional revealed religion to a common center, and so this transformation came about passively rather than actively. Its internal coherence was not articulated, and Mendelssohn did not shed light on the influence that religious natural truths and revealed legislation had upon each other, nor on the interaction between his naturalistic rational God-man correlation and his supernaturistic practices, where the rational connection to God was removed. Reggio, by contrast, arrived at the dialectical principle actively. He faced the mutual centering of reason and revealed faith directly, and identified areas of coincidence between revelational belief and rational cognition, describing how each evoked the other. Krokhmal did so actively as well, by demonstrating the synthesis of faith (thesis) and reason (anti-thesis) in terms of philosophical theology.

1.1. MOSES MENDELSSOHN (1729-1788)

Mendelssohn occupies a special position in the historical development of modern Jewish thought. He was a participant in the process of emancipation, which continued to evolve as Judaism shifted towards the German non-Christian world, and the German non-Christian world gravitated towards Judaism. In his own personality and work, the dynamics of interchange between the formerly boundaried realms of the autonomous Jewish community and that of Christian society converged. Mendelssohn served as the receptacle for the yearnings of those disposed to enter the territory between the two formerly distinct realms, and he became the exemplar for synthesis between German (Christian) *Aufklärung* and Jewish *Haskalah*. He would come to be regarded as both the progenitor of the synthetic process during the decades to follow and a "lightning rod" for criticism of that process. And finally, he would become the ongoing frame and point of reference for post-emancipation Jewish philosophical thinkers.[1]

Mendelssohn's early training, his relationship with Gotthold Ephraim Lessing, the Lavater affair, the publication of *Jerusalem*, and the path of his scholarly work all illustrate the nature of his participation in the process of emancipation.

1.1.1. The Enlightenment Personality

Born in Dessau, Mendelssohn studied *Talmud* with his father and with Dessau's rabbi David Fränkel, and took it upon himself to read Hebrew literature of a cosmopolitan character, a combination typical for the *Haskalah*. His reading included Eldad Ha'dani's travel reports, David Gans' astronomical and geographical treatises, Menahem Graf's *Va'yakhel Mosheh* (a commentary on the *Zohar*'s doctrines of emanation) and Maimonides' *Guide to the Perplexed*.[2] He moved to Berlin in 1743 to study *Talmud* in the yeshiva which Fränkel now headed. In 1754 he met there the great literary figure Gotthold Ephraim Lessing, who helped him

---

1 In an earlier study, I suggested that Mendelssohn held together the divergent urges latent in Jewish thought through the emancipation. His demise catalyzed a "*shevirat ha'kelim*" (shattering of the vessels)-like explosion, and different pieces were picked up and made into cornerstones by his successors. See Gershon Greenberg, "Nineteenth Century Jewish Thought as '*Shevirat Ha'kelim*'," in *Jewish Philosophy and the Academy*, eds. Emil Fackenheim and Raphael Jospe (Madison: Fairleigh Dickenson University Press, 1996), 100-114. See also Raphael Jospe's review of *History of Jewish Philosophy*, eds. Daniel H. Frank and Oliver Leaman, *Routledge History of World Philosophy*, vol. 2, in *Jewish History*, vol. 12, no. 2 (Fall 1998): 137-142.
2 Alexander Altmann, "Years of Growth," in *Moses Mendelssohn: A Biographical Study* (London: Routledge, 1973), 3-15; David Sorkin, "Foundations," in *Moses Mendelssohn and the Religious Enlightenment* (Berkeley: University of California Press, 1996), 3-14; Feiner, *The Jewish Enlightenment*, 115.

publish *Philosophische Gespräche* ("Philosophical Conversations," 1754). Mendelssohn subsequently defended Lessing's positive portrayal of Jews against Johann David Michaelis' attack in *Die Juden*. In a letter to his mentor, the scholar Aaron Solomon Gumpertz, Mendelssohn asked how anyone with the least sense of honesty could deny Israel the possibility of having a single honest man—the very nation from which all prophets and the greatest kings arose. Was it not enough that the Jews had to suffer such cruel hatred at the hands of Christians? Were those injustices now to be vindicated by defamation? Let the Christians continue restricting the Jews' existence as free and happy citizens, even go on exposing them to derision and contempt, he declared, but they must not deny the Jews their virtue—their only solace and refuge.[3] In 1755 Mendelssohn and Lessing collaborated on an essay about the English Age of Reason poet Alexander Pope, and the next year, upon Lessing's suggestion, Mendelssohn translated Rousseau's *Discourse on the Origins and Foundation of Human Inequality* into German.[4]

In 1763/64 Mendelssohn expressed his philosophical respect for Jesus' moral character to the Swiss Calvinist preacher Johann Caspar Lavater, letting him believe that he, Mendelssohn, might convert to Christianity—a conversion that could set off the messianic process itself. In 1769 Lavater translated the Christian apologist Charles Bonnet's *La Palingénésie philosophique ou idees sur l'état passé et sur l'état futur des êtres vivans*, refuting the view in Mendelssohn's *Phaedon* (1767) that only revelation could provide certain knowledge of the immortality of the soul. Lavater also praised Mendelssohn's love of truth, profound discernment, and incorruptible impartiality, and then offered Mendelssohn a "golden bridge" from Judaism to Christianity. He challenged him to read Bonnet's treatise with philosophical impartiality and either publicly refute Christianity if the arguments for it were incorrect, or act with prudence, love of truth, and honesty, and do what Socrates would

---

3   Letter of Mendelssohn to Aaron Solomon Gumpertz, June 1754, in Gotthold Ephraim Lessing, *Theatralische Bibliothek* (Berlin: C. F. Voss, 1754-1758), as cited by Altmann, *Moses Mendelssohn*, 41.

4   Lessing, *Pope ein Metaphysiker!* (Danzig: Johann Christian Schuster, 1755). Jean-Jacques Rousseau, *Johann Jacob Rousseau Bürgers zu Genf Abhandlung von dem Ursprunge der Ungleichheit unter den Menschen, und worauf sie sich gründe: ins Deutsche übersetzt mit einem Schreiben an den Herrn Magister Lessing und einem Briefe Voltairens an den Verfasser vermehret* (Berlin: Christian Friedrich Voss, 1756).

have done if they were correct, and convert. Mendelssohn responded in 1770, explaining that there were truths that existed which were available to everybody through rational insight. These included God's omnipotence over all creation, God's creation of man in His own image, and man's capacity to nevertheless sin and die. Because of its own special limitations, Judaism required a revealed body of law for its people to reach salvation. These laws were not subject to human understanding, and were binding until revoked by God. Ultimately, however, all mankind would acknowledge the identical truths about God and man. At that point, the distinctions between nations regarding access to these truths would no longer be binding.[5]

Lavater's challenge resurfaced in 1782, when Mendelssohn published a preamble to the German translation of Manasseh ben Israel's plea for readmission of Jews to England. An anonymous author writing under the title *Das Forschen nach Licht und Recht* (*The Search for Light and Truth*) pointed out that according to Mendelssohn, conversion to Christianity did not require abandoning the principle of one God, or the principle of the gathering of all nations into one flock with the advent of the messiah. If so, Mendelssohn should affirm Christianity and even lead other Jews to baptism. True, the "ecclesiastical system" with its punitive force would have to be abandoned, but this should not be a problem, for Mendelssohn had renounced all religious coercion in the name of religious freedom and reason. Unaware that the author was August Friedrich Cranz (a minor scribbler) and not the respected Christian statesman Josef Edler von Sonnenfels (a Jewish convert to Roman Catholicism), Mendelssohn took it upon himself to respond. He did so with *Jerusalem* (1783).[6]

---

5   Charles Bonnet and Johann Caspar Lavater, *Herrn Carl Bonnets ... philosophische Untersuchungen der Beweise für das Christentum. Samt desselben Ideen von der künftigen Glückseligkeit des Menschen. Aus dem französischen übersetzt, und mit Anmerkungen herausgegeben von Johann Caspar Lavater* (Zürich, 1769). Mendelssohn, *Schreiben an der Herrn Diaconus Lavater zu Zürich von Moses Mendelssohn* (Berlin: F. Nicolai, 1770). Altmann, *Moses Mendelssohn*, 209-263. Sorkin, *Moses Mendelssohn and the Religious Enlightenment*, 24-25.

6   *Manasseh Ben Israel, Rettung der Juden. Aus dem englischen übersetzt. Nebst einen Vorrede von Moses Mendelssohn. Als ein Anhang zu des Hrn. Kriegsraths Dohm Abhandlung: Über die bürgerliche Verbesserung der Juden* (Berlin and Stettin: Nicolai, 1782); [August Friedrich Cranz], *Das Forschen nach Licht und Recht in einem Schreiben an Herrn Moses Mendelssohn, auf Veranlassung seiner merkwürdigen Vorrede zu Manasseh ben Israel* (Berlin: F. Maurer, 1782); Altmann, *Moses Mendelssohn*, 464. Sorkin, *Moses Mendelssohn and the Religious*

Jerusalem offered an interpretation of Judaism's principles in a political context, and in this way his work resembled Spinoza's *Theological-Political Tractate* and anticipated Saul Ascher's *Leviathan* (1792). In the first section of this book Mendelssohn analyzed relations between church and state, and in the second he delineated three levels of Judaism. As portrayed by Simon Rawidowicz, the structure resembled that of a house.[7] The ground level was inhabited by all of humankind, who shared a general religion consisting of eternal, universal, and necessary truths. These included God's governance of the world, the immortality of the soul, and the Noahide laws (Genesis 9:18). Human reason had the capacity to produce these principles, and did so—although their natural presence ultimately came from God. These eternal truths could be comprehended by the human intellect, demonstrated and verified by human reason, even be produced by reason, and did not require the revelation of a Mt. Sinai. In fact, had these essential truths been unknown before the Sinai event, God's proclamation there that He was the cause of all reality would have been meaningless. Although God had to be the ultimate source for these truths, since they were innate tenets of the world which He created, they were inherently rational and completely accessible through, and expressible by, reason. Indeed, they were not changeable by God—if only because God Himself was rational. Above these truths, on the second floor, there were historical, temporal truths which dealt with how the Jewish nation should relate to the conditions in which it found itself at any particular time. Only Jews lived on this floor. Its structure was permanent, while the legalistic content could be removed without causing the floor to collapse. Thus, the laws tied to life in the Land of Israel were no longer binding once the people had left their land. While in the Land, there was a theocracy, a convergence between the people's relationship to society and the relationship to God. Civil acts were invested with sacred significance, and an offense against God, e.g., of the Sabbath, was also a political crime; likewise, defiance of state authority was also an offense against God. Outside the Land, religion separated from the state. Laws pertaining to the relationship between the polity and God no longer applied, and thus there was no place

---

Enlightenment, 464.

7   Simon Rawidowicz, "Ha'filosofiah shel Yerushalayim," in *Iyunim Be'mahshevet Yisrael*, ed. Benjamin Ravid (Jerusalem: Reuven Mass., 1971), 70-117.

for religious coercion. The third floor of the house was also for Jews only. Here, there were eternal, contingent truths, laws (largely ceremonial), judgments and commandments which originated in God's will. The ceremonial laws functioned as symbols or religious conceptualization of the truths down below on the ground floor. As they originated in God, and were not rational, only God could change these truths. While the Jew could reflect upon them, it was impossible to enter into the will or mind of God and look for some basis to change them.

In the decades to come, *Jerusalem* generated much attention, as well as criticism. There were several potential problems. For one, third floor laws were rooted in the eternal truths of the ground floor, yet no matter what reflection those truths might generate, the laws were not to be altered—that is, unless God Himself changed them with another Sinai revelation. Thus, commenting on Exodus 23:19, Mendelssohn explained that the Jew was not to explore why God prohibited eating milk and meat together. God did not make the reasons for His commandments available, through revelation, for man to probe; the Jew needed to know only that God commanded the obligation. Once the people of Israel accepted the yoke of God's kingdom, the Jew was obliged to follow the expressions of His will by action. The purpose of the law coincided with its implementation as a divine commandment—and did not involve the Jew's knowing the reason.[8] There was, to extend Rawidowicz's metaphor, no staircase in the house from the first to the third floor. A second problem was that Mendelssohn did not reconcile his religious-philosophical (naturalistic) disposition, where the God-man correlation was rational, with his supernaturalistic approach to practice, where the rational connection to God and His laws was removed. A third problem was that while all nations shared eternal truths theoretically, only the Jews had the legislation to actually access them. Nor did he believe that the nations would unify around the truths in anticipation of a messianic end to history, where the legislation would ultimately be marginalized. Without the legislative instrument, however, the concepts were undefined to the point of being meaningless. Essentially, in responding to

---

8   Mendelssohn, *Derekh Selulah: Hu Hibur Kolel Hamishah Humshei Torah*, vol. 2 (Fürth: D. Zürndorfer, 1823), 73[b]. For a new perspective on this problem as related to the biblical tabernacle, see Elias Sacks, "Ethics, Politics and Jewish Practice: Revisiting Mendelssohn's Hebrew Writings," paper delivered at the Association of Jewish Studies conference in Boston, December 19, 2010.

the needs of modernity and reason on the one hand and the needs of traditional Judaism and revelation on the other, Mendelssohn retreated to a middle ground—where the center remained in an unsettled condition. (Selections from *Jerusalem* reflecting the dialectical tension between the Mendelssohn's personas as both the "Socrates of Berlin" and as "Moses Dessau" are included below.)

The swerving path of Mendelssohn's writings reflected his dialectical interests in German philosophical thought and traditional, revealed Judaism. In the spirit of the *Haskalah* and the *Aufklärung*, he wrote in the short-lived journal *Kohelet Musar* (*Tribune of Morals*, 1750) about humanistic ethics and the return to a life of nature, in an effort to reshape the moral outlook of those Jews learned in traditional texts. In *Philosophische Gespräche* (*Philosophical Conversations*, 1754) he affirmed his commitment to rationalism, while simultaneously denying the possibility of accessing the truths of God's mind and locating revelation beyond the reach of rational philosophy (which was subordinate to piety and observance). *Beur Milot Ha'higayon* (*Commentary on the Terminology of Logic*, 1760) was a philosophical work, as was *Phaedon* (1767), in which he probed the practical use of reason by Socrates, as distinct from the Sophists' involvement with theoretical issues. He also provided a rational affirmation of Socrates' doctrine of the soul's perfection and immortality—showing how philosophy itself constituted a training for death, and justifying God's existence. In *Beur Li'megilat Kohelet* (*Commentary on the Scroll of Ecclesiastes*, 1769-1770) he combined a literal approach to Biblical exegesis with a discussion of the immortality of the soul and providence as ideas of natural religion. The *Sefer Ha'nefesh* (*Book of the Soul*, 1769, published posthumously in 1787) was a philosophical work drawing on classical Hebrew texts to amplify on the *Phaedon*'s proof for the soul's immortality. *Ritualgesetze der Juden* (*Ritual Laws of the Jews*, 1778), written within the framework of traditional Judaism, affirmed the unchanging authority of the literal meaning of Jewish law, whereas *Beur Sefer Darkhei Shalom* (*Book of the Paths of Peace*, 1783), a translation of the Pentateuch with commentary by a team of scholars led by Mendelssohn, combined *Haskalah* scholarship with traditional commentary. It included a German translation in Hebrew letters, and a Hebrew commentary blending rabbinic exegesis with rational philosophical discourse. In a similar vein, *Jerusalem* (1783) affirmed both the authority of Sinai-revelation with practical application of divine legislation and naturally accessible doctrines of the religion of reason. It coupled supernaturally revealed commands for action with rationally perceived eternal truths. Finally in *Morgenstunden* (*The Morning Hours, or Lectures on God's Existence*, 1785) Mendelssohn carried forward his theme of the value of practical reason over theory.[9]

1.1.2. Progenitor, Exemplar, and Frame of Reference

The historians of the period, from Isaac Euchel in 1788 through David Sorkin in 1996, agree on Mendelssohn's position as progenitor and exemplar. They differ, however, about whether tension or harmony prevailed in his mediating position. Euchel, writing of Mendelssohn as exemplar, declared that his "life should be our standard, his teaching our light," as he stood at once in Jewish culture and the new European environment in harmony.[10] More than a century later, Max Wiener spoke of the dialectical character of Mendelssohn's project. Mendelssohn's Judaism, Wiener wrote, was a self-contained, religio-national unity, grounded in revelation, with ceremonies and rites which constituted a specific unifying character. Having accepted revelation at Mt. Sinai, Israel was bound to this revelation forever—or until a new revelation would come about to displace it. At the same time, Wiener declared, Mendelssohn's teachings of Judaism had a spiritual dimension of rational form. This rationality nourished Mendelssohn's Jewish consciousness and the bond to his Jewish heritage.[11] Julius Guttmann stressed that Mendelssohn successfully balanced the conflicting forces of philosophy and Jew in his soul. Mendelssohn lived in two worlds, Guttman wrote: in his belief, a child of the universal religion of reason; in his observance of religious laws, a member of the Jewish community. Devoted to both, he experienced no conflict or tension between them. The idealism of religion of reason and the priority of Jewish sentiments were together genuine components of Mendelssohn's spiritual essence, Guttmann asserted.

---

9   The description of Mendelssohn's works is based on Sorkin, *Transformation of German Jewry 1780-1840* (Oxford: Oxford University Press, 1987), *passim*; Schweid, *Toledot Ha'hagut Ha'yehudit*, 126; and Heinz Mosheh Graupe, "Moses Mendelssohn," in *The Rise of Modern Judaism: An Intellectual History of German Jewry, 1650-1942* (Huntington, NY: R. E. Krieger, 1978), 81-82.

10   Isaac Euchel, *Toledot Rabbeinu Ha'haham Mosheh ben Menahem* (Berlin: Hinukh Ne'arim, 1788), 113, as cited by Sorkin, *Moses Mendelssohn and the Religious Enlightenment*, xviii.

11   Wiener, "Mendelssohn and the Religious Forms of Judaism in the Nineteenth Century," in *Studies in Jewish Thought: An Anthology of German Jewish Scholarship*, ed. Jospe , 404-416.

Mendelssohn's system of thought adapted one to the other, and their joint occupancy in his soul did not affect his personal integrity. The two aspects of his existence, therefore, remained separate but together in his consciousness, saving him from inner turmoil.[12] On the same topic, Altmann wrote that Mendelssohn's personal conviction held together the dichotomy between the particular-revelational dimension of his life and work and the universal-rationalistic dimension. As such, he represented a blissful moment in intellectual history; only later would the inner tensions fully surface. While the appearance of unity might not have reflected fully what went on inside, the degree of harmonization that he did achieve was astonishing.[13] Heinz Mosheh Graupe, for whom Mendelssohn symbolized the era of assimilation, emancipation, and Jewish enlightenment in Western Europe, thought the two sides were in harmony. Mendelssohn could endure Lavater's challenge (1769) to refute either Christianity or Judaism, maintain his equilibrium, and proceed to write philosophical works.[14] Katz took the view that the neutral society created by rationalists of the day, where human principles had intrinsic value and religious differences were non-existent, enabled Mendelssohn to exist simultaneously in the traditional Jewish religious community and the world of rationalism with its Christian point of departure.[15] Schweid wrote that despite the tension, Mendelssohn was still able to successfully serve as mediator. With one leg remaining in the vestiges of the Jewish *Kehillah*, and the other in German culture, he was, in fact, in continual tension, but he was able to remain true to Judaism while maintaining social ties with the intellectual elite, approaching the issues of the day (the place of the Jewish community in the national state; Christianity and tolerance; *Torah* authority and *Wissenschaft*; the faith of Judaism *vis-à-vis* the humanistic ideals of Europe) from a dualist perspective. At the same time, for Schweid, the mediation was one-sided, because the Christian community did not accept Mendelssohn's mediation. To be part of enlightened humanistic culture meant,

---

12   Julius Guttmann, *Philosophies of Judaism*, trans. David Wolf Silverman (New York: Holt, Rinehart, & Winston, 1964), 300.

13   Altmann, "Moses Mendelssohn's Concept of Judaism Re-examined," in *Von der mittelalterlichen zur modernen Aufklärung* (Tübingen: J. C. B. Mohr, 1987), 244, 248.

14   Graupe, 71-84.

15   Katz, *Tradition and Crisis*, 255-257.

to them, to be Christian.[16] Shemuel Feiner, on the contrary, viewed Mendelssohn's dialectical orientation as successful. He was accepted into the German intellectual elite—enabled by the presence of a social, religious, and national neutral zone and a common social-cultural *milieu* of the intelligentsia.[17] Sorkin, for his part, wrote that emancipation ideologues viewed Mendelssohn as the great progenitor of the generation. This was in keeping with the *Aufklärung* idea of the genius's role in history—a role earlier assumed by Luther *vis-à-vis* the Reformation. To them, Mendelssohn was the sole figure responsible for introducing Jews to a culture of historical change and regeneration.[18] Mendelssohn's dual success as full believer in revealed religion and full participant in enlightenment thinking was, Sorkin wrote, attributable to the "missing link" of a religious enlightenment-grounding which enabled the interface between the Socrates of Berlin and Moses Dessau. In fact, while other representatives of the religious enlightenment reconciled faith and reason by drawing from the German *Aufklärung* (circa 1720-1770), Mendelssohn personified the Jewish version of religious enlightenment, the *Haskalah*. He became the exemplar, the ideal figure for members of the German Jewish subculture, the prototype of the man of *Bildung*; this group read the history and activities of the subculture into his work and life. It was natural, Sorkin added, that the premises of his *Jerusalem* were followed by the intellectual leadership of the Assembly of Jewish Notables in Paris (May 1806). Specifically, they concurred with its assertion that Judaism did not clash with the secular state, and that political and ceremonial laws belonged to separate spheres.[19]

In his capacity of progenitor, exemplar, lightning rod, and receptacle for the yearnings of others who entered the corridor between the formerly boundaried realms of the autonomous Jewish community and that of Christian society, Mendelssohn came to serve as an ongoing point and frame of reference for Jewish philosophical thinkers, from Ascher through Franz Rosenzweig. Wiener concluded that the origins

---

16   Schweid, *Toledot* 122-125, 148.
17   Feiner, *The Jewish Enlightenment*, 206, citing Katz, 254.
18   Sorkin, *Transformation of German Jewry*, 97. On the role as progenitor see also Allan Arkush, *Moses Mendelssohn and the Enlightenment*. See also Schweid, *Toledot*, 126 and Graupe, 81-82.
19   Sorkin, *Transformation of German Jewry*, 8-9, 79, 97, 100; *Moses Mendelssohn and the Religious Enlightenment*, xviii.

of many different dimensions of modern Judaism were traceable to
Mendelssohn—intellectually, although not historically. In fact, the
religious, national, Orthodox, and liberal strands of the fabric of Jewish consciousness were anticipated and recorded by him.[20] According
to Schweid, Mendelssohn both initiated modern Jewish thought and
influenced most of its streams—and nineteenth-century Jews considered him the founder of their endeavors, even while they differed with
him. The study of the essential problems of modern Jewish philosophical thought, Schweid continued, rightly returned to his thought as the
point of departure.[21] In a similar vein, Sorkin wrote that as the embodiment of the relationship between German philosophy (the "Socrates
of Berlin") and traditional Judaism ("Moses Dessau"), Mendelssohn
himself is the entry point into modern Jewish thought—for which the
answer provided by his identity was an integral part. Specifically, he
turned out to be the "magnetic pole" to the "compass" of nineteenth-
century Jewish thought.[22]

Mendelssohn's role as progenitor, frame of reference, and point of departure for modern Jewish thought may be illustrated with statements
by the authors whose texts are included in this volume. Reggio, called
"the Italian Mendelssohn," praised him for awakening the Jewish world
to scientific study—as if God Himself had sent him to remove the darkness over Israel's intellect. Reggio emulated the *Book of the Paths of Peace*
and translated Scripture into an Italian that was written with Hebrew
letters.[23] Salomon Maimon acknowledged how Lavater, and then Jacobi
with his claim that Mendelssohn's friend Lessing was a Spinozist intellectual pantheist, exposed the ambiguity in Mendelssohn's work between
faith and reason, but praised him for responding to them. Maimon himself preferred Maimonides' negation of attributes to God over Mendelssohn's affirmation of the different aspects of God's reality; Maimonides'
view that the highest good coincided with knowledge of the truth over
Mendelssohn's inclusion of natural impulses in the idea of perfection;
and Maimonides' view that the soul's immortality was a matter of in-

---

20   Wiener, 417.
21   Schweid, *Toledot*, 122.
22   Sorkin, *Moses Mendelssohn and the Religious Enlightenment*, xvii, 152.
23   Jakob Goldenthal, "Beiträge zur Literatur der jüdischen Religionsphilosophie,"
Allgemeine Zeitung des Judentums: Literarisches und Homiletisches Beiblatt 1, no. 36 (27
December 1838): 163-166.

tellectual knowledge of eternal truth and of union with universal spirit, over Mendelssohn's idea about the ongoing individuality of the immortal soul. But Maimon agreed with Mendelssohn that the fundamental laws of the Jewish religion were properly the fundamental laws of the Jewish state, to be obeyed by all citizens—while a Jew separated from the state was under no such obligation. He also agreed that conversion to Christianity did not free a Jew from observing the laws of Judaism—as Jesus himself had demonstrated.[24]

Salomon Formstecher credited Mendelssohn with moving Jews out of their dark, medieval hermitage into the light of reason. By providing credibility for religious truths, he assured Judaism's spiritual vitality in modernity. Mendelssohn also enhanced Judaism's role in world history by reining in pagan-philosophical tendencies. Formstecher spoke of a world-historical struggle between the pagan universe of nature (unfree, unconscious) and the Jewish universe of spirit (free, self-knowing). Kant posited a vision where spirit conquers nature; his successors (Fichte, Schelling, Hegel) diminished this victory by defining absolute existence in terms of a pagan-philosophical "I" vis-à-vis "not-I." By restoring limits to philosophy when it came to comprehending God's essence, Mendelssohn renewed spirit's dominance over nature. Formstecher credited Mendelssohn with helping Israel to share the rational light of modernity, and assuring its spiritual vitality by affirming God as transcending human intellectual assertion and philosophical inquiry.[25] Samuel Hirsch commended Mendelssohn for exposing Judaism to Christian humanistic education, as well as to the challenges of philosophical rationalism. He identified Mendelssohn's work as the turning point between old and new cultural history, notably through his success in having Jews study the German language (*Book of the Paths of Peace*). But Hirsch also criticized Mendelssohn, both for advocating free thought about God and divine providence on the one hand, and for speaking of obligations to divine legislation until God Himself revoked it on the other. Hirsch disagreed with Mendelssohn's conviction that ceremonial legislation could be emp-

24 Salomon Maimon, "Mendelssohn: Ein Kapitel dem Andenken eines würdigen Freund gewidmet," in *Salomon Maimons Lebensgeschichte*, vol. 2, ed. K. P. Moritz (Berlin: F. Vieweg, 1792), 168-186.
25 Salomon Formstecher, "Moses Mendelssohn, ein Philosoph auf dem Gebiete des Judentums," in *Gedenkblätter an Moses Mendelssohn* (Leipzig: Verein zur Förderung geistiger Interessen im Judenthume, 1863).

tied of the doctrines of God, and appreciated the fact that in his time it was necessary to bring Judaism into a universal context. By 1841 (when Hirsch was writing), however, the primary need was to preserve Judaism on its own terms. Ceremonies, for example, had to be revitalized.[26]

Like Formstecher, Salomon Ludwig Steinheim recognized the pivotal role of Mendelssohn's work in Judaism's passage into modernity. Mendelssohn also liberated it from oppressive Orthodoxy. Like "volcanic lava" that acts to cultivate the "plains" below, he served as the harbinger of the fourth, final, adult stage in Israel's history. But Steinheim criticized Mendelssohn for compromising Scriptural revelation by attributing commandments related to God's existence and man's moral character to human nature, and by trying to prove God's existence mathematically—as if God's existence depended on whether or how human thought could account for it. Mendelssohn did turn to revelation, not for spiritual truths, but for *Mishpatim* and *Huqim*. And his motivation was unauthentic: it was his fear of the sacred in history and political moral deterioration. Additionally, there was the contradiction between philosophical grounding on one side and revealed legislation on the other. Mendelssohn was aware of the contradiction, but he preferred to leave the matter to his successors.[27] Franz Rosenzweig praised Mendelssohn for helping in Judaism's transition into the modernity that would give rise to these successors—specifically, by explicating the relationship between Judaism and world culture, and forging a *Deutschjudentum*, Jews who considered themselves German. But *Deutschjudentum* also compromised Judaism's doctrines and present historical reality. Rosenzweig noted that Mendelssohn's efforts were suitable for the emancipation era and the transition—but not for later times. As the situation now stands, "From Mendelssohn on... the Jewishness of every individual has squirmed on the needle point of a 'Why.'"[28]

---

26   Samuel Hirsch, *Die Religionsphilosophie der Juden* (Leipzig: Heinrich Hunger, 1841), 9-10. See further, Samuel Hirsch, *Das Judenthum, der christliche Staat und die moderne Kritik: Briefe zur Beleuchtung der Judenfrage von Bruno Bauer* (Leipzig: Heinrich Hunger, 1843), 19, 23-24, 112-113.

27   Salomon Ludwig Steinheim, *Moses Mendelssohn und seine Schule in ihren Beziehung zur Aufgabe des neuen Jahrhunderts der alten Zeitrechnung* (Hamburg: Hoffmann und Campe, 1840).

28   Franz Rosenzweig, "Die Bauleute," "Vorspruch zu einer Mendelssohnfeier [Fall 1929]," and "Der jüdische Mensch," in *Der Mensch und Sein Werk: Gesammelte Schriften* (Dordrecht: Martinus Nijhoff, 1984), 699, 457, 566-567. See Paul Mendes-Flohr, "Mendelssohn and Rosenzweig," in *Der Philosoph Franz Rosenzweig* (1886-1929), vol. 1 (Freiburg: K. Alber,

In his *Leviathan*, Saul Ascher criticized Mendelssohn for redefining Judaism in reaction to, and in terms of, external forces. Like Maimonides who sought to blend Judaism with Aristotle, and Spinoza who built up Judaism's rational content to the exclusion of revelation, Mendelssohn was an apologist. He sought to copy what in his era were Judaism's antagonists, Christianity and German culture, by eclipsing his own religion with legislation. If Mendelssohn wanted to maintain the patriarchal roots of wisdom and the vital historical truths held by the Israeli memory, why did he have legality imprison reason and belief, which served those goals? Mendelssohn also confused *Mishpatim*, the essential legislation which held religious truth—which remains eternal irrespective of being written down in *Torah*—and *Huqim*, the ordinances of expedience which were decreed by God. By including the *Mishpatim* in divine legislation, he subjected necessary truths to God's arbitrary action and limited access to them through law and symbol. Further, Ascher claimed that, by tying legislation to the specific function of the Mosaic state-constitution, Mendelssohn indicated that legislation would lose its function once that constitution was no longer in place. Ascher coupled Mendelssohn's view that Judaism's particular character was not spiritual but a function of ceremonial law and rabbinic stipulation with Spinoza's view that the essence of Judaism was revealed law—and if that was Judaism's character, it made the religion vulnerable to irrelevance once scientific study took hold. Finally, Ascher objected to Mendelssohn's exclusion of dogma on the one hand, and giving prominence to liturgy and ritual on the other. Without dogma, religion became a matter of performance.[29]

Nahman Krokhmal, according to Solomon Schechter, was an admirer of Mendelssohn, while Joseph Klausner characterized Krokhmal as the "Galician Mendelssohn."[30] Einhorn joined those who credited Mendelssohn's work with playing a pivotal role in Judaism's passage into modernity. Specifically, he did this by breaking the spell of an exclusivistic Judaism and raising consciousness concerning Judaism's sharing universal elements of religion; his ideas for reform in the name of reason and freedom shattered petrified Judaism. But Einhorn also criticized Mendels-

---

1988), 213-223.

29 Shaul Ascher, *Leviathan* (Berlin: Frank, 1792); *Napoleon* (Berlin: G.A. Lange, 1808), 156-160.

30 Solomon Schechter, "Nachman Krokhmal and the Perplexities of the Time," in *Studies in Judaism* (New York: Macmillan, 1896), 46-72. Joseph Klausner, *Historiah Shel Ha'sifrut Ha'ivrit Ha'hadashah*, vol. 1 (Jerusalem: Ahiasaf, 1952), 148.

sohn for his ambiguity, introducing reason into Judaism while restraining it. On the one hand, he spoke of natural and rationally apprehensible truths, and on the other of a revealed legislation which was to be enacted irrespective of rational grounding. Mendelssohn's God, Einhorn pointed out, originated in reason while relating to Israel in terms of a-rational revealed legislation. While ceremonies were to evoke the natural and eternal truths, they themselves were a-rational in character.[31]

Hermann Cohen praised Mendelssohn for his disposition towards Christianity. Mendelssohn himself resisted attempts to relate Judaism and Christianity, which he felt was necessary, lest he ignite the conflict about Christian messianism. This caused him to retreat from the important issue of historical progress, lest the issue of Christian supercession come to the forefront. But he faulted Mendelssohn for letting legislation eclipse the faith-doctrines in divine revelation, since his legislative truths were in fact matters of religious knowledge. Moreover, by making legislation Judaism's *raison d'etre*, and thereby isolating it from the broader society, Cohen argued that Mendelssohn compromised his overall effort to enhance Judaism's cultural and political life in Germany. Still, Mendelssohn was to be credited with striking the proper balance between retaining Jewish identity and fostering a mutually beneficial interaction between Judaism and Germany. Specifically, the German-Hebrew translation in his *Book of the Paths of Peace* drew Jews to the German language, helping to liberate them from their ghettos and into the Germanic mindset. Overall, his work likewise helped to enlighten German culture about Judaism.[32]

I.I. Selections from *Jerusalem*, translated by Allan Arkush[33]

Summary

Mendelssohn stipulated universal truths which were independent of time, which were necessary, and that did not change. These eternal truths did not

---

31   See Greenberg, "Mendelssohn in America: David Einhorn's Radical Reform Judaism," *LBIY* 27 (1982): 281-294.

32   Hermann Cohen, "Deutschtum und Judenthum [1915]," in *Jüdische Schriften*, vol. 2 (Berlin: C.A. Schwetschke, 1924), 267

33   Translations are from Moses Mendelssohn, *Jerusalem or on Religious Power and Judaism*, trans. Arkush, with an introduction and commentary by Altmann (Hanover, NH: University Press of New England, 1983), 94-97; 97-99; 118-119; 126-128; 128-130; 133-134.

require revelation—the revelation at Sinai was not about the eternal truths. Secondly, he specified truths which were particular to Israel and contingent, originating in and subject to God's will and subject to His will (and His will alone). Thirdly, he listed truths of time, which were tied to historical events. The first category related to reason, the second to observation, and the third primarily to testimony of others. God provided the means for understanding these three truths: the capacity for reason, the aptitude for observation, and the credibility of the narrator.

[Eternal and Temporal Truths]

One calls eternal truths those propositions which are not subject to time and remain the same in all eternity. They are either *necessary*, in themselves *immutable*, or *contingent*; that is, their permanence is based either on their *essence*—they are true in this other way—or on their *reality*: they are universally true, they exist in this and no other way because they became *real* in this and no other way; because of all the possible [truths] of their kind they are the *best*, in this and no other way. In other words, necessary as well as contingent truths flow from a common source, the source of all truth: the former from the *intellect*, the latter from the *will of God*. The propositions of necessary truths are true because God *represents them to himself* in this and no other way; the contingent, because God approved them and considered them to be in conformity with his wisdom in this and no other way. Examples of the first kind are the propositions of pure mathematics and of the art of logic; examples of the second are the general propositions of physics and psychology, the laws of nature, according to which this universe, the world of bodies and the world of spirits, is governed. The former are immutable even for the Omnipotent, because God Himself cannot render his infinite intellect changeable; the latter, however, are subject to the will of God and are immutable only insofar as it pleases his holy will, that is, insofar as they are in accord with his intentions. His omnipotence can introduce other laws in their place and can, as often as it may be useful, allow exceptions to occur.

Besides these eternal truths, there are also *temporal, historical truths*; things which occurred once and may never occur again; propositions which have become true at one point in time and space through a confluence of causes and effects, and which, therefore, can only be conceived as true in respect to that point in time and space. Of this kind are all the truths of history, taken in its broadest sense; things of remote ages, which once took place, and are reported to us, but which we ourselves can never observe.

Just as these classes of propositions and truths differ by nature, so, too, do they differ in respect to their means of persuasion, or in the manner in which men convince themselves and others of them. The doctrines of the first kind, or the necessary truths, are founded upon *reason*, that is, on an immutable coherence and essential connection of ideas, according to which they either presuppose or exclude one another. All mathematical and logical proofs are of this kind. They all show the possibility or impossibility of thinking certain ideas in association with others. Whoever wishes to instruct his fellow man in them must not commend them to his belief, but should force them, as it were, upon his reason. He should not cite authorities and invoke the credibility of men who maintained exactly the same thing, but dissect the ideas into their essential elements and present them to his pupil, one by one, until his internal sense perceives their junctures and connections. The instructions which we may give others are, in Socrates' apt phrase, but a kind of midwifery. We cannot put anything into their minds which is not actually contained there already; yet we can facilitate the effort it would cost to bring to light what was hidden; that is, to render the unperceived perceptible and evident.

Besides reason, the truths of the second class require *observation* as well. If we wish to know what laws the Creator has prescribed for his creation, and according to what general rules the changes in it take place, we must experience, observe, and test individual cases; that is, we must, in the first place, make use of the evidence of the senses; and next, determine by means of reason what many particular cases have in common. Here, we shall indeed be obliged to accept many things, on faith and authority, from others. Our life span is not sufficient for us to experience everything ourselves; and we must, in many cases, rely on credible fellow men; we must assume that their observations and the experiments they profess to have made are correct. But we trust them only insofar as we know and are convinced that the objects themselves still exist, and that the experiments and observations may be repeated and tested by ourselves or by others who have the opportunity and the ability to do so. Indeed, if the result is important and has a considerable influence on our own felicity, or on that of others, we are far less satisfied with the report of experiments; but we seek an opportunity to repeat them ourselves, and to become convinced of them by their own evidence. Thus, the Siamese, for instance, may by all means trust the reports of the Europeans that in their part of the world water becomes solid and bears heavy burdens at certain times. They may accept this on faith, and, at all events, present it in their physics text books as an established fact, on the assumption that the observation can always be repeated and verified. But should there be any danger of lives being lost, should they have to entrust themselves or their kith and kin to this so-lidified element, they would be far less satisfied with the testimony of others, and would seek to convince themselves of its truth by various experiences, observations, and experiments of their own.

Historical truths, however—those passages which, as it were, occur but once in the book of nature—must be explained by themselves, or remain incomprehensible; that is, they can only be perceived, by means of the senses, by those who were present at the time and place of their occurrence in nature. Everyone else must accept them on authority and testimony. Furthermore, those who live at another time must rely al-together on the credibility of the testimony, for the thing attested no longer exists. The object itself and the direct observation of it, to which they may wish to appeal, are no longer to be found in nature. The senses cannot convince them of the truth. In historical matters, the author-ity and credibility of the narrator constitute the only evidence. Without testimony we cannot be convinced of any historical truth. Without au-thority, the truth of history vanishes along with the event itself.

As often, therefore, as it accords with the intentions of God that men be convinced of any particular truth, his wisdom grants them the most appropriate means of arriving at it. In the case of a necessary truth, it grants them the requisite degree of reason. If a law of nature is to be made known to them, it gives them the spirit of observation; and if a historical certainty, it places the narrator's credibility beyond all doubt. It seems to me that only where historical truths are concerned does it befit the supreme wisdom to instruct men in a human manner, that is, through words and writing, and to cause extraordinary things and miracles to occur in nature, whenever this is required to confirm authority and credibility. Eternal truths, on the other hand, insofar as they are useful for men's salvation and felicity, are taught by God in a manner more appropriate to the Deity; not by sounds or written characters, which are comprehensible here and there, to this or that individual, but through creation itself, and its internal relations, which are legible and comprehensible to all men. Nor does He confirm them by miracles, which effect only historical belief; but He awakens the mind, which He has created, and gives it an opportunity to observe the relations of things, to observe itself, and to become convinced of the truths which it is destined to understand here below.

I therefore do not believe that the powers of human reason are insufficient to persuade men of the eternal truths which are indispensable to human felicity, and that God had to reveal them in a supernatural manner. Those who hold this view detract from the omnipotence or the goodness of God, on the one hand, what they believe they are adding to his goodness on the other. He was, in their opinion, good enough to reveal to men those truths on which their felicity depends, but not omnipotent, or not good enough to grant them powers to discover these truths themselves. Moreover, by this assertion one makes the necessity of a supernatural revelation more universal than revelation itself. If, therefore, mankind must be corrupt and miserable without revelation, why has the far greater part of mankind lived without *true revelation* from time immemorial? Why must the two Indies wait until it pleases the Europeans to send them a few comforters to bring them a message without which they can, according to this opinion, live neither virtuously nor happily? To bring them a message which, in their circumstances and stage of knowledge, they can neither rightly comprehend nor properly utilize?

According to the concepts of true Judaism, all the inhabitants of the earth are destined to felicity; and the means of attaining it are as widespread as mankind itself, as charitably dispensed as the means of warding off hunger and other natural needs. Here men are left to brute nature, which inwardly feels its powers and uses them, without being able to express itself in words and speech except in the most defective manner and, as it were, stammeringly. In another place, they are aided by science and art, shining brightly through words, images, and metaphors, by which the perceptions of the inner sense are transformed into a clear knowledge of signs and established as such.

I return to my previous remark. Judaism boasts of no *exclusive* revelation of eternal truths that are indispensable to salvation, of no revealed religion in the sense in which that term is usually understood. Revealed *religion* is one thing, revealed *legislation*, another. The voice which let itself be heard on Sinai on that great day did not proclaim, "I am the Eternal, your God, the necessary, independent being, omnipotent and omniscient, that recompenses men in a future life according to their deeds." This is the universal *religion* of *mankind*, not Judaism; and the universal *religion* of *mankind*, without which men are neither virtuous nor capable of felicity, was not to be revealed there. In reality, it could not have been revealed there, for who was to be convinced of these eternal doctrines of salvation by the voice of thunder and the sound of trumpets? Surely not the unthinking, brutelike man, whose own reflections had not yet led him to the existence of an invisible being that governs the visible. The miraculous voice would not have instilled any concepts in him and, therefore, would not have convinced him. Still less [would it have convinced] the sophist whose ears are buzzing with so many doubts and ruminations that he can no longer hear the voice of common sense. He demands *rational proofs*, not miracles. And even if the teacher of religion were to raise from the dust all the dead who ever trod the earth, in order to confirm thereby an *eternal truth*, the skeptic would say: The teacher has awakened many dead, yet I still know no more about eternal truth than I did before. I know now that someone can do, and pronounce, extraordinary things; but there may be several suchlike beings, who do not think it proper to reveal themselves just at this moment. And all this is still far removed from the infinitely sublime idea of a *unique, eternal Deity* that rules the entire universe according to its unlimited will, and discerns men's most secret thoughts in order to reward their deeds according to their merits, if not here, then in the hereafter.

Anyone who did not know this, who was not imbued with these truths indispensable to human felicity, and was not prepared to approach the holy mountain, could have been stunned and overwhelmed by the great and wonderful manifestations, but he could not have been made aware of what he had not known before. No! All this was presupposed; it was, perhaps, taught, explained, and placed beyond all doubt by human reasoning during the days of preparation. And now the divine voice proclaimed: *"I am the Eternal, your God, who brought you out of the land of Mizrayim, who delivered you from bondage, etc."* A historical truth, on which this people's legislation was to be founded, as well as laws, was to be revealed here—commandments and ordinances, not eternal religious truths. "I am the Eternal, your God, who made a covenant with your fathers, Abraham, Isaac and Jacob, and swore to make of their seed a nation of my own. The time for the fulfillment of this promise has finally come. To this end, I redeemed you from Egyptian slavery with unheard-of miracles and signs. I am your Redeemer, your Sovereign and King; I also make a covenant with you, and give you laws by which you are to live and become a happy nation in the land that I shall give you." All these are historical truths which, by their very nature, rest on historical evidence, *must* be verified by authority, and *can* be confirmed by miracles.

Miracles and extraordinary signs are, according to Judaism, no proofs for or against eternal truths of reason. We are, therefore, instructed in Scripture itself not to listen to a prophet if he teaches or counsels things contrary to established truths, even if he confirms his mission by miracles; indeed, we are to condemn to death the performer of miracles if he tries to lead us astray into idolatry. For miracles can only verify testimonies, support authorities, and confirm the credibility of witnesses and those who transmit tradition. But no testimonies and authorities can upset any established truth of reason, or place a doubtful one beyond doubt and suspicion.

Although the divine book that we received through Moses is, strictly speaking, meant to be a book of laws containing ordinances, rules of life and prescriptions, it also includes, as is well known, an inexhaustible treasure of rational truths and religious doctrines which are so intimately connected with the laws that they form but one entity. All laws refer to, or are based upon, eternal truths of reason, or remind us of them, and rouse us to ponder them. Hence, our rabbis rightly say: the laws and doctrines are related to each other, like body and soul.

We have seen how difficult it is to preserve the abstract ideas of religion among men by means of permanent signs. Images and hieroglyphics lead to superstition and idolatry, and alphabetical script makes man too speculative. It displays the symbolic knowledge of things and their relations too openly on the surface; it spares us the effort of penetrating and searching, and creates too wide a division between doctrine and life. In order to remedy these defects the lawgiver of this nation gave the *ceremonial law*. Religious and moral teachings were to be connected with men's everyday activities. The law, to be sure, did not impel them to engage in reflection; it prescribed only actions, only doing and not doing. The great maxim of this constitution seems to have been: *Men must be impelled to perform actions and only induced to engage in reflection.* Therefore, each of these prescribed actions, each practice, each ceremony had its meaning, its valid significance; each was closely related to the speculative knowledge of religion and the teachings of morality, and was an occasion for a man in search of truth to reflect on these sacred matters or to seek instruction from wise men. The truths useful for the felicity of the nation as well as of each of its individual members were to be utterly removed from all imagery; for this was the main purpose and the fundamental law of the constitution. They were to be connected with actions and practices, and these were to serve them in place of signs, without which they cannot be preserved. Man's actions are transitory; there is nothing lasting, nothing enduring about them that, like hieroglyphic script, could lead to idolatry through abuse or misunderstanding. But they also have the advantage over alphabetical signs of not isolating man, of not making him to be a solitary creature, poring over writings and books. They impel him rather to social intercourse, to imitation, and to oral, living instruction.

Now I can summarize briefly my conceptions of the Judaism of former times and bring them into a single focus. Judaism consisted or, according to the intention of the founder, was to consist of:

1. Religious doctrines and propositions or *eternal truths* about God and his government and providence, without which man cannot be enlightened and happy. These are not forced upon the faith of the nation under the threat of eternal or temporal punishments, but, in accordance with the nature and evidence of eternal truths, recommended to rational acknowledgement. They did not have to be given by direct revelation, or made known through *word* and *script*, which are intelligible only *here* and *now*. The Supreme Being has revealed them to all rational creatures through *things* and *concepts* and inscribed them in the soul with a script that is legible and comprehensible at all times and in all places. For this reason our much-quoted poet sings:

> The heavens declare the majesty of God, And the
> firmament announceth the work of His hands;
> From one day this doctrine floweth into another;
> And night giveth instruction to night.
> *No teaching, no words,*

Without their voice being heard.
Their choral resoundeth over all the earth,
Their message goeth forth to the ends of the world,
To the place where He hath set a tent for the sun, etc.

Their effect is as universal as the beneficent influence of the sun, which, as it hurries through its orbit, sheds light and warmth over the whole globe. As the same poet explains still more clearly in another place:

From sunrise to sundown
The name of the Lord is praised.

Or, as the prophet says in the name of the Lord: *From the rising of the sun to its setting, My name is great among the heathens, and in every place frankincense is presented unto My name, even pure oblations, for My name is great among the heathens.*

2. Historical truths, or records of the vicissitudes of former ages, especially of the circumstances in the lives of the nation's forefathers; of their having come to know the true God, of their way of life before God; even of their transgressions and the paternal chastisement that followed them; of the covenant which God concluded with them; and of the promise, which He so often repeated to them, to make of their descendants, in the days to come, a nation consecrated to Him. These historical records contained the foundation for the national cohesion; and as historical truths they can, according to their nature, not be accepted in any other manner than on *faith*. Authority alone gives them the required evidence; these records were also confirmed to the nation by miracles, and supported by an authority which was sufficient to place the *faith* beyond all doubt and hesitancy.

3. Laws, precepts, commandments and rules of life, which were to be peculiar to this nation and through the observance of which it should arrive at national felicity, as well as personal felicity for each of its individual members. The lawgiver was God, that is to say, God not in his relation as Creator and Preserver of the universe, but God as Patron and Friend by covenant of their ancestors, as Liberator, Founder and Leader,

as King and Head of this people; and He gave his laws the most solemn sanction, publicly and in a never heard-of, miraculous manner, by which they were imposed upon the nation and all their descendants as an unalterable duty and obligation.

These laws were *revealed*, that is, they were made known by God, through *words* and *script*. Yet only the most essential part of them was entrusted to letters; and without the unwritten explanations, delimitations, and more precise determinations, transmitted orally and propagated through oral, living instruction, even these written laws are mostly incomprehensible, or inevitably became so in the course of time. For no words or written signs preserve their meaning unchanged throughout a generation.

The written as well as the unwritten laws have directly, as *prescriptions for action* and rules of life, public and private felicity as their ultimate aim. But they are also, in large part, to be regarded as a kind of script, and they have significance and meaning as ceremonial laws. They guide the inquiring intelligence to divine truths, partly to eternal and party to historical truths upon which the religion of this people was founded. The ceremonial law was the bond which was to connect action with contemplation, life with theory. The ceremonial law was to induce personal converse and social contact between school and teacher, inquirer and instructor, and to stimulate and encourage rivalry and emulation; and it actually fulfilled this mission in the early period, before the constitution degenerated and human folly again interfered to change, through misunderstanding and misdirection, the good into evil and the useful into the harmful.

Summary
In Israel's original constitution, God was the sovereign and civil acts had sacred significance. Violations of the religious law were civil violations as well, yet the religious institution could not punish violations of belief. Turning to modern society, Mendelssohn advised adaptation to the constitution of the country, while continuing the religion of the fathers.

In this original constitution, state and religion were not conjoined, but *one*; not connected, but identical. Man's relation to society and his relation to God coincided and could never come into conflict. God, the Creator and Preserver of the world, was at the same time the King and

Regent of this nation; and his oneness is such as not to admit the least division or plurality in either the political or the metaphysical sense. Nor does this monarch have any needs. He demands nothing from the nation but what serves its own welfare and advances the felicity of the state; just as the state, for its part, could not demand anything that was opposed to the duties toward God, that was not, rather, commanded by God, the Lawgiver and Regent of the nation. Hence, in this nation, civil matters acquired a sacred and religious aspect, and every civil service was at the same time a true service of God. The community was a community of God, its affairs were God's; the public taxes were an offering to God; and everything down to the least police measure was part of the *divine service*. The Levites, who lived off the public revenue, received their livelihood from God. They were to have no property in the land, *for God is their property*. He who must sojourn outside the land serves *foreign gods*. This [statement which occurs] in several places in Scripture cannot be taken in a literal sense. It actually means no more than that *he is subject to alien political laws which, unlike those of his own country, are not at the same time a part of the divine service.*

The same can be said of the crimes. Every sacrilege against the authority of God, as the lawgiver of the nation, was a crime against the Majesty, and therefore a crime of state. Whoever blasphemed God committed lese-majesty; whoever sacrilegiously desecrated the Sabbath implicitly abrogated a fundamental law of civil society, for an essential part of the constitution was based on the establishment of this day. *"Let the Sabbath be an eternal covenant between Me and the children of Israel,"* said the Lord, *"a perpetual sign that in six days the Eternal, etc..."* Under this constitution these crimes could and, indeed, had to be punished civilly, not as erroneous opinion, not as *unbelief*, but as *misdeeds*, as sacrilegious crimes aimed at abolishing or weakening the authority of the lawgiver and thereby undermining the state itself. Yet, nevertheless, with what leniency were even these capital crimes punished! With what superabundant indulgence for human weakness! According to an unwritten law, corporal and capital punishment could not be inflicted unless *the criminal had been warned by two unsuspected witnesses with the citation of the law and the threat of the prescribed punishment*; indeed, where corporal or capital punishment were concerned, the criminal had *to have acknowledged the punishment in express words, accepted it and committed the crime immediately afterwards in the presence of the same witnesses.* How rare must executions have been under such stipulations, and how many an opportunity must the judges have had of avoiding the sad necessity of pronouncing a sentence of death over their fellow creature and fellow image of God! *An executed man is*, according to the expression of Scripture, *a reproach to God*. How much the judges must have hesitated, investigated, and considered excuses before they signed a sentence of death! Indeed, as the rabbis say, any court competent to deal with capital offenses and concerned for its good name must see to it that in a period of *seventy* years not more than one person is sentenced to death.

This clearly shows how little one must be acquainted with the Mosaic law and the constitution of Judaism to believe that according to them *ecclesiastical right* and *ecclesiastical power* are authorized, or that temporal punishments are to be inflicted for unbelief or erring belief. *The Searcher for Light and Right*, as well as Mr. Mörschel, are therefore far removed from the truth when they believe I have abolished Judaism by my rational arguments against ecclesiastical right and ecclesiastical power. Truth cannot be in conflict with truth. What divine law commands, reason, which is no less divine, cannot abolish.

Not unbelief, not false doctrine and error, but sacrilegious offenses against the majesty of the lawgiver, impudent misdeeds against the fundamental laws of the state and the civil constitution were punished; and these were punished only when the sacrilege exceeded all bounds in its unruliness, and came close to rebellion; when the criminal was not afraid to have the law quoted to him by two fellow citizens, to be threatened with punishment and, indeed, to take the punishment upon himself and commit the crime in their presence. Here the religious villain becomes a sacrilegious desecrator of majesty, a state criminal. Moreover, as the rabbis expressly state, *with the destruction of the Temple, all corporal and capital punishments and, indeed, even monetary fines, insofar as they are only national, have ceased to be legal. [Shabbat 15ᵃ].* Perfectly in accordance with my principles, and inexplicable without them! The civil bonds of the nation were dissolved; religious offenses were no longer crimes against the state; and the religion, as religion, knows of no punishment, no other penalty than the one the remorseful sinner *voluntarily* imposes on himself. It knows of no coercion, uses only the staff [called] *gentleness*, and affects only mind and heart. Let one try to explain rationally, without my principles, this assertion of the rabbis!

And even today, no wiser advice than this can be given to the House of Jacob. Adapt yourselves to the morals and the constitution of the land to which you have been removed; but hold fast to the religion of your fathers too. Bear both burdens as well as you can! It is true that, on the one hand, the burden of civil life is made heavier for you on account of the religion to which you remain faithful, and, on the other hand, the climate and the times make the observance of your religious laws in some respects more irksome than they are. Nevertheless, persevere; remain unflinchingly at the post which Providence has assigned to you, and endure everything that happens to you as your lawgiver foretold long ago.

In fact, I cannot see how those born into the House of Jacob can in any conscientious manner disencumber themselves of the law. We are permitted to reflect on the law, to inquire into its spirit, and, here and there, where the lawgiver gave no reason, to surmise a reason which, *perhaps*, depended upon time, place, and circumstances, and which, *perhaps*, may be liable to change in accordance with time, place, and circumstances—if it pleases the Supreme Lawgiver to make known to us His will on this matter, to make it known in as clear a voice, in as public a manner, and as far beyond all doubt and ambiguity as He did when He gave the law itself. As long as this has not happened, as long as we can point to no such authentic exemption from the law, no sophistry of ours can free us from the strict obedience we owe to the law; and reverence for God draws a line between speculation and practice which no conscientious man may cross. I therefore repeat my earlier protestation: Weak and shortsighted is the eye of man! Who can say: I have entered into God's sanctuary, gauged the whole system of his designs, and am able to determine its measure, goal and boundaries? I may surmise, but not pass judgment nor act according to my surmise. If in things human I may not dare to act contrary to the law on the mere strength of my own surmise and legal sophistry, without the authority of the lawgiver or custodian of the law, how much less may I do so in matters divine? Laws that depend on the possession of the Land [of Israel] and institutions governing it carry their exemption with them. Without Temple and priesthood, and outside Judea, there is no scope for either sacrifices or laws of purification or contributions to the priests, insofar as these depend on the possession of the Land. But personal commandments, duties imposed upon a son of Israel, without regard to the Temple service and landed property in Palestine, must, as far as we can see, be observed strictly according to the words of the law, until it shall please the

Most High to set our conscience at rest and to make their abrogation known in a clear voice and in a public manner.

Summary

Mendelssohn was not historically-minded. He wrote to Probst Thomas Abbt, for example, that neither natural history, history of earth, nor political history interested him. In response to Lessing's work on the education of the human race (1780) where Judaism yielded to Christianity, and Christian revelation yielded to reason alone, Mendelssohn wrote that he perceived no overall cultural progress. Cultures grew and faded, and individual progress did not produce any general historical advance. Mendelssohn did recognize the historical character of oral law as developing in the context of changing circumstances, and he rejected Lessing's contention that rabbinic deliberations stretched biblical content beyond its time. To the contrary, it brought it into time. Christian dogma, however, appeared to be immune to historical progress.

HISTORICAL CONCEPTIONS

As often as it was useful, Providence caused wise men to arise in every nation on earth, and granted them the gift of looking with a clearer eye into themselves as well as all around them to contemplate God's works and communicate their knowledge to others. But not at all times is this necessary or useful. Very often, as the Psalmist says, *the babbling of children and infants will suffice to confound the enemy.* The man who lives simply has not yet devised the objections which so greatly confuse the sophist. For him the word *nature*, the mere sound, has not yet become a being that seeks to supplant the Deity. He still knows but little of the difference between direct and indirect causality; and he hears and sees instead the all-vivifying power of the Deity everywhere—in every sunrise, in every rain that falls, in every flower that blossoms and in every lamb that grazes in the meadow and rejoices in its own existence. This mode of conceiving things has in it something defective, but it leads directly to the recognition of an invisible, omnipotent being, to whom we owe all the good which we enjoy. But as soon as an Epicurus or a Lucretius, a Helvétius or a Hume criticizes the inadequacy of this mode of conceiving things and (which is to be charged to human weakness) strays too far in the other direction, and wants to carry on a deceptive game with the word *nature*, Providence again raises up other men among the people who separate prejudice from truth, correct the exaggerations on both sides, and show that truth can endure even if prejudice is rejected. At bottom, the material is always the same—there endowed with all the raw but vigorous juices which nature gives it, here with the refined good taste of art, easier to digest, but only for the weak. On balance, men's doings and the morality of their conduct can perhaps expect just as good results from the crude mode of conceiving things as from these refined and purified concepts. Many a people is destined by Providence to wander through this cycle of ideas, indeed, sometimes it must wander through it more than once; but the quantity and weight of its morality may, perhaps, remain, on balance, about the same during all these various epochs.

I, for my part, cannot conceive of the education of the human race as my late friend Lessing imagined it under the influence of I-don't-know-which historian of mankind. One pictures the collective entity of the human race as an individual person and believes that Providence sent it to school here on earth, in order to raise it from childhood to manhood. In reality, the human race is—if the metaphor is appropriate—in almost every century, child, adult, and old man at the same time, though in different places and regions of the world. Here in the cradle, it sucks the breast, or lives on cream and milk; there it stands in manly armor, consuming the meat of cattle; and, in another place, it leans on a cane, once again without teeth. Progress is for the individual man, who is destined by Providence to spend part of his eternity here on earth. Everyone goes through life in his own way. One man's path takes him through flowers and meadows, another's across desolate plains, or over steep mountains and past dangerous gorges. Yet they all proceed on their journey, making their way to the felicity for which they are destined. But it does not seem to me to have been the purpose of Providence that mankind as a whole advance steadily here below and perfect itself in the course of time. This, at least, is not so well settled nor by any means so necessary for the vindication of God's providence as one is in the habit of thinking.

That we should again and again resist all theory and hypotheses, and want to speak of facts, to hear nothing but of facts, and yet should have the least regard for facts precisely where they matter most! You want to divine what designs Providence has for mankind? Do not frame hypothesis; only look around you at what actually happens and, if you can survey history as a whole, at what has happened since the beginning of time. This is fact, this must have been part of the design; this must have been decreed or, at least, admitted by Wisdom's plan. Providence never misses its goal. Whatever actually happens must have been its design from the beginning, or part of it. Now, as far as the human race as a whole is concerned, you will find no steady progress in its development that brings it ever closer to perfection. Rather do we see the human race in its totality slightly oscillate; it never took a few steps forward without soon afterwards, and with redoubled speed, sliding back to its previous position. Most nations of the earth live for many centuries at the same stage of culture, in the same twilight, one which seems much too dim for our pampered eyes. Now and then, a dot blazes up in the midst of the great mass, becomes a glittering star, and traverses an orbit which now after a shorter, now after a longer period, brings it back again to its starting point, or not far from it. Individual man advances, but mankind continually fluctuates within fixed limits, while maintaining, on the whole, about the same degree of morality in all periods—the same amount of religion and irreligion, of virtue and vice, of felicity and misery; the same result, if one compares like with like; of all these goods and evils as much as is required for the passage of the individual man in order that he might be educated here below, and approach as closely as possible the perfection which is apportioned to him and for which he is destined.

1.2. ISAAC SAMUEL REGGIO ("YASHAR" OF GORIZIA, 1784-1855): REASON AND REVELATION, DIALECTICALLY RELATED[34]

Reggio was born near Italy's northeastern border, in Gorizia. He studied Bible and *Talmud* with his father Avraham Hai ben Azriel (1755-1846), the rabbi of Gorizia and author of pedagogical texts on the *Mishnah* and the Bible (*Eshel Avraham: Ben Eser Shanim La'mishnah* and *Eshel Avraham: Ben Hamesh Shanim La'mikra*). He attended Gorizia's public school where he studied various sciences, and the local *Gymnasium* where he focused on mathematics. Reggio married Rahel bat Shelomoh Halevi in 1808, and in 1810 was employed as an instructor in literature and geography at the *Gymnasium* that he had attended. In 1813 the Austrians took control of Gorizia from the French, and Reggio was dismissed on the grounds that Christians should not be learning from a Jew.

Supported by his wife's family, Reggio dedicated himself to scholarship. An admirer of Mendelssohn, he emulated the *Book of the Paths of Peace* and translated Scripture into Italian in Hebrew letters (1818-

---

34   Reggio apparently referred to himself as "Yashar Mi'gorizia" to connect himself with Joseph Solomon Delmegio, "Yashar of Candia." Goldenthal, "Beiträge zur Literatur der jüdische Religionsphilosophie: *Ha'torah Veha'filosofiah...*," *Allgemeine Zeitung des Judentums: Literarisches und homiletisches Beiblatt* 1, no. 35 (15 December 1938): 160-162. See Simon Bernfeld, *Dor Tahapukhot* (Warsaw: Schuldberg, 1897), 114. On Reggio's life see Klausner, "Yitshak Shemuel Reggio," in *Historiah Shel Ha'sifrut Ha'ivrit Ha'hadashah*, vol. 4 (Jerusalem: Ahiasaf, 1953), 10-37; Raphael Kirchheim, "I. S. Reggio," *Volkskalender für Israeliten* 19 (1861): 23-30; Yitshak Hayyim Castiglione, *Toledot R. Avraham Hai Reggio U'veno R. Yitshak Shemuel Reggio* (Cracow: Fischer, 1891); Henry Samuel Morais, "Isaac Samuel Reggio," in *Eminent Israelites of the Nineteenth Century* (Philadelphia: Stern, 1880), 296-301; Giuliano Tamani, "I. S. Reggio E L'illuminismo Ebraico," in *Ebrei A Gorizia E A Trieste Tra 'Ancien Régime' Ed Emancipazione* (Udine: Del Bianco, 1984), 29-40; David T. Malkiel, "New Light on the Career of Isaac Samuel Reggio," in *The Jews of Italy: Memory and Identity*, ed. Bernard D. Cooperman and Barbara Garvin (Maryland: University of Maryland Press, 2000), 137-159; and "The Reggios of Gorizia: Modernization in Micro," in *The Mediterranean and the Jews: Society, Culture and Economy in Early Modern Times*, vol. 2, ed. Elliott Horowitz and Moises Orfali (Ramat Gan: Bar Ilan University, 2002), 67-84; and Marco Grusovin, "Isacco Samuele Reggio, rabbino e filosofo," *Quaderni Giuliani di Storia* 17, no. 2 (1996): 7-20. Also Marc Shapiro, "Isaac Reggio and the London *Herem* of 1842," *Jewish Culture and History* 4, no. 1 (2001): 97-106. The JNUL Archives in Jerusalem hold the Reggio-Zunz correspondence, June 1836 – April 1838, 792/G20.

1821).[35] He began his work with a deliberation about the dialectical relationship between rational proof and the divine authority of *Torah* revelation and a discussion of the philosophical approach to *midrash* in Rambam's *Guide to the Perplexed* (vol. 3, ch. 43).[36] In 1821, when the Austrian authorities ordered rabbis to have doctorates in philosophy, Reggio proposed the establishment of a rabbinical college dedicated to that end. Students would be trained in Scripture, *Talmud*, and Hebrew literature, as well as in philosophy. To justify and support the endeavor, he published *Torah and Philosophy* in 1827. Then, with the help of Samuel David Luzzatto (they worked together on the journals *Bikurei Ha'itim* and *Kerem Hemed*), the college was established in 1829.[37]

In *Torah and Philosophy*, portions of which have been translated for this volume, Reggio spoke of how the potentially beneficial mutual relationship between revelational and philosophical truth had been frustrated in the course of Jewish history. Out of zeal for the *Talmud*, some traditionalists suppressed philosophical reason; out of their opposing zeal, the rationalists suppressed the literature of revelation. In the first section of the book Reggio criticized the categorical opposition by the rabbinic sages to all external, apocryphal literature, while he praised the support for philosophy on the part of the medievalists Maimonides and Moses Almosnino (1515-1580) and modernists Mendelssohn and Naphtali Herz Wessely (1725-1805). He also clarified a distinction between the rabbinic attitudes towards physical science and towards metaphysics. There was nothing in Jewish sources to prohibit philosophical inquiry into subjects on the physical level, he declared. The prohibition was limited to metaphysical topics as identified by Aristotle (notably

---

35   Reggio, *Torat Ha'elohim Meturgemet Italkit* (Vienna: G. Heltsinger, 1818) and *Sefer Torat Ha'elohim: Kolel Hamishah Humshei Torah: Meturgamim Italkit U'mevoarim Beur Hadash Kefi Peshatei Ha'ketuvim U'kelalei Ha'lashon*, 5 vols. (Vienna: Anton Strauss, 1821).

36   Reggio, "Hakdamah," in *Sefer Torat Ha'elohim: Kolel Hamishah Humshei Torah*, vol. 1 (Vienna: Anton Strauss, 1821), 1-13.

37   Philippson remarked that "What Krokhmal and Rappaport meant for the east, Reggio and Luzzatto meant for the south." See Martin Philippson, *Neueste Geschichte des jüdischen Volkes*, vol. 1 (FaM: J. Kauffmann, 1922), 199. On Reggio and Luzzatto, see Reggio, *Katuv Yashar: Sefer Kolel Igerot Le'shadal Im Ezeh Shirei Yashar*, ed. Castiglione (Cracow: Y. Fisher Ve'sason Printing, 1902); Marco Grusovin, "La risposta del giudaismo italiano all'a haskalah berlinese; alcune considerazioni su Isacco Samuele Reggio e Samuele David Luzzatto," *Studi Goriziani* 78 (1993): 11-23; "Correspondence," in *Kokhavei Yitshak* 24 (1858): 25-32; and Nikolaus Vielmetti, "Die Gründungsgeschichte des Collegio Rabbinico in Padua," *Kairos* 13, no. 1 (1971): 38-66.

God's incorporeality and the immortality of the soul), where the interests of religion and philosophy coincided.

In the second section Reggio addressed that aspect of the dialectical relationship where non-revelational wisdom strengthened the revelational. In the area of natural sciences, physics stimulated awareness of the laws which governed nature, the perfection of nature, and the wisdom that had to exist in order for the world to be created. The study of pharmacology added knowledge to the system of Jewish laws pertaining to food, and the study of astronomy was helpful in Jewish calculations regarding the new moon and holidays. Reggio held that ethical philosophy could deepen the understanding of the spiritual dimensions of Scripture's positive commandment. Metaphysics could also help to remove negative accretions to revealed Scripture, namely superstition and pilpulistic adventures, by focusing on the themes underlying rabbinic texts and making positive contributions to understanding the matter of God's incorporeality. Reggio questioned contemporary rabbinical prohibitions against philosophical inquiry into metaphysical subjects, alleging that political and financial motives were involved.[38] When the "Russian Mendelssohn" Isaac Baer Levinsohn (1788-1860) learned of this, he attacked the book as a whole and demanded that Reggio ask for forgiveness from contemporary rabbis for the insult.[39]

In the third section Reggio addressed other aspects of the dialectical relationship. Advocates of revelation alone discredited philosophy on the grounds that philosophers disagreed so much among themselves. To the contrary, Reggio responded, such disagreements evidenced the seriousness with which philosophers probed their respective positions. Those revelation advocates also contended that the intellect was essentially unreliable. If so, Reggio countered, why were they using their intellect to make such a judgment? In principle, as demonstrated in Mendelssohn's *Morgenstunden*, while the truths of *Torah* were beyond intel-

---

38 Reggio, *Ha'torah Veha'filosofiah* (Vienna: Anton Schmid, 1827); Goldenthal, "Beiträge zur Literatur der jüdische Religionsphilosophie," *Allgemeine Zeitung des Judentums: Literarisches und Homiletisches Beiblatt* 1.35 (15 December 1838): 160-162; and Joseph Derenbourg, "*Ha'torah Veha'filosofiah*: Torah und Philosophie in ihrer Versöhnung," *Wissenschaftliche Zeitschrift für Jüdische Theologie* 2 (1836): 331-350.
39 Isaac Baer Levinsohn, *Yehoshofat: Hu Bikoret Al Sefer Torah Veha'filosofiah Leha'hakham Yitshak Shemuel Reggio, Ha'mekhuneh Yashar* (Warsaw: David Baer Natanson, 1883), 8; Editor, "Isaac Baer Levinsohn," in *The Jewish Encyclopaedia*, vol. 8 (New York: Funk and Wagnalls, 1901), 43-45.

lectual reason, they were not opposed to it. Indeed, philosophy provided reasons which substantiated the authoritative truths of belief. Specifically, scientific research involved the "intrinsic" proof of individual reason and direct observation, while beliefs involved the "extrinsic" proof of drawing credible testimony from others. Philosophy offered rational criteria for evaluating that testimony. It also offered creative hypotheses, to be proven in the course of time, on the basis of the historical data provided by the believers' traditions and *Torah* prescriptions based upon divine authority.

In the fourth section, Reggio applied philosophical methods to understanding original human perfection, transgression, punishment, death, and redemption. He also returned to the theme of *Torah* truth as being beyond (but not opposed to) the rational intellect. While some other nations were confined to a natural relationship to God, a relationship within the bounds of natural events, Israel's relationship to God fell within the category of the supernatural, in the realm where human reason did not overlap with revelation. As such, Reggio faulted Rambam for seeking to rationalize positive commandments and implying that reason could replace the command; these were rather given by God forever, to distinguish Israel with its messianic destiny from other nations. He also criticized Mendelssohn's student David Friedländer (1750-1834) for his Deism, and Herz Homberg (1749-1841), Peter Beer (1758-1838), Joseph Johlson (1777-1851), and Isaac Mieses (1802-1883) for limiting revelation to the role of educating humanities to certain truths.

In 1833 Reggio published an edition of Elia Delmedigo's (1460-1497) *Behinat Ha'dat* (*Examination of Religion*), and the next year the letters of Joseph Solomon Delmedigo (*Yashar Mi'kandia*, 1591-1655).[40] He succeeded his father as rabbi of Gorizia upon his death in 1841. Then in 1849 he published his autobiography, which listed one hundred and three published and unpublished works (*Minhah Le'ohavav*, "Offering to the Beloved"). His publication of the *Kol Sahal* and *Sha'agat Aryeh* manuscripts of Leon da Modena (1571-1618), entitled *Behinat Ha'kabbalah* (*Examination of Tradition*, [Gorizia: Seitz, 1852]), elicited Zechariah

---

40   Elia Delmedigo, *Behinat Ha'dat*, ed. Reggio (Vienna: Anton Edlen v. Schmid, 1833). See Reggio, "Ha'arah Nishmetet Min Ha'sefer Behinat Ha'dat" in *Yalkut Yashar* (Gorizia: Seitz, 1854), 32-40. Reggio, *Igerot Yashar* [Mi'kandia, Yosef Shelomoh Delmedigo] *El Ehad Mi'meyode'av*, 2 vols. (Vienna: Anton Edlen v. Schmid, 1834). See Isaac Barzilay, *Yosef Shelomoh Delmedigo, Yashar of Candia* (Leiden: Brill, 1974).

Frankel's strong objections. Leon da Modena, Frankel complained, lampooned rabbinical teachings with a "burlesque frivolity which shut out everything holy." For Reggio "to intentionally disperse the material just to pander to the masses and create a religious scandal, indicated a loss of religious and ethical sanity."[41] His *Guide for the Instruction of Jewish Youth* appeared in his last year of life. It contained essential elements of Jewish theology, published with the hope that a successor would come to develop them enough to provide a refuge for Israel's youth from "storms of doubt, unbelief and irreligion." N. H. Picciotto, the translator, added that the *Guide* enlarged the student's view of religion, took him to his heavenly source, and guided him to admire and comprehend the objects of religion with virtue and love.[42]

I.II. Selections From *Torah and Philosophy:* Section 3. Chapter 1

Summary of translated passages
Responding to claims made by Torah scholars against philosophy and scientific research, Reggio maintained that belief and philosophy-scientific research were not opposed but rather complementary. On the one hand, they took different paths. Philosophical proofs were intrinsic in character and had objective truth. For example, an equidistant triangle has three angles. Belief, however, was based upon the observations of others about specific objects. The observations were conditioned by the process of the believers' subjective reception (extrinsic proofs). On the other hand, they contributed to one another. To dispel fantasy and contradiction, the believer could employ rational criteria. These included the original source's moral standing, self-interest, intelligence, and tendency to fantasize. They also incorporated the nature of

---

41 Zechariah Frankel, "Critique of Reggio's publication of the work of Leon da Modena," *Monatsschrift für Geschichte und Wissenschaft des Judenthums* (1855): 467-468. See also Abraham Geiger, *Leon da Modena, Rabbiner zu Venedig (1571-1648) und seine Stellung zur Kabbalah, zum Talmud und zum Christentum* (Breslau: J. U. Kern, 1856); and David Einhorn, *"Behinat Ha'kabbalah (Prüfung der Tradition) enthaltend Kol Sakhal und Sha'agat Aryeh*, von Leon da Modena, herausgegeben und mit kritischen Anmerkungen versehen von Reggio, Görz 1852," *Der Israelitische Volkslehrer* 4 (1854): 97-101, 123-139, 186-197, 221-229, 247-256. Kirchheim countered in 1861 that Reggio had no intention of helping the ignorant to undermine Judaism, but that he merely wanted to publish an interesting work. See Kirchheim, "I. S. Reggio."
42 Reggio, *A Guide for Religious Instruction of Jewish Youth Proposed to Teachers by Isaac Samuel Reggio*, trans. from the Italian by H. M. Picciotto (London: Simpkin, Marshal, 1855).

experience with the object of belief involved, and the logic of the testimony.
At the same time, the scientific researcher relied on the testimony of others,
and so depended upon belief. A believer who employed scientific proof did not
weaken belief, but strengthened it. Scientific research also removed obstacles
to belief. These included physical lust, pride, and temptation. Reggio set God-
given ordinances of Torah apart from reason, since they were based upon
a wisdom which transcended intellect and human wisdom, and the doubts
which reason might have about them were not relevant.

[Excessive Claims Against Philosophy]

The way of researchers who proceed fairly does not only involve checking
and looking for reasons and proofs to establish the truth of some object.
It also involves submitting claims which the disputant maintains must
be considered to judgment. We who want to apply true judgment to the
discipline of philosophy, having dealt briefly with the applications of this
discipline, now turn to deal with the many claims lodged [on behalf of To-
rah] and expressed against philosophy by the doomsayers. We will weigh
their claims fairly, to observe whether or not the reasons stand. This inquiry will shed light upon, and instruct us about, the path of judgment.
If we are capable of refuting those claims with correct proofs (*mofet*), we
will understand how the aforementioned philosophical application flows
from the very existence of this wisdom (*hokhmah*), a wisdom which is
in itself good and upright. Philosophy's defects, as detailed here, come
from improper use. As a corollary, it may be stated that no fault remains
with the wisdom of scientific research (*hokhmat ha'mehkar*), as long as
one stays within the boundaries drawn around this wisdom, according to
its character. It would be impossible to deal with all the claims which the
opponents could make. For who could guess what is in their hearts? They
would come up forever with ideas (*deot*) from their hearts. Every day,
they would wage new wars against philosophy. Here, I will try to list only
the major, more prominent complaints.

1. Does Scientific Research (Hakirah) Oppose Faith?

The first and strongest claims which *Torah* scholars usually make against
philosophical study is that faith and scientific research are opposed, and
that they can never reside together in any human heart. Before accepting something as true [they explain], the scientific researcher always
looks for different sorts of proof. The believer relies on the words of the

trusted narrator, who tells him that it is correct to believe such and such, and then gladly accepts all principles of faith without feeling compelled to review the proofs. Therefore, the *Torah* scholars say, it is impossible to instill faith in the heart of someone who covenants with scientific research. As soon as scientific research enters in, faith leaves, for they are opposites. It follows, for those who say this, that the children of Israel, believers who are children of believers, are obliged to keep their distance from scientific research, to keep it distant lest they fall in love with it and hate the faith which is the heritage of their forefathers. Were this claim to be authentic, it would completely vitiate what we have written so far. All our efforts and labors to defend philosophy and reconcile it with divine *Torah* would come to naught and be pointless. But it is not so! If you, enlightened reader, would approach the issue carefully and sensitively, and give your heart to what is prepared in answer to this claim, you would agree that the claim is as chaff scattered by the wind (Psalms 1:4).

[Cognition and Belief/Faith]

At birth, man is empty of all cognition (*yediah*). As he gains in years, uses his senses daily and hears words from those who are more intelligent than he, becomes enlightened about the things he has seen or heard, combines one concept (*musag*) with another, and draws consciousness from premises and the like, his cognitive knowledge (*yediotav*) slowly increases. He ascends higher and higher, and comes closer and closer to perfection every day. He acquires two types of cognitive knowledge:

[First] there are objects which a person knows in terms of their authentic existence, in that the reasons (*ta'amim*) and proofs (*mofteha*) within the thing itself have become known to him. The term cognition (*yediah*) applies here. Thus, a person knows that in an equal triangle, angles are equal to each other, each with sixty degrees—if he also knows the premises upon which this statement is based. That is, if he knows that the three angles of the triangle total one hundred and eighty degrees and that all triangles with equal sides have equal angles. He must also know the reasons for these premises—e.g., that two parallel lines intersected by a third line will have two interior angles totaling one hundred and eighty degrees. He must also have the right proofs. Then, it can be said of him he has knowledge of the object. For these premises and examples come to hand, by observing lines, angles, and triangles in nature. All these objects (*devarim*) are in the thing itself which he interprets.

[Second], a person may also recognize the truth of something—not in terms of knowing the reasons in the thing itself; but because it is told to the person by someone who is trusted and would surely not lie. This understanding (*hakarah*) is not cognition but belief (*emunah*). The one who recognizes such a thing is called a believer. Anyone who relies upon that someone is called one who trusts in that someone. For example, a person hears from geometricians that each angle in an equilateral triangle has sixty degrees. He considers it proper to take this truth from them, as they already checked into it and properly investigated its truth, and they are worthy of being relied upon. Then it is said that a person believes in the object (*davar*). If so, the cognition is the agreement by the soul to this one object among other objects, on the strength of having examples which prove the truth of the object. Thus, faith is the soul's agreement with one object among many objects on account of witnesses before us.

[Validating Belief]

But if you proceed more closely and penetrate the interiority of this matter, and observe the foundations upon which the believer builds his faith, you will find that reality always agrees with what the person conjectures in his soul to be true in terms of belief. At times, those in whom he trusted tell him something deceptive. This is what happens when someone does not have the criteria to verify whether the teller is trustworthy or not. The fool cited in Proverbs 14:15 believes everything—some of which is undoubtedly false. Were it not so, King Solomon, peace be upon him, would not have called him foolish. It would be correct to say that belief does not always apply to an object which is true. It sometimes applies to a lie. This also appears within the definition of faith—as in the *Guide to the Perplexed* (part 1, chapter 50), the words of which are interpreted by Efodi [Profiat Duran, 1350-1415, author of *Ma'aseh Efod*]:

> The definition of faith is this: One believes that the object outside the soul is as the soul conceptualized it even though the person did not interpret the object with

proof. As such, the definition of faith would apply *even to deceptive faith* ["Efodi" *ad Moreh Nevukhim, Helek Rishon, Perek* 50].

The pious author [Bahyah Ibn Pakudah, eleventh century] of *Hovot Ha'levavot* claims as follows:

> ... the believer having faith in those from whom he has received the traditions, but without knowing the truth by the exercise of his own intellect and understanding; such a person is like a blind man led by one that can see. It is also possible that he is receiving the tradition from one who himself has only learned it traditionally. This suggests comparison with a company of blind men, each of whom has his hand on the shoulder of the one in front of him, and so on until the row reaches the person who is at their head and acts as their guide. Should this seeing person fail in his duty and neglect to watch over his company or should any of them stumble or meet with any other mishap, the misfortune would affect them all. They would all miss their way, fall into a pit or ditch, or encounter an obstacle that would prevent their further progress. [*Perek* 2, *Sha'ar Ha'yihud*, trans. Hyamson]

The [introduction to Joseph Albo's] *Sefer Ha'ikarim* teaches a similar definition of faith. Rabbi Menahem [ben Avraham] Bonafos thinks likewise. In the beginning of his *Book of Definitions (Sefer Ha'gedarim)* [ca. 1400] he says "Faith is something (*Inyan*) conceptualized in the soul. Something is believed in, in the way it is conceptualized. *That which is conceptualized may be either true or not true.*" Experience also determines that the matter is so. How many times does one believe something being told and which is considered true, and then some days after realizes that it is a lie and that one's faith was misdirected? Besides, it is known that there are many religions in the world, in terms of divine worship. They are different from one another, and each religious person thinks that only his kind of worship is true and pleasing to God. This is so, even though we know clearly that it is totally impossible for them all to be true and pleasing to God. Accordingly, we said correctly that faith is not always supported by truth, but sometimes by falsehood—when the believer does not differentiate or lies to himself and lets himself think that something is true [when it is not].

> Note: It is not my intention to speak here of the nature of faith, which Holy Scripture greatly glorifies and praises. It states, 'I have chosen the path of faith' [Psalms 109:30], 'and who can find a faithful man' [Proverbs 20:6]; 'the just shall live by his faith' [Habakkuk 2:4], etc. It is right that you know, that the Scriptures use the term FAITH solely to express true faith—not faith which, God forbid, is based upon lies. This is also how Scripture uses the word wisdom (*hokhmah*)—solely to express the wisdom of *Torah* and correct behavior. This is explained at length in the work *The Locked Garden (Gan Na'ul)* [1765/66] by the great rabbi Naftali Herz Wessely. It is known that authors sometime use the term "*haham*" (wise person) even for a plowman, a weaver, an embroiderer, anyone with some skill or someone who understands medical science, or natural science, or the like. On account of this, would you say that such cognitive knowledge is what King Solomon, peace be upon him, meant when he said, 'Happy is the man who finds wisdom' [Proverbs 3:13], for 'wisdom is better than pearls' [Psalms 8:11]? This is how you should evaluate the term faith, if you see how Scripture praises greatly the one who walks the path of faith. Properly, you should think that the intention has to do with someone worthy to conceptualize objects in his soul as they truly are outside the soul. This is a great achievement. You will find this explained nicely in the *Book of Attributes* [1786], part 2, chapter 5 of Rabbi Naphtali Herz Wessely [*Sefer Ha'midot Vehu Musar Ha'sekhel, Helek Sheni, Perek Hamishi* (Berlin, 1786), 53^b-65^a]. But here we use the term faith according to its customary meaning for everybody. Therefore we said that at times, it also rests on a lie. And understand. [End of Note].

In regard to this issue, it would be proper to inquire about the criteria which distinguish true faith from false. Our answer is that the believer who properly employs intellect will apply seven initial tests: Does the source for what is heard include all the conditions required to assume its truth? Once the believer finds that all these conditions are assembled, it will become clear to him that the source is true and not false. He then judges what he is told to be clearly true. This is so, even if proofs for the object itself remain unknown to him. Were these [internal] proofs known to him, he would already have left the confines of faith and entered into the confines of cognition, as stated. From this, understand that both knower (ha'yodea) and believer will need proofs. The knower seeks internal proofs, i.e., those taken from the object itself (intrinsic arguments). The believer pursues external proofs, outside the object (extrinsic arguments), that is, reasons which inhere to the one telling him something. Ultimately, both use proofs.

We must say, that were it not for the fact that the believer is obliged to pursue some kind of proofs, his faith would be null and void. For even if some liar or crazy person would come and tell him that clouds rain gold coins on his town every day, or that he saw a donkey flying in the air, or similar nutty things, if the believer accepts all this in full faith and does not react with objection, he is guilty. This is a vexation of spirit [Ecclesiastes 1:17] and unacceptable to intelligence. One is oneself guilty, if one is told of two objects which seriously contradict one another, and nevertheless believes both to be true. It would be absurd and unacceptable to assume that no reason need be sought for the belief. Therefore, it is all the more necessary for the believer to have a brain in his skull, to always require reasons upon which to build his faith, and to check the source for what he hears. For example, [1] One should check whether the person telling him something is a good and upright human being who loves truth, or is an evil doer out to deceive others. Further [2], whether that person has anything to gain personally for telling something untrue—such that he might switch truth for lie for some personal advantage. Moreover [3], one should check whether the person is alert and intelligent, or a dullard, dunce, or simpleton. In this case, it is highly possible that [the teller] was led astray by others. [4] Is [the teller] wise and knowledgeable, or ignorant about the subject he spoke about? [5] Is his mind always on the right track, or does the power of imagination sometimes take over—such that he imagines that objects exist, which never do? [6] Did he perceive the objects by sense, or did the object reach him via hearsay? [7] Did he reflect carefully upon his perception, or act hastily and sloppily? [9] Do the parts of the story fit together, or are they perhaps contradictory?

[The Role of Scientific Research in Belief]
There are similar tests for checking the veracity of witness statements. Judgment depending on witnesses—justifying a just person or convicting an evil person by means of their testimony—falls under the definition of faith, as explained, to the extent that the faith is based upon reasons. If there is still any doubt about this, take a look at the opinions of Maimonides, *Rav* Bahyah Ibn Pakudah, Joseph Albo [1380-1444] and Rabbi Menahem ben Avraham Bonafos [14ᵗʰ/15ᵗʰ century]. Consider the words of Rabbi Solomon ben Abraham Adret, in his *She'elot U'teshuvot* [*She'elah* 548, p. 75ᵃ, col. 1]. "The children of Israel will not be convinced (*le'hitpatot*) [Reggio's term *yitpesu* is apparently an error] of something, until they arrive at truth through much scientific research and complete scientific research." All our great wise men took this path, teaching us that believers too will lean towards reasons. After this is clear to you, the problem is solved. The claim I introduced at the beginning of the chapter disappears by itself. For how could the believer discover the external proofs needed, unless his intellect used logical principles? How could this take place, without the methods of scientific research? The believer himself becomes a scientific researcher, and insofar as scientific research helps faith to provide with external proofs, faith and scientific research cannot be opposites. Those who say they are do not speak the truth.

Do not rush in anger and say they are still opposed; that the scientific researcher will not be satisfied with external proofs in ascertaining the truth of objects, will always seek internal proofs from the object itself; that the believer's methods are incorrect in the eye of the philosopher and that there will forever be intense animosity between scientific research and faith. If you would but reflect on my points [you would see] that this is a lie.

[The Role of External Proof (Belief) in Philosophy]
Not every scientific researcher is a philosopher just like that. In truth, the individual who proceeds solely in terms of internal proofs, and is not anxious to gather ideas founded on understanding the substance of things, will not reach the high degree of true philosophy. To the contrary, he has many disadvantages. The human being is limited in his faculties, by the years of life, and does not have the power to research everything and know clearly all the objects needed for his perfection.

He cannot reach some objects, whether because of intellectual limitations, time pressures, or the pursuit of a livelihood. He will need to accept some objects from others, for he cannot look and check every object, everywhere, and every time! Often, he needs the support of external evidence, for he does not have the strength to perform all the experiments which others have done, in order to establish the truth of some particular object! Have not all world events of earlier days, all wisdom created by people in the past, all laws of nature disclosed on the basis of experience, reached us only through writing? Each piece of writing is external evidence, and evidence is accepted on faith alone. The term "cognition" would not apply, for no piece of writing contains internal proof for its truth. If the scientific researcher rejected data like this, because it contained only external proof, he would be left without the knowledge necessary for completing the research. For example, it would be stupid to say that Rambam did not write the *Guide* attributed to him, or that in reality there is no place in the world called "America" because one has no proof that these are true facts. Is there not enough to external proofs, to ascertaining the truth through them? Are not the two kinds of proof we cited both born out of intellect (*sekhel*)? The more they proceed correctly according to laws of logic, the more they contain enough to provide confirmation and proof of the truth of the object. Also, the common sense rooted in us often compels us to pursue external proofs and to accept truths founded upon them. Insofar as all laws of true philosophy revolve around judgments of common sense, it is obvious that the true philosopher will accept both kinds of proofs. If the left hand accepts internal proofs regarding objects suitable to this path, then the right hand will embrace the external, when the philosopher understands that he reaches what is sought also through the external proofs. In this respect as well, there is no conflict between truth and scientific research.

[Faith and Command]

Given all that's been said, it seems to me that the claim of those opposed to scientific research, who hate it, is still not silenced—because of their love for faith. My ears quiver as they shriek:

Do not your words uproot the duty of faith, leaving neither root nor branch? According to your words, even if the believer relied on proofs, it still would not be possible to command him to faith. No command is enough to bring him under the yoke of faith. This is the job of external proofs. If this is so, what the *Posekim* taught us, that it is a command to believe this or that, or that the Israelite is obliged to believe, is in vain! The *Great Book of Commandments* (*Sefer Mitsvot Ha'gadol*) [by Moses ben Jacob, of Coucy, 1250], begins sections one and two on positive commandments with the statement, 'The command to believe' ["*Mitsvat aseh leha'amin,*" in *Mitsvot Aseh: Miha'sefer Mitsvot Gadol* [Venice, 1547], 96ª]. Your words, according to which there is in reality no such duty, clearly eliminate this. If we listened to you, and let people be free, not to listen any more to the voice of command which obliges belief, faith would lose all root. Faith would cease in the land.

To this I reply: Let us say that it is true, that faith is the foundation of human prosperity. That once the bonds [of faith] of the people are broken, they grope around at noon as if it was night, without knowing why they fail. Accordingly, it would be proper for anyone who yearns for true bliss to adhere to faith and walk the path of faith. As King David, may peace be upon him, said, "The path of faith I have chosen" (Psalms 119:30). But even I, God forbid, did not advise moving away from faith. To the contrary, I said that its presence was necessary for anyone who covenanted with philosophy. And I will prove this below. But in terms of the duty to believe, i.e., whether or not the command falls upon faith or not, I see that there is some misunderstanding. I think that neither those who endeavor to uphold the commandment, nor their opponents, have probed the context of the matter properly, or at least they did not explain their views very well. I, in my simplicity, will try to plunge into these mighty waters, and explain how the duty to have faith is to be understood. With God's help I will strive to reconcile the two explanations [that faith cannot be commanded; that faith can be commanded]—with God's good help. Perhaps God will make my path successful. You, the reader, may scrutinize and judge my words.

According to the first view, it appears totally impossible to command a person to believe one thing or another. Even the most stubborn person would have to confess that faith is founded upon reasons, as we explained earlier. It is therefore impossible for faith to be commanded. For if reasons are strong, faith will enter the heart by itself, even without a commandment. This is because a person cannot remove what his intellect has ascertained to be true. And when the reasons are weak, faith will not be formed in his heart even if a hundred commandments and warnings supported it. For how could someone accept as true, what one's knowledge (*da'at*) determined to be false? Even were his mouth to declare "I believe," would he not be a hypocrite if his intellect refused to accept it? What is the point of lip service, if the heart remains aloof? How could hypocritical talk and deceptive language be pleasing to the God of truth? Experience testifies that it is impossible to compel any person to believe in one object among [many] objects. Even if they bound him in chains and tortured him until his soul reached *Sheol*, his heart could not be forced to have faith until those aforementioned proofs became clear to him. Even if at moments his mouth declared "I believe" in order to be saved from harsh suffering—as happened so frequently with survivors of the House of Israel who remained in Spain after the expulsion—who could tell me what was in his heart? Is it not possible, that he still refused to believe in his heart, and that he was only making a false declaration with his lips?

It is well known to anyone intelligent that the human being is free in his actions—and all the more so in his thoughts, and that his free will would not be inclined to one side above all others, except for the power of evidence (*re'iyot*), for he knows by his reason to bring one side near, and keep the other at a distance. Were it presupposed that a person was forced to believe in something by the power of the order of the command, then the power of choice would already be annulled for him. Therefore, it may properly be said that faith does not submit to command. Our opinion is reinforced by *Torah* itself. Nowhere do we find any command to believe. The *Torah* does not say, "Believe, Israel, the Lord our God, the Lord is One," but "Hear." Not "And have faith that the Lord your God is God," but "Know." Judge according to the passage "Know the God of your fathers" [I Chronicles 28:9] and many other passages. All our great scholars, such as Rabbi Sa'adiah, Maimonides, and Bahyah Ibn Pakudah, sustained this insight. Rabbi Obadiah Sforno [1475-1550] states in the introduction to *Light of Nations* (*Hakdamah*, in *Or Amim*),

> the blessed God did not specifically command any principle in the theoretical area [of belief]. But He did com-

mand us to know, in observing statements purely about His justice. Whoever is a teacher [so to speak] like God, certainly knows that it is incorrect to say that we have no choice [when it comes to] believing what the commandment commands us.

In a nearby passage [Obadiah Sforno states]:

It is obvious to any investigator, that it is an error to think that the Bible says nothing about how knowledge is acquired. Every philosopher would mock at references to objects, in which the faithful one believed without knowing about them, and every opponent sneer. As if the [divine] Righteous Teacher commanded in vain when He said, 'Know this day, and lay it to thy heart, that the Lord, He is God... [Deuteronomy 4:39]. There are many such passages in the *Torah* and prophets, commanding or eliciting cognition and intellection. There is not a single command to believe. God has not commanded us to believe in His existence or any other or providence. Faith does not fall under the will and therefore does not fall under command.

The author of *Sefer Ha'yashar* (*The Book of the Righteous*) seems to have the same opinion. At the beginning of Gate 3 he wrote "know that faith will be of the intellect...," etc. [Source uncertain; *Sefer Ha'yashar* of Jacob ben Meir Tam has no "*Sha'ar* 3"]. In his commentary on the *Torah* portion *Yitro*, Rabbi Isaac Abarbanel argues that the term "commandment" does not apply to faith. ["*Ve'lo tipol ha'mitsvah be'emunot,*" "*Yitro ... Ve'amnam,*" in *Perush Al Ha'torah*, vol. 2 (Jerusalem, 1964): 182ª]. In *Behinat Ha'dat* (*Examination of Religion*), Elia Delmedigo wrote: "Our *Torah* does not oblige us to believe at all in contracting objects, or to deny first axioms. There is no divine punishment for not believing what our intellect (*sekhel*) with its God-engraved nature, cannot accept or believe." Given all this, it may be properly concluded that a command to believe is impossible as a matter of principle. [If it existed] the heart would turn away, the claim described at the beginning of this discourse [about the mutual intolerance between belief and research] would take over, the spirit of faith would be driven from the land and believers obliterated.

[On the Duty (or Obligation) to Believe]
My heart therefore tells me to affirm and keep the duty (hiyuv) to believe unconditionally, when duty is understood solely in these terms. The obligation does not apply to the intellect. For the intellect is active only in terms of proofs and reasons as demonstrated. [This obligation] applies instead to the realm of the will [and not to faith]. The purpose of the duty is for a person to try to utilize any means to bring him to faith, and to distance anything which prevents him from using those means. If a person does try, then faith will surely enter his heart. Scholars of ethics have said that a person's first obligation is to know one's duties, in order to be able then to carry them out. So it is with the matter of faith. One is obliged to prepare oneself in such a way that faith could enter one's heart. This means employing all activities needed to bring faith within oneself, and removing all impediments which obstruct faith.

Let me offer an example. If a person tells me that I will see a certain tower, first there really has to be a tower. It also has to be accessible to me. Sparks of light have to fall upon it. I have to have healthy and good eyes. And none of this would be enough, if I closed my eyelids or turned around. I have to face in the direction of the tower, direct my eyes to where the tower is, and remove any obstacles between my eyes and the tower. The evidence (re'iyah) will surely come by itself. It will rest on principles known to the science of optometry, on laws which the blessed Creator impressed upon the nature of light, and upon the nature of the eye. It is similar with faith. To say a person is obliged to believe this or that from the mouth of others does not mean one must accept everything without any examination or intellection—or without seeking external proofs. This is as impossible as seeing something with one's eyes closed. The intention is that one is obliged to try, with all the strength at one's disposal, to gather proofs upon which one builds one's faith. Even though one does not have the power to make the proofs strong rather than weak, one does have the power to go back to the proofs, learn what they are, think about them at length, hear words of the wise, and reflect upon works of *Torah* and wisdom—and seek all means which lead one to faith. One's heart is obliged to love truth and hate lies. One must have a great yearning to find the truth—and not to say, "What use is there in finding it?" One is obliged to remove everything which moves one from the path of faith. This includes physical lust; someone sunken into it will not yearn for truth. Pride is also included. Someone with pride about one's delicate intellect and broad understanding will sometimes think that it compromises one's glory, that it is humiliating to accept things in which the multitudes believe. To a proud person, it seems proper for a person of intellect to reduce one's faith, so as to distinguish oneself from the credulous crowd. Further, one is obliged to be free of all the enticements and incitements contained in the words of the *Apikorsim* (heretics) and their books, for they are detrimental to one's good disposition towards faith.

It is true, that anyone who seeks truth also needs to incline their ear to the disputants as well: One needs to research proofs for their merit and their vulnerability, so as to deduce the true judgment. In order to do this without risk, it is proper for the person to be pure of all alien thinking, and devoid of all disgraced qualities—so that arrogance, pride, pursuing the sensational or [responding to] other enticements of the inclination, do not incite one to exchange truth for falsehood. But who can boast of being [totally] free of all these obstacles? It befits a person to be of a great intellect, to be sure never to fall into error, lest it become possible to hold onto imaginary proofs as if they were true. One should not be so impudent as to rely entirely on one's intelligence and think oneself immune to error. Given this, clearly, the more one is intellectually limited, and the more evil characteristics struggle within, the more one should be extremely wary of non-religious people and not go a-whoring after them. For by nature the heart is inclined to evil, as we demonstrated (*Ma'amar 2, Perek* 2). Given all this, the disposition for faith is liable to be lost. Take into account, that a person has a great obligation to [endeavor] to believe, as understood from our earlier exposition. There is no doubt, that the rabbinical sages had that kind of [qualified] obligation in mind, when they said we need to believe, that we are obliged to believe, or something similar. After we grant that this [sort of] obligation exists, the claim cited [i.e., that belief is commanded] becomes void. Then you will no longer be opposed to what we have established. For so it is said: [Through] the obligation to believe and through the quest for reasons for believing in something, a person will help his brother. Together they will be whole, as brothers dwelling together.

[On Torah, Faith, and Deliberation]

Examine and know from what is said here, how high is that degree of true faith which is so greatly praised in Holy Scripture. For the ordinances of holy *Torah* rest upon the prescription of that holy wisdom which is hidden from the eyes of all living beings. Human intellect cannot probe the ultimate reaches of *Torah's* perfection. And the human mind is impatient to grasp the grounds of *mitsvot*, to their very source. Since it is impossible to accept the *mitsvot* by means of cognition, as we shall explain below (*Ma'amar* 4, *Perek* 5), we need to receive them on faith. Given the absence of internal proofs, we have to rely on external ones. There is no disadvantage to this. To the contrary, these external proofs are as good as the others—if not more. Insofar as everything we know about internal proofs is based only upon the intellect, what we know has many limitations—as you will realize from the next chapter. But what we receive from the mouth of the most faithful, that the blessed Creator has given *Torah* to be the inheritance of Jacob, is beyond all suspicion and doubt. Besides this, there is in reality nothing as trustworthy as the ordinances of divine *Torah*. As King David, peace be upon him, said many times, the "testimony of God is reliable" [Psalms 19:8]. "Your testimonies are very reliable" [Psalms 33:5]. "All His ordinances are reliable" [Psalms 101:7]. "All Your commandments are reliable" [Psalms 109:86]. It is most correct to walk the path of faith, not only regarding the acceptance of the yoke of *Torah's* commandment. At times, it is also possible to choose the path of faith regarding other matters, where the researcher negotiates intellectually, endeavoring to reach internal proofs. This is particularly so in the case of plain folks with concerns for worldly matters and who are quite limited in terms of intelligence (*binah*). Nature blankets them with the spirit of slumber and shuts the eyes of the intellect, to the point of making it difficult for them to delve into subtle research. And they cannot complete deliberations (*iyun*), even with much labor. Thus, it is proper for them to depend upon trustworthy preachers—who tell them what they should know.

Know, my reader, that my discourse on faith could not be completed properly in just a few pages. For not even extensive interpretations and many books would exhaust the subject. Still, even the few things written in this chapter should suffice for anyone interested in proving that there is no opposition between scientific research and faith. In the beginning (*Ma'amar* 1, *Perek* 3), I let it be known how many select scholars and leaders in Israel, whom God enlightened, traveled the waters of scientific research and prevailed over the waves. No flood carried them away, no abyss swallowed them up. Their righteousness rescued them from all obstacles. Their faith helped them and saved them. Were it to be demonstrated that scientific research opposed faith, they would not have succeeded in mixing two such opposites together. From this, a person of intellect should conclude, that bliss stands upon two pillars, tradition and deliberation. Therefore, do this yourself my son, and be rescued. Arise, emulate those perfect individuals. They are exemplary. And if God gave you eyes to see, hearts to know, and a yearning to hear the teachings and to act wisely (I do not address those of weak intelligence, for they do not have the ability to enter the palace of research), then you will follow the advice of that One who is wiser than any mortal man before you: "It is good to hold onto one thing and not to lose hold of the other. For a man who fears God will succeed both ways" [Ecclesiastes 7:18]. For if so, you will be careful in your action. When you walk, your step will not become entangled. If you run, you will not stumble. For God will be your trust and will keep you from falling into a trap.

1.3. NAHMAN KROKHMAL ("RANAK," 1785-1840)

Nahman Krokhmal used dialectical logic to reconcile faith and reason. He regarded the slavish obedience to commandments, especially when to the exclusion of intentionality and rational explanation, as poisonous. Nor was rationalistic scientific study on its own the solution, for in his view faith was also essential. A person who engaged in *Torah* study as an ecstatic, he held, would die from the heat. If one studied solely as a rationalist, one would freeze from the snow. The right path was down the middle, one of religious philosophy or philosophical theology. In the texts translated for this volume, Krokhmal elaborates upon his concept of philosophical theology (*hokhmat ha'emunah*) as the synthesis of pure faith (thesis) and reason (anti-thesis). He delineates three levels of philosophy: logical philosophy, concerned with the relationships between ideas of reason; the philosophy of nature, concerned with the idea-itself, the idea-as-object, and the dialectical relationship between the two; and the philosophy of spirit, concerned with the soul and its faculties. This third level, the arena of philosophical theology, engaged in ideas which transcended the intellect, primarily the ontological idea of God. Here, the data of the soul, available in representative images, were transformed into logical ideas. These ideas included being and nothingness, related dialectically and synthesized into becoming; being-of-itself *vis-à-vis* being as other; and quality and quantity.

Krokhmal was born on the Austria-Hungary border in Brody, Galicia, a trade city that had access to the enlightenment of Western Europe.[43] With the Austrian Kaiser Joseph II's 1781 *Edict of Toleration*, sec-

---

43   On Krokhmal's life and thought, see Roland Goetschel, "Au carrefour de la tradition et de la modernité; le penser philosophique de Nahman Krokhmal," in *La Storia Della Filosofia Ebraica*, ed. Irene Kajon (Milan: CEDAM, 1993); Jay Harris, *Nahman Krokhmal: Guiding the Perplexed of the Modern Age* (New York: New York University Press, 1991); Klausner, "Hashpa'ato Shel Hegel Al R. Nahman Krokhmal," in *Ve'zot Li'yehudah: Kovets Ma'amarim Be'hokhmat Yisrael Mugash La'yovel Ha'shishim Shel Ha'rav Ha'rashi Yehudah Leib Landau* (Tel Aviv: Va'ad Ha'yovel, 1936), 71-81; and "Rabi Nahman Krokhmal," in *Historiah Shel Ha'sifrut Ha'ivrit Ha'hadashah*, vol. 2 (Jerusalem: n.p., 1952), 148-165. Also Yehezkel Leib Landau, "Nahman Krokhhmal ein Hegelianer" (Ph.D. diss., University of Berlin, 1904); Meyer, "Nahman Krokhmal: A Philosophy of Jewish History," in *Ideas of Jewish History* (Detroit: Wayne State University Press, 1987), 189-214 (includes translation of historical portions of the *Guide*); Shimon Rawidowicz, "Hayei Ranak," in *Kitvei Rabi Nahman Krokhmal* (Berlin: n.p., 1924), 17-98; "War Nahman Krokhmal Hegelianer?" *Hebrew Union College Annual* 5

ular studies became available to Brody's Jews. Nahman's father Shalom Krokhmalnik was a well-to-do businessman who traveled to Berlin— and had contact with Moses Mendelssohn and David Friedländer. He had Nahman attend *Heder* and then the *Beit Midrash* for flour makers— where he studied Bible, *Talmud*, and Talmudic commentaries. Although the Austrian government required study at a government school, his mother Miriam was able to pay the tuition, and not have him attend. He learned German by himself, from reading newspapers. At fifteen, Nah- man married Sarah Haberman, from a rich Zolkiew family, who sup- ported his scholarly work.

The couple moved to Zolkiew on the Sivan River, a town of four hun- dred (out of a total eighteen hundred) Jewish families. As described by Krokhmal's student and biographer Meir Halevi Letteris, it was sur- rounded by the mountains (where the military hero King Johann III So- biesky had a summer home) and walls—which protected Jews during the 1648-49 Chmielnicki massacres. The *Beit Midrash*, next to a beauti- ful synagogue Sobiesky had built out of respect for the ancient kings of Israel, was filled day and night. Some studied ancient theology, while others escaped the winter cold and recited Psalms and *Zohar* passages without understanding them.[44] Krokhmal dedicated himself to study, reading Maimonides' *Guide to the Perplexed* with the interpretation of Moses ben Joshua of Narbonne (died 1362); the Biblical commentary and philosophy of Abraham Ibn Ezra (1092-1167); Mendelssohn's *Book of the Paths of Peace* and the texts of German *Haskalah*. He also studied Spinoza, Kant, Leibniz, Wolff, Mendelssohn, Salomon Maimon, Fichte, Schelling, and Hegel; Hebrew poetry; and works in mathematics and

---

(1928): 535-582; and "Rabi Nahman Krokhmal: Ke'hoker U'mevaker ... Yahaso Le'hasidut, Le'haskalah Ulile'umiut ... Rabi Avraham Ibn Ezra Beha'arato Shel Ranak ... Geulat Demut: Ranak Ve'hegel ... Kelitat Ranak Ve'hashpa'ato ... Rabi Yitshak Abravanel Ve'ranak: Al Ha'ruhani Ha'muhlat Le'ranak," in *Iyunim Be'mahshevet Yisrael*, vol. 2 (Jerusalem: Reuven Mass, 1971), 163-292; Rotenstreich, "Muhlat Ve'hitrahashut Be'mishnato Shel Ranak," in *Kenesset: Divrei Sifrut Le'zekher Bialik*, no. 3 (1941): 333-344; Margarete Schlüter, "Jüdische Geschichtskonzeptionen der Neuzeit: Die Entwürfe von Nachman Krochmal und Heinrich Graetz," *Frankfurter Judaistische Beiträge* 18 (1990): 172-205; Ismar Schorsch, "The Production of a Classic: Zunz as Krokhmal's Editor," *LBIY* 31 (1986): 281-315; and Jacob Taubes, "Nahman Krokhmal and Modern Historicism," *Judaism* 12 no. 2 (1963): 150-164.
44   Meir Letteris, *Zikaron Ba'sefer* (Vienna: n.p., 1886): 8-10, as cited by Rawidowicz in "Hayei Ranak"; Samuel David Luzzatto, "Mikhtav 5: Aharei avor za'am," *Kerem Hemed* 3 (1838): 61-76; Luzzatto, "Mikhtav 20: Samahti me'od," *Kerem Hemed* 4 (1839): 131-147; and Nahman Krokhmal, "Mikhtav 27: Hetavta Hasadekha," *Kerem Hemed* 4 (1839): 260-274.

natural sciences. He learned Latin, Syriac, and Arabic, and learned about current events from newspapers.

Krokhmal fell sick in 1808 (from the stomach ailment which might have been what finally killed him) and had to lighten his reading. He turned to historical material (including Jacques Basnage, *L'Historie des Juifs*, 1706-1711) before he had to abandon study altogether. He began to teach in 1814, and founded an "academy without walls" (Rawidowicz) outside Zolkiew. The program included Goethe, the Kabbalist Mosheh Hayyim Luzzatto (1707-1740), and the *Maskil* exegete Naphtali Herz Wessely (1725-1805). Letteris described how Spinoza's *Ethics*, Reuven ben Hoeshke's (d. 1673) *Yalkut Reubeni*, Azariah Rossi's (sixteenth century) *Me'or Einayim*, Kant's *Critique of Understanding*, the Biblical commentary of Moses Alshech (sixteenth century), the *Zohar*, *Talmud*, Roman poetry, and the work of the Greek satirist Lucian of Samasota all rested together on Krokhmal's desk. A visitor by the name of Hillel Lokhner reported that Krokhmal composed the *Guide to the Perplexed of Our Time* (originally entitled *Sha'arei Emunah Tserufah, Gates of Pure Faith*), by putting his thoughts down on paper after his post-lunch rest, and collecting the pieces in a chest.

Krokhmal had problems with Zolkiew's conservative, anti-*Haskalah* Jews. When illness caused his face to turn sallow, they claimed he was being punished by a dark piece of the vessel which had shattered in the catastrophe of beginning the universe (*kelippah*). When he wrote to Rabbi David of the Karaite community in Kokusow, *Hasidim* spread the rumor that he'd become a Karaite. He responded by declaring his own commitment to *mitsvot*, pointing out that Karaites observed *kashrut*, were worthy of contact with rabbis, and merited a place in the world to come. He accused *Hasidim* of passing the very persecution they suffered at the hands of *Mitnagdim* on to others.[45] When his *Maskil* student Avraham Goldberg Meraveh was threatened by the Orthodox with excommunication for reading *Haskalah* literature and ordered to burn it, Krokhmal assured him that the attackers would eventually ruin themselves—and advised Meraveh to appeal to the government.

In 1816, when his father-in-law's fortunes declined, Krokhmal tried to help by joining him in the wine business. He also became a communal leader in Zolkiew—seeking to have Jews excused from the military be-

---

45   Krokhmal, "El ahuv ha'nikhbad [Ze'ev Dov Shif]," in *Kitvei Rabi Nahman Krokhmal*, 413-416.

cause of their Sabbath and *kashrut*, and to have the government assist impoverished Jews. When his wife died in 1826, he immersed himself in philosophy, especially Hegel's, and had the first chapter of the *Gates of Pure Faith*, entitled "Poisons" (translated below), printed by Meraveh. He wrote anonymously, in fear of the Orthodox.

Krokhmal returned to Brody in 1836, to work as an accountant. He declined the opportunity to serve as rabbi, lest he arouse Orthodox antagonism; he did not teach, he said, lest *Torah* be diminished by using it to earn a living. In the summer of 1838 he left for Tarnapol. There, he responded to Samuel David Luzzatto's attack in *Kerem Hemed* on the rationalistic theories of religion of Maimonides and Abraham Ibn Ezra (these texts have been translated for this volume) and asserted that wisdom intensified communion with God. It was also false to accuse them of substituting the ideals of Greek philosophy for those of Judaism. Such attacks, he added, only provided enemies of Jews the weapons to vilify Israel. Why would Luzzatto "shoot such a poison arrow?"[46]

In the last four years of his life Krokhmal worked on the *Guide*, and arranged to have it published posthumously by Leopold Zunz. He declined an invitation to serve as rabbi in Berlin, feeling unfit to advise people about matters of conscience. Had there been an institute for the scientific study of Judaism, he remarked, he would have joined it. He died in July 1840. His younger daughter Raysa died shortly thereafter; the older one Konya, who shared his philosophical spirit, raised one son who assimilated and another who converted; his son Joseph, a medical doctor, converted to Christianity and raised two sons who became antisemites. The younger son Abraham followed in his father's scholarly footsteps.

Shimon Rawidowicz imagined Krokhmal with shoulders bent from the weight of all the Jews he carried, while trying to diminish their perplexity about religion, liberating those who felt imprisoned in their religion, and guiding them back to their roots. These interests of his led Joseph Klausner to identify Krokhmal as a "Galician Mendelssohn."

---

46   Luzzatto, "Mikhtav 5: Aharei avor za'am," *Kerem Hemed* 3 (1838): 61-76; Luzzatto, "Mikhtav 20: Samahti me'od," *Kerem Hemed* 4 (1839): 131-147; Nahman Krokhmal, "Mikhtav 27: Hetavta Hasadekha," *Kerem Hemed* 4 (1839): 260-274. See also Guttmann, *Philosophies of Judaism*, 327-328; Morris B. Margolies, *Samuel David Luzzatto: Traditionalist Scholar* (New York: Ktav, 1979), 159-163.

I.III.I. Selections From *Guide to the Perplexed of Our Time*

Translator's summary

In chapter or "gate" one, Krokhmal identified the sick and poisonous forms assumed by contemporary Jewish faith. The first form was ecstatic separation from the world of sense and intellect. Its first level involved imagining all sorts of new powers; its second, visions of angelic beings teaching the secrets and inner meanings of the world; its third, deranged enthusiasms. The enthusiast thought of himself as co-creator with God and above all law. The second poisonous form was disgust with allegedly natural evil and the attempts to defeat it through prayer by invoking angels and ancient pious figures, and through magic and idolatrous manipulation of the imagined good and evil spirits running one's life. The third poison was slavish obedience to commandments to the exclusion of inner intention, of duties of the heart and soul, as well as of rational explanation. Each of these three exaggerated expressions yielded its opposite. The result was that enthusiasm catalyzed denial of spirituality. Superstition brought on doubts about sacred texts and venerated personalities. Atrophy of intention catalyzed abandonment of pious acts, and conversely but with similar results, intention supplanted practice and rebelliousness and arrogance took over. However, by identifying the sickness, in the manner of Maimonides' "Eight Chapters on Ethics," Krokhmal at least had the basis to try to provide a cure.

1. Gate 1: Poisons[47]

"Open the gates, that a righteous people may enter, which keeps the faith" (Isaiah 26:2). The one who deserves it, receives the elixir of life.... The one who does not deserve it, receives deadly poison (*Yoma* 72[b]).

Faith is agitated by three [dialectically connected extremes], by means of which the pillars of correct worship will be shaken. Each begins with [one] straight path, and end with [many] paths [akin to] death. The three are based upon perverted inclinations and the crudeness of the deceitful heart.

A. When the believer inflames his soul (*nefesh*) to worship and abstracts his thought from worldly concerns and the desires of life, he will come to despise all which falls into the [category of] the senses.

---

47   Lawrence Kaplan worked through my translation of "Gate 1" and made several important corrections.

Thereafter, in his eyes, intellectual understanding—whose uses are defined in accordance with logical and critical examination—will become insignificant. He will turn his eye all day long to the condition of his inflamed soul and to nothing else. He will dream that his soul has powers of new comprehension and has strength from above. And this is the first step. [If he takes] the second step, he is already [in the realm of] evil. He will seem to see with his inner eye, angels of God or substances which are pure or devoid of matter. He will seek out a stratagem to approach them. When he intermingles with them, they [supposedly] make known to him every secret and the entire future. And in order to verify these pronouncements, which [in truth] are the fruit of his inflamed imagination, he will seek evidence from holy books, which he will read not only in terms of the phrases and words, but by means of letters, vowels, accents and crownlets [of letters].

The last step: He will be deranged [to the point of] thinking of himself as an associate of the Blessed Creator, and as having the power to change nature according to his desire, to give orders (Psalms 19:4) and to move nature away from its laws—the technical term for which is arresting the act of creation. Afterwards, he will imagine himself to be elevated above the rational and traditional commandments of *Torah* [which are accepted because they are transmitted empirically from generation to generation, as described in Sa'adiah Gaon, *Book of Beliefs and Opinions* III, 1-2]—in accordance with his elevation above the world of separation and restoration, for only there are the forbidden and permitted differentiated, as are the fit and unfit, suitable and unsuitable. Finally, his derangement will reach the point where he describes himself in terms of attributes elevated beyond those of human beings and spirits—and becomes extremely close to making himself into a false God. How strange is this extreme. Common sense would certainly not tolerate that something like this would [actually] exist in the world. Nevertheless [its existence] is confirmed by experience, doubled and tripled and multiplied many times. A little of [this aberration] is known to all, but the rest to experts alone. The beginning of this inclination in the soul of the faithful, we call by the Arabic name *haziah*—enthusiasm (*shvermeray*). A believer who is strong-hearted and spirited is especially susceptible to this. The situation is especially dangerous for those who [have the condition of] sanguinic temperament and for someone whose soul has not yet acquired reverence, humility, and the rest of the commendable qualities.[48]

B. And there is the believer who finds that his heart is inclined to detest good and choose evil. He feels in his soul the deficiency and the wickedness of his disposition, and since it has already been implanted in his heart that faith and worship bring him happiness, he will imagine finding help and a remedy[49] for his sickness in the greatness of faith and the increase of worship. He will multiply prayers and supplications [Genesis 25:21, Daniel 9:3]. Because he feels unworthy of receiving any response on account of his evil disposition, he looks for defenders—angels on high and the pious of past generations—[to help him] before the righteous judge. He will call them by true or fabricated names. He will consult the dead, will build gravestones (*nefashot*)[50] for them, light candles for them, and so forth. From here, he will branch out into believing in [angelic] princes in charge of all the foundations of creation, its powers and events, and good and bad spirits which warn and mock and accompany each thing. He will labor to find favor in the eyes of those who are good and to appease, or to hide from, the evil ones. And the deceived heart will incline him to achieve his desire by means of strange acts which are incompatible with nature—as strange as are those substances towards which his worship is directed. Like the enthusiast, he will strive to approach spiritual entities. But [unlike him he will do so] by an abhorrent and perverted method and for a purpose deficient in virtue—for his own benefit and to save himself from evil [Jonah 4:6].

And he does all this without deliberation, but rather on the basis of feeling and of the flux of his soul, inasmuch as it is difficult for him to improve his acts and purify his heart; he finds that the vain beliefs and the rituals arranged for it, despite their strange features, are easier for him. The beginning of this disposition in the soul is called by the name superstitious—*Abergloyben*. Those weak of knowledge and strong of imagination among the common folk are especially susceptible. And it is dangerous, because it obfuscates the brightness of religion. It makes man similar to a monkey and equates pure commandments with mere dreams and magical acts. And at its ultimate extreme, he who succumbs to it ends up a real idolater. Giving lip service to unity, he believes in

---

48 Cf. "Ha'aderet veha'emunah lehai olamim," *Mahzor*, vol. 2 (Sulzbach: n.p., 1795): 29[b].
49 Cf. "Ha'aderet veha'emunah lehai olamim," *Mahzor*, vol. 2 (Sulzbach: n.p., 1795): 58[a].
50 Cf. *Erubin* 55[b].

and worships all powers and acts of nature—and even more, the fabrications of his corrupt imagination.

C. There is also the believer who, seeing the damaging consequences of the two aforementioned examples, will refuse to seek the great things [Psalms 131:1]. He will prepare his heart only to fulfill the commandments according to their structure and application, and according to how they are ordered and valued. Such [an approach] is good in itself, and perhaps the best approach for most men. But it is difficult for man—be he great or small, heartless or full of heart, to keep to one straight path, without addition or subtraction or without adding contrivances from his reason—and the reason for this having to do with the individual's drive to actualize those powers that lie deep within him. The believer will therefore multiply elaborate performances and stringencies and [pay very close attention] to the ways in which they are to be fulfilled. He will busy himself with those things, with their derivatives and extensions, without end.

But the great evil will branch out, so that his heart will turn slowly from the inner intention—which is truly the soul (neshamah) of the commandment, as the act is its body. Even worse, he will also lose the primary and venerable commandments that do not involve performance at all, and are known [in the words of Bahyah Ibn Pakudah] as the "duties of the heart." Their foundation is the holiness and pureness of thought in opinions and in ethics. They become for him as though they never existed, inasmuch as his thought has become coarse and no longer capable of receiving [duties of the heart]—although his intellect remains keen regarding other inquiries. He will be immersed in this path, to the point where he makes a division, even in deeds, between *hukim* and *mishpatim* (non-rational and rational commandments).[51] He will neglect rational commandments, and will expend his energy on the pursuit of the traditional (non-rational) commandments, for he believes [with reference to the traditional commandments] that since his intellect (*sekhel*) cannot establish their binding character and since Gentile nations criticize them, the rewards [for observing them] will, so he believes, be much greater than for observing rational commandments.

This sickness of the soul can be characterized as the *multiplication of*

---

51   Cf. Leviticus 18:4, *Yoma* 65ᵇ, *Midrash Ba'midbar Rabbah* 19.

deeds which destroys the intention, or the holiness of the act and the profa-
nation of the thought (Verkhayligkayt). Our ancients referred to this [pre-
dicament] *as the plague of the Pharisees*, whom they divided into the
seven individual types.[52] Especially susceptible [to this extreme] are the
so-called experts and those who are low in rank among the ones who
apply themselves to *Torah*. The danger of this [sickness of the soul] is
very great, even though it is not manifest [to] superficial observation.
For it drags the great purpose of worship into the dust. This purpose
is to raise the soul of man to a realm of metaphysical reality (*tushya*),
and that his soul should be spiritual (*lehiyot ruhani*) while at the same
time being kept out of the trap of enthusiasm. This inclination makes
him bit by bit into a black slave standing ready and calling out, "What
is my duty? I will do it," his hand open all day to receive a reward for his
hard work.

"When there was confusion in Israel" [Judges 5:2], many fell into the
three extremes cited. Then there arose in the nation men with eyes open
to the wrongs that had been done. Now, since according to the laws of
ethical existence exaggeration to any degree will be the cause of bringing into being a quality opposite to itself, indeed at its opposite pole,
there arose those who adhered to an extreme that was opposed to the
three respective extremes. These [opposing extremes] are also evil and
absolutely destructive.

Opposed to this enthusiasm [A], there arises the *denial of spiritual ex-*
istence, until those who espouse [this view] will aggressively despise the
human image and will consider the substance of one's soul and its wondrous faculties to be the effects of some [kind of] heat, some natural,
material humidity. Opposed to superstition [B] there arises *the absence*
of faith and the doubting of all witnesses to inner feeling and common
sense, and even of the traditions of the fathers. This reaches the point
where some become so deranged as to doubt, for example, the existence
of the faithful shepherd Moses our teacher and that the *Torah* was given

---

52   The seven types of Pharisees are: (1) The *shikmi* who was circumcised for an unworthy
motive (Genesis 34); (2) The *nikpi* who walks with exaggerated humility; (3) The *kizai* who
in his anxiety to avoid looking at a woman dashes his face against the wall; (4) The "pestle,"
whose head is bowed like a pestle in a mortar; (5) The one who says "What further duty is
there for me to perform it?" as though he has already fulfilled every obligation; (6) The one
who loves the rewards promised for the fulfilling precepts; (7) The one who fears punishment
for transgressing precepts (*Sota* 22[b]).

through him; and to wonder whether the books of prophecy [*Nevi'im*] and those inspired by the holy spirit [*Ketuvim*] were composed by some deceitful teacher. Opposed to the deed which destroys the intention [C], there arises the *abandoning of all acts*. Those who espouse this view glorify themselves on the basis of their [supposedly] great knowledge of intention of the commandments, whether in accordance with [philosophical] wisdom or in accordance with esoteric [mystical] doctrine. These latter [i.e., those who glorify themselves on the basis of their supposedly great knowledge of the intention of the commandment in accordance with esoteric mystical doctrine] are close to the enthusiasts. These [intentionalists] begin [with abandoning] the [symbolic] commandments of remembrance, and this then spreads from this point to [abandoning] the rest of the commandments. Ultimately, they [i.e., the intentionalists] reach the point of thinking that all sins and improper conduct do not by themselves constitute rebellious or high-handed behavior. That is, except when it comes to those whose knowledge is weak or entirely lacking. [That is, those] who lack the ability to comprehend the intention of the legislator of the commandment and the commandments' deep purpose within the political community [as do the philosophical intentionalists] or its effects upon supernal realms [as do the mystical intentionalists]. And they, the sages [the philosophical intentionalists] and the knowers of esoteric doctrine [the mystical intentionalists], grasp the purpose [of the commandments] and attain [their] goal by means of paths special to them.

[To summarize], these three [antithetical] extremes—denial of the spiritual, absence of faith, and abandonment of deeds—are not as natural, neither to individual man nor the social group [as the first set of extremes]. Therefore, they always come later in time than the first entrapments cited. From the reality [of the antithetical extremes] we can derive testimonies and proof that those causes [namely the first set of extremes] which gave rise to them [to the antithetical extremes] have already been in existence for a long time. Now since it is very difficult with regard to hidden sicknesses like those we discussed above [namely, the first set of extremes] to become aware of the illness, in this respect can we say that the two opposing [sets] of extremes will [serve as] balm and medicine for chronic and deep leprosy. But aside from this aspect, one cannot cure a sickness of the soul by [the method of] curing one extreme by [going to] the opposite [extreme]. A great wise man already answered this question.[53] What is more evil to the individual or group—heresy or false superstitious faith? He said: The difference between them is similar to that between those who have cancer and those with consumption. The man who desires life will seek deliverance from both (Psalms 34:12).

Translator's summary of untranslated passages
In chapters two through five Krokhmal specified the need for defining essential religio-philosophical terms—metaphysics, the relation between God and man, right and wrong, and the inner meaning of law. He identified his approach as that of religious philosophy: "The [way of approaching] Torah may be compared to two paths. One is ablaze with fire, the other is covered with snow. If a man enters [the study of Torah] by the former path [of ecstasy], he will die from the heat. If he proceeds in the latter path [of rationality] he will be frozen by the snow. What he must do, is walk in the middle [i.e., the philosophy of Torah] (Yerushalmi Hagigah, ch. 2, Halakhah 1)."[54]

In the sixth chapter Ranak described the tripartite, cyclical pattern of various ancient nations. In the first period of growth, absolute spirit assumed the historical form of a particular, dominant "Volksgeist" (ruah ha'umah) (national spirit), e.g., law, which was also projected onto an individual leader or deity. In the second period, this feature and the nation supporting it became powerful. In the last stage, this power turned materialistic, sensuous, and arrogant, and eventually destroyed itself. The subjective aspect of spirit, the identifiable layer of Volksgeist, atrophied along with the nation. However, human history was in God's image. God, as absolute spirit, was the source and totality of all existence (intellectual and material). The absolute spirit inherent to the nation remained. It retained an imprint from the temporary national immersion, and then was sublimated into the path of humanity's positive resolution and ultimately into Israel.

In chapters seven through ten, Krokhmal described Israel and its history. Judaism was the embodiment par excellence *of absolute spirit. Because it was directly involved in it, Israel could and should proclaim this absolute spirit to the rest of the world. Since God chose Israel to teach others, Israel was, in one respect, adaptable everywhere. But Israel was also isolated, to the extent neces-*

---

53   Lawrence Kaplan informs me that the "wise man" referred to Moses Mendelssohn. On this theme, see also Maimonides' *The Eight Chapters of Maimonides on Ethics* (*Shemonah Perakim*), ed., annotated, and trans. with intro. by Joseph I. Gorfinkle (New York: Columbia University Press, 1912).
54   Krokhmal, "Sha'ar 2," in *Kitvei*, 10.

sary to distinguish its task. The task was an a priori *totality into which all other aspects of Jews and Judaism were sublimated. Israel was rooted in absolute spirit at the beginning and to the end. In between, it was subject to the tripartite cycle of growth, flowering, and decline. Israel's historical vacillations were defined in terms of closeness to, and distance from, God; at no one time would all the people be wholly isolated from God. Israel was uniquely indestructible, and at its very moments of ultimate decline, it rose up once again. The presence of universal spirit prevented its dissolution. Other nations disappeared from history as identifiable entities, at the third point of the cycle. Israel transcended the natural cycle. Its first cycle began with Abraham, who developed a refined concept of deity which was strengthened by revelation. The concept was developed concretely by Abraham's successors, in Egypt and later through the granting of* Torah. *The following period, which went through David and Solomon, was the stage of power. The period from 586 BCE through Gedaliah, who was appointed by Babylon to rule Judah after the first exile and then shortly thereafter assassinated, was the period of decline. Renewal began with the ascent and development of absolute spirit, in the years up to the destruction of the Temple in 70 A.D. A new cycle began with Yavneh and its yeshivah life. The stage of power continued throughout the Moslem period and Maimonides. Decline took place in the seventeenth century with Chmielnicki.*

Bible, Halakhah *and* Aggadah *were analyzed and evaluated from the historical perspective in chapters eleven through fifteen.*

Chapter sixteen, translated below, presented the philosophical dimension to Krokhmal's interpretation of Judaism. The method was dialectical, a process which was itself implicit in absolute spirit.[55]

I.III.II. Gate 16: "Definitions and Proposals for a Theology (Hokhmat Emunah) Derived from Logical Philosophy"

Translator's summary
Theology melded the spiritual and the logical. It utilized data from the philosophy of spirit which were available in representative images. It transformed them into ideas of logic, such as being and nothingness, finite and infinite.

---

55   Ranak's position in this chapter on reconciling opposites evokes the view of Schelling and deserves analysis. See, for example, F. W. J. Schelling, *Bruno or On the Natural and the Divine Principle of Things* [1802], trans. Michael G. Vater (Albany: State University of New York Press, 1984).

Theology's thesis was faith, its anti-thesis was reason, and its synthesis was philosophical theology. Jews resisted the entry of scientific study into theology, the condition which generated this synthesis, out of fear that values of alien nations would be imported into Jewish belief. This fear should be overcome: "The Lord possessed me as the beginning of His way, before his works of old" (Proverbs 8:22).

A. DEFINITIONS OF QUALITATIVE (*EIKHUT*) BEING

[Theology and scientific study]

We already said that the subject (*noseh*) of theology (*hokhmat ha'emunah*) is essentially religious faith, but specifically as it is comprehended by understanding. That is, the content found in faith, in a representative image (*tsiyur mahshavi'i*) and in psychic emotion, is the content found in theology—although transferred from forms of feeling and representation alone, to the form of general concepts (*musagim*) of understanding. This is because in religious faith and the hearts adhering to it, there are already representations and feelings of God. [They are] of His attributes and of His relation to the entire world, and to man's soul (*nefesh*) and its particular functions such as good and evil. The practice of theology is nothing but the understanding of those representations in their truth, namely, [the act of] abstracting from their particularities and making them into universal concepts of understanding. Our ancients began to dwell upon the roots of religions and secrets of *Torah* (in an esoteric and sketchy fashion, at any rate, from the middle of the Second Temple period on, and openly and in a systematically consistent method from the days of *Rav* Saadia Gaon and the first Kabbalists). Our ancients produced new speculative (*mahshaviot*) concepts in accordance with their insights. They were obliged to define and determine these notions with terms like infinite and finite, necessity and possibility of existence, the eternal and temporal, the existent (*yesh*) and nothingness, material and spiritual, free choice and predestination, becoming (*kiyum*) and destruction, and thousands of other terms like them. All are found potentially in religious faith and are not truly new, but they are new to our scientific study. Here, scholars have abstracted them and transformed them into universal thoughts of understanding. Faith, both in name and doctrine, is undoubtedly the beginning of man's scientific study, learning, and education. Because of this, faith has priority in time and nature. Theology is last in [subjective] time but has priority in terms of [objective] status. Reason (*binah*), i.e. the universal divine understanding rooted in man, has a higher rank than the representations [which are found at] the beginning of speculation. But that does not mean [that it has] a rank higher than that of internal feeling.

Theology truly encompasses all significant scientific study and epistemology (*hasagah*); it includes them in their universality. The Sages never refrained from taking the concepts and terms we cited which they needed for their inquiry, from other disciplines—especially from logical philosophy. Each principle in the realm of theology is a unity and differentiation between ideas (*mahshavot*) and concepts of understanding (*musagot ha'sikhli'im*).[56] For generations, the Sages had to present studies and premises which had already grown and ripened in [different forms in] other fields of intellectual (*ha'ruhani*) inheritance. [These materials were] given to humankind as a totality, at large, and to the particularizations of mankind. The Sages used them in order to reveal through them the hidden things of *Torah* and its secrets, as well as *Torah*'s method and ultimate intentions. That is just what theology is. Know and understand, that one does not diminish the dignity of *Torah* if one first has to learn the forms of the letters and vowel sounds and their pronunciations, verb usages and declensions of nouns. All together, these are the concern of grammar. Thus, it is inappropriate to be surprised if we consider only the definitions and presuppositions drawn from the discipline of philosophy prior to [studying] pure theology. This priority does not encroach upon the dignity of *Torah*. So spoke the Rabbi [Moses ben Maimon] of blessed memory, about his honored book [*Moreh Nevukhim*]: "The subject of this entire book and everything derived from it, pertains truly to the wisdom of *Torah*"—although [admittedly] there are also many chapters in the book which are exclusively philosophical.[57]

But what turns the heart of the believer away from this method [to which I have subscribed] even more, is truly due solely to coincidence—that those premises and studies made themselves known in some nation other than our own. It must be strange in that other nation's eyes,

56 Cf. Immanuel Kant's distinction between *Vernunft-begriffe and Verstandesbegriffe*. Rudolf Eisler, *Wörterbuch der philosophischen Begriffe*, vol. 1, 796-799; and vol. 3 (Berlin: E. S. Mittler, 1927-1930), 406.
57 Maimonides, *Moreh Nevukhim: Beha'atakat Shemuel Ibn Tibbon* (Vilna: Y. Punk, 1909), 4; *Guide for the Perplexed*, trans. M. Friedländer (New York: Pardes House, 1946), 2.

for us to use the same words for subjects of religious faith. The response
to this apparent strangeness is this: Who knows if there were not in our
nation, at times, the same scientific studies and philosophic definitions?
If they were lost to us in the course of the terrible affliction which pursued us, because they were a part and portion only of individuals and
obtained only orally? *Rav* [Mosheh ben Maimon] saw fit to apologize for
this difficulty in the special chapter which begins "Know that the wis-
doms which were in our nations," etc. (*Moreh Nevukhim*, Part 1, section
71).[58] That is point one.

Moreover, the sciences, especially philosophy in these days of
ours—have been assisted a great deal by principles of religious faith
received from us; we, the chosen part of the human species for a period
of almost 2000 years. Likewise, we know clearly that the philosophical
wisdom of the Greeks began during the time of Cyrus, King of Persia.
Its original source is in the Orient—[meaning] Israel and environs. The
researcher who understands will deliberate and calculate how much
[philosophy] has been influenced, in terms of assistance and power, by
[our] revealed religion (*ha'emunah ha'tori'im*) and [our] prophetic simili-
tudes. Also, in the late Greek period, all the [Jewish] prophetic books
were edited and made known to the Greeks. Scholars of our nation authored many books in the Greek language on theology—a few of which
are still available to us.

In short, let us say this: According to the principle of revealed religion, all humankind together is one habitation in the mind of God,
albeit [this will be known] at the end of days (and as much as this enters
assurances and prayers). It is also so in theology. It is improper for us
already to grant any place to this [nationalistic] envy. And furthermore,
our ancients often stated the principle of condensing philosophical deliberations of inferior imitators into more sophisticated [and concise]
statements of truth. The one who checks in depth will be amazed. He
will admit that those who come later [often] have no advantage other
than the expansion and clarification of the subject. At the same time,
one may also thank and praise those who come later. Because of them

---

58 "Know that many branches of science relating to the correct solution of these problems
were once cultivated by our forefathers, but were in the course of time neglected, especially
in consequence of the tyranny which barbarous nations exercised over us" (*Guide for the
Perplexed*, 7-8).

we concentrated on discovering the same subject in our ancestors. They saw it in general [and] with their clear observation. But they did not have the facility, or enough distinct words and terms, to be able to clarify for themselves or for us, the concept and what it represents. This will be explained by us with straightforward proofs in what follows in this essay. Let us begin with what we have designated, and know that what we today call philosophy is divided into three primary parts.

Translator's summary
There were three parts to philosophy. First came logical philosophy, which dealt with the origin, nature, and relations of ideas of reason or understanding. Second was the philosophy of nature, which was concerned with the correspondence between the idea itself and the idea in an object as abstracted from sensibility and imagination. Third, the philosophy of spirit or ideal philosophy, which was concerned with the soul and its faculties—feeling, imagination, will, reason, and understanding. In this chapter, Ranak limited himself to logical philosophy.

A. Logical Philosophy
Its topic [consists of] ideas of understanding, i.e., representations of the beginning of ideas, [*a priori*] concepts of understanding and ideas of rationality. Here, we research the nature and essence of all of these to the extent that they are ideas alone. We look critically at what is found in these ideas, [i.e.] the order and relation found among them, and how they were produced and correlate to one another.

B. Let us look at what is found, to be [*a posteriori* or] external and corresponding to these ideas—which ideas are outside the soul, i.e., in [the] world and in nature. We find the same ideas of understanding in nature. We understand by means of them the truth of the world, as it is to the eyes of understanding abstracted from sensibility (*hush*) and imagination. And this is called *philosophy of nature*.

C. The soul and its primary powers: Sensibility and imagination, the understanding, will and rationality. All these are included under the same ideal, divine scientific study (*ha'mada ha'ruhani*) within the realm of the ideal. This study's correlations, its levels and stages, its universality and unity are included in *ideal* philosophy (*filosofiah shel ha'ruhani*). [Included as well is the phenomenon of] the singularity of the rationality of rational beings within the world-totality, in religion and various scientific studies, as well as in all activity of thought and critiques of the human species. Ideal philosophy's particulars constitute many sections according to the many subjects cited, concerning all parts of wisdom—as mentioned. We will speak [of this] in later chapters, as required according to our primary inquiry and according to our ability, with the help of [the One who] bestows knowledge and language of study [Isaiah 50:4].

Until now we have only dealt with the first part [on logical philosophy]. It explains the becoming of and [what is] characteristic to ideas, insofar as they are only ideas, as well as the words which are supposed to signify them. Know and understand that a great gate includes all this. The one who considers them carefully, will comprehend the coherence of the chapters on attributes [*Moreh Nevukhim*, chs. 51-60] of the *Rav*, and the rest of esoteric chapters similar to them. Likewise they stand alone, and there is nothing besides them. They are the key for maintaining the fundamental roots of ancient wisdom of Israel, the wisdom of *Sefirot*. What will be explained by us in these coming chapters is the touchstone and important cornerstone for everything said about those subjects cited.[59]

After this slightly too long, but in our judgment necessary proposal, let us come to the topics to be explored. We already explained that what is [found] in faith, in ideas and feeling of the soul, is itself the content found in theology—albeit changed from the form of thought and feeling into the form of intellectualizing (*Haskalah*). [In the Rabbinic period] the intellect reached the point of abstracting and intellectualizing the representations of faith. The Sages were obliged to use in theology such words as spiritual, infinite, will and choice, and their opposites: material, purposeful, necessary, predestination, being and nothingness, will and purpose, becoming and destruction, and many subjects like them. These words were abstracted from faith and its accepted vocabulary. Already, then, the Sages were obliged to explain these words with definitions and what they implied. This is the topic of logical philosophy.

Translator's summary
The initial ideas of understanding were existence (which was general), and quality (which was delimited). In turn, each idea included principles of being and delimitation. But universal being was prior to all ideas of existence,

---

59 Gap in text.

including delimitation. It was also prior to privation. The idea of nothing-ness was also included in the idea of universal being, insofar as it meant that which did not exist.

[*Being, Existence and Quality*]

We have already explained that theology's subject is the subject of faith itself as understood by the intellect (*sekhel*). Theology must therefore, in proposing faith, explain the subject of the ideas of understanding, both in general and in particular. Let us begin by saying that the begin-ning of the ideas of understanding is apparently the [general] idea of *existence* (*yeshut*) and the [particular] idea of *quality* (*mahut*). That is, understanding decides about something it has, asks what it is, and the answer comes back that it is *such and such*. We have here two aspects (*behinot*). This [general] subject and *such* a [particular] subject. And if we abstract them into universal ideas we will find that any idea of existence (*yesh*) or of quality is [in turn] composed of two parts:

A. The being (*heyot*) common to all ideas;

B. The *delimitation* of a special attribute, through which the idea of being [is understood to have separated itself off and then] returned to existence (*yeshut*), or [has become a] conceptualized quality.

And according to this direction of inquiry, the ideas of "being" are first intellectual ideas (*ha'mahshavot ha'sikhliyot*). And we will see what there is to understand about the truth of this idea [of being]. It is, in actuality, universal, and it is prior not only to all ideas of existence, but also to all delimitation and all unity. It includes even privation, such as darkness, blindness and foolishness. We will think about all of this in terms of the idea of being, and we will say that darkness *is* privation alone. It therefore cannot be said that in this idea there is neither qual-ity nor attribute. We cannot designate it with one name from among the delimitations of understanding, identifiable in terms of named state-ments, which our ancestors included in the ten [categories of Aristotle] and which were subsequently [included in] other numbers. *Being* is ab-stracted from all of them. Since the representation [of existence and of delimitation] does not grasp this being at all, [the being] is the founda-tion and beginning [only] of all ideas which come after it.

Translator's summary

Being and nothingness were related dialectically. They were opposites, yet

one. The beginner could not appreciate this. To arrive at an authentic rep-
resentation of being, one could not just rush over to the representation of
change. Nor was change merely an issue of switching one form for another
while matter remains identical. What was sought after, in speaking of the
relationship between being and nothingness, was being-in-and-for-itself.

[Being and Nothingness]

We will understand further, that the idea of *nothingness* or non-being
is undoubtedly also opposed to the idea of being. [But this opposition
must be viewed in] the same way that [the idea of being] is grasped, by
ideas. That is, we have ideas about nothingness, devoid of all substance
(*etsem*) as well as the rest of understanding's delimitations. From this
perspective, [the idea of nothingness or non-being] is one with the idea
of being and is included in it. It is said about nothingness, for example,
that it does not exist. And this investigation is not insignificant. We assert that it is true that *being* and *nothingness* are opposites, and nevertheless are one. No difference between them is represented, insofar
as there is no delimitation in either of the two ideas, such that an idea
could grasp them in terms of any sought-for distinction (with the other). This may look [insignificant] to the beginning observer who rushes
towards what is highly objectionable. The beginner would [find it difficult to accept] the fact of two opposites [being elements] in one subject.
His understanding would also be prevented from accepting the fact that
being is nothingness, and nothingness is being.

[Change]

And truly, the contradiction and opposition between being and nothingness, insofar as it is the first opposition in ideas and is not mediated, remains very apparent. [But something more emerges when] thinking has
enough strength to hold on to the representation of being. One should
not [merely] pass [over being with] the representation of nothingness,
in order, one imagines, to get to the representation of change where
one thing becomes something else. In the representation of change, one
thing decays and the other becomes. In order to represent the change,
one imagined that matter which is material (*ha'homer ha'hiyuli*) remains
forever. It only divests itself of one form and dresses in another form.
But this representation of matter is not the authentic being that is abstracted from all unity and delimitation and which we seek. For this be-

ing [namely representation of matter] is already delimited; it remains in view amidst all changes and passing forms. We want being in-and-for-itself (ha'heyot be'atsmah)[60] without delimitation.

Translator's summary
Being and nothingness were only points of departure. Their contradictoriness would be removed through the idea of becoming. Through this unifying idea, they achieved metaphysical reality. As parts of becoming, being and nothingness were each combinations of static and dynamic dimensions.

[Becoming as a Metaphysical Reality]
Truly, being and nothingness are weak ways of viewing. They are exclusively points of departure [of thought]. Because of this, [logical] common sense by itself is liable to go from here to there, namely, to the ramifications of ideas which are born and disappear. The ideas are understood to be abstract and empty. [However], metaphysical reality and actuality [the first part of reality] are ever [becoming] more manifold in them. Behold, the idea of becoming (havayah), the same strange one-ness [as described above, also prevails] between being and nothingness. All men have a representation derived from becoming. They acknowledge that [this representation] is solely of a simple idea, and that in [the idea of becoming], nothingness and being are together at one glance. It is similar with the idea of beginning. The idea is that the thing begins, is no longer, and has already [passed]. But [beginning also means the] relationship to what comes later. It will not be called [only] the beginning of a thing; it is [known] in regard to its continuity as well. The idea of becoming itself implies stages. It will not remain [as is]. It will rather become something which [will be] present (hoveh). This is existence. Know this as well. We speak of the one-ness of being and nothingness, without negating their difference. [But it is also true that the fact] that being and nothingness are two different things rests on words alone.

The truth is that both thoughts [of being and nothingness] are only abstractions of the understanding, abstractions which are not existent (nimtsa'ot) entities. They are not fully understood.[61] Thought cannot re-

---

60   See Hegel, *Encyklopädie der philosophischen Wissenschaften im Grundrisse*, ed. Georg Lasson (Berlin: L. Heimann, 1870), section 91.
61   For the distinction between *noumena* and *phenomena* see Kant, *Kritik der reinen Vernunft*

main with them, for truly, they are only abstract. They are devoid of all metaphysical reality (*tushiah*) and actuality (*kinyan*). They are only at the beginning of our ideas and the first grasping on the part of the understanding mind (*ruah*). From these ideas, [understanding should] proceed to all the ideas and representations and [objects of] understanding which come after them. [Ultimately, these] are *metaphysical*, i.e., the fullness of actuality, substance. What is [in the end] understood is to be contrasted with those first ideas whose principle is the abstraction from *metaphysical reality*.

Because of this, the contradiction and negation can be explained and revealed by those [first thoughts] at the beginning of the examination. Our philosophers said: Make *there is not* into there is.[62] They spoke of nothingness by the way of *being*, [transposing categories of being into the realm of nothingness]. Thus, when they said "better[63] that man were not created," they spoke of being by way of nothingness. For the contradiction between these two ideas to be revealed, behold, ideas should proceed to link them together. Ideas should arrive at the idea of *becoming*. This is the [dialectical] truth of the two of them. In this idea there is *nothingness* which returns to *being*. Over-against this [idea] is the idea of *non-existence* (*hefsed*), [namely] being which returns to nothingness.

[Dynamics]

And one will observe movement and energy in this idea [of becoming]. And that is what is said in Scripture—"All things are energetic" (Ecclesiastes 1:8). In the beginning, the ideas [of being and nothingness] rest calmly in their places. They do not come near one another and so they are opposed to one another. However, in the idea of *becoming* they return to be parts of one complete thought. They are no longer parts which rest beside one another, but parts in motion. To designate the parts separately, we may use the name *moments* (*rega'im*) [combining static and dynamic dimensions][64] in the idea of *becoming*. Here this word means movement and rest together (moments in time are also of this sort. The small part takes [for itself something] from time which always

---

(Leipzig: Philipp Reclam, 1878 rpt. [1781]), 231.

62   Rawidowicz cites *Sefer Yetsirah*, ch. 2, *Ma'amar* 6.

63   Rawidowicz points out the error. Ranak's text has *tov* instead of *noah* (as in *Erubin* 13[b]).

64   Cf. Eisler, *supra*, 814.

flows continually and which is arrested here by the idea. Also, [this small part] by itself is synonymously present and absent, i.e., composed of being and nothingness). It becomes clear to us, that being and nothingness are both abstractions resting in themselves. Because of this, both are negation and empty. Their truth [and metaphysical reality] is the *becoming*, wherein they are moments.

Translator's summary

The idea of quality referred to delimited being. This limit was imposed upon the universality of the idea of being, upon being-in-and-for-itself. It placed a certain boundary upon being, such that a negative "other" emerged which was beyond the boundary. The delimitation had being on one side, and the privation of being on the other. Insofar as being was recognizable only in its delimitation, it involved the transition from nothingness to being and being to nothingness. That is, it involved changeability, or becoming.

[Quality]

The second idea is that with which we began above [b], the idea of existence as quality. Let us understand what this idea consists of. It too rests quietly and there is no movement in it, no passage from one subject into its opposite component. But after our deliberation we will find that this idea, as we have already indicated, is composed of the idea of being. Here the idea of being has a special delimitation, namely qualitativeness (*eikhut*). That is, we will not be able to have an idea of any quality or being except when we delimit it qualitatively: red, white, long, heavy, good, necessary, and the like. All are answers to questions about what the thing is.

When we speak of *quality* with any delimitation, which is the [specific] quality of the being, we understand the being as if it is a substance symbolized by this word. It should be evident what the being and the quality with it is. It is the existent itself in its image of itself, in regard to quality or the *existent* (*yesh*). After appropriate consideration, we will find that all delimitation is, as its name [implies], a limit or negation which we give to the idea of being—an [idea itself] which is universal and not grasped by any idea. [Delimitation is] some limit which negates the universality of being, in order to grasp in this thought the *being* of the special quality. Therefore, the definition of quality or existence [applies to] that in which actuality and privation exists. [We have here] being which [functions as] actuality, and quality which [functions as] negation.

Let us consider the existent in our inquiry about being. There exists through the quality in being, the being which is therein and another being which is not therein. This [outside] being is the *other*. If we observe it in the inquiry into its designation, there exists in this quality itself, the actuality of being—like the substance of reddishness. But in order to grasp [that reddishness] in ideas, it [must be] delimited by privation. [This privation] is the limit and end of all quality itself. And because of this, the doctrine has emerged among us that all "existence" which is grasped in thought is

a. Delimited, i.e., it includes being, and privation of being.

b. Changing, i.e., in the [act of] grasping the idea, its being is already contained, as is another being other than it. This [brings us to] is the idea of "changeability." This idea becomes clear to us from [the fact] that from the becoming, which is movement, the idea proceeded to the existence, which rests quietly without passing outside itself. This idea appears as though it is only one moment among the moments of becoming, i.e., [universal] being. But in truth, insofar as it is being, [here] it is recognizable only in its delimitation. Already united in it, as said, are the two moments—being and nothingness [e.g., by saying something is red, one says it is not white].

Translator's summary

Delimitation took place as an endless process. Being was always itself, remaining in itself, yet it also always passed into its other and then negated the other. Limitation was always involved in becoming something else. Quality was ever in process. Being which was without limitation would be called being-in-and-for-itself, and was also referred to as universal being.

[Endlessness]

Let us deliberate on the idea of limit and of changeability. What is the idea of this topic (*inyanah*)? Quality (*ha'mah*) passes from a delimitation that has unified it in its qualitativeness (*be'eikhuto*) into a second being [which is also subject to unified deliberation]. And this is truly the root of the term *changeability*. The thing turns into that which is second to it [e.g., milk becomes butter; water becomes ice]. But this second-to-its being is also situated in a special delimitation, that is, it is composed of being and nothingness. It too will necessarily pass over the limit which separates it from one *being* [which is] secondary to it. And so the [process] will always proceed endlessly.

We will see that associated with the idea of change, there is the thought of *endlessness* and its opposite, *end*. To be sure, after authentic deliberation, we will see that this process does not give us truly endless. Existence or quality, which is being with limit, is always made into something else which is limited and which does not emerge without [an] end. The process considered here includes only the topic *proper* to us, whereby we seek what is endless in order to be extricated from the contradiction between being and nothingness. But we never achieve that. The contradiction in our operation remains forever. [There never is authentic endlessness]. Inasmuch as it is existence which has come into being, it is limited and at the same time transcends its limitations.

Indeed, if we add the deliberation about change and what is included in this idea, we will find immediately that in the first change—when we say that quality is changed into [something] second to it, and this second again into [something] second to it—being will not change, except [into] something which is other, and second again to its other. And [that] all being is made other and this other changes itself [into an] other. Nevertheless, being [from the universal perspective] remains and stays in its [own] self (*me'eino*) and within its self-examination of itself. It is in-and-for-itself (*hu bifnei atsmo*), and the other passes over it mystically [outside of our own thoughts], one after another.

Let us grasp this passage in [terms of] ideas. We do not remain only at the being without its change, nor at what is known from the change, but rather at the joining of these two manners of examination [namely, the viewpoints of being and non-being], which are moments of the [universal] being which changes. Here, we remain with the idea of the true infinite (and it is called *indifferent one-ness* by the first Kabbalists), which is indifferent to the thing and to its opposite (*temurah*).[65] Or in short, the quality (*ha'mah*), (being), is being with a limitation, and the limitation separates between it and other beings. [That is, determina-

---

65 Cf. Schelling, "It is not itself the object thought about prior to the process, or in and at the same time below itself. But precisely because of this, it is also not subject over-against itself. It is thus also relative to itself, the indifference of subject and object." Schelling, "Hegel," in *Sämmtliche Werke* vol. 1, part 10 (Stuttgart and Augsburg: J. G. Cotta, 1861), 130.

tion is the logical counterpart of limitation]. If the limit is so assessed, it [means] that it is in relation to being-as other (*heyot ha'zulat*).[66] Therefore, when we say that the limit already was, we say that the something is other. That is a negation, inasmuch as all limit is negation. When we say that the change already [was], we negated that other, i.e., that same negation, and after? Negating the negation there remains true existence [e.g., wood is not a stone]. This is the infinite or endlessness, which we see in the negation of the negation.

With this, we have arrived at the true subject in the idea of the infinite or endlessness, which idea is the third [moment] in ideas. Namely, that the idea of being is determined by negation, until it returns to the idea of quality and being. And through such delimitation and change, which is negation of negation, being returns [dialectically] to itself. And so we have a third idea, namely, being which returns to itself by finding the being and quality. This return is without end, inasmuch as something which wants to determine its being, and thereby its quality and the grasping thereof, has always to negate something of itself [e.g., by being about to become an oak tree, the acorn precludes becoming something else]. Because of this, we will call this being-which-continues-towards-itself, continuity without end. It is what is known as the idea of being-in-and-for-itself.

This is the difference between the beginning of ideas of being alone—which is only *itself* alone [regarding] its first being, and not mediated by another—and being for itself (*heyot bifnei atsmo*) which is already mediated by itself. This [latter] being is something other in thoughts of quality [than what it was before]. [This happens] through its returning to itself by negating the determination and change. This is the being and the nothingness which are united in the quality of the thing [e.g., in describing a table as white, it is stated that it is not black].

Translator's summary
Being-in-and-for-itself was mediated by a concatenation of ideas which explained the activity. The third link was being-in-itself. This was one simple idea, in which the first two links were included. For example, it was an idea of man rather than ideas about human parts.

---

66   Cf. Hegel, *Encyklopädie*, section 91.

[The One Simple Idea]
Because of [the fact that] this idea [of being-in-and-for-itself] is a subject only in itself, it is mediated by the concatenation of ideas:

[1] its non-mediated being

[2] its being-as-other (*heyot ha'zulat*)

[3] its being-in-itself (*heyot bifnei atsmo*).

The concatenation of ideas of something is a moment of this last idea. [Similarly], common sense also knew that in regard to action, there is a reflexive subject. There is a special conjugation even in grammar, which likewise includes three criteria:

[1] the verb before it has acted [future]

[2] the verb when it is acting [present]

[3] the verb after it has received action [past]

But this is not described in being. In common understanding (*ha'sekhel ha'meshutaf*), being rests quietly without activity. But to the idea of rationality (*mahshevet ha'binah*), the being which rests quietly is none other than an abstraction of mere understanding. Therefore, it is like naught. It has no truth, except [the truth] that it is mediated through being [with respect] to the other and through the return to being-in-itself. It is naught in truthfulness [if truthfulness means] actuality without any abstraction. [Here, truthfulness is limited to process] mediated by its moments, as we have explained. The topic of the idea of activity and of reception of activity and reflexive activity in itself, are terms of mediation of the [processes] and thoughts as well, as we shall explain later. Accordingly in truth, there is no being without some activity. And if we have an idea of being alone, without any activity, it is truly only a fantasy of the understanding—i.e., only abstraction.

At this point we have arrived at a new idea. This is the idea of *being-in-itself* or *being-by-itself* (*heyot le'nafsho*). Let us examine its connotation. It is what we understand by a thing which is being in itself and alone. It is not like other being, and no other being has any connection with it. Therefore, we will not think of being-in-itself as having any continuity or part. And we do not partition it into [spatially] extended parts—inasmuch as these parts already [have] another being. Rather, we turn backward and continue the being-in-itself (*heyot le'atsmo*) and to-itself alone.

Because of this we have also reached the *simply* one idea. For example, in our idea of man we do not have an idea of man together with ideas about parts of his body and his many limbs. Rather, we return from them and their being, to the one idea of man's being. And so, whenever we spoke of a "composite thing" the word "composite" implied that we will still have an idea of the many parts which are the constituents of the compositions. In saying "thing" (*davar*), we have already shifted the parts and returned them to the simple being—and this is a thing. And because of this, this being is called being-in-itself or being-by-itself. And it is also the idea of the simple one.

Let us deliberate more about this [process of] returning. We find therein, that the one returns to itself and repels from itself all other being outside it. In this activity-in-itself, there already rests being-as-other, i.e., other being, each one of which is also being-to-itself or one.

Translator's summary
When being proceeded into its other and then returned to itself, some units of being-as-other were repelled, while others were integrated. Attraction and repulsion mediated being-in-itself. But the idea of something included the two forces in one-ness. The medieval Medaberim *contended that all substance could be separated into simple parts which had no composition, quantity or connection. That is, they separated repulsion from integration. This was false. Even on the level of simple understanding, the term "many" indicated combination and separation together.*

[Attraction and Repulsion]
We have thus come to many ones. This is the idea of *many-ness*. But we are here within the gate of first ideas. We still do not know any other difference between the things, other than [that between] being and existence. [Existence] is being with delimitation which [also] goes forth to another being—it changes—and returns to itself; which is the one. Therefore the other individualities, which it rejects when it returns, are wholly equal and similar to it [in terms of beings and individuals]. An idea has no ability of differentiation [and therefore cannot claim that the entities are not equal]. In thought, the individualities [appear as] one together with the first one. That is, just as being-in-itself repels the others, so being attracts the others to itself. They are made [into] one idea, namely the idea of *attraction and repulsion*, of *separation and joining*. We understand this idea [to be characteristic] in existences (*be'nimtsa'ot*). Let us say we have an idea about something which is said to be a cubit

long or composed of elements (*yesodot*)[67] or that it bears qualities or that it bears such and such attributes. We already understood that it is one being. That is, we discuss the separation and joining as one. And they, as we recalled, are two moments of this idea which are opposed to one another. We will understand them only [in terms of] the one-ness and the shifting of one to the other.

[*The* Medaberim]

And from here you will comprehend the separate substance, or the part which is not divided further. Rabbi [Moses ben Maimon] attributed [this interpretation] to the *Medaberim* [in *Moreh Nevukhim*, Part 1, 73].[68] They said, that regarding all substance which is composed necessarily, we can in any case divide it through speculation until we reach the simple parts which compose it. Everything which extends itself in its association [with other parts], we can always separate. We therefore reach individual, simple substances—i.e., those which have no composition and therefore no connection at all. But not one of the simple substances has any quantity at all. The *Medaberim* took being-in-itself as it was in *representation*—i.e., being quietly at rest, unmediated by its moments. Because of this, they determined such parts indirectly. They abstracted the moment of repulsion from the moment of combination which is in the idea of being-in-itself.

But in truth, the two moments are combined as one in the subject (*benose*) [and the separation is an artificial abstraction]. Existence is found mediated by moments of being and nothingness. It is represented in thought by means of determination. The limit is mediated by negation of the limits and represented as being-in-itself. This being-by-itself is mediated by activities of repulsion of other units—which activity itself includes the beginnings as well as the relation which one unit has with the others. It is represented in [terms of] attraction and connection.

[*The Many as One*]

Because of this, the two factors of one and many, of separation and connection, are not truly separated. And even simple understanding comprehends that we cannot say "many" about things which are totally dif-

---

67 Cf. Isaac Israeli (ca. 832-932), *Sefer Ha'yesodot* (Drohobyc: n.p., 1900).
68 The *Medaberim* were exponents of Arabic scholastic theology, the *Kalam*.

ferent, except [to the extent] that they are one. We do not say that a horse, camel, or donkey is many, even if we think of them as such. In being, each of them has a one-ness [and we cannot count each as many]. And some will not understand any separation without connection. When we say separation we imply connection. Conversely, when we understand connection we imply separation. But simple understanding cannot comprehend the truth of the idea. It cannot comprehend that being-in-itself is in itself this transition [between] two moments. Nor can it comprehend that being-in-itself returns from existence to being-by-itself, and is now one; and that from this one being-in-itself returns to existence—which existence is multiplicity and extension and connection. [E.g., the one concept of a donkey implies a non-donkey, and hence plurality. The dialectic between unity and plurality in the same concept cannot be grasped by simple understanding.]

Note: We speak of an elementary idea which is simple without mediation by its moments. We mean [this] only in relation to the power of representation, for which this idea is still simple. This will not contradict whatever is in relation to us. It does not contradict the stance of deliberation of our understanding in which we find ourselves. We find in the idea the composition of the ideas we cited. And we have called the representative image of this thought simple and unmediated, only until these moments cited [will also become manifest] to the intellectual faculty, in the process and ramification of ideas. Only until these moments are actually resting in the intellectual faculty, i.e. in special representations. Whatever they are in the [intellectual] faculty, was also [accessible already] in simple thought. This was seen in our deliberations about the representations.

Translator's summary

Quantity referred to the growth and diminution of the delimitation's magnitude. An idea of quantity simultaneously involved attraction and repulsion of units. In the case of simple ideas, the idea of quantity involved discrete and continuous quantity together.

[Quantity]

Until now we have spoken of the idea of being as it is a kind of *qualitative* limitation. As such, being will reach full unity with itself in the idea of the one. But by means of the negation implicit to it, it returned to [the situation of] opposition with multiplicity. Because of this we have reached a new category of thought—and this is *quantity*.

We already explained that the subject of existence or of quality, is being with a qualitative limitation. The limitation will be [affirmed] in reality (*kiyum*) or even in negation, such as with the idea of blindness, coldness and foolishness. But if the being will be delimited in this kind of way, then its delimitation is not necessary. Rather, we can remove it and exchange it with one which is lower than it. [We can do this] until the limitation will not be totally denied, but will rather be transitory and changing. This limitation is called quantity. Geometricians have already defined that magnitude which has the ability to receive addition or diminution.

In sum, the idea of the house or of red will remain in [the thought], whether we add to or diminish from the building or reddishness. We have seen, that quantity is truly the idea mediated by two moments. [One] is quantity's return to itself by itself, or negation of each single unit. This is *repulsion*. [The second is] quantity's relation with this single unit [in terms of, quantity's] negation. This is *attraction*. And quantity is mediated by these two moments. But if the representation of being is a simple idea, then this idea becomes manifest—namely in its representation—in two sorts of quantity:

[1] *Discrete quantity (Hakamah ha'mitpared)*—as numbers of apples, whose connection into a unity can occur only in idea. [That is, cognitively and not perceptively.]

[2] *Continuous quantity (Hakamah ha'mitbadek)*—as the line, area, and body, whose parts are continuous with one another. They cannot be described as one (or many), except [in an] idea.

But in truth, the two moments cannot be separated. For their mediation is the verification of the idea. Any discrete quantity which is represented is also continuous. [For example], the apple's parts [together] also bear continuous magnitude, as does each part [by itself]. We understand continuous quantity, as a continuity (*divuk*) of parts. If so they are [the continuity's] units. And discrete [quantity] is discrete only in its relation to the units. And this is its continuity with them. And all continuity is continuity of units. It is impossible to understand the idea of one-ness, without our understanding its opposition, along with it.

Honestly, the discrete and the continuous are not two sorts which are distinguishable in terms of quantity. Rather, the truth of the matter is that the one idea is mediated in its totality by its two moments. The idea is taken by representation and understanding at one time in [terms of] one of their [qualitative] characteristics (*tekhunatav*), namely, the moment of one-ness and repulsion. At the other time the idea is taken [in terms of] the second of its characteristics, namely the [quantitative] moment of multiplicity and connection.

Translator's summary
The Medaberim contended that matter, time and space were divisible into parts up to a certain point, where they became indivisible. Their opponents contended that the division proceeded endlessly. Ranak combined discrete and continuous quantity, such that quantity was ever in the process of division and succession. Their division amounted to nothing more than an abstraction of understanding.

[Note on Time, Space and Matter]
This idea of quantity as over-against quality is found outside understanding, [and] in the idea of [spatial] distance, time and matter. With regard to space, [we refer to] our idea of space in itself, as over-against the things which fill it. And equally so, in time. That is, time represented in itself, without the present in it. It is similar, with matter, where we do not examine the form in it, but rather the extent that matter is solely abstraction. All of these [space, time, matter], are quantity devoid of quality.

And here lies the difficulty and contradiction known from the controversies. Should we determine that the division within the idea will [a] necessarily reach [the point where] simple parts are not further divisible, or [b] that [the division] will proceed endlessly? A few will go along with the [first position, espoused by the] *Medaberim* quoted by Rabbi Moses ben Maimon (*Moreh Nevukhim*, Part 1, 73). [In their view] matter, which is composed of small parts, cannot be divided [endlessly] into smaller atoms. [No part] is quantifiable [because infinite division is not possible]. They had the same opinion about time. [In their view] time is composed of time-atoms, which on account of their short duration cannot be divided. They said the same about space, which is a combination of such [indivisible] points. The *Medaberim* themselves brought proper proofs showing how it is impossible to call something finite, in the sense that matter or a part of space and time would [imply] the inclusion of parts without end.

The [second] opinion maintains, to the contrary, that the division will necessarily proceed, in ideas, without end. We will never arrive [finally] at separate substances, periods and points, as cited. Their proofs also appear valid. According to them, the *Medaberim* are obliged to recognize [endlessly] separate substance and great distances. [The inference by the *Medaberim*] that the diagonal of the square is equal to [one of] its side[s], and all such geometrical phenomena are [theoretically] annulled, since all [the proofs of those opposed to the *Medaberim*] take the road where endless division is possible. Cf. *Moreh Nevukhim* (Part 1, 73, end of third proposition), where the *Rav* says "it would fill days to [refute all of the *Medaberim*'s] presuppositions."

[Discrete and Continuous Quantity]

How may the contradiction in understanding be explained? The two parts of the contradiction [are identified and the *Rav* offers] suitable and strong proofs at the onset of his investigation. The solution to contradiction should be obvious from what we explained. [Let us reiterate:] With regard to the two moments, mediated [and] combined quantitative being, one passes to the other. Accordingly, it is honestly not possible to separate them or to connect one with the other. Let us take the first, [mediated] moment for itself. No combining or spatial extension will exist. The endless combining is always denied, in order to reach the simple one. In this way, all is discrete quantity, composed of separate substances, and there is no continuous [quantity] at all. Let us now take hold of the second moment of quantity. All will be continuous quantity. We are unable to comprehend the particular magnitudes; [or distinguish] the magnitude of its continuous quantity and the magnitude of its discrete quantity. Two parts will never exist for us, where we could discern between them not even a small part which would be self-sufficient and could be combined with the second. In this moment the quantity is successive and without any parts. To summarize: If we were to take discrete quantity only, there would be for us only units or the separate substance cited. If we take [quantity] only as continuous, it will always be continuous. That is, the dividing will proceed endlessly. These two paths are only abstractions of understanding, and the separation is without verity. The verification of these two factors and their passage into one another is in fact the verification of quantity. And this is so because we cannot understand the one-in-itself without taking the other into account. That is, continuous quantity as a continuity of many, i.e., many one-ness. Discrete quantity is also continuous. That is, that in order for us to reach the idea of the one, we repel the other. And so it is always. Everything which is rejected is also one. This one-ness [of the one and the other] is what is continuous between them.

[Mathematics and Geometry]

The verification of the one-ness of discrete quantity and continuous quantity may be understood further. It is said at the initial stages of knowledge, that we will reach the unity of discrete quantity in mathematics, and unity of continuous quantity in geometry. But in truth, geometry will only teach us to compare and evaluate among continuous subjects— e.g., sides and angles which face one another from a distance. For completely perfect determination, we must still unite them by numbers. And if the unity of a circle is solely geometrical—i.e., all points in the circle are equidistant to the one central point and through this it is completely united—then this unity will not be increased to become a triangle or a square. For their total unity, we in any case need numbers. The definition of line—namely that it is the principle of continuous quantity—is one point which moves into the distance. Because of this, the point is the first unity in terms of continuity, just as the one is the first unity in terms of the discrete. The point, truly, is the being-in-itself, as we have explained. But when we say there is self-activation in it, it already has left being-in-itself. Its unity has disappeared into the distance. It has now a relation to another being. Because the point came outside itself, the line is necessarily described as if it were many points, and needs to [establish] limits between the units. The one and the many will be equal with regard to discreteness. And so it is in the rest of the unities and delimitations of distances, regarding both areas and bodies.

Translator's summary

All quantity had magnitude, which is to say delimitation. Quantity could be counted. Counting involved attraction (summing up) and repulsion (separation into units) together. Quantity could be extensive, referring to fixed points outside each other in space and time, or intensive, referring to collective unfixed points. Here too, however, one could not be understood rationally without the other.

[Numerical Quantity]

According to what has been explained concerning quantity, the being of quantity consists in removing the designation of quality. This being bears some quality, although we have left it and stopped observing it. All quantity is therefore, *magnitude*. That is, a being unique in its delimitation. Accordingly, all quantity has some magnitude—i.e., the quantity which is unique in its delimitation. And it necessarily has limit. As Rabbi [Moses ben Maimon] said (*Moreh Nevukhim*, Part 2, preface, proposition 1), the existence (*metsiut*) of an infinite magnitude is an error. The unity of quantity is the *number*, and its foundation is oneness and enumeration. That is, we summarize part of quantity in our ideas, we have an idea of it as oneness, and this is the limit to summation.

For example, we measure a hand breadth, and some numbers—i.e., thirty—and this makes the limit of separating. [I.e., we discontinue individual numbers] and we say that the quantity of its number is thirty hand breadths. If we call the sum of the three hand breadths a cubit, then the numerical quantity is "truly" equal to the first [i.e., thirty hand breadths]. Because of this, all accounting is but the value which [prevails] between oneness and multitude and their limitation. Both are from the activity of the moments which are in quantity, as we cited. Were it not for the moment of continuity, which is attraction, we would not have reached [the point] of summing up the hand breadth or cubit. All would be separate units, not a *number*. Were it not for the moment of separation, which is repulsion, there would have been no counting. Again, all would be the quantity of oneness—not a number.

There are two kinds of quantity: the determined [with two fixed points] or magnitude [with unfixed points].

A. *Extensive*—Here, parts are beside one another in space, or after one another in time.

B. *Intensive* alone—for example, the quantity of heat whereby we distinguish more or less; or great or little reddishness; or speed of movement. All are quantities, but the parts are not found outside each other. Rather, they are changing amounts measured by understanding—in the sense that if we compose lesser degrees of heat which are found in actuality, an equal degree with which to sum them up will not become manifest. It will be found likewise in actuality. For if we pour water of one degree of heat into other [water] which has one degree, we will not end up, because of that, having both degrees—except if they were of the same degree [to begin with]. Whereas a quantity of water which is extensive (*mitpashet hitsoni*) is added, a quantity of heat which is intensive (*mitpashet penimi*) is not added. Therefore, *degree* is defined as a quantity of quality, not as a quantity of the essence of the thing.

Thus, understanding separated absolutely between two kinds of quantity. However, after this rational deliberation, we will find that they are likewise combinations of moments. One cannot be understood rationally without the other. Here we saw that the number which makes itself present, through the *one* and the multitude, turns out to be one in its universality. And this we already see when we deliberate about the passage from enumeration which always goes out of itself, to a limit which is one and simple. However, in the representative image as well, the magnitude will return to the oneness in the inner magnitude cited—in which a limitation is [connected] with the magnitude. This, as cited, is called "degree."

Translator's summary
Logical philosophy treated ideas of understanding. Philosophy of nature encompassed the external "topic" (as object and subject) to the idea, and the dialectical relationship between a thing and the thought of it. Philosophy of spirit involved the relation between logical philosophy and philosophy of nature.

[Logic, Nature, and Spirit]

Note: It is explained above that the one who understands knows that the spirit of *logical philosophy* is only ideas, [and only] insofar as they are only ideas of understanding [or cognitive ideas]. And we thereupon explore their nature and quality. We critically examine what is found in these ideas alone, as well as how they made themselves present to one another. But whether and in what manner, an external topic parallel [to these ideas] is found; and [whether] these ideas are [in turn] found in the external topic[69]—this [namely, the correspondence between thing and thought] is the topic of the *philosophy of nature*. The soul and its primary

---

69   Cf. Isaac Israeli, *Sefer Ha'gevulin* on the doctrine of truth and the conformity of the thing with the thought. [Isaac Israeli], *Isaac Israeli, A Neoplatonic Philosopher of the Early Tenth Century*, translated with commentary by Altmann and S. M. Stern (Westport, CT: Greenwood, 1979).

faculties—feeling, imagination, intellect, will, and understanding—are the subjects of the ideas cited. The relation between these faculties of understanding and nature, that is external to them, is the topic of the *philosophy of spirit*. We will explain these two disciplines in special gates, if God gives us strength. But here we are engaged only with *logical* ideas and with the words presumed to signify them. Comprehension of everything we have said about this will provide the key to comprehending the chapters of Rabbi [Moses ben Maimon] on attributes [part 1, chapters 53ff], and the remainder of esoteric chapters in the *Moreh Nevukhim*. It will also provide the key to comprehend the primary roots of the philosophy of Israel, the wisdom of *Sefirot*. And may we be able to distinguish all on the critical scale, if God so grants.

Translator's summary

Krokhmal defined the finite and infinite logically, as intellectual ideas. He did not define them ontologically, as ideas which transcended intellect—e.g., God, which belonged to the philosophy of spirit. The idea of the infinite could not be understood as outside the finite. For this would limit it. Nor could it be understood as the extension of the finite, into which the finite opened up. That would make the finite infinite. To represent the infinite at all would limit it, just as would understanding it in any finite terms. To let the finite touch the infinite or to enlarge into it, destroyed the infinite. The infinite had to be open on both sides. In the case of being, one began by considering its qualification negatively. One then negated this negation, and so on, endlessly. Meanwhile, being remained and comprehended everything. Similarly, one began to "grasp" the infinite by denying that it was finite. We negated that finite which was, in turn, negation of the infinite. Meanwhile, infinity stood above all.

[Finite and Infinite]

We will return now to the topic at hand, namely the idea of the *finite and infinite*. We have not engaged in these subjects to the extent that they are topics existing outside the understanding [i.e., ontologically]. ["Outside the understanding" applies to] the substance which is absolutely highest, God. [It applies] to the substance of everything which is outside Him and exists from Him. This [realm] belongs to the *philosophy of spirit*, to which we have referred. At this point the deliberation about the infinite and finite is under the scrutiny of their [logical] being, solely as ideas which make themselves present in, and exist in, the intellect.

Let us explain them further. Let us take these two ideas as they are at the beginning of representation. Each one of them has an existence (*metsiut*) in-itself, in [our] understanding. That is, the finite is real in-itself (*kayem be'atsmo*). The infinite is outside the finite and secondary to it. Here we truly do not have the idea of the infinite in this at all. There are two possibilities. If the idea is partial, this infinite is such that [it belongs to the sphere of] the finite. The finite divides it and limits it. It is finite in-itself and has an end. It is not the idea which we meant by it. On the other hand, the representation [catches] the beginning of the finite, as it stands permanently in one corner. This point could be the beginning of the corner of the infinite. Then [the finite] would be absolute reality, equal in its status to the idea of the infinite for it would have complete and absolute being. [I.e., we can have an idea of the infinite. If we have a representation thereof, it is *de facto* not the infinite.][70]

If [those who object] say that the being of the finite depends upon the infinite, then there is a contradiction. Their heart does not understand what they say with their mouths. Reference to the beginning of the representation states that there is no mutual entry between these two ideas. [That is, they are not commensurate. The infinite is open on both sides. If there is a point which enlarges into the infinite, it can no longer be the infinite]. In this manner, the finite returned to nothingness. Because of this, there will be the idea that there is a broad and deep limit between the two ideas. These two ideas stand uniquely within their limitations. It will be considered wise [to say], that the finite cannot attain the infinite, that it cannot come close to it or enter into its realm. Given this, it is acknowledged that the finite is nothing. It is the shadow which passes and does not stand still. It is a child of change and a disappearing vapor. The contradiction is clear to [those who oppose this view]. [By contrast], the representative image affects therein such a reversal of intention, that it totally separates the infinite from the finite. It makes the infinite a bearer of limitation and finitude, and also makes the finite stand in-itself and in absolute being. This is the opposite of the intention of the infinite.

---

70   Cf. Kant, "No sensible form can contain the sublime property so-called. This concerns only ideas of the reason, which, although no adequate presentation is possible for them, by this inadequateness that admits of sensible presentation, are aroused and summoned into the mind." Kant's *Critique of Judgment*, trans. J. H. Bernard (London: Macmillan, 1891), vol. 1: 23, 103).

Indeed, according to our path above, when *being* is grasped, namely when it is a quality, it is [grasped] in the negative. When quality changes itself into another quality, the negation is negated here into another negation, and so on forever. [I.e., we have the real meaning of infinite, when the finite is explained as its denial.] What truly occurs is negation of negation, while being always remains. Because of this, being does not vanish or end, and is infinite. Because of this, it is truly unjustified to speak of the unity of finite and infinite. For in this statement we would, God forbid, make the infinite into the finite. Can we even say that the finite already changed itself in its being, to be one with the infinite? [No, because] this [means that] the infinite also changed itself somehow internally from what it was previously.

The truth is that the infinite stands. The finite vanishes and passes. It remains within the infinite only as a representative image which annuls itself. [I.e., the infinite is not an extension of, nor comprehended by, the finite. The finite is given its place in the infinite.] And in order to show the substance of this deliberation....[71]

The final chapter of Krokhmal's "Moreh Nevukhei Ha'zeman," chapter 17, consistes of a general introduction to the philosophical thought of Abraham Ibn Ezra.

---

71   Gap in text.

Chapter Two

INTELLECTION AND DEVELOPING CONSCIOUSNESS

2.0. INTRODUCTION: MAIMON, FORMSTECHER, HIRSCH

A second point of departure within the territory between the formerly boundaried areas of the autonomous Jewish community and the Christian world was that of rationality—in the forms of intellection and self-consciousness. Salomon Maimon spoke of the Jewish religion as an expression of the union between finite intellect (human) and divine intellect (infinite), of the quest for perfection in terms of adherence to the divine mind. This was the proper quest of both philosophy and the Jewish religion—the latter found at Sinai, in the *Zohar*, and in early Hasidism. Maimon's introduction to *Gibeat Ha'moreh*, translated for this volume, identified perfection with the emergence from potentiality to actuality. Actuality was achieved when the intellect reached an infinite dimension. This activity fell within the discipline of metaphysics.

Samuel Hirsch's Judaism was grounded in the development of the human being's consciousness and its self-consciousness. Considered anthropologically, religious consciousness involved the passage from abstract freedom to freedom-with-content, a passage enabled by the higher presence of absolute, divine freedom. The process broadened into world-history as religion moved from a focus on concrete religious content (paganism) to the spiritualizing of external reality through revelation (Judaism and Christianity), to the complete absorption of concrete religious content into religious consciousness (the messianic age centered in Judaism as exemplified by Abraham). In the passages from Hirsch's *Religious Philosophy of the Jews* translated for this volume, Hirsch identified religious consciousness as a necessity of human spiritual nature. According to him, religious consciousness was rooted in consciousness of the self and the freedom it generated. This freedom (developed in dialectical relationship to necessity) became actualized as consciousness-expanded across the concrete environment. The process was enabled, and ultimately guaranteed, by God. Each human being was faced with a choice between actualizing sensuous naturality or actualizing freedom. The former choice constituted sin—which, Hirsch stressed, carried no ontological value and did not affect God. The latter constituted the core of Judaism, which developed the concepts of human freedom and the consciousness of God.

Whereas Samuel Hirsch understood Judaism in terms of anthropology and world-historical dimensions of religious consciousness and freedom, Salomon Formstecher understood it in terms of cosmic and national contexts for religious consciousness. God's world-soul, a harmony of nature and spirit, manifested itself in history as spirit that was separate from nature. The human being participated in divine self-consciousness and was therefore able to reconcile nature and spirit, and to do so in terms of spirit. The nation of Israel was positioned to lead the world in this effort by using reason to bring forth the revelation of the world-soul's ideals—which it alone could access in history.

In the texts translated for this volume, Formstecher wrote of the two dimensions of the world soul, nature (of necessity and the earth organism) and spirit (of freedom), and of the self-conscious human mind/spirit which is capable of spiritualizing the earth organism. The people of Israel were uniquely capable of using the self-consciousness that all human beings possess as images of the divine, to confront the choice between nature and spirit which came at the beginning of human history, and to reconcile them according to spirit. That is, the people were able to channel the nature-spirit equilibrium of pre-historical, objective revelation into historical, subjective revelation. At Sinai, they had accessed the eternal ideals of the world-soul through revelation and had brought them to self-consciousness, through reason. For both Hirsch and Formstecher, Scriptural history demonstrated how Judaism was essentially a unique vessel providing access to the higher sources of self-consciousness and freedom. These qualities were natural to all humankind, but the people of Israel were a collective exemplar, able to lead the rest of humanity to a state of ultimate freedom. For both Hirsch and Formstecher, the dynamic of self-consciousness and freedom provided a basis for the philosophical interpretation of history, in terms of Israel's internal development and in terms of the world.

2.1. SALOMON MAIMON (1754-1808): INTELLECTUAL PERFECTION[1]

Shelomoh ben Yehoshua—he assumed the name "Maimon" when he was thirty, in honor of Rambam—was born in Sokoviborg in Polish Lithuania. He learned Hebrew scripture, rabbinic commentaries, and *Talmud* from his father, and had limited exposure to scientific literature (namely, to David Gans' *Nehmad Vena'im* on astronomy) and the German language, both through his own initiative. Maimon developed the reputation of a Talmudic prodigy, making him a sought-after husband. He married at age eleven, a son was born in 1768, and he worked as a private tutor to support the family. He traveled to find texts of Hebrew philosophy and German science, and also to meet with Dov Baer, the Maggid of Mezeritch, a student of the Ba'al Shem Tov (1773). At age twenty five, abandoning his family, he traveled to Königsberg—supporting himself there, in part, with his translation of Mendelssohn's *Phaedon* into Hebrew (prompted by Jewish students)—and then to

---

1   There is extensive scholarship about Maimon. This includes: Samuel Atlas, *From Critical to Speculative Idealism: The Philosophy of Salomon Maimon* (The Hague: Nijhoff, 1961); Arkush, "Solomon Maimon and His Jewish Philosophical Predecessors: The Evidence of His Autobiography," in *Renewing the Past: Reconfiguring Jewish Culture. From al-Andalus to the Haskalah*, eds. Ross Brann and Adam Sutcliffe (Philadelphia: University of Pennsylvania Press, 2004), 149-166; Bergman, "Sefer Ta'alumot Hokhmah Shel Shelomoh Maimon," in *Sefer Ha'yovel Le'profesor Shemuel Kroys* (Jerusalem: Reuven Mass, 1936), 255-259; Solis Daiches, "Maimon and His Relation to Judaism," *Jewish Review* 5, no. 26 (July 1914): 152-172; Feiner, "Salomon Maimon and the *Haskalah*," *Ashkenaz* 10, no. 2 (2000): 337-359; Gideon Freudenthal, "A Philosopher Between Two Cultures," and "The Published Works of Maimon," in *Salomon Maimon: Rational Dogmatist, Empirical Skeptic* (Dordrecht: Kluwer, 2003), 1-17; 263-272; Geiger, "Zu Salomon Maimons Lebensgeschichte," *Jüdische Zeitschrift für Wissenschaft und Leben* 4 (1866), 189-199; Noah I. Jacobs, "Salomon Maimon's Relation to Judaism," *LBIY* 8 (1963): 117-135 and "An Annotated Bibliography of Salomon Maimon," *Kiryat Sefer* 41, no. 2 (1966): 245-262; Friedrich Kuntze, "Grundzüge der philosophischer Entwicklung Maimons," in *Die Philosophie Salomon Maimons* (Heidelberg: C. Winter, 1912), 18-28; Fabius Mieses, *Korot Ha'filosofiah Ha'hadashah* (Leipzig: n.p., 1887), 100ff; Christoph Schulte, "*Kabbalah* in Salomon Maimons Lebensgeschichte," in *Kabbalah und die Literatur der Romantik*, eds. Eveline Goodman Thau, et al. (Tübingen: Max Niemeyer, 1999), 33-66, and "Salomon Maimons Lebensgeschichte: Autobiographie und moderne jüdische Identität," in *Sprache und Identität im Judentum*, ed. Karl E. Grözinger (Wiesbaden: Harrassowitz, 1998), 135-150.

Berlin.[2] He reached the gate of the city, but when he shared that he intended to issue a commentary of Rambam's *Guide to the Perplexed* (he had a digest of the *Guide* with him) he was turned away—Rambam was linked to reforming Judaism, and Orthodox Jews saw him as a threat. Maimon then went on to Posen. There, supported by the family of the (then absent) Chief Rabbi Raphael Kohen (an opponent of Mendelssohn), he dedicated himself to compiling *Heshek Shelomoh*.

The *Heshek Shelomoh*, never published, included commentaries on the fourteenth century philosophical sermons of Nissan of Gerona (*Derashot Ha'ran*) and on Abraham Ibn Ezra's commentary on the thirteenth century mystical *Torah* commentary of Rabbenu Bahyah Ibn Asher; a study of *Kabbalah*; and a Hebrew text book for "higher algebra." It also included a probe of Rambam's philosophy, *Ma'aseh Livnot Ha'sapir* (About the Sapphire Stone) and the *Guide* digest. As described by Abraham P. Socher, human perfection for Maimon consisted of human intellectual cognition of, and cleaving to, God's active intellect. This was derived from Rambam—whose *Guide*, he said, was a memorial to the spirit's quest for perfection. For Aristotle, passive intellect included the potential of human thought to become actually thinkable, and the active intellect actualized this potential in the form of thinking. Man's ultimate goal, for Maimon, was to bring intellect from potential to actual, and thereby to cleave to the active intellect—and become immortal through its immortality. The ennobling of man's intellect by the active intellect was like "the lighting of one candle from another, in which nothing is gained [or lost]" (*Heshek Shelomoh*, folio 8). Once the human intellect cleaved completely to the active intellect, to become immortalized in noetic terms, the individual soul would no longer exist. As Maimon later wrote, "the soul with its attainment of this high immortality must lose its individuality."[3]

Maimon returned to Berlin in 1781 or 1782, and this time succeeded in entering the city. He gained Mendelssohn's attention by writing a Hebrew essay refuting Christian Wolff's "principle of sufficient reason"

---

2   The *Phaedon* translation has been lost. Maimon also translated *Die Morgenstunden* into Hebrew, which has also been lost (except for some excerpts in *Gibeat Ha'moreh*). See Bergman, *The Philosophy of Salomon Maimon.*, trans. Noah I. Jacobs (Jerusalem: Magnes, 1967), 4.

3   Maimon, *Autobiography*, 163. Abraham P. Socher, *The Radical Enlightenment of Salomon Maimon* (Stanford: Stanford University Press, 2006), 65, 68-69, 128.

for demonstrating God's existence. But Mendelssohn, embroiled in the controversy over his Judaism *vis-à-vis* Christianity brought on by the anonymous *The Search For Light and Truth*, and possibly concerned with Maimon's scandalous behavior towards his family, advised him to leave, and he went on to Amsterdam. There, he made a half-hearted attempt to kill himself by leaping from a bridge during Purim. His motive could have been anything from an attempt to unite with God (as the active intellect or *Shekhinah*) through the destruction of the individual self, to responding to his failure to participate in the *Bildung* of Western European Jews that was underway, to a Purim-like ritual of reversing values, replacing life with death. After that incident he went on to Hamburg, where he attempted a religious form of suicide, by converting to Lutheran Christianity. He related his story to the first clergyman he could find. He told the minister that he was a Polish Jew destined by training for the rabbinate, when he felt a ray of light pierced through the darkness of superstition and the ignorance of his world. He sought to free himself from the darkness by coming to Berlin, where the support of some enlightened individuals enabled him to search for knowledge. He found all this to be useless, however. To be happy (temporally and eternally, both of which depended upon intellectual perfection) and to become a useful human being, he felt that he needed to embrace Christianity, he said. While it was true that Judaism came closer to reason, he admitted, Christianity had advantages on the practical level. Hearing this tale, the pastor nonetheless turned him down. Later on, Maimon explained this scenario differently: He was too enlightened (*aufgeklärt*) to return to Poland and too ignorant of the manners and customs of those he wanted to join in Germany, and so had no alternative but to embrace Christianity.[4] Following the attempt to convert, Maimon enrolled as an adult student (he was now thirty-one) in the *Gymnasium Christianum* in Altona (Steinheim would enroll there about a quarter

---

4   Maimon, *Lebensgeschichte*, 182-183. Saul Ascher spoke of Maimon's relationship to Polish culture:

> I know Maimon personally and well. He received a copy of Kant's *Critique of Pure Reason* from my hands—which he returned years later and which I still have in my bookcase. I was the one who encouraged him to go to the author [Kant], who often helped him with advice. I can therefore judge his literary character properly, and the good-natured way in which he presented things. As a born Pole, he only had Jews

of a century later), and studied English, German composition, and mathematics. Meanwhile, his private life returned to the fore. Rabbi Raphael Kohen approached him, with the threat of excommunication, about either divorcing his wife or returning home to care for his family. Maimon spurned the overture, pointing out that his conduct was "as little opposed to religion (properly understood) as it was to reason."[5]

In 1785 he returned to Berlin for one year—this time successfully integrating into the circle of *Maskilim* (among them, Mendelssohn's disciple David Friedländer). His scholarship included a partial Hebrew translation of Jacques Basnage, *L'Histoire des Juifs* (Rotterdam, 1706-1711), of which Mendelssohn reportedly approved, an algebra text in Hebrew (unpublished), and *Ta'alumot Hokhmah*, an account of Newtonian mathematical physics (unpublished). He continued on to Breslau, and while supporting himself as a tutor in Hebrew, mathematics, and physics, he presented a set of aphorisms on the impossibility of establishing a first cause from Leibniz's "principle of sufficient reason" to Christian Garve (the first reviewer of Kant's *Critique of Pure Reason*). He returned to Berlin—by this time divorced from his wife—and completed *Versuch über die Transcendentalphilosophie*, a commentary to Kant's *Critique of Pure Reason*. Kant praised it: "A glance at it enabled me to appreciate its excellencies at once, and to recognize that not only have none of my opponents understood me and my essential meaning as well as Maimon—but also that only a few possess the subtlety necessary for such profound investigations."[6]

---

who lived in the former Poland in view when he prepared his *Autobiography*. Like the Polish state itself, they presented a special aspect of culture. Everything Maimon said applies to these Jews. They had their own [constitutional] system, among themselves. The state itself had none, and therefore felt even less called upon to provide one for the Jews. Maimon's well-intentioned articulations about his countrymen, as well as his malicious ones, should not be taken seriously as rational conclusions to solid principles. Like most Poles, or Poles who were clever but not refined, Maimon had mood swings which determined his judgment. I often witnessed how his best friends would get offended when this happened—and this delighted him. There is a little evil which sticks to the human conscience. Cultured people know how to conceal it. Maimon often unintentionally expressed it, and this made many enemies.

Saul Ascher, *Die Germanomanie* (Berlin: Achenwall und Campe, 1815), 55-56.
5 Maimon, *Lebensgeschichte*, 19.
6 Kant, Letter to Markus Herz (26 May 1789) as cited by Bergman, *The Philosophy of Salomon Maimon*, 5.

He also wrote his *Autobiography*.[7]

Socher wrote that Maimon was animated by his quest for noetic perfection and to cleave to the active intellect. He strove to be of the immanent, infinite intellect—or the "world-soul" of Giordano Bruno, the universal intellect, or the *Ruah Ha'olam (Weltseele)* as the (Aristotelian) form of the entire world.[8] The quest lay in philosophy, but also in the pure Judaism of Sinai or early Hasidism. Hasidism's *devekut* (cleaving) to the *Shekhinah* (divine presence) was a form of union with active intellect—to which the *Shekhinah* (the lowest of the kabbalistic *Sefirot*) corresponded. In his commentary on *Derashot Ha'ran* Maimon wrote that a great act of cleaving (*devekut*) could be understood in terms of (Aristotelian) matter and form. In creation, God first prepared matter, and then form. The former was the *Shekhinah*, the latter the "Holy One Blessed be He." God (form) and the universe (matter, *Shekhinah*) were unified, enabling *devekut*. According to Dov Baer, the *Maggid* of Mezeritch, there was no place in the universe devoid of God, and cognition of anything meant cognition of God.[9] To achieve the highest perfection, one had to regard oneself as an "origin of the God-head," no longer as a self-existing being.[10] To receive the Holy Spirit, an emissary of the *Maggid* told Maimon, one must become an instrument, purely passive, rather than self-active.[11]

Religion for Maimon was an expression of gratitude and reverence towards the ultimate source of human benefit.[12] Idolatrous religion drew similarities between cause and effect. For example, it attempted to arrive at God's perfect essence by concentrating all conceivable perfections together and projecting the resulting concept into infinity. To the extent that the idolater sought to initiate divine perfection, God was limited to being a model for man.[13] For Maimon, Spinoza's God as the

---

7   This section is based upon *Salomon Maimon: An Autobiography*, ed. Moses Hadas, trans. J. Clark Murray (New York: Schocken Books 1947); Salomon Maimon, *Lebensgeschichte*, ed. Jakob Fromer (Munich: Georg Muller, 1911); and Socher, *The Radical Enlightenment of Salomon Maimon* (Stanford: Stanford University Press), 1-142.

8   Maimon, *Gibeat Ha'moreh*, 110.

9   Maimon, *Maggid Devarov Le'ya'akov* (1781), 26[b].

10   Maimon, *Lebensgeschichte*, 102-103.

11   Socher, 76-77, 95-96, 132-133.

12   *Autobiography*, 11.

13   Maimon, "Abgötterei," in *Philosophisches Wörterbuch oder Beleuchtung der wichtigsten Gegenstände der Philosophie in alphabetische Ordnung* (Berlin: Unger, 1791), 6.

identifiable ultimate cause fell into this category:

> [Spinozism] supposes one and the same substance as the immediate course of all various effects, which must be regarded as predicates [i.e., attributes] of one and the same subject. Matter and mind [i.e., extension and thought] are, with Spinoza, one and the same substance [i.e., God], which appears, now under the former, now under the latter attribute. This single substance is, according to him, not only the sole being that can be self-dependent, that is, independent of any external cause, but also the sole self-subsistent being, all so-called beings besides it being merely its modes, that is, particular limitations of its attributes. Every particular effect in nature is referred by him, not to its proximate cause (which is merely a mode) but immediately to this first cause which is the common substance of all beings.[14]

For the authentic religious personality, Maimon wrote, the ultimate cause (God) could not be identified from a human perspective. God's reality was a perfect, infinite essence, as the ideal of infinite perfection was inherent in Him. It was not added to Him, by man or any outer cause which has been derived from the human world. Not even the terms "is real" or "is not real" are applicable to God. "Is" applies to sensible objects and "real" is observable, while God's inherent reality is an idea. Maimon used the analogy of a beard and an angel to illustrate this. An angel cannot be described as bearded or not bearded, because an angel has no body.[15]

Given the disjunction between human understanding (tied to sensible perception and time) and God's inherent reality, how could the authentically-religious person relate to God? Maimon delineated two levels of understanding: a lower one of multiplicity and temporality, and a higher one beyond both. The idea of the power of infinite understanding, the infinite ability to know, is available to the human being, bridg-

---

14 *Autobiography*, 113. See Bergman, "Spinoza and Maimon," in *The Philosophy of Salomon Maimon*, 216-228, and Socher, 9-10.
15 Maimon, "Atheist," in *Philosophisches Wörterbuch*, 25-27.

ing the two and relating the human being to the reality of God. Specifically, consciousness which is of time and space can attach itself to an infinite ability to know. When this consciousness becomes an object for reflection, the difference between finite and infinite can be overcome, and the divine ideal of infinite perfection grasped.[16]

For Maimon, original Judaism was the true religion. When Moses was atop Sinai, he had a contract-like experience with the supreme being (equivalent to a rational, metaphysical idea of unidentified ultimate cause) in a moment of silent stillness. As he began to descend, the silent moment became symbolized as a covenant with *YHWH* (*Yod-Hay-Vav-Hay*), which transmitted the apprehended metaphysical idea without obstructing it. What philosophers would describe in terms of the infinite ability to know, Moses provided through symbol. Maimon wrote:

> ... Judaism consists in a contract, at first merely understood [i.e., silent stillness], but afterwards expressed, between man and the Supreme Being, who revealed Himself to the patriarchs in person (in dreams and prophetic appearances) and made known by them His will, the reward of obeying it and the punishment of disobedience, regarding which a covenant was then with mutual consent concluded. Subsequently, through his representative Moses, He renewed His covenant with the Israelites in Egypt, determining more precisely their mutual obligations; and this was afterwards on both sides formally confirmed on Mount Sinai. ... The representation of a covenant between God and man is to be taken merely analogically, and not in its strict sense. The absolutely Perfect Being can reveal Himself merely as an idea to the reason. What revealed itself to the patriarch and prophets, suitably to their power of comprehension, in figure, in an anthropomorphic manner, was not the absolutely Perfect Being Himself, but a representative of Him, His sensible image. The covenant, which this being concludes with man, has not for its end the mutual satisfaction of

---

16   Maimon, "Gott," in *Kritische Untersuchungen über die menschlicher Geist oder das höhere Erkenntnis und Willensvermögen* (Leipzig: Gerhard Fleischer, 1797), 245-247.

wants. The Supreme Being has no wants, and the wants of man are satisfied not by means of this covenant, but only by observation of those reactions between himself and other natural objects which are founded on the laws of nature. This covenant, therefore, can have its foundation nowhere but in the nature of reason, without reference to any end.[17]

Beginning with the completion of Moses' descent, continuing with Jewish history and individual Jewish experiences, the covenant granted by *YHWH* entered daily use. This undermined the function of the symbol as an expression and sign of the silent moment, for the symbol became its own reality—thereby blocking the Jewish mind from access to that moment. The quest for the metaphysical idea relocated itself from the infinite to the finite, and thereby defeated itself. For example, the symbol of Sinai was expanded into Mosaic legislation and the Temple of Jerusalem. The Temple was destroyed and eclipsed by mystification, and then Mosaic legislation was eclipsed by *Mishnah* and *Kabbalah*. The infinite core was lost, and finite mystery and rabbinic legalism took over.

Gibeat Ha'Moreh

Gibeat Ha'moreh *was an interpretation of Part I of Rambam's* Guide to the Perplexed. *It appeared anonymously in 1791, a year after the* Versuch über die Transcendentalphilosophie, *although the publisher, Isaac Euchel, knew the author's identity. The text was issued by the publishing arm of the Free School of Berlin, which also published the leading* Haskalah *journal,* Ha'measef *(published by Euchel as well). Its theme was the achievement of noetic perfection: "Know that the true good is the attainment of perfection; i.e., the emergence of that which is potential to that which is actual"* (Gibeat Ha'moreh, 35). *Maimon posited that the finite and infinite intellect were of the same kind, differing only in degree* (Gibeat Ha'moreh, 34). *It was necessary for the infinite to shed its finitude and to conceptualize the infinite intellect, and this came about through shedding the very concept of limitation* (Gibeat Ha'moreh, 29). *The shedding of the concept of limitation, uncovering the continuum between finite and infinite and the fact that they were of the same kind, is enabled by God. God is infinite intellect, as well as the intellectualizing*

---

17   *Autobiography*, 177-178.

subject and intellectualized object (Gibeat Ha'moreh, 105).

In the "Introduction," translated for this volume, Maimon defined perfection in Aristotelian terms, as the emergence from potentiality to actuality.
Each species has its own kind of perfection, and that of the human being is
intellection (Haskalah). The central aspect of intellection is knowing the reality of perfect, infinite substance. Accordingly, the highest discipline is metaphysics, which transcends the finite empirical world and the disciplines tied to
it, such as natural science. As an example of metaphysical judgment, Maimon
pointed to the *a priori concept of causality, which enables the connection between fire and the warmth of a substance next to it. Maimon regarded the*
Guide to the Perplexed *as a compendium of metaphysical intellection.*

II.I. Introduction to *Gibeat Ha'moreh* (Berlin 1792), translated by Gershon Greenberg[18]

Summary of translated passages

[Perfection: Animal and Human]
*Perfection was a matter of emerging from potentiality to actuality, and hu-
man perfection was intellection. The animal had its own perfection, which
was natural to it. Human perfection was potential, and requires education
and adaptation to be actualized. The perfection of the intellect was not to be
confused with other forms of human perfection.*

The *telos* (*takhlit*) of man's activities, in the aspect (*behinah*) of having
will and choice, is the ultimate human good (*ha'hatslahah ha'enoshi'it*).
This excellence necessarily comes after the attainment of perfection. It
is thus proper for us to research: What is the nature (*inyan*) of attaining this perfection? What are the means for possibly reaching (*nagia*) it?

---

18 The significance of the title is unclear. It might have been to praise Rambam, by speaking
of the "elevation" (*givah*) of the *Guide*; or referred to King Saul's home (*gibeah*) (I Samuel
11:11). Maimon may also have been emulating the title *Gibeat Shaul* (1645) by his predecessor
Shaul Morteira. I used the text edited by Samuel Hugo Bergman and Nathan Rotenstreich,
"Hakdamah Ha'hakham Ba'al Gibeat Ha'moreh," in Shelomoh ben Yehoshua Maimon, *Divrei
Mavoh Le'Gibeat Ha'moreh* (Jerusalem: Ha'hevrah Ha'filosofit Bi'yerushalayim, 1952), 5-14,
and took into account the translated terms in Bergman, "Ha'munahim Ha'filosofi'im Ha'ivri'im
Shel Maimon," in *Ha'filosofiah Shel Shelomoh Maimon* (Jerusalem: Hebrew University Press,
1932), 168-170 and Bergman and Rotenstreich, "Milon Ha'munahim," in *Gibeat Ha'moreh
Li'shelomoh Maimon* (Jerusalem: Israel National Academy of Sciences, 1965), 190-192.

Let us say: The perfection of anything which exists consists of emerging from potentiality to actuality. The tree's perfection, for example, is that of bearing fruit.[19] Man's perfection is intellection (*haskalah*). So it is in similar cases. In this respect, man is far from all the animals outside of himself. Each special (*me'yuhad*) species of animal has its necessarily special activity, in terms of its being of that respective species. Thus, the chameleon's perfection is digging into the earth; the spider's is weaving, etc. Moreover, the perfection of all the respective species of animals is not acquired through education and adaptation. Rather, the perfection exists (*nimtsah*) in each species with the onset of its being. It is also impossible for us to rob it of that activity which is special to it, or that it will acquire another [special] activity through education and adaptation.

This is not so for man. No special activity is imprinted upon him with the onset of his being (*heyoto*). Rather, he is prepared (*mukhan*) by nature for many and various activities. These are only potentially inherent to him at the onset of his being. They emerge gradually into actuality when causes challenge him. In addition, man's perfection is acquired by him through education and adaptation. Perfection is not imprinted upon him, as is the case with other living beings. We find that man's being is naturally prepared to acquire many kinds of perfection. Or, the being of man possesses many potentials (all disposition to perfection is called potential)—for example, the potential for feeling, for imagination, for memory, for understanding (*Verstand*), and so forth. Besides, it is proper for man [*qua* man] to direct all his aims towards actualizing all these respective potentials. This requires making efforts within various disciplines. While all the respective potentials extend to any sort of discipline, we will also apply the special sort of discipline to the potential special to it. As law is an allocation of activities (*Verteilung der Geschäfte*), it is also the foundation of the special discipline of politics. That is, it cannot be assumed that each member of the state satisfies his needs by himself—that he prepares his own food, weaves his clothing, and builds his house, etc. Rather, it is necessary for each and every one

---

19 *Takhlit* referred to Aristotle's *entelecheia*, *shleimut* (perfection) to *arete*. See Maimon, "Hakdamat Ha'hakham Ba'al Gibeat Ha'moreh," in *Gibeat Ha'moreh Li'shelomoh Maimon*, eds. Bergman and Rotenstreich (Jerusalem: Israeli Academy of Science, 1965), 1-5, and "Hakdamah Ha'hakham Ba'al Gibeat Ha'moreh," in *Divrei Mavoh Le'Gibeat Ha'moreh*, eds. Bergman and Rotenstreich (Jerusalem: Ha'hevrah Ha'filosofit Bi'yerushalayim, 1952), 5-14, 40-41 (henceforth noted as "B-R").

to specialize in one special activity.

From this ensues the perfection of each respective occupation. Each special man is prepared by nature for a special occupation. By concentrating on one occupation, it is possible for him to reach a great degree of perfection at it—something which is otherwise impossible. The single man, by himself, is analogous to a small town, where each special potential needs to become a special actuality. Then it is possible for him to reach a great degree of the [respective] perfection. For example, the potential of imagination needs to be special to the occupation of drawing or to [composing] a melody, etc. Reason (*tevunah, Vernunft*) needs to be special to logic. Intellect (*sekhel, Verstand*) combined with reason needs to be special to geometry and general philosophy. Man should not want to philosophize with imaginary drawings, or analyze the delight of the melody with his intellect.

Summary of translated passages
The various disciplines shared the laws of intellect and reason, while differing in terms of subject and content. Metaphysics pursued intellectual concepts and universal forms imprinted upon the substance of intellect—as related to universal subjects. While the discipline of logic compared the concept of subject and the concept of predicate of each judgment, metaphysics connected the concepts into a single judgment. It also posited its own, a priori reality, because matter was taken up into form, and was outside experience. An example is the concept of causality, prior to the experience of fire vis-à-vis warmth. This made metaphysics superior to the natural sciences.

[*The Distinctive Disciplines: Natural Science, Logic and Metaphysics*]
It is appropriate that you know that all kinds of various disciples (*hakhamot*) have both a common nature (*inyan*) and a nature where they vary from one another. The nature in which they all share, is their alignment and agreement with the laws of intellect and reason in general. This is what I will call the form (*tsurah*) of the disciplines. The nature whereby they differ from one another is that subject (*nose*) of each, which is separate from the subject outside it in other disciplines—which is to say, from the aspect of the content (*homer*) of the disciplines. For example, the discipline of geometry and the discipline of science have in common that they both necessarily agree to the methods (*darkhei*) of universal intellect and reason. That is, in every judgment of theirs, there

must be a predicate of the judgment which does not contradict the subject. And we assume nothing without sufficient cause, etc. And they are mutually exclusive, insofar as the subject of geometry is the quantity as abstracted from quality; and the subject of natural science is the quality as abstracted from quantity. This is so with everything.

There are two sorts of disciplines which exist, whose subjects, that is to say, whose contents, are [also] the forms of the rest of the disciplines. They are logic and metaphysics. These are mutually exclusive, insofar as logic is a negative form, and metaphysics is positive.[20] Logic only compares between the concept (*tsiyur*) of the subject and of the predicate of each judgment. When the respective concepts agree, the judgment is defined as being positive. When the concepts are mutually contradictory, the judgment is defined as being negative. Logic by itself adds no further concept. Metaphysics, however, explores the intellectual concepts. That is, searches after the universal forms (*tsurot*) imprinted upon the substance (*etsem*) of intellect as related to all universal subjects (transcendental forms); and after the conditions for their application (*die Bedingungen ihres Gebräuchs*), so as to thereby connect the given (*munahim*) concepts of the subject and the predicate. For example, the judgment 'Special subject A is the cause for another special subject B" does not only follow the law of contradiction (*das Gesetz des Widerspruchs*). For despite B's not merely contradicting A, A does not posit the cause for B. It is clear from this, that besides the concepts of A and B, it is necessary for there to be an intellectual concept, i.e., the causal concept. By means of it, we can connect both given concepts into one judgment. It is the same with similar cases. This explains the high level of metaphysics, relative to other disciplines. The reality of no other discipline comes close. Metaphysics posits its own reality by itself, insofar as it is form. In other disciplines, matter (*homer*) is also of concern. In metaphysics, form and matter are one.[21] [Matter is pres-

---

20 Logic as a negative form meant as an analytical form; as a positive form, metaphysics was synthetic. Maimon used the traditional distinction between logic and metaphysics, and infused it with Kantian content. Logic was formal logic, metaphysics was transcendental logic (B-R).

21 All the sciences needed to be supplied with matter. In metaphysics, i.e., transcendental philosophy, matter and form were found together. Maimon was influenced by Spinoza's distinction: Where reason was outside (here, the material sciences), it was not necessary. Where reason was within (here, transcendental logic) it was necessary (B-R).

ent, only as form.] Besides, metaphysics is not derived from experience (miha'behinah, aus Erfahrung), as is the case with natural science.
Metaphysics also excludes itself from experience. It is the opposite [of
experience, as form is not material]. There is no place for experience
except in the *a priori* reality of the metaphysical principle.[22]

An example will make this clear: "Fire warms the substances
(gashmi'im) close to it. This includes, by itself, the concept of cause. If
this concept did not inhere in the intellect, it would not be possible for
this judgment to be necessary. Even if we comprehended (hisagnu) fire a
thousand times and afterwards, in time, the warming of the substances,
a fire which warms substance would not necessarily follow. What we
come to know (ha'noda) is not from this experience, but from what we
conceptualize. Namely, that the reality of warmth in substances follows,
in time, the reality of fire. It was already possible for us to conceptualize
in our consciousness (da'atenu) that at times fire would exist. Nevertheless, the warming of substances afterward in time would not follow [the
conceptualizing of fire—unless we already had a concept of cause].[23] But
according to what we have explained, the concept of cause is imprinted
upon our intellect prior to our experience, with regard to the form of
hypothetical judgments (hypothetischen Sätze). If we assume A in our
experience,[24] we must necessarily assume B—whatever A and B are (for
logic will only present its analysis in forms of judgment). That is, in defining methods which connect subject and predicate as abstracted from
their materiality (special subject and predicate). To this class belong the
respective methods of connection, which include whatever types of subject and predicates there may be. There is also the judgment mentioned
above: "The fire warms the substances close to it," with the material
[component] of judgment. That is, the subject and the predicate (the
fire and the warmth of the substances) are special things (devarim) tak-
en from experience—a necessarily inclusive judgment. [Materials, e.g.,
fire, are provided by experience. The form of the causal connection is *a
priori* and inclusive.] This judgment has conditional forms taken from
logic. It is inherently possible. Nevertheless, it is clear that the discipline

---

22 That is, there was no place for experience (behinah) without assuming, a priori, the
realities of the principles of metaphysics (Kant's condition of experience) (B-R).
23 This epitomized Kant's claims, to the benefit of the *a priori* (i.e., necessity) of the law of
causality. See Maimon, *Versuch über die Transcendentalphilosophie*, chapter 2 (B-R).
24 That is, through our will, in an arbitrary manner (B-R).

cited [logic] does not instruct us about the possibility of connecting the form with the material, [while metaphysics does]. The conditions which ensue will be suitable to all the respective connecting. [By itself, logical form does not indicate conditions for its application to the materiality.] Also, metaphysics explores the possibility of the respective judgment and its use regarding things which exist universally and in actuality— not the experience of things existing in particular actuality[25] (since this is the subject of natural science and not of metaphysics). It instructs us that all of this necessarily follows from the nature of the intellect and the methods of its application.

From this it may be explained that despite natural science's being prior in time to metaphysics, metaphysics is prior to natural science in essence (be'teva).[26] Should our consciousness conceptualize an annulment of metaphysics, there would be no place for nature (teva), or for natural science. In general, no place would remain for any discipline at all. Indeed, man would have no advantage over animals (see Ecclesiastes 3:19). These very profound matters will be explained in their proper place, in light of the venerable text [of Rambam] which follows. But this expresses the intention sufficiently.

What is still to be accounted for is the essence (otsem) of the dignity of metaphysics and the superiority of metaphysics over all other disciplines. It teaches us, through definitive examples (mofet), about the reality (metsiut) of the perfect, infinite substance—and what we should ascertain, positively and negatively, about it.

[Guide to the Perplexed]

Summary of translated passages
The Guide to the Perplexed included the principles of metaphysics, and discussed proofs for the reality of God, His unity and incorporeality. It discussed theology as an intellectual pursuit, and of the soul. The text did not follow the order of other disciplines; it proceeded according to issues selected by Rambam. It was its own compendium, leading to human perfection. The people

---

25   In particular actuality, i.e., in real actuality, in a concrete way. This was a subject for the material sciences (B-R).
26   Maimon distinguished between priority in time and priority in nature, following Aristotle (B-R).

of Israel have been too intellectually weak to appreciate the work. But also, Rambam chose to be concise. The work needed to be grasped as a whole, on its own terms—outside of which everything was doubtful. Also, by later standards, the sciences were lacking in complexity.

The venerable book, as its name indicates, is a *Guide to the Perplexed*. It includes principles of the discipline of metaphysics and its primary doctrines. This is followed by proofs (*perakhim mofti'im*) for the reality of the Name, His unity, and negating His corporeality (*gashmiut*). Then, in general, what is needed for faith in Him. Or, what cannot be attributed to Him without impairing His perfection. The work also explains to us the nature of prophecy and interprets the books of prophecy. It shows us how theology does not contradict the human intellect, as the uneducated have thought. Rather, it fills the deficiencies of intellect. In addition to this, the *Guide* concerns itself with issues (*inyanim*) of great usefulness from other disciplines—natural science, astronomy and similar disciplines, in particular the science of the soul and its faculties. None of [what the *Guide* does] follows the learning-order of those respective disciplines; as it was not the intention of the teacher-author, may his memory be blessed, to copy the texts of those disciplines. [Rambam] himself, may his memory be blessed, explained that. He rather proceeds according to what follows from the nature (*teva*) of the issue (*inyan*), each issue in its proper place, in a manner suiting his intention. My essay (*ma'amar*) will be lengthy where Rambam, may his memory be blessed, dealt briefly. And it will fill the deficiencies in the disciplines of his age, judging by today's standards.

The treatise (*hibur*) [of Rambam] is an independent compendium of precious disciplines and lofty ideas (*yediot*) leading man to perfection. And it is proper that we give credit to the teacher-author, may his name be blessed, who left us a blessing which "might keep us alive, as it is today" [Deuteronomy 6:24]. This is after our long exile, with our becoming a disgrace [in the eyes of] our neighbors, an object of derision and mockery for those around us. The wisdom of our scholars was lost, and the reasoning (*binah*) of the insightful was hidden. Then the teacher, may his memory be blessed, shed light upon our vision with this venerable work. The treatise has its unique reality. Neither before nor after the teacher has anything like it been written. Anyone who studies it devoutly will recognize that, although we have been privileged to have the book for many centuries, we have not been worthy [enough to receive] its light. Our eyes [remain] dark in their sockets. They are so weak, that they cannot look at the resplendent light shining from the treatise.

There are several reasons for this: [1] The author, may his memory be blessed, was concise where he might have [expounded at] length. As will be explained, he himself, may his memory be blessed, composed his essay (ma'amar) only for those who philosophized and intellectualized (hiskil) about the disciplines. His words remain as a sealed volume for anyone else studying it. [2] The deficiency of the disciplines of his day, as measured by today's standards. This is especially so in natural science altogether, and its division established for astronomy, that is, for the concept of cosmic structure, in particular the order of the parts of the cosmos in relation to one another. The student will see this in my interpretations of the respective passages.[27] [3] The [perceived] deficiency in the order—simply because Rambam composed the treatise with a special scope in mind. The principal intention is lost, namely to understand (havanah) his knowledge (da'at) at a single glance, outside of which everything could be doubted. To be sure, some later interpreters tried to supplement all of this. Let the intellectual (maskil) see for himself and judge whether or not they fulfilled their intention.

Since I have "great zeal" [I Kings 19:19] for the honor of the venerable author, I took it to heart to interpret this venerable text anew, elaborating where he, may his memory be blessed, was concise. I will explain by example every judgment which exists, adding to the example found in the essay; calling the students' attention to analogies between the views (deot) of Aristotle and his followers, and the views of outstanding contemporary philosophies. "Let me not be prejudiced to anyone or flatter anyone" [Job 32:21]. As the wise man said, "Love Socrates, love Plato, and love truth more than either" [Aristotle, Nichomachean Ethics 1096a:16].

Summary of translated passages
The telos *of* Gibeat Hamoreh *was perfection, going beyond even universal judgments according to laws of intellect and forms of comprehending truth. This pursuit was active, and involved bringing the potential into the actual.*

---

27   For this reason, Maimon proceeded to provide an outline of the history of philosophy, concerning astronomical questions (B-R).

[Judgements]

It is proper for you to know, intellectual reader, that our *telos* is not to comprehend (*hasagat*) the truth, or have ideas of some universal judgments according to laws of the intellect which agree with the universal forms of comprehension. Truly, our intention here has the *telos* of comprehending perfection. This is not possible, without bringing potentiality to actuality. This is achieved only actively (*bi'feulah*) and not passively (*kabbalat ha'peulah*).[28] There is no activity in having ideas about some judgment and trusting in that judgment. There is activity [however,] in having ideas of the methods leading to the judgment.

A judgment [regarding] truth, whatever it be, has no advantage for the believer. It turns against the believer, in experiencing the matter (*inyan*) in itself. To give an example regarding experiencing the matter in itself: Someone who believes the earth is global has no advantage over the one who believes it is flat. Both pictures are equally possible, so that one has no advantage over the other. The advantage of the first judgment comes from its accordance with laws of universal motion. Because of this, it is connected with other judgments. And comprehending the connection between the judgments is the substance of the activity of the intellect. While the second judgment is of itself possible, it still is not from the activity of the intellect—as the second judgment is not connected with other judgments. It is also possible for someone to know all the judgments which exist in scholarly texts, without thereby achieving any perfection. Another person might know [only] a few judgments, but with examples; that is, in their connection to other judgments. The degree of perfection is according to the degree of comprehension in connection with the judgments.

Besides, it does not behoove you to intend to comprehend the truth, to have ideas of judgments which agree with the truth in the texts of the disciplines. It is rather proper for you to have ideas of the methods, through which discoveries are made in the disciplines. This way, you yourself will discover from experience. Obsolete words will be explained, with God's help, in another place. This is what I wanted to [offer by way of] preface, concerning the *telos* of comprehending the truths

---

28   The activity of the intellect, which was man's perfection, was also the condition for having real ideas, and was the source for the doctrine of understanding (*hakarah*) and justifying it (B-R).

and the paths of achieving it universally. It is the *telos* of my intention, my method of interpreting the venerable text.

Before I begin to explain the words of the *Rav*, may his memory be blessed, I deemed it proper to introduce the history of philosophy, from its beginning to our own times, for the sake of all intellectual readers. It would not have been honest to say that only disciplines in Aristotle's times were in some aspect deficient. For in the time of the *Rav*, may his memory be blessed, as he himself noted, they were also deficient in some aspects—by comparison with our own times. [The claim that] "Anything I say is right" [is relative].

> My beloved, intellectual reader,
> Know my name, and the name of my father.
> In your hearkening to the words in me (*she'bi*).

2.2. SALOMON FORMSTECHER (1805-1889): CONSCIOUSNESS, SPIRIT AND NATURE[29]

Formstecher characterized the residents of his birth place, Offenbach am Main, as provincial, and he was critical of how the different religious communities shut themselves off from one another. His father, a wood engraver (*Holzformstecherkunst*), provided tutors for his son to study Hebrew and *Talmud*, while he studied the regu-

---

29   Formstecher's works include: *Zwölf Predigten gehalten in dem Israel. Gotteshause zu Offenbach* (Würzburg: C. C. Etlinger, 1833); *Israels Klage und Israels Trost: Zwei Predigten* (Offenbach: n.p., 1835); "Über Stabilität und Fortschreiten im Judentum," *La Regeneration—Die Wiedergeburt: Eine Monatsschrift zur Beförderung religiöser Aufklärung und moralischer Bildung, von Simon Bloch* 1 (1836), 111-116; *Die Religion des Geistes* (FaM: Joh. Chr. Hermann, 1841); *Divrei Shalom Ve'emet: Aussprache des israelitischen Gemeindevorstandes zu Offenbach am Main an seine Gemeindegliedern über dessen Anordnungen und Einrichtungen seit 1821 bis auf die Gegenwart* (Offenbach am Main: n.p., 1843); "Philosophie des Judentums: Beleuchtung des im *Literaturblatt des Orients* ... erschienenen Aufsatzes 'Philosophie des Judentums' ... von Dr. S. Hirsch," *Literaturblatt des Orients* 20 (16 May 1843): 314-316; 21 (23 May 1943): 327-331; "Was ist Sünde? Predigt am Versöhnungstage," *Israelitischer Volkslehrer* 2 (1852), 194-202; and "Über das Wesen und über den Fortgang der israelitische Gottesverehrung," *Die Synagoge* 2 (1839): 87-107.
   Studies of his life and thought include: Bernard Bamberger, "Formstecher's History of Judaism," *Hebrew Union College Annual* (1950/51): 1-35; Greenberg, "Zur Verteidigung Formstechers," *Judaica* 29, no. 1 (March 1973): 24-35; Samuel Hirsch, "Rezension von S. Formstecher, *Die Religion des Geistes*," *Literaturblatt des Orients* 28 (9 July 1842), 435-442; no. 36 (3 September 1842): 563-566; *Beilage* 38 (13 September 1842): 3-8; Isaak Markus Jost, "Rezension von S. Formstecher, *Mosäische Religionslehre*," *Allgemeine Zeitung des Judentums: Literarischer Wochenbericht* 24 (1860): 707f and "Rezension von S. Formstecher, *Die Religion des Geistes*," *Israelitische Annalen* 41 (1841): 327; 42 (1841): 335f; 43 (1841): 343f; Leo Lichtenberg, "Salomon Formstecher's Concept of Judaism as Presented in his *Die Religion des Geistes* with Special Consideration of his Sources," (Hebrew Union College rabbinical thesis, 1940); Ignaz Maybaum, "Samuel (*sic*) Formstecher: Ein Beitrag zur Geschichte der jüdischen Religionsphilosophie im 19. Jahrhundert," *MGWJ* (1927): 80-99; Meyer, "Reform Jewish Thinkers in Their German Intellectual Context," in *The Jewish Response to German Culture*, eds. Jehuda Reinharz and Walter Schatzberg (Hanover: University Press of New England, 1985), 64-84; Hans-Joachim Schoeps, "Salomon Formstecher," in *Israel und Christenheit: Jüdisch-christliches Religionsgespräch in neunzehn Jahrhunderten* (Munich: Ner Tamid, 1961), 128-137; Leopold Stein, "Rezension von S. Formstecher, *Israelitische Andachtsbüchlein*," *Israelitischer Volkslehrer* 3 (January 1853): 74-75.

lar subjects at the Duke's Free Latin School.[30] Formstecher studied classics, political science, Hebrew Scripture, Christianity (including New Testament, church history, theology) and philosophy, under the Hegelian Joseph Hillebrand (1788-1871), and learned philosophy at the University of Giessen. After he received his doctorate (no dissertation was required) he returned home to serve as the *Prediger* (preacher) of the Israelite (i.e., Reform) community and, in time, as Offenbach's chief rabbi.

In *Twelve Sermons* (*Zwölf Predigten*, 1833) Formstecher described Judaism as a living organism with a particular process of development. He wrote that uniformity and elements of stagnation undermined it. At each stage of history, he proclaimed, Judaism needed to realize itself anew and to do so in terms of the respective contemporary condition—lest it be undermined by uniformity and, with it, stagnation. The enlightenment and emancipation of the current era demanded a categorical departure from the Judaism of the dark Middle Ages. Specifically, once the ghetto walls had fallen and civil equality had been achieved, Judaism was to maintain itself as a religious community only, and not to seek to establish itself as a state within the German state. Formstecher conceived of the human being as being located between God (spirit) and animal (nature); created in God's image, standing above the animal world, the human being possessed an immortal soul which protected it against descent to the animal level, and sin.[31] In 1838 and 1839 Formstecher published scientific studies about the immortality of the soul, eschatology, angels, and demons as they were

---

30   Formstecher, "Tischrede," in Leopold Stein, ed. *Festbericht über das fünfzigjährige Dienstjubiläum des grossherzoglichen Rabbiners Herrn Dr. S. Formstecher (Oktober 1882 zu Offenbach am Main)* (Offenbach: C. Forger, 1883), 37-40; and Meyer Kayserling, "Salomon Formstecher," in *Bibliothek jüdischer Kanzelredner* (Berlin: J. Springer, 1872), 137-152. Hillebrand succeeded Hegel at Heidelberg in 1818. See Ludwig Noack, "Hillebrand," in *Philosophie-Geschichtliches Lexikon* (Leipzig: Koschny, 1879), 384-386; and Hans-Ulrich Schreiber, *Joseph Hillebrand: Sein Leben und Werke* (Giessen: n.p., 1937).
31   Bettina Kratz-Ritter, "Zwölf Predigten (1833)," in *Salomon Formstecher: Ein deutscher Reform rabbiner* (Hildesheim: Georg Olms, 1991), 66-71.

conceived of according to Judaism.[32]

Formstecher's major work was *The Religion of the Mind/Spirit* (*Die Religion des Geistes*, 1841). In it, he described how the universe began with God's spiritual attribute of the world-soul, of which He (a pure mind/spirit) was conscious. The world-soul manifested itself in the earth organism, where it assumed the form of spirit as distinct from nature. While the two realms (of nature and spirit) began in equilibrium, they were potentially opposed. Nature was unconscious and followed laws of necessity, while spirit was conscious and aligned with the ideals of freedom. Nature moved in circles, ever repeating and reproducing itself, while spirit moved in a line, ever developing itself anew. Nature manifested itself as complete, while spirit presented itself as ever-striving towards realizing the ideal of freedom.

The human being was a spiritual power of the manifested world-soul, but as it was drawn from the world-soul it was also related to nature. Man occupied a unique position, bridging the world-soul and its self-manifestation as spirit *vis-à-vis* nature amidst the earth organism. He had the ability to reconcile the spirit-nature duality in terms of spirit, and to participate in raising the realms of nature and spirit back to the realm of the world-soul. As the image of God who thereby shared the self-consciousness of the divine, the human being could spiritualize the earth-organism. The human being could become aware of the origin and destiny of the world, blend nature into spirit through spirit, and raise nature and spirit to the world-soul, going even beyond merely an equilibrium between the two. While the human being could ignore self-consciousness and sink into nature for a time, self-consciousness would ultimately burst forth.

Formstecher posited that the cosmic structure had a historical dimension. The initial manifestation of the world-soul in the earth-organism was one of harmony or equilibrium between nature and spirit (the stage

---

32   Formstecher, *Israelitischer Andachtsbüchlein zur Erweckung und Ausbildung der ersten religiösen Gefühle und Begriffe: Ein Geschenk für gute Kinder* (Offenbach: C. Wächtershäuser, 1836); *Torat Mosheh: Mosäische Religionslehre für die israelitische Religionsschule* (Giessen: n.p., 1860); "Beitrag zur Entwicklungsgeschichte des Begriffs der Unsterblichkeit der Seele in Judentum," *Wissenschaftliche Zeitschrift für Jüdische Theologie* 4 (1838), 231-249; "Zur Geschichte der Eschatologie im Judentum," *Wissenschaftliche Zeitschrift für Jüdische Theologie* 4 (1839): 239ff; and "Beiträge zur Entwicklungsgeschichte der Angelo—und Dämonologie in Judentum," *Israelitische Annalen* 1, no. 46 (15 November 1839): 361-362 and 48 (29 November 1839): 371-378; no. 51, 403-404; no. 52, 411-413.

of pre-historical revelation). This was followed by a division between nature and spirit (the stage of historical revelation)—which is when sin began. This development, in turn, precipitated the emergence of consciousness and self-consciousness (which were grounded in, and drew upon,
the world-soul) *vis-à-vis* nature and pre-historical revelation. Insofar as
the recollection of pre-historical revelation was a function of consciousness, it also enacted man's identity as the image of God. From an ontological perspective, the recollection unfolding on the anthropological
level was already complete. Man would necessarily become conscious of
pre-historical revelation, because that consciousness was a higher level
of truth. In the course of time, the line between human consciousness
and pre-historical revelation became progressively thinner, until it became transparent.

The goal of *The Religion of the Mind/Spirit* was to explain Judaism's
reality in and for itself, as well as the absolute necessity of its appearance before and acceptance by other nations in order to bring about a
universal religion. In and for itself, Judaism was categorically distinct
from paganism. For the pagan mind, spirit was consumed by nature.
The pagan mind brought the world-soul (nature and spirit), which was
sui generis, into the world of nature. God and the world-soul were tied
to nature, and no higher realm existed into which man could emerge in
an act of freedom. Nor did human beings have a place in which to position themselves so as to look upon nature, enabling self-consciousness.
The pagan mind was characteristically aesthetic, and its *Weltanschau-
ung* was a matter of nationalism, racism, mythology, and geography. In
the mind of Judaism, the spiritual world-soul of God extended into the
earth-organism's phenomenal world of nature. But the spiritual realm
persisted—both above as the prime attribute of God and as a reality
parallel to nature below. The presence of a spiritual dimension is what
assured the option of freedom and self-consciousness.

In its historical development, Judaism moved the activity of spirit
in stages from a revelational ("objective") form at the beginning to a
rational ("subjective") mode at the end. In the objective period (that
of the prophets), Jews received God's revelation (heteronomous *Torah*-
instructions), and sought to convert ancient slavery into freedom, in
addition to transforming physical monotheism (in Egypt) into spiritual monotheism. In the subjective-objective period (rabbinic era), the
revelation from above was articulated in terms of *Halakhah*, applying

human reflection to the enthusiasm of the first period's prophets. The rabbinic sages brought revelation into consciousness by applying reason to temporal conditions. In the objective-subjective period (the first dimension of the medieval era), the subjective, autonomous thrust yielded compounded rituals. In the subjective-objective period (the second dimension of the medieval era), revelation became rationally comprehensible. Maimonides, for example, maintained that supernatural phenomena did not testify to beliefs and that a truth's credibility depended upon its rationality. In the subjective period (the modern era from Mendelssohn on) divine revelation became rationally comprehensible; self-sufficient knowledge and philosophical self-consciousness dominated. Overall, the progressive subjectivizing belonged to the larger cosmic process of the inevitable blending of pre-historical with historical consciousness.

Judaism appeared to mankind as the instrument of the absolutely necessary process of nature's rise into the spiritual realm and the extraction of spiritual reality from out of the confines of nature. Given the spiritual grounding of the universe, its spiritual destiny was a certainty. Christianity and Islam served as bridges to bring Judaism to the pagan world—while protecting Judaism from the dangers of contact with the pagan mind. In the north, Christianity extracted the spirit from nature through grace; the death and resurrection of Jesus returned spirit from out of the nature which consumed it, back to the world-soul and the religion of spirit developed by Judaism. It did so through the instruments of monasticism, original sin, and holy trinity—all forms of spirit which the pagan mind could understand. In the south, Islam released spirit from nature through acts of non-reflective devotion—using fantasy, poetry, oppression, and materialism to do so. Ultimately and inevitably, the spiritual content would be released and, along with Christianity and Islam, blend into Judaism. As with Judaism in particular, the historical, global encounter between nature and spirit would ultimately be synthesized into spirit and reflect the world-soul.[33]

Historians of modern Jewish philosophy have routinely identified Formstecher's *The Religion of the Mind/Spirit* with Friedrich Wilhelm

---

33   Formstecher, *Die Religion des Geistes* (FaM: Joh. Chr. Hermann, 1841); Hillebrand's *Philosophie des Geistes oder Encyclopädie der gesammten Geisteslehre* (Heidelberg: n.p., 1835) could have inspired Formstecher's title.

Joseph von Schelling (1775-1854), the principal philosopher of German Romanticism.[34] In reaction to the perceived absence of comprehensive spiritual unity of all things in Kant's analytical work and critical philosophy, the Romantics sought a single absolute principle, such as an infinite life in which all forms of life were phases—including the conscious life of the individual, the historical life of the race, the life of nature, religious faith, and artistic creation.[35] In *The Ages of the World* (1811) Schelling spoke of the absolute, divine unity of two dimensions. In nature (of necessity and self-sufficient being) God evolved self-consciously in pre-historical eternity; in the reality-principle of pure freedom, organic beings developed in history. The divine unity, in addition to self-consciousness, also contained three potencies. One prefigured each moment of creation; another brought universality to particularity and unreason-unconsciousness to reason-consciousness (the human being); and the third developed dualisms between nature and history and between nature and mind/spirit into eschatological unities.[36]

But the identity of Formstecher's thought with Schelling's needs to be qualified. First, while Schelling's world-soul was a realm tied to nature, in which imperceptible spirit (non-visible nature) and perceptible nature (spirit made visible) were related in terms of absolute identity, for Formstecher the world-soul was a divinely grounded imperceptible spiritual source of being which existed independently, whether or not it manifested itself in perceptible phenomena. Second, Schelling's world-soul, simultaneously mind/spirit and nature, served as the grounding for a Judaism tied to paganism, while Formstecher's purely spiritual world-soul provided grounding for a spiritual Judaism distinctly separated from paganism. Third, their views of the historical roles of Judaism and Christianity were reversed. Formstecher's Judaism functioned as Schelling's Christianity, and his Christianity as Schelling's Judaism. According to Schelling, Judaism was a transitional phenomenon between paganism and Christ's revelation. In "supra-history" man had immediate consciousness of God and the concept of world-soul that is

---

34   Julius Gutmann, Albert Lewkowitz and Nathan Rotenstreich identify Formstecher's thought with Schelling's.

35   See Harald Höffding, "The Philosophy of Romanticism," in *A History of Modern Philosophy*, vol. II (New York: Dover, 1955), 139ff.

36   Frederick de Wolfe Bowman, "The Character and Significance of *The Ages of the World*," in Schelling, *The Ages of the World* (New York: Columbia University Press, 1942), 66-79.

included in God. In "pre-history," beginning with Adam's sin, most nations of the world expressed divine revelation through myth. Judaism, however, retained the concept of the primordial God in immediate consciousness ("*YHWH*"). But it also had to struggle against paganism, and because of this became bound together with paganism, while Christianity was able to recapture the original immediate consciousness of God. To participate in history, according to Schelling, Jews would have to become Christians. Conversely, for Formstecher, "pre-historical revelation" meant the period before the fall into sin, when the world-soul manifested itself in the world in such a way that spirit and nature remained in harmony. "Historical revelation" meant man's (Adam's) awareness of his creaturehood, i.e., when nature and spirit separated and human consciousness sought to reconcile them by bringing nature into the realm of spirit. While Judaism (the religion of the spirit) was responsible for carrying out this reconciliation in Israel, Christianity was to redeem the spirit out of paganism, so as to bring the rest of the world, as well as itself (Christianity) within the harmony of nature and spirit and towards the spiritual reality of God's world-soul.[37]

Formstecher later published a study of Mendelssohn as a philosopher within the Jewish context, and he served as editor (with Leopold Stein) of the journals *Der Freitagabend* and (with K. Klein) of *Die Israelitische Wochenschrift*).[38]

---

37 Schelling, "Von der Weltseele," in *F. W. J. Schelling's Sämmtliche Werke* I, vol. 2 (Stuttgart: J. G. Cotta, 1856-1858), 347-351; *Aphorismen zur Einleitung in die Naturphilosophie*, part 1, vol. 7, 146-148; *Bruno oder über das göttliche und natürliche Prinzip der Dinge*, part 1, vol. 4, 297-298; *Ideen zu einer Philosophie der Natur*, part I, vol. 2, 57-73; "Philosophie der Mythologie" in *F. W. J. Schelling's Sämmtliche Werke* II, vol. 1, 156-174. See Paul Tillich, "God, World and Man," in *The Construction of the History of Religion in Schelling's Positive Philosophy*, trans. Victor Nuovo (Lewisburg, PA: Bucknell University Press, 1974),54-76. Kuno Fischer, "Die Grundidee der Naturphilosophie," in *Schelling's Leben, Werke und Lehre* (Heidelberg: C. Winter, 1923), 323-324; Bergman, "Friedrich Wilhelm Schelling," in *Toledot Ha'filosofiah Ha'hadashah* (Jerusalem: Mosad Bialik, 1984), 125-137. See also Victor C. Hayes, "Schelling and the Christian Tradition," in *Schelling's Philosophy of Mythology and Revelation* (Armidale: Australian Association for the Study of Religion, 1995), 35-46.
38 Formstecher, "Moses Mendelssohn, ein Philosoph auf dem Gebiete des Judentums," in *Gedenkblätter an Moses Mendelssohn: Verein zur Förderung geistiger Interessen im Judentum* (Leipzig: n.p., 1863): 5-21.

II.II. Salomon Formstecher, *The Religion of the Mind/Spirit: Presenting a Study of Judaism in Terms of its Character, Path of Development, and its Calling in Humanity. Judaism and Scientific Study.*

Summary of untranslated passages
Judaism, older than the civilizations of Greece and Rome, was a timeless monument upon which nations engraved their impressions in the context of their respective eras. It endured on the world-stage into the present, ever committed to its ideas despite overwhelming enemies. Christianity and Islam emerged from the source of Judaism and they remained aware of their dependence. Now that Judaism had become a subject for non-Jews to study, Jewish scholars and spiritual leaders had to become involved in the scientific study of Judaism. Specifically, the difference between external (non-Jewish) and internal (Jewish) perspectives had to be recognized and articulated. The outsider focused on Judaism as an original and indispensable ingredient of the (Christian) religious structure, while the Jew viewed Judaism as an ingredient of the human organism which had a calling related to all humankind. The specific task of The Religion of the Mind/Spirit was "to present Judaism as an absolutely necessary phenomenon in humankind, to demonstrate that Judaism was still to be considered as such, and to show that in its essential development Judaism grew into the universal religion of civilized mankind." Judaism was both an entity which was complete and integrated in itself, and one related to humankind in terms of mutual interchange. In this work Formstecher would probe Judaism's relation to paganism; Judaism's relative and absolute truths; delineates Judaism's unbroken quest to realize an absolutely true ideal; and explicates Judaism's relations to other religions.

The scientific method would be used: Subjective judgments conceded to objectively provided sources. Judaism was to be judged without presupposition by the Jew, just as it should be by the non-Jew. As such, its approach was unlike the Christian. While evil, fanatical hatred towards Judaism had disappeared from most Christian hearts, Christian understanding was still not devoid of prejudice. In the Jewish approach, the factual events of Jewish history and their truths (notably about the single God and His relationship to the world) ruled. There was no obligation to believe in God's immanence in order to receive God's grace; no requirement to believe in any anti-rational mystery. Unlike Christian theology, the Jewish approach did not require belief at the beginning and end of scientific research. It was foreign to Judaism to believe out of religious duty; to accept religious truths, even if they contradicted reason, solely because they were communicated by divine authority. That God concluded a covenant with Israel, for example, was believed on the basis of the reliability of the narrator's communication. It was a matter of reason and historicity, not any inspiration.

Formstecher would endeavor to (1) shed light on Judaism in and for itself and (2) on its relationship to humankind. The former was a matter of Judaism as an idea and in its purity. The latter was a matter of Judaism's appearance, and involved both inherent-absolute truths and relative truths which entered Judaism from the outside. Formstecher wrote that in its essence (idea) Judaism did not develop, while in terms of its appearance it did, with its "garments" changed over the course of time. With its shell ever changing, Judaism's core remained ever vital. While at some point it was necessary for Judaism to garb itself in a "frightening burial shroud" to protect the seed of life within from the "winter storms" of world history, as soon as the "spring sun of tolerance, civilization and humanity allowed," fresh garments were found. Essentially, Judaism belonged to the dynamic, lively organism of humankind, stepping back and forth with it, sharing its errors, weaknesses, discoveries and strengths.

Summary of translated passages

In chapter one Formstecher wrote that behind the particular sensible data which constituted the earth-organism was a world-soul from which they came and to which they returned. That source was God. The essence of the world, its bearer, remained the same. The forms, which had their own reality, changed. That essence produced the sensibly perceptible powers. The human being was unique among these powers, because it possessed self-consciousness. God was to be understood as totally other than creation, as existing whether or not the world-soul became perceptible, whether or not the earth organism came into existence.

CHAPTER I: GOD AND THE WORLD

The sense organs of human experience are sensitive to impressions. There must be something there to produce these impressions. There exists a world that offers itself to sensible perception, and so there must [already] be a world there. This world presents itself to sense perception not as an unbroken whole, but as a great variety of particulars next to one another and in ever-changing and alternating sequences.

The perception of particular parts next to one another forms the concept of space. The apprehension of these parts in their succession forms the concept of time. In the course of time, or within the two boundaries offered by the varieties of time and space, an ongoing surfacing and immersion of particular parts is perceptible. Mountains rise up and then collapse. Plants germinate from a realm beyond perception, they grow for a time, wither, and disappear from view. Members of the human species appear as newly created essences, wander about for a number of years, and then say to the globe: Live well forever! Everything which offers itself to the senses changes and then ceases to be available to sensible perception. Something which exists cannot become a nothing; once an existence comes about it must exist forever. Only the forms and formations change. The bearer of the form, color, smell, taste, brittleness, elasticity and so forth, remains unchangeable, stays ever the same. In this way, the world divides itself into form or attribute, and the bearers of the form or essence.

All phenomena which are sensibly perceptible and subject to change belong to the attributes of the world, and these include solid matter. Anyone who accepts the eternity of solid matter would, by the same reasoning, have to assert the eternity of color, smell, and sound. Why would the object of the sense of touch possess less eternity than the object of hearing, of seeing, of smell, and of taste? Solid matter is also an attribute of [prior, ongoing] essence. As a *Hyle* [something existing of itself] it would be an absurdity, while a dualism [between essence and appearance] would be a half measure. The essence of the world is not sensibly perceptible, but a *Pneumatikon* (spirituality). The form in-and-for-itself can not have an existence in-and-for-itself; only the bearer of the form in-and-for-itself can [have such a reality]. A form-in-itself, as an attribute, is a nothing. It exists only in terms of the essence of the bearer of the world—and in the [subjective] representation by the perceiver. As it presents itself to the sensible organs, the entire world is but a phenomenon of its bearer which is its essence. The world is the perceptible covering of its imperceptible soul.

The particular parts of the world present themselves to sensible perception in a variety of ways. These various representations could not depend upon the different [subjective] ways of apprehension by the senses, for then one and the same thing could be apprehended in a variety of ways, depending upon caprice. Rather, these representations must be the product of various [objective] impressions upon the senses. The essence of the world must therefore bring forth different [objective] impressions, or, which is the same, the world-soul must be able to present itself according to a variety of [objective] impressions. As soon as the imperceptible world-soul presents itself to the senses in a discernable manner, it presents itself as moving in some way and it reveals the power which brought forth that movement and the phenomena itself. Each and every appearance is a [different] sensibly perceptible power. The appearance and the sensibly perceptible power are one and the same, separated by our ability to make that knowledge or observation abstract. Because the appearances are varied, so are the powers.

The world-soul manifests itself as [different] powers, but it also has its own existence. [In itself] the world-soul is not [just] an aggregate of powers; its powers constitute its abilities, but not its essence. All powers which are perceived as phenomena are in fact powers of the world-soul. The plant which offers itself to my senses is an embodied power [or ability] of the world-soul. The entire species of animals is the hypostasis of a power of the world-soul. Our earth, our solar system, the whole Milky Way system, the infinite universe, are all revelations of *one* single organism of the powers of the world-soul. The earth is the disclosure, the divestiture of the world-soul's abilities [or powers]. The world-soul itself must be thought of as always existing, even if not perceptible, and whether or not it discloses and divests itself of its abilities [or powers]. In itself, the bearer of the world is neither life nor death. It asserts [its own] existence in a way which we cannot grasp. Oppositions between life and death can be applied only to the [perceptible] phenomena of life and death.

A phenomenon is created at the moment the world-soul manifests one of its powers, and the phenomenon lives as long as this manifestation is sensibly perceptible. It dies when our perception disappears. As a manifestation of the world-soul, the whole world is alive. What is dead for us is that which we no longer are able to perceive. The bearer of all phenomena would have, and has, existence even if all appearances would be, or are, thought away.

The human being belongs to the powers of the world-soul which appear upon the earth. In terms of quality, the human being is surely the highest apparent power. As a physical organism, the human being stands upon the highest rung of the ladder of all earthly phenomena. While it belongs to the phenomena, because of the human being's psychical properties, it is [also] situated beyond them all. The human being knows itself, it possesses self-consciousness. Through self-consciousness it becomes acquainted with itself as a revealed power of the world-soul. The human being alone, and no other power of the world-soul manifest on earth, knows about itself. The human being, the [only] earthly power able to achieve self-consciousness, constitutes consciousness within the earth organism. Through the human being the earth organism comes to know itself and also to know itself as over and against all other phenomena of the world-soul....

The world-soul presents itself in the human being as self-consciousness and as self-determining when it comes to the world-soul's activities. For such [human] properties to be able to appear as perceptible powers, the world-soul must [already] possess them for itself, and whether or not the properties are revealed in the human being. The bearer of all phenomena is accordingly not only the physical world-soul which produces all movement. Through its self-consciousness and through its self-determination, the [world-soul] bearer is a self-sufficient, free spirit. It is *God*.

God is independent of all phenomena, a self-conscious and free essence. The [phenomenal] world is not something next to God. It rather unveils, and enables perception of divine qualities or attributes. Accordingly: Without God, there is no world. But not: Without world, there is no God. God is God, even without revealing His qualities. World-creation repeats itself daily, [and] as often as a new generation enters into existence. It is not an act of necessity but of freedom. God, as a free, self-determining essence, wills—to use an anthropological expression, which is all that is possible for us—to present divine qualities to us perceptibly. The will, as a divine idea, becomes the world. The world is a perceptible idea of God. The human mind/spirit exists, even if it does not present itself in pictorial ideas. Likewise, God is to be thought of as existing, even were He not to think of any world; even were He not to allow creation to exist.

God's qualities [or attributes] are perceptible for us, to the extent that the phenomena of the world-creation which are perceptible to us present themselves to the human being. The human being displays itself as the highest of these phenomena, and we can name no higher qualities [or attributes] of God than those which are presented by the most perfect human being. We also think of the qualities [or attributes] quantitively, according to measures of augmentation. Still, the portrayal of God within the scope of human definition always remains only an apotheosis of the human being, and as soon as we might [attempt to] articulate a definition of God we would commit the sin of anthropomorphism. This can be seen by anyone who clearly recognizes the relationship between God and the world. God cannot be [comprehended] without self-consciousness and freedom, lest He stand lower than the human being and not the creator of the human being. But who would contend that God possesses these attributes in the way that we possess them? The creator must be considered totally different than creation, both quantitatively and qualitatively.

How could even the highest philosophical consciousness of the human being be called the absolute consciousness of God? How can it be possible for the human being to recognize God and, since human consciousness differentiates itself into subjective and objective, and also construct the Absolute, according to the laws of thought? The human mind/spirit, even at the culmination point of its perfection, is self-consciousness of the earth, not of the universe. Who can conceive of the properties which God revealed on other planets and suns? If the human mind/spirit does not want to deceive itself and make the product of its fantasy into existent realities, it must humbly recognize the limits to its knowing-ability. The human mind/spirit should be convinced that it has a dilemma which, at least in this world's reality, it cannot solve. The human mind/spirit is left with great questions: What is God according to His essence? Why does He reveal Himself in the world? Was there a period of creation in which God existed without a world? Why does God manifest Himself in this way and not in any other? There are many such questions. Unless we deceive ourselves, we can never answer them (17-22).

Summary of translated passages
The earth organism, a power or ability and expression of the world soul, consisted of infinite powers and appearances. Each appearance was both an individual entity and part of the universal reality of the earth organism. When the appearance followed the laws of the earth organism (universal) it acted necessarily (although the appearance was rooted ultimately in the freedom of the world-soul). When it did not follow the laws it was free (individual). As an appearance of the earthly organism, the human mind/spirit participated in an earthly mind/spirit. But it was also individually self-conscious

of the earth organism and knew its laws. The human mind/spirit was both
part of the earthly mind/spirit and its laws and an individual human mind/
spirit which contained ideals for measuring the truth of other phenomena.

CHAPTER II: NATURE AND SPIRIT

The *Pneumatikon* [i.e., world-soul], which is perceived sensibly as the
[apparent] world, reveals its multiple powers as multiple phenomena.
One phenomenon is also only one power. In turn, one power reveals
itself in many individual powers. Then in turn, each individual power
manifests itself as a defined phenomenon. In the entire solar system,
the bearer of the universe (*Weltall*) reveals only one of its powers. Likewise, we perceive only *one* defined power as the individual earth. *One*
power manifests the individual creation on the earth. And finally, *one*
power manifests each individual part of creation.

The manifestation of the world-soul in the earth as an epitome of all
powers is *universal life*. Any part of this is an *individual life*. The world
[i.e., the earth] is *one* organism, and each of its parts, in turn, is an independent organism in itself. Each and every part of the world has a
double life, participating in the cosmic universal life of the world and
representing its own individual life for itself. In turn, each and every
power includes [its own] individual powers. Each and every individual
life, taken for itself, is to be regarded as a universal life which in turn
itself includes several individual lives. As a part of the cosmos, our solar
system is an individual life. But as a solar system, as a self-subsisting
organism for itself, it is a universal life. Likewise, our earth or any plant
upon the earth is apprehended both in [its wider] context and as singular existence for and of itself.

That each phenomenon participates in universal life and in individual life [is something which is] perceptible. The phenomenon is displayed as universal life in terms of the endeavor to maintain the species and in individual life in terms of the endeavor to maintain itself.
We perceive in the two discernable forms of this double life a fixed
regularity and stereotyped formation. We can determine in advance
how each form of life must present itself. We call this regularized way
of presenting life *the law*. The laws of life which pertain to the phenomena initially presented to us portray themselves as abstract and
as formed out of generalized perceptions of our experience. The necessity which philosophical thought postulates for a world constructed by

philosophical thought has solely subjective and never objective validity. The laws, which to our perception are products of necessity, are [ultimately] manifestations of the absolute product of divine freedom. [Universal and particular] life presents itself in the way it does, not because it must present itself *so*, but rather because it should present itself *so* according to the divine will. We recognize this *so*, which God wills, as true. This true knowledge provides us with established laws and with logical necessity.

Every single phenomenon, as a manifestation of both universal and individual forms of life, submits to laws of life which human thought has formulated. Comprehended subjectively, the laws appear to be products of necessity. For example, the major laws to which each and every phenomenon of our solar system and earth are subjected are those of centripetal and centrifugal powers. As long as a movement displays both these powers in their respective ways, the movement seems normal to us. The movement becomes abnormal as soon as the laws which we have established are not conformed to. But each and every anomaly which we stipulate about the phenomena is only subjectively an anomaly. For all necessity is subjective. Objectively, each and every appearance is a consequence of divine freedom, and freedom excludes anomalies. Also, a phenomenon can be an anomaly only insofar as it contradicts the laws of individual life. As a participant in universal life, it would have to be considered completely normal. Several terrestrial diseases cease to be objectively considered diseases, once it is seen that they are normal participants in the universal life of the solar system, or that, together with universal life, they belong to the cosmic universal life of all existence. While they will always continue to be abnormal subjectively, they cannot be so objectively. For in this operation the human being is the planetary consciousness of the earth.

All the phenomena of the world which reveal themselves to us with fixed regularity, whose movements must follow the laws established by us, belong to necessity—albeit only as we subjectively apprehended it. We call these phenomena by the universal name *nature*. We also perceive phenomena in human life which directly contradict these laws. These should not be regarded as the consequence of coercion, but the consequence of *freedom*.

An individual may, contrary to laws of universal and individual life, surrender the quest to preserve the species and the self. It may reject such universal or individual egoism in order to make life's endeavor possible or just easier for some other unique individual. It may believe that surrendering the egoistic endeavor through self-conquest brings it to the goal that it set for itself. Such an individual is not subjugated to regular necessity, but stands beyond its natural law and is free to do as it chooses. As found in the human being, we call this freedom *mind/spirit*. As a phenomenon that is sensibly perceptible, the human being obviously belongs to nature and reveals its movements according to the laws of universal and individual physical life. But it does so with self-consciousness, according to recognized grounds of appropriateness. The human being can suppress the endeavors of both [universal and individual] forms of life, should this facilitate someone else's reaching a goal. Nature recognizes only the two quests [universal and individual], the two forms of the double life. But *the mind/spirit* can annul both forms of life in order to achieve the goal of a third quest which is unique to it. That is, the mind/spirit can momentarily suppress nature, which strives for independence, if the mind/spirit wants to validate itself. Such a quest by the mind/spirit is the exact opposite to that of nature.

The human being, with its mind/spirit, inherently belongs to the earthly organism. Thus, when the mind/spirit stands outside the nature of the earth, it nevertheless does not stand outside the earthly organism [itself]. As a participant in terrestrial universal life, the human being is both human mind/spirit and earthly mind/spirit—although obviously not in the mystical-astrological sense. Were we to think of the human being as not intrinsically part of the earth it would have to have changed both quantitatively and qualitatively, ceasing to be human mind/spirit and ceasing to be planetary earth-mind/spirit. As earthly mind/spirit, the human being carries the self-consciousness of earth. It does not need to have some prestabilized [other worldly] harmony in order to conceive of a recognized external world. Human knowledge of earth does not involve discerning anything strange or other, for it is self-knowledge. Human knowledge is, in fact, wisdom of the earth about itself. Knowledge of phenomena outside the earth would require wisdom about the human being's own relationship to the phenomena of [another] world.

Despite all the human knowledge about astronomy and astrology, the mind/spirit is capable of grasping only the earth's relationship to the solar system, and not laws about individual life in some other part of the solar system. As the self-consciousness of the earth, the mind/ spirit must have wisdom of the laws of nature. Although the mind/spirit stands above these laws of nature, the laws still remain the directives of the mind's/spirit's own organism. Laws learned through experience are not a matter of some abstract perception. As proper to the mind/ spirit, they must be regarded as idea-images or ideas original to the mind/spirit. The apprehension and formation of a law remains always a product of our sensible faculty of knowledge, a result abstracted from experience. Without our experience of them, they never would have entered our consciousness. When the human mind/spirit perceives a regular phenomenon as a law, it is conscious of the original idea-image that it inherently possesses as self-consciousness of the earth. The human mind/spirit perceives and finds an inborn ideal for the law in itself. This ideal serves as a criterion for evaluating the phenomena of the outer world and can raise these phenomena to the level of objective truth by identifying them with the archetype [or ideal].

It is self-deceptive to try to construct a world *a priori*. Without experience, deprived of objects, our consciousness remains empty of content. [At the same time], purely empirical knowledge, which excludes all inborn ideas, remains a subjective version of truth without any objective grounding. As the human being apprehends the outer world, that human being must be regarded not only as a human mind/spirit but also as an earthly mind/spirit. As part of the earth which has wisdom about itself, the human being possesses knowledge of the laws of nature's perfection as concrete images of thought and ideals of human life. The human being compares perceived phenomena with this ideal, and when they agree, the perceived phenomena are called *truth*.

In its universal life, the human mind/spirit is the self-consciousness of the earth. This consciousness is what makes ennoblement of nature and new artistic creation possible. Were the human being to stand outside all relation to earthly life, without any original knowledge of the laws of nature, this would not affect the laws of nature or lead the laws of nature on a path to a higher perfection. Were the human to stand outside, it would recognize neither the path nor its perfection! But when the universal spiritual life of the human being is a self-consciousness of earth, the human being will know the laws and the ways according to which and upon which nature as a necessity must manifest itself....

While both nature and mind/spirit belong to the individual life of the earth-organism, they are still diametrically opposed. Nature manifests itself unconsciously according to the laws of necessity, while the mind/spirit manifests itself consciously according to the ideals of freedom. Nature moves in circles, continually repeating itself and always reproducing itself. Mind/spirit moves forward in a line, continually developing and creating itself anew. Nature manifests its completion and its perfection, and is an object for description. Mind/spirit, on the other hand, presents itself as striving to realize the ideal, as incomplete, as open, as offering potential paths to history (22-29).

Summary of translated passages
The scientific study of physics dealt with consciousness in terms of the universal life of nature. The study of aesthetics dealt with the realization of nature according to the ideal of beauty. Logic dealt with laws of knowledge in terms of natural phenomena, and ethics with the harmony between laws of knowledge and the ideal of the "good" in individual life. The bearer of the cosmos (the world-soul) provided ideals of beauty and good to the human mind/spirit. These ideals (or idea-images) reached self-consciousness when the human being was provided with nature and perceptible content, who then was capable of "understanding" integrated phenomena conceptually, and using reason to compare the concepts with the ideals. As an objective position of original being provided by the bearer of the world, the ideal did not develop. Rather, reason brought the ideal into self-consciousness, where it developed subjectively. In turn, this belonged to the process of revelation—revelation being the good ideal which God created within the human mind/spirit.

CHAPTER III: REASON AND REVELATION

Like any point of existence, the mind/spirit presents itself to us as a representative of a two-folded life. It proclaims itself as the consciousness of both its universal and its individual life. The self-consciousness of universal life, where earthly mind/spirit is portrayed by the human being, is objectively manifested as the scientific study of *physics*, understood in its widest sense. The laws for realizing an ideal of universal life, once the human being's nature reaches consciousness, are covered by the scientific study of *aesthetics*. In both these scientific studies, physics and aesthetics, mind/spirit manifests itself not as human mind/spirit but as earthly mind/spirit, as a consciousness of the earthly organism. The mind/spirit must know *all* the constituents of the earthly organism, one of which is the human being itself. Likewise, mind/spirit must also know about itself as a human mind/spirit. It must itself become an object of knowledge, which has stepped out of the realm of universal life and included itself within the borders of individual life.

In its individual life, mind/spirit knows itself in a double way. [First, it functions] as an organ for knowing all the world's phenomena. Here, mind/spirit knows the laws for evaluating the knowledge as true or untrue. This is the wisdom of the scientific study of *logic*. [Second], mind/spirit knows itself as manifesting a power of primordial existence, which an individual life, i.e., an endeavor which exists for-itself, has; this is an endeavor which mind/spirit recognizes as directly opposed to the undertaking belonging to natural phenomena. Laws for the individual life of the human mind/spirit cannot be natural laws. They are, properly, laws of the human mind/spirit or moral laws. Wisdom about these laws appears to us as the scientific study of *ethics*. *Logic* and *ethics* are to human individual life what *physics* and *aesthetics* are to universal life. Logic brings out the [knowing] mind/spirit with regard to phenomena. Ethics brings out the [knowing] mind/spirit with regard to the ideal.

A phenomenon in nature or in art which is in harmony with the *ideal* of the universal life of the mind/spirit is called *beautiful*. A phenomenon which is in harmony with the ideal of the individual life is called *good*. Beautiful and good are predicates attributed to phenomena which are appropriate to the respective ideal, such that the two types of phenomena are often confused, and those that are part of universal life are called "good," and those in ethics of harmony with the individual life are called "beautiful." The mind/spirit possesses ideals, original idea-images, for the beautiful and for the good. Through experience, these ideals are brought into an object of knowledge. Here, mind/spirit is self-consciousness; mind/spirit manifests itself in its two-folded life. But mind/spirit is not led by experiences as something strange or outside of itself. The experience must be regarded, rather, as a property belonging to mind/spirit.

The ability of the mind/spirit to compare phenomena with its inborn [ideal] archetypes and to discern and evaluate them as objectively true or untrue is called *reason*, that which discerns. Reason is not to be confused with another capability of the soul, which we call understanding. In understanding, the mind/spirit steps out of itself. There it remains permanently, ever outside itself, among the phenomena perceived by the mind/spirit. The mind/spirit distinguishes particular features of phenomena, gathers together those which are similar, forms concepts, and subordinates particular phenomena to a concept and thereby draws conclusions. In reason, however, the mind/spirit, enriched by perception, turns back towards itself. It compares the perceived image with the mind's/spirit's original idea-image [or ideal] to determine its truth. Reason is the ability of the mind/spirit to accept perceived phenomena as true or not, before the judgment seat of the ideal. Reason can emerge as the judge in the realm of aesthetics, as well as of ethics. There it assumes another name. In the realm of aesthetics reason expresses its universal life under the name *artistic taste*, objectively considered. In the realm of ethics, reason expresses its individual life under the name of *conscience*.

The two-folded [universal and individual] self-consciousness of mind/spirit presents itself in terms of the two ideals of the beautiful and the good. As long as the perception does not bring the object corresponding to the ideal to consciousness, the mind/spirit does not know about the ideal which exists within it, for the mind/spirit can only have an ideal of what is there. It can only know originally, what is there, and cannot conceive of that which does not exist; it cannot have an ideal for it. Mind/spirit knows that it possesses an ideal of the beautiful, because nature, the perceptible object, offers the idea of the element of the beautiful to the mind/spirit. The ideal reaches self-consciousness through the apprehension of the perceptible object. Similarly, the ideal of the good needs a perceptible object which gives content and substance to the empty form of the ideal. Reason can certainly evaluate a phenomenon, as to whether or not it is good, but in and for itself reason is devoid of content. Without a given object, it has nothing to evaluate. Along with the creation that represents the ideal of the beautiful, there must be a creation for the ideal of the good. The [world-soul] bearer of the world-all must manifest itself in the earth-organism not only as the beautiful, but also as the good. The bearer of the world-all places the object of the beautiful into [the realm of] nature and places the object of the good in the [realm of] the mind/spirit. An activity of the mind/spirit which is formless, an existence which is not sensibly perceptible, cannot be called aesthetically beautiful. The process of attributing this description requires a free self-consciousness, which deviates from nature as such.

The creation of the good lies only in the mind/spirit. It becomes the object of which the mind/spirit should become conscious *vis-à-vis* the ideal of the good. This manifestation of primordial existence, the good creation, is called general *revelation*. Anthropomorphically expressed, it is the communication of what God has made good into the human mind/spirit. The content of nature is the manifestation of the objectively beautiful, which is brought to consciousness in the mind/spirit as the ideal. This manifestation of beautiful is known ever more clearly, the more plainly the ideal presents itself with superfluous details. Similarly, the content is the manifestation of the objectively good. This good comes to consciousness in the mind/spirit as ideal. It is known ever more clearly as it develops as a phenomenon.

As points of primordial existence, both the good creation and the creation of the beautiful are completed objectively. As a divine communication, revelation [of the good and the beautiful] cannot become more perfect, any more than nature. But nature can always be further researched, and revelation can always be more clearly known. Revelation cannot develop, but our knowledge of revelation can. Through the perception of a revelation, reason can bring the ideal of the good to self-consciousness. The more extensive and freer the perception, the more purely will reason grasp revelation and the more clearly know the ideal. As an objective point of primordial existence, revelation has no developmental path. But the subjective knowledge of this objective position is also called revelation, for revelation's content is first truly revealed to us through this subjective knowledge. Here, revelation does have a progression, a perfecting. Objective revelation, as the absolute good, is complete and stable. Subjective revelation, as object of our knowledge, is incomplete and in process.

Reason and revelation are completely different sorts of manifestations in mind/spirit. Reason [in itself] is without content; it can evaluate the perceived good but not create it. Revelation in itself has the content of the good; it is a complete, real, spiritual creation. Reason without revelation is a human power of the soul. But without an object of the good for the good [ideal] and therefore, necessarily, without a beautiful object for the beautiful [ideal], reason slumbers idly and provides no hint of [the content of] its existence. Without reason, revelation is objectively present but not subjectively known. For the human mind/spirit [to be vital], reason and revelation must be bound together: Revelation must provide reason with a substance for the ideal of the good, and reason must bring objectively-provided revelation to consciousness. Reason mediates the revelation which lies imperceptibly in mind/spirit with perceptible phenomena, and mediates the subjective ideal with objective reality (29-34).

Summary of translated passages
Objectively, the divine ideal was beyond space and time. Subjectively, it was within them. Within the bounds of nature, which proceeded unconsciously towards its own destiny, the divine ideal was apprehended in terms of necessity. To the extent that the human being belonged to nature, it did so as well. Insofar as the human being was mind/spirit, it became conscious of its destiny and thereby free. Ultimately, the nature-mind/spirit dualism of the earth-organism would be unified in terms of mind/spirit. The human being, situated on the border between them, could and should unify the two realms under the mastery of mind/spirit.

CHAPTER VI: THE DESTINY OF THE HUMAN BEING

The world is the perceptible garment of divine power [i.e., the world-soul]. We find a mind/spirit in the world which displays itself in activities solely according to the laws of a known ideal. It is unimaginable that the thought of that [divine] absolute essence which is manifest in mind/spirit, although not *only* in mind/spirit, was more limited than mind/spirit itself. Rather, we must assert in human language (which is all we have at our disposal) that the self-conscious absolute [essence] presents itself in its manifestations according to a known ideal and that all phenomena of existence are small, indispensable parts of this idea-image [or ideal] of God. Objectively considered, the reality of the God-ideal, a reality lying outside the borders of time and space, is always to be acknowledged as free. Subjectively considered, within the frameworks of space and time, the human being must regard this reality as absolutely necessary. Our thinking must affirm that everything which happens must therefore happen. For the God-ideal must realize itself.

Nature, a creation which does not have wisdom about itself, is realized with necessity. It is subordinate to the law of the God-ideal, and is destined to realize that ideal at some point. Thus, nature has a destiny. Insofar as it belongs to nature, the human being is subordinate to this destiny. All nature's products must be given to the human being; the human being cannot make these products by itself. As a natural creation, the human being must also kneel before the throne of fate and accept with resignation the lot granted to it from the urn of eternity. Still, the human being, as bearer of the mind/spirit, is free—it can create a happiness for itself, a happiness which nature of itself mercilessly denies. Paying a small toll to nature, the unchained human being crosses the border of nature's territory and ascends freely and happily into the sphere of mind/spirit.

The God-ideal of world-creation is realized by nature unconsciously and of necessity. It is realized by mind/spirit consciously and with freedom. Since the mind/spirit and its manifestations belong to the world, and as such is an indispensable part of that eternally complete God-ideal, there is also a plan for it, according to which it should realize itself, a destiny—even though it is [still] free and, subjectively considered, not destined. Mind/spirit knows its destiny, while nature does not; spirit *should*, nature *must*. About mind/spirit we may ask: *Why* is mind/spirit destined? About nature we may only ask: *How* is it destined? The "why" is blended into nature's existence.

The human being stands on the boundary between [the realms of] nature and the mind/spirit and is at home in both areas. It therefore exhibits a two-folded destiny. It must display its destiny as a creation of nature with necessity, and should display its destiny as a creation of mind/spirit with freedom. The idea of nature is complete and [already] realized in nature. The idea of mind/spirit is perfect as well, but not yet realized. To be realized, the idea must become conscious. The human being, as a creation of nature, is not capable of knowing its destiny, because nature manifests its destiny in its existence. As bearer of mind/spirit, however, the human being must be able to know this destiny clearly. The destiny of the mind/spirit is the God-idea for the mind/spirit, the ideal for the mind's/spirit's universal and individual life. To say that the mind/spirit knows about its destiny would be like saying that mind/spirit knows about itself.

The content of our destiny is the content of our ideal. The earth, as nature, has come to consciousness in the universal life of mind/spirit. The earth constitutes itself as an artistic creation and realizes its ideal in that universal life through aesthetics: In the individual life of the earth, the mind/spirit appears diametrically opposed to nature. Nature is characterized by mutual exclusion, self-validation, and individual conquest. Individual organisms collide into, destroy, and swallow up one another. They maintain their existence through bitter struggle. The character of mind/spirit, over and against this, displays itself as individual self-denial, ego-suppression, and self-dissolution into the all. The individual of nature sacrifices the neighboring creature for its own self-preservation, and builds its own existence by destroying it. The individual of mind/spirit sacrifices itself for the neighboring creature, seeks to preserve it, know it, and dignify its existence. The effort of the individual of mind/spirit is diametrically opposed to that of nature.

The earth shows this dualism. But because there is *one* earth organism, the dualism is brought into unity. Mind/spirit, which as consciousness of this earth-organism, knows about this dualism, must seek to represent the higher unity, and of course in the mind's/spirit's bearer, the human being. Reconciling the opposition between nature and mind/spirit, bringing them into unity in such a way that neither of the two perishes, is an ideal which human mind/spirit seeks to realize. This task is our destiny. If *nature and mind/spirit form a unity in the human being under the mastery of the spirit*, then we may say: "Human being, you may rest from your striving. You have reached your destiny. You stand upon the culmination point of your perfection." As long as the two opposites strive to preserve themselves at the cost of the other, as long as the body's self-validation means suppressing the mind/spirit, or the mind/spirit, steadfast in its opposition, requires the killing off of sensuality, the earth-organism will not attain consciousness of its unity, and the earth-organism will remain imperfect, incomplete.

In the perfect human being nature may not perish. Nature is as an essential part of the earth-organism, and as such is divine. It must be ennobled and enspirited. It must show in its activities that it has achieved self-consciousness, a self-consciousness realized of course through the mind/spirit—so that nature also bears the impression of the mind/spirit and is completely submissive to it. The realization of the ideal of human universal life and of human individual life appears to us expressed as opposites, just as nature and mind/spirit appear that way to us. The realized ideal of universal life is nature as it proceeds further in its own sphere, while the realized ideal of individual life portrays nature as totally subordinate to mind/spirit. But at their points of departure, the respective realizations appear as products of one and the same mind/spirit, and as unified in one and the same self-consciousness of the earth-organism (46-49).

Summary of translated passages.
Pre-historical revelation was located beyond time and space, where nature and mind/spirit remained indistinct. Historical revelation involved human beings in choosing between mind/spirit and nature. As history progressed, the human being distinguished between and reconciled the realms of nature and mind/spirit in an ongoing process. The human being could either remain on a physical level, knowing itself as a natural creature, or become a creature of spirit and ennoble nature. By becoming sensitive to spiritual creation, mind/spirit tapped into human destiny. As this process progressed, the increasingly self-conscious earthly mind/spirit transformed pre-historical revelation, which was objective, into the subjective realm of historical revelation.

CHAPTER VII: PRE-HISTORICAL AND HISTORICAL REVELATION

The unconscious monad of the earth-organism presents a dualism, that of natural creation and spiritual creation. As unveilings of the divine [world-soul] power which lies outside the boundaries of time and space, they are both perfect. Both creations should be known by the mind/spirit, and receive their identity [with one another] in [human] consciousness. [Specifically], mind/spirit should recognize nature as its self [which participates] in mind's/spirit's universal life, and also recognize mind/spirit as its self which participates in mind's/spirit's individual life. Differences between subjectivity and objectivity are resolved when the mind/spirit becomes conscious of the essence of nature and of its self (mind/spirit), and in the absorption of the known object by the knower. As this takes place, the earth-organism becomes a self-knowing monad of existence. Like the real content of natural life, the spiritual creation or the real content of spiritual life, is fulfilled as the realization of a divine power in terms of the development of the earth organism. We call this spiritual creation revelation. Revelation was co-created with the earth. This pre-historical revelation was provided to the human species objectively. It came into being outside of time, and outside the arena of history.

As the consciousness of the earth, the mind/spirit must know about its self. Through wisdom about objectively given revelation, the mind/spirit brings revelation into [the range of] subjectivity. The mind/spirit can acknowledge that this revelation exists only at the moment it knows this same revelation. This becoming-conscious of an objectively-given revelation, which is also the mind's/spirit's knowledge of its God-given destiny, is historical revelation, for the moment of knowledge takes place in the course of time and within the field of history.

Pre-historical revelation, objectively given, is perfect. Historical revelation, the object of the knowing mind/spirit, is imperfect. This is because the mind/spirit gathers knowledge about its own content only when stimulated by perceptions and experiences. Also, because the mind/spirit is capable of having these perceptions only in space and these experiences only in time, it can only gather the knowledge sequentially.

As knowledge about objective revelation forms and perfects itself gradually, it is impossible to fix the moment of historical revelation [in time] with mathematical precision. Nevertheless, it can be identified as the moment when pre-historical revelation, as the destiny given to the human being by God, is brought to human consciousness. Historical revelation presupposes natural human existence, because this revelation, as the content of our destiny, needs a nature through which to become powerful and inspired. Historical revelation also presumes a wisdom about the distinction between nature and mind/spirit, between earth and heaven. Lastly, it assumes a feeling that the status of mind/spirit is above nature, heaven above earth. The human being in the period before historical revelation should not be thought of as a totally natural creation without any discernible spiritual spark. Instead, the complete image of the human being's ideal was presented at the beginning of the period. Nature and mind/spirit exhibited themselves in the human being as complete creations which were in perfect, albeit unconscious, harmony. This was the paradisical life of the golden age.

At that moment, [before historical revelation], neither nature nor mind/spirit reached human consciousness. Human beings felt both drives with equal power, and found themselves in the equanimity of union. Adam would have remained in this garden of Eden, had he not eaten of the tree of knowledge. Once he ate of it, his eyes opened and he became ashamed of himself as a natural creation. This meant that the human being should know mind/spirit and nature in their duality, in order to reconcile these differences in human consciousness. Knowledge in terms of both its universal life and its individual life is indispensable to the human being in order to reach perfection. This knowledge is awakened by perception and experience and enables the human being to find itself, first in its universal life and then in individual life. Nature must display itself to the body's eye before revelation displays itself to the spirit's eye, because the human being must already know itself as a natural creation if the human's historical revelation wants to destine it to ennoble this nature into the creation of mind/spirit.

The original point of indifference between nature and mind/spirit lies in the unconscious human disposition and presents itself in the perfect harmony of activities. The point must be differentiated for there to be self-knowledge, which is characteristic of and indispensable to the human being. Nature and mind/spirit must enter into consciousness separately. The human being's consciousness as a natural creation forms itself first. The human being must know itself as nature before it can understand that mind/spirit is destined to conquer nature. But mind/spirit is not [totally] absent from the formation of the natural human condition. Rather, mind/spirit shows traces of its unconscious existence as though slumbering in feeling. It is awakened into perfect self-consciousness when the human being knows itself completely as a natural creation and has thereby thoroughly transformed the object of the processing mind/spirit.

At this point, when the human being's mind/spirit is awakened to self-consciousness, the mind/spirit knows its destiny as a revelation given by God—as distinct from something which originates in the "I's" own content. The knowledge which comes to the human being is called divine instruction. The moment of its entry [into consciousness] is called (historical) revelation. The character of this revelation, a consequence of the perfected natural condition and a product of free perception and experience, is [for the human being] completely subjective and individual. The revelation does not come to all human beings at one and the same point of time. The [idea] of perfecting the natural condition, along with the freedom that entails, does not present itself to everyone simultaneously. Revelation is not complete at the first moment of entry into existence. It perfects itself ever more and more, according to the conditions of human perception and experience. Nor does revelation finally complete itself at the same pace for all those human beings who know about it; this is because the conditions for this completion do not take place uniformly for everyone.

Pre-historical revelation, the objectively given content of mind/spirit, is unique. Absolutely true, historical revelation is likewise unique, and consists of clear knowledge about objectively given content. But [from the subjective perspective] there are several relatively-true historical revelations. A historical revelation is relative and not absolutely true when the mind/spirit does not acknowledge the [presence of the] absolute ideal of humankind but rather acknowledges the goal as an ideal to be realized, which is conditioned by temporary and local circumstances.

In its natural condition, the human being is the product of climate and time. Only in the spiritual condition does it find itself beyond spatial and temporal limits. The revelational moment [of history] finds the human being in its natural condition, within the limits of space and time. Each revelation must therefore treat the human being according to the local and temporary context. Each revelation must qualify itself according to that context, and to carry out its task it must utilize the means required by the respective context. When it enters into existence, each historical revelation can only be relatively true, for it finds each natural human being formed differently by local and temporary conditions. These conditions should educate natural human beings and serve as manifold means for realizing their ideal. Each historical revelation has objective [pre-historical] revelation as its substratum. Certain elements enter into consciousness from out of the objective [pre-historical] revelation, in accordance with the context of the human being who is being educated. These elements of objective revelation also form a natural garment for the human being who is situated on the border of the natural realm, serving as a symbol which satisfies the senses. The elements of objective [pre-historical] revelation allow the advancing human spirit to separate the symbol's relative truth from its absolute truth more and more and appropriate absolute truth for itself (the human spirit). The relative truth of a historical revelation is conditioned by the actual situation of the human being now [in the process of] reaching self-consciousness. The ladder of this relative truth has higher and lower rungs. The differences reflect the natural situation as conditioned by local and temporary circumstances. Accordingly, the substratum of objective [pre-historical] revelation must present itself in the subjective revelation in an endless series of stages, advancing from a barely noticed little spark to the brightest flame.

Historical revelation at the lowest stage has the smallest value of relative truth. It finds the human being nearly immersed in natural life, where it is barely able to awaken the slumbering mind/spirit. It has to be satisfied with bringing the human being to the point of just having an inkling of the existence of a creator in creation, where the human being deifies nature and thought itself is subordinate to deified nature. The first appearances of historical revelation take place in natural worship, in bowing down before a stone, tree, river, animal, or even before the sun and other heavenly bodies. This is because the content of deified nature is the ideal of that human being who is still situated in nature. With fetishism, the earth-organism knows itself only as nature. The mind/spirit is still completely asleep in its individual life; even in its universal life, it is not yet awakened to consciousness of its absolute ideal. There is still no hint of the aesthetic. The creativity of human life is shown only in imitating an as-yet unacknowledged physics. Natural worship reaches the highest stage when nature achieves knowledge and realization of its ideal by virtue of the universal life of the mind/spirit. At that level, the human being knows humans as the highest essence of existence—albeit only as the highest natural creation, since they are still found in natural life. Upon this highest stage of natural worship, the human being finds its own apotheosis. It knows of statues that correspond to the ideal of spiritual universal life and to the objective laws of aesthetics—for example, the image of its Zeus, of the deity of deities.

The historical revelation which presents itself in natural worship is indicative of the graded value of historical revelation's relative truth within the respective ascending stages. In terms of its universal life, mind/spirit ascends from the stage of unconsciousness to clear consciousness, and to cognition of the mind/spirit's aesthetic ideal. Historical revelation begins with the veneration of raw natural stuff and ends with adoration of the realized ideal of art. It cannot raise itself higher, because the universal life of the human mind/spirit is not capable of higher development.

The truth of this historical revelation, which presents itself in natural worship, always remains relative. Even at its highest level, historical revelation cannot achieve absolute validity. Remaining within nature, it is never capable of bringing the duality of nature and mind/spirit or of objectivity and subjectivity into union. The only revelation which can achieve absolute truth is that which strives to realize not only the ideal of spiritual universal life, but of spiritual individual life as well; and therefore situated in the realm of nature as well as in that of mind/spirit; recognizes both sides of the earth-organism separately, and deems the goal of its striving, through mind/spirit, to raise nature and mind/spirit into harmonious union.

The mind/spirit wanders across the entire field of natural existence in order to grasp the ideal of its universal life. It must begin at the lowest stage, that of fetishism, and can rest only at the highest stage of artistic development. Likewise, in order for mind/spirit to grasp the ideal of its individual life, it totally shuns the realm of nature as its opposite. It holds in regard only the knowledge of its nature—and establishes the overcoming of self as the goal of its endeavor. In natural worship, mind/spirit strives for knowledge and for the presentation of the objectively beautiful—however, it allows the objectively good to be ignored completely. In spiritual worship, mind/spirit strives after the knowledge and presentation of the objectively good—whereby the objectively beautiful remains totally foreign.

Mind/spirit strives to realize each ideal of its universal and individual life separately. In their relationship of firm opposition, natural worship and spiritual worship are both one-sided. Each must acknowledge the other as its negation, as its opposite pole. Natural worship bears the character of nature; concrete natural forms are the symbols transmitted by knowledge of natural worship's ideal, which is expressed as polytheism. In spiritual worship, the mind/spirit knows itself in its individual life. It also wants to serve its self, and absolutely rejects each and every perceptible form as belonging to nature. It rejects natural worship as idolatry, as an inspiration of the devil. Because mind/spirit knows itself only as a formless unity, absolute monotheism is its manner of presentation. Natural worship portrays itself as multi-dimensional because it is influenced totally by local and temporary conditions, whereas spiritual worship is one-dimensional, because mind/spirit must find the formless ideal of its individual life, even at the lowest stage of knowledge, as something unique.

As it enters into existence, the revelation of natural worship, like the revelation of spiritual worship, is valid only as relative truth. For the revelation of both these worships seeks to bring the human being out of its unconscious natural condition and into the conscious condition of spiritual life. Each worship seeks to further the ideal of spiritual universal life or spiritual individual life which is special to it, into knowledge and presentation. But the two revelations are distinct with regard to their claims to validity in terms of absolute truth. The revelation of natural worship carries out its task when the mind/spirit knows and presents the ideal of its universal life, when it observes itself as the consciousness of nature. It does so when nature manifests itself in its highest beauty, in the aesthetically perfect, plastic presentation of the human form; and when it manifests itself in action according to the most perfect symmetry, earning the name of an aesthetic rather than ethical action. But even here, at the culmination of its path of development, natural worship cannot claim validity in terms of absolute truth. Even here, mind/spirit does not recognize itself in its total life. The dualism between mind/spirit and nature persists, and reconciliation of nature with mind/spirit through the mind/spirit can never be achieved.Once natural worship reaches its culmination point and has brought mind/spirit to knowledge of the ideal of universal life, as a transitory element in the mind's/spirit's path of self-development it must fall apart as nothing; it must always come to an end. The revelation of spiritual worship, however, makes a proper claim to validity in terms of absolute truth. To be sure, only relative truth's validity applies to revelation's entry into existence. For revelation must pay heed to the local and temporary circumstances in which it finds the human being who is to be educated. Revelation seeks to grasp those symbols which are indispensable to the achievement of its goal. Also, revelation is intended to be the realization of only one dimension of the spiritual life, that of individual life. It seeks to establish the dualism of the earth monad. Only spiritual worship can achieve absolute truth, for once it reaches its culmination point and is capable of recognizing and presenting the ideal of its individual life, it realizes that which is objectively good. The objectively good consists of the reconciliation of nature with and through the mind/spirit. This reconciliation comes, namely, at the moment when the earth-organism in the human being knows itself as a unity and presents itself as such through the ethical harmony in the human being's way of proceeding. At the culmination point of spiritual worship, historical, relatively true revelation becomes absolutely true. For then revelation is the wisdom of the human mind/spirit about objectively given pre-historical revelation and about the content of the human mind's/spirit's own self. It is the knowledge about the destiny of the human mind's/spirit's own life which is to be represented.

The more spiritual-worship advances the more it can be reconciled, not with natural worship, but with nature, as an essential part of the earth monad, and the more it will grant nature its own right. It ennobles natural worship's drive by impressing the ethical stamp of mind/spirit upon it, and by raising nature from raw animalistic movement to purified human life.

Accordingly, pre-historical revelation displays itself as the complete manifestation of the absolute, just as nature displays itself as one single manifestation thereof. Perfectibility is unthinkable for either. But just as mind/spirit reaches knowledge of nature through the perception of nature, it achieves knowledge of revelation through the perception of revelation. Or—because revelation rests in the mind/spirit itself—through self-perception. That moment, when the eye of the mind/spirit becomes sensitized to the existence of this spiritual creation, is the beginning of the chronological era of historical revelation. From this moment on, spiritual creation is ever more clearly known, and the eye of the spirit rests ever more upon this spiritual creation.

The mind's/spirit's path of development is not mechanical, such that experience comes from the outside, enriching mind/spirit with gifts and expanding it with outwardly apportioned flourishes. The path of development is purely organic. As the seed unfolds into root, stem, leaf, blossom and fruit because of its inherent power; so the mind/spirit develops because of its inherent power. Through perception of the world, the mind/spirit is stimulated to present its ideal. Through self-contemplation, the mind/spirit finds a two-fold ideal in itself, that of its universal life and that of its individual life, and finds itself as a spiritual creation. Similarly, a two-fold historical revelation must take place. By knowing that two ideals, that of the universal life and that of the individual life, constitute the content of one and the same "I," the mind/spirit dissolves their separateness and identifies them [with one another]. Similarly, the revelation of the spiritual individual life must recognize the revelation of the spiritual universal life as a necessary phenomenon with relative truth, while it must simultaneously negate it as its opposite. It must dissolve the spiritual universal life into its self and validate its self as the total manifestation of mind/spirit with absolute truth (53-63).

2.3. SAMUEL HIRSCH (1815–1889): CONSCIOUSNESS AND FREEDOM[39]

Samuel Hirsch was born in Thalfang, near Trier in Rhenish Prussia—

---

[39] Hirsch's major works are: *Das System der religiösen Anschauung der Juden und sein Verhältnis zum Heidentum, Christentum und zur absoluten Philosophie. Erste Hauptabteilung. Die Apologetik. Erster Teil: Die Religionsphilosophie der Juden* (Leipzig: Heinrich Hunger, 1841); *Die Messiaslehre der Juden* (Leipzig: Heinrich Hunger, 1843); *Das Judentum, der christliche Staat und die moderne Kritik: Briefe zur Beleuchtung der Judenfrage von Bruno Bauer* (Leipzig: Heinrich Hunger, 1843); *Die Reform im Judentum und dessen Beruf in der gegenwärtigen Welt* (Leipzig: Heinrich Hunger, 1844); *Die Humanität als Religion* (Trier: C. Tröschel, 1854); and *Systematischer Katechismus* (Philadelphia: Hirsch und Larzelehre, 1864).

On his life and thought see: Fackenheim, "Samuel Hirsch and Hegel" in *Studies in Nineteenth Century Jewish Intellectual History*, ed. Altmann (Cambridge: Harvard University Press, 1964), 171-201; Judith Frishman, "True Mosaic Religion: Samuel Hirsch, Samuel Holdheim, and the Reform of Judaism," in *Redefining Judaism in an Age of Emancipation: Comparative Perspectives on Samuel Holdheim (1806-1860)* (Leiden: Brill, 2007), 278-305; Greenberg, "*Religionswissenschaft* and Early Reform Jewish Thought: Samuel Hirsch and David Einhorn," in *Modern Judaism and Historical Consciousness* (Leiden: Brill, 2007), 106-139; "Religion and History According to Samuel Hirsch," *Hebrew Union College Annual* 43 (1972): 103-124; "Samuel Hirsch's American Judaism," *American Jewish Historical Quarterly* 62, no. 4 (June 1973): 362-382; and "Nineteenth Century Reform Religious Thought and Religionswissenschaft," in *Modern Judaism and Historical Consciousness*, eds. Andreas Gotzmann and Christian Wiese (Leiden: Brill, 2007), 105-139; Kenneth Koltun-Fromm, "Public Religion in Samson Raphael Hirsch's and Samuel Hirsch's Interpretation of Religious Symbolism," *Jewish Thought and Philosophy* 9 (1999): 69-105; Meyer, "Reform Jewish Thinkers and Their German Intellectual Context," in *The Jewish Response to German Culture*, eds. Jehuda Reinharz and Walter Schatzberg (Hanover and London: University Press of New England, 1985), 64-84; Aharon She'ar-Yashuv, "Ha'datiut Shel Avraham Be'filosofiat Ha'dat Shel Shemuel Hirsh," in *Avraham Avi Hama'aminim: Demuto Bi're'i Ha'hagut Le'doroteha*, eds. Mosheh Halamish, Hannah Kasher, and Yohanan Silman (Ramat Gan: Bar-Ilan University, 2002), 247-256; Manfred Vogel, "Does Samuel Hirsch Anthropologize Religion?" *Modern Judaism* 1, no. 3 (1981): 298-322; and Wiese, "Samuel Holdheim's 'Most Powerful Comrade in Conviction': David Einhorn and the Debate Concerning Jewish Universalism in the Radical Reform Movement," in *Redefining Judaism in an Age of Emancipation: Comparative Perspectives on Samuel Holdheim (1806-1860)* (Leiden: Brill, 306-373), 306-374; "Von Dessau nach Philadelphia: Samuel Hirsch als Philosoph und Reformer," in *Jüdische Bildung und Kultur in Sachsen-Anhalt*, eds. Giuseppi Veltri and Christian Wiese (Berlin: Metropol, 2009): 363-410. The lectures by Paul Rousseau, Christian Meyers, Laurent Mignon, Irene Kajon, Christian Wiese, Renée Wagener, Wolfgang Alt, Stephanie Schlesier, Thorsten Fuchshuber, Judith Frishman, Gershon Greenberg and Ken Koltun-Fromm at the recent conference at the University of Luxemburg ("*Samuel Hirsch: Religionsphilosoph, Emanzipationsverfechter und radikaler Reformer: Jüdische Identität im 19. Jahrhundert am Beispiel von Werk und Wirkung des ersten Oberrabiners Luxemburg*," 17-19 October 2010) will appear in the conference's forthcoming volume.

where the Jews, who were mainly country farmers and craftsmen, got along so well with their Christian neighbors that they participated occasionally in each others' worship services. When he was three years old, his father, a businessman, sent him to study at the town's *Heder*. He then went on to yeshivas in Metz and Mainz. Hirsch remembered the atmosphere there as stifling, with Hebrew Scripture, on the one hand, taught thoroughly, but secular literature, on the other, excluded from the program. After studying secular subjects at, and graduating from, the Mainz *Gymnasium*, Hirsch enrolled at the University of Bonn. His main instructor there was the Protestant theologian Karl Immanuel Nitzsch, with whom he studied Biblical theology, theological morality, history of Christian dogma, and an "encyclopedia of theological scientific studies." He transferred to the University of Berlin, where he continued his study of Hebrew scripture and took philosophy courses with the Hegelians Karl Ludwig Michelet (Aristotle's metaphysics, logic, natural philosophy, and the history of recent German philosophical systems from Kant through Hegel) and Friedrich Adolf Trendelenburg (pedagogy and the ethical systems of Schleiermacher, Hegel, and Herbart).[40]

Hirsch was intending to become a book dealer when a chance event turned him towards the rabbinate. On his way home after the summer 1838 semester in Berlin he stopped off at Dessau. He was recruited to serve as *Prediger* (preacher) for *Rosh Hashanah* services at its Great Synagogue—Joseph Wolf had already delivered sermons there in German in 1805. Despite having neither rabbinical ordination nor a doctorate (something the congregation would bring up later in a contract dispute), he was offered a position as their rabbi. Following his appointment he received both ordination from Reform-leader Samuel Holdheim (Frankfurt on the Oder), and a doctorate from the University of Leipzig. The doctorate was granted for the sermons that he published in *Peace, Freedom and Unity* (1839) and *The Messianic Doctrine of the Jews* (1843). He also included the first parts of *The Religious Philosophy of the Jews* (1841),

---

40   See Emil A. Hirsch, "My Father and Teacher," *The Reform Advocate* (29 May 1915), 297ff. See also Henning Theurich, *Theorie und Praxis der Predigt bei Carl Immanuel Nitzsch* (Göttingen: Vandenhoeck und Ruprecht, 1975). Salomon Ludwig Steinheim also studied under Trendelenburg, as did Hermann Cohen—who used Trendelenburg's motif that the common element of "movement" mediated between thought and reality. See Michael Zank, *The Idea of Atonement in the Philosophy of Hermann Cohen* (Providence: Brown University Press, 2000), 1n.

which he described in an April 1841 letter to the founder of the Historical School Leopold Zunz as the philosophical portion of a larger system delineating boundaries between Judaism, Christianity, and paganism. The first of a projected series of volumes (only one was published), it brought together materials from his courses at the universities of Bonn and Berlin and Hirsch's own independent studies of Far Eastern and Middle Eastern religions, and was structured according to Hegelian dialectical logic. Hirsch did not last in the position of rabbi—whether because of problems surrounding *Schutzjude*-status required by the state, or his congregants' Sabbath and *Yom Kippur* desecrations. Nor was he appointed to teach at Leopold Zunz's Jewish teachers' institute in Berlin as he had wished. But he did receive enough financial support from Moritz Mayer Junior of Leipzig to complete and publish *The Religious Philosophy* and *The Messianic Doctrine of the Jews*, as well as a response to Bruno Bauer's attack on the Jews.[41]

In *The Religious Philosophy* Hirsch complained that after a full half-century of formal emancipation in Germany, Jews were still only being tolerated. Instead of being treated as spiritual equals with Protestants and Catholics, they were considered disposable. To achieve proper respect, Hirsch believed, Judaism needed to be subjected to scientific study. To him, this meant addressing issues of Jewish religious consciousness philosophically; specifically, applying the human spirit/mind (*Geist*) to the substance of Judaism as found in Hebrew Scripture. Initially, these matters and their necessity were merely felt, creating a tension or contradiction between the non-spiritual and the mind/spirit-in-itself. Then, mind/spirit became aware of the contradiction, bringing it to consciousness and also reproducing the content of Scripture

---

41 Editor, "Dessau," *Allgemeine Zeitung des Judentums* 6, no. 9 (26 February 1842): 122-123. See Samuel Hirsch, "Vorwort," in *Die Religionsphilosophie*, vii-x. Samuel Hirsch, *Gedächtniss Rede auf den verewigten Dr. Moritz Mayer gehalten in der Synagoge der Ref. Gem. Keneset-Israel zu Philadelphia* (Philadelphia: Stein und Jones, 1867). Hirsch-Zunz correspondence of 10 June 1839, 4 August 1840, 16 April 1841, 15 September 1841, 2 November 1841, 21 December 1841 and 21 December 1841 (*JNUL* Manuscript Division, 40792-G14). The records of an 1839 controversy between Hirsch and the administrators of the Franz school in Dessau in 1839 are held in Staatsarchiv Magdeburg (Abt. Dessau C15 no. 21 Bd. 6 Bl. 63 *Rückseite*, 50 pages in length). When Hirsch studied at the University of Berlin, he did not enroll in Bruno Bauer's courses. See also David Sorkin, "Preacher, Teacher, Publicist: Joseph Wolf and the Ideology of Emancipation," in *From East and West: Jews in a Changing Europe, 1750-1870*, eds. Frances Malino and Sorkin (Oxford: Basil Blackwell, 1990), 107-125.

for consciousness. Ultimately, the entire material of Scripture would and should be reproduced for consciousness, which would totally dissolve the contradiction. The process of the scientific study of Judaism also would involve the philosophical treatment of the essence of religious consciousness on a universal basis. According to Hirsch, in the first stage of religion, that of paganism, the mind/spirit did not apply itself to content, and concrete religious issues remained apart from consciousness. In the second stage, that of the religions of revelation (Judaism and Christianity), mind/spirit applied itself to the external realities of religious life and established their contents in terms of absolute spirit/mind and the absolute necessity it entailed. In the last stage of religious development, messianism, spirit/mind manifest itself universally. All contents changed their position from otherness *vis-à-vis* the mind/spirit to presence within religious consciousness in terms of absolute necessity.

For Hirsch, the core of religious consciousness was rooted in the individual relationship to God. In Judaism in particular, and within human history from paganism to revelation to messianism in general, this relationship was a matter of self-consciousness and freedom. Specifically, the human being was a microcosm of the prior stages of nature, and distinct from other creation by its self-consciousness. In the embryo, the fetus passed through vegetative stages. After birth the child passed through levels of animal consciousness, where distinctions were drawn between it and other created entities. In the beginning, the child's freedom was abstract, empty of positive content. With no inner direction, the child only reacted to external nature. As the child employed nature in a process of self-objectification, freedom became concrete during the process by which the child became an "I." Namely, faced with choices between true life (real freedom and virtue) and death (illusory freedom and sin), between life's essence (spiritual) and what was external to essence (naturality), the child's self-consciousness emerges as choices are made.

Every choice for real freedom implies the existence of a permanent ontological source for the actual freedom, of a grantor who is free. This source is God, whose freedom is ideal, absolute, and the culmination to humankind's endless series of choices to be really free. God also sets the process of human freedom into motion. The individual life of freedom is rooted in God, as the grounding for a relationship between what the human being is potentially and what it should be actually. The human being does not affect God by remaining passive or not choosing freedom; God cannot be not-God. Hirsch was convinced that ultimately, the individual, Judaism, and world-religion would spiritualize natural, eternal freedom and become free, for the world is of God, and so its ultimate being is of freedom.

In 1843, thanks to the efforts of a relative of the king of the Netherlands whom Hirsch had tutored, Hirsch was offered and accepted an invitation to serve as Chief Rabbi of Luxembourg. He held the position for twenty-three years, during which time he was able to release the Luxembourg Jewish community from the tight hold the Trier rabbinate had exerted upon it. He led Jewish army recruits in a protest against the requirement of *more judaico*, the medieval oath affirming their inferior status which Jews were still compelled to take in lawsuits with non-Jews. He also defined his own path within the growing Reform movement. In the name of tradition he stressed the importance of Hebrew prayer, while in the name of change he installed an organ in his synagogue, eliminated a number of *Piyutim* from the *Rosh Hashanah* service, and supported Holdheim's Breslau rabbinical conference (1846) proposal to move Sabbath to Sunday in order to increase observance. In *The Reform in Judaism and its Calling in the Contemporary World* (1844) Hirsch evaluated cultic symbols according to current values and in terms of the religious truths they expressed. He discredited those he considered mysterious, that he felt were kept only in an attempt to manipulate the divine. He was opposed to political restoration of the Land of Israel, and focused on a spiritual-centered nationalism, independent of geography.[42]

In 1866 Hirsch accepted David Einhorn's invitation to succeed him at Keneseth Israel Congregation in Philadelphia. He had many reasons to agree to this move. Jesuits had attacked his affiliation with the Free Masons Lodge in Luxembourg, and German anti-Judaism was undermining the messianic character he associated with Jewish presence in

---

42   See Charles and Graziella Lehrmann, *La Communauté Juive du Luxembourg dans le Passé et dans le Present* (Esch-sur-Alzette: n.p., 1953), 63ff.; Katz, "Samuel Hirsch—Rabbi, Philosopher and Freemason," *Revue des Études Juives* 125 nos. 1-3 (January – September 1966): 8-20; Greenberg, "The Historical Origins of God and Man: Samuel Hirsch's Luxembourg Writings," *LBIY* 20 (1975): 129-148 and "The Reformers' First Attack on Hess' Rome and Jerusalem," *Jewish Social Studies* 35 nos. 3-4 (July-October 1973): 175-197.

Germany. His concept of history was anchored in the future with its possibilities, and America was filled with opportunities—he later spoke of the messianic ramifications to the emancipation of the slaves and the opening of the western frontier.

America would also be able to accommodate his version of Reform Judaism's principles, as articulated in the following principles: (1) Once a state advanced freedom of conscience, the religion of Judaism should find a way to coalesce with the state. For example, recitation of prayers for Zion, which to Hirsch amounted to treason against the American flag, needed to be eliminated. (2) Religious truths lay within the human heart, so supernatural revelation was superfluous—neither Scripture nor the *Talmud* were of supernatural origin. (3) While principles of Jewish law were to be retained, specific laws themselves should be changed according to historical conditions. (4) History expressed the active revelation of God's will in time, and it contained and furthered the moral category of freedom. (5) As religious ceremonies were intended to evoke consciousness of man's relationship with God, the forms should adapt to circumstances as necessary. (6) Prayer, the highest form of religious devotion, should be in the language best understood by the worshipper.

In 1888 Hirsch was dismissed from his Philadelphia position, purportedly because of his old age and his German accent. He died at his son Emil's home in Chicago.[43]

II.III.I. Selections from *The Systems of the Religious Perceptions of Jews and its Relationship to Paganism, Christianity and to Absolute Philosophy*.

Section I: Apologetic. Volume I: The Religious Philosophy of the Jews.The Principle of Jewish Religious Perception and its Relationship to Paganism, Christianity and to Absolute Philosophy. With Explicit Prooftexts from Holy Scripture as Interpreted in the Tamud and Midrash.

Summary of untranslated passages
For fifty years since liberation from the ghetto, Jews absorbed the culture around them. But the Christian church and the state which it influenced still did not recognize Judaism, only tolerated it. Efforts at emancipation were perversely misunderstood as an attempt to gain political or professional sta-

---

43   Leo Kaul, *The Story of Radical Reform Judaism* (Los Angeles, CA: Leo Kaul, 1951).

tus or political equality, or prevent state influence upon Jewish religious institutions. Instead, it was a matter of higher necessity, something accountable to God. Indeed, Judaism required Jews to serve the state. Toleration rather than recognition meant that the state wanted to rid itself of Judaism and had been unable to do so, but would still work at it. Jews who valued their religion must not stand by as it came to be regarded as some ungodly and sickly influence on contemporary humankind.

The church applied the precept of extra ecclesiam nulla salus (outside the church there is no salvation) to Jews. While Protestants would object if the Church applied that principle to them—e.g., with regard to mixed marriages—they seemed oblivious when it was practiced on Jews. Instead, the church should add the phrase nisi Judaeis in religione eorum (unless those [outside the church] were of the Jewish religion). Such mutual recognition would bring both peace and a sort of emancipation which would be accountable to God.

Recently, the state spoke on behalf of Jewish nationality. But this was only an attempt to clarify Jewish particularity so that Jews would become aware of the curse which hung over them and rush into the womb of the blessed church. Even Paul left salvation to God, not to the human will ("For he saith to Moses, I will have mercy on whom I will have mercy, and I will have compassion on whom I will have compassion." Romans 9:15). Jewish salvation did not need the help of the church. It should be understood that Jewish nationality—and Jews constituted a nationality, not a confession—was purely spiritual, not a matter of civil or political conditions. The rebuilt Temple, for example, would be a house of prayer for all peoples.

The key to transforming the situation was scientific understanding. At the moment, Judaism mistrusted scientific study, because contemporary conditions were identified with those of Mendelssohn's school. At that time, rationalist philosophy dominated, Jews sought humanistic training equal to that of the Christian, and Judaism's exclusive characteristics were viewed negatively. Now it was important to grasp what was exclusive about Judaism, its positive world-perception, the particular ceremonies and customs—and all in terms of their absolute necessity. Scientific study of Judaism should now be addressed towards building Judaism on its own terms, not tearing it down.

Scientific study belonged to the philosophy of religion, the aim of which was to explore the entire content of religious consciousness philosophically. While Hegel's philosophy of religion employed representative images as a "sop" to the church as he himself wreaked havoc with the content of Christi-

anity and other religions, Hirsch's philosophy of religion would explore religious content without compromising the integrity of any religion.

Summary of translated passages

Hirsch's religious philosophy was a philosophical treatment of the content of religious consciousness. Although religious consciousness was necessitated by human spiritual nature, the necessity came from this nature and so felt as if it was free. Once expressed, the truths of religious consciousness had a quality of immediacy—for the mind/spirit (Geist) testified to them immediately. Hirsch rejected Hegel's view of religious truths as representative images (Vorstellungen), sensible representatives of the sensible that was no longer there and of the spiritual which was not yet there, because God, as mind/spirit, could not be a representative image. Religious truths were rather religious perceptions (Anschauungen) of the "eye" of the mind/spirit. With these perceptions, the mind/spirit provided witness that the mind/spirit necessitated its own content. At this point, Hirsch used the terms "religious philosophy" and "philosophy of religion" interchangeably.

THE CONCEPT OF OUR SCIENTIFIC STUDY

The general name of our scientific study is *philosophy of religion*. Religious philosophy is a particular part. The purpose of religious philosophy is *to treat the entire content of religious consciousness [and knowledge] philosophically.* The highest [level] of religious consciousness achieved by the human mind/spirit cannot be *accidental.* For the human being to have religious consciousness or not cannot be by chance. Necessity which [is inherent to] the human being's spiritual nature forces it to have religious consciousness. The human being is forced by the necessity [inherent to] its spiritual values to have religious consciousness. But because it is the mind/spirit forcing the human being, the human being has no knowledge of any necessity. This necessity is not some foreign essence forcing the human being towards religion. In that case, it would have to know about the force, would struggle against the yoke—and seek to be irreligious instead of religious. Since the human being's own mind/spirit compels it towards religion, the human being feels itself *free* and *well.* Normal consciousness does not perceive any necessity of the mind/spirit for religion.

Normal consciousness knows religious truths immediately. It is of no matter that truths of religious knowledge came first as mediated by school, religious instruction, home education, or the Church. As soon as knowledge can express the religious truths, the knowledge is immediate. Religious knowledge does not sense that the truths it expresses are foreign, and acquired only by study. Mind/spirit provides religious knowledge with itself as witness. The mind/spirit testifies immediately that these truths are knowledge's own, the truths of the mind/spirit.

Mind/spirit relates in the same way to everything else it knows. The mind/spirit knows what it does immediately, from the highest to the lowest, at the moment when it names it. The language itself must first be learned and acquired by study, as can be observed with any child. But it is still purely spiritual; the animal cannot speak because it has no mind/spirit. Also, language itself is purely immediate. Further, the human being is aware of a great distinction between areas of its knowledge. The knowledge about God has infinitely more value than does knowledge about normal conditions of life. This distinction is known immediately. It is of *potency* and *degree*. Both belong to immediate knowledge, and in that sense are equal. Speaking Platonically, there is only memory [on the part of] the mind/spirit, and what the mind's/spirit's essence tells the human being is [already] found in the human being.

Hegel used *representative images* as an appropriate term for immediate knowledge. But he chose the term only because he needed a *reservatio mentalis*. According to his method, philosophical knowledge must provide the thing-itself. But Hegel could not conceal from himself, that [when his philosophy] applied the thing-itself, namely *the doctrines of the church, to his system*, he imputed decidedly anti-church meaning to church terminology. Luckily, the term *representative image* was coined, which held a way open for retreat. The representative image is situated between the sensible, which is *no longer there* and merely represented as something sensible, and the spiritual, which is *not there yet* and is nonetheless represented as something sensible. The representative image is a seemingly unstructured mixture of the sensible and the spiritual. I can have a representative image of God, as if He has a body. But I cannot think of Him as such. The thing-itself provided by philosophy could not be expected to agree with the representative image. Justifiably, the church rejects the insult of having doctrines of accidental character [i.e., those tied to representative images] imputed to it. [Contrary to Hegel], immediate religious knowledge of the Church or of Judaism knows nothing about God in terms of representative images.

Indeed, immediate religious knowledge knows that God cannot be a representative image, because God is mind/spirit. I call immediate religious knowledge *religious perception*. The truths of religion are apprehended directly through the eye of the mind/spirit. The knowledge of the sensible is perceived through the eye of the body, while the mind/spirit provides instantaneous testimony to both. In the former, it is the spiritual that is perceived immediately; in the latter, it is the sensible that is perceived immediately.

What is this witness of the mind/spirit? What brings the mind/spirit to testify to this content [of religious consciousness]? The fact *that it bears witness that the mind/spirit is its own content, the content of the mind/spirit. The mind/spirit necessitates itself to have this content, because it always had it.* In normal consciousness, the content [of mind/spirit] is known; but the necessity of the content is merely felt. Philosophical wisdom not only wants [to know] the content, it wants to know the necessity which the mind/spirit has for this content. This is the concept behind philosophy of religion. It wants to grasp the necessity for the mind/spirit [to have its content]. Philosophy of religion can provide nothing more, neither in terms of the content or its form, than what is already available in immediate religious knowledge. Philosophy of religion can provide no other content, because its substance is the same as that of mind/spirit. Philosophy of religion can provide no other form for this content, because the content is not assigned capriciously by the mind/spirit, but by its own necessity. The issue is therefore set by the mind/spirit in the only form proper to it, a form which is necessary to the mind/spirit and also to its content. But philosophy of religion also provides something new. In normal consciousness this necessity of content and of form is only *felt*, only presumed. Philosophy *seeks to know this* necessity. Even in normal consciousness, the truths of religion are not *separated* out. The mind/spirit is necessitated to have these truths and has them all together. Philosophical knowledge does not first bring them together; the truths were already formed by their imminent necessity. True philosophy can provide no form to any individual truth, other than what it already had in religious consciousness, according to its basic necessity. True philosophy just brings this necessity-at-its-basis to light. *Sham philosophy* places itself in the middle between immediate religious knowledge and true philosophy. It tears individual truths away from the totality of truth, and gives both of them false content although in appropriate form. Neither immediate religious knowledge nor true philosophy can agree with such sham philosophy—also called philosophy of understanding. It *rather builds the necessary bridge from immediate religious knowledge to philosophy* (xv-xviii).

Summary of untranslated passages
Philosophy of religion presupposed the necessary content of mind/spirit and sought to grasp this necessity. The religious mind/spirit brought its own content to consciousness, but the necessity of it remained only felt. That content consisted of religious texts which had endured over the course of the religious mind/spirit's development. The necessity by which that content developed was reproduced by philosophy of religion for thought and knowledge.

Specifically, as long as the necessity behind producing the content of the mind/spirit for consciousness was only felt, it remained unspiritual. Mind/ spirit regarded holy scriptural material as unspiritual and opposed it. This left the mind/spirit in contradiction with itself, having itself produced both the spiritual and the unspiritual dimensions of religious content. The mind/ spirit accepted this contradiction and established an adjoining space next to it which was empty of contradiction. The spiritual (truth) and the unspiritual (lie) now stood side by side, and the contradiction between truth and lie reached consciousness. The mind/spirit sought to transcend the contradiction and expressed its invalidity as a religious and spiritual feeling, a sentiment that is immediate and raised above contradiction.

Holy scripture corresponded to the feeling of spiritual necessity. The feeling, in turn, contradicted the claim of the mind/spirit to know itself. The content of immediate religious knowledge had to be identified with the content of philosophical knowledge, thus removing the contradiction. The mind/ spirit, using the contradiction as an agent of spiritual necessity, reproduced the entire content of the religious consciousness through consciousness, and removed the contradiction. By producing its own content, mind/spirit moved from spirit-in-itself (necessity that is felt, freedom empty of content) to spirit-for-itself, concrete freedom.

Philosophy of religion as Hirsch described it dealt with the sub-section of philosophy called philosophy of mind/spirit. It began with the contradiction between the felt necessity of the content of the mind/spirit (religious knowledge) and the mind/spirit in-itself (with its freedom), between the unspiritual (feeling) and the spiritual (thought). The mind/spirit set a place for itself next to this antithetical juxtaposition, creating another contradiction.

By acknowledging the mind/spirit's necessity to become knowledge, knowledge became an abstraction. This was spirit-in-itself, the internality of mind/spirit. Spirit-in-itself moved to reverse itself into spirit-as-other or nature, and to return to itself to be spirit-for-itself; from logical philosophy to natural philosophy to the philosophy of mind/spirit. At this point, philosophy of religion entered in (xxiii-xxv).

Summary of translated passages
Hegel arrived at the Vorstellungen *of religious truths only after grasping the mind itself as psychology, morality, philosophy of law, philosophy of history, and then absolutely, as aesthetics. Only then did it comprehend itself as religious philosophy. For Hirsch, the disciplines of psychology, morality and aesthetics were inseparable from the religious mind/spirit and belonged under the category of philosophy of religion. Nor were religions different stages of the absolute mind/spirit as it moved to being-in-and-for-itself (Hegel), but rather philosophy of religion was the final stage.*

> *Note*: According to Hegel, as is known, even when the mind/spirit conceptualized itself, it had a long way to go before it acknowledged itself as religious. First, the mind/spirit grasped its existence as a particular spirit (psychology). Then it realized itself as this particular spirit (morality). Then it understood itself as the mind/spirit of the nation (philosophy of law) and finally as the mind/spirit of the nations (philosophy of history). At this point, the mind/spirit knew itself as absolute. First it did so directly (aesthetics), then as mediated in terms of representative images (religious philosophy). Finally, the mind/spirit comprehended itself as being-in-and-for-itself. At this stage, the mind/spirit is mediated in its immediacy (history of philosophy).
>
> We cannot take this path. For us, all disciplines fall under the philosophy of religion. Hegel himself says that a nation's morality and ethics, even national history, can be conceptualized only after understanding the people's religious mind/spirit. Aesthetics was as little independent of this religious mind/spirit as the history of philosophy. Psychology belonged, actually, to the other-

existence of mind/spirit—for here the mind/spirit was completely abstract—that is, to the philosophy of nature, which was presumed by the philosophy of religion. Insofar as psychology was to be apprehended/realized as the mind/spirit's other, as the housing in which the mind/spirit provides a dwelling for itself, it constituted a part of the philosophy of religion. For Hegel, philosophy of religion was not final or absolute, while for us it contained the totality of philosophy of the mind/spirit. For Hegel, religion proceeded from the individual to the general, from fetish to God or mind/spirit. Paganism was not established by the mind/spirit, but was rather a wrong, capricious descent of the mind/spirit from itself. It manifests itself as self-conscious alienation of the mind/spirit from itself. Hegel conceptualized the mind/spirit of religion in terms of initial and final [stages] in the absolute totality of mind/spirit [as being-in-and-for-itself]. This is not our path at all (xxv-xxvi).

Summary of translated passages

After rejecting Protestant theologian Friedrich Schleiermacher's "consciousness of dependence," Steinheim's "shibboleths," and Neo-Orthodox thinker Samson Raphael Hirsch's obliviousness to non-rabbinical sources, Samuel Hirsch wrote that for authentic scientific study of religion, the object of study was purely spiritual. The scientific comprehension of religion focused on the human mind/spirit. It began with the human being. The human being was a microcosm, blending vegetative and animal life in its own way and transcending them with the "I" of self-consciousness. The "I" expressed formal freedom, and it gained substance as it objectivized itself in nature.

Note: We have in mind *the shibboleths of Dr.* [Salomon Ludwig] Steinheim and *Ben Ussiel's Letters* and *Israel's Duties* by Mr. [Samson Raphael] Hirsch in Oldenburg. We will deal with Steinheim in the second section of this volume [on passive religiosity or paganism's self-destructive dialectic]. Samson Raphael Hirsch is not aware that he contradicts himself. He wants to know Judaism only from its literature—*Pentateuch, Prophets, Writings, Talmud* and *Midrash*. In doing this he in fact initiates an old principle initiated by Christians,

not Jews, mediated by a spiritual epidemic and taken over unknow-
ingly by Jews. It has been echoed thousands of times from Paul to
Hegel. Compare [Samson Raphael] Hirsch's *Israel's Duties* (viii) with
the well-known [Pauline] idea that the Jews *stand under the curse of
the law* or with the *abstract* Jewish God of the Hegelians.

[*The Emergence of the "I"*]

We want to find the beginning of scientific knowledge of religion.... At first,
we have nothing more than our interest in knowledge about religion.
The question therefore arises: From where does this interest come? Is
the interest just something *accidental*? Can it be something else? Does
our innermost nature *necessitate* this interest? Accordingly, *our nature
itself* becomes the object of our inquiry. The entire presumption we
have made, consists of this: We, who have this interest in religion, constitute an axiom which *not even the most skeptical doubter can doubt*. If
a person doubts his/her own existence, the person doubts that he/she
doubts and thereby doubts no more. *Who, then, are we? How do we come
to this interest?*

ESSENCE OF RELIGION
[*Freedom and religion*]

It is rightly asserted that the human being is the superior creation
of the earthly organisms, as it *sublimates* into itself all prior stages of
earthly development. The human being unifies in itself the lives of all
earthly essences, and they run through life anew in the human being.
But the human being is more than a *complex of earthly life*. It is not
merely the *microcosm* which reflects in miniature the life of all prior
creatures. The human being forms an *essentially new stage* in the sequence of creation.... The human fetus lives through the stages of inor-
ganic and vegetative life. The sequence of animal life begins with birth.
The human being then proceeds from the lowest to the highest stage,
and does so in a very short time. At first the human being leads a life
of dull feeling and sensation. Then it distinguishes things from one another, and establishes and recognizes them as distinct. That is, it has
consciousness of the outer world. But it remains at the animal level, for
animals, especially the higher species, also have world-consciousness,
consciousness of the outer world. They recognize objects previously encountered, etc.

When does the human being emerge as something special? Not before the child stops calling itself in the third person, and begins to call itself "I." That is, when it lifts itself out of *world-consciousness and into self-consciousness. Only when the human being learns to call itself* "I," is it really a human being. It tears itself away from everything natural, from all earlier stages of existence and becomes a proper essence [for-itself].

THE I, OR SELF-CONSCIOUSNESS

The human being first becomes uniquely human with the word "I." In what does this so meaningful *"I"-statement* consist? In *freedom* itself. We can articulate what is unique to the human being by saying: *the human being is a free essence, born to freedom. Freedom is what first makes the human being into the human being.*

Initially, the *"I"-statement* expresses only a *principle,* a *beginning,* freedom that is *abstract* and *empty*—not to be confused with *real freedom.* The *"I"-naming* at first consists of this: I am *an essence other* than the entire outer world. Its laws are *not* mine. Unlike the animal, I am not driven by instinct. The animal *must* comply with its instinct, *not knowing that it is [complying with] its own essence.* It views its essence as *something foreign* to itself, as a necessity coming to it from the outside. I, to the contrary, need not comply with *anything external.* I can resist everything that comes from the outside and surrender my life to my own will.

Still, this *freedom is but a word without content or substance.* It is only spoken. All I know about it, is what *it is not* [i.e., not something necessary from the outside]. I do not know *what it is.* But freedom cannot remain without content or substance, lest it switch into its opposite, *un-freedom.* As long as it is completely empty of content, it is [only] *caprice,* or only a receptacle for *accidental content.* There is no internal basis of determination. Any such foundation comes to this un-freedom from the outside. I do not know by myself what I should and will do. My action depends solely on what the world outside offers me. This accidental and unfree action is characteristic of the child. The child's behavior is not a *procedure,* but a *game.* The child is controlled completely by its mood. Who knows whether the game it is playing now will last? Will that which is fun now turn boring in a moment? This is because the child's freedom, its I, does not yet have a fundamental nature to satisfy it.

This freedom is only formal. I am *next* to everything that I do; but *only* next to it. What I do is not *I*, [in the sense that] it is not set by me and does not return to me. I do not recognize what I do as the *revelation, testimony, activity* of my innermost essence. What I do remains alien to me and to my innermost core. It is given to me by the outer world and remains so. I am not conscious of my action, *so as to make it mine*. Instead I act without consciousness, I act solely according to the conditions offered independently of me. This empty, abstract freedom is *self-contradictory*. In saying "I," I express that I *should* be and want to be free, while my action shows that I remain at the *should* [stage]. Instead of being free, I am unfree.

This contradiction is rooted in the way in which the human being came to abstract freedom. Nature led the human being to the point where it said "I" without its own input. Abstract freedom was a gift of nature. That is, *the human being is free by nature*. This is the contradiction, because nothing can be free by nature; naturality and freedom are mutually exclusive. Freedom, rather, is to be earned. It is to be transparent and clear, and include nothing foreign to what it would be of itself.

There is [real] freedom when the human being utilizes what nature provides to objectify its (the human being's) own content; when it integrates its content into what nature offers from the outside. The human being cannot receive itself or its content from the hands of nature [and be free]. The human being is not free by nature, it must make itself into what it is by nature [in its otherness], that is, *it must first make itself free*. My essential task, the essence of the human being, is to make myself into what *I should be* by nature but am not already. It is to raise myself up to true freedom, which means that I am not only *with* my activities but that my activities, my *entire existence, my actions as well as my thoughts* are set exclusively and solely *by me*. My activities should testify to and produce nothing but my freedom: Circumstances should not determine my acts but should be utilized by me. I should impress *my* essence on them, and bring *my* thoughts and the purposes of my innermost existence into perception through them. In every moment of my life I should do nothing but *raise abstract freedom into true and real freedom*; make that which is offered *by nature into what is mine*; utilize what is offered to me by integrating my I, my freedom, into it. This is what is essential and the true concept of freedom. It is also the essential and one true concept of religion. Religious life [consists of] nothing other than *eternally real* and *eternally self-realizing* freedom. Religious life is the life in freedom. In it, I *am* already free, as I am already raising abstract freedom into real freedom and perpetually making myself free, as I am perpetually active. Freedom without self-conscious activity is never freedom, but of nature. The mind/spirit never stands still in using what nature offers to bear continual witness to human freedom.

Note: The word "religion" is not biblical. It is taken over from paganism, where it does not include the factor of freedom. People disagree as to whether it is derived from *religere* or *relegere*; about whether its basic meaning is *to be bound* under the will of the gods, or amounts to *making present* the *essence* of the gods. It would be a wonder for Holy Scripture, undeniably a treasure of religious expressions and indications, not to contain an equivalent expression for religion. But neither *religere* nor *relegere* correctly and completely expresses what the essence of religion [is for it]. Holy Scripture defines the essence of the human being in terms of *the religious life*. Religion in Holy Scripture means the *essence of the human being*. The two concepts [religion and the essence of the human being] coincide. The human being ceases to be human as soon as it sets out to be other than religious. How does Holy Scripture express itself about the human being?
[For example]:

> And God said, Let us make man in our image, after our likeness; and let them have dominion over the fish of the sea, and over the fowl of the air, and over the cattle, and over all the earth, and over every creeping thing that creepeth upon the earth. (Genesis 1:26)
> Much has been said about the matter of the human being's similarity to God, but the verse makes it clear. The similarity consists of freedom. Not in the *abstract*, but as realized and ever *self-realizing*. The term "let them have dominion" is to be thought of only in terms of true freedom, not external mastery. The author of Genesis obviously knew that the human being never had, nor ever could have, dominion over all the fish in the sea, the fowl of the air, and over all animals including the worm

which creeps on the earth. It follows from Genesis 1:29-30 that only vegetation, not animals, are provided for the human being's immediate use.

This creation history is based on the perception that the human being sublimates into itself all prior stages of earthly development (and again, this is not the microcosm of paganism). Intentionally hidden in the verse is the perception that to be truly free the human being must first *turn against itself* the animalistic in *itself*. Not *annihilate* it—not lead a purely spiritual, non-sensual life; not kill off sensuality, but rather *master* the sensual and the animal in itself, using it as a means for *realizing* the human's freedom. This was intentionally hidden in the verse, so *the true meaning of the mastery would become clear for the human being only in the course of subsequent history*. Only the literal, outer meaning, that of external *mastery* over the environment, came to consciousness for the first human being. (Hegel knows this passage very well and often refers to it. It is hard to imagine why this *passage alone was not enough* to show him the error of his apprehension of Jewish religiosity) (8-15).

Summary of translated passages
Religion did not involve a God-man relationship (Verhältniss), which implied that God had limits. The God-man encounter which existed revolved around freedom. The human being had a natural potential freedom. It was to be actualized by the expansion of human consciousness across its environment. This implied a grantor who was absolutely free, namely God. Religious life was centered around the divine ground and human actualizing of freedom. Hirsch criticized Hegel's view, where religion was the human being's attempt to become conscious of its essence in a process which contained God but where God was not the foundation. Hegel also compromised the respective integrities of the religions of the world by imposing his philosophical logic upon them. Philosophy is properly only one part of human life. When it came to religion, it serves to conceptualize religious perceptions. Hirsch also rejected the anti-Hegelian position that religion was a matter of feeling.

ABSTRACT CONSCIOUSNESS OF GOD

On the basis of speculative reason and Holy Scripture, we have found that the *essence of religion* is *equivalent* to the *essence of the human being*, which is to say, equivalent to *human freedom*. But this overlooks something very important, namely the matter of connection or relationship to God being included in the concept of religion.

One cannot speak at all of a relationship to God. Only *finite things* relate to one another. In one sense finite things, where one thing stands here and the other there, have a relation to one another, and in another sense they do not. They relate to one another but each also remains independent in itself. One is the border to the other; where one is the other ceases, and *vice versa*. They relate to one another precisely in this mutual bordering. *All relational words* are originally spatial and temporal designations: e.g., before, after, under, upon, over, etc. In this sense, the human being does not have a relationship to God, because where the human being is, God is also and God has no border. Other relationships are not spatial and temporal. The son stands in a relationship to the father, the citizen to the fatherland, the servant to the master. But this does not apply to God either. When the father and son have a relationship, they are *mutually dependent*. The son needs the love of the father, and the father needs the love of the child. The same applies with civil relationships. Mutual dependency is the main condition for any relationship. *God, however, is not to be thought of in terms of a relationship of dependence.* While this most simple sentence would be conceded by anyone, it still needs to be stated. The essential error of the religiosity of our time consists precisely in the fact that religion is thought of solely as a *relationship of the human being to God*.

Contemporary Jews may be divided into two parties. The essential mistake they have in common is to think of religion as a relationship of the human being to God. The *first* group [the Orthodox] places so much weight upon the externals of Judaism—ignoring the warning of the venerated Jewish sage R. Hiyya, "Do not make the fence greater than the main thing, lest it collapse and destroy the plants" (*Bereshit Rabbah* ch. 19)—that it recognizes as pious and authentic Jews only those who hold fast to the externals. The externals alone are enough to be a pious Jew, by their account. By *external action*, which is not and cannot be grasped, the Jew enters into a *relationship of service with God*.

The second tendency imagines that it can disregard the externals of

Judaism, since it is inconceivable *that God could be served by such trivial observances*. While far apart from the first, the second tendency is rooted in the same soil. [The fact is, however, that] *God is not served by any of our activities*, neither trivial observances, nor important works of compassion, etc. We cannot speak of a relationship of service or any relationship of the human being to God. At most, we can do so only figuratively.

> *Note*: The sickness of contemporary Judaism does not implicate Judaism's mind/spirit. The fact that the *contemporary Jew* thinks that he/she serves God by his/her activities, does not prove that the Jewish religion knows God only as the master. This is what is *sick about contemporary Judaism*. Health is something else, but it does display itself *vis-à-vis* the sickness. The eternal law of the mind/spirit applies: When there is an opposition, neither side is totally true. The so-called *pious Jew* of our time has no advantage at all over the so-called non-pious—unless the non-pious belong to an indifferentist category. The "pious" is not the true Jew, and does not belong to the *ancient old ones*, to *the religiosity of our forefathers*. Instead, the "*pious*" *are unconsciously infected by Christian perception*. This "pious" Jew has lost the [authentic] mind/spirit and now wants to impose that *spiritlessness* onto Judaism. *Our forefathers had the mind/spirit and its form was also alive*; they characterized themselves as *modest, merciful and compassionate (Yebamot 79ª)*. What could be more *insolent* and *shameful* than what is seen daily on the part of the self-appointed ancient ones? For them, *any means* is right, be it lie or slander, to achieve the goal. Is religion for them anything but a tool of passion? We have proof enough of *their mercy* and their *considered judgment*. Happy are they who are not on the receiving end of the sort of compassion that these have towards the dead (*hevrah di'gemilut hasadim*, i.e., charitable societies) and beggars!

The concept of religion does not include the factor of a *relationship of the human being to God*. No objection can be raised against us for not having included such a relationship in our deliberations. But I have included *a consciousness of God*. While religiosity is not a *relation of the human being to God*, it is *the human being's relation to itself*. The grounding, the root of *the human being's relation to itself*, must *be God*. Such a consciousness of God [i.e., that God is the ground of the human being's relation to itself] has been implied in what I have said until now. We have become acquainted with the human being as being initially *free abstractly*. The human being's relationship to itself, i.e., all its omissions and commissions, can first be only one of abstract freedom. As such, the human being's knowledge of God must be the knowledge of an *Abstract Beyond*.

When I express myself as an "*I*," I express myself as a master of everything, and that *absolutely nothing* I know about has the value of my "*I*." Nothing entering my consciousness can force me absolutely to something I do not want. I recognize the height, the superiority of my essence, to be such that I cannot be forced to do anything. The human being can yield its life *to freedom*. But the human being does not have this power over everything, this *harmony*, even if at first only negative, *between human freedom and the all:* A power such that absolutely nothing can force it to do anything to itself. Nor did the human being earn this power. The human being *finds the power in itself*; and accepts it as a *gift* which reached it somehow. The human being therefore looks to the essence *above itself* which granted it this freedom and is the principle of its freedom. This spirit provided the human being with power over everything. It must therefore be *omnipotent, that which has absolute power over everything*. The human being calls this force God. Thus, humanity knows of God as the principle and cause of its freedom. God wants the human being to be free. The abstract concept of God is conferred immediately with abstract freedom. This does not mean that the human being enters into a relationship with God, for it does so only with itself. Insofar as a person knows itself as free (here, abstractly free) it corresponds with its own nature, even if it must consider this nature a gift from that which is the principle of its freedom, a gift from God.

Note: For a long time, the conceptual definition of religion for Christian theology has been, 'Religion is a way of knowing and honoring God' (*religio est modus dei cognoscendi aque colendi*). That is, Christianity has been in conflict with philosophy from the very beginning. Religion for Christianity is *one way* of knowing God. There is another way of knowing God next to it, philosophy. In most recent times, it has been recognized on scientific grounds that the human mind/spirit is *united*. The one mind/spirit cannot have two ways of truth. [It follows that] nothing validated by philosophy could be false in theology, and *vice versa*. Attempts are made to get beyond the issue of conflict between faith/belief and knowing. The Hegelians modify the ancient [Christian] explanation. Religion is only *one way* of knowing God. Therefore, there is another beside it, and it is *better* and *more complete*. Religion is the mind's/spirit's striving *to become conscious of its own essence, the process of objectifying itself before itself.* (Hegel's philosophy really knows no God other than the *essence of the human mind/spirit.* The essence of God is thus *completely clear, transparent* and revealed. Philosophy, however, *knows perfectly what God is.*) But religious striving is incomplete. It is only about the *representative image*; and brings the human being no further than making its essence [available in terms of] *representative image.* The human being must therefore begin the process over *again.* The human being succeeds in truly conceptualizing its essence only in philosophy. For Hegel, *religion is shattered philosophy.* It follows that the history of religion must be grasped as *history of philosophy.* Its task is no longer for the human being to transplant itself into the mind/spirit of earlier nations, feel with them, and look with them upon the divine. The whole aim now is to extract *the thoughts, i.e., the logical scheme,* out of the religion.

For example, take Hegel's religious philosophy and his treatment of the religion of India and of the Jews. His pre-supposed scheme turns out to be a childish game, and affects the form of presentation. *The concept for each respective stage of religion* is a given. Concrete presentations of the religions themselves follow, as if they were tests for what was figured out in advance. *This contradicts Hegel's own method.* Absolute method should have each element develop *on its own terms* and no foreign criteria may be introduced. Hegel protests against schemes that propose advance categories, into which material has to be subsumed, as if being stored in a closet. But because of his own false presupposition (that the concept of religion is exhausted with the declaration that religion is the striving of the mind/spirit to grasp its essence in thought) he falls into the very error in the field of religious philosophy to which he objects.

The anti-Hegelians rightly reject this theory of Hegel's, where religion strives after something which it cannot possibly achieve, trying to accomplish what is possible only for philosophy. They turn the matter around. Or, better expressed, they return to an old definition. Namely, that religion is the *best* way to know God and that philosophy is a lesser way. For them, religion is inborn in the human being. It is a feeling, a consciousness, *an unnamable something* which cannot be compared with anything else. It is an X. Thought and activity surrender to this X. Insofar as all of life *refers to God* through this X, life is religious. X is the conscience for the activity, and it is a theoretical conscience, an inborn idea for securing thought before philosophy. Without the activity of the X there can be *much assurance* but little faith/belief. And with the X there can be much faith/belief but little assurance. By accepting the inborn idea, the X, it is believed that the area of religion is secured from being overtaken by philosophy. Having found the formula for making it impossible for philosophy to take over, one can now play around with philosophy, take an interest in and be influenced by it. Wherever philosophy is not in harmony with the *inborn idea*, i.e., that which is religious, especially *Christian consciousness*, philosophy is rejected. But philosophy is like an adolescent. It is curious and is not afraid to ask questions. What is this X? What sort of inborn idea is it? Is it more than an *affirmation*? Is it true that such an *inborn idea* is available in the human mind/spirit? Philosophy asserts: The human being has a sense for truth—it has [general] reason. Reason is inborn in the human being and strives to develop and unfold. But X should *be more* than general human reason, for *without the X there is much assurance but little faith/belief*. This "more" is *called* philosophy, and is also to be *traced* to *human nature*.

But to begin with, religious life does not refer to God. Reference to someone is always a [matter of] *relationship* to that someone. Obviously, the expression "to want to have a relationship to God" is a distortion. Religious life cannot be comprehended either as a matter of knowing, as with Hegel, or a matter of feeling, as it largely is for other thinkers; or finally, as with the new practitioners, conceptualized primarily as activity. Religion is nothing more or less than the human being's life *which is appropriate to itself and makes itself proper to itself.* When a human being lives *in a manner fitting to its essence*, it lives in a way proper to the essence of the creator. *The conflict between faith/belief and wisdom* is not originally present in religion, and it first has to be introduced to it. When one asks what religion is, one should *for the moment* forget this conflict. Philosophizing is as much a human activity as other activities of the mind/spirit. They all belong to religion, they are not *beside* or beyond it.

As with any body of knowledge, for example, linguistics, humanity first reaches religious knowledge through *perception, poetic instinct*—or whatever it may be called, but something other than immediate knowledge. Philosophy *conceptualizes* these perceptions. If they are correct, philosophy *does not change them.* (Hegel, of course, supposedly does not want to change the original religious representative images. But this is no more than a juggling act, a verbal trick. No true shepherd of the Church should be deceived. Hegel has no intention of changing the *philosophical content* upon which the religious representative images are grounded, and this is his entire concern. He ends up throwing religious representative images into a melting pot and leaving the leftover sediment for the masses. If Hegelians knew more than just how to swear to everything their teacher said [*in verba magistri jurare*], they would ask whether religious truths could in fact be these *shattered* philosophical thoughts he calls *representative images*. Hegel's palliative distinction between *religious representative images* and *religious thoughts* is utterly false— although it has confused so many.) But when, and only when, these perceptions are false, they cannot withstand the test of philosophy. If they are false it is the fault of the human being. It is obviously dishonest to say *that much conviction and yet little religiosity can be present* [together]. Do not misuse this holy word conviction. Do not call only *imitated words* conviction. Where there is true conviction, there is also true faith/belief; faith/belief gives strength and moves mountains. It overcomes difficulties of any kind and knows how to bear patiently and to pity. But this I concede: *Much conviction can be present* together with *very little faith/belief in your dogmas.* But true conviction without religiosity is as little possible, as religion is without conviction. [End of note] (25-34)

Summary of translated passages
Human essence was characterized by a contradiction. It was free by nature, while this could not be truly freedom, because freedom meant self-determination. Awareness of the contradiction led to a new contradiction. The first contradiction should have been unbearable and have necessitated its own negation, but it had to remain to participate in resolving the inconsistency. There was a further contradiction. Formal freedom was not to be forced to do anything, while it appeared to be forced to endure this contradiction. Finally,

formal freedom endured, but also emerged from the contradiction.

In Hegel's system, formal (natural) freedom contradicted concrete freedom, and the human being clung to concrete freedom because formal freedom is unbearable. Hegel failed to see that when the opposition forces the shift from formal to concrete freedom, the uncompelled character of human essence is removed. Hegel had a second contradiction, that of holding onto an untenable contradiction-of-the-contradiction, remaining formally free while rejecting concrete freedom. A disharmony between formal freedom and freedom's natural content annulled concrete freedom. But it also provided form with appropriate content and harmonized them. Hirsch observed that this excluded the factor of freedom which was present in the disharmony, and led to the annihilation of form.

[CONTRADICTION ON THE ROAD TO REAL FREEDOM]

A contradiction constitutes the essence of the human being. On the one hand, the human being is initially free only *by nature*. On the other, the human being cannot be free by nature. Because freedom is *self-activity* and *self-determination*, freedom's presupposition and content should be itself, not nature. This opposition is initially only *in-itself*, not *for-us*. We become aware of it only by observing *the essence of this natural freedom*. It must come to the attention of *the human being*, to human consciousness, whether or not the human being is a philosopher. Each person must experience this contradiction in itself, and be stimulated to resolve it, stepping out of natural freedom and rising to authentic freedom. In turn, however, this involves a new incongruity.

The first contradiction, that freedom remained *formal, natural, and empty of content*, should be *unbearable* and must *necessitate* its own negation. On the other hand, the freedom [empty of content] must not be *destroyed* by negating the contradiction [between freedom as nature and freedom as self-determination]. Freedom that is empty-of-content must participate essentially in the process of annulling the contradiction and cooperate *in resolving it*. But freedom empty of content means *the inability to be forced to anything at all*. If it contributes to resolving the contradiction, it must never be *forced* to do so. The freedom empty-of-content [side to] contradiction must appear to be *bearable*, it *must be equally able or unable to bear the contradiction*. But if it can endure, how can it emerge? And if it cannot endure, it ceases to be freedom, and becomes *forced* by the *natural* factor adhering to it to become something other than it is already. This contradicts its own essence, much as the first contradiction. It turns out that (1) freedom that is empty-of-content contradicts itself in its *original existence* and (2) the endeavor to come out of this contradiction contains its own contradiction.

The [path of] incongruity can also be expressed in this way: At first I am only formally [and naturally] *free*, I find myself to be the master of my own doings, bound by *absolutely nothing*, not law and not anything else. Here, freedom is still *empty of content*. This formal freedom, precisely because it is only the *word which is empty of content*, contradicts itself. This contradiction comes to consciousness. I feel myself unlucky in and through this formal freedom. In turn, this formal freedom constitutes an essential factor for my progress. No one else can help me out of this contradiction. I must be my own doctor. I must redeem myself, precisely because I am formally free. This formal freedom is my last stronghold. I alone have a key and nothing can enter without my approval.

My formal freedom, my immediate existence, must be unbearable. Otherwise, I would remain in this immediate natural existence as an animal would, in terms of the law of preservation. I would never try to come out of it. On the other hand, I must be able to remain in natural freedom, lest it is not "I" who seeks to come out of it, *free* in the endeavor to redeem myself out of the bonds of nature: If not, an external power, foreign to me, would be forcing me to come out of it. Then again, if I should keep myself at the point of *immediate naturality*, there is absolutely no way to [make progress and go beyond this point]. If the contradiction of the first immediate naturality is *endurable* for me, should I just not tolerate it [and preclude my self-determination]? And if it is not bearable for me? Then I cease being free, driven by the contradiction of grasping for a condition which is appropriate to me, without attaining it freely. How is the bridge between *formal* freedom empty-of-content and *real freedom* to be found?

[*Note*]: This point has been thoroughly overlooked until now. Even Hegel only brings up formal freedom's contradiction: With him, formal freedom suddenly shifts into concrete freedom *only through* *their* contradiction. For Hegel, there are two conditions of the human mind/spirit: (1) Natural freedom and (2) Concrete, fulfilled freedom. The human being cannot bear the first and so reaches for the second.

Hegel failed to recognize that although the first contradiction was *unbearable*, it may not *force* the human being to shift directly into the second. If it did, the very *lofty and excellent quality*, which comes with natural freedom, that the human being cannot be compelled, would be *surrendered* and *annihilated*, rather than *retained* or *sublimated*.

Hegel's second contradiction is not the *negation of negation*, nor *contradiction of contradiction*. If it were, it would immediately be true freedom. Rather, for him it is the *contradiction* of having to reach towards the *contradiction of a contradiction*, even when this contradiction of contradiction became unendurable. As it is impossible for the human being to persist in the contradiction of formal freedom and remain formally free, it must still be capable of saying "*No*" to concrete freedom. For Hegel, the human being cannot *do away with* everything when it comes to formal and concrete freedom. As formally free [however], *the human can do away with everything determinate*, including concrete freedom. Logically, formal freedom only has the value of *abstract possibility*. But it is impossible for freedom to remain only formal, and it may not remain solely possible for formal freedom to grasp onto concrete freedom.

Hegel's concrete freedom obviously also contradicts the first contradiction. But it contradicts only what is bad about abstract freedom. The *disharmony* between the *form of the freedom* and the *natural content* [of freedom] annuls concrete freedom, such that it provides the form of the freedom with an *appropriate content* and evokes harmony and accord between the form and the content. But the *obligatory coming* out of this disharmony into harmony negates and totally excludes precisely what should remain. Namely, the factor of the form, the factor of the *freedom* available in the disharmony. Hegel provided *form* with appropriate content. But *form* itself is *annihilated*, and not merely as *empty form*/distinction whereby the form, previously without real content, could now maintain such content—but now totally. For Hegel, the transition from formal to real freedom is a necessity. The *essentiality* of formal freedom disappears. This essentiality constituted the sole "content" of freedom's lack-of-content, namely that *it necessitates itself to nothing*. (35-37)

Summary of translated passages
At the onset of history, according to Hegel, the human being sinned and

thereby created a split within itself between good and evil. The sin, however, was necessary for human development. For Hirsch, the human being was faced with a choice between realizing potential freedom and realizing potential sensuous naturality. Sin was neither inevitable nor necessary. It could and should have always remained a possibility. Nor did sin have ontological reality. It had no effect upon God, who remained the ground for realizing freedom whether or not the human being sinned. As the human being pursued freedom it became increasingly conscious of God and of itself as God's image.

THE POSSIBILITY OF SINNING

Sin is not [equivalent to] natural, finite life. By nature the human being is not sinful; no sin adheres to it naturally. Neither vice nor virtue is inherent to what is natural. Each natural inclination is, for-itself, neither evil nor good. But the human being cannot remain in this [condition of] *pure naturality*, and *never* does. The natural condition [of the human being], the first, immediate condition, has a contradiction, one *that the human being cannot endure* and *must* get beyond. Why is the human being placed immediately into a condition [of contradiction]? Because it is essential to the concept of freedom *for the human being to be indebted to itself for everything*. The human is, clearly, the first [creation] *to make what it is, out of itself*. This immediate natural condition [may] also push itself too far; but it *only* is doing the pushing. To where? That is life to the human being.

The human being is not just left to choose among all the *conditions which are offered to it accidentally* [from the outside]. This is just the initial self-contradicting natural condition which the human *must go beyond*. If all that was offered anew to the human being was merely *accidental*; if the human being only had to *capriciously choose* among the multiple conditions offered to it, it would still be at its original point of departure. All the *content* is provided from the outside. All there is, is a form of freedom empty of content, where the human being chooses randomly *one* from among all the conditions offered to it accidentally. But just as little may only *one* condition beyond the natural condition, supposedly appropriate to it, be offered the human being, namely that of *freedom-being-realized*. For then the human would then be *forced* to realize the freedom, and this contradicts freedom's essence.

How to go beyond the first natural condition and *thereby maintain human freedom*, which is the only reason the human being was placed into this contradiction in its original natural condition? The human being must be offered two essentially new conditions to choose from. Two such circumstances are indeed offered to the human being. *One* is the path to true life and is true life itself. The *other* is the path of illusory life, to death, and is death itself. One is the path to virtue and real freedom; the other is that of sin. They offer themselves to the human being directly, although they do not have *the same* value. The human being knows that it must take the first path only, that it alone is appropriate to it, that it alone has the true significance for the freedom which [at this point] is still empty of content. The human being knows that it *can* take the other path, and that it should not.

The human being does not first come to consciousness of sin through real sin. It does not first come to *consciousness of virtue through realized virtue.* Before the human has even sinned, and before it has yet become virtuous, it knows both and their value to the human being.

The human being's original natural circumstance contained two factors: 1) *Freedom.* 2) *Naturality*. The contradiction between the two factors reaches human consciousness. Freedom cannot come into its own because of the *naturality which adheres* to it externally, while naturality cannot validate itself because of the freedom which adheres to it. To get beyond this mutual struggle between freedom and its naturality, the human being must achieve victory for one or the other. Either freedom is achieved at the cost of the naturality adhering to it externally or naturality is achieved at the cost of freedom. The human being knows that its freedom, its "I," is *its most characteristic essence*, and that naturality, by contrast, is only *external* to it. It knows that it is appropriate to obtain victory for freedom. The human being also knows that its naturality seeks victory over the freedom opposed to it. And not in such a way that naturality *remains with its regular activity*—where its power is equal to freedom's and was not victorious. Rather, where it elevates its regular activity, feverishly advancing it. *Naturality*, that is, *wants to preserve sensuous lust.*

Achieving victory for freedom is not a matter of *leaving freedom as it is*, and weakens the power of the naturality opposed to it. This never succeeds. The freedom before the human being is empty. It needs content. As long as freedom has no content *of its own*, it must draw content from the naturality which contradicts it. Freedom achieves victory *where it elevates its own activity*. It is secured only where the human being yields totally to freedom; seeks the content of its activity in free-dom itself; seeks to realize freedom's content and purpose; and where the naturality opposed to freedom is used as the necessary and *wholly appropriate material* for achieving human freedom. Freedom is not a *one-time* action but a *perpetual activity* of life. The free human being is *always* active in freedom. It is always striving, not to *exclude* the sensu-ous, but to use it as the means for service to freedom.

But the human being could also take the other path. Sensuality and naturality are recognized as external to the human being, but they seek to make themselves [internally and] *exclusively* valid, and do so at the *cost of freedom*. They seek to elevate their normal activity, offering the human being *increased sensual lust*. If the human being takes this direc-tion, lust will achieve the value of "I," of the human being's freedom. This is sin.

The human being is originally offered two continual paths for going beyond self-contradictory *natural freedom*. One is in the *direction of free-dom*. It makes freedom's activity the human being's own activity and reduces the sensuous into the service of freedom. *Here the human being makes itself truly free.* Through *its own action*, the human being helps its freedom become its sole appropriate content. With the other, the hu-man being goes in the direction of *naturality*, letting naturality's activ-ity increase, and reduce human freedom into the service of naturality. Here *the human being also makes itself into what it is*, [namely unfree]. The essence of the human being is *to make itself free*, and this necessity includes the possibility of making *itself unfree*. This unfreedom cannot persist in pure naturality any more than freedom can. Pure naturality is *given* to the human being and the human being finds naturality before it. *But the human being makes itself free or unfree.* Accordingly, *the possibil-ity of sinning, just as the possibility of virtue, should be viewed as necessarily wanted by God*. For only if there is this possibility can the human being go beyond natural freedom [in a way which is] *appropriate to its essence and without contradiction. But this possibility for sinning should also remain a pure possibility and never become a reality.*

Note: The point about the *possibility of evil*, that evil is *necessary as a possibility* in order to preserve the factor of formal freedom for the human being, but *should remain only a possibility*; never *become a real-ity*, but nevertheless could become a *reality*, is the turning point, the crossroads, where our path separates off from that of the most recent [i.e. Hegelian] philosophy. It is the *theme* of Judaism, the shibboleth, by which Judaism is distinguished from paganism and Christianity.

For Hegel and many who emulate him, sin is a *necessary pathway* to the good. Not *just possible sin, but real sin,* he proposed, is necessary in order to reach the good. In the beginning, idyllic, natural situation, the human being was *one* with *mother earth, one* with nature, and know neither good nor evil. Then, humans led a *happy dream life.* The *contradiction* between good and evil had to enter into such a childlike natural condition, because humanity should not remain *in this* naïve condition. A necessary division within the human breast occurred. People viewed division, which negated the non-viable condition, *as the result of the guilt of human sin.* When humans achieved consciousness of good and evil, or found their natural condition in a state of division, they believed that this came from sin. This is the Hegelian theory.

According to Hegel, evil differentiates itself from the good, in that it is the [ground for the division between good and evil] and the *necessary means* of becoming good. Initially, there was an abstract *union between the human being* and its own nature. Humanity lived unconsciously. Like the animal, it was *at one* with itself and with the outer world. But this union could not remain; the human being [according to Hegel], unlike the animal, should not live in union with its own nature. That union must display itself as *that which it [really] is,* namely the *contradiction* [between good and evil] in the human breast. The human being separated itself from nature, and entered into *opposition* with it. Divided within itself, it looked upon the division—which, as the *first negation* of the first inappropriate condition, was—as the consequence of guilt or of sin, and as itself, sinful. The *negation* of this *first negation* followed. That is, the division—a necessary point of passage—was in turn annulled. According to Hegel, virtue was a higher form of union. It was *only dreamed* of as being the first union, and not present in reality, because as soon as the human being came to consciousness, it went beyond the first union. The human being was already divided and, according to Hegel, already caught in sin.

It is easy to see why philosophy had to arrive at this theory. Philosophy wants to conceptualize everything, and conceptualization means *perceiving something in its necessity.* This includes the *necessity* of sin. Philosophy makes this easy for itself by *calling sin something which is not sin at all* [but only a division in human consciousness, or the root of this division]. What *really is sin is totally ignored*. The human being may view the division [between itself and nature, between good and evil within itself], as neither its fault nor its doing. This is *because the human being [finds itself facing] the division*. By nature, the human being is divided, without its own input. [Real] sin first enters in, depending upon *the manner and way in which the human being seeks to get beyond the division*.

The consequence of the Hegelian theory is pantheism. [For Hegel], at all times, the *one divine life* divides from its self within nature. Divine life comes to consciousness of this division *in the human mind/ spirit*, where the separation is affirmed, negated and sublimated. I am convinced that Hegel can only be overcome if precisely this *point is kept in view*. Hegel's theories of *negation* and *negation-of-negation* are wholly applicable in nature, where everything *follows the law with necessity*. But as we have seen, the human mind/spirit must have two paths in order to go beyond *the first negation and reach the negation of negation*. We will see to what one-sided and false understanding of Genesis (chapters two and three) this Hegelian theory leads.

According to Judaism's basic doctrine, sin is not only the *passage point to the good*. It remains *possible* throughout life. God desires sin as a pure *possibility* so that the human being can appropriate piety for *itself* in a *free manner*. In reality sin is always accidental, and the human being need never sin [See *Nidda* 16ᵇ].

Judaism knows nothing of Christianity's *inherited sin*. Hegel considers it a *conceit* for the pious human being to claim that it *could always be something else if it wanted, that it could also be bad*. [To the contrary], the consciousness—*that the human being could also sin*, or better, *that the human being could fall into sin*, stays with the human being forever, and does not forsake it until the dying day. Far from being *a conceit*, it is a *source of all humility*. This must not be expressed incorrectly by adding: "If *the human being wanted*." The pious person never speaks so. Piety is not some *stubborn* child's play, as if I would be happy if it were possible to go beyond it. Or I would want to have myself reflected in mastery, even over piety, always having the *power* of my "I" in view, never piety. This is conceit, sin, not piety.... (38-48)

CONCRETE CONSCIOUSNESS OF GOD

Only when the human being *realizes* its freedom, *makes itself truly free*, only when it reduces the life of naturality into a *means for* spiritual life—ever conscious that it *could* fall into sin, but that it neither *should* nor must—does the human being arrive at true consciousness of God. Here, the human being knows itself as *concretely free* and *master over everything sensuous*. Not only is sensuality unable to force the human to do something it does not want; the human being appropriates this sensuality into its service and fully masters it. This freedom, in principle as well *as being a possibility for the human being's appropriation*, is God's gift. God made it possible for the human to become free. *God must therefore be truly free, the true master over everything.* "Everything has been created in a way to serve God's honor" (*Yoma* 38^{b}). Here, God is not a "*Beyond*." Insofar as the human recognizes itself as free, it knows itself as God's *image* and *beloved child*. God is *eternally free*. God granted the human being the possibility to raise itself to divine freedom. In its freedom and continued possibility for freedom's realization, the human being recognizes itself as part of divine life, *as ascending to and sublimated into divine life. Here the will of God and the will of the human being are absolutely one. The human being lives in true union with God*, with itself, and with [sensuous] nature which has now yielded totally to it.

But the human being also recognizes that divine life is absolutely independent of its own. The human being could sin by realizing what should remain only *possible*; and insofar as it opposes and falls away from God. (Not in the sense of the Hegelian schools, where the fall is a *necessary* factor of opposition. Ours is only a figurative fall). The human being knows that by *realizing* its "could" in this respect, it turns itself against *itself*. It has not damaged divine life in the slightest. *God does not fall away from God*. The human being *falls away from God,* and does so without changing divine life in the slightest.

Out of His love for the human being, God wants to know it as truly free. This divine love also gives the human being the possibility to sin and not reach towards true freedom. But divine love does not change even if the human being truly sins. God really remains the same, and God's love for the human being remains the same. The love *shows itself now in the punishment of sin,* which brings the knowledge of what real sin is in fact to the sinners' consciousness. Namely: *contradiction-*

in-itself, the contradiction of the human being against its own essence, the contradiction within the human breast. It is not a contradiction within God. With this we have already shifted to an entirely different ground, namely to the concrete (48-49).

Chapter Three

HETERONOMOUS REVELATION

3.0. INTRODUCTION: SALOMON LUDWIG STEINHEIM; SAMSON RAPHAEL HIRSCH; FRANZ ROSENZWEIG

The thinkers presented so far breathed the air of the emancipation-world's universalistic values. They participated in the move from inviolable tradition, with its metaphysical bases, to *Wissenschaft*'s rational assertions and theories of knowledge. They subscribed to the shift from a cosmically-structured, absolute reality which was regarded as independent of human consciousness to structures which were internal to that consciousness. They shared as well in the ideological shift from asserting Judaism as being metaphysically true, to the relative truth of Judaism as seen *vis-à-vis* other religions.

Specifically, in the first chapter I presented thinkers for whom the dialectical principle governed encounters between revelation (belief) and reason (philosophy). Mendelssohn withdrew from the two, as from two poles, towards a center which remained unclear. Reggio endeavored to explore and explicate the centered interchange. Krokhmal engaged in constructing the discipline of philosophical theology. In the second chapter I described thinkers who grounded the Jewish religion in rationalist, primarily autonomous human endeavors, which I have identified as intellection and self-consciousness. In this group, Maimon asserted the perfectibility of the human intellect through adherence to the divine mind (active intellect). Samuel Hirsch identified self-consciousness with the development of freedom, in the dual contexts of the God-man relationship and of religious history, while Formstecher focused on self-consciousness as a form of human participation in God's world-soul, and as the driving force for spiritualizing nature.

In this third section I offer another point of departure, that of revelation, to which history adapts. The grounding of thought in revelation belonged to pre-emancipation thought. Our thinkers adhered to this model as well, but they also engaged the values of the post-emancipation world. Notably, they factored history and rationalism into their frameworks. Steinheim took the position that the basis of Judaism was revelation, and that revelation was mutually exclusive with reason (a position that was demonstrable by self-critical reason). Revelation was also central for Samson Raphael Hirsch. While he did not regard revelation and reason as mutually exclusive, he did relegate reason to the periphery. According to both Steinheim and Hirsch, human (Jewish) history has adapted, and must adapt, to revelation. In their view, revelation did not develop according to history (as it did for Ascher and Einhorn). Rosenzweig likewise considered revelation to be central, but also viewed it as extending into history through Christianity (a theme anticipated by Samuel Hirsch in 1841).

SALOMON LUDWIG STEINHEIM

For Steinheim, reason's highest achievement was the recognition of the superiority of revelation—the recognition of reason's limits in the face of the reality of Sinai revelation, just as it recognized its limits before the realities of nature. Steinheim separated reason from revelation entirely, the one being autonomous and anthropocentric and the other heteronomous and theocentric. The very content of revelation (unity of God, human freedom, world-creation) was antithetical to rational deliberation. Nor did revelation belong to history. It rather burst into history for history to adapt to it. The texts selected and translated for this volume illustrate these principles.[1] In his attack upon Mendelssohn, Steinheim claimed that Mendelssohn's thought aligned itself with the pagan-philosophical position, where the God of revelation was brought down to nature and reason, depriving Israel of its pure source from Sinai. In his response to *The Religious Philosophy of the Jews*, he criticized Samuel Hirsch for setting aside revelation and developing a doctrine of Judaism out of the human mind/spirit and inborn reason, one that was dialectically articulated. Steinheim placed Formstecher's dialectical approach alongside Hirsch's, and associated both with the errors of Men-

---

1   Parts of Steinheim's *Die Offenbarung* have been translated into English. Joshua O. Haberman, *Philosopher of Revelation: The Life and Thought of S. L. Steinheim. Including an annotated translation with a biographical and analytical introduction of the entire first volume of his four volume work, and selections from volumes 2, 3 and 4* (Philadelphia: JPS, 1990).

delssohn. In *Neither Right, Nor Left*, Steinheim recognized that reason could be used for establishing ethics, even for understanding belief, but asserted that the content of revelation remained inaccessible to it. He drew categorical distinctions between paganism and revelation with regard to history. The one moved from an era of purity to apocalypse, the other from sin to redemption. While the pagan-rational mind was about finitude and relativity, the revelational experience was of infinitude and absolute reality. After distinguishing Judaism's creation from that conceived of by Kant, Steinheim charted the categorical distinction between the realms of philosophical formulation and revelation.

SAMSON RAPHAEL HIRSCH

A year after Steinheim published the first volume of his *Revelation*, Samson Raphael Hirsch (1808-1888), founder and leader of neo-Orthodoxy, published his *Nineteen Letters on Judaism*. The next year he published *Horeb: An Essay on Israel's Duties in the Dispersion*. Hirsch had studied in the Mannheim yeshiva under Jakob Ettlinger and Isaac Bernays (1792-1847), and then at the University of Bonn, where he took courses in Greek, Latin, history and philosophy. He first served as rabbi in Oldenberg, Emden, and from 1851 on in Frankfurt am Main.[2]

For Hirsch, *Torah*-revelation at Sinai, the essence of Judaism, was a heteronomous act, an absolute fact which remained outside historical change. Revelation was its own testimony, and was to be accepted on its own terms as an act of divine will—to which reason was applicable only after the fact. As with natural science, where nature was first recognized as established independently and only then studied by scientific methodology, so revelation was to be accepted according to its own terms and only then tested through the use of reason. Hirsch described nature and *Torah* as two *a priori* revelations, to which reason applied in an *a posteriori* way. He wrote that:

---

2   Samson Raphael Hirsch's *Nineteen Letters*, *Horeb* and *Chumash: The Five Books of Torah*, which are his main works, are readily available in English. On Hirsch's life and thought see Noah H. Rosenbloom, *Tradition in the Age of Reform: The Religious Philosophy of Samson Raphael Hirsch* (Philadelphia: JPS, 1976); Robert Liberles, *Religious Conflict in Social Context: The Resurgence of Orthodox Judaism in Frankfort am Main 1838-1877* (Westport: Greenwood Press, 1985); Yitshak Heinemann, "Studies on R. Samson Raphael Hirsch (Hebrew)," *Sinai* 24 (1949): 249-271.

In nature, all phenomena stand before us as indispensable facts, and we can only endeavor *a posteriori* to ascertain the law of each and the connection of all.... The
same principles must be applied to the investigation of
the *Torah*. *Torah* is a fact to us, like heaven and earth....
In the *Torah*, even as in nature, God is the ultimate
cause. In the *Torah*, even as in nature, no fact may be
denied even though the reason and the connection may
not be understood. What is true in nature is true also in
Torah; the traces of divine wisdom must ever be sought
after.... The ordinances of *Torah* must be law for us, even
if we do not comprehend the reason and the purpose of
a single one.[3]

Accordingly, biblical criticism, generated from the humanistic, secular
world of belief and opinion, was extraneous to Jewish belief, since the
Torah was the objective reality of the revelation given by God, and not a
human creation. Just as nature could not be reduced to the point of being grounded upon the rustlings of the human heart, *Torah*'s truth could
not be established on the basis of man's subjective reflection. Biblical
criticism, which purported to evaluate *Torah* from the outside, compromised that objectivity.[4] However, while Sinai revelation was a *sui generis*
supernatural event, an incursion of eternity into time and space, there
was also a type of revelation that was within the Jew. Truth and justice,
Hirsch posited, were God's revelations within the inner self; justice was
an expression of a person's recognition from inner revelation. That is,
human conscience served as an instrument through which divine will
disclosed itself. This did not imply autonomy. It meant, rather, that ex-

---

3   Hirsch, *Igeret* 18, footnote 6, in *Igerot Tsafon: Neunzehn Briefe Über Judenthum* (Altona:
Johann Friedrich Hammerich, 1836); and *The Nineteen Letters*, trans. Karin Paritzky,
revised and with a comprehensive commentary by Joseph Elias (Jerusalem: Feldheim,
1995), 271-272.
4   Rotenstreich, *Ha'mahshavah Ha'yehudit Be'et Ha'hadashah: Toledot U'mamashut* (Tel Aviv:
Am Oved, 1966), 114-115; Schweid, "Gilui Hama'or Ha'penimi Shel Ha'torah: Mishnato Shel
Ha'rav Shimshon Rafael Hirsch," in *Toledot Filosofiyat Ha'dat Ha'yehudit Bi'zeman Ha'hadash*,
vol 2, *Hokhmat Yisrael Ve'hitpathut Ha'tenuot Ha'moderni'ot* (Tel Aviv: Am Oved, 2002), 108-
119; and "Ha'yahadut Ke'mahut Al'historit: Mishnato Shel Shimshon Rafael Hirsch," in
Toledot Ha'hagut Ha'yehudit Be'et Ha'hadashah: Ha'meah Ha'tesha Esrei (Tel Aviv: Ha'kibuts
Ha'meuhad, 1978), 291-391.

ternal, supernatural revelation had a dialectically related counterpart with the Jew. While revelation ultimately came from without, it also resided within.[5]

In *Der Jude und seine Zeit* (1854) Hirsch wrote that while Judaism's role was to educate the times of history, the times were not to educate Judaism. God established Judaism, from its very beginning, in opposition to historical times. Thus, for thousands of years Judaism was a singular protest against the pagan world. When this opposition was removed, it was not because Judaism had adapted to the non-Jewish environment of the era, but because sparks of revelation were entering the non-Jewish world. Were Judaism to form itself according to the times, there would, Hirsch declared, no longer be any need for it.[6] In principle, he was opposed to historicizing Judaism. Its law could not be restrained for him by the limits within historical process and temporality. Temporal changes did not master the law, nor crack apart its integrity; what lasted was preferable to what changed. The true essence of Judaism was removed from historical process; revelation was absolute, and stood opposed to the subjectivizing of religion. Similarly, the inner life of the Jew remained untouched by the historical process; the Orthodox Jew prayed outside the world in which he lived—and then returned to a world to which his prayer did not pertain.[7] Hirsch's Israel, Schweid explains, functioned in terms of two histories, inner and outer, which blended at the end of time. The truths of *Torah* revelation did not change. Israel's temporal history from the patriarchs through exile and on to redemption was a matter of becoming educated to eternal *Torah*, and reverting back to *Torah*. Thus, on Passover, each celebrant saw himself as leaving Egypt, and on *Shevuot* as receiving *Torah* on Sinai. Israel was also involved with the nations of the world, but as an example of the life of *Torah*, and in order to declare that God was the sole creator and that the goal of life was to fulfill His will. The *Torah* did not change, but

5   Hirsch, *Horev: Versuche Über Jissroels Pflichten in der Zerstreuung* (Altona: Johann Friedrich Hammerich, 1837), para. 325 and 328; Walter S. Wurzburger, "Samson Raphael Hirsch's Doctrine of Inner Revelation," in *From Ancient Israel to Modern Judaism: Intellect in Quest of Understanding. Essays in Honor of Marvin Fox*, vol. 4 (Atlanta: Scholars Press, 1989), 3-12.
6   Hirsch, "Der Jude und seine Zeit [Oktober 1854]," in *Gesammelte Schriften*, vol. 1 (FaM: J. Kauffmann, 1902), 148-159.
7   Rotenstreich, *Ha'mahshavah Ha'yehudit*, 114-115; and *Tradition and Reality* (New York, 1972), 113.

rather, the nations came closer to it. The *Torah* Jew was not the child of time; he stood above it, to influence it. The inner realm of Israel's history was of the eternal *Torah*, the unchanging ideal. The outer realm, surrounding it, involved interaction with the surrounding culture and defective history. At the end of time, Israel's absolute and relative existences would blend.[8] Hirsch wrote:

> When the scales have ceased to swing, the spirit which understands itself, its history and its law will have pervaded all the members of Israel. When the branch gone forth from Israel shall have accomplished its mission and fought to victory a battle of another kind in the midst of our non-Jewish brethren; when the free gaze uplifted to the All-One, and the awareness of inner moral power shall have conquered whatever dims the eye and corrupts noble vigor—then the book of history, with its conclusive lesson, will also penetrate the spirits of all men.[9]

FRANZ ROSENZWEIG

Franz Rosenzweig's life and thought centered on revelation. His personal experiences on *Yom Kippur* in 1913 and during World War I led him to believe that revealed Judaism was immune to historical events, and his study of Jewish religious texts provided access to revelation. He came to see the Jewish people as a single entity, in harmony, rooted in that revelation. In the course of his long confinement with paralysis, he studied the biblical book of Isaiah as a focus of Scriptural revelation. He replaced Mendelssohn's use of *"der Ewige"* with "I shall become what I shall become," in order to convey the act and principle of revelation. He also wrote of Israel's residing in the light of eternal life, apart from history, through the presentness of the *Tenakh*.

Rosenzweig articulated the meaning of revelation, the central concept of his religion, in terms of tensions. While universally available, it was also a particular event of the past for Judaism and Christianity. A

---

8   See especially *Igeret* 7. Schweid, "Gilui Hama'or Ha'penimi," in *Toledot Filosofiyat Ha'dat* and "Ha'yahadut Ke'mahut Al-historit," in *Toledot Ha'hagut Ha'yehudit*.
9   Hirsch, *Igeret* 18, in *Igerot Tsafon*.

single occurrence which transformed the individual, it was also a continuing process of God's bestowing His love. Though spoken in dialogue, it was a mystical union. God initiated and dominated the love, yet the individual was responsible for upholding it. And God was revealed in time, but also in eternity. The God of revelation perceived by temporal man was inseparable from historical moments. The Jew of blood perceived immediately the purely eternal God from within the fiery eternity which the Jew alone endured.

For Rosenzweig, revelation related constructively to history, through Christianity. While for Hirsch and Steinheim the history of Israel in time and world events needed to adapt to absolute revelation, for Rosenzweig Israel remained eternal while Christianity channeled Israel into time. Israel resided ecstatically within God's light, the light of His countenance shining eternally within each Jew. The nation resided at the trans-temporal *eschaton* of history, where creation and revelation became subsumed into redemption. Thus located at the center of the star, Israel resided outside history, as the Jew was tied eternally to redemption. Christianity, rooted in redemption, nevertheless moved into history, and so conveyed Judaism into time. Christianity's mediation, for Rosenzweig, was a constructive process, integral to the world's entering redemption.

3.1. SALOMON LUDWIG STEINHEIM (1789-1866)[10]

Steinheim, for Hans-Joachim Schoeps, was the first Jewish theologian of the modern age. He was born in Bruchhausen bei Ottbergen, Germany, attended the *Gymnasium Christianium* in Altona, and studied at the universities of Kiel and Berlin (Like Samuel Hirsch, he studied Greek philosophy under Christian August Brandis), and then returned

---

10   Steinheim's work includes: *Die Offenbarung nach dem Lehrbegriff der Synagoge*, vol. 1 (FaM: Siegmund Schmerber, 1835); vol. 2 (Leipzig: Leopold Schnauss, 1856); vol. 3 (Leipzig: Oskar Leiner, 1863); vol. 4 (Altona: Gebrüder Bonn, 1865); "Von dem Gedanken eines Volkes Gottes und einer Offenbarung: Einige Bedenken über die Rezension von Nitzsch, *System der christlichen Lehre* in der *Allg. Lit. Zeitung* nr. 38 vom März 1838, soweit sie das Judentum angeht," *Allgemeine Zeitung des Judentums* nos. 74, 77, 80, 81, 85 (1838); *Moses Mendelssohn und seine Schule in ihrer Beziehung zur Aufgabe des neuen Jahrhunderts der alten Zeitrechnung* (Hamburg: Hoffmann und Campe, 1840); "Synagoge und Tempel: Ein modernes Schisma," *Allgemeine Zeitung des Judentums* 6, no. 38 (17 September 1842): 562-569; 6, no. 39 (24 September 1842): 578-583; "Religionsphilosophie: *Die Religionsphilosophie der Juden* ... von Dr. Sam. Hirsch, Rabbiner," *Literaturblatt des Orients* 20 (14 May 1844): 308-313 through 31 (30 July 1844): 483-487; "Die Zukunftslehre der Offenbarung und die Messiasidee," *Der Israelitische Volkslehrer* 5 (1855): 345-357; "Weder zur Rechten noch zur Linken," *Der Israelitische Volkslehrer* 7 (1857): 57-62; 79-87; 119-125; 154-162; 182-191.
       On Steinheim's life and thought, see: Hans Andorn, "Die problem-geschichtlichen Zusammenhänge von S. L. Steinheims Offenbarung nach dem Lehrbegriff der Synagoge," *Monatsschrift für Geschichte und Wissenschaft des Judentums* 74, nrs. 11-12 (November/ December): 437-457; Isaac Eisenstein Barzilay, "Moses Mendelssohn," *Jewish Quarterly Review* 70, no. 1 (July 1961): 69-93 and 70, no. 2 (October 1961): 177-186; Heinz Mosheh Graupe, "Steinheim und Kant," *LBIY* 5 (1960): 140-176; Avraham Yitshak Horowitz, "Darkhah shel Torah," in *Emek Yehoshofat* (St. Louis, MO: Moinester, 1917/18): 39-44; Gary Lease, "Salomon Ludwig Steinheim's Influence—Hans-Joachim Schoeps, A Case Study," *LBIY* 29 (1984): 383-404; Benjamin Rippner, "Salomon Ludwig Steinheim," *Monatsschrift für Geschichte und Wissenschaft des Judentums* 21, no. 8 (August 1872): 347-357; no. 9 (September 1872): 395-407; Hans-Joachim Schoeps, "Salomon Ludwig Steinheim," in *Israel und Christenheit. Jüdisch-Christliches Religionsgespräch in neunzehn Jahrhunderten* (Munich: Ner Tamid, 1961), 138-146; H. J. Schoeps, H. M. Graupe, and G. H. Goeman, *Salomon Ludwig Steinheim zum Gedenken* (Leiden: E. J. Brill, 1966); Julius H. Schoeps, Anja Bagel-Bohlan, Margret Heitmann, and Dieter Lohmeier, *Philo des 19. Jahrhunderts, Studien zu Salomon Ludwig Steinheim* (Hildesheim: Georg Olms, 1993); Mosheh Schwarcz, "Musag Ha'herut Be'dat Ha'filosofit Shel Schelling Ube'dat Ha'torah Shel Shelomoh Shtaynhaym," in *Safah, Mitos, Omanut* (1966), 89-142; Aharon She'ar-Yishuv (Wolfgang Schmidt), "Steinheim's Beziehung zur jüdischen Tradition," *Zeitschrift für Religion und Geistesgeschichte* 46 no. 1 (1994): 1-14; "Salomon Ludwig Steinheim, ein deutsch-jüdischer Polyhistor im 19. Jahrhundert," *Menorah* 1 (1990): 47-65, and *The Theology of S. L. Steinheim* (Leiden: Brill, 1986). Steinheim, *Shelomoh Levi Shtaynhaym: Iyunim Be'mishnato* (Jerusalem: Magnes, 1994) and *Shtaynhaym Al Hitgalut Ve'teokratiyah: Mivhar Ketavav Shel Shelomoh Levi Shtaynhaym* (Jerusalem: R. Mass, 1989), both works translated and edited by Aharon She'ar-Yishuv.

to Kiel. His degree was in medicine, which he practiced in Altona from 1814 until he moved to Rome in 1845. Steinheim's writings covered a broad area, ranging from medicine and politics to his area of primary interest, Jewish religious philosophy and theology. He had no formal training in Judaism, and little knowledge of Hebrew. His Jewish sources were limited to Hebrew Scripture in translation, selected medieval philosophers, and Mendelssohn's *Book of the Paths of Peace*.

Steinheim lived and thought across a spectrum, with Judaism related to the outside world at one end and Judaism generated from within itself on the other. Thus, on one hand, his early academic world was Christian; he had considered conversion to Christianity, and when he died in Zurich he was buried in a Protestant church cemetery—though later he was reinterred in the Jewish cemetery in Altona. He was dedicated to Jewish emancipation, an active participant in the effort to gain Jewish rights in Schleswig-Holstein, and an admirer of Gabriel Riesser (1806-1863), a champion of Jewish emancipation in Germany. He also supported the Reform movement and scientific study, and criticized the neo-Orthodox leader Samson Raphael Hirsch for indiscriminate veneration of anything that had been accrued to Judaism over the centuries. At the other end of the spectrum, he hoped that emancipation would turn Jews back to the Jewish moral and religious centers of life. He advocated neo-Orthodoxy's commitment to absolute revelation, an approach that sought to clear rationality away and make room for revealed religion.[11]

Steinheim's turn to an internal Jewish center and to absolute revelation was tied to his understanding of Judaism *vis-à-vis* paganism. While the pagan deity was created by human beings and developed by his reason, Judaism's God was independent of man and his world. According to paganism, all effects had causes and the deity was the ultimate cause. According to Judaism, God created the causal sequence itself. While for paganism the deity was subordinate to nature, acted within the boundary of materiality and causality, and man was a naturalistic mechanism, according to Judaism God and man created freely and ethical life was possible. For paganism the world was eternal and being could not come from nothing (*ex nihilo*), while for Judaism the

---

11   See Schweid, "Ha'hitgalut Shemi'ever Li'tevunat Ha'adam: Mishnato Shel Shelomoh Ludvig Shtaynhaym," in *Toledot Ha'hagut Ha'yehudit Be'et Ha'hadashah: Ha'meah Ha'tesha Esrei* (Erets Yisrael: Ha'kibuts Ha'meuhad, 1978), 281-282.

world had a beginning and an end and being could come out of nothing. Paganism proposed that this world was the best possible, but Judaism did not take this for granted. And finally, while for paganism the source for knowledge was the world, for Judaism it was God. Steinheim included idealist philosophy as part of the pagan realm, for its deity belonged to man's epistemological processes, did not have its own center, and human consciousness was a condition for the deity's self realization; this worldview was anthropocentric as opposed to theocentric. He viewed Formstecher and Samuel Hirsch as idealist (hence pagan) philosophers, as they made rational necessity ultimate and their God was inherent to human reason and logic.

Revelation was at the heart of Steinheim's religious philosophy. He focused on separating reason from out of revelation, and he identified reason's greatest achievement as the recognition of revelation's superior status. Referring to Kant's antinomies (i.e., contradictory ideas about one and the same object of thought that were nevertheless equally necessary), he demonstrated how, in the end, reason proved impotent in grasping reality. For example, when water cooled to four degrees it condensed, but when it froze it expanded.[12] According to reason, therefore, the world ran according to causality, but according to experience there was free will. While the pure idea of God meant the unification of infinite multiplicity, this was logically impossible. Reason could not conceive of the world not having a beginning; since matter could only come from other matter the world had to be infinitely old. In the end, then, reason could not bring man to understand reality, either sensible or insensible. Its greatest achievement would be to recognize that the truth about reality had to be drawn from another source and to set limits for itself, to "imprison" itself and open the way for revelation. Steinheim waited for revelation to burst into his experience from the outside, to become the presupposition for the rational process. He adapted Kant's distinction between "legislative" reason (deductive, *a priori,* and constructive in terms of unifying doctrine into system) and "critical" reason (inductive, *a posteriori*, and destructive in terms of examining the faculty of knowledge), saying that legislative reason injected concepts, produced from out of itself, into consciousness. Critical reason utilized experience, recognized reason's limits, and held revelation to be true precisely

---

12 Steinheim, *Die Offenbarung,* vol. 2 (Leipzig: Leopold Schnauss, 1856), 45-47.

because it was not produced by legislative reason.

Revelation, for Steinheim, was characteristically by other-than-reason. It was dramatic and communicated through speech. It belonged to a territory which man did not know by himself and which he could not produce autonomously. According to revelation: 1) God was a simple, single unity, not in terms of abstract, infinite multiplicity, but in terms of a unified personality which addressed man and the world. 2) Man was not doomed by his natural condition but free to respond to divine commands. 3) The world was created, not self-generated, and created by God's will. According to the categories of reason, by contrast, there was either unity of multiplicity or multiplicity of unity; subjection to law or self-obligation to reason; and either the world was infinitely old or it was self-generated.

Judaism's special revelation, rooted outside human history with its rational and autonomous dimensions, burst into historical time with the patriarchs and remained until Sinai. While revelation remained unaffected by history, history adapted to it. There were four historical eras, resembling the stages identified by Fichte: Childhood (patriarchs through Judges), when the Israelites blindly obeyed revealed commandments as appropriate to nomadic life; Youth (Judges through first exile), when the imposition of leadership was resisted by efforts to restore the unlimited freedom of earlier times. Adolescence (rabbinic period) when the sense of self grew and the spirit searched out reasons for revelation—although, in the face of the rabbinic authority of the yeshiva, in vain; adulthood (modernity), when the "father" who was revelation could be understood and appreciated, and the commandments of *Torah* could be obeyed out of a sense of family loyalty.[13] Steinheim characterized the adaptation of history to revelation thusly: Like an indissoluble crystal, the revealed idea of God (which involved a moral principle according to which human holiness and freedom should overcome the environment and God's spirit overcame chaos) came from beyond history and entered the life of Israel. Over the generations, drawing upon the soul of Israel on an unconscious level, the revealed idea bound the people together. Because the idea conflicted with the realm of reason

---

13   Fichte, "Die fünf Grund-Epochen des Erdenlebens," in *Die Grundzüge des gegenwärtigen Zeitalters* (Berlin: Realschulbuchhandlung, 1806), 4-15. See Hans Andorn, *Sal. Ludw. Steinheim's "Offenbarung nach dem Lehrbegriff der Synagoge"* (Giessen: Thuringia, 1930), 23-27.

and its empirical dimension, other peoples despised and persecuted Israel. Nonetheless, the idea survived and the people who were rooted in it as well. In the end, Steinheim assured the reader, the realm of reason would negate itself, and revelation would become universal.[14]

III.I. Selections from *Moses Mendelssohn and His School as Related to the Problem of the New Generation of the Old Era* (1840), translated by Gershon Greenberg

Summary of translated passages
Steinheim distinguished the pagan-philosophical and rational mind from the mind receptive to revelation. While reason remained vague about the future, for revelation the future was clear: History surged forward to the kingdom of God and the domain of revelation. Imbued with the desire to pursue freedom within history, Israel was committed to working towards that kingdom. Steinheim criticized Mendelssohn's work as a reflection of the pagan-philosophical temperament and as an attempt to derail the pure revealed doctrine of God. Mendelssohn's charismatic act of the shattering of the old to introduce the new was valuable, but the substance of his thought was destructive. He attempted to prove God's existence on the basis of rational evidence and he thus opened a threshold for compromising God by elevating humanity. The thin tree of revelation, however, remained standing after him—a testimony to the strength of the original Moses and against the contemporary Moses. Steinheim looked hopefully towards the return of Judaism to its origin at Sinai.

...Mendelssohn identified rational monotheism with the monotheism of our holy sources, as analogous to commandments which could be understood in themselves and derived from the human mind. This monotheism did not require revelation (*Jerusalem* ch. 2). In his philosophical work *The Morning Hours* he ascribed knowledge about God's existence to reason alone—revelation about it was superfluous or even false. I was unaware that somewhere he had acknowledged the principle of [Reimarus'] *Wolfenbüttel Fragments* that "the books of the Old Testament were not written to reveal religion" (Hermann Samuel Reimarus,

---

14   Steinheim, "Was knüpft den Juden an seinen Volk und seiner Glauben?" *Allgemeine Zeitung der Judentums* 3 nos. 8, 10, 13, 17 (1839): 30-58, *passim.*

Fragmente des Wolfenbüttelschen Ungenannten [Berlin: A. Weyer, 1784, fragment 4], 154). In any case, the entire *The Morning Hours* testifies so definitely to that principle that it could have been his own.

Mendelssohn expelled what was essential from the [Biblical] *Codex*, namely, revelation in its absolute sense. This meant he drove out the sole authority which commanded the aggregate of religious activities— activities which were too often either opposed to the dictates of reason or completely violated the grounds required for a critique of understanding. Obedience to the commands was assured solely and exclusively by veneration for that authority. Mendelssohn thereby became the instrument for the collapse of those very activities he should have commended to his community as duties to God. A thinker of such broad scope, who closely followed the footprints of rationality and proceeded from idea to action, could not have been unaware of the consequences for authoritative ceremony once free use of reason was justified (8-12).

...Our religious knowledge is not pagan-philosophical knowledge— to which the newest school [i.e., Mendelssohn's] ascribes conceptual structures in various stages of development. From now on, for those in the house of Israel, thought about God must reveal itself in its sublime uniqueness to the human capacity for thought. It is to be recognized in its characteristic individuality as *different* than, not merely *distinct* from, all the myths, cosmogonies, philosophies and theologies of common sense or the varied forms of natural human understanding. "You shall *know* today and *take it to your heart*" [Deuteronomy 4:39] says the holy source. It presses upon the human being something which is unnatural and contradictory, the *duty* to *believe*. This is the living faith/belief, the faith/belief in the light of the established wisdom recommended to us and which constitutes our spiritual legacy.

It will not be long before this beatifying faith/belief will be revitalized in Israel's community and regain its stature. The ancient wine will acquire a new and appropriate vessel as beautiful as the mind/spirit which is its internal, ennobled essence. For here, if anywhere, is to be found the vocation of the house of Israel. The "You shall know today and take it to your heart" is the central flame of Israel's national life. It is the seed which Israel sows among the nations of the earth for knowing and truly serving God and developing a kingdom of justice and love upon earth. The contradiction between worldly goods and higher salvation is resolved only by a kingdom of God which is realized on earth. The Old

Testament theocracy based upon the covenant with Jehovah was such a kingdom. The idea of a holy kingdom of God remains the ultimate point of reference to which all spiritual and fruitful reactions of human history are directed. As expressed nowadays, it is the kingdom of freedom of thought and conscience. But our planet is young and the human species is barely past adolescence. Human history has a long way to go before it sees the point of light of that kingdom. There may be a lengthy path before this point of light is formed into the sunlight of the Lord. Meanwhile, this point of light remains, always and forever, the goal towards which the crowded masses move. Only foolish conceit regards the darkness in which the fool is found as being the designated condition of the human species from eternity and for eternity. [No,] this kingdom is the *meta* towards which all of history, with all its ephemeral politics and power manipulations, is thrust....

What reason anticipates about the misty future, the revealed word presents to us with complete clarity and makes into a present program. Rational anticipation draws a picture of a cloudy future. Revelation depicts a two-thousand year past in terms of a perpetual present. With reason, there is presentiment and questioning. With revelation, there is perception and answers. An empty image of thought, a mirage of our fantasy, is distinct from the essential, natural object offered to the human-sensible ability. Given the same evidence and the same degree of certainty, the representative image of God and His relations with the world that is produced and deduced by our natural power of thought is distinct from the representative image we receive exclusively through audible words....

[Creative and Receptive Reason]

Reason clearly has two sorts of functions: a formative, creative one; and a receptive, grasping one. Reason has the means and characteristics to distinguish between the appearance and the object, between the image of a rose projected into the air out of a concave mirror and the real rose which brought this appearance about. Reason has equally certain criteria and distinctive signs for recognizing what is not sensibly perceptible—and whether it is essential or a mirage. Accordingly, reason clarifies whether the idea of God is received from the outside or constructed from out of our capability for thought.

[But] human reason [also mistakenly] purports to be a creative ability in the highest stage, which is related to the idea of God, even though it is forced to concede the absurdity of such pretension in terms of the visible world. This is because of insufficient reflection about the nature of the "facts of consciousness." None of the serious contradictions into which human reason must necessarily fall when it constitutes itself as a creative ability, not solely a perceptive one, have been considered. It has long been known how grossly unsubstantial and contradictory reason can become when it endeavors to construct a world of visible things which is other than the reality found before it. The same exact thing happens with the concept of God. When explicated [rationally], this concept is transformed into a mass of contradictions and quickly annuls itself. The concept loses its conceivability, it becomes an impossibility, as the constituent parts work against each other. The result is a non-existence.

We have already contrasted all creation on the part of reason, creation on the part of so-called rational religion, with the essence of revelation, which does not contradict itself and is authentically and truly existent. The creation of reason and the essence of revelation relate to one another as the magical world of poetic fantasy relates to the real world, as the spiritual object relates to the material object. What is really essential always comes to us from the outside. The history of the Old Testament gives us the revelation which in fact has the character of reality, in contrast to analogous sources, myths, legendary cycles, and doctrines of creation from across the pagan world. The latter carry signs on their brows of having been derived from reason, of agreeing sufficiently with our thinking capacity. They manifest the conceptual process of the human being and allow for the application of the very newest schemes of concept, idea and spirit. The naïve monotheism of the Brahman-doctrine became manifest through Buddhism as essentially polytheistic, as an abstraction, as a conceptual unity. When it comes to Old Testament monotheism, by contrast, there are immediate insurmountable obstacles to any attempt to displace it with philosophical-mythical elements (50-56).

Nature (to use one of my most beloved expressions) has given none of its creatures any ability without simultaneously providing [the means] of realizing it in deed and action. Nature created no need without simultaneously creating its [means of] satisfaction. Every quest and every endeavor [of nature] presupposes its object and confidently expects [that it will be achieved]. Similarly [on the spiritual level], no empty fantasy will cloud out the highest moral striving of the human soul, the deep, sacred endeavor [which resides] within history. To the contrary, the highest moral striving is portrayed in exemplary manner in the Old Testament and partly achieved in its system of theocracy. That theocracy had the best state constitution, a genuine republic and, as that perceptive writer (Karl Gutzkow [1811-1878]) was aware, one given by God: The sole object of the legislation [of the Old Testament theocracy] was that the human being would be free in yielding to the command of the highest eternal freedom, the command of the genuine father of spirits and bodies. The people who presented this idea of acquiescing to the authority could not release themselves from the idea. As long as the human species existed spiritually, i.e., existed at all, no earthly power could liberate the people from that command. Israel takes pleasure in the "yoke of the kingdom of heaven." This yoke is Israel's life-point, the internality to its externality, its truly special position and its stability, until that day, seen in advance and with certainty by the prophets, when the kingdom of God will be realized on earth.

Whether the presentation of this idea will have the power to win over our sages of the west, epigones of pre-revolutionary French free-spiritedness; or convince Berlin philosophical rationalism how false and empty it is, remains uncertain. But I no longer doubt that there is a solid group of scholars among us who do not consider it utterly silly to speak about the ancient revelation as literally true, nor entirely ridiculous to submit heart and soul to it. Gradually, here and there, the clear-sighted eye finds it conceivable not to ridicule and make fun of those "ancient follies which were long-abandoned during the nineteenth century" and even to believe that religion is not only for the masses but, to the contrary, for the most refined of the nations. Then again, it is true that religion is for the masses. There was the rabble driven out of Egypt on account of its "leprosy" (as it was called), filthy within and without, a slime-covered gray shell which hid the royal pearl between its lids. A mangy mob followed its shepherd though the desert, "a land which was not sown" [Jeremiah 2:2], to Sinai. This rabble remained in its compact block, and as the servant of God, was wiser than all the wise people of the west who smirked at its teaching. This suffering, pathetic mob was the *uniquely free people in the shape of the slave.* Until today it carries humankind's salvation around in its tattered cloak. The high aristocracy of the enlightenment, the propagandists of healthy human understanding, probably have difficulty contemplating this (58-60).

The Synagogue never included the sad, pathetic thought of teaching about a revealed God who was disconnected from world and history—as did Epicurus, the Stoics and the noble Asian Brahmans. We teach and believe in one God, this-worldly and other-worldly, father of body and spirit. This God is engaged with the world. His holy will directs the world with the guiding bond of prophecy. He "leads the sun from its dwelling and the moon from its resting place" as the Israelite says (58-59). The Israelite recognizes and knows that his/her God is a God of the living. For out of trust in the living God the Israelite calls out with the Psalmist, "Had the Lord not been for us"—so the Israelite may speak—"had the Lord not been for us: They would have swallowed us alive" [Psalms 124]; "Our soul is rescued as the bird out of the nest of the fowler; the nest is torn apart and we have escaped! Our salvation is in the name of Jehovah, the creator of heaven and earth" [Psalms 124:7-8]. We believe in a "this worldly God who looks upon us, as upon all His works, with grace, love and compassion; whose eye never slumbers and sleeps, the guardian of Israel" (58-59). Even should the Israelite walk into the valley of the shadow of death, he/she trusts in Him, full of hope, and fears no evil. For us, God is therefore a truly this-worldly God. For He is engaged in everything in this universe and watches over and leads everything this-worldly (83-84).

...We have the concept of an "other-worldly" God, as over against paganism's "this-worldly" deity. We believe in a God who has nothing in common with materiality or the stuff of the world; who does not differentiate Himself into two modifications, those of mind/spirit and of body (to describe this according to an ancient, somewhat modified, doctrine). But the moment we speak of God's world governance we [also] have a complete concept of a "this-worldly" God. We have the very special conviction that God is not only the orderer of the world, but its real creator; that He created out of nothing in a way that the human being cannot grasp; that He also made the stuff necessary for His work of creation. This conviction, which sounds so strange to pagans and philosophers, is the midpoint of our whole doctrine of revelation. Our entire theory of human responsibility and of freedom of the mind/spirit, not some theorem about which many could be indifferent, depends upon this conviction. Without it, we could not arrive at the concept of duty, or at ethics.

Were our God not completely free, we, His children, could surely not be free. If we were not free, we could not be responsible. We would not be able to develop our life at a level any higher than that of some special clock mechanism. It would not be a truly human life, where mutual well-being, love renunciation, and the lofty command of duty govern.

All these words would ring hollow and false without this very singular doctrine of creation. We know as well as the pagans do how reason teaches: Out of nothing, nothing comes! This is the well-known ancient refrain, which paganism and its philosophy have continued to repeat until this very day. But to us simple human beings, the "necessary god" of the philosophers amounts to "no god." This expression is contradictory, and the contradiction has often been thrown into the face of paganism and philosophy. It has nevertheless always reproduced itself anew in different forms, and each new philosophical formulation was able to deceive for a time. We have taught about faith/belief [in the other-worldly God] for 4,000 years and have been ridiculed and mocked for doing so. The honor bestowed upon our professorship has been death and banishment. We continue to teach and preach this faith/belief despite the ridicule and scorn. The founder of the New Testament taught it when he was asked for the highest prayer (Mark 12:29-30; Matthew 22:37; Luke 10:27). The great scholar [of science] Galen considered [our] faith/belief foolish, the great poet Horace found us despicable because of our faith/belief, and Tacitus called our way a plague. All of this was because of our "other-worldly" God. Nevertheless, perhaps even the most profound Hegelian could still benefit a little by giving this special thought further attention. Hegel's great predecessor Kant at least did not consider Moses' doctrine of creation tasteless. Compared to similar tenets, he thought it was the most rational (87-89).

I must endure in silence, if critics object and say that I dwell too much on the doctrine of the new school [of Hegel's disciples, notably Wilhelm Vatke]. This school represents the newest threat to our simple doctrine. Leading a revolt against long-term attempts to derail and confuse the pure doctrine of God should be totally unnecessary. But at the same long time, the enemy is still busy—albeit with changed tactics—generating a mystical cloud, gray and composed of light and shadow, in our souls; and diverting our mind/spirit from Him in whose "light we see light."

Let us look at the path of development of our [Jewish] community in Germany over the last half-century and at Mendelssohn, the pinnacle of this spiritual development, the master in Israel of the time. This entire epoch must be designated as negative and destructive. Mendelssohn endeavored to prove the existence of the Almighty *more mathematico* conclusively, totally renouncing the innocent and revealed doctrine of God. He still acknowledged legislative tradition because of a deep moral need to avoid inner degradation. Perhaps along with this there was reverence towards a sanctuary of great divine history and towards external, distinctive signs for recognizing actual divine leadership and governance. But he destroyed the root of the palm tree. He bore out the pulp, and eventually the crown which gave shade withered! The thick undergrowth around the roots, the paradisical greenery around the stem, (most probably) would not have been destroyed for a long time. But "an axe" was taken to the "roots" and what was external and perishable was scattered. Still, the slender palm remained standing, striving towards heaven as always, as during the time of the purest, noblest expressions of the soulful Psalms and Isaiah's prophetic voice.

The mission of Moses Mendelssohn is complete. Like a first king, Mendelssohn stood in history with head higher than the entire nation. The world mind/spirit concentrated itself on him and began in him. Let us concede: The mind/spirit of the development of the new "work" of our community began with him. When it started, Mendelssohn effectuated the painful convulsion, the birth pains of new thought, the difficult beginnings of rejuvenating an ancient time. As Plato would describe it, this was the sprouting of wings of the soul. Like with children and new teeth, there were pains and aches. It was exactly the new thought which impelled Mendelssohn and beyond his generation and raised him like a new volcano above the landscape. From the tip of the new height, the fertile springs streamed into the landscape below. The soil of culture rose under the feet of the new generation: Layer after layer of new riches of the earth covered one another, until the insignificant generation rose up to the same level as that of the noble thinker. The abundance spread around the young streams, blossom upon blossom, seed upon seed. Now the harvest is complete. "What was being contested is now understood by itself, and the new stage of education has begun."

But the height towards which Mendelssohn's era strove was reached some time ago. Were it our generation's ultimate summit, we would quietly occupy it, and build our huts on the new Mt. Tabor. But we are still too distant from the peacefulness of that promised day, from that "peace on earth." Division without and within [Judaism] presses a new [religious] era upon us and tells us that our path of development cannot end with this [Mendelssohnian] accumulation of fertile soil. To be sure, Israel has no figure of Mendelssohn at this time, no human peak from which a similarly fertile Nile could pour out over the contemporary landscape. But Israel does have an ancient, eternal chain of Alps. It has shining summits which tower up to heaven before the eye of the soul. They are the doctrine of the first Moses, the word of revelation. From this clear height, that word will never cease to flow into a thousand brooks. Never, at least as it looks now, will the valley below rise to that height. This highest of all measurable spiritual points of the earth is the outline of an authentic theocracy. [From it] the doctrine and worship (*Torah ve'avodah*) of the single God, in God's purely elementary form and without pagan-philosophical modifications, permeates throughout civilization. If we could present that epoch symbolically, we would present it in the biblical terms of reconciling Abel and Cain; the shepherd and landowner; monotheism and polytheism; the entry of God's state in place of legislation (Nomocracy); and the doctrine of revelation in place of paganism.

We have attempted to trace the origin of true principles which struggle with increasing intensity against each other in human history. Discord in thought manifests itself as soon as the human being goes beyond its spiritual boundary to claim a position of equal standing with God, by bringing the ground and essence of existence, not just existence's cause and circumstances, into scientific study. The very antinomies of finite and infinite, movement and rest, of necessity and will, etc. now enter the life of politics, with its secrecy and openness, and war, with its standing army and the destruction war brings. The curse of thought which has lowered itself to the doctrine that *only contradiction is truth*, has thrown its deep, long shadow over the history of mankind. Its practical doctrine has become: *Like a cloudburst, war is beneficial*; certainly against the endless, languishing sultriness; certainly against the accursed tension of the antagonistic atmosphere of hidden resentment and restrained animosity—an animosity armed with weapons beaten with demonic force into iron. Until now, this has been the sad picture of civilization: People disdain serving God and instead become tenant farmers to human beings. People reject God's command and exult over tyranny of earthly creatures. All that is conceivable is the permanent power of the one now with power and permanent resistance by his servants. Power and cunning, and mistrust and meekness, reign.

Now, just at the heights of the human society and divine peace, the blazing heavenly fire is stolen. But now, in reverse, it is diverted from the depths into the [alleged] heights. The new Prometheuses, plunderers in reverse, are much more evil than any people "who wander around in the night of the shadow of death." At the earth's heights the eager offspring, Deukalion and Pyrrha [son and daughter-in-law of Prometheus who survived a flood and provided for the creation of men and women], smile at each other with friendly glances outside and hate within their hearts. The wars of kings over property, glory, stolen goods and plunder have finally emerged into the language of the common man (87-95).

III.II. Selections from Samuel Hirsch's *Religious Philosophy of the Jews* (1844), translated by Gershon Greenberg

Summary of untranslated passages
Hirsch had accused Steinheim of failed understanding, and Steinheim pointed out to this "defender of rationalism" that the history of philosophy was impotent. Kant, Steinheim continued, demonstrated how reason was insufficient for knowing the essence of the phenomenal world, while real knowledge about the invisible (noumenal) world (soul, freedom, God) was not possible; his noumenal-phenomenal distinction showed the contradiction between things-in-themselves and real empirical data, which reason recognized. Then Hegel condensed the world into an ego, which knew itself and provided the essence of all things. Schelling posited the objective world outside the activity of thought, and Johann Friedrich Herbart's pure thought created its own world. Philosophy's history, therefore, in Steinheim's view, pointed to its denial of its own viability, and the need for the rational approach to surrender to revelation. God's existence was simply beyond the human mind and its productions. The human mind could not know God. Instead, it should open itself up to the distinctive realm of God and His creative and self-determining freedom.

Steinheim identified the contradictions between a priori *scientific constructions and the phenomena of nature. For example, the* a priori *doctrine arrived at mathematically, that the atmosphere was infinitely high (Pierre Bayle, Ediné Marcotte), contradicted the conclusion arrived at inductively and experimentally, that the atmosphere was limited from above (Pierre Si-*

mon Laplace). Or, a priori reason concluded that a space could not contain two different bodies at the same time, while inductive research concluded that it was possible to compress a cubic mass of atmospheric air into an area half its size. A priori, a body was infinitely divisible, while inductively the whole was greater than its parts—a part of a cubit inch, for example, would not be as divisible into infinity as the whole inch.

Summary of translated passages
Content reduced the power of thought, in the sense that the thing-in-itself could not be grasped. Something's essence always contradicted the a priori concept. The contradictory relationship between the visible world (reality) and a priori knowledge (concept) extended to God's relationship to the world vis-à-vis a priori knowledge—in the form of revelation (which is learned) vis-à-vis reason (which involves memory). Samuel Hirsch's work did not account for revelation in the strict sense; his concept of God was remembered rather than learned. While the results of Hirsch's work differed from Hegel's when it came to Old Testament doctrine, the dialectical method was the same.

Every truly given content has a force, a power which reduces the pure process of thought. As bitter as it may be for thought to do so, it is obliged to *believe* in *irrational* dimensions and to get used to phenomena which take place in direct contrast to the higher rationalism of the thought process.... I arrived at the certainty that the *rerum Natura*, Kant's *thing-in-itself*, is not just something that our reason is incapable of grasping. The *essence of things* stands adversely and in contradiction to the *a priori* concept which our reason develops out of itself with a presumed creative power—where reason accepts the concept of *cogito* as an unmediated primary [fact]. *The critical ability of reason finds itself obliged to surrender its own dogma and construction, and to consider facts which contradict their truth.* This goes one step further than Kant's not-knowing. Ever since the deep probe into so-called exact sciences began, true physicists have distanced themselves from the "logical pride of the system." They have proceeded alongside philosophical dogmatism, without really paying attention to that rigidity. By contrast, philosophical dogmatism utilized the discoveries of the exact sciences with gusto. It has processed them for its own purposes, often quite clumsily, in order to boast about how it had figured everything out by itself. For all that, no sensible researcher of nature would be deceived by Hegel's recent natural philosophy—as malicious as it is misguided—and substitute a blown up world-sized ego for what is actually a cuckoo's egg.

After proving as clear as day that it was impossible for human reason to know the thing-in-itself, the immortal Kant demolished his mortal tribute by accepting a part of the existence of God as a postulate, namely, the one given necessarily along with the moral law. He demolished that tribute by undertaking the construction of the material thing-in-itself, the body, in a genuinely dynamic way—something directed by his attempt at evaluating physical powers. The latter undertaking may well have its cause in the fact that Kant did not recognize the contradiction between the physical and the *a priori*. In this respect, what the most recent school [of Hegel] teaches, namely that contradiction is truth, may prove true, though in a totally different sense. Namely, the truly real is what is opposed to our reason's pure concept of what is truly real....

The Critical School [of Kant] extends the impossibility of a purely rational knowledge of the thing-in-itself to the facts of the spiritual world, to the *soul, freedom* and *God*. According to Kant's method, the principle of contradiction between reality and the conceptual thing should be extended equally to the world of the invisible, to the *mundus noumenon*. This is the content of the "Prolusion to the Second Section" in my *Revelation According to the Doctrine of the Synagogue*, a piece considered offensive by the defenders of rationalism.

I found that the *a priori* knowledge of *God and His relationship to the world* had a quality inherently the same as that of *a priori* knowledge of the visible world. In the visible world *"knowing or remembering"* stands over against *"not-knowing and learning,"* and it is the same with spiritual nature. In the spiritual world this *learning, experience, reception of something new* (synthesis) is called *"a revealing, revelation."* I have sought to show how revealing and revelation extend beyond the content and dogmatism of our reason, which is what happens with the phenomena of the visible world. I found that the God who reveals Himself to the human being has the same relationship to the God constructed rationally by the human being, as a real natural essence does to a pure concept. I discovered a fixed characteristic in this relationship which distinguishes the truly existing God from the dogmatic God-of-appearance. The truly living God appears before my soul as a mind/spirit, above and beyond the world. Without that real communication, without the true teaching (*Torah*) before my soul, I could have either only a vague presentiment of, and some (*a priori*) untruth, about God. Through *Torah* I could have what God's wisdom found proper to communicate with me. When it comes to my knowing ability, then, *revelation* parallels the gradual knowledge of phenomena of the sensible world. *A priori* knowledge provides a full concept of God, but this God is an empty pattern, a shadow image of my self. The *Torah* does not provide a full concept of God, but it does give me a personally real God. What I ... may consider to be my own meager reward consists in bringing out this comparison and proving those features—those of *real learning* vis-à-vis *remembering*, or of a *truly existing, real essence* vis-à-vis the *phantom of a self-overtaking dialectical,* a priori *spurious* wisdom—and moving our previous knowledge a bit forward.

Transferring a method from the *sensible* to the *trans-sensible* world of things is, to be sure, not as easy as applying the formula of knowledge just to the sensible world. But the transfer is still necessary. At some time it has to be completed, if we want to escape the perdition of eternal banter by proteus-like rationalism and the shadow-boxing of dogma. It is necessary, in order to be able to look down at caricatures of constructing God as assuredly as the physicist who smiles upon caricatures of constructing nature. It is also necessary to do this in order to divide the wheat from the chaff, reality from appearance, truth from lie, Judaism with its revelation from paganism with its claim to revelation.

The division is not without difficulties. The unclean spirit of confusion still bursts out in theology, despite Moses and the prophets. In physics, the seriousness of the research never succumbs to the arrogance of dogmatic reason. This obviously lies in the difference between [sensible and invisible] objects. There are five simultaneous witnesses for any *sensible* object; all our feelers are stretched out to encompass the material of the visible world. But we have only *one* sense for the *invisible* world, that of *hearing*. The *mind/spirit* whose acquaintance we should make is [in some respects] similar to us (even something similar to us which we could grasp if necessary) and so it must communicate with us through the *word*, through the *spoken* thought. It must *make itself audible.* Let us assume that creation does not end with the human being's mind/spirit. Rather, that the presentiment expressed by the poet is correct: "He does without a stairway deep beneath him" and *has a presentiment of a stairway high above him.* This "*stairway high above*" keeps pace with the staircase of the gloriously-shining world bodies above the small planet which we presently inhabit. So it is indeed not "*good-naturedness*" in the sense of Mr. [Samuel] Hirsch, i.e., not foolishness; and it is no "*identification of Judaism with lack of understanding*" to expect that our intelligence about the mind/spirit over us is possible *only* through a communication, a proclamation from outside, through a revelation in the absolute sense of the word, and that such a proclamation constitutes the content and value of our Holy Scripture (340-343).

[In response to Samuel Hirsch's criticism] let me offer the words of Professor Friedrich Adolf Trendelenburg, one of the leading critics and philosophical scholars of the present, in his *Logical Inquiries*:

> The dialectical method has been applied primarily to theology. In physics and natural sciences, which deal with *factual certitude* and sensible meaning, there are barely any examples.... Given its special objects, theology does not have the certainty of perception which exists in other scientific studies. In theology, dialectic gives an appearance of internal proof and so has been especially welcome. Those [theologians] who have trusted the dialectical method have gotten differing results with regard to essential doctrines. This has generated divisions. [In *our* recent philosophical dogmatic, the division between doctors *Salomon Formstecher* and *Samuel Hirsch*], which appears to verify that subjective perspectives play a role in objective dialectic, and that unlike other proofs dialectic cannot possibly achieve comprehensive clarity.] Dialectic has been received most favorably in theology, where it has received an almost unique positive response. But even here it has experienced lively contradictions, as should be observed by anyone who has noticed the ongoing interchange between theological perspectives and philosophical systems. [By contrast], there are scientific studies which must set the dialectical method aside, because *it wants to teach without learning; because, fancying itself in possession of the concept of the divine,* it obstructs

the certain path of painstaking research.[15]

Such are the words of a sound and sincere thinker, one who knew about the character of Old Testament revelation only as it was compounded with the admixture of a neo-Platonic philosophical formulation and so one who did not [really] know that revelation. The evangelist Mark preserved the Christianity of the founder's teaching, which recognized the declaration, *"Hear O Israel, the Lord our God, the Lord is One"* as the epitome of the law. But Matthew mutilated that epitome, Luke forgot it, and John exchanged it for the doctrine of the trinity. Otherwise, Trendelenburg [would have known about revelation] and adopted the same procedure for theology, with the same reagent and tests, which every kind of physicist easily accepted and daily applied.

My critique of Dr. Samuel Hirsch's *The Religious Philosophy of the Jews* should be understood and seen from the standpoint of my view of the essence of revelation. Given Hirsch's standpoint, he either had to reject or (at least) deliver a negative judgment about my work. And given my standpoint, I must deliver a similar judgment about his work. It comes down to this: *Which standpoint is correct? And is the standpoint true to the Old Testament canon?* I hardly need to remind anyone that no mediation is possible between the two basic views about the essence of knowledge, [those of Plato and Aristotle]. There is no bridge leading from Plato's essential view *that all our learning is only remembering*, an explication of what is internal to us, to the view of *Aristotle, that we know of nothing which is not available to us in sensible perception*. The two essential views are complete opposites, struggling over existence and non-existence. They will continue struggling until one wins.

It is clear that abstract concepts contradict the facts of physics (which increase infinitely amid the phenomena of natural history, especially the

---

15 According to Trendelenburg:

> The dialectical movement is nothing else but reason grasping itself. The entire cycle which it describes is therefore *a priori* knowledge. Whether or how far this concept rests upon previous experience is forgotten. Experience itself obviously presumes creationist thinking. All things come from creation. This is the *Prius*.

Logische Untersuchungen, vol. 1 (Leipzig: S. Hirzel, 1870): ch. 3, 90. Steinheim cited the 1840 edition, vol. 1, ch. 3, 90-91.

facts of organic nature). It is therefore justified to conclude *that* a priori *construction, the pure concept, does not know of the thing-in-itself. Indeed, it knows precisely the thing-in-itself's opposite.* Kant proves that *a priori* reason has no concept of the essence of things. I am obliged to confirm his judgment [and declare]: for reason to *recognize what is presented from out of itself as truly real is a lie, something non-existent, an untruth.* This is totally within the range of Kant's critique of reason.

This is our conviction, and there can be no other: any system or doctrine about the spiritual and God which brags about having been acquired *without revelation and instead through the human mind's/spirit's own work,* through the reason of the human being, which brags about having been *remembered* but not *learned,* is either an illusion or a lie. Its deity is an idol, a false deity. Having expressed my opinion about the content [of Hirsch's *Religious Philosophy of the Jews*] I am now obliged to give reasons for sentencing the text's philosophical dogmatism to death....

Perhaps Dr. Samuel Hirsch would not concede at all that he denies revelation in its true and literal sense. In fact, one might be convinced of this on the basis of some later places in his text.... But in terms of the spirit of the whole work, and the main features of his dogmatic, it cannot be denied that it is *against* the view of authentic communication from without, and against revelation *stricto sensu.* The concept of God praised by Hirsch does not come to the human mind/spirit from outside, and is not *learned.* It is within the human mind/spirit and developed out of it, it is *remembered.* In a word: our author is, successively, a rationalist, a believer in reason, a believer in thought, i.e., in the dogmatically philosophical sense and, as will soon be shown, in the dialectical-Hegelian sense. To be sure, the result which he turns out is very much different from the result drawn by Hegel about the significance and position of the doctrinal concept of the Old Testament. But it is nothing new to see how a spiritual phenomenon, here the Old Testament, is treated like a wax nose: turned inwards, outwards, flattened and pointed all at the same time.

Summary of translated passages
Hirsch advocated scientific study with a particularistic emphasis which was absent from Mendelssohn's humanistic direction. Still, Hirsch's world view of Judaism belonged to necessary knowledge and absolute reason—making it different from the pagan-philosophical perspective only on a modal level. The views of Mendelssohn and Hirsch were distinct only when it came to the

non-Jewish philosophy each utilized—Leibniz-Wolff or Schelling-Hegel. In-
stead of an authentic revelation of God, for Hirsch the concept of God was
inborn in human reason and dialectically developed. Hirsch did not separate
his unmediated knowledge of the world from unmediated knowledge about
God. Instead of grasping the essence of the authentic God, Hirsch grasped
his own mind/spirit. Instead of learning, he only remembered. Ultimately,
Hirsch faced a choice: To acknowledge creatio ex nihilo *and with it unop-*
posed freedom of mind/spirit, or take the (Spinozistic) path of mathematical
demonstration and conservation of what already existed.

We should not overlook the "Preface" to *The Religious Philosophy of the Jews* (p. 9) which explicates the struggle within the Synagogue. After the author finds fault with the unfortunate attitude of tolerance on the part of the Church *vis-à-vis* the Synagogue, he lays claim to the notorious *extra ecclesiam nulla salus* for the Synagogue. Hirsch expresses himself thusly:

> A scientific understanding is more important for our in-
> ner life than for our relation to what is outside. It has
> been much contested in our midst and has reached
> the point where any rabbi trained in scientific study is
> viewed in advance with mistrust. It is undeniable that
> much malice, lust for power, etc. is involved. But some-
> how [this scientific approach] must indeed be legitimate,
> for otherwise it would not have such power over our con-
> science [and generate such antagonism]. I believe [the
> reason for the mistrust] is this: *Contemporary [scientific]*
> *endeavors are confused [by critics] with those of Mendels-*
> *sohn's school.* [That school wanted to bring Christian and
> Jew] to the same level of humanistic education.... The
> contemporary concern should be *precisely the particular-*
> *ity, the positive world view of the Jewish religion ... and the*
> *forms which the Jewish religion gives to itself in order to*
> *continually bring this positive world view into the present.*
> *Specifically, the concern should be to grasp the ceremonies*
> *and concepts of the Jewish religion in their absolute neces-*
> *sity and raise* them again to living fact of the heart.

This passage, printed in a font that emphasizes the point, contains

Hirsch's promise to maintain and present the characteristic, positive world view of the Jewish religion, "and its essential difference with the efforts of the *Mendelssohn* school." Mendelssohn's efforts are described as destructive, "tearing apart, surrendering."

With regard to the first point about grasping the "positive world view of the Jewish religion," the question is this: if the world view of Judaism is one which is to be grasped as absolutely necessary, then it falls—and the author is happy to concede this—within the rubric of "necessary knowledge." It is therefore only a revelation of reason, and to be sure a revelation of human, conceptual and absolute reason. The *specific* difference between Judaism on the one side, and paganism and philosophizing on the other, is annulled: Only a *modal difference* is conceded. The difference is a matter of whether we comprehend the Jewish world view in terms of the conceptual system of Leibniz-Wolff dogmatism, Schelling's doctrine of identity or finally Hegel's dialectic.

Mendelssohn wanted to conceptualize the Jewish world view according to the dominant principles of his time. He denied God's revelation, because for him the concept of God was an inborn idea of the human being. What is the difference between Mendelssohn and contemporary Jewish theologians [such as Hirsch and Formstecher]? [Just that] they want to conceptualize the Jewish world view according to the philosophical system of *their* time and to identify their concept of God with that of *Schelling* or *Hegel*. Whether expressly or *sub rosa*, they deny the authentic revelation of God. Instead, the true concept of God is now expressed either by Schelling or Hegel. It is inborn in human reason and develops fully through a dialectical process. Any reflective person would agree that in terms of this maxim the Jewish world view is no different from that of the [pagans and the] philosophers. The two differ only in terms of the respective systems which form and house them. As to the *Mendelssohn* school, one can [also] find fault with it. Like any other school, depending on the sort of stream, it became increasingly shallow and finally dispersed into silt.

Does the Jewish world view differ from the *essential* teachings of paganism and philosophizing? Then it is not "*to be grasped in its absolute necessity.*" The moment it becomes a necessary concept, it has to become identical with one of the current, former or future philosophies and cease to be a "characteristic" religious world view. It would be transformed from a *doctrine* into *a priori* wisdom.

If the *Mendelssohnian* (rationalistic) school is accused of being de-structive, then devotees of subsequent philosophical systems should be blamed for the contemporary destruction. Anyone who has or will claim *wisdom which is prior to all proper revelation* destroys the deep internal grounding of this revelation. They resemble those who used some facile demonstration from the conceptual world to make exact sciences into something superfluous. Whenever they are unable to fit the absolute concepts together with experimental sciences to claim true knowledge for themselves, they either deny or overturn the outcomes and results of physics, chemistry, etc (361-365).

The author maintains that "the unmediated mind/spirit knows not only about religion in an unmediated way." It "relates to everything else it knows in the same way." This, regrettably, is only too true! [It reflects the fact that for Hirsch] *unmediated knowledge of the world* is worth exact-ly as much as *unmediated* knowledge of God and divine matters. Neither world nor God are worth a straw. In knowledge, there is a "distinction only of potency, according to degree." Regarding both the knowledge of God and knowledge of normal life conditions, whatever the mind/spirit's essence expressed in the mind/spirit is to be found in mind/spirit itself.

It is certainly an impressive beginning to have the human mind/spirit reject all *learning* and seek to draw the quintessence of all essence from out of its own mind/spirit. It is never that way! Hirsch should only be lucky enough to be a theologian able to teach the scientific study of reli-gion, a scientific study in which absolute knowledge would be capable of boasting about memory. Indeed, there was good fishing for the absolute idea in his nebulous heavenly atmosphere, in his spiritual cloud. But if the theologian [Hirsch] looked just once out of the window into the free world of God, and did so seriously rather than with that well-known "logical pride," he would most likely have had a different disposition. The theologian would then have the insight that the characteristic obstinacy of *the essence of things* cannot be dissolved through any "remembering" and brought to consciousness. At that point, [Hirsch] might well arrive at the thought, so certain and so near, that what we know about [his sort of] God and what we grasp about such a God's essence *is nothing more than our own mind/spirit*. Were God even slightly richer in content, more powerful, more knowing, than the human mind/spirit, how would it be possible to have adequate knowledge about Him and His action? How could the little- or unknowing human mind/spirit grasp the much-knowing or all-knowing God and His knowledge? Would that not be a contradiction? Only paganism, and dogmatic philosophy with its principle that the human being is the measure of all things, have philosophies of religion and know God in His internality. But this known God is just that! God is known, just as the acknowledged *"known* world" of natural philosophy is known. This world is known to be at one with necessity, and to proceed simultaneously according to necessity (376-377).

The doctrine that God made the world out of nothing is outwardly ignored and basically disclaimed by every philosophical dogmatic and by all pagan and philosophical schemes. *True freedom,* i.e., resemblance to God, is denied. It is *united with necessity.* That is, indirectly but nevertheless completely (along with more rigorous concepts), true freedom is erased from the book of life. It will avail nothing, to hear all the talk about freedom of the will and self-determination. For if freedom is completely at one with necessity, it amounts to declaring: *There is not [any] freedom.* Further, if God is no longer a thoroughly free spirit, He is no longer a creator but only an orderer of matter. God is therefore unfree, which is what paganism and all philosophy have taught until today and still teach. World stuff and the world's inertia constitute hindrances to His will which need to be overcome. Nor could any other mind/spirit contain *libertas indifferentiae,* absolute freedom, power, cause, indeed the first cause to become a new act. With the collapse of this freedom, a second main pillar of the religious view of the Jew collapses [in addition to *creatio ex nihilo*] and it can hardly be replaced with the reed-like support of so-called "fulfilled or concrete freedom."

But theologians once again face a bitter choice. Should they acknowledge the inexplicable, unopposed freedom of the mind/spirit, and with it the doctrine of creation out of nothing? If they did they would be one of ours, believing Israelites, *who have learned something* which scientific study cannot grasp. Scientific study only seems to grasp onto something—like a youth grasps the butterfly only to crush it. The other choice is for theologians to make a commitment to conceptual absolutes, to *Spinoza's demonstratio more mathematico* (mathematical demonstration). Away with the term freedom! Bring on the *conatus suum Esse conservandi* (conserving of the impulse to be oneself); or Johann Friedrich Herbart's [1776-1841] closely related self-preservation. Just no *"striding between two waves."* Doctrine has to be pure! (434-435)

III.III. Selections from *Neither Right, Nor Left*, translated by Gershon Greenberg

Summary of translated passages
Mendelssohn asserted that Hebrew scripture did not reveal God but did reveal commands and statutes. He remained a Jew in practice. Eventually, however, the revealed commands and statutes would have to be surrendered, for without the revealed God they were untenable. Steinheim acknowledged the role of rationalism as a grounding for ethics and a means for understanding faith/belief. Indeed, what was true in religion was also true in philosophy. But reason could not measure the truth of data of itself, only how data measured against the standards of truth.

In theory, opposites move away from one another and confront one another destructively simultaneously. In practice, it takes decades, centuries, for them to eventually arrive at antagonistic, polar positions. The theoretical opposition-become-practical is portrayed today in most spheres of religion, and this includes Judaism....

The opposition was initially expressed seven decades ago by the philosopher Moses Mendelssohn in his *Jerusalem*. He asserted: *Holy, Old Testament scripture was not given to reveal a God, rather only certain commands and statutes.* This is the opposite (antithesis) of the older formulation (thesis): *In Holy Scripture, God revealed Himself, in terms of His essence and His will, to the human being. Legislation, in its narrow sense is subordinate*, a consequence. With Mendelssohn's assertion, subordinate legislation became the main thing, and not only the main thing but the sole purpose. The sole purpose, if not the highest aim until then, [namely God's revelation to the human being], was set aside completely. The proclamation in Mendelssohn's *Jerusalem* was the strict consequence of his *Morning Hours*. Anyone who found God in a mathematical manner (*more mathematico*), even if only through a calculation of probability, hardly needed a revealed God. Such a God could only be a burdensome and bothersome supplement.

This is generally well-known. Also familiar is how the originator of the contradiction to the ancient *doctrine* [that God revealed Himself] knew to observe the doctrine's *practice* [i.e., its commands and statutes]. Mendelssohn clung firmly to the revealed laws and ceremonies lest the totality [of Judaism] be surrendered. He urged his fellow believers to adhere to them. But his closest disciples implemented the obvious consequence to his principles and statutes. The statutes did not suit the *rationalist* God and so were quickly sent after the expelled God of revelation. The very thin and fragile shell of ancient tradition which remained, surrendered early on to the pressure of outside impetus and broke into pieces. Why, it was asked, did God give us reason? It was no more difficult for reason to shake off the strange, old Franconian synagogue services, than to shake off their supposed [divine] director—who was already set to the side. Had the philosopher Mendelssohn lived longer, he certainly would have seen with his own eyes the inevitable repercussion to his unexplained dependency upon a Jewish-rabbinical statute about a second manifestation of God [upon redemption]: the abolition of revealed law so fully implied in his premise [about the revealed God].

...But what stopped the great thinker from carrying out the natural consequence himself? Neither the *argumentum a tuto* (argument from the whole) of cowardice (where he was out to secure his position) nor the lazy *Logos* of custom. *Moses Mendelssohn* shared the noblest temperament of his people and of his time! Much earlier, he let it be understood that he feared specific and strong reaction [to his work] on the part of his fellow believers and was anxious lest a condition of demoralization result directly from the sudden light which he believed he had spread. These moved him to a characteristically practical approach. On the one side, he understood how the reaction of fellow believers would have consequences for him [personally]. On the other, the disintegration of education at that time in Judaism was so widespread that a person of Moses Mendelssohn's piety had to retreat before going any further. He proceeded, therefore, to free the mind/spirit bound by traditional statutes, without becoming unbound or unstable.

Mendelssohn, that is, was at least able to achieve a short-lived delay of the consequences to the dreaded implementation of his theory. It took two generations for his theory to be implemented in its extreme form within the structure of a free Jewish community. That objectionable contradiction between doctrine [about the revealed God] and life [in terms of obeying commands and statutes] has [perhaps] fortunately, been neglected. We would [like to confront it and work towards an] honest realization and restoration of their inner harmony. But only if the real central-point of the issue, "theoretically, is *rationalism really grounded as Moses Mendelssohn believed and taught it?*" is deeply probed.

A careful and thorough investigation is a solemn obligation. Especially since the Mendelssohn-[Christian] Wolff proof for God's existence was destroyed irretrievably long ago by the "all-pulverizing" *Kant*....

We hardly need to be afraid of cogent objections to presenting our thesis as an axiom. As *the human being is essentially mind/spirit, surely its purest and highest expression must be formed by and preserved in the laws belonging to what is spiritual.* The essence of this forming consists in this: *the human being's conduct, as expression of its existence, is to be the authentically true expression of this spiritual nature, a product of the human being's mindset and free self-determination in action.* If *rational thinking* is, consequentially, the human being's first motive, the second motive is ethical willing as derived directly from the first. *The human being's pure thought is the ground of its free conduct.*

So we say: *the reason of the human being is unified.* Human beings can therefore only think *really*, i.e., *correctly*, in one way. A variety of thinking would be ambiguous and erroneous, something strange, not sane. Something cannot be the truth here and illusion or untruth elsewhere. Therefore even the *pious lie* is still a lie, and there is no certainty about whether it is true. Despite its name, it may be more deserving of condemnation than something profane, for it is the lie of the highest order. Only strictly consequential thinking earns the name of truth. All else is drivel. Therefore, something cannot be recognized as true in religion and a lie in philosophy. Only that which is preserved as true before reason can be true as well in religion, in what we really hold as *our faith/belief.* Reason has the calling and role *to perceive.* It is called upon to examine all doctrines of faith/belief, i.e., to examine according to the same innate standards of truth and laws of criticism which reason applies to other areas of knowing. These [standards and laws] are the pillars, the eternal bearers and keepers of all true knowledge. True knowledge has to preserve this position of judgment and not retreat quietly into higher questions. The more intensively and sharply reason exercises its analytical chemistry, the nobler the regulus whose authenticity and value reason is to determine. Reason does not *create* this regulus; it only *evaluates* it, it only *tests* its purity. Reason itself registers the content of the true and the false. A doctrine of faith/belief should no more withdraw itself from this judgment than should any philosophical formulation or doctrine. Were it to withdraw and hesitate to speak or answer in any way, it would invoke the judgment of rejection upon itself and, [so to speak] break a staff over its own crown. It would voluntarily renounce any claim to the truth. There is nothing more ridiculous than to bring the comprehensive critical apparatus to bear upon trivial problems of scientific study, and then deflect the most important questions. The strictness of an inquiry grows with the difficulty of the question. The more unbelievable the expression and the more presumptuous the claim, the sharper and stricter the interrogation should be. *Nowhere is the critique of reason to be elicited to such an extent, nowhere is it more in place and have more right, than in the matter of faith/belief.* As with any place else, however, reason may not make itself into the measure for the truth of the data. It measures according to the laws of truth alone. Reason will not be asked whether a particular expression *agrees* with reason's own findings, rather only *whether or not it contradicts reason's findings, i.e., whether it withdraws from the standards for truth.*

...I am making a claim, already made by Kant, with intentional emphasis. *On the one hand*, I am doing this to secure the agreement of the rationalists, without responding to their specific claims about material agreement between the results of reason and the dogma of faith/belief. *On the other*, to win over the faction which opposes the rationalist. Like Kant, I maintain an essential limit [to reason], and defend myself against the anticipated objection that I expected something other than just control or teaching pure critique from rational activity. However, if instead of earning approval from the rationalists and their opponents I offend them, I would be consoled by the fact that it seldom goes differently for the judge of peace.... (57-62)

NOR TO THE RIGHT, TO RABBINIC ORTHODOXY

Summary of untranslated passages
Steinheim accused Rabbinic Orthodoxy of covering the sublime words of revelation with abstruse veils, of falsifying the content of revelation with pagan-philosophical ingredients, and of identifying the outer shell with the core to the point of giving them equal status. Many Jews were offended and abandoned Judaism.

With regard to paganism: Mosaism opposed its appeal to natural instincts, with its attention to sensual lust and promises of the world beyond, and spoke of knowing God as eternal and creator of heaven and earth. Moses warned against seduction through the heart and eye, but paganism's appeal persisted.

It was easily grasped, made nature attractive, demanded little of the human being and reduced or even annulled ethical requirements. In Egypt, for example, Jews were drawn to the myths of Egypt and Canaan with their raw and sensual worship. In the Land of Israel and Babylonian exile they were drawn to the Bactrian magical doctrine of light and the Zoroastrianism myths and their tenets of fire or light. The Old Testament stipulated, "Thou shalt make no graven images," but Zoroaster's refined artistic expression of the sensuality of the soul and the rational construction of a double-principle of deity (through statement-counter statement, and something contrary to revelation) still seeped into Judaism (see Isaiah's protest. Isaiah 45:5-7). Over time, different ingredients entered in. Jews depicted the physical device of a divine chariot of Ahura Mazda (even though Ahura Mazda was to be venerated in terms of mind/spirit). Jewish prayers were populated by weird personalities. Magical rings and amulets infiltrated spiritual devotion. Lilith Eilithyia and Militta (or Molidita) appeared in the rooms of women about to give birth. Contrary to Scripture ("Surely there is no enchantment against Jacob, neither is there any divining against Israel." Numbers 23:23), rabbis performed exorcisms. During the sounding of the Shofar, it was imagined that Satan sat in the horn, secret formulas were directed to Metatron and other angels. During the Dukhan *service, mystically-veiled priests whispered horrid words against bad dreams. There was the mysterious custom of the Hoshanah service or Hoshanah Rabbah. All of this undermined the revealed core of Judaism. But it became so deeply interwoven with rabbinism that any changes at this point would shake the synagogue to its deepest foundation (79-87).*

Summary of translated passages

Paganism's doctrine of the future was opposed to revelation's. For paganism, history began in purity and ultimately descended into an apocalyptic conflict between darkness and light. Given the development of the world according to natural laws and towards a "physiological" future, the conflict was inevitable; an overarching dynamic left individual choice impotent. For revelation, history began in sin and advanced to future redemption, moving from loss of innocence to consciously regaining it. The future was ethical and free will played a central role. In the biblical period, for example, ethical messianism represented by the prophet Isaiah was compromised by elements of heredity and political kingship concerning Samuel but these were, in time, extracted out of Judaism.

NEITHER TO THE RIGHT NOR TO THE LEFT

Let us compare revelation's doctrine of the future with that of paganism. For the doctrine of revelation, eschatology, the doctrine of the future of the human species on earth involves educating the entire species into perfect humanity according to the primordial *image of divine origin and divine destiny*. All of humanity rises from the lowest position of organic-animalistic rawness to the highest possible level which wisdom and freedom can achieve on earth. It means *the gradual development of all the spiritual talents and germs of the human souls and their redemption from the bonds of unethical drives into free and rationally appropriate self-determination, comparable to the holy creative genius in the image of whom the human soul was created. The kingdom of God of the future, the messianic era, is simultaneously the end and the conclusion to earthly days.* This is the conclusive solution to the great problem of the humanizing of our species. The redemption is two-fold. One redemption is from the necessary *laws of nature*, and the other *from external, imposed legislation of state law by means of factual inner sanctification and ethical self-determination.* This higher future, which we confidently expect for our successors and which was promised with great clarity by the prophets, is the kingdom of peace. The *innocence* necessarily lost when the human being first emerged from the condition of unconscious organic life, with its blindly-effective laws of instinct, *the unconscious, original innocence*, is now *regained with consciousness*. The possibility of deviating from the straight path came with the eligibility to choose. *Sin* entered the history of mankind. Human history is the history of the higher drives, the quest and press towards the final goal of life on earth. With the achievement of that goal, history will have resolved its problem and thereby annulled itself.[16] / According to the doctrine of revelation and the faculty of the noblest prophecy, the culmination point, true blessedness, and the paradise of the human species, is *the future goal which lies before us*. And this is also the interpretation according to the rabbis. *Sin*, bound to *distress*, is *the beginning and advance* of our history. *Redemption and blessedness is history's goal, and sanctification and peace is its end.*

In paganism it is reversed. Paganism's doctrinal point is totally the opposite. The *end* for revelation is the *beginning* for paganism. Pagan-

---

16   In the original text, a new paragraph begins at this point. In the interest of clarity, I have in the following chapters represented some paragraph breaks with a slash.

ism's *beginning is of perfect purity* (the aboriginal light), *its continuity is of gradual darkening*, and its *conclusion is of world decline*. / At the beginning everything was good and pure. Then everything became increasingly darkened and impure, the total opposite of the primordial light, material devoid of light, pure evil, and everything was dissolved into the "Indifferent." The *darkening*, the *spoiling*, was provided along with the world's coming into being, so that the fall from pure primordial light was a necessary result of the world's creation. Thus, for the world to *become* was equivalent to the *fall* of the world....

If we look more closely at this ancient pagan doctrine of faith/belief, we will discover with some certitude the basic element from which this doctrine of faith/belief arose and formed itself. It is none other than our *creative, architectonic reason*, with its unmistakable, characteristic form of *statement, counter-statement* and *mediation* (copula). Paganism, be it mystical-symbolic or mathematical-constructive, cannot transcend this point of culmination. The *abstract doctrine of unity* of *primordial substance* is diametrically opposed to the *individual, personal unity* of revelation. This unity is exactly what forms the vital point of Old Testament doctrine. Through it, everything achieves a new formation over-against ancient paganism. The doctrine of a free *creation out of nothing* is the main signpost of revelation. Entwined with various derivative teachings it overturns the pagan teachings which run parallel to it—as I believe I have already shown with regard to the dogma of the idea of the future.

The *idea of the messiah* is closely connected with the doctrine of the future. Paganism's *physiological* doctrine of the future is diametrically opposed to revelation's ethical doctrine of the future. In *paganism* the *unshakeable natural law* of cause and effect rules with inflexible results. In *revelation* the act of the *ethically free will* rules. The physical opposition between light and darkness, creation and destruction, good and bad, the fall of the originally pure from itself through internal opposition—all these physically-polar contradictions disappear. In their place, *a uniform will of a single mind/spirit* enters in. In revelation, the idea of a fall, of a complete transformation of inner nature, turns itself around into [an act of] lewdness and disobedience against divine command. The fall thereby becomes a punishable act of the free will. Directly with the first exile, the *doctrine of freedom* according to the word of revelation entered into close contact, and thereby conflict, with the externally related but internally distinct pagan *dogma of Parsee doctrine*. We find this conflict clearly expressed at the end of the book of Isaiah, and at the beginning of the exile with Jeremiah—in Aramaic, the conflict is sharpened (Jeremiah 10:19). / But objections by two of the first prophets was not enough to protect such a sublime doctrine—one as distant from the natural human being as *the messianic doctrine of the Old Testament*— from contagion. / Gradually, the representative images of the doctrines of *emanation* and *incorporation* stole their way into the sphere of revelation. The *messianic idea* was added as a *principle of legitimation*. Out of the pure ideal of the kingdom of peace and justice, a legitimate kingdom formed with *earthly* succession to the throne. Even Isaiah was not free of this mixture of spiritual and earthly.

We must return to this point of history and probe the significance of this addition to the idea of the heavenly kingdom. *The idea of a heavenly kingdom*, i.e., of God's dominion over, His commands to earth without any human mediator, was the prototype for the Israelite national constitution until the last days of Samuel. The people finally urged Samuel *to establish himself as a king, just as the pagans around them.* Samuel had to yield. Simultaneously, *the earthly monarchy was regarded as a total fall* away from God and His rule over Israel (I Samuel 8:6). The descent was equated with the idolatry of the desert. The over-emphasis of Holy Scripture on establishing the first inherited monarchy is explained by the facts of actually abandoning the existing divine reign and falsifying the doctrine of the future with pagan legitimation.

If the pagan liked to express him/herself so strongly against *human* mastery, against *worldly* monarchy; how much sharper the judgment had to be when a *theocracy* actually shaped the statute and God Himself was the real sovereign! This monarchy [of Samuel] was modeled after those of *surrounding* peoples. Israel borrowed it from paganism. It became the basis for Israel's doctrine of the future, where the representative idea of an anointed one (*mashiah*) was legitimately derived from kingly seed. The pure, divine doctrine of the future of revelation was mixed with the wretched doctrine of the future according to the pagan tradition, with its dominance of corporality and the preponderance of the organic act of procreation. This produced a mixed, impure dogma. It has been objected, that rabbinism brought crude, worldly materialism from the outside into the doctrine of the messiah, and I share this objection. But it is a wonder that this objection came from that [very] side which pushed this wretched doctrine to its extreme.

The legitimate messianic idea, the pure, ennobled idea of the future, already found in Isaiah, bears an ancient Asian imprint. When it became combined with the theocracy of the Old Testament, its purely ethical ingredient became seriously compromised. In general, a combination between something worse and something better drags the better down, and this happened here. The touch of sloth masters what is healthy. The smallest addition of paganism with the prophets was transformed by those who came later as the main idea in the further construction of the messianic doctrine. Accordingly, not even the smallest pagan ingredient should have remained within the pure concept of revelation. The concept of monarchic heredity should have been definitively extracted from Judaism's doctrine of the future and the doctrine's pure content restored. If we consider Samuel as an inspired prophet who spoke from God, we cannot doubt that what he said was true. *The monarchy he instituted, demanded by Israel, contradicted theocracy.* It meant a fall away from the living God. If this is to be understood as complete monarchy, nothing good, only something bad, could come from perpetuating it. Matters would only get worse! We cannot let our holy *doctrine of the future*, this hope and this consolation for the entire human species, tainted and diminished by some sort of favoritism and hereditary nobility—among a people for whom moral and legal equality of everyone before God and the law was and is an essential principle.

This consoling promise [of the messiah] penetrates like a spring of light through the desolation and the confused life path of the body of qualified nations of the earth. Even today it constitutes the pillar of cloud during the day and the pillar of fire at night in the desert of wandering towards lands of freedom and the tranquility of nations. Unperturbed by the pygmy-like thought of human leadership, this promise appears as the holy banner delivered to us by providence to carry at the head of the procession of the nations. At the same time, it is the distant point of light, the eternal goal towards which the procession strives. Its faithful banner-bearers have been filled with certainty of victory [as they trod] their thorny path through the world and maintained their courage through difficult sufferings. Through this messianic promise we [were able to] achieve a miraculous joyousness. Through this promise we have become an entire nation of witnesses to truth and the salvation of the human species. Despite diversionary aberrations, the spring of this promise has not been blocked up. It has bubbled forth with powerful surges from the depths of revelation, pushing away all the mud of mis-understanding which pollutes the spring, and it restores the soul of the pious pilgrim with its pure balm (119-125).

Summary of translated passages
The finite rational mind was unable to accommodate infinite reality or probe the divine essence of things. It produced God by itself, claiming there was no need for anything outside or beyond it. Rationalism's a posteriori method had failed to prove God's existence, because God did not resemble experience. Its a priori proofs (ontological, teleological, physio-theological and Kant's ethical proof) have been, respectively, easily refuted. Reason could not explain divine freedom because—unlike human freedom—it was absolute. And since for reason out-of-nothing, nothing came and world stuff was eternal, there was no room for an absolutely free God who developed the world. Nor could reason establish ethical legislation. With regard to Mendelssohn in particular: He left the matter of reconciling reason (philosophy) and revelation to his students—lest he had to renounce revealed legislation and the doctrine of creation out of nothing.

Nor to the left, to the faction of rationalist enlightenment.... Now we turn against the declared enemy of revelation, against rationalism, against the outspoken heterodoxy of the enlightenment. It was first introduced into our generation by Moses Mendelssohn, and carried to the extreme by his successors. We must analyze this defection from revealed doctrine, its tendency towards atheism, and demonstrate how baseless it is.

Rationalism in Judaism has denied and cast off revelation as such. Through Moses and the prophets God made Himself known in a miraculous way to our predecessors. In place of this, rationalism instituted a God that it invented and constructed out of its operation of reason. The work at the beginning of the century and earlier has been carried on and perfected into the present. Many masters in Israel have thought that if a person sensed the inclination and sufficient power within him/herself alone, no help from the outside need be accepted. Who needs crutches, as long as one has good legs? Who needs glasses when he still has good eyes?

It could be that presenting a harmony between philosophical formu-lation and the doctrine of revelation, or bringing the doctrine of revela-tion into genetic relation with philosophical formulation was not part of [Mendelssohn's] considerations and intentions. It is my contention, however, that Mendelssohn [consciously] held this [matter] in suspension and left it to his students to carry out the task [of resolving it]. He knew exactly about the infinite cleft between what *was proven* and what was *revealed*, even if he was not inclined to measure or account for it. Instead, he gave preference to his dogma of reason. Had he considered the cleft, he would have had to explain what prevented him from sending divine legislation after the God [of revelation] who was expelled. There would have been no grounds not to overlook the pregnant doctrinal point of a *"creation out of nothing,"* the cardinal dogma of revelation. He could no longer deem it too insignificant to mention the difference between the philosophical God and the God of revelation.

Unless he was ready to yield his basic stance, he had to ignore the doctrinal point of creation out of nothing. For revelation's axiom, *"Everything out of nothing,"* stands in sharp contrast to reason's axiom, *"Out of nothing, nothing comes."* It is as essential to revelation as is the representative image of "first cause," which contradicts reason's axiom of *"no effect without a corresponding cause."* Mendelssohn was surely aware of this essential difference, as it constituted [one of] the main confessional dogmas according to the great synagogue authorities *Maimonides* (*Thirteen Principles*), Menasseh ben Israel (in his *Book of Creation*) and *Rabbi Abraham Ben David* (Rabad). It remains incredible how he was able to withdraw from this discussion. More incredible, even, than his hollow form-worship which set essential content aside. Still, we should be grateful to him for such manipulation, as well as for the rest of his *rational thoughts and proofs*. For they position us to probe his true conviction concerning the essence and significance of the ancient canon. Otherwise, we could only have conjectured about it.

Human reason has neither the calling, the ability nor the assignment to resolve the problem of the essence of things. It has even less ability to establish knowledge about the mind/spirit of all minds/spirits, namely God. It is not capable of constructing divine things, namely ethical legislation, on an immovable basis in order to produce the idea of God out of that legislation. Once I prove this, it will become evident that so-called natural or rational religion is an illusory mirage, and that the God of rationalism is without essence. To provide this proof, I offer this proposition:

Reason has a certain presentiment of the existence of God. Nevertheless, any attempt to ascribe this presentiment with

the character of scientific knowledge will necessarily fail.
Just as much as the attempt will fail to determine the char-
acteristic distinctive sign of this singular essence scientifi-
cally or characterize that of which there is a presentiment.

Scientific knowledge can be acquired either through experience (*a poste-*
riori) or *developed out of the concept* (*a priori*). Obviously we can have no
knowledge about God which resembles experience, or could be raised
through inference to exact scientific study. God is a trans-sensible essence, while experience obtains information only through sense in the
world of senses. *We have to verify that we can obtain just as little* a priori
knowledge about God. The well-known *a priori ontological* proof of God
("Anselmian") is the oldest. It deduces existence out of the *impossibil-*
ity that there would be nothing; out of this it posits *the existence of God.*
Generally understood as only existence; bare, naked existence of existence.
This proof for the existence of God proves nothing but this: *if we pre-*
sume that our own existence is real, there must be an ultimate ground for
all existence. But that presumption must itself first be proven. Because
the old *cogito, ergo sum* (I think, therefore I am), which transforms and
messes up its frail descendants into *amo, ergo sum* (I love, therefore I
am), is miles apart from any pretention of proof. It is only the *feeling of
existence*, contained in a word, and provided with language. All such *facts
of consciousness* are only axioms out of which a proof can be derived, but
are themselves incapable or unreceptive to proof. Should our existence
become the sole surety for God's, then His surety must stand on weak
legs. We can only share the naïve indignation of the child we know who
found a notebook of a young philosopher on a desk entitled "*Proof for
the existence of God*," and called out involuntarily: "The doctor would be
better off first proving his own existence."

The other proofs are basically only grounds for persuasion, not proofs:
Not the proof from the purposefulness of the world order (teleological).
Not the one derived from the greatness and loftiness of the world order
(physico-theological), usually connected to the former. Least of all the
ethical proof, which the author himself (*Kant*) called only a postulate. It
relied for its subsistence upon a *moral world order*, upon *ethical legislation*
and upon the postulate of a legislator. Still, the postulate of [the ethical
proof], arrived at through the postulate's power of demonstration, is
significantly weightier than the proof which appears with the preten-

sion of mathematics: the *ontological* proof. The ontological proof relates only to our inner consciousness' presupposition of a real existence, an existence which still remains very disputable. The ethical proof rests on the indestructible ground of consciousness *of being able to choose between two paths*. It rests on the *consciousness of freedom in* the human mind/spirit....

Let us consider, first of all, how deeply subordinate a thinking mind/spirit such as ours must be to the mind/spirit in which the world plan can be formed and carried out. It appears to us that it would be impossible to try to squeeze this infinite essence into our tiny, pygmy-sized ability-to-comprehend! We know the old saying of the Sophists: *The human being is the measure of all things*. But at that time the human being still had an equally extensive and false concept (as time would tell) of the place in which it lived as well as of itself. In ancient paganism this saying was correct. But in the new world, the mouth of the poet responded to Protagoras: "The human being is only the measure of the human being. Yet the heaven is endless."

If we look at our anthropomorphic rationalism more closely, we will become aware of the difficulties in which it entangles itself. An either/or choice must be made: One choice is to deprive the highest and primordial grounding of all things free and even of consciousness. Here, rationalism gives the most perfect essence a quality which is less than that of the very imperfect human being, whose mainstay of existence is the powerful, inexhaustible feeling of freedom. The other choice is to ascribe the feeling of freedom to the highest and primordial grounding, and to do so in terms of how [feelings] are found in us. Or to ascribe to God the same spiritual quality, which is found in us, and on the same terms—except with the negation of their limitations, i.e., *unlimited freedom*. Were the human being to attribute only restricted freedom to the highest of all essence, it would encroach upon the character of the most perfect essence. It would reduce it to an essence which, no matter the measure of power towering above tiny human power, would still not be essentially different from the human. Like the human being, this perfect essence would be condemned to the slavery "of the pitiless unalterable fate." That such a deity is nothing but a pathetic idol, a mockery of Promethean character, is obvious. But if rationalism in fact extended absolute freedom to such a deity, it would become entangled in a new, unresolvable contradiction with its own axiom, "*Out of nothing, nothing* comes." The *eternity of matter* is thereby accepted, and *world stuff is as eternal* as God. This world stuff is insubordinate and resistant to God's absolute will, it restrains God's power. One can see how rationalism pulls the rope back and forth while the knots it wants to loosen become only stronger.

To bring rationalism back from its presumption that it offers an accurate idea of God through its own reflection, we only have to direct it to a similar failure in a much narrower realm, and in a stratum closer to it. We say: the rich, talented human mind/spirit can make itself and its profusion of power known to the neediest mind/spirit in two ways only. Through its *work* and through its *word*. Through work it provides those subordinate to it with a presentiment of its abundance. Through the word the human mind/spirit explains its abundance and thereby its all-powerful essence.

Let us take the case of the inventor of a wonderful machine, a [James] *Watt*. Let us say that he decided to communicate something useful about his invention to someone less informed in physics and mathematics, which was of use to that person. To do so Watt would communicate something of physics and mechanics, so as to introduce the person to the knowledge needed about these exact sciences in a way in which the knowledge would be generally comprehensible. But for this student to acquire a correct concept of the great master's intention, the master would have to communicate the grounds through which he was moved to creation, and the purpose he set for himself, through *words*. These intentions would remain unknown and not understood even by someone deeply into physics and mechanics, unless the person received the necessary disclosures about them from the mouth of the inventor.

Let us say that the student learned everything required and of value from the master, and gained insight into the entire mechanism through self-study. Should he then ask the master: "Master: Did you also invent the material for the machine, the wood, the brass, the steam and the water?" Wouldn't this be the question of someone insane and worthy of piteous contempt from the master? Nevertheless, in deeply discrete tones we ask a question—which would be insane to direct to a mortal master—of the world-architect, when we pose the question about the origin and essence of matter! We ask the unnameable architect: *Did you also create the stuff for Your world structure?*

This specific question now constitutes the life-death question and

central point of our knowledge of God. Having long ago renounced probing the range and content of even one significant portion of God's work
with our intellectual power, now we want to procure vague information
about that master who produced *such great work and about whether God
was an infinitely powerful essence similar to us, which we could therefore
grasp, or a spirit possessing the unique, inconceivable power to produce something out of nothing.* As we shall soon see, the entire success of our hopes
in the domain of the spiritual world depends upon the outcome of this
question—a question which makes no sense *vis-à-vis* the mortal master.
We must learn whether *we want to deal with one who is similar to us or one
who is an incomprehensible creator of all.*

This much is incontrovertibly certain: *If God was directed to available
stuff for building the world, like a potter and clay, this would make His will
imperfect. For God's will would then be carried out only to the extent the clay
allowed. He could not select the purely good, but only the best possible good
from the less good, and bring it to bear.* This is the true meaning of the
ancient pagan-philosophical doctrine: *God produced the best of all possible
worlds*—a leading motif in *Leibniz's* theodicy....

The correct concept of a God, the perception of a God who, as expressed by a certain overpowering person among our contemporaries
and fellow believers (Heinrich Heine, "Nachworte," in *Romanzero*, 305),
"*has the elbows free*," is to be found where *a true doctrine of creation* exists
and is recognized. Over against this there is nothing but narrow minded
idolatry, whether in refined or crude dress. The product of *rationalism*,
i.e., the God-creating reason of human beings, is nothing other.

This is the *theoretical* aspect! Now the *practical* has to be discussed. *Is
it up to our will to choose between the two world views? Or: in the interest
of freedom and of true human essence, are we not practically forced to choose
and decide—contrary to the basic axiom of our reflective reason—for that
incomprehensible dogma of creation out of nothing?* (154-162).

Summary of translated passages
Kant's proof for the existence of God related to the ethical, not the world of
sensible appearance. He also set aside the principle of created ethics, something rooted in his Germanic antipathy to anything Jewish. For Kant, creation was a physical dogma. For Judaism, creation was centered on God's
freedom and ethics. Steinheim reiterated his parallel between the contradiction between a priori *reason and empirical reality, and* a priori *construc-*

tion and trans-sensible reality. For Judaism the act of physical creation of the world transcended all the antimonies which belonged to the world of thought. Judaism's creation excluded the thought of causality, as a physical category inapplicable to the spiritual and trans-sensible reality, and one applicable only to the axiom that out of nothing, nothing came; and that matter was eternal.

The deep thinker of Königsberg, having shown the emptiness of trying to prove God's existence in terms of the sensible world, sought to prove God's existence in the ethical world as an irrefutable postulate. Kant found the lost God again in His freedom. [But God was] bound together with coercive moral law, to some extent denying reason both its self-sufficiency and basis to capture its own essence. The fact is that Kant would have been less the philosopher, consciously possessing his very own power and firm will, had he not attempted to make reason the creator of reason's God. On the other hand, he isolated the ethical from the sensible world [of appearance] order to an extent which could have [damaging] consequences for moral legislation. What Plato carried out long ago in the theoretical arena, Kant carried out in the practical. Kant reduced the entire realm of appearance to one of indifference and non-existence. He did so while having to actively prove the practical in, and according to, the realm of appearance and to affirm the realm of appearance as a power of free causation. Kant's doctrine resulted directly in excessive idealism and absolute egoism, the reverse of what he sought. The self-legislative reason of the real legislator, whose reason Kant sought but could only postulate and *never find*, placed itself without further ado on the throne of the world. Self-legislative reason ultimately deteriorated into the madness of *"I would be the true God."*

The greatest of all thinkers of recent times suffered from one purely German weakness—which is perhaps the sole *reason* for this blunder. Because this blunder is a fixed national idea, it should not be made into something overly individualistic. This blunder is a *certain natural trait, the inner resistance to everything which somehow heroically stems out of Judah.* He indicated this himself. This little cloud darkened this hero-of-thought's otherwise very clear view. He saw the light and was close to knowing it. He was so near that he discovered the expression of what was uniquely true in the Mosaic doctrine of creation. Nevertheless, on account of this black cloudy spot, he did not recognize the deep meaning of the doctrine of creation, which pointed to the truly ethical.

Kant took the true doctrine of creation merely as a physical dogma. According to its essence [as enunciated in Judaism], the dogma is purely ethical. It teaches the truly real existence of freedom in the trans-sensible world. It teaches that a God who was active in the sensible world was the first of all causes [but not in an Aristotelian sense]. Creation is a simple fact and whatever is created [in particular] is the simple effect of that fact. It exists absolutely, outside the thought-form of thesis, antithesis and copula. (It is not like a necessary result of thought, whose non-existence is impossible. It could also not be.) Through this we receive a new grounding for the ancient character of what is really essential, the *absence-of-opposition*—which is found often in Aristotle's logic and other writings. It states: *There is no opposition when it comes to the essential.* Along with this, what is *essential* is simultaneously the *non-thinkable*, it is only knowable. Everything *thinkable* is subjected to antinomy. Each *statement* has its counter-statement. This is the granite-like, eternal sign of distinction between the *independently existing* and every corresponding *thing of thought*: *Everything truly real is free of opposition.*

We have already deliberated about the basic axiom and the norm for distinguishing essence from appearance in *Revelation According to the Doctrinal Concepts of the Synagogue*. We have probed it in terms of several doctrines of physics. For example, we demonstrated the validity of this axiom in terms of opposing results *concerning the height of the earth's atmosphere*: According to [Pierre Simon] *Laplace*, the result is achieved mathematically, in an *a priori* way: *The earth's atmosphere is without limit.* According to [Jean Andre] *de Luc*, directly contradicting it, the result is achieved *a posteriori. The height of the earth's atmosphere is strictly cut off and limited to a defined, not too lofty height, as with oceans.* There could be no more radically opposed opinions about the same question. Let us first consider that the judgment arrived at through mathematical calculus, which asserts the infinity of the atmosphere, suffers from the internal schism of transforming a *finite* into an *infinite*. The judgment arrived at through induction, by contrast, views the atmosphere as a given finitude, as something defined by air, and subjects this finite to the experiment of weighing and measuring in terms of barometric height. Secondly, we should consider how natural science's judgment is cast straightaway towards the side of *reality devoid of opposition,* and how the mathematical result of the "gradually disappearing and never ceasing *infinite finite*" has been decisively rejected. We *believe,* or rather we *know* with categorical (not apodictic) certainty, that our atmosphere is limited by a surface, without ever having seen or hoping to see it.

This brings us to our general judgment. *What our* a priori *construc-tive-demonstrative reason declares about the essence of things in sensible nature contradicts what we find before us in reality and are forced to rec-ognize as true and real. The same must be valid for trans-sensible nature. Our* a priori *construction stands in contradiction with the thing in terms of reality. The sign of distinction is also here: Namely, the opposition [tied to] the product of reason and the absence of opposition [when it comes to] real essence.* From now on, we have to apply the formula of knowledge and distinction to the authentic object of the doctrine of faith, as a test of the doctrine's genuineness.

There is no better way to begin than with the profound statement of [George Christoph] *Lichtenberg*:

> We know with much more clarity, that our will, like any-thing which happens, must have a cause. Could one, therefore, suddenly turn the argument around and say: Our concept of cause and effect must be very incorrect, because if it is correct our will could not be free? (*Ver-mischte Schriften*, ed. Friedrich Christian Kries, vol. 2, [Gottingen: 1801], 38-39)

And in the same sense [Lichtenberg continues]: "It was a great er-ror on the part of [Christian] Wolff's philosophy to apply the theme of contradiction to *the knowable.* It really applied only to what could be thought." Clearly the misunderstanding lies in the ambiguity of the word "cause." We take this word at one time in an *inclusive* sense—and in another in a *narrower* sense. First we grasp it as that which *generally produces an effect,* and then we grasp it as *sufficient,* as *adequate,* as the producer in connection with what is produced (sufficient cause, *causa sufficiens*). In the first version, the statement: *Every effect has its cause* is completely valid. In the second, there is the important restriction to physical succession of effects from their causes—e.g. place, movement, etc.,—to heavenly bodies in connection with the central body; the cause of freezing, of moisture, of rain, etc. in the atmosphere. Here the con-cept of cause and effect is significant only in the regulated, governing nature of things, in the visible world. Not in the *trans-sensible*. As we step forth beyond the sensible into (transcendental) *spiritual* nature—the *sufficiency, the adequacy of causality* ceases, and is no longer adequate. The impact of the spiritual upon the physical is no longer to be grasped as adequate causality. For the spiritual does not *touch* the physical, such as to constitute a necessary claim as sufficient cause. Whether or not it is my power of mind/spirit which now raises and carries my hand [with] the pen or any other outwardly heavy body contrary to the law of falling, does not matter. My will—[which is] *inadequate to the adequate power of gravity*—is to a certain degree a stronger cause than is natural law. These effects are facts of the *experience*, of simple *knowledge*. We only know that these effects are available. In no way do we explain them in terms of adequate causes. As *Lichtenberg* correctly and incisively recognized, it was a basic error for the philosophy of *Wolff (Mendelssohnian)* to over-look this incongruence, and to extend law and *norms of what is thinkable* to what is solely *knowable*.

This rationalistic axiom of reason, that *no effect is without sufficient cause*, stands very close to the second axiom that: "*Out of nothing, nothing comes*." The axiom's next consequence is the *eternality of world stuff, of matter*. We would immediately hold that the consequence is a *denial of creation*. We will discuss *the denial of freedom*, which follows directly from it. In any case we are already in a position, the extensive sphere of negation having been set aside, to survey rationalism as over-against our consciousness of freedom and the doctrine of revelation. We want to try to measure and determine this as exactly as possible.

Summary of translated passages

Kant's antimony regarding finite and infinite accurately indicated the limits of a priori *reasoning in coping with the problem of the world's creation. But Kant's God of rational apprehension could not be the creator of matter. The rationalistic God was necessarily bound to and limited by matter. Further, by making the ethical law in man an eternal postulate of a legislating God, God's freedom was limited. In Judaism, the absolutely free God created the world and He created ethics.*

The acceptance of the infinity and eternity of matter stands on the same level as the acceptance of *the unlimited atmosphere*. It contains its own antimony and is a contradiction in terms (*contradictio in adjecto*), the *unthinkability of a finite infinite*. But this is one of the main antimonies on the Kantian tablet. Both *infinitude and finitude of matter cannot be thought of simultaneously. The truth must be one of the two, because the third is not given (tertium non datur). It follows that* a priori *reason cannot resolve and demonstrate this world problem.*

If this is already certain for the material world, it will confront us much more intensively in the spiritual and [intellectual] world. The God [of Kant] who produces pure rationality for us, the *God of rationalism*, of the lower or higher level; the God of *so-called healthy human understanding*, and the God of the *most sublime speculation*, can never be grasped as the *creator of matter*. For the conception of creator of matter repudiates the irrefutable axiom, "Out of nothing, nothing comes." The rationalistic deity in its purest formation, e.g., in Leibniz's theodicy, is conditioned by, and assigned to, a material which is equally eternal. Deity does not create its world. It only constructs and builds it out of stuff, which allows only for the most possible good and not the absolute good. Whatever deity could make from the stuff found before it, is what deity makes correctly. But deity *could* not have made everything as perfect as it would have wanted, given its absolute goodness. The material was too *raw*, too *brittle*; too *inert*. This is the highly rational god. This god cannot do what it wants; resistant matter impedes its action. This God of rationalism is like the potter bound to his clay. The potter depends upon the clay, along with his artistic power. *The rationalist God is unfree* in carrying out its work.

If we draw a conclusion from our consciousness of freedom similar to that which *Plato* drew for the existence of the world soul from the soul in the [human] organism, what would it be? Plato called out: "How could we come to [our] soul, if the All was not ensouled?" *"How could we come to [our] freedom, if the spirit of spirits was not free?"* One could then object: "Why not just as well grant to the world creator the freedom we keep in ourselves—a freedom clearly restricted by the stuff upon which it works. Indeed, what is more! Such [Platonic-like] consciousness of freedom shows itself, upon closer inquiry, to be a self-deception. For everything must have its own sufficient ground, and will alone does not lift weight off the ground. Consistent rationalism is finally pushed to the extreme of denying the entire will of human beings and conceiving of a solely mechanical automaton. But therein there also lies the resolute negation of the ethical law and at the same time all law, the basis of human society.

For Kant the sublimity of *"the ethical law in us,"* more than *"of the starry heavens above us,"* was an eternal, indestructible postulate of a law-giving God. In [Judaism] this categorical command of ethics became a postulate in ourselves [as God's creation], indeed an axiom of the absolute *freedom of God*. Like the human being who knows itself as the cause of its creations, and who *atones* appropriately before the internal judge, God knows Himself as the cause of His action, cause of the world. In the doctrine of revelation [of Judaism] God lets Himself be known as creator, who in His omnipotent freedom made even the stuff [of the universe] according to His will.

This is the step we take beyond *Kant's Critique*: we find in the Mosaic doctrine of creation not only the phrase which most precisely expresses the relationship of God to the world. We also find the ultimate ground of all freedom and morality. The first biblical verse, the dogma *"God created the world,"* is not only a *physical* but an *ethical* axiom. This provides a common standpoint which Kant and his successors sought for in vain for so long. In [Judaism's] dogma of creation, world orders, *sensible* and *trans-sensible* world-orders, *physical* and *moral*, come together. Let us therefore accept the revealed teaching as what is really true, over-against our own rational axiom, and cast off [rationality's] eternity of matter. Let us grasp this dogma as the single basis, as the one characteristic dogma of revelation, and now call out: *extra ecclesiam nulla salus*, that outside this dogma no morality exists, and therefore no salvation, no blessedness. [When we do so, it is not a matter] of blind, faithful acceptance of some kind of beloved dogma of the church. It is rather a result of [earnest] conviction according to the firmest grounding and [strength] of our principles. We have tried seriously to acquire the *object* of faith/belief in the [realm of the] doctrine of faith/belief, as the object is acquired and affirmed through induction in the exact sciences, and *thereby raise theology from the sphere of feeling up to the dignity of exact scientific study.*

Our faith/belief is well grounded upon our pregnant-with-meaning dogma of creation, which contradicts the hypothesis of eternal matter and the law of eternal necessity flowing out of it. It is based upon the eternal rock of rational knowledge about all real, essential things, which have permanence in and for themselves, outside our thinking. Each of the world views, *on the one hand* the rationalistic-demonstrative and *on the other* the revealed doctrine of creation, produces a characteristic expression about the configuration of the entire human life. We can indicate this impression and expression of *rationalism* here, and in revelation there, in threefold stages, from general to particular in the following way: I. As theory; II. As practice, and finally; III. As fact. The following table indicates how this may be grasped.

A. *Opposites of the Widest Range, in Theory*	
Philosophical Formation	*Revelation*
Doctrine of Unity	
1. Oneness of the abstraction, Divinity or polytheism	1. Oneness of the person, with full self-consciousness of itself
Doctrine of Creation	
2. a. Eternality of matter. b. God as merely orderer. c. World soul.	2. *God made the world and the stuff for it.*
Eternal Law of Necessity	
3. Consequences of cause and effect. Fate.	3. *Absolute freedom.* Prophecy.
B. *Opposites in the Narrower Range, in Practice*	
1. The *human being* must. He is subjected to the law of necessity, as is his god. 2. *The human is an insubstantial individuality.* Only the species means something and counts. 3. The *species sinks ever deeper.* (the four or five ages)	1. The *human being* is created free, in the image of his creator. 2. *The human being is a self-sufficient individuality within its species.* 3. *The species ever develops itself to higher perfection* (Kingdom of Messiah).
C. *Oppositions in the Narrowest Range, in Fact*	
1. The state is an organic construction and historical state of law, monocratic or polycratic aristocracy. 2. The state of castes, status, serfdom. Property and propertylessness. 3. *Noble and ignoble*, as the effect of the organic act of fathering. Animalistic viewpoint of the races.	1. *The state a state of God*, founded upon *theocracy*. 2. *The state is of citizenry. Equality of all before law and enjoyment of rights.* 3. *Childhood of God*, according to the exemplary state of Palestine, until the time of kingdom. (182-190)

3.2. FRANZ ROSENZWEIG (1886 - 1929)[17]

17 For a bibliography of Rosenzweig's work see L. Anckärt and B. Casper, *An Exhaustive Rosenzweig Bibliography: Primary and Secondary Writings* (Leuven: Bibliotek van de Faculteit Godgeleerdheid, 1995).

Rosenzweig's works include *Der Mensch und sein Werk. Gesammelte Schriften, vol. I. Briefe und Tagebücher. 1. Band, 1900-1918. 2. Band, 1918-1929*, ed. Rachel Rosenzweig und Edith Rosenzweig-Scheinmann unter Mitwirkung von B. Casper (Den Haag: Martinus Nijhoff, 1979); *Der Stern der Erlösung (SE)* (FaM: J. Kauffmann, 1921); *Franz Rosenzweig: Briefe*, eds. Ernst Simon and Edith Rosenzweig (Berlin: Schocken Press 1935); *Kleinere Schriften* (Berlin: Schocken Press, 1937); *On Jewish Learning*, ed. Glatzer. (New York: Schocken Press, 1955); *Hegel und der Staat*, 2 vols. (Munich and Berlin: R. Oldenbourg, 1920); *Understanding the Sick and Healthy*, translation of *Das Buchlein vom gesunden und kranken Menschenverstand*, by T. Luckmann, ed. Glatzer, (NewYork: Noonday Press, 1953); *Sechzig Hymnen und Gedichte des Jehuda Halevi* (Konstanz: O. Wöhrle, 1924); *Die Fünf Bücher der Weisung, verdeutscht von M. Buber gemeinsam mit F. Rosenzweig* (Berlin: Schocken Press, 1934).

On Rosenzweig's life and thought see Leora Batnitzky, *Idolatry and Representation: The Philosophy of Franz Rosenzweig Reconsidered* (Princeton: Princeton University Press, 2000); Haggai Dagan, "The Motif of Blood and Procreation in Franz Rosenzweig," *AJS Review* 26, no. 2 (2002): 241-249; Ya'akov Fleischmann, "Shenei Ha'nitsahim," *Iyyun* 5 (January 1954): 72-82; Else Freund, *Franz Rosenzweig's Philosophy of Existence* (The Hague: Martinus Nijhoff, 1979): 115-189; Barbara E. Galli, *Franz Rosenzweig and Jehuda Halevi* (Montreal: McGill-Queen's University Press, 1995); "The New Thinking: An Introduction," in *Franz Rosenzweig's "The New Thinking,"* eds. Alan Udoff and Galli (Syracuse: Syracuse University Press, 1999): 1-41 and "Time, Form and Content: Franz Rosenzweig and the Secret of Biblical Narration," *Judaism* 44, no. 4 (1995): 467-476; Robert Gibbs, *Correlations in Rosenzweig and Levinas* (Princeton: Princeton University Press, 1992); Nahum N. Glatzer, "Was Franz Rosenzweig a Mystic?," in *Studies in Jewish Religion and Intellectual History Presented to Alexander Altmann*, eds. S. Stein and R. Loewe (Birmingham: University of Alabama Press, 1979); Yudit Greenberg, *Better than Wine: Love, Poetry and Prayer in the Thought of Franz Rosenzweig* (Atlanta: Scholars Press, 1996); Will Herberg, "Rosenzweig's Judaism of Personal Existence," *Commentary* 10 (1950): 541-549; Rivka Horvits, "Tefisut Ha'historiah Ha'yehudit Be'mahshevet Frants Rosentsvayg," *Proceedings of the American Academy of Jewish Research* 37 (1965): 1-24; Reinhold Mayer, *Franz Rosenzweig. Eine Philosophie der dialogischen Erfahrung* (Munich: Kaiser, 1973): 37-53; Mendes-Flohr and Jehuda Reinharz, "From Relativism to Religious Faith: The Testimony of Franz Rosenzweig's Unpublished Diaries," *LBIY* 22 (1977): 61-174; Mendes-Flohr, "Rosenzweig and Kant: Two Views of Ritual and Religion," in *Mystics, Philosophers and Politicians: Essays in Jewish Intellectual History in Honor of Alexander Altmann*, eds. Reinharz and Daniel Swetschinski (Durham, NC: Duke University Press, 1984): 315-341; and "Mendelssohn and Rosenzweig," *Journal of Jewish Studies* 38, no. 2 (Autumn 1987): 203-211; Stephane Moses, *Systeme et Revelation. La Philosophie de Franz Rosenzweig* (Paris: Sevil, 1982); Michael Oppenheim, *Revelation in Modern Judaism* (Lewiston, NY: Mellen, 1985): 34-44; R. Schäffler, ed., *Offenbarung im Denken Franz Rosenzweigs* (Essen: Ludgerus, 1979); Mosheh Schwarcz, *Safah, Mytos, Omanut* (Jerusalem: Schocken Press, 1967); Eliezer Schweid, "Ha'filosofiah Ha'datit Shel Franz Rosenzweig Mul Etgar Ha'hilonit," *Da'at* 6 (Winter 1981): 111-124; W. Strolz, "Offenbarungsglaube im Denken von Franz Rosenzweig," *Offenbarung im jüdischen und christlichen Glaubensverständnis*, eds. J. J. Petuchowski und W. Strolz (Freiburg: Herder, 1981): 180-212; and Manfred Vogel, *Rosenzweig on Profane and Secular History* (Atlanta: Scholars Press, 1996).

3.2.1. Life Through Revelation

Note: Citations from Rosenzweig's letters and diary entries are from Nahum N. Glatzer, *Franz Rosenzweig: His Life and Thought* (New York: Schocken Press, 1953).

The "Archimedes fulcrum" of Rosenzweig's thought was God's act of turning to man with revelation. Rosenzweig's orientation towards the world was derived from revelation, the events of his life took place according to it, and his writing was its exegesis.

Rosenzweig was brought up in a well-to-do, assimilated household in Cassel; he was exposed to traditional Judaism by his uncle Adam Rosenzweig. After graduating from the local *Gymnasium* in 1905 he studied medicine for two years at the universities of Göttingen, Munich and Freiburg. Over the next five years he took courses in history, philosophy, theology, art, literature and classical languages at the University of Berlin and the University of Freiburg. His most influential teacher was political theorist Friedrich Meinecke. In 1912, in Berlin, he completed his dissertation on Hegel's political theory. He was quickly drafted into the army, but discharged a few months later for a minor injury.

Beyond conversion (1913)

Rosenzweig had considered baptism as a youth. In 1913 his jurisprudence professor at the University of Leipzig, Eugen Rosenstock, himself a convert from Judaism to Protestantism, brought him to the brink of carrying it out. During their discussions Rosenzweig found himself theologically impotent, which he attributed to the absence of absolute positions in Judaism:

> In that night's conversation at Leipzig, in which Rosenstock pushed me step by step out of the last relativist position which I still held and forced me to take an absolute standpoint, I was inferior to him from the start—because I had to affirm for my part too, the justice of this attack. / If I could then have buttressed my dualism between revelation and the world with a metaphysical dualism between God and the Devil, I should have been unassailable. But the first sentence of the Bible prevented me from doing this. This piece of common

ground forced me to face him. This has remained the unmovable point of departure even later in the weeks that followed. Every relativism of world-outlook is now impossible for me.[18]

Rosenzweig asked Rosenstock what one could do when all answers failed, and Rosenstock replied, "I would go to the next church, kneel and try to pray." Compared to Rosenstock's concrete faith, Rosenzweig's own religion of abstract philosophical orientation felt empty to him. He faced a choice: Either the Judaism he knew or Rosenstock's Christianity, with its absolutes, its faith experience, and its revelatory relationship between God and man and man and his fellow. He chose to convert. But the conversion would be through Judaism itself and not out of some neutral, rationalistic ground. Specifically, it would entail a process of liberating himself from *mitsvot*. This took him to High Holiday services at a small Orthodox synagogue in Berlin. There, he experienced how on *Yom Kippur* the Jew:

> Confronts the eyes of his Judge in utter loneliness, as if he were dead in the midst of life.... Everything lies behind him. Then 'God lifts up his countenance to this muted and lonely pleading of men' and grants man a part in eternal life. Man's soul is alone with God. Everything earthly lies so far behind the transport of eternity, that it is difficult to imagine that a way can lead back from here into the circuit of the year.[19]

Alone with God, bearing "a testimony to the reality of God which cannot be controverted," conversion became neither possible nor necessary:[20]

> Yes, what the church means to the world is that no one can reach the Father save through Jesus. But the situa-

---

18   Rosenzweig, "An Rudolf Ehrenburg: 31.10.1913," in *Franz Rosenzweig: Briefe*, 71-72.
19   Rosenzweig, *SE*, vol. 3, 85-86.
20   Rosenzweig, "Fragmente aus dem Nachlass," in *Almanach des Schocken Verlags auf das Jahr 5699* (Berlin: Schocken Press, 1938/39): 60.

tion is quite different for the one who does not have to *reach* the Father because he is already with Him.[21]

In 1914 Rosenzweig dedicated himself to reading Jewish texts, which provided access to revelation, and to a critique of the contemporary Jewish and Christian theology which endeavored to eliminate revelation.[22] The same year, he discovered Schelling's outline for a complete system of Idealistic philosophy—which he would publish in 1917.[23]

War: September 1914 – November 1918

In September 1914 Rosenzweig volunteered for the German army. He worked as a male nurse in German-occupied Belgium, attended ballistics school in France, joined an anti-aircraft unit in the Balkans, and finally served in an officers' training camp near Warsaw. He was not, however, taken hold of by all this turbulent history. He wrote his friend Hans Ehrenburg.

> The war itself in no way represents an epoch to me: [On *Yom Kippur*] in 1913 I had experienced so much that 1914 would have had to produce the world's collapse to make any impression on me.... Thus I have not experienced the war.... I neither expect nor hope anything from it, but carry my life through it like Cervantes his poem (not even in the left but in the right hand; with the left I master as much of the war as I can).[24]

From the Balkan front in 1917 Rosenzweig wrote an open letter to Hermann Cohen on the need to integrate the Hebrew texts of Judaism into Jewish education.[25] During the war years he learned directly about other types of Jews and their practices, and integrated this broader knowledge into his thought. In Yugoslavia he encountered

---

21   Rosenzweig, "An Rudolf Ehrenburg: 1.11.1913," in *Franz Rosenzweig: Briefe*, 73.
22   Rosenzweig, "Atheistische Theologie," in *Kleinere Schriften* (Berlin: Schocken Press, 1937), 278-290.
23   Rosenzweig, "Die älteste Systemprogram des deutschen Idealismus," in *Kleinere Schriften*, 230-277.
24   Rosenzweig, "An Hans Ehrenburg: October 1916," in *Franz Rosenzweig: Briefe*, 123.
25   Rosenzweig, "Zeit ists," in *Kleinere Schriften*, 56-78.

Sephardic Jews, and their Judaism impressed him with its natural, integrative quality, as compared to the assimilated Judaism he knew at home. When he read Salomon Maimon's *Autobiography* in 1916, he reacted by saying that it was nonsense for Maimon to brand Eastern European Jews of his time as barbaric: "It's really an integrated culture; it's only the individual (Maimon, for instance) who becomes a barbarian by relinquishing it."[26] When he met Eastern European Jews in Warsaw in 1918, he observed:

> The Jewish boys are splendid and I experienced something I rarely feel, true pride in my race, in so much freshness and liveliness. Driving through the town, too, I was greatly impressed by the masses of Jews.... In general, what among us [German Jews] are only (or again) qualities of the intellectual stratum are here typical qualities: absolute alertness, the ability to place every trivial detail in interesting contexts.... I well understand why the average German Jew no longer feels any kinship with the Eastern European Jew. Actually he has lost it; he has really become philistine, bourgeois; but I and people like me must feel it keenly.[27]

Rosenzweig was confined to military hospitals in Leipzig and Belgrade in 1919. There, he completed the *Der Stern der Erlösung (SE)* manuscript he had started at the Balkan front in 1918.

Freie Jüdische Lehrhaus, Frankfurt 1920

To bring the *SE* text into life, Rosenzweig worked to establish the *Lehrhaus*.[28] Its purpose was not to promote European *Bildung*, but to provide a place for all Jews to live an authentic Jewish life in communion with their predecessors and successors. At its 17 October 1920 open-

---

26 Rosenzweig, "An die Eltern: 9.7.1916," in *Franz Rosenzweig: Briefe*, 97.

27 Rosenzweig, "An die Mutter: 23.5.1918," in *Franz Rosenzweig: Briefe*, 319-320. The subject of Rosenzweig's reception in Eastern Europe has yet to be explored. See Ya'akov Landau, "Di Shabbes-dike velt: Loyt Frants Rosentsvayg. Dray shterns balaykhtn dem yidishn himl: Di bashefung fun himl un erd, di antflekung fun g-ts torah, di derloyzung fun der velt...)," *Beit Ya'akov* 8, no. 7 (June-July 1931): 8.

28 Rosenzweig, "An Martin Buber: August 1919," in *Franz Rosenzweig: Briefe*, 123.

ing, Rosenzweig spoke of returning to the central source of Judaism.

> The old learning had its starting point in *Torah* and was designed to lead into life. The new learning will lead from wherever we stand in life back to the *Torah*. We lead everything back to Judaism. From the periphery where we stand we feel [it] is still Judaism. Not apologetics, but clarification with ourselves.[29]

The *Lehrhaus* was to be a modern *Beit Midrash* (house of learning) where the Bible, for example, was not to be a matter for Higher Criticism but studied as part of Jewish life through the ages:

> Not what caused the word of the Bible [is important] but the effect it had on the reader. If I study the old Hebrew commentaries, I see what happened to the text in the course of our Jewish life. This too, is a study of history, and one free of hypothesis.

By instilling the students with texts and inspiring a communion between Jews of the present and Jews of the past, the *Lehrhaus*, Rosenzweig hoped, would help to consolidate the Jewish people and neutralize the apologetic character of post-Emancipation Jewish identity. Further, Rosenzweig sought to set a dynamic in place where sacred learning extended into the secular world, and abstract intellectual activity was enacted in *mitsvot*. He also wished to remove the regional division between Eastern and Western European Jews; specifically, to minimize the a-rabbinical and anti-ghetto tone of progressive western Jewishness.

The faculty included Martin Buber, who lectured on *I and Thou*; Erich Fromm on the Karaites; Leo Strauss on Cohen's *The Religion of Reason*; Nathan Birnbaum on Orthodox Judaism; Gershom Scholem on the *Zohar*; Ernst Simon on nineteenth-century German philosophy of history; and Leo Baeck on worship. Rosenzweig lectured on the psychology of the Jew after the Emancipation, and trends in German idealist philosophy from Kant through Hegel. Despite the initial great appeal, student

---

29   Rosenzweig, "Neues Lernen," in *Kleinere Schriften*, 94-99.

interest in the *Lehrhaus* dwindled and Rosenzweig found himself ready
to employ even "crude and cheap methods: famous names, sensational
topics, elegant programs, high admission fees and rough treatment" to
attract enrollment.[30] It closed in 1932, but reopened in November 1933
for several years until this sort of public Jewish activity was no longer
possible in Germany. After Rosenzweig died in 1929, an hour was set
aside every year at the *Lehrhaus* in his memory.[31]

Paralysis, 1921-1929

Within a year of the opening of the *Lehrhaus*, Rosenzweig was struck
with paralysis. While the disease spread relentlessly, death did not come
quickly, as predicted. He remained in the attic of his home in Frankfort,
where he was assisted by his wife Edith Hahn, whom he had married
in 1920. The attic became the central gathering place for German Jewish thinkers, and on Sabbath and holidays worship services were held
there. The poet Karl Wolfskehl described how the room offered relief,
freedom and community to Rosenzweig's guests:

> Behind the desk, in the armchair sat, not as one had
> imagined on climbing the stairs, a mortally sick, utterly
> invalid man, almost totally deprived of physical force,
> upon whom salutations were lost and solace shattered.
> Behind the desk, in the chair throned Franz Rosenz-
> weig. Throned and showered bounties. The moment our
> eyes met his, community was established. Everything
> corporeal, objects as well as voices and their revelations,
> became subject to a new order, were incorporated with-
> out strain, conscious effort or need for readjustment,
> into that wholly genuine, primordially true kind of
> existence irradiated by beauty. It simply couldn't have
> been otherwise, for what reigned here was not pressure
> and duress, but utter freedom ... in the presence of this
> man, *well* in the fullest sense, one's own welfare was as-
> sured, wholly and in accord with the spirit. Near Franz
> Rosenzweig one came to oneself, was relieved of one's

---

30   Rosenzweig, "An Rudolf Hallo," in *Franz Rosenzweig: Briefe*, 466.
31   Glatzer, "The Frankfort *Lehrhaus*," in *Essays in Jewish Thought*, 261-262.

burdens, heaviness, constriction. Whoever came to him he drew into dialogue, his very *listening* was eloquent in itself, replied, summoned, confirmed, and guided, even if it were not for the unforgettably deep and warm look of the eyes.[32]

During 1922 and 1923 Rosenzweig translated the poetry of Yehudah Halevi. In 1923 he wrote an open letter to Martin Buber on how the hyphenated Jews produced by the nineteenth century ("Christian Jews, national Jews, religious Jews, etc.) could return to being full Jews,[33] and also wrote an introduction to Cohen's *Jewish Writings* with an essay tracing Cohen's development from a neo-Kantian academic philosopher to a warm, believing Jew. Rabbi Leo Baeck of Berlin arranged for Rosenzweig to receive the rabbinical title of *Moreinu* the same year—a fact which remained secret until after his death. In 1925 Rosenzweig authored "Das neue Denken," epitomizing his *SE*. He also began a new German translation of Hebrew Scripture with Buber; they were able to complete the books of Kings and Isaiah.

The last year

Rosenzweig's life represented his thought and also blended into them as well. His experiences on *Yom Kippur* in 1913 and in World War I spoke to a concept of eternal revelation and the belief that Judaism was immune to historical events. He asserted that learning Jewish texts provided both access to revelation and a means for revelation to enter the life of the people. His opposition to assimilation and promotion of the concord of the different cultures of Judaism spoke to his idea of an internally-centered Jewish people, a people harmonized into a single entity that was rooted in revelation. During the eight years of his paralysis, Rosenzweig became a crucible for his own thought, a Jew whose life was filled with revelation, text and peoplehood. Nahum N. Glatzer wrote that during his last year, 1929, Rosenzweig journeyed back through his past, recapitulating his life so as to purify and spiritu-

---

32   Glatzer, "Franz Rosenzweig: The Story of a Conversion," in *Essays in Jewish Thought*, 230-242.

33   Rosenzweig, "An Eugen Rosenstock: 25.8.24," in *Franz Rosenzweig: Briefe*, 507-508. Rosenzweig, "Die Bauleute: Ueber das Gesetz," in *Kleinere Schriften*, 106-121.

ally refresh it, and bring it to a perfect conclusion.[34]

Thus, Glatzer explains, Rosenzweig prepared a second edition of *SE*, with chapter headings, index and identification of Jewish source material. He endeavored to have it translated into Hebrew, under the title *Magen David* or *Kokhav Miya'akov* and arranged for Joseph Rivlin of the *Lehrhaus* to begin the process.[35] His interest in the *Tenakh*, whose ideas involving revelation and tradition were strange to him as a youth, and later (along with prayer) became the center of *Lehrhaus* study, now became focused on the book of Isaiah.[36] He absorbed Isaiah's themes of Israel's selection, hope for a covenant of peace, Jerusalem as the heart of all nations, and the knowledge of God. He experienced these subjects simultaneously through the *persona* of the suffering servant (Isaiah 52:53)—and when he read the portion he cried even though his mouth could not open. In 1929 Rosenzweig also arranged for his son to have a *Torah* teacher.

Rosenzweig had thought of God's name as being revealed upon the culmination of creation, penetrating the void and becoming the source of world history.[37] Now, he replaced *"der Ewige"* (the eternal), Mendelssohn's German philosophical translation of *YHWH* in the *Book of Peace and Truth*, with "I shall become what I shall become." Though it conveyed the act and principle of revelation, the phrase did not emphasize the essential aspect of God (*Sein*) but rather God's reaction to man (*Dasein*), and also expressed God's hidden-ness in the distance and revealed-ness in nearness. Unlike Mendelssohn, Rosenzweig would not use one term for God in his translation while employing another for personal worship.[38]

For Rosenzweig, the Jewish nation before Emancipation had had its own center and had appropriately born the eternity implanted within it. After Emancipation, amidst/in the prevailing apologetic atmosphere, Jewry lost this center, and its central beliefs were weakened.[39]

---

34 Glatzer, "Shenat Ha'ahronah shel Franz Rosenzweig," in *Essays in Jewish Thought*, 274-283.

35 Rosenzweig, "An Hans Ehrenburg: 6.7.1919," in *Franz Rosenzweig: Briefe*, 365-366; "An Joseph Rivlin: 24.10.1926," in *Franz Rosenzweig: Briefe*, 566.

36 Rosenzweig, "An Rudolf Ehrenburg: 23.2.1917," in *Franz Rosenzweig: Briefe*, 160-163.

37 Rosenzweig, "An Gertrud Oppenheim: 30.5.1917," in *Franz Rosenzweig: Briefe*, 211.

38 Rosenzweig, "Der Ewige: Mendelssohn und der Gottesnahme," in *Kleinere Schriften*, 182-198.

39 Rosenzweig, "Neues Lernen," in *Kleinere Schriften*, 94-99.

The *Lehrhaus* steered away from Enlightenment *Bildung* and back towards *Yeshivah* learning. In the last year, in contrast to Mendelssohn's
Biblical translation which sought to integrate Jews into German culture by using the German language, Rosenzweig's Biblical translations
opened a way for those who wished to return to Jewish sources. For the
Mendelssohn jubilee in October 1929, he wrote that although Mendelssohn succeeded in preserving the integrity of both Germany and
Judaism in his personal synthesis, he did not teach his successors how
to emulate him. The synthesis was in fact dangerous, and his inheritors
often left Judaism altogether.[40]

Earlier, Rosenzweig wrote about Israel residing in the light of eternal
life apart from history.[41] An accurate "historical" study of Judaism, he
said, should point to Judaism as over and against the passing, historical character of other nations.[42] The authentic present was offered by
Tenakh, not by developing history.[43] Yehudah Halevi, for example, used
Scripture to purify his Judaism of the immediate exilic environment. In
his last year, Rosenzweig rejected the term *Bible* as used by the authors
of *Encyclopaedia Judaica*, vols. 3 and 4, where it meant "New" Testament and "Old" Testament, as a resistance to historical judgment.[44] A
few days before he died, the actress Hannah Rovina brought the Second
Book of Samuel into the present by reading the story of Amnon and
Tamar. Rosenzweig responded:

> You have brought into my narrow room / That re-
> freshment, tragic catharsis, / With which you regale
> thousands outside.
>
> The father was deeply moved and so was the son. But
> the latter, his tears streaming, left
>
> The room, protesting angrily, / Thus renewing for
> you the triumph / Of the most ancient of all tragedies:

---

40   Rosenzweig, "Vorspruch zu einer Mendelssohnfeier" (Autumn 1929), in *Der Mensch
und sein Werk. Gesammelte Schriften, 3. Band, Zweistromland* (Den Haag: Martinus Nijhoff,
1984), 457.
41   Rosenzweig, "Zeit ists," in *Kleinere Schriften*, 56-78. Rosenzweig, *SE*, vol. 3, 95.
Rosenzweig, "An Rudolf Ehrenburg: 28.12.17," in *Franz Rosenzweig: Briefe*, 275.
42   Rosenzweig, "An Gertrud Oppenheim: 1.5.1917," in *Franz Rosenzweig: Briefe*, 201.
43   Rosenzweig, *SE*, vol. 3, 53.
44   Rosenzweig, "Zur *Encyclopaedia Judaica*," in *Kleinere Schriften*, 521-538.

Thespis' play, the Fall of Miletus / So incensed the
Athenian citizenry That it arrested the poet.

Scion of our old race / Founder of Hebrew tragedy,
/ Thanks for the refreshment I received at your hand.[45]

Collectively, Glatzer wrote, the activities that Rosenzweig participated in during his last year distilled his life up until then, and did so in
such a way that he was able to transcend the past and move from time
and into eternity. Specifically, his final thought about death reached
the center of the All. In 1907 Rosenzweig acknowledged that he had
no relationship to the problem of death.[46] In 1908 he wrote that "he
alone is truly blessed who is able not only to experience consciously
this daily reawakening, but also in the moment of death to remain conscious and make the step from this world to the next with his senses
still intact."[47] In the course of time he understood death as the hidden
root of thought.[48] When death actually came, Rosenzweig the person,
not Rosenzweig the expositor of philosophical system, had already
overcome it. In his final moment he thought of his *Berit milah* and *Yom
Kippur* 1913, both expressions of the apperception of God from within
eternity. Rosenzweig had discovered that his Hebrew name, taken from
his grandfather, was not Levi but Yehudah. Yehudah ben Shemuel was
also the name of Yehudah Halevi, of whom Rosenzweig said:

> The tension between man and God is irreconcilable—
> then man himself, in the sight of God, gives the an-
> swer which grants him the fulfillment of his prayer of
> return.... In this manner, he is as close to God ... as it is
> ever accorded man to be.[49]

Rosenzweig instructed that his gravestone should read "I am ever
with you," expressing that moment of overcoming death and sharing
eternal life.

---

45 Rosenzweig, "An Channa Rowina," in *Franz Rosenzweig: Briefe*, 1235-1236.
46 Rosenzweig, diary entry of 15 December 1907, in *Der Mensch und sein Werk*, 1. *Band*, 74.
47 Rosenzweig, 10.8.1908, as cited by Hermann Badt in *Der Mensch und sein Werk*, 1. *Band*, 85.
48 Rosenzweig, *SE*, vol. 2, 2.
49 Glatzer, "Franz Rosenzweig: The Story of a Conversion," in *Essays in Jewish Thought*, 230-242.

3.2.2. New Thinking

Rosenzweig's biography reflected the themes of *SE*. In this text he separated traditional thought from his own "new thinking." In traditional thought, God, man and world were sublimated into each other with one dominating the other two. Thus, ancient philosophy was cosmological (world-dominated), medieval religious thought was theological (God-dominated) and modern Idealism was anthropological (man-dominated). The Idealism to which the process had led, however, had proved empty. It swallowed up individual death in its philosophic whole, but death in reality lost none of its poisonous sting. In Rosenzweig's "new thinking," each of the three entities retained its respective integrity. Once isolated, the entities were able to share in each other and relate dialogically. Man remained man but also transcended himself. He died, but through death also encountered life in God. From the grandest standpoint, God and the world related in the dialogue of creation. Man and God related in revelation, and man and the world in redemption. In the messianic universe, the three dialogues would be orchestrated into a single "trialogue." In it, God, man and world would "touch" one another without losing themselves.

In revelation, God broke through to man in love. He asked man, "Where art thou?" Man responded, reaching into eternity, and answered "Here am I." An endless dialogue began. God approached man from an infinite, transcendental distance, and also withdrew so man could step towards Him. Man endeavored to love infinitely, although he could in reality only do so finitely. The dialogical event was defined from within itself. No previously fixed ideas determined it. Dialogue awaited and "depend[ed] upon" time. Its proper vehicle was speech, for while thought was independent of time, speech was bound to temporality. In the dialogue of revelation, Rosenzweig claims, all that was revealed was God revealing Himself:

> All that God ever reveals in revelation is—revelation. Or, to express it differently, he reveals nothing but Himself in man. The relation of this accusative and dative to each other is the one and only content of revelation. Whatever does not follow directly from this covenant between God and man, whatever cannot prove its direct bearing on this covenant, cannot be a part of it.

The problem has not been *solved* for the visionary who beheld the vision; it has been *dissolved*.[50]

Man's experience could not be communicated by him afterwards, even if he is able to extend God's love that he has shared in revelation into his own love for his fellow man.

In creation, God's infinite substance broke into the cosmos. The cosmos responded by becoming defined into particular entities, whereupon each new creation would evoke new entities. The process was completed when revelational love flowed through all humanity. This was redemption. Divine creation was realized as revelation evoked redemption.

Judaism and Christianity worked together to bring redemption about. Judaism resided in the "center of the star," in the realm of being which was outside of history. The Jew was constantly, indeed eternally, tied to redemption. A born Jew shared in that flow of blood through the "veins" of the generations. Christianity conveyed Judaism into time. While rooted in redemption, Christianity was also capable of moving into and with history. It could and did extend Judaism to all mankind. The Christian thereby built the bridge of love between creation and redemption. This bridge was an eternal way.[51]

3.2.3. Revelation and its "tensions"

In *Understanding the Sick and Healthy* Rosenzweig renounced the philosopher's "sick" understanding which did not trust in experience but

---

50   Rosenzweig, *Sechzig Hymnen und Gedichte des Jehuda Halevi* (Konstanz: O. Wöhrle, 1924), 174, as cited in Glatzer, *Franz Rosenzweig*, 285.
51   Rosenzweig spoke of Samuel Hirsch as his "*Vorplagiator*" with regard to his theory of Judaism and Christianity:

> Steinheim—und 1918 schrieb ich dasselbe in den Stern, irgendwo in die Mitte; ich kann die Stelle wohl kaum rasch finden, aber es steht da: Kind ist mehr als Geschöpf. Steinheim kannte ich damals auch noch nicht, während ich Samuel Hirsch, den Vorplagiator des Gedankens der Juden—und Christentumstheorie meines dritten Teils, schon 1913, unmittelbar nachdem ich diesen damals für mich rettenden Gedanken gefunden hatte, entdeckt hatte.

Rosenzweig, "An Martin Buber...21.5.24," in Franz Rosenzweig, *Der Mensch und sein Werk*, 2. Band, 1918-1929, 963.

relied on reason and was unwilling to wait to meet with God. He affirmed, instead, the "healthy" understanding of religion, where the individual was open to the world and allowed the stream of experience to inform him.[52] Revelation was the "central concept" of Rosenzweig's religion, and its dialogical basis was "the centerpiece, as it were, of this entire book."[53] It was experienced as dialogue between God and the individual personality. The dialogue was spoken, since for Rosenzweig, speech was the only act which was parallel for God and man: "The word of God and the word of man are the same. What man hears in his heart as his own human speech is the very word which comes out of God's mouth."[54]

Rosenzweig's concept of revelation unfolded in a series of sets of apparent tensions. It was a present personal experience, universally available, but was also a past public event for Jewish and Christian communities in particular. It was a distinct, single occurrence which transformed the individual, but also a continuous process where God bestowed his love as long as the individual was able to receive it. Revelation was spoken in dialogue, yet it was a mystical union where the human soul was overcome by God's love. "In love, the I which would otherwise bear the attributes disappears totally in the instant of love." In revelation God initiated and dominated: "It is love which meets all the demands here made on the concept of the revealer, the love of the lover, not that of the beloved."[55] Yet the human soul remained responsible: "If ye acknowledge Me, then I am God."[56]

Rosenzweig also described a tension between the revealed God of time and the revealed God of eternity. As a Jewish "existentialist" he perceived God from within a historical standpoint. This was the God of revelational experience and love, tied to a temporal context. Revelation was eternity in, and as, time. It was an effulgence which irradiated the temporal facts of creation. It uncovered the life within, prevented its death and made it "audible." Revelation flowed, ever afresh, from

---

52   See Oppenheim, *What Does Revelation Mean for the Modern Jew?* (Lewiston, NY: Mellen, 1985): 34-44.
53   Rosenzweig, "'Urzelle' der Stern der Erlösung," in *Kleinere Schriften*, 357-372.
54   Rosenzweig, *SE*, vol. 2, 80-81.
55   Rosenzweig, *SE*, vol. 2, 96, 97.
56   Rosenzweig, *SE*, vol. 2, 121.

thing to thing in the fullness of time.[57] In the moment of revelation, man stretched forth from secular history to share eternity and all of time, which was concentrated in an eternal moment. But time was not erased. There was no *ecstasis* from history. Man's successive, momentary loves rose out of the static historical plane. But as a born Jew, Rosenzweig also had an apperception of God from within eternity. This God, of the innermost reaches of the star of redemption, was detached from historical time. Israel's creation preceded time and remained, unchanging, as long as the cosmos did. The people resided in collective ecstasy within God's sacred countenance, and blended into its light. In the star's center, Israel survived death and led a sacred life. It resided at the trans-temporal *eschaton* of history, where creation and revelation were subsumed into redemption. The blood of Israel carried eternity through the generations, and spiritual ecstasy became deep reality. Through Israel's blood, the light of God's countenance shone eternally within each Jew. Sacred time, Israel's events, laws, language and prayer, blended into this light, and each born Jew's God was of this eternity. God was apperceived solely from within the eternal in terms which transcended time. Rosenzweig endeavored to relate lovingly to God, to whom felt that his Jewish blood permittedhim exclusive access. These joint endeavors meant a split in his experience, between one position in the rays of God's star, and one in the fire's center. The God of revelation perceived by man-as-temporal was inseparable from historical moments. The Jew of blood immediately apperceived the purely eternal God from within the fiery eternity which the Jew alone endured. The reader of *SE* waited in vain to reconcile the temporal God of love with the eternal God of blood.[58]

The translated selections are from Rosenzweig, Franz, THE STAR OF REDEMPTION. Translated by Barbara E. Galli. Copyright 2005 by the Board of Regents of the University of Wisconsin System. Reprinted by permission of the University of Wisconsin Press.

---

57   Rosenzweig, *SE*, vol. 2,.29-30, 93-94.
58   Greenberg, "Franz Rosenzweigs zwiespältigen Gottesicht: Von der Zeit und in Ewigkeit," *Judaica* 34, no. 1 (March 1978): 27-34 and 34, no. 2 (June 1978): 76-89.

III.II. Selections from *The Star of Redemption* (Part Two, Book Two), translated by Barbara E. Galli

Summary of passages translated by Barbara E. Galli

Discussing creation and revelation, Rosenzweig wrote that God disclosed Himself in creative activity. The disclosure began when His wisdom surfaced as the self-negation of His Nought. This was the affirmation of the world. Within this "first revelation," the utterly concealed God became manifest as creation. Out of the darkness there emerged at once an infinity of acts of bare creative power. These were captured in visible form. With this visibility, God could not retreat back to concealment, and the "first revelation" was secured against retrogression into the mysterious night. This implied the "second revelation," revelation as distinct from creation. Here, God became transfixed into the unconcealed present. Creation was confirmed at every moment by the revealer.

Love is as strong as death. As strong as death? Against whom is it that death shows its strength? Against the one whom it seizes. And love—certainly, it seizes both, the lover as well as the beloved. But the beloved differently from the lover. It is in the lover that it originates. The beloved is seized; her love is already a response to the being-seized, it is Anteros the younger brother of Eros. It is true first for the beloved that love is as strong as death. Moreover, nature has given only the woman, and not the man, the capacity to die of love. What has been said of the twofold encounter of the man with his Self applies strictly and universally only to the masculine. Thanatos can approach her, too, in the sweet name of Eros, and most often the most feminine woman. Therefore, because of the absence of his opposition, her life is simpler than that of the man. Her heart has already become firm in the tremors of love; it no longer needs the tremor of death. A young woman can reach her maturity for eternity, whereas a man can reach it only when Thanatos crosses his threshold. No man dies the death of Alcestes.[59] Once touched by love, a woman is what a man will only be at the centenary age of Faust: ready for the final encounter as strong as death.

Like all human love, this is only a simile. As keystone of Creation,

---

59   Reference to *Alcestes* by Euripides (438 BCE). Alcestes, ready to sacrifice herself for her husband, was saved by Hercules.

death imprints everything created with the indelible stamp of its condition of creature, with the words "has been." But love declares war on it. Love knows only the present, it lives only out of the present, aspires only to the present. The keystone of the dark vault of Creation becomes the foundation stone of the bright house of Revelation. For the soul, Revelation is the lived experience of a present that, though resting on the existence of the past, does not dwell in it; on the contrary, this present walks in the light of the divine countenance.

The Revealer. The Hidden One

It is to God the Living One that the pagans cry, insofar as he is not sleeping, or has gone up hill and down dale; in the powerful wisdom of his creative act, he appeared as the God of life. That limitless power, hidden in the mythical vitality of God, came forth again, but it changed from arbitrariness, a prisoner of the moment, into a wisdom resting by nature on duration. What had struggled forth out of God's "nothing" as a self-negation of this nothing, had entered into the living "something" of God and emerged from this no longer as a self-negation, but as affirmation of the world. As it were, God's vitality once again became the nothing, a nothing of a higher degree, a moment which only had been related to that which escaped from it, but in itself, this was a nothing full of character, not a nothing exactly, but a something. This vitality was a nothing only in the fact that, when it appeared on the outside, it broke apart into new figures: one of these is already familiar to us, the essential power; for these new figures do not have behind them anything nameable, or anything from which they might have emerged; if we wanted to designate as God's vitality this sort of backdrop of the power to create which has been revealed, then we would rightly have to object that such an emergence could not occur out of the mythical vitality of the hidden God, but only out of its reversal in Revelation, but for this reversal there is no name; it is only the geometric point as it were out of which the emergence occurs.

Of course, "before" this reversal, too, it was only a geometric point, the meeting of the two segments, that of the original Yes and the original No in the divine nothing; and the reversal is only comprehensible in the reversal of the directions: in one case, their rays meet, in the other, they diverge. But the result of the meeting of two lines is only a point; yet, as a conceived point, it can be named, determined, it is a something, like the point x and y of a system of co-ordinates. On the other hand, the point that is uniquely determined as the starting point of directions is fixed like the starting point of a system of coordinates, but it is not determined: it is only origin of the determination which takes place in the system of coordinates. Hence it happens that the God of paganism has a very lively and visible face and is not at all experienced as a hidden God, while faith proves very clearly that it knows absolutely nothing of a God who would not be revealed: for God in himself is a "hidden God," the same God who, before his reversal from obscurity, in order to become manifest, did not appear hidden at all to unbelief. It is precisely at this different relationship to Revelation that one recognizes the anchoring-place of paganism such as we defined it very clearly throughout Part One: the difference between the original nothing as the original founda-tion of the something of the origin, and this something at the origin as result of that original nothing, not a manifest result of course, but veiled in itself and yet visible. Visible though not manifest, that is to say, visible for the one whose eyes are enveloped by the same dark-ness where that something of the origin is veiled, and so are adjusted to this darkness.

The Revealed One

For faith, apart from Revelation—and later we shall find analogous points also as regards the two other elements of the primordial world—for faith then, God is purely and simply a hidden God, but in the framework of Revelation, he at once becomes manifest and con-sequently fragmented in order to form the figures of his becoming-manifest: but if he is thus manifest in them, don't we now lose what we believed was already in our hands: the elemental "factuality" of God? If God is only hidden origin of his manifestation, then where, in Revelation, has the outright tangible reality gone which God already possessed in paganism? But did he really possess it? Wasn't it bro-ken into a hundred pieces by the omnipotence of the perhaps which remained unshaken? Certainly, the factuality does not seem directly affected by the "perhaps," but after all, a factuality such that it will not answer any questions about its "how" surely does not have much self-confidence. One may presume that, in its affirming its inability to recognize the elemental actuality of God, and in distancing this God because he is "hidden," Revelation would instead strive for its own appropriate factuality founded not on the elements but on the one path of the one reality itself which would be raised above every [?] perhaps to the height of absolute certainty.

And so it is. God, having emerged from his nothing of the primordial world, had only become result; so, too, the hidden God, who alone gives belief a glimpse of that result of the primordial world, is only the beginning of a process of which we have seen the first act, the Creation of the world by God. For God, Creation is not merely Creation of the world, but it is also an event which takes place within himself, as the hidden one. In this sense, we had to mark Creation already as a Revelation of God. And indeed he does reveal himself in Creation as Creator, that is to say in the multiple works which no longer grow and which no longer increase; on the contrary, they are in the beginning and hence once and for all, and so, as far as this concerns God, they are attributes and not acts. The rest, that which emerges from the hidden God, "outside" of Creation—must God complete this infinity which is once and for all liberated, this unlimited infinity of the creative power of God, in the direction that would gather this infinity into actual unity? It would then be a matter of a reality that possesses in itself the drive gradually to traverse the entire infinity disseminated from the divine power, hence of a reality which grows in itself, capable of exceeding itself. How and where it realizes this drive, we won't yet talk about here; but about this point we do have to be clear, that it has this drive.

Love

Just as before, it was the original freedom, the unsubdued passion of the mythical God that broke into the light of the new day from out of the hidden God as divine creative power; henceforth it is the divine essence marked by destiny, the *Moira*, which seeks a path out into the open. Without a doubt, God's inner "nature," the infinite oceanic silence of his being, had coalesced and consolidated as fate under the impact of the divine freedom of action inherent in God; but fate is always something that endures. The *Moira* did not change her decree; it might well be that this is disclosed only in the course of time, but it is in force from the beginning; fate is the original law, its messengers are the oldest ones among the race of the gods; and it is not by accident that they are mostly women; for the maternal is always that which is there already, the paternal is only an addition; for man, the woman is always mother. But fate must lose this permanent and primordial trait when it now breaks into the light, outside of the obscurity of the divine hiddenness. The freedom to act in the creative power of God had become manifest as essential being, being which is attribute. Now being, tied to destiny, must reveal itself in a corresponding reversal, in order to reveal itself as a process that has arisen in the moment, as a happened event. What is this fate that breaks in eventfully with the full brunt of the moment and is not destined from the very beginning, but is on the contrary precisely negation of everything valid from the very beginning, even as negation of the very moment immediately preceding this one: in its very own narrow space, the moment which preserves the entire weight of destiny; of a destiny that is not "decreed," but suddenly present and which, in its suddenness, is yet impossible to ward off, as if it had been decreed from all eternity—this fate and this moment—what is it? A look at the creature, created in the likeness and image of God, teaches us the only name we can and must give to this internal fate of God which has become affect. Just as God's arbitrariness, born of the moment, had turned into lasting power, so, too, his eternal essence had turned into—love at every waking moment, always young, always first. For love alone is at the same time this fatal violence that beleaguers the heart in which it awakens, and yet so newly born, so devoid of a past—for the time being—so surrendered to the moment it fulfills, and to that moment alone. It is an intrinsic necessity, entirely "*dues fortior me*"—to use the words of the great lover[60] who upheld his love and whom his love upheld through hell, world and heaven;[61] and yet going back to what immediately precedes this, in its violence, the love is not sustained by a decree created from all eternity, which would be a perpetual "for a long time" preceding its "already-being-there"; rather, it is sustained by the ever new "in the moment" of its "having-come-precisely-in-this-moment": *ecce dues fortior me "qui veniens dominabitur miht"*. Love is nothing other than the decree of fate, on which the arbitrariness is broken in the mythical God himself; and yet it is as distinct from this decree as the heavens are from the earth; for that

---

60   The great lover Dante.
61   The great lover Dante.

decree had emerged from the nothing as simple Yes, a simple "it is so," "it was decreed so"; but love reversed this decree into a necessity that breaks into the revealed world, from out of the night of the hidden God, as a No, as a perpetually new self-negation, unconcerned about everything, about everything that came before and about everything that will follow, entirely birth of the immediately and presently experienced moment of life.

Here begins that supplement which is the Revelation of God, merely ushered in the acts of Creation of which we spoke above. In order to retrieve the "factuality" of God which risked being lost in its hidden nature, we must not stay at his first Revelation in an infinity full of creative acts; there, God threatened to be lost again behind the infinity of Creation; he seemed to become mere "origin" of Creation, and hence to become again the hidden God, just what he had ceased to be in creating.

From the night of his obscurity something other has to emerge than his mere creative power, something that would keep visible the vast infinity of the creative acts of his power, such that God could no longer once again take refuge in the secret, behind these acts. The upholding of such an infinity, its vast expanse, will only be able to happen in such a way that the whole vast expense be entirely traversed; but as infinite expanse, it will only be able to be traversed by a force of infinite breath, a force which is never exhaustible. And it goes without saying that this force also must spring up directly from the depths of the divine obscurity; for only then will it be able to realize what we expect of it: to protect Revelation which takes place in Creation from a backwards fall into the night of the secret. So, precisely for the sake of its revelatory character, the first Revelation in Creation requires the breaking in of a "second" Revelation, of a Revelation that is nothing but Revelation, of a Revelation in the stricter sense of the word, or rather in the strictest sense.

So this must be a Revelation that "does not posit" anything, that which does not create anything outside itself by setting it into the void; certainly, this last mode of manifestation was also Revelation, but only "also"; essentially and above all, it was Creation; the Revelation that we are seeking must be quite essentially Revelation, and nothing else. But that means: it can be nothing other than the self-negation of a merely mute essence by a word uttered out loud, the opening up of something locked, of a silently reposting permanence by the movement of a blink of the eye. In the illumination of such a blink of the eye there resides the force to transform the created-being that is touched by this illumination by turning the created "thing" into the testimony of a Revelation that has come to pass. Every thing represents such a testimony already because it is a created thing, and the Creation is already itself the first Revelation. But just because it is a created thing from all eternity, this fact that it is a testimony of a Revelation that has already occurred remains behind it, in the darkness of a first beginning; it is only when, at some point in time, it is illuminated by the rays of a Revelation that has not taken place once and for all, but which takes place at this moment, it is only then that the circumstance that brings it about that it owes its existence to a Revelation becomes more than a "circum-stance": it becomes the inner core of its factuality. It is only in this way—when it is no longer a testimony of the Revelation that occurs "just now" at this moment—it is only then that the thing steps out of the past of its essence and enters into its living present.

In the course of time, this "illumination" diffuses always anew from thing to thing, and in this way it frees things from their pure created-being and at the same time it rescues Creation from the fear, perpetually hanging over it, of sinking back into its origin from out of the nothing on the one hand, and from out of the hidden being of God on the other. Just in its absolute emergence from out of the moment, Revelation is the means of fortifying Creation in its formative arrangement. The Creator could still withdraw behind Creation into its obscurity of a wealth of figures, hence into a darkness itself without figures; in some way, there always remained for him the flight into the past of the "origin" where he "could modestly hide behind eternal laws"; but in his eternal presence, the Revealer can at every moment capture the origin in the brightness, in the manifest, in the non-hidden, precisely in the present; and in so doing, he lets the hidden being of God permanently sink into the past; from now on God is present, present like the moment, like every moment, and so he begins to become that which he had not yet been as Creator and which he only now begins to become: "factual," like the pagan gods in the fortified castle of their myth.

Summary of passages translated by Barbara E. Galli
God's sacrificial love: The "second revelation" was an act of self-sacrificial love, for it drew from the very marrow of God's self. In denying concealment and in affirming creation, God gave Himself away. God's love was rooted in the complete moment of its origin, in the entirety of created life. Conversely, God loved everything, and all the dead past and future which was no longer alive would one day be devoured in the victorious today of God's love. On the path to victory, death submitted at every instant to creation.

The Love

All the demands put on the concept of the Revealer converge toward love: the love of the lover, not that of the beloved. Only the love of the lover and this giving of self once again in every moment, only this love gives itself in love; the beloved receives the gift; her receiving of it is her return gift, but in the receiving she does not remain any the less close to herself and she becomes complete serenity and a blissful soul in itself. But the lover—by sheer fighting, he uproots his love from the stem of his Self, just as the tree bursts forth its branches from out of itself, and just as each limb breaks out from the trunk, no longer remembering it, and denying it; but the tree stands there, adorned with the branches which belong to it, though they all deny it; it has not set them free, it did not make them fall to the ground like ripe fruit; each twig is the tree's twig while being entirely a twig for itself, having broken through in its own place, and exclusively in its own place, enduringly bound to this place. Likewise, the love of the lover is implanted in the moment of its origin, and because it is so, it must deny all other moments, it must deny all of life; in its essence, it is unfaithful, it must renew itself every moment, and every moment must become the first glance of love. Only through this totality in every present moment can it grasp the whole of created life, but through this, it really can do it; it can do it by travers-ing this whole with ever new meaning and by shining its rays and its life upon now this and now that single thing—a progress that begins anew every day, and never needs to come to its end; at every moment, because it is wholly present, it thinks it has reached the height beyond which there is none higher—and yet, each new day it learns again that it has never loved as much as today the part of life which it loves; every day love loves a little more that which it loves. This constant increase is the form of permanence in love, in that and because it is the most extreme non-permanence and its fidelity is devoted solely to the present, singular moment: from the deepest infidelity, and from this alone, it can thus become permanent fidelity; for only the non-permanence of the moment renders it capable of living every moment as new and thus of carrying the flame of love through the vast nocturnal and twilight-kingdom of created life. It increases because it does not want to cease being new; it wants always to be new in order to be able to be permanent; it can only be permanent by living entirely in the non-permanent, in the moment, and it must be permanent so that the lover may be not merely the empty bearer of an ephemeral emotion, but living soul. This, too, is the way God loves..

Present

But does he love? May we attribute love to him? Doesn't the concept of love imply a need? And could God need something? Haven't we denied that the Creator could create through love in order not to have to attribute a need to him? And now is the Revealer nonetheless supposed to reveal himself through love?

But why had we denied a need to the Creator? Because his Creation must not be arbitrariness, a sudden impulse, a necessity of the moment, but enduring attribute and essence. Whatever happens, the need must be neither a quality of God, nor his permanent essence. And indeed, this is not the case for love. It is not a quality of the lover, it is not a man who loves. The fact of loving is precisely not a determination in the definition of a man. Love in the man is ephemeral self-transformation, a self-renunciation; he is no longer anything other than lover when he loves; the I, otherwise the bearer of the attributes, disappears entirely in the moment of love. Man dies in becoming lover and is reborn as lover. Need would be an attribute. But how would an attribute find room in the narrow space of a moment? Could it be true that love means a need? Perhaps the need precedes love? But what does the lover know of what precedes it? Its first moment is the one that awakens it; seen from the outside, it may well be that one finds a need at its origin—but what does that mean except that the point of created existence that has not yet been touched with its glance still lies in darkness, the darkness of Creation precisely? This darkness is the nothing that resides at its origin as created "foundation." But, in it itself, on the narrow plank of its momentariness, there is no room for a need; in the moment where it is, it is perfectly fulfilled; the love of the lover is always "happy"; who would go and tell him that he still needs anything other than—to love?

So love is not an attribute, but event, and there is no place in it for an attribute. "God loves" does not mean that love belongs to him like an attribute, like the power to create, for instance; love is not the fundamental form, the solid, immovable form of his countenance, it is not the hardened mask which the one who has molded it removes from the countenance of the dead person, but the evanescent, never exhausted change of expressions, the always new light that shines upon the eternal features. Love balks at making a portrait of the lover; the portrait would harden the living face into a dead one. "God loves": this is purest present whether it is going to love, or even whether it has loved—what does love itself know of this? It is enough for it to know one thing: that it loves. It does not extend into the immensity of infinity, like the attribute; knowledge and power are omniscience and omnipotence; love is not all-love; Revelation does not know of any father who is universal love; God's love is always wholly in the moment and at the point where it loves; and it is only in the infinity of time, step by step, that it reaches one point after the next and permeates the totality with soul. God's love loves whom it loves and where it loves; no question can touch it, for each question will one day have its answer in that God loves, too, even the questioner who thinks he is forsaken by God's love. God always loves only whom and what he loves; but what separates his love from an "all-love" is only a "not-yet"; it is only "not yet" that God loves everything besides what he already loves. His love traverses the world from an always new impulse. It is always in the today and entirely in the today, but every dead yesterday and tomorrow are one day swallowed into this triumphant today; this love is the eternal victory over death; the Creation which death finishes and completes cannot resist it; it must surrender to it at every moment and thus also ultimately in the plenitude of all moments, in eternity.

Summary of passages translated by Barbara E. Galli
Into dialogue: Revelation was of words, "and what cannot become word is either prior or posterior to this world." God and man were brought together by speech. Speech made God fully alive as the revealer, and man fully alive as the one who accepted God's words and helped to establish them in the world. It began with the monologue upon the act of human creation, when

a Thou responded to an I within God's interior. With revelation, the Divine I acknowledged the human Thou as external and there was dialogue. It started with God's "Where art Thou?" The dialogue of revelation began when God expressed His love for man, calling him into relating. At first man hid, but then he came out of hiding to respond "Here I am." Then the only commandment, one which was purely present, was enunciated. "Thou shalt love the Lord thy God with all thy heart and with all thy soul and with all thy might."

Grammar of Eros (The Language of Love.) Root Word

"I" is always a No become audible. With "I," an opposition is always set up, it is always underlined, always stressed; it is always a "but as for me." Even if it wants to remain unknown and wraps itself in the modest cloak of obviousness—when, for instance, Luther acknowledges before the Imperial Diet his stand, his firm certainty and his firm hope, and all three as "his own"—even then the sparkling eye betrays the king in disguise, and world history draws three bold lines under that threefold I in the hour where the mask is lifted. The I, whether it wants to be or not, is always the subject in all the sentences where it appears. It can be neither the object nor passive. One might ask in all honesty, in the sentence "You are beating me" or "He beat me"—obviously not when reading it but when saying it—whether really You or He is the subject and not rather the I, as already betrayed by a conspicuous stress in intonation, a stress that is absent for a normal object. But from the original word itself, from the "not otherwise," via which the original No accompanies every word, saying it aloud leads directly to the I. Indeed, only now do we see why we could not be content, in the manner of the scholastic model, with a *sic et non*, and why we had to assert a "so and not otherwise," and thus replace the non through the double negation of a not-otherwise.

Dialogic Form

The "not otherwise" is immediately beset with the question: "Not otherwise than what exactly?" It has to answer: "Not otherwise than all." For it is quite simply against "all" that it must delimit what is designated as "so and not otherwise." And it is "not otherwise" than all. Otherwise than all: already the so posited this conclusion; the "and not otherwise" that followed the so means precisely that, though otherwise, the so is not otherwise than all, that is to say that it is capable of relationship with all. In this sense, what is it then that is "not otherwise" than all? Than "all," therefore than "the All." Only "thinking" which is identical to the "being" of the All and of every singular object, hence "thinking" which is at once identical to it and opposite to it—the I. In the "I," a word within its own linguistic class, we have not discovered the No become audible, like in the preceding book, where the "good" was the so become audible, but in the game of questions and answers inherent to thinking, we discovered it as a singular answer to a singular question. And so let us not continue, like with Creation, to proceed from linguistic category to linguistic category, but in accordance with the entirely real linguistic expression of language where, because for us it is the central part of this whole work, we are going to stay, we shall proceed from real word to real word. Only reflectively—it is only through reflection that we shall be able—and that we shall, of course, be compelled—to recognize also in the real word the representative of its linguistic category. But as such, we do not discover a representative of a category: we discover it directly as word and answer.[62]

Monologue

To the I there answers,[63] in the innermost of God, a You. It is the mutual accord of I and You in the divine monologue at the time of the Creation of man. But just as the You is not an authentic You, seeing that it stays in the innermost of God, likewise the I is not an authentic I, for it has not yet encountered a You facing it. It is only when the I recognizes the You as something outside it, that is to say when it grows from monologue to genuine dialogue, that it becomes that which we have just defined as saying aloud the original No. The I of the monologue has not yet become a "but as for me," it is not an emphatic I, an I that obviously speaks only for itself; actually, as we already saw in connection with the "let us make (man)" in the narrative of Creation, it is not yet a manifest I, but an I still hidden in the secret of the third person. The I, strictly speaking, the I that is not obvious, the emphatic and underlined I can become audible only with the discovery of the You. But

---

62   *Wort und Ant-wort*: "word and answer," a play on words difficult to render in English.
63   *Ant-wortet*: "answers"; see previous note.

where does this autonomous You exist which stands freely facing the hidden God, and upon facing him could discover itself as I? There exists a world of objects, there is the Self that is enclosed in its closure; but where is there a You? Indeed, where is the You? This is the question that God himself asks.

The Question

"Where are you?" This is nothing else but the question about the You. Not a question about the essence of the You: for the moment it is not even within our range of vision; and we are asking only about the "Where?" Where, then, is there a You? This question about the You is the only thing that we already know about it. But the question is enough for the I to discover itself; it does not need to see the You; by asking about it, and by testifying by means of this question that it believes in the existence of You, even when it is not within sight, it addresses itself and expresses itself as I. The I discovers itself at the moment where it affirms the existence of the You, through the question where it is.

The Call

It discovers itself—and not the You. The question of the You remains a mere question. The man hides, he does not answer, he remains mute, he remains the Self as we know it. The answers that God finally gets to his questions are not answers; the answers to the divine question of the You are not an I, not an "It is I," nor an "it is I who did it"; rather, instead of the I, it is a He-She-It that comes out of the answering mouth; the man objectifies himself in order to become "the male human"; the woman, for her part, totally objectified as woman who is "given" to the man, is the one who did it, and she then throws the guilt on the last It: it was the serpent. The Self needs to be charmed by a more powerful spell than the mere question about the You for it to open its mouth saying I. In the place of the indefinite You, in the place of mere allusion to which man only answers by mere allusions—the woman, the serpent—the vocative now appears, the call; and so every exit to objectification is cut off to the man; in the place of his general concept, which can take cover behind the woman or the serpent, there appears that which cannot run away and is simply called the particular, that which has no concept and slips away from the domain which both articles, the definite and the indefinite, rule, a domain which nevertheless includes all things, even if simply as objects of a universal Providence, and not of a particular providence: the proper name. The proper name, which is not exactly a proper name, not a name which was given arbitrarily to the man, but the name that God himself took for him and which for this reason only—to be a creation of the Creation—properly belongs to him. To God's question: "Where are you?" the man still remained a You, as a defiant, obstinate Self; when called by name twice, with the strongest fixity of purpose to which one cannot remain deaf, the man, totally open, totally unfolded, totally ready, totally—soul, now answers: "I am here."

Listening

Here is the I. The individual, human I. Still totally receptive, still only opened, still empty, without content, without essence, pure readiness, pure obedience, all ear. There falls into this obedient[64] listening, as first content, the commandment. The invitation to listen, the call by the proper name and the seal of the divine speaking mouth—all this is only introduction, the preliminary to every commandment, fully articulated beforehand only so that it can precede the one commandment, which is not the highest of the commandments, but is really the only one, the sense and essence of all the commandments that ever may have come out of God's mouth. What then is this commandment of all commandments?

The Commandment

The answer to this question is known to everyone; millions of lips testify to it evening and morning: "You shall love the Eternal your God with all your heart, with all your soul and with all your might." You shall love—what a paradox n these words! Can love be commanded? Isn't love destiny and being deeply touched, and if it is free, isn't it a free offering? And now it is being commanded? Surely, love cannot be commanded; no third party can command it or obtain it by force. No third party can do this, but the One can. The commandment of love can only come from the mouth of the lover. Only the one who loves, but really he can say and does say: Love me. From his mouth, the com-

---

64   *Gehorsam*, "obedient"; play on *Hören*, with the same root: "to hear, to listen."

mandment of love is not a strange commandment, it is nothing other than the voice of love itself. The love of the lover has no other word to express itself than the commandment. Everything else is already no longer immediate expression, but explanation—explanation of love. The explanation of love is very deficient, and like every explanation, it always comes after the event; and therefore, since the love of the lover is in the present, it really always comes too late. If the beloved, in the eternal faithfulness of her love, did not open her arms to receive it, the explanation would fall completely into the void. But the commandment in the imperative, the immediate commandment, springing from the moment and already on the way to being said aloud at the moment of its springing up—for saying aloud and springing up are one and the same thing in the imperative to love—the "Love me" of the lover, this is the absolutely perfect expression, the perfectly pure language of love. Whereas the indicative has all the circumstances behind it that established the objectivity and whose purest form seems to be the past, the commandment is an absolutely pure present for which nothing has prepared it. And not only has nothing prepared it; it is absolutely unpremeditated. The imperative of the commandment makes no forecast for the future; it can imagine only the immediacy of obedience. If it were to think of a future or an "always," it would be neither a commandment nor an order, but a law. The law counts on periods of time, on a future, on duration. The commandment knows only the moment it waits for the outcome right within the moment of its growing audible, and when it possesses the spell of the genuine tone of a commandment, it will never be disappointed in this awaiting.

Present

The commandment is thus—pure present. But, whereas every other commandment, at least when considered from the outside and as it were after the event, could have been just as well law, the commandment of love alone is absolutely incapable of being law; it can only be commandment. All other commandments can pour their content into the form of the law; this one alone refuses to be decanted, its content tolerates only the form of the commandment, of the immediate presentness and unity where consciousness, expression and waiting for fulfillment are gathered together. So, as the one pure commandment, it is the highest of all commandments, and where it takes the lead as such, then all that could also be law by another route and seen from the outside also becomes a commandment. God's first word to the soul that is united with him is the "Love me"; so everything that he could still reveal to it otherwise under the form of law, is transformed without further ado into words which he commands it "today"; all this becomes the setting forth of the one and first commandment, the commandment to love him. All Revelation is placed under the great sign of the today; it is "today" that God commands and it is "today" that his voice is to be heard. It is the today in which the love of the lover lives—this imperative today of the commandment.

Summary of passages translated by Barbara E. Galli
The beloved's response to "I:" "I the Lord" sealed the negation of God's concealment. It would accompany revelation through all individual commandments, for only an "I" could command "love me." The beloved human soul responded in the present, conscious of wanting nothing in the future but to remain beloved. Man was also conscious that he did not love as much as he was loved by God. To acknowledge his love, man had also to acknowledge his weakness. Acknowledgement—"I have sinned"—abolished this weakness of the past and purified the present.

Revelation
This imperative can only come from the mouth of the lover, and from this mouth can come no other imperative than this one; likewise, the I of the speaking one, the root word of the whole dialogue of Revelation, is also the seal which is set upon every word and characterizes the singular commandment as commandment of love. In the words: "I, the Eternal,"[65] this I is the great No of the hidden God, which negates his own hidden nature and begins and accompanies Revelation through every singular commandment. This "I the Eternal" creates, for the Revelation that takes place in the prophet, an instrument and style of his own. The prophet is not mediator between God and man, and he does not receive Revelation so that he can transmit it further; on the contrary the voice of God comes from him immediately, out of him God speaks immediately as I. In contrast to the master who com-

---

65   Rosenzweig is using Moses Mendelssohn's German Bible translation for God: *Der Ewige*, The Eternal One.

mitted the great plagiarism of Revelation, the true prophet lets God speak and transmits to the amazed audience the Revelation that took place in secret. Strictly speaking, it is not at all that he lets God speak, but at the moment where he opens his mouth, it is already God who is speaking; the prophet scarcely has time to start with the formula: "Thus speaks the Eternal One" or with the still briefer and quicker formula that dispenses even with the verbal form, "Word of the Eternal One," and before God has taken possession of his lips. The I of God remains the root word resounding through Revelation like a pedal-note, it rises in protest against any translation by He, it is I and must remain so. Only an I and not a He can speak the imperative of love; it must never say anything else except: love me.

The Receiving

In the uttermost of silence—what can it reply to the commandment of love? For there must be a response; the obedience as regards the commandment cannot remain mute; it must in its turn speak aloud, become spoken word; actually, in the world of Revelation everything becomes word, and that which cannot become so is either before or after it. The soul, then—what does it reply to the demand to love?

Shame

It is the beloved's confession of love that replies to the lover's demand of love. The lover does not confess his love—how could he, he has no time for that; before making his confession, his love would already have vanished, it would no longer be present; if he nonetheless tries to, it gives the lie hidden in the present confession. For that which was once known is already known, and hence this sinks back into the past and is no longer the present that was intended in the confession; so the confession of the lover is at once changed into a lie, and it is only right—and also a sign that shows how deeply all this is anchored in the unconscious—if faith rejects the mere confession and if the already open soul of the beloved closes again. The lover really speaks only in the form of the demand of love and not in that of the confession. It is otherwise for the beloved. For her part, recognizing his love is not a lie. Once born, her love is a love that holds, a perpetual love, and so she can hold on to it, she can confess it. Her love, too, is in the present, but not in the same way as that of the lover, it is in the present only because it is lasting and faithful. In the confession, it is recognized as this love that has duration and wants to endure. To the confession everything appears bright and shining for the future; the beloved is conscious that she wants in the future simply to be what she is: beloved. But before, in the past, is a time where she was not yet that; and that time where she was not loved, that time without love, seems to her overlaid with a deep darkness; indeed, because love becomes enduring for her only in faithfulness, that is to say only in relation to the future, that darkness pervades all the past until the exact moment of the confession. Only the confession ravishes the soul in the blissfulness of feeling loved; before this, everything is enveloped in the lack of love, and even the readiness in which this Self has been called by its name and has opened up to the soul still remains in that shadow. So the soul meets with difficulties in the confession. In the confession of the love, it lays itself bare. It is sweet to confess that one loves again and that in the future one wants nothing but to be loved; but it is hard to confess that one was without love in the past. And in spite of all, love would not be that which jolts, startles, enraptures, if the jolted, startled, enraptured soul was not conscious that it had not been jolted or startled until this moment. So there had to be a jolt in order for the Self to become beloved soul. And the soul is ashamed of its past Self and of not having, with its own strength, broken this spell whose captive it was. This is the shame that spreads over the beloved mouth that wants to confess; it must acknowledge its weakness both past and present, where it would like already to acknowledge its bliss both present and future. So the soul is ashamed of confessing its love to God who calls out to it his commandment of love; for it can acknowledge its love only by also acknowledging its weakness, and by replying to God's "Thou Shalt Love": I have sinned.

Reconciliation

I have sinned, says the soul, and gives up its shame. By speaking like this, it looks purely back into the past and purifies the present of the past weakness. I have sinned means: I was a sinner. With this confession of the past sin the soul clears the way for the confession: I am a sinner. But this second step is already the full confession of love. It casts afar the constraint of shame and fully surrenders to love. The fact that man was a sinner is washed away through the confession; for this confession he had had to overcome his shame, but it stayed by his side during the time of his confession. It is only now, when he recognizes himself, even though he has cast away his past weakness, as always a sinner, that the shame leaves him. Indeed, the fact that he dares to venture into the present is the sign that he has overcome his shame. As long as it stayed in the past, he did not yet have the courage to express himself fully and confidently; he could still doubt the answer he would be given; for from God's mouth the soul had till now heard only the call by his name and the commandment demanding love, it had not yet received any "explanation" or any "I love you," and, as we know, this could not be forthcoming, for the sake of love's bounded-ness to the moment on which authenticity of the lover's love rests, and in the confession, in the explaining always made up of sentences, it would run aground, really aground, due to "grounds"; for the lover's love in contrast to the beloved's love, which rightly has its ground in it, is groundless. So the soul, which wanted to make its confession, still hesitated, not knowing whether its confession would be accepted. It is only when it ventures out from the confession of the past to take a risk in the confession of the present that its doubts fall away; by confess-ing its fallibility as always present, and not as a "sin" that took place formerly, it becomes certain of the answer, so certain that it no longer needs to hear it aloud, it hears it within itself; God does not have to purify it of its sin but in the face of his love, it purifies itself; at the same moment when the shame has left it and where it is surrendered to the free confession in the present, it is certain of God's love, as cer-tain as if God himself had whispered into its ear, "I forgive," that which was so desired beforehand when it had confessed to him the sins of the past; now it no longer needs this formal absolution, it is rid of its bur-den at the moment when it dared to take it entirely upon its shoulders. In the same way, the beloved no longer needs the lover's confession, a confession so very desired before she recognizes her love; when she herself risks making the confession, she is as certain of his love as if he were whispering his confession into her ear. The recognition of her still present fallibility is the only reason for which the past sin in gen-eral is confessed; this is no longer the recognition of a sin—that has also passed, as has the confessed sin itself—one does not confess the absence in the past, rather the soul declares; even now, even in this moment present of moments, I am far from loving in the way I—know myself to be loved. But this confession is already its highest bliss; for it includes the certainty that God loves it. It is not from God's mouth, but from its own, that this certainty comes to it.

Chapter Four
HISTORY

4.0. INTRODUCTION: SAUL ASCHER; DAVID EINHORN; ZECHARIAH FRANKEL; ABRAMAM GEIGER; HEINRICH GRAETZ; MOSES HESS

The fourth point of departure was that of history, where thought was tied to historical events and historical process. Coming out of the emancipation-world of values, all of our thinkers were in some way historically-oriented. Mendelssohn coped with the issues of historical progress in his encounter with Lessing.[1] Cyclical historical development was an essential subject of Krokhmal's philosophical theology. For Samuel Hirsch and Formstecher, world-history overlapped with developing self-consciousness. For Steinheim and S. R. Hirsch, history was a function of the reality of revelation, and for Rosenzweig the God of revelation perceived by temporal man was inseparable from historical moments. Historical reality played the central and definite role, for those whose departure point consisted of the events and process of history.

SAUL ASCHER
Saul Ascher regarded post-Napoleonic history and the emancipation, with its rationalism and tolerance, as Judaism's definitive ingredients. He delineated three stages in the history of religion: natural, revelational and rational. In his view, Judaism was the exemplar of revelational religion, and was now passing into the rational stage. Ascher proposed to guide the passage. He did so by extracting the essence, consisting of the God-man relationship and Israel's "core beliefs" (which were "regulative" as distinct from rabbinic or "constitutive"), opening Judaism's con-

---

1   See Hans Liebeschütz, "Mendelssohn und Lessing in ihrer Stellung zur Geschichte," in *Studies in Jewish Religious and Intellectual History: Presented to Alexander Altmann on the Occasion of His Seventieth Birthday*, eds. Siegfried Stein, Raphael Loewe, and Arkush (Tuscaloosa, AL: University of Alabama Press, 1979): 167-182.

stitution to intellectual progress, and thus suiting it to the universalism and enlightenment of modernity.

Ascher's attention to historical events extended to Christian anti-Jewish attitudes, which had to be corrected for Judaism to complete its passage into the post-Napoleonic rational stage. He attacked Kant for his triumphalist Christianity. Kant's Jew-hatred blinded him to Judaism's morality (for him, Christianity alone was truly moral) and violated the modern principles of tolerance and universal morality. Ascher attacked Fichte for his exclusivist Christian revelation, and his Eisenmenger-like notion of removing all Jewish ideas from the culture by removing Jewish heads in exchange for granting civil emancipation and alignment with the post-French Revolution world.

DAVID EINHORN

Einhorn identified Judaism's inner principle as a dynamic process of centralizing polar differences (e.g., transcendental *vs.* immanent deity; *YHWH vs. Elohim*). While it was able to fuse these elements, their respective polar identities were not annulled. The revelatory dimension of Judaism united with the human, rational dimension, such that revelation became effective in a rational context. In turn, reason required the experience offered by history in order to develop. For Einhorn, history reflected God's presence, and through it the human being could relate to divine revelation. Specifically, Sinai revelation was to be brought to rational consciousness, removing the (solely subjective) perception of separation between rational thought and revelation. Historical experience (itself reflecting the divine) provided the time and material for doing so. Einhorn was eager to seize new encounters, and thereby expand the rational articulation of revelation. The people of Israel, having been at Sinai, were pivotal for the world's enlightenment—although that revelatory enlightenment was present for and available to all mankind. Once Israel succeeded in opening the pagan mind to enlightened spirituality, Judaism could dispense with all ceremonial means of self-identification.

For both Ascher and Einhorn, historical realities outside the sphere of Judaism were critical to Israel's identity. Ascher aligned the nation's regulative and constitutive formations with post-Napoleonic enlightenment and emancipation, after history reached the rational stage. To belong to this advance, Judaism needed to formulate a new constitution, one which reflected its essence, rather than holding on to that of the rabbinic constitution which, over time, had come to eclipse its core meaning. Einhorn thought in terms of a triangular relationship between revelation, reason and history, where reason accessed revelation by means of historical data entering from the outside. As history moved forward, further access to revelation became possible. Einhorn looked to the future to provide the material which reason needed to advance its access.

ZECHARIAH FRANKEL

Zechariah Frankel (1801-1875) shared Einhorn's triangular mindset. Divinely-revealed content joined the historical dimension, as Israel's human creativity explicated the *Torah*'s content and testified to the trans-human source. The people of Israel had the ability to bridge what was beyond history and what was within it. Their creativity mediated revelation and history and produced oral law. While revelation (embodied in *Torah*) transcended history and was inherently permanent, oral law (both a product of the historical nation of Israel and the crucible of Israel's interaction with revelation) belonged to history and changed. Neither revelation alone nor oral *Torah* was exclusively true. Truth came at their points of agreement, as the people caused the two to interact dialectically. For Frankel, such a truth did not compromise revelation, but rather revealed the divine will. During the period between the Second Temple's destruction and emancipation, the historical dimension was internal to the Jewish nation, who lived according to their own truths and were separated from the political realities of world history. With emancipation, a political dimension entered in from outside, providing a potentially enriching path to world-historical consciousness.[2]

Einhorn and Frankel worked with different components and inter-relationships in their respective three-pronged structures. Einhorn found truth in progress itself, in events as they moved into the future. Frankel looked for truth in the interstice between *Torah* and the nation (as well as the oral law produced by the nation). For Einhorn, what revelation, reason and history produced was, by definition, truthful. Frankel, for his part, maintained that whatever truth was produced at the interstice was required to comply with *Torah*, the transcendental source which the

---

2   Schweid, "Ha'torah Veha'am: Mishnato Shel Zekhariah Frankel," in *Toledot Ha'hagut Ha'yehudit Be'et Ha'hadashah: Ha'meah Ha'tesha Esrei*, 314-321.

historical nation unveiled. It followed that while for Frankel the oral law mediated history and revelation, for Einhorn they were mediated by reason.

ABRAHAM GEIGER

Abraham Geiger (1810-1874) shared Ascher's attentiveness to emancipation as a touchstone for restructuring Judaism. But while Ascher's "thesis" (or basis) was the historical event (involving the French Revolution on one side, and Jew-hatred on the other), Geiger's "thesis" was Judaism. Similarly, Geiger had an enthusiasm for historical progress corresponding with Einhorn's, but Jewish "tradition," not world-history, was the "thesis." He concurred with Frankel's focus on interstitial activity—for Frankel it was between *Torah* and nation, however, while Geiger identified it with Israel's "genius" for tradition.

Religion for Geiger came from the feelings of limitedness and dependence upon an absolute power beyond human grasp. These feelings moved the individual to come close to the divine creator of the universe and instilled a yearning to join the universe. Israel had an aptitude for this. The people, he believed, possessed an original force which enlightened their eyes, enabling them to look into higher realms of spirit and discern the close relationship between human and divine (universal) spirit; to grasp the higher challenges to human existence and to clearly perceive man's ethical character. With this, Israel's revelation, an all-encompassing force illuminated individual minds and enabled them to break the barriers of finitude.[3] The capacity for this was concentrated in the biblical prophets, who had experienced this illumination intensely and shared it with all the people.

The substance of the first period of Jewish history, the biblical era, was revelation. In the second period, that of "tradition," the revelation of Scripture was processed, shaped, and molded for life. Rooted in the spiritual heritage of the past, Judaism approached the heritage freely. This period extended from the completion of the Bible to the completion of the Babylonian *Talmud*. The third period, that of "legalism," was one of preserving the spiritual heritage without further development; there was neither authority nor desire to go beyond its established

---

3 Geiger, "Die Offenbarung," in *Das Judentum und seine Geschichte* (Breslau: Schletter, 1864), 33-34.

limits. Devoted to summarizing what the tradition handed down, it ran from the completion of the Babylonian *Talmud* to the mid-eighteenth century. The fourth period (the modern era) was that of "critical study." Through reason and historical research, the effort was made to become liberated from the letters of the previous era, but without severing the bond to the past. The intention in this era was to revitalize Judaism and have the stream of history flow once again.[4]

The idea of ethical monotheism became historicized, then, in an ongoing spiritual process, according to the four stages. None of these stages was normative; whatever developed in the respective period had relative, not absolute, value. The process was facilitated by the religious genius that stemmed from the original illuminations. Internally undefined, the genius became knowable *a posteriori*, with new expressions of revelation, as appropriate to the age—ever-centered on the idea of ethical monotheism. It became visible as the content of Israel's past was brought into the present, revitalized, and prepared for the future. The process was that of "tradition," which was Geiger's "daughter of revelation," the soul which animated the body. He described this as an evolutionary force, an invisible creative power which was continually at work and never finalized. In accordance with need, and situations emerging from contact with the outside world, it continually gave birth to new forms.[5] For Geiger, the outside world was essential to the dialectic, constituting the very air and light which Israel needed to go on existing—and which nevertheless had to breathe and shine according to the ongoing idea of ethical monotheism.[6]

---

4 Geiger, "Lectures Delivered at the Academy for the Science of Judaism (Berlin 1872-1874)," in Max Wiener, *Abraham Geiger and Liberal Judaism: The Challenge of the Nineteenth Century* (Philadelphia: JPS, 1962), 155-157.

5 Geiger, "Exil und Ruckkehr," in *Das Judentum und seine Geschichte* (Breslau: Schletter, 1864), 71-72.

6 Meyer, "Abraham Geiger's Historical Judaism," in *New Perspectives on Abraham Geiger*, ed. Jacob J. Petuchowski (Cincinnati: Hebrew Union College, 1975), 3-16; "Abraham Geiger," in *Ideas of Jewish History* (New York: Behrman House, 1974), 161-172; "Recent Historiography on the Jewish Religion," *LBIY* 35 (1996): 3-16; and "Universalism and Jewish Unity in the Thought of Abraham Geiger," in *The Role of Religion in Modern Jewish History*, ed. Katz (Cambridge: Association for Jewish Studies, 1975), 91-101. See also Schweid, "Ha'kera Bein Ha'avar Veha'hoveh: Mishnat A. Geiger," in *Toledot*, 263-272; Ken Koltun-Fromm, "Historical Memory and the Authority of Religious Judaism," in *Abraham Geiger's Liberal Judaism: Personal Meaning and Religious Authority* (Bloomington: Indiana University Press, 2006), 12-39.

HEINRICH GRAETZ

Heinrich Graetz (1817-1891) shifted the dialectical dynamic used by Frankel and Geiger from its grounding within Israel's history into an *a priori* tripartite idea to which Israel's history conformed. Jewish identity coincided with the totality of Jewish history, not with any one part, as a reflection and counterpart to that idea. Graetz rejected Samuel Hirsch's understanding of Judaism as an embodiment of speculative theology, a kind of incipient Hegelianism which traversed a variety of dialectical levels. He also dismissed Steinheim's Judaism as an *a posteriori* revelation of anti-rational dogmas, which were so clear that they compelled recognition on the part of speculative reason. He found Samson Raphael Hirsch's Judaism, as a systematic program for cultivating an obedient disposition, a submissive subordination to God's absolute will—where the ultimate goal was to inculcate religious feeling—unconvincing. To Graetz's mind, all these represented only portions of the Jewish experience.[7]

Graetz also spoke of a set of ideas at the heart of Judaism, with which it could be identified, as opposed to paganism. For paganism, out of nothing, nothing came. Its vocabulary was that of nature. Consciousness of God and nature blended, such that laws of necessity reigned, and there was no freedom. According to the idea of Judaism, the world was created *ex nihilo*. Its vocabulary was that of spirit. Nature came to exist only through God's creation; God could remove nature from existence; and nature was related to man by its consecration. In the one, God was seen. In the other, God was heard.

The *a priori*, tripartite idea of Judaism was materialized by passing through the political, religious and reflective stages of history, and then into a fourth stage (the Jewish state), in which the three coalesced. In the first, which ran through 586 BCE, the idea was to be made into a state institution—with the monotheistic idea serving as a foundation for political and social unity. But the process remained incomplete—whereupon the prophets projected the matter into the future. The second, religious, stage ran through 70 AD. Ezra made the *Torah* available to all, the Maccabees protected the nation from paganism, and the Pharisees sought to shape life to religion and purify it according to

---

7   Heinrich Graetz, "The Structure of Jewish History," in *The Structure of Jewish History and Other Essays*, Trans., ed. and introduction by Ismar Schorsch (New York: JTS, 1975), 63.

Torah. In the third stage, Israel moved from the political and religious to the reflective level. The nation retreated from the real world and fled into the *Beit midrash*. Religious life became subsumed into theoretical debates and Judaism sought to grasp its set of ideas in consciousness. While persecution intruded from the outside, the *Talmud* acted as a buffer against foreign elements and the people remained sufficiently apart to advance their self-consciousness. Because the Land of Israel was isolated (surrounded by sea, desert, mountains), a diaspora was necessary for the Jewish set of ideas to flourish; the nation and its ideas needed to be compared with others, to become enriched by the world. Reflection and self-consciousness served to secure and advance the progress towards the kingdom—which remained incomplete during the political stage. With the state, the *a priori* tripartite idea would be historicized—as well as brought to consciousness. Further, with the "seed" growing into a "tree," the fact that Israel has contained the *a priori* idea from its very origin will become evident.[8]

Saul Ascher conceived of Jewish history in terms of an interstice between (1) the progress of world religion from natural to revelational to rational stages; (2) Israel's progress from regulative to constitutive character, and then to constitutive within the regulative framework; and (3) the impact of the French Revolution. For Einhorn, Jewish history was the decisive and material factor in centralizing reason and revelation. For Frankel, Jewish history was an evolving dialectical interchange between *Torah* and nation. For Geiger, it was the "history of the idea of ethical monotheism."[9] For Graetz, Jewish history was the unfolding of an *a priori*, three-dimensional idea of political, religious and reflective stages, culminating in the comprehensive stage of a Jewish state. Moses Hess retracted away from abstractions and external groundings, and enclosed his thinking within the boundaries of the empirical Jewish people.

MOSES HESS

In *Rome and Jerusalem* (1862) Hess described mankind as a living organism with a sacred history. Within the organism, each *Volk* retained its

---

8   Heinrich Graetz, *Die Konstruktion der jüdischen Geschichte* (Berlin: Schocken, 1936), Trans. by Schorsch, *The Structure of Jewish History*, 63-124.

9   Meyer, *Ideas of Jewish History* (New York: Behrman House, 1974), 29.

identity while recognizing its function within the whole organism. The Jewish people, the most creative of national organs, were a race—from which the individual was inseparable. The race executed its own mental activities, from which it formed its social institutions according to inborn instincts. From this life-forming racial source, the people created their own sacred territory. Religion and nation were inseparable; national religion coalesced with national consciousness into one organic whole. The religion was also historical; Hess called Judaism a "cult of history." Its history blended dimensions of the material and the spiritual, the spirit becoming absorbed in the body, and the body in the spirit. Israel's history brought life and death together. Everything developed in an original way, achieved its life goal, died—and then released itself again to a new life in an eternal cycle of infinite (yet somehow unified) and godly life. In the Jewish religion, life was united with death, death with life, and both were of equal value. The nation of Israel (and it alone) was ever-reborn and self-productive; its history embodied the very idea of indestructibility. When the people first began to feel the onset of a national decline, they bound themselves to the belief in the messiah. They found refuge in the knowledge that their race was a source for immortality, spanning back to the patriarchs and forward to the messiah.

Given Judaism's organic character, there was no single abstract belief that could become frozen. Israel's uniqueness was not a matter of some overriding theoretical content. Its religious knowledge grew from the life of the spirit, found within the nation, and its beliefs belonged to ever-developing history. Its many sects and movements were transitory phenomena of the eternally developing organism, and the different world views articulated by the people over the centuries, at times even contradictory, coalesced into certain ever-present conceptual traits. These included the prophetic longing for the perfection of human activity, creatively modified by inner and outer experience to the point of breaking through to redemption and fulfilling the prophetic vision of the unity of mankind. Judaism also claimed the heritage of the concept of ethical monotheism, and of divine unity as manifest in the people and unified mankind. These traits belonged to Israel's sacred territory, to the religious dimension of race and culture. Rather than abstract or self-defined, they were ever-present, yet elastic enough to be part of Israel's organic identity.

The nation of Israel, Hess wrote, was the core of the human family.

Israel's history was linked to mankind's, and through it the history of all mankind would become sacred. The organic process of human development, centered in Israel, would be complete when all humanity became a single family, its members bound together by the sacred spirit of the creative genius of history. Israel's religion was destined to become the common property of the civilized world, when at the end of days the knowledge of God would fill the world. At the end of days, the people of the God of history would announce the Sabbath of history. Social life would be complete, and world social harmony created. For its part, Israel would transcend itself, attain a level of self-consciousness of its history. It would return to its *Urquelle*, of prophecy, to its racial instinct and *Volksgeschichte*, so as to participate again with vitality, in its own sacred spirit. Once this was achieved, the people would have to struggle for their own national rights, for only within their own land could the *Urquelle*-grounded regeneration unfold. Providence, Hess remarked, would not have prolonged Jewish existence up to this point had this most sacred of missions not been reserved for it. With Israel's return to its national roots, Jews, together with Europeans, must recognize the divine plan behind all the (organic) nationalisms—to coalesce into one sacred world history so that history and eternity will coincide.[10]

---

10   Greenberg, "The Reformer's First Attack Upon Hess' Rome and Jerusalem: An Unpublished Manuscript of Samuel Hirsch," *Jewish Social Studies* 35, nos. 3-4 (July-October 1973): 175-197; Isaiah Berlin, *The Life and Opinions of Moses Hess* (Cambridge, Jewish Historical Society of England, 1959); Ken Koltun-Fromm, *Moses Hess and Modern Jewish Identity* (Bloomington: Indiana University Press, 2001), 9-10, 34-37, 100-109.

4.1. SAUL ASCHER (1767-1822): JEWISH IDENTITY

Ascher's family was permitted to reside within the boundaries of Berlin by virtue of its high economic and social status ("*Schutzjuden*").[11] He studied Hebrew as a child and excelled in the study of *Talmud* to the point of teaching others. Aside from his self-referential "Dr.," no data about his education is available. He grew up with some sense of alienation from the Berlin Jewish community:

---

11   On Ascher's life and thought see Ya'akov Fleischmann, "Dat Ha'nisim Ve'dat Ha'aritsut: Shaul Ascher," in *Be'ayat Ha'natsrut Be'mahshavah Ha'yehudit Mi'mendelson ad Rozentsvayg* (Jerusalem: Magnes, 1964), 22-27; Walter Grab, "Saul Ascher, ein Jüdisch-Deutscher Spätaufklärer zwischen Revolution und Restauration," *Jahrbuch des Institut für Deutsche Geschichte* 6 (1977): 131-180; Heinrich Graetz, *Geschichte der Juden von den ältesten Zeiten bis auf die Gegenwart*, vol. 11 (Leipzig: Oscar Leiner, 1900), 141, 159, 234, 343; Michael Graetz, "The Formation of the New 'Jewish Consciousness' in the Time of Mendelssohn's Disciples: Saul Ascher" [Hebrew], *Studies in the History of the Jewish People and the Land of Israel* 4 (1976): 219-237; Peter Hacks, *Ascher gegen Jahn: Ein Freiheitskrieg* (Berlin: Aufbau-Verlag, 1991); Gerald Hubmann, "Völkischer Nationalismus und Antisemitismus im frühen 19. Jahrhundert: Die Schriften von Rühs und Fries zur Judenfrage," in *Antisemitismus-Zionismus-Antizionismus, 1850-1940*, eds. Renate Heuner and Ralph-Rainer Wuthenow (FaM: Campus Verlag, 1997), 10-34; Hubmann, "Saul Ascher-ein früher Kritiker des deutschen Nationalismus," *Diskussion Deutsch* 114 (1990): 3; Katz, "Kant Veha'yahadut," *Tarbits* 41 (1972): 219-237; Hans Liebeschütz, "Mendelssohn und Lessing in ihrer Stellung zur Geschichte," in *Studies in Jewish Religious and Intellectual History Presented to Alexander Altmann*, eds. Stein and Loewe (Tuscaloosa: University of Alabama Press, 1979), 167-182; Ellen Littman, "Saul Ascher: First Theorist of Progressive Judaism," *LBIY* 5 (1960): 107-121; Meyer, *The Origins of the Modern Jew* (Detroit: Wayne State University Press, 1967), 122-125; Fritz Pinkuss, "Saul Ascher, ein Theoretiker der Judenemancipation aus der Generation nach Moses Mendelssohn," *Zeitschrift für die Geschichte der Juden in Deutschland* 6 (1935): 28-32; Paul Lawrence Rose, "The German Nationalists and the Jewish Question: Fichte and the Birth of Revolutionary Antisemitism," in *Revolutionary Antisemitism in Germany from Kant to Wagner* (Princeton: Princeton University Press, 1990), 117-132; Christoph Schulte, "Saul Ascher's 'Leviathan,' or the Invention of Jewish Orthodoxy in 1792," *LBIY* 45 (2000): 25-34; Klaus von See, *Die Ideen von 1789 und die Ideen von 1914: Völkischer Denken in Deutschland zwischen französischer Revolution und erstem Weltkrieg* (FaM: Athenaion, 1975), 36-42; Uriel Tal, "Young German Intellectuals on Romanticism and Judaism: Spiritual Turbulence in the Early 19th Century," in *Salo Wittmayer Baron Jubilee Volume, on the Occasion of His Eightieth Birthday*, 2 vols., ed. Saul Lieberman (Jerusalem: AAJR, 1974), 919-138; Wiener, "Shaul Ascher un di teorie vegn yidntum vi a religie," *Yivo Bleter* 23, no. 1 (1944): 55-79; Wiener, "Moses Mendelssohn und die religiösen Gestaltungen des Judentums im 19. Jahrhunderts," *Zeitschrift für die Geschichte der Juden in Deutschland* 3 (1929): 201-212; and Heinrich Zschokke, *Eine Selbstschau* (Aarau: Heinrich Remigius Sauerländer, 1843), 35.

Do not think of me as the strictest apologist for the Jews, or that I want to play that role. I have never worked for the Jews' approval, nor do I expect to get it. I am convinced that the way in which I have lived among the Jews and the unrestrained character of the judgments I've made upon their actions and intents have incurred more resentment than trust. When it comes to their fakery, which I have seen closely and often, I could even cry out with Juvenal, 'It is hard not to write satire.' [*Satire I*, beginning][12]

In his 1930 dissertation, Fritz Pinkuss concluded that Ascher's religious philosophy appeared to have as little approval among Jews as recognition among Christians. This could be attributed, Pinkuss speculated, to his minimal religious attachment—he had attended Easter services to learn about the spiritual and intellectual level of the Christian sermon.[13]

But despite the alienation, Ascher did identify himself as a Jew. He aligned himself with the Jewish revolutionary tradition of Maimonides, Spinoza and Mendelssohn, writing that:

Maimonides was inclined to find all of Aristotelian philosophy in Judaism. Spinoza wanted to upset all revealed religion through Judaism, and Mendelssohn sought to weaken the obtrusiveness of an opponent. / My intention, however, is to present Judaism in such a way that every enlightened person could acknowledge that Judaism could be the religion of a member of any society, and that it has principles in common with every religion.... / I do not know what good genius encouraged a Maimonides to bring Judaism back to its pure principles. I

---

12   Ascher, *Die Wartburgs-Feier: Mit Hinsicht auf Deutschlands religiöse und politische Stimmung* (Leipzig: Achenwall und Coup, 1818), 27-28.

13   Pinkuss, "Saul Ascher, ein unbekannter Theoretiker des Judentums und der Juden-Emanzipation" (Rabbinical dissertation, *Hochschule für Wissenschaft des Judentums*, 1930), 6-7, citing *Eisenmenger der Zweite* (Berlin: C. Hartmann, 1794), 68. I am grateful to Dr. Pinkuss for providing a copy of his dissertation. Ascher, *Bemerkungen über die bürgerliche Verbesserung der Juden* (Berlin: Kunze, 1788), 17, 32, 59; and Ascher, *Der Falke* (1818), 65.

do not know what evil genius let a Spinoza fall away, to the point of transforming Judaism into a nothing. I do not know what indifferent genius led a Mendelssohn to want to overcome his opponent but in fact let himself be overcome. / This I do know: That I am indebted to these men for [the fact] that I demanded of myself that I take a step which was perhaps contrary to the entire direction of the human spirit/mind of our time. It obliges me to climb to higher sources and to descend from them.[14]

He likewise affirmed his Jewish identity with his defense of Judaism against the Germanic attacks by Johann Gottfried Fichte, Ernst Moritz Arndt and Friedrich Ludwig Jahn.

4.1.1. Ascher and Kant

Ascher's thought was significantly influenced by Kant. Heinrich Heine, in fact, thought of Ascher as a personal embodiment of Kantian rationality. He cited a meeting in Berlin, when Ascher was in his late fifties. Ascher had told him that fear came only if reason decided that something was scary. It was reason that had power, not conscience. After demonstrating the superiority of reason, Heine related, Ascher checked the time and concluded the encounter with "Reason is the highest principle." Heine ended up having a nightmare about the encounter:

> Once in Goslar, after going to bed, it became deathly still. I suddenly heard the sound of an old man dragging his feet outside my room. The dead doctor Saul Ascher entered. A cold fever ran through my bones. I shook like a leaf.... In his usual easy-going and friendly way he said, 'Be not afraid, and do not believe I'm a ghost. That is only your fantasy. What is a ghost? Define it. Deduce the conditions for its possibility. What is the relation of its appearance to reason? Reason, I say reason.' The ghost then analyzed the distinction between phenomena and noumena as in Kant's *Critique of Pure Reason*.

---

14   Ascher, *Leviathan oder über Religion in Rücksicht des Judentums* (Berlin: Frankeschen Buchhandlung, 1792), 60-161, 239-240.

He analyzed the problematic of belief in ghosts, set up syllogisms and proved logically that there could be no ghosts.[15]

Ascher's Kantian mindset came to light in a variety of ways. Kant's free will was determined by reason, independently of sensible drives, and Ascher in a similar vein associated Judaism with a concept of will determined solely by reason and understanding: "A rule of the will which is determinative through a form of reason would be sufficient for Judaism. There was no point in having objective rules which failed to raise the human above its rank—which was the point of religion."[16] Kant identified belief as subjective truth, and Ascher wrote that the subjective requirement of Judaism was belief, while revelation was the objective requirement.[17] Kant identified reason, understanding and sensibility as functions of knowledge, while Ascher in a related manner identified principle (reason), doctrine (understanding) and law (sensibility) as the components of revelation—with the principle recognized as the aim to be led to God's essence; the doctrine drew attention to the highest being, and to the law that symbolized revelation and belief.[18]

---

15   Heine, "Reisebilder: 1 Teil: Die Harzreise," in *Heinrich Heine: Historisch-kritische Gesamtausgabe der Werke*, vol. 6, ed. Manfred Windfuhr (Hamburg: Hoffmann und Campe, 1973): 102-105, in "Die Harzreise" Heine cited Ascher's *Ansicht von dem künftigen Schicksal des Christentums* (Leipzig: n.p., 1819) as an expression of particular malice against Christianity. Pinkuss, "Saul Ascher, ein unbekannter Theoretiker."

16   Kant, *Kritik der Reinen Vernunft: nach der ersten und zweiten Originalausgabe* (Riga: J.F. Hartknoch, 1787), ed. Raymund Schmidt (Hamburg: Felix Meiner, 1956): 726; or *Zweiten Originalausgabe* (Riga: J. F. Hartknoch, 1787), 830 as cited in Heinrich Ratke, *Systematischer Handlexikon zu Kants Kritik der reinen Vernunft* (Hamburg: Felix Meiner, 1965), 309. Ascher, *Leviathan*, 109.

17   See, for example:

> The holding of a thing to be true, or the subjective validity of the judgment, in its relation to conviction (which is at the same time objectively valid), has the following three degrees: *opining, believing* and *knowing*.... If our holding of the judgment be only subjectively sufficient, and is at the same time taken as being objectively insufficient, we have what is termed *believing*."

Kant, *Critique of Pure Reason*, trans. Norman Kemp Smith (London: Macmillan, 1929), 646; or *Kritik der reinen Vernunft. Zweiten Originalausgabe*, 850.

18   "All our knowledge starts with the senses, proceeds from thus to understanding, and

Kant distinguished essence (the primary internal principle of some-thing) and form (the appearance of something), while Ascher wrote that religion was grounded in the idea of a higher essence and also the means of relating to it. Though the idea and the relation, the essence, always remained the same, the forms in which the idea and relation appeared varied.[19]

Kant, on his part, inter-related duty, freedom and reason. Duty was a moral necessity (or force) which flowed out of free will, which belonged to reason's essence and to human autonomy, while free will set the pur-pose of the legislation from which duty emerged. For Ascher, legislation was needed only to have human beings adhere to duties for which they felt no inner calling. Duty, which was general, was contrary to inclina-tion, and legislation, which was addressed individually, was contrary to reason. One acted freely with duty only insofar as the action accorded with reason-provided legislation.[20]

According to Kant, a regulative principle systematized empirical knowledge, while a constitutive principle made the constitution of *a priori* concepts possible. For Ascher, a religion was regulative when it relied on the empirical experience of faith/belief, and this led to revela-

---

ends with reason." See Kant, *Kritik der reinen Vernunft*, ed. Raymund Schmidt (Hamburg: Felix Meiner, 1956), 338. Or Kant, *Zweiten Originalausgabe*, 355. Ascher, *Leviathan*, 23. Pinkuss, "Saul Ascher, ein unbekannter Theoretiker," 11.

19   "Essence is the first inner principle of everything which belongs to the possibility of a thing." See Kant, *Metaphysische Anfangsgründe der Naturwissenschaft*, ed. Konstantin Pollack (Hamburg: Felix Meiner, 1997), 31.

> The essence of a thing exists in the form, insofar as the essence should be known through reason. If this thing is an object of the senses, then it is the form of the thing in perception (as appearance); and even pure mathematics is nothing other than a doctrine-of-forms of pure perception; just as metaphysics, as pure philosophy, grounds its knowledge above all on forms of thought, under which each object (the material of knowledge) may later be subsumed.

Kant, "Von einen neuerdings erhobenen vornehmen Ton in der Philosophie," in *Immanuel Kants Kleine Logisch-metaphysische Schriften*, ed. Karl Rosenkranz (Leipzig: Leopold Voss, 1838 rpt.), 639-640. Ascher, *Leviathan*, 20.

20   Kant, *Über den Gemeinspruch das mag in der Theorie richtig sein, taugt aber nicht für die Praxis* (FaM: Vittorio Klostermann, 1946 rpt.), 24. Kant, "Metaphysik der Sitten: Tugendlehre," in *Metaphysik der Sitten in Zwei Teilen und Pedagogik* (Leipzig: Leopold Voss, 1838 rpt.), 222. Ascher, *Leviathan*, 61-62.

tion. It was constitutive when it relied on trans-empirical revelation, leading to faith/belief. Regulative religion involved a total amalgamation of religion and society; constitutive religion involved their partial blend. Regulative religion therefore depended upon the mind/spirit of a nation, while constitutive did not. Faith/belief was regulative insofar as it made revelation possible; when faith/belief was the consequence of the revelation, revelation was accepted as a totality, it was constitutive.[21]

But Ascher also criticized Kant. In his translation of Mandeville's *Fable of the Bees* he wrote that Kant's practical philosophy failed to provide a systematic foundation for the rigors of duty, or a rational basis for ethical relationships. In *Eisenmenger the Second*, he asserted that the concerns of Kant's "esoteric" philosophy should never "be applied to general, popular, i.e., human life or to fixed events which provided philosophy with a sort of transition." When Kant attempted to correlate philosophy to reality, he ran into inevitable practical difficulties. It was, in fact, impossible for Kant to justify his attempt to demonstrate an ethics involving the manifoldedness of reality on the basis of established philosophical principles. Ascher wrote an extended critique of Kant's triumphalism regarding Christianity's succession of Judaism—that, he claimed, improperly disregarded the moral principles of Israel.[22]

4.1.2. Judaism and Modernity

Ascher believed that the French Revolution released the force of rationalism to the whole world, and that this force included morality-centered Jewish monotheism. He became part of the process by his own commit-

---

21   Ascher, *Leviathan*, 37-38, 72-73.

22   Bernard Mandeville, *Bernhard von Mandevilles Fabel von der Bienen. Aus dem englischen übersetzt und mit einer Einleitung und einen neuen Kommenter versehen von Dr. S. Ascher* (Leipzig: n.p., 1818), 20 as cited by Pinkuss, 34-35; 47 note 29; Ascher, *Eisenmenger der Zweite, Nebst einem vorangesetzten Sendschreiben an den Herrn Professor Fichte in Jena* [1794], in *4 Flugschriften* (Berlin: Aufbau Verlag, 1991 [1794]), 43-46, 53-71. See also Ascher, *Leviathan*, 108-109.

Heine's biographer regarded Ascher as a sober critic of Kant. See Adolf Strodtmann, *H. Heines Leben und Werke*, vol. 1 (Hamburg: Hoffmann und Campe, 1884), 444 and vol. 2 (Hamburg: Hoffmann und Campe, 1884): 400 as cited by Pinkuss, "Saul Ascher, ein unbekannter Theoretiker," 47, note 29. In *Ideen zur natürlichen Geschichte der Revolutionen* (1802) Ascher rejected Kant's reduction of human forms of behavior to a categorical imperative, because the social dimension of personal behavior was severed through the emphasis on individual behavioral decisions. See Jörn Garber, "Revolution als geschichtsphilosophische Kategorie: Saul Ascher," in *Revolutionäre Vernunft* (Regensburg: Scriptor Verlag, 1974), 209-213.

ment to enlightenment, reason and equality; his effort to extract the "constitutive" layer of rabbinic legislation (*Halakhah*) from Judaism's essence; and his vehement rejection of Germanic nationalism.

Ascher's writing career began in 1788, when he criticized the Austrian Emperor Joseph II's recruitment of Jewish soldiers for Austria's war against Turkey. Jews, he objected, should not accept military responsibility, let alone do so to enhance social recognition, until they received equal civil rights. Moreover, the Emperor manipulated the fact that some Jews bought their way out of military service to accuse poor Jews who did not enlist of being unpatriotic.[23] Ascher went on to write on many issues concerning the nature of Judaism and matters of political culture. *Leviathan* became his most prominent work.

Ascher dedicated his *Leviathan* to Friedrich Wilhelm II, King of Prussia, with the note that "Human reason is now being diverted by delusions of an over-heated power of imagination. There seems to be a conflict between reason and humankind." The volume dealt with religion in general and Judaism in particular.[24] All religions involved two elements—a highest essence and a communal structure, differing only in their expression, Ascher wrote. There were three stages: Natural religion (where the deity was the epitome of nature), revelational religion (where the deity related to supernatural events) and rational religion (where reason provided testimony for the deity). Judaism was the paradigmatic religion of revelation—which Christ would subsequently convey to the nations and from which Mohammed drew, along with his extractions from Christianity. Judaism's God was a trans-natural, metaphysical reality and the source of ethical values, Ascher declared. However, He was tied to a community, and this community suffered political misfortune because of His presence. God also intervened into history, and the points of intervention mapped memory and history. Revelation of these religious truths was subjective in terms of the beliefs it required, and objective in terms of the principles, doctrines and laws which ensued from it. Ascher distinguished between two dimen-

---

23   Ascher, *Bemerkungen über die bürgerliche Verbesserung der Juden, veranlässt bei der Frage: Soll der Jude Soldat werden?* (Berlin: Kunze, 1788) as cited by Pinkuss and Grab.

24   It is unclear whether the *Leviathan* title of Hobbes, used by Friedrich Buchholz, *Der neue Leviathan* (Tübingen: n.p., 1805) and Andreas Klein, *Leviathan oder Rabbiner und Juden* (Jerusalem: n.p., 1801), was in Ascher's mind. See Reinhold Lewin, "Die Judengesetzgebung Friedrich Wilhelms II," *MGWJ* 58 (1913): 74-98, 211-234, 363-372, 461-481, 567-590.

sions of Judaism: One included the belief in God, a "thing-in-itself," the essence of the religion embodied in the people ("regulative"). The other included the display of this essence in laws, ordinances and rules ("constitutive"). The former unfolded during the era of ancient Israel in the Land of Israel, when human and national needs were addressed ("regulative"), and the latter with rabbinic law and Israel's mission to spread moral monotheism to the world, accompanied by its associated dangers ("constitutive"). Over time the constitutive dimension blended with the essence, such as to resist change. But emancipation now provided the opportunity to extract the essence through scientific study. Ascher hoped for a mutual effort, where rabbinic forms would be extracted from the essence and set aside, and nations would adopt an enlightened attitude towards Judaism. Judaism could then participate in political structures.

In *Eisenmenger the Second* (1794) Ascher attacked Johann Gottfried Fichte's portrayal of Jews as inherently depraved and therefore impossible to emancipate, comparing him to Johannes Eisenmenger (the seventeenth century orientalist who attacked rabbinic Judaism), and blaming him for reviving medieval religious persecution. To Fichte's acknowledgement in *Contribution to Correcting the Public's Judgment of the French Revolution* that "I for one see no other way to provide [Jews] with civil rights than this: Cut off all their heads overnight and replace them with others which contain not a single Jewish idea," Ascher commented, "Given the recent events in France ... who would have thought there would be those in Germany who believed that an entire nation would be improved by *cutting off heads?*"[25] In *Ideas Concerning the Natural History of Political Revolution* (1799) Ascher observed that following the first stage of history, where freedom was associated with pleasure, and the second, where freedom was associated with reason and opinion, thanks to the French Revolution and Napoleon, history was now at

---

25 Ascher, *Eisenmenger der Zweite: Nebst einem vorangesetzten Sendschreiben an den Herrn Professor Fichte in Jena* [1794], in *4 Flugschriften* (Berlin: Aufbau, 1991), 34. Johann Gottlieb Fichte, *Beitrag zur Berichtigung der Urteile des Publikums über die französische Revolution*, ed. Reinhard Strecker (Leipzig: Meiner, 1922 [1793]), 114-116 and Ascher, *Die Germanomanie*, 61.
  Leopold Zunz, who met Ascher, said he was impressed by his moral character and his opposition to fanatical Germanism. Ascher, he said, was an enemy of all enthusiasts (*Feind aller Schwärmerei*). See *Leopold Zunz: Jude-Deutscher-Europäer*, ed. with introduction by Glatzer (Tübingen: J. C. B. Mohr, 1964), 95-97.

the third stage, that of moral freedom. This meant the spread of Israel's moral monotheism, *via* Christianity, through the world, was possible.[26] In *Napoleon. Or, Concerning the Progress of the Government* (1808) Ascher identified Napoleon with a revolutionary spirit which converted chaos into the highest form of social order.[27]

In 1810 Ascher was jailed for a few weeks for his journal articles attacking government economic policy and bureaucracy. He was accused of being "a disruptive and disobedient citizen whose essays, both domestic and foreign, seriously undermined the state's stature and reputation.... Under current conditions they are dangerous. An example is needed to shock anyone else so disposed."[28] In 1811, in a series of articles for *Miscellanies About Recent News About the World* (published in Aarau, Switzerland by Heinrich Zschokke, who had studied Scriptural and Talmudic prescriptions concerning running a household with Ascher), Ascher attacked the Christian German Table Society (which included Fichte, military strategist Karl von Clausewitz and legal philosopher Carl von Savigny) for displacing enlightenment, equality and tolerance with medieval nationalism, and in *The Germanic Mania* (1815) he denounced the paroxysms of German nationalistic messianists (e.g., of Ernst Moritz Arndt and Friedrich Ludwig Jahn), who were out to make Jews the first branch in the fire destroying everything foreign—all as manifesting values and thought diametrically opposed to the French enlightenment.[29] When *The Germanic Mania* was burned, Ascher said it was

> because I maintained in it that the German was constructed like every other human being; that Christianity was not the German religion; that Germany was not the assigned possession of the aboriginal German; and that the [divine] creator did not deny prosperity in Germany to any person who did right before Him.[30]

26 Ascher, *Ideen zur natürliche Geschichte der politischen Revolutionen* (1799) as cited by Grab. See Ascher, *Der Falke: Eine Vierteljahresschrift. Der Politik und Literatur gewidmet* (Leipzig: n.p., 1818/19) and Ascher, *Der deutsche Geistes-Aristokratismus. Ein Beitrag zur Characteristik des zeitigen politischen Geistes in Deutschland* (Leipzig: n.p., 1819) as cited by Grab.

27 Ascher, *Napoleon, oder über den Fortschritt der Regierung* (Berlin: G. A. Lange, 1808).

28 Cited in Pinkuss, "Saul Ascher, ein unbekannter Theoretiker," 52-53.

29 Ascher, *Die Germanomanie: Skizze in einen Zeitgemälde* (Berlin: Achenwall und Comp, 1815). Zschokke, *Eine Selbstschau*, 35.

30 Ascher, *Die Wartburgs-Feier: Mit Hinsicht auf Deutschlands religiöse und politische*

Ascher further explained in *The Wartburg Celebration* that Jews wished to share the enlightenment theme of human equality and cooperate with the government on equal footing but were rejected because of certain mystical concepts that supported German antisemitism and myths of German supremacy. He railed against the mercenary spirit and selfishness manifest in the anti-Jewish propaganda of the Hanseatic states, where Christian Germanity/Germanic Christianity was undermining the human and civil rights of all Germans.[31] In 1819, writing in *View of the Future Destiny of Christianity*, he reiterated that Christianity served to make revelation universal, as part of the inevitable spiritual advance of humankind.[32]

IV.I.I. Selections from *Leviathan*, translated by Gershon Greenberg

Summary of translated passages

BOOK I: OF RELIGION. CHAPTERS 1-3

Ascher presumed that all human beings were to some degree religious. All religions related to an essence which was higher than the human being's, and differed only about the respective forms. There were three stages, which progressed with history. In natural religion, divine essence was the epitome of natural perfection. In the religion of revelation, which for Ascher was the authentic religion, supernatural events revealed the highest essence, and inspired the veneration which came upon recognition that the highest essence could not be completely known. Each of the three had a societal character. In natural religion, spirit ensouled and united all of society. In revealed religion, society excluded individual autonomy. In rational religion, society was an aggregate of individuals, and then activities, together with temporal and eternal salvation, were integrated.

Natural religion was always regulative, relying upon the nation's intellect and mind, and rational religion was always constitutive, a matter of an unchanging whole. Revealed religion, however, moved from a regulative to

---

Stimmung (Leipzig: Achenwall und Comp, 1818), 34.

31   Ascher, *Die Wartburgs-Feier*, 25-27.

32   Ascher, *Ansicht von dem künftigen Schicksal des Christentums* (Leipzig: n.p., 1819) as cited by Grab.

a constitutive character. In revealed religion, the regulative condition was the authentic juncture for knowing the religious essence. Ascher addressed himself to those who opposed Judaism in terms of its constitutive dimension alone, that of the building erected atop the essence of Judaism.

CHAPTER 1: THE PURPOSE OF ALL RELIGIONS

... When it comes to religion, one can determine the usefulness only if the effort is made to trace human nature. This is a truth which in our time deserves perhaps the greatest consideration. / One should not think that this applies only to those religions which are developed out of the principles of reason. The existence of each and every religion, be it rational, natural or revealed, is indebted to the needs of a society which reached a certain degree of development [to bring that religion about].

The diverse forms which different nations have with respect to religion may still appear quite puzzling. One must be able to analyze these forms through a method, and thereby come to know the general purpose of religion which is present in all of them. The diverse means which the crudest and most undeveloped nations used to achieve this general purpose may be very striking to educated and civilized people. Still, the thinker must indeed return to those diverse means, and regard them merely as attempts which the human mind/spirit makes here as anywhere else. For a variety of motives, the human mind/spirit will eventually, and finally as with all things, strive to ennoble and elevate these diverse means.

If one wishes to concede some degree of validity to this anthropological rule, then one must inevitably return to this: Each and every religion, to the extent that it is developed and perfected by the human being, is grounded in a principle or idea of an essence higher than and more superior to the human being. The relationship between us and this essence, and the means of achieving this relationship and being able to maintain it, is what *religion* indicates to us. If one analyzes this general concept of religion, one will recognize that religion simply indicates the means by which we should or could pursue this essence on a path to happiness, where the essence directs us in its mysterious and very diverse ways. / There are different stages to the manner in which this direction takes place. If the purpose of that religion amid whose shape and form the stages may appear is always the same, then we can take into consideration only those various stages or forms which the most educated human beings accept or preserve in order to sufficiently produce the general purpose of religion. / The purpose which we thereby achieve is important enough, if I just say that all claims for preference in such a probe by any single religion are removed. If one always holds to the form of any single religion, that religion will furnish an agreeable aspect from a certain perspective and the dispute will never be settled or cleared up.

All that we can present here in advance, as prolegomenon, comes to this: Religion is the need of the human being, insofar as the human being is a rational essence. In this respect, no human being was ever without religion. If a human being ever became a heretic, it happened only through *religion* (17-21).

CHAPTER 2: ON THE DIVERSE FORMS AND RANGE OF RELIGION
[Natural, revealed, and rational religion]

When we observe things as they really appear to us, we are engaged with the truths of nature. When we imagine how things once were, we are engaged with truths of history. When we think of how things can or should appear, we are engaged with truths of reason. / These three sources are sustained by us in order to enrich and nourish our mind/ spirit. The more a truth lets itself bring these three sources back, the greater the objective validity the truth has for us. / If we take religion as an object, one which awakens a general interest in human beings, we find that: One society abstracts religion from the events of nature, another society establishes religion upon the authority of historical oc- currences, and a third society analyzes religion out of itself, out of [its own] principles of reason.

To the extent our experience suffices, we have always perceived that, insofar as the mind/spirit rushes towards formation, there is a drive in the human being which develops the idea of a source for all good and evil, the concept of a cause. This source and cause sets into motion everything we see living and becoming around and next to us. If the human being is placed into the great drama of nature with such an idea, it becomes impossible to engage in observations about nature without eventually giving content to this idea in nature. If the human being knows this essence in nature, that it should be the epitome of all perfec- tion, then nature must also finally become a means, one which teaches the human being to venerate and worship this essence. The origin of natural religion refers to this.

It is, however, possible for there to be experiences which surpass the events of nature in terms of energy or magnitude; or which are capable of concentrating in themselves the entire interest we have, by nature, for such an essence. These events could also move the human being to a point where it finds the essence to which it wants to dedicate respect and attention in those events. In this alone I acknowledge the source of everything which is called *revealed* religion.

But if there are internal grounds for movement which hold more interest than all external grounds, reason leads us on a path which it has abstracted out of experience. If it does not find evidence of a highest essence in nature or in an event but rather locates it in itself, so be it. Then reason has opened a path, about which reason alone can teach, which I call *rational* religion... (23-25).

Revealed religion is a property of the orient. With their livelier mind/spirit and stronger imaginative power, the people under this heavenly expanse did not have enough patience or tenacity to recognize the highest essence, in all its glory, in nature. Besides, nature was not so inviting, so hospitable to the human being. A person of great spiritual gifts, lively power of imagination, and lasting perseverance, needed to arise among these people. That person had to know how to present the greatness and power of a higher essence to them in a sufficiently florid way. The person needed their respect, so that when he presented the greatest miracles and supernatural events which could fit nicely into their way of thought (if he did not point to them himself, he presented their authenticity through witnesses), the people did not hesitate to regard them as true and sufficient. These activities alone convinced them for the first time of the existence of a God. Through them the people arrived at the right way of constructing a concept of authentic religion. This religion is not formed according to nature. Rather, the more supernatural or the more unnatural the act of revelation, the more the people were inclined to a religion which was completely contrary to the purpose of nature. One sees the people always following the will of the highest essence. It always leads them on a special path, and had to prescribe the most intricate norms to keep their lively mind/spirit active and dependent. / One therefore saw these people always composing their own very special entity. Their manner of thought and way of conduct were not that of ordinary people, but rather similar to those of the higher, holier and enlightened essence.

The adherent of *rational religion* takes a totally different path. This advocate also seeks a highest essence, which he/she believes is owed veneration and respect. But he/she finds this essence neither in nature nor in supernatural activity or event. All of these things express too feebly the outline of that image which creates the adherents' fantasy as regulated by rational principles. The only veneration which this supporter believes that he/she owes to that image is grounded on the thought that the vision exists. The only respect which the adherent can express to that image consists in the confession: that he/she cannot grasp the essence and cannot know it in its entire magnitude (28-31).

CHAPTER 3

Up until now we have considered religion insofar as it develops directly and makes the greatest possible impression on the human being. But the influence of each respective form of religion must have something special, and it must give rise to something among the people themselves, which has influence on their political and societal circumstances.

Let us take *rational religion*. We find that the people who subscribe to rational religion conduct themselves according to their own discretion and express religion solely through their activities. Society comes together; each person provides him/herself with a calling, and each member shows what he/she in particular could accomplish as a human being for the society. The society as a whole decides what each member should accomplish. To the extent that the society thereby institutes an order, it seeks to bring itself together with religion into a community where the society becomes a symbol of its religion. Simultaneously, the public constructs a *societal* religion, or establishes a rule of reason according to which it decides the legality or illegality of its activities.

The defenders of *rational religion* assert that it is the only way for people to unify. Rather than disintegrating on account of interest in temporal and eternal prosperity, people unify, as it were, through a necessary and subjective restriction. Opponents of rational religion assert that people differing in physical constitution, with propensity for, passion about, and interest in truth, could never tolerate a general restriction. Such a restriction would be grounds for anarchy, both in thought and action. For the most part, separatism and bold egoism, which become the first sources for the decline of human society, usually result.

Let us look now at *natural religion*. It develops directly among human beings and builds and expands itself according to the extent they lift themselves out of barbarism—such that it almost becomes more and more a need of society. The legislator, the artist, the intellectual and the common man all form their concepts according to the natural religion such that if their religion were to be removed, the mind/spirit which ensouled them would be scared off at the same time. No one would be able to provide adequate grounds for his/her behavior. Religion comprised the principles for all their scientific studies and activities, in short, for their entire mindset. They simultaneously form a *religious* society, a society which does not seek to unite through religion, which knows no other standpoint for its unification, but rather is already fused with religion and determines its conduct only out of religion.

Nothing shocks me more than when one objects to a Plato for not wanting to know about matters of religion being changed according to principles of reason. Plato was himself an adherent of natural religion. He knew of its influence on society. For Plato, to remove a society's religion meant taking everything from society. This is why his conclusion corresponded completely with the institutions of an ideal state that breathe with the spirit/mind of natural religion (*Republic* 50:4).

Only the short-sighted person would pose the question: How could the ancients have had the best legislation, and yet a religion of superstition? Cornelius Pauw (in *Recherches philosofiques sur les Egyptiens et Chinois*, Part 2, 194 [1795]) seeks the causes (for this combination) within the crude and uncultivated ancestors of the religions of well-developed nations. It seems to me, rather, that the influence of religion among the ancients was so powerful, that I could discover the true mind/spirit of their legislation only by means of this view, or, rather, could [accurately] realize [the character of] their religion by means of their mindset and way of conduct.

Generally, legislators of natural religion looked for any way to avoid collision with religion, but rather clung to it. One could see this with the legislator Solon. As Cornelius Pauw says, Solon did not change anything about their [the Greeks'] religion and only improved their laws. The Spartan legislator's institutions expressed the mind/spirit which completely ensouled the Greeks, namely their religion.

Essentially, nothing can be changed about a natural religion. While it is inherently subject to modification, his modification is not conferred upon it but must develop naturally. Natural religion expands or contracts in terms of the manner of thought, range of intellectual power, the progress of morality and the impulse to act. There were epochs when the venerators of natural religion were more dependent on certain parts of their religion than others. This is totally confirmed by the Egyptians, Greeks and Romans. Each and every provincial city, every spot, had its respective center of religion upon which it especially depended. Yet without exception the Egyptian, Greek and Roman venerators possessed one religion respectively.

Advocates of natural religion sought means to denigrate human spirit as weak and to regard natural religion, in its highest form, as the single object, and the sole reality for the human mind/spirit. The enemies of the religion of nature found that means to consist of something which degraded human reason, and was unworthy of adherence.

If we consider *revealed religion* more closely, one finds that it does not develop of itself, but is rather given to the human being. It is therefore either overwhelming, negating the human being's entire autonomy; or it is totally isolated from the person's other spheres of activity, so that the human being's activity now takes a completely different path.

With the religion of revelation, the human being is only a believer or an essence which is mechanical. In a society in which revealed religion is given, there therefore can be no artists, no legislators, no intellectuals and no ordinary men. Each person is content with what is given to him/her. Each remains standing at his/her designated boundary. Should adherents of the revealed religion step outside the boundary and search for a path of activity in the thousand-fold plan instilled into them by nature, they would burst apart the whole [societal] bond and often choose a way having no trace of what was called their religion.

Revealed religion is therefore either everything for its adherents or it stands isolated. In short, the adherents build either a *religious* society or a *societal* religion. In the first instance I call the religion *regulative*, in the other, *constitutive*. / A religion is regulative insofar as it depends upon the intellectual tone and mindset of the nation. A religion is constitutive insofar as it forms itself into a totality, modified neither by thought nor by custom. / As far as I know, this special character of revealed religion has not been taken into consideration in our sense. That is why we often hear that its friends proclaim that revealed religion is the best way to make people happy, because it can let us have complete autonomy. Its opponents blame revealed religion for placing us in chains, robbing us of all autonomy, suppressing our reason and disposing our heart to mystical feelings. / This discovered characteristic of revealed religion distinguishes it from other religions. Rational religion is always constitutive and natural religion remains ever regulative. Only revealed religion moves from a regulative condition to a constitutive one.

Each religion therefore has its friends and opponents and they do not agree about the *essence* of religion itself. The adherents and opponents of revealed religion often agree about the *essence* of revealed religion. But they have differing opinions about its *form*. / I have therefore dealt here only with those opponents of revealed religion who take into account only the building which is erected on the basis [i.e. essence] of religion. That is, with those who take the constitution of the religion into account more than the point in time in which it developed itself or was still regulative. / But the regulative condition of religion is the authentic juncture for knowing the religion's aim and its essence. This has led me to probe deeper into the essence of revealed religion and develop its manifold form up to its constitution and then apply this to Judaism and outline a structure for it which we can find unopposed in every society and that can silence all its opponents (32-39).

Summary of translated passages
Revelation came directly to human beings or was mediated by an individual. The mediator was initially trusted as a reliable transmitter, who was confirmed once the recipients were convinced that the mediator's source was the highest essence. In the revealed religion of Judaism, the highest essence guided the people's actions, and became the exclusive source for legislation (the regulative period). Christ conveyed the revelation that was available to the Jews to all nations. Mohammed drew from both Jewish and Christian revelations, and brought Jews and Christians under one shepherd.

BOOK I: CHAPTERS 4-7
On the Purpose of Revelation
We have said that predispositions for the development of a religion were available in the power of the mind/spirit, and that according to these dispositions either a natural, revealed or rational religion develops. / But what purpose can we now ascribe to revelation? For we do not perceive anything in the general course of things, in all nature,

which could be absorbed into the sum of our knowledge, and which could prepare for revelation.

Revelation is the perception of something which is withheld from our perception within the general course of nature. If we were to go through the history of all revealed religion we would find that the highest essence always reveals itself to human beings, or through one of its immortal mediators, if not in all its glory, then with as much glory as is bearable. (Note: One could accuse me of a *petitionis principii* here, if one wanted to believe that I desired to establish the objective possibility of revelation. But since one can easily determine that I seek to establish only the subjective possibility, I could properly proceed from what one may view in philosophy as only a hypothesis.) This step could not be without consequences for the people. They received an impression of that essence to which their reason led, or which they were inclined to imagine as ideal. Once they thought that the most real and most powerful essence created all of nature according to the essence's unlimited will, none of the promises or commitments could make the people distrustful. Why should they have misgivings? After all, the essence revealed everything to these people because they were better and more dignified creatures. And if the essence did not transform nature into something better, it could still provide the people with a representative image of its higher omnipotence and glory.

The people harmonized this thought with higher sentiments. They strained all their powers of mind/spirit to a more elevated level and invigorated the flourishing power of imagination with increased passion. Thus, a little strain could upset all their powers. The playing space of nature became too small. The human mind/spirit found direction and nourishment only from miracles, supernatural events and extraordinary appearances.

Thus we see how all revealed religion made progress. The germ of the Jewish religion was already present in the times of the patriarchs. At that time it still was not *constitutive* religion, but only *regulative* religion. The highest essence revealed itself to the patriarchs. And from now on the human being could take no step, undertake no action, indeed preserve no thought, without divinity's expressing its opinion about it. The germ was planted, but later the family increased and successors saw frequent displays of nature's accidents and destiny's moods. The successors had to rely more and more on the help of the higher essence. They became increasingly unaccustomed to using their own powers. Rather, the will of divinity was allowed to lead them, and its silent stillness placed them in the greatest confusion, which generated revolt, disorder and occasioned mutiny. Finally the decisive moment came, when divinity made a complete system known to them. The people were disposed to conduct themselves according to this structure, and divinity wanted the nation to behave according to it.

It was the same with the Christian religion. Christ did not arise to preach the truth of a God. Christ did not need to, because this truth was instilled among Jews everywhere. Christ might not have gone so far for this truth, had he not been persecuted. The persecution brought Christ to the great plan of teaching all nations. For this he had to appeal to revelation or take refuge in miracles, which fit the manner of the revealed essence of whose existence the people were already convinced. / Likewise, Mohammed's purpose was not to teach a special religion. Instead, it was to bring the Jews and Christians of that time under a single shepherd. One sees that his religion borrowed something from the mind/spirit of both. He had influence only in the Orient, and there is, unmistakably, no other reason for this than the fact that by this time Christianity had already struck roots all over. It would have been impossible for Christianity to concede a place to someone who was so distant from the manner of thinking of non-Oriental people.

Since these religions are the main pillars of revelation, not to mention that we know them precisely, I cannot restrain myself from making a remark to confirm my opinion. / When it comes to the history of Judaism, we find that divinity revealed itself directly. With the introduction of Christian faith divinity revealed itself through a mediator, and with the introduction of the Mohammedan faith divinity revealed itself through the prophet. Everything was first communicated to the prophet by the angel Gabriel, as stated in the respective *Surah*, and in this manner divinity dignified the human being with a higher teaching. / It may be unmistakably surmised: [1] That five hundred years after the Christian era the idea of divinity must have been very refined. [2] That one could not be convinced that divinity would still dignify the best human being, after the human had brought about so much evil, and converse with it face to face... (40-44).

Summary of translated passages
Revealed religion involved the perception of objective, extraordinary events,
and also subjective drives and truths. The subjective truths contained pre-
scriptions and ordinances leading one close to God, which in turn led to legis-
lation. In Judaism, legislative similes eventually overcame the mind/spirit of
faith/belief. The dead letter, thoughtless word and activity-without-internal-
calling ended up taking over.

There are certain truths of whose existence we are convinced, either
by objective presentation or by perception. There are others of which
we are convinced, either by subjective presentation or through rational
grounds. / Let us apply this to revelation. Revelation involves objective
truths, i.e., conditions in which direct perception is involved. That the
Eternal spoke with Moses is an objective truth. Revelation likewise
contains subjective truths. For these, we can produce no other witness
than the internal impulse to receive them. That we should venerate God
is a duty which has truth for us. But in no case can we prove that it is
a general rule in nature. / The sum of all the objective truths in revelation contains, for the most part, important events, incidents, and
extraordinary appearances. They should lend their weight to the aim of
revelation, and really instruct us about the entire process: They constitute what I call *the doctrine*. / All the subjective truths which constitute
the special purpose of revelation, contain prescriptions, restraints and
ordinances. They should lead us on a path which brings us closer to divinity, by means of which we can live in a manner pleasing to God. These
truths constitute what I properly call *legislation*. / It is obvious that with
revelation, legislation must always be the consequence of doctrine. A
solely objective truth, in and for itself, cannot determine our behavior
unless it has an agreeable influence upon us, any more than we could
provide a basis for a particular act which evokes no interest on our part.
    With revelation, therefore, all subjective truths are grounded on
objective truths. Revelation leaves no place for an internal calling to activity, to the extent it has not at the same time prescribed rules for this
activity. / Understood most generally, revelation can touch the manner
of thinking and behavior, in short all commission and omission, of human beings. But one must assume that such persons could only be those
who let themselves be led by an authority, of whose [specific] purpose
they had no idea. One must assume that these are people to whom all

the means through which revelation has elevated them, as it were, to heaven, appeared, as it were, weak—in order for them to be able to reach the true purpose intended for them in nature by the creator.

If not a political move, then it was always at least wise foresight not to liberate humanity from the delirium in which they found themselves, but rather to quickly set into motion all means necessary to hold society together. Society had to be unquestionably ordered in such a way that it would not be overtaken by this delirium; or in a way that opportunity would be provided to maintain people properly in the society. / This was also a wise foresight which the creator had to have bestowed upon the Jews in full measure: He revealed laws to them in order to keep those who did not know how to lead themselves on the path which He indicated to them in the general order of things.

This was the real aim of revealed legislation [in Judaism], but regrettably it has been falsified. Dead letter, word without thought, activity without calling, all replaced the entire meaning which lay in the law. We therefore saw how the people often fell away and lost all interest. This was because legislation eventually let the mere simile (*Bild*) overcome the mind/spirit of faith/belief. ... If we want to come as close as we can to the real purpose of revelation, we must take all those side paths to it, which were only outlined. In this way we will return to the truths; which are that revelation never bestowed subjective truths or rules for determining our will. Revelation's only purpose was to bring us to a greater conviction of that to which reason could lead us, or to inspire an earlier interest in that conviction through an act of great solemnity (40-48).

Summary of translated passages
Judaism was a vessel of divine blessedness, which was as a seed prepared to blossom forth in history when opportunity arose. The blessedness was given in a region of the world in which conditions were best for Judaism to provide this blessedness to others, and in the form most appropriate to the region.

BOOK II: CHAPTER 1: THE PURPOSE OF JUDAISM

Having laid out for the reader my thoughts about religion, revelation, and faith/belief, their manifold aim and their various components, I now consider myself competent to apply all this to Judaism.

First, I pose this question: What is the real purpose of Judaism? We view Judaism as something [of the] divine. According to His great plan, the creator inserted the seed of Judaism into the course of things, to break forth when opportune, blossom and remain standing in all its brilliance. Judaism was a vessel for the blessedness which God prepared for a portion of His creatures, while He created other vessels with other forms for other creatures. / Let us consider Judaism as a higher means provided by the creator to a human society, in order for it to partake in blessedness. We perceive that the human being already has enough inherent talent, in and for itself, for bringing happiness to the world. Accordingly, the primary intention of the creator with these higher means must have been to acquaint this human society with a level of blessedness, achievable only after a major revolution of its talents.

The unfathomable activities of the Highest for advancing His creatures in blessedness are as different as [the various] vessels for blessedness are according to climates and territories across the horizon. We can therefore assert that Judaism, above all, is given in a region where the main intent and ground principle of Judaism could contribute the most to the blessedness of [all] human beings. / Human beings were universally created according to a basic principle of blessedness. They deviate one from another only in terms of the form of blessedness, as conditioned by the climate. The creator had to select a form for the Jews which was appropriate in terms of climate-conditioned nature, to lead them to a path on which they found a level of blessedness—one which He showed to other people through His unfathomable decisions in other ways. / I can therefore find the real purpose of Judaism only in this: Judaism should be a means of making those human beings to whom it was designated live up to their spiritual talents, and as receptive as possible to the happiness of society (91-93).

Translator's summary of untranslated passages
The path towards Judaism's blessed society was depicted in the book of Genesis. The pious Noah, unique to his generation, let himself be led by divinity and was exempted from humankind's fall. Those among Noah's descendants who built the tower of Babel were excluded from the divine plan, while the line from Shem through Peleg and Terah to Abraham was included. God extracted Abraham from a nomadic, unstable people with His plan for a blessed and stable society. In response to Abraham's hesitation, God repeatedly promised land and heirs. From Abraham's side, the covenant of circumcision and the binding of Isaac demonstrated fidelity to God.

God clarified that the lineage ran through Isaac rather than Ishmael. He assured Jacob of the land (Genesis 29:13-15; 35:9), and when famine forced the people to leave, God assured him that the people would endure. In Egypt, the heirs of Isaac and Jacob resisted adjustment and persisted in hoping to return to their land. When they were eventually incorporated into Egypt's economy, mistreatment restored that hope. Ascher wondered whether the divine plan would have been compromised, had the people not suffered. ("Had the Egyptian kings or their advisors not exhausted the multitude with despotic behavior and excessive discipline, would divinity have carried out its plan? Who knows? Would the multitude have been inclined to build a country for itself, had it faced the prospect of becoming equal citizens of Egypt? Who knows?") But the issue was moot. The Israelites in fact suffered, they longed for freedom, and God intervened in history. Filled with gratitude, the people memorialized the liberating events with the national festival of Passover. Since their energy was depleted (they grumbled at scarcities, lost confidence in their strength) and legislation could have further sapped their energy, the festival was only an ordinance, the Sabbath was proposed mildly (Exodus 16:25) and God sought to educate the people towards societal life (91-104).

Summary of translated passages

BOOK II: CHAPTER 2: ON THE ESSENCE OF JUDAISM

Faith/belief was the pre-condition for the religion of revelation—as exemplified by the life of Noah. Faith/belief in Judaism was originally regulative, a dominant mind/spirit among the people who were directed by God. Through revelation, God taught the people according to a collective form of truths, a collective conceptual basis. Revelation instilled truths which could not be reached by reason. Judaism provided a transcending central conception, and as such was better able to provide a universal religion than was Christianity. Christianity provided a rule for the will, which left the human being as it already was—without raising it to a new level.

In Judaism, regulations were provided to enhance national-historical development. When the weakness of people so required, God also provided ordinances to carry out that goal. There were subjective and objective components to Judaism's revealed religion: (1) The subjective condition was faith/belief. Originally regulative and according to the people's will, covenantal ordinances created faith/belief as constitutive. Rules became legislation and the people's will was subjected to control. (2) The objective condition was

revelation. It included: (a) Principles or subjects of faith/belief, known from
purposes and activities related directly to God's essence, which comprised
the material of revelation. (b) Doctrines or "objects" of faith/belief, which
included the forms of revelation and involved activities focused on obeying
God. (c) Legislation, the "predicate" of faith/belief, which utilized revelation
symbolically. It shared in the composition of faith/belief.

If one considers it exactly, what we have just explained from the Bible confirms what we maintained at the onset: [First:] Faith/belief is the pre-condition of all religion of revelation. / We find that with the exception of a certain number, faith/belief was maintained by Noah's linear descendants. The Bible characterizes Noah simply as a man who walked in God's way. He must therefore have had an extraordinary talent for faith/belief by nature. This talent became the absolute pre-condition for the revelations shared with him and [for the fact that] he did not have the slightest opposition to living up to these revelations.

Second, we see from what we have explained until now that a real *religion* lies at the basis of Judaism. That is, Judaism contains the method, or has the basis, whereby a society of people becomes accustomed to certain concepts, which they all should grasp in a similar form. The real and highest purpose of all religion is to make human beings knowledgeable of certain truths, and to present the truths to them in a more intelligible way than they, in their childhood, were capable of doing.

Third, we see that divinity chose revelation as the primary means of instilling truths. The people could not grasp these truths directly through reason, while revelation instilled a great interest in truths and imparted a great devotion to the truths.

Fourth, we see that up to this point in the history of Judaism, faith/belief, which was the pre-condition of revelation, was only regulative. [Faith/belief] was a dominant mind/spirit among the people. They all had the one same talent, they knew only one path upon which to walk. They knew no other. Up to that point, accordingly, divinity did not find it necessary to maintain the nation's faith/belief through threats. Divinity only pointed a finger. An event, an appearance, could strengthen their faith/belief. We see that when they saw the Egyptians lost in the Red Sea behind them while they made their way through the sea, the Bible used the expression, "They *believed* the Lord and His servant Moses" (Exodus 14:31).

This sheds light on the fact that Judaism is a proper revealed religion. That is, the Eternal chose Judaism as a means of teaching a number of people to think according to one [comprehensive] form. This is the proper meaning of revealed religion. I doubt whether anyone has penetrated so deeply as to be able to stipulate the concept of it in this way. / I therefore owe the reader a more extensive explanation. As I see it, Judaism as a revealed religion has the special advantage of getting people accustomed to thinking according to a single [comprehensive] form. I do not understand how thinkers engaged primarily with this material have lost this point of view. / If we take into account the respective situations of nations for whom [revelation] was designated, I am convinced that no other revealed religion has had the influence which Judaism has. I therefore maintain that the method used to educate humankind in their childhood was appropriate only to Judaism.

According to the purpose of the Christian religion, for the most profound thinkers, Christ arose solely to teach people moral truths. If I hypostasize to this purpose—which to be honest I cannot accept—not something lower but something nobler, I would ask: Would the better method not be to provide a person with a basis for all its concepts and leave it up to the human being to prescribe its own norm of behavior? Which is what every revealed religion, if it is to be generally applicable, must do? / Christ's principles, one will say, are for all peoples. But would not one main point, which is the source for all these principles, be preferable? And does not Judaism provide this main point in the proper sense? / As we have seen until now, Judaism provided only a rule for the understanding, while Christianity provided a rule for the will as well. Accordingly, should not primitive Judaism sooner be able to provide a universal religion than Christianity, given that Christianity is seen in terms of a rule for the will? Since a rule of will contains a determination through rational form, wouldn't Judaism already be adequate? Why specify objective rules [of will] which would not, as religion properly should, raise the human being above its status, but rather leave it as human as it already is?

It is true that according to the terms of Judaism's faith/belief, Judaism is at first only regulative. This leads to the obvious question: Can we preserve Judaism up to when we let it step forth as a constituted religion, even after such a deduction (105-109)?

BOOK II: CHAPTER 4

... First, Judaism has a *principle* which it reveals through its activities. Out of it, a *doctrine* emerged, which simultaneously summoned obedience. Out of the doctrine, *legislation* emerged. / The primitive *aim* of Judaism was exclusively to make people happy through the bond of society. The Eternal sought to accustom people to thinking according to a single [comprehensive] form, so that they would be suited to thinking in the same way about their noble aim. The faith/belief was *regulative*. / The Eternal concluded a covenant with the people. In order to maintain the people's faith/belief He bestowed certain ordinances. They were to be the symbols of the purposes. The *faith/belief* became *constitutive*; that is, each person had to submit him/herself to a certain bonding in order to become included in [carrying out] the intended purpose. Besides, *religion* was only *regulative*; that is, one was a Jew whether or not one acted according to an as-yet unavailable constituted norm. One behaved completely according to one's own discretion. Reason was reined in, and will alone remained the arbitrary master. / Without doubt, circumstances made it necessary to submit to these certain regulations, which conclusively became legislation. One was not merely tied to being importuned by the symbols of one's faith/belief, one was forced to act through prescribed norms. As these norms became accepted in their proper order, *faith/belief* became *dogmatic* and *religion* became *constituted*. That is, faith/belief observed the will, and the will was obliged to be guided by general, revealed laws.

The subjective condition for Judaism is faith/belief; the objective is revelation. The components of revelation are 1) the principle, which we know from the purpose which leads us directly to the essence of God; 2) the doctrine, which include the activities or the dogmas which make us directly aware of our relationship with the Highest; 3) the legislation, which is either used as a symbol in respect to revelation or helps to constitute the symbol in regard to faith/belief.

The laws therefore have a two-fold designation. They are to help constitute the objective as well as the subjective condition for Judaism. They therefore do not constitute the real *essence* of Judaism. They are merely the *predicate* of faith/belief, the *means* of maintaining revelation in Judaism as constituted religion. In what follows we will be able to easily determine whether or not Judaism was a *revealed* legislation.

As over against this, the *doctrine* is the proper *object* of faith/belief.

It is the entire *form* of revelation, insofar as it presents the activities of God methodically. Doctrine teaches about the influence of God's activities on the people. Through this influence: First, the purpose of God could be presented in a more sensible, clear and graspable way. Second, because of its individuality the doctrine is valid only as an article of faith. The doctrine therefore simultaneously provides objects for proper faith/belief, and simultaneously constitutes it, insofar as no devotion to faith/belief can take place without doctrine. ... But the *principle* is the proper *subject* of faith/belief. It is the *material* of revelation which we recognize from the form or the doctrine. The material of revelation allows us to comprehend divinity further, insofar as revelation could determine the noble aim which divinity wants to achieve with us; and insofar as the material of revelation wanted to maintain divinity's influence on us (121-125).

Summary of translated passages
The principle provided by regulative belief and the doctrine provided by regulative religion comprised the essence of Judaism. In turn the essence, which encouraged freedom of thought and moral action, produced constitutive belief. "Laws," "ordinances" and "rights," the constitutive layer of religion, were mistakenly substituted for the purpose of religion, and now had to be removed. As long as Jews accepted the religious constitution they were duty-bound to live with it. But the time had come—following the spirit of Maimonides, Spinoza and Mendelssohn—to oppose it. Scientific study was the instrument. Ascher would begin with the core, the organon *of Judaism, consisting of fourteen elements in the form of beliefs. Once the constitutive shell was removed and the core asserted, a way between Judaism and mankind would open up—and all this, without compromising the covenant.*

BOOK III: CHAPTER 7
The reader will not be able to grasp our entire system, unless my distinction between regulative and constitutive faith/belief, and regulative and constituted religion is followed precisely. Constitutive faith/belief follows purely regulative religion directly, and constitutive religion follows constitutive faith/belief.

Now we have shown that constitutive religion never grasped the non-mediated purpose of religion, but only something functional. Also, that regulative faith/belief contained the essence of religion, while constitutive faith/belief presented the essence of religion in its full scope. / Since we can change nothing about the form of faith/belief, regulative religion in Judaism remains firm. We must develop a [newly] constitutive faith/belief out of Judaism—something that has been neglected in Judaism until now—and thereby [re-]constitute the essence of our religion. We must present what is proper to our religion and establish its [new and true] constitution. / Regulative faith/belief brought us to an object of faith/belief, i.e., the principle, just as regulative religion brought us to truths of faith/belief, i.e., to the doctrine. / Principle and doctrine also constitute the essence of Judaism. They base themselves directly upon the condition, i.e., the faith/belief, and they definitely give that condition to constitutive faith/belief. What, then, is proper to faith/belief?

Faith/belief does not upset the autonomy of our other powers. It does not constrict our freedom to think or act. To the contrary, faith/belief imparts even greater strengths to us, if we regard it as purely regulative for reason and for will. Faith/belief then endows reason with the noblest ideas, which are analogous to it. It awards the will with the finest morality and the drive to action which are parallel to it. Should we now apply faith/belief, in partnership with both powers [i.e., reason and will], we must bring forth legislation which makes a constitution of religion directly available or which forms a fruitful symbol of our faith/belief.

Regarding the latter: we will retain from the legislations, ordinances and laws that which should represent a symbol of our constituted faith/belief: That which encompasses what we have also involved in the widest possible range of religion: namely, the legislation. / This is also appropriate to human nature. The person, such a varied and active creation, can only maintain order in his/her activity if he/she seeks rules, laws, ordinances and signs, according to need. Religion must also have laws, *et al*. It must construct an external function that contains the inner function. Legislation is the predicate of religion and the means by which to constitute it. In this way we will have affirmed what we assert about every positive reformation, that it annuls the constitution but does not totally destroy its ingredients.

Judaism provides us with the entire range of any revealed religion in terms of principle, doctrine and legislation. In order to maintain order herein, Judaism must arrange certain scientific studies. / [First:] Judaism must take on the job of developing its sources, history of formation and principles according to our system. A *theoretical dogmatic* or the scientific study of the sources of our faith/belief would emerge from this. / Second, the talent must be acquired to teach religious truths in context, consistently and intelligibly. A *practical* dogmatic or a scientific study of the constitutive faith/belief of our religion would emerge from this. / Third: A power must be established to maintain symbols of faith/belief, and through which the legislation will be implemented and explained. This would provide a *symbolism* or a scientific study of the constitution of religion.

With such a religion no abuse can occur. Reason includes the freedom to think, the will to act. A negative reformation must develop from this. The form of religion would then be gradually adapted, clarified, corrected and grasped with a critical eye *vis-à-vis* the constitution. / Through such a constitution we would be able to form a bond among ourselves and a bond among human beings. Our faith/belief would stand there, pure and noble. No antagonist would have the audacity to pollute its sanctuary or act against any adherent of its constitution.

But our form of faith/belief must be displayed plainly and openly, like the book of nature before the world and future generations. No one should blame us for misusing faith/belief. Let us bring the witness to faith/belief forward.

1.I believe in one God.

2.In one single God who revealed Himself to our forefathers Abraham, Isaac and Jacob and promised them our salvation.

3.Who chose for Himself Moses and other men who pleased Him and bestowed upon them the gift of prophecy.

4.Who gave laws to our forefathers on Mt. Sinai.

5.We believe that the observance of the laws was holy to our forefathers. This kept them upon that path which we now walk upon with open faith/belief in God and His prophets.

6.We believe that this God is a God of love.

7.He will reward the good and punish the evil.

8.He governs the world through His foresight and omnipotence.

9.He will also direct our misfortunes towards the good.

10.We hope in redemption through His messiah in this life, and in our grave with those whom He will respectfully dignify at the resurrection.

11.We obligate ourselves to keep the covenant which the Eternal concluded with our fathers, through circumcision.

12. To celebrate the Sabbath as a day holy to God.

13. To renew the memory of His good deeds through festivals.

14. And implore grace and purification from Him, through atonement.

This is the *organon* of Judaism, and there is no other. One must elucidate it and explain it through the aids provided by Scripture and tradition. Faith/belief, trust and obligation form the bond which links us and holds us together. What unites us, or should unite us, with other people? Judaism has hinted at this in the purposes located in it. The rest remains engraved in our hearts, and develops in the point of a thousand feelings.

It is true that as long as we remain with this constitution, it is disloyal to oppose it. I have shown the way to rightly annul this constitution and introduce a new one. In this way we do not act like children who have forgotten their duty to the faith/belief of our forefathers. We are stirring up against God-like creatures who are arbitrary and trust only in their own power. Nor does forgetfulness dispel all which has happened. Our way does not cause the ruin of the covenant through unbelief. / Your present constitution certainly undermines this purpose of our faith/belief. Perhaps this is still not noticeable by all of you. But time will teach differently, and then woe to our faith/belief, woe to our vocation as people/human beings.

Had one been concerned earlier with the proper purpose and the essence of Judaism, one would have returned to these truths long ago. I cannot repeat this enough: To take the constitution of religion for its essence, for its function, engenders all sorts of harm, separating us away from all societies, hindering us from choosing professions in them, inducing us ultimately to concentrate all active powers upon a single point. Precisely because of this, religion itself became a motive to fixate our mind/spirit on a point about which we had more talent for speculation than for solid thinking according to principles. Withdrawn away from any acquaintance with humanity's progress in the arts and scientific studies, we slumbered dreamily.

Humanity let us sleep for a long time and meander around in our idealistic world. I do not know what good genius encouraged a Maimonides to bring Judaism back to sure principles. I do not know what evil genius let a Spinoza desert and transform Judaism into a nothing. I do not know what indifferent genius led a Mendelssohn to want to overcome his opponents, only to be overwhelmed himself. / This I do know: That I have these three men to thank for motivating me to take a step which is perhaps contrary to the entire direction of the human mind/spirit of our times. I therefore had to ascend to the exalted sources and descend again from there (233-240).

IV.I.II. Selections from *Eisenmenger the Second*, translated by Gershon Greenberg

Translator's summary
Opponents of Judaism were either religious or political. In the political group, some taught that Jews could not improve their own political situation while others alleged that Jews did not want to. Johann Gottlieb Fichte represented another trend. He sought to universalize authentic revelation through the principle of practical reason and its corresponding moral legislation. Fichte mistakenly sought to apply Kantian philosophy, which was intended to be solely speculative. He avoided its pivotal issue, that the eternal collision between moral legislation and will could never free us from the chains of necessity on the one side and the temptations of immorality on the other. Ascher questioned the viability of Fichte's inter-relation between revelation, its concept, and moral legislation. He asserted that Fichte's purportedly universal revelation was in fact a particular revelation of the Christian Fichte, which excluded the revelation of Judaism.

Unmistakably, one can divide the opponents of Jews in Europe into two classes, *religious* and *political*. In earlier times, where each state set out to embrace religion, Jews were persecuted on account of their religion. Later, people began to separate the interest of the state from religion, and they paid more attention to the principles of Judaism's adherents [themselves]. The spirit of the era misled thinkers into regarding these adherents not only as crazy Pharisees but also as scary cannibals. In most recent times, as people have begun to seek different ways of supporting the principles of a good state-system, Jews have been reprimanded only for their negative political side. / The *political* opponents of Jews are the ones who have recently raised their voices and incited against them. They do not all proceed from a single principle, but rather divide into two factions. / One faction asserts that the Jews will not improve politically, because they *cannot* improve their political situation. The other asserts that they cannot improve their political situation because they do not *want to* improve it. For the former, the Jew is burdened by foolishness and laziness of spirit. For the latter, the Jew is evil and self-aggrandizing. For the former faction, the Jew does not *know* what is better. For the latter, the Jew does not *want* what is better. / As offended as one is, one still tries to convince these opponents about the facts and about the insufficient data for their judgment. Any reasonable or honorably thinking person is justified, perhaps more than justified, in believing that the Jew *can* and *wants to* improve politically. This fact cannot elude the observer.

[Amidst these attacks] a totally new species of opponents develop before our eyes, armed with more terrifying weapons than the others. Their principles are first grasped after they germinate. As far as I can tell, they are intimately connected to [Fichtes'] remarks about Judaism and Jews [in *Contribution to Correcting the Judgment About the French Revolution*]. Perhaps these principles led him to attack the [Jewish] nation and its beliefs in ways usually associated with earlier times.

I am proud to count myself among those who venerate recent developments in philosophy. I certainly do not fail to recognize the value which the mind/spirit of critical philosophy has for our exciting age. I do not overlook how it reduces the arrogance of despotic and anarchic thinking, and how it brings mutually specious assertions of the various contesting parties to the surface. But what should I think when those who present themselves as the apostles of critical philosophy, who consider themselves invigorated by it, blindly impute a particular purpose to the spirit of critical philosophy which I would never ascribe to its greatest teacher [Immanuel Kant]?

As much as has been made of the *esoteric* and *exoteric* philosophy of the ancients, I believe that its real perspective has generally been missed. The ancients, I suspect, perceived that certain speculative views of the universe could not be applied to the real world; and that such views could occasion damage and indescribable conflict, rather than order and improved conditions [in the real world]. The ancients never sought to apply the subjects of esoteric philosophy generally and popularly, such as to change human life and particular events. They let these subjects stand as distinct monuments, and anyone who felt called upon to at least think about how to act could [if they wanted,] apply their mental powers to them. / Their successors turned what their great teachers used as a means of spreading wisdom into an end. Once the students settled on how to think [about how to act], the most absurd activities and opinions ever encountered in the ancient history of philosophical understanding emerged.... [The situation is similar in modern times.] In solving certain problems of philosophy, the great thinker Kant presented specific outlines for thought and used them to propose a certain philosophy. These outlines were intended more as a stimulant for speculation than as a firm, insurmountable structure. I wish he had not also intended to see his ideas realized in the real world at all—which now appears to be so, given the motives for the ideas (41-44).

Summary of untranslated passages
Kant's disciples failed to recognize that his philosophy was an outline for thought that was inapplicable to reality. One difficulty was the collision between moral legislation and will, which was bound by necessity on one side and temptations of immorality on the other. The disciples weighed everything according to their respective contexts and principles. They judged history, politics, laws of nature, religion and even revelation in partisan fashion. Once all this manifested itself, Kant was accused of skepticism and materialism, as well as of destroying morality and religion.

Fichte entered into the fray and presented the rationality of the concept of revelation, in his "Attempt at a Critique of All Revelation" *(Versuch einer Kritik aller Offenbarung, 1792). Not only did revelation not contradict the principles of reason; for Fichte it was universally valid with respect to those principles. Fichte transformed revelation itself into a concept. He determined what revelation was according to laws based on principles of practical reason, and concluded that the concept of revelation corresponded to moral legislation. Ascher objected: Was revelation thinkable without some perception preceding it? If so, revelation could not be utilized conceptually. Fichte for his part demonstrated what kind of revelation was desirable in terms of moral legislation. But which was prior, revelation or moral legislation?*

Fichte's (unnamed) cohorts endeavored to decide with certainty which revelation was of divine origin. But this, Ascher pointed out, required determining which revelation was universally valid, and he noted that any revelation acceptable to a thinking person involved the purpose of human existence; therefore, revelation and truth coincided. A universally valid revelation had to be suitable to the human way of thinking, as it deduced the essence, the content of each real revelation. Any critique of revelation had to take the essence of revelation into account—and this concerned the role of faith/belief, that in turn involved determining the purpose of revelation—which would annul the revelation itself.

In the end, Ascher concluded, revelation, whether as such or as an object of faith/belief, could not be thought of as agreeing with reason. Although Fichte purported to offer a critique of revelation, he in fact was out to prove that only Christian revelation was factual. This was also behind his remark about "decapitation" regarding Jews in his Contribution to Correcting the Judgment About the French Revolution. *In Fichte's mind, the emancipation of the Jews, tied up with the French Revolution, clashed with the exclusiveness of Christian truth. As with Kant, the only faith grounded in divine revelation was the Christian faith (see* Religion Within the Limits of Reason Alone*).*

Summary of translated passages
Kant articulated a statutory ecclesiastical faith, a church which united people in terms of a moral legislation awakened by revelation. The Christian church, and it alone, for Kant, was based upon morality. Ascher observed that Kant recognized how Judaism prepared for Christianity physically and empirically, but ignored Judaism's faith/belief and morality.

Thank heavens! Controversial sermons having been banned from the pulpit, and philosophers direct them to their university chairs. No matter that people still complain about the evil influence of the enlightenment.

Is it any less a controversial sermon when a philosopher, a transcendental thinker [i.e., Kant], undertakes measuring revelation and religion according to his fixed principles? He can [justifiably] determine the possibility of universally valid revelation and generally determine the purpose of a [specific] religion. But is he able to justifiably assert from the data of a [specific] revelation, that this revelation is universally valid? And that a religion built upon it generally corresponds to the purpose of a religion? Will he be able to do that? Consider this: In the hands of reflective, contextual thinkers these data support any sort of form with as many purposes as one may wish. Like puppets, these purposes could be turned around and applied to any principle one may capriciously stipulate. Is the type of data presented by Christian faith/belief any different than the type of data offered by any other religion?

Let me first introduce Kant's principles: [According to him] religion consists of the veneration of God as the legislator of all our duties.[33] Laws are either *statutory* (following certain prescriptions without regard to their inner-moral value) or *purely moral*. Only the statutory laws are capable of a diversified form. Revelation alone can determine the selection of the form for us. Purely moral laws are recognized through reason and [the form] is simple (*vis-à-vis* the moral law). Statutory laws comprise a *historical* rational belief. Purely moral laws are the basis of a *pure rational faith*. / To the extent that human beings unite into a common essence under moral legislation as commanded by God, a *church* comes about: It is *invisible*, insofar as it cannot be realized as pure idea. In certain case, however, human beings strive to draw near to this idea, they unify to spread that thought [or idea], and the Church becomes visible. / Because human beings are generally not ready for purely rational religion, a worshipping faith/belief will likely develop among them. Since reason cannot respond in terms of how we are to behave as citizens of this divine state on earth [i.e., the Church], a Church is formed that is based upon a statutory, historical faith/belief awakened by revelation. As opposed to pure religious faith, the Church can be described as ecclesiastical faith/belief. / There is only *one* (true) religion, but various sorts of faith/belief can lead to it. One should therefore always speak of "the faith/belief" of the Jews, Mohammedans, and Christians; not of "the religion" of each, from which each forms a Church. The Church's faith/belief in the pure faiths/beliefs of religion has an interpreter. In order to be introduced, this interpreter must serve that faith/belief.[34]

Each statutory ecclesiastical faith/belief is maintained through *Scripture*. Scripture becomes more capable of establishing the general purpose of a pure religious faith the closer the statutory ecclesiastical faith/belief is brought to the principles of a pure religious faith/belief. / The higher the degree to which a statutory ecclesiastical faith/belief draws attention to general faiths/beliefs of religion through the means at the disposal of the statutory ecclesiastical faith/belief (as a higher knowledge of a pure faith/belief of religion in rational expression, in seeking rational expression in historical monuments), the closer the

---

33   Kant, *Die Religion innerhalb der Grenzen der blossen Vernunft. Ersten Auflage* (Königsberg: Friedrich Nicolovius, 1793), 139.
34   *Ibid.*, 142.

faith/belief gets to the general public, the more it can be named the *true* Church. A true Church [is one] which, in maintaining the means to the general religious belief/faith, can *become triumphant* and, ultimately, *exclusively salvific*.

I will not contest the principle Kant stipulates for a pure faith/belief of religion. I have already expressed myself about this, and I reserve the right to introduce the data in a more appropriate place as a basis for my remarks. I will only shed light on the results, which are based exactly on the course of ideas upon which Kant was focused. Kant provides the idea of how a *systematic* Church history can be sketched out to show how the moral principle lying within us could eventually weaken a particular faith/belief of the Church and end up forming a universal Church intended to become permanent for all peoples and all times. The history also presents the struggle between a religious faith/belief of divine worship and a moral religious faith/belief [and the anticipated victory of pure morality]. Kant asserts that this history can only produce unity when applied to that portion of the human species where a predisposition for the unity of the universal Church is already well developed: "Because the history of different nations whose faiths/beliefs have no bonds with one another preserves no unity."[35] Kant expounds upon the one faith/belief in which there is an underlying moral principle. He discusses how faith/belief prepares for the final victory of pure morality in the struggle between religious faith/belief of divine worship and moral religious faith/belief. He further elucidates the one faith/belief which, in and for itself, spreads the kingdom of the true Church on earth, and, rising above its companions, exalts pure religious faith/belief.

It is Judaism's destiny, for which Christianity should undoubtedly be the most grateful, that no advocate of Christianity can present his credentials without destroying Judaism's deeply-rooted right to those credentials by means of all sorts of dexterity in philosophical politics. / It first became evident that the Jewish faith/belief had no essential bond with the (Christian) ecclesiastical faith/belief which Kant wanted to discover, even if that Jewish faith/belief was the *physical* cause for the grounding of the church. Physical cause? This probably means revelation, as what is physical about faith/belief, insofar as it is empirical.

---

35   *Ibid.*, 185.

Thus only revelation, but not the moral aim of Judaism, provided the cause for the development of Christianity? Let us hear (53-57).

Summary of translated passages
According to Kant, the Jewish religion was produced by a national stock which unified into a political institution. Morality was only an addition. Ascher countered that as explained in Leviathan, *Judaism was originally regulative and not constitutive. Kant also asserted that Judaism was not a matter of moral conscience, but of external observance of commands given in terms of reward and punishment and in the context of its particular political institution. In fact, Ascher countered, ancient Judaism's relationship with proselytes contained the seed of a universal church.*

Purely in terms of its original institutional arrangement [according to Kant], Jewish faith/belief should contain the quintessence of statutory legislation, upon which to establish a state-system. But surely Kant is thinking here of the first [statutory arrangement], not the original system of government of Judaism. Initially, Judaism did not have a (constitutive) institutional arrangement. As indicated at length elsewhere, it was *regulative* (*Leviathan*, 106). I could assert the same about Christianity, which became statutory only long after its regulative existence.

Further [according to Kant], the moral components which Judaism had already at the time of its establishment, or which became attached to Judaism, did not belong to Judaism. Judaism, Kant continues, is no religion, and consists rather of the uniting of a special stock into a common entity in terms of political legislation. As such, it does not have the constitution of a Church. The intended theocratic system (or aristocracy of priests), where God was venerated purely as a world regent and which made no claim related to conscience, did not make the system religious.

With this argumentation, Kant thoroughly emulates Judaism's theological opponents. If you speak only about the *foundation* of a religion, Christianity in this respect seldom deviated from Judaism. But if you speak of the real purpose and spirit/mind of Judaism, then surely Judaism could be brought closer to the purpose of Christianity.

But then, should one not consider that the motive and the purpose, which must be moral, ought to be expressed in such maxims as Kant elicits so beautifully from the Apostles? To the contrary, I find the spirit/mind of each respective religion precisely at the moment of its germination, when the inner dignity of the spirit/mind animated the people to adhere to the religion.

If you believe that the Apostles were already inspired by Christianity, so I deem that the Patriarchs (or our Emir) were already ensouled by Judaism. But that Christ accepted the apostles for himself solely through His activities, through the noble draw of His heart, and not at all through his moral maxims, which the Apostles registered for themselves, is a matter of consensus. Could the special destiny of antiquity not have made Judaism's first adherents attentive to the wiser steps of divinity? Understood in this way, not even Kant could assert that Judaism did not include a Church.

In the sense in which Kant takes the Church:

> It could best of all be likened to that of a household (family) under a common, though invisible moral Father, whose holy son, knowing His will and yet standing in blood relation with all members of the household, takes His place in making His will better known to them; these accordingly honor the Father in him and so enter with one another into a voluntary, universal, and enduring union of hearts.[36]

Judaism would perhaps better realize this odd idea of a Church in a (not unknown) [Hebrew scriptural] father who did everything possible to invite and educate his family in terms of wise intentions for a lasting heartfelt unity and the like. Should one still see Christianity as opposed to this authentic church [of Judaism], one need not also conclude: Because the [Jewish] church does not occupy Judaism and because Judaism veered away from it in so many ways to the point of deviating from it, therefore Judaism would never constitute a church, and could never have a religious constitution.

When Kant speaks more openly, saying that Judaism can have no religious unification, he first alleges the ancient assertion that Judaism consisted solely of commands. They were given not for the sake of moral conscience but solely for external observance. Temporal reward and pun-

---

36   Kant, *Religion Within the Limits of Reason Alone*, trans. with an introduction by Theodore M. Greene and Hoyt H. Hudson (La Salle, IL: Open Court, 1960), 93.

ishment were apparently established on that basis, while faith/belief in future life and heaven and hell passed over the Jews, as [they do] with the most primitive people. A political, rather than ethical (i.e., determined by the legislation of virtue) entity, [Kant continued] was to be established. Out of this, a universal Church could never emerge, for the entity excluded the human species as a whole from its community. No matter that the entity fixed upon a God, who could not be represented by any visible picture, who was the universal lord of the human species as a whole; because God bestowed a mechanical cultus, the idea [of God] resembled, or was even pursuant to, the polytheistic idea of other peoples.

One sees how the author [Kant] twists and turns just to bring his opinion forward. If there is not attention to religious postulates (future life *et al.*) in the constitution of Judaism, this is because they simply did not exist. But Judaism and Christianity show that a religious purpose is not achieved through these postulates. After they already adopted them, neither Judaism nor Christianity changed into an ideal religion— as Kant presumed to outline. It follows that, given the lack of postulates or the still silence when it comes to them, there is no basis at hand to maintain that Judaism intended a purely political system.

If it is asserted [by Kant] that no universal church can arise from the political system of Judaism, based upon commands and external observance, [then] the blame should not fall upon Judaism. Circumstances alone caused an intelligent man like Moses to take the precaution of erecting a wall around his constitution. I rather believe that one side of the wall was to cut off any intercourse between the Jews and the proselytizing-related spirit of Egyptian and other priests. On the other side, it was to serve as a means of subjecting those who offered themselves to the Jews as proselytes (whom the Jews made infallible) to as many tests as possible—in part as a means to become convinced of the converts' devotion; in part as a means of having the proselytes become inclined to Judaism's purpose and be earnestly concerned about it. The proselytes and the purpose of which they became aware now seem to disclose that Judaism was in no way grounded upon the *hatred of the entire human species*, [but] rather, that Judaism is supposed to contain the seed of a universal church. After all these remarks, even the objection that the idea of divinity in Judaism, because it was venerated purely as a mechanical cult, was not to be highly regarded, falls aside. It would indeed be rash for someone to draw conclusions about regulative application from the constitutive application of this idea. This would, however, indeed be the case, if one were to assert that the idea of divinity was merely invented to keep up the mechanical cult. This is an opinion with which surely no thinking person could agree.

At the same time, this entire argumentation may well show Kant that I too could use the politics so useful to him in presenting Judaism—as he sneaks off the stage to present Judaism *per se* as a misanthropic creation.

Before going any further let me explain. If I seek to equate Judaism's purpose with the purpose which Kant discovered in Christianity, this is only to shed light on the controversy. I am not convinced at all that these or any other religions are based upon their [respective] proper purpose. I rather imagine that with the help of scriptural interpreters and those learned in Scripture, I could refer any religion to the aim of Christianity as Kant defines it. / At the same time, I wanted to see Judaism set upon a firm basis no less than I wished Kant to seek out a firm basis for Christianity. For how does it help to fight over priorities, which are valued according to each respective eye? (57-62)

Summary of translated passages
For Ascher, until the kingdom of God arrived, no one religion was to be exalted above any other. Kant's assertion that Jesus annulled circumcision in order to make his (Jesus') religion universal was questionable. The annulling came only with the Apostles, after non-Jews began to join Christianity outside the land of Palestine. Kant's contention that Jesus' religion of morality appeared suddenly, as though Jesus invented it, was also questionable. Jesus drew his religion of morality from Judaism.

But as long as conditions remains the same, as long as the kingdom of God has not arrived through Christianity, Judaism or any other religion, no truth-loving and right-minded person should be allowed—in order to avoid the practical consequences for society and state—to exalt one faith/belief at the cost of others. Now let us hear what Kant says about Christianity.

Christianity, Kant asserts, provided the idea of a system of Church history based upon an entirely new principle. Whatever the Apostles brought from time to time from Judaism to Christianity carried implications for *introducing* Christianity. The subsequent abrogation of circumcision [according to Kant] surely showed that Christianity comprised a religion which was valid for all people. [For Kant] *Christianity arose suddenly, albeit not unprepared*, not out of the Judaism constituted by Moses, but out of a Judaism enlightened by a moral philosophy which accrued to it from the outside. The teacher of the Gospels declared *himself* as one sent from heaven. For he explained that moral faith/belief was alone salvific. Through His life's journey, the teacher of the Gospels demonstrated his authenticity. Through teaching and the suffering of his person, the teacher provided the archetype for the only mankind satisfactory to God.[37] Speaking without bias, far from all predilections, without hypocrisy and obliged to state the truth: It is not audacious on my part to assert that the moment Kant wrote this he undermined his entire philosophy—as a thinker who, proper to his calling, searched out the causes and consequences of all phenomena. / Consider this, dear reader! Suddenly Christianity is elevated. Suddenly a principle emerges —I really have no words for it—upon which Christianity should base itself. Suddenly Jesus stands there, proclaiming Himself to be sent from heaven. What a philosophical *Deus ex machina*! What a philosophical *Saltus mortalis*!

But Christianity was not so *sudden*. In which political system did the Jews at the time of the birth of Jesus of Nazareth find themselves? Which culture did the nation have by itself? And what did it acquire from outside the land? What influence did this nation's culture have upon the nation's religion and customs? Anyone who answers these questions with critical spirit/mind will not see Christianity emerging [so] suddenly. To the contrary, Christianity's entire spirit/mind is to be discovered in the Judaism of the time. One would have to concede: Like Moses, Jesus of Nazareth was not merely a thinker but a doer. With this distinction: Moses only had [a mass of] *people* before him. They did not yet reach a degree of development which would summon them to proper activity. Moses, rather, led them according to his will. Jesus had a *nation* before Him, one skilled in the arts of the priests and therefore the more distrustful. The nation upset all Jesus' undertakings. They persecuted Him everywhere. They finally brought an end to His noble intention through His death. From this it is evident that the number of adherents in His [own Jewish] nation was very small.

I gladly concede that the divinity of the founder of Christianity was helpful in insisting that Judaism should be given a different direction

---

37 Kant, *Die Religion*, 74-77.

through the genuine moral doctrine which the Apostles had him express. But I will not concede that this moral doctrine was invented by him to share with *the world.* / It follows that Judaism would only be transformed into Christianity, not that Christianity in and for itself was supposed to oppose Judaism. / What Kant, by the way, calls *Introduction* is a method, which was not instituted only for Christianity to obtain entry into Judaism. Moses already used this method when he sought to introduce Judaism. He said it already existed before Judaism's constitution. In doing so, Moses retained much of the Egyptian religion. This was to avoid offending the disposition of Jews who stuck to Egyptian superstition.

The Apostles observed how their teaching had very few adherents among the Jews, and that these few Jews were not permitted to express themselves. The Apostles were therefore obliged to leave *Palestine.* I certainly believe that they were not so short-sighted as to carry forward the truths articulated for the Jews by Jesus outside the country with the limitations of the main pillars of the Jews' religious system—which Jesus himself always took into account. I rather believe that the Apostles sought to spread precisely those truths which were stripped of all their pedantic interpretations. Jesus was not out to annul circumcision for Jews—nor could he have done so. The Apostles could not, and did not, want to make its cancellation a condition for the faith of the Apostles outside the country. Only gradually, as the faith of the Apostles added foreign adherents, could the Jewish-Christians risk discontinuing circumcision.

Thus, on the basis of the subsequent abolition of circumcision, Kant would not be able to assert that Jesus intended to establish a world-religion. The persecution of the Apostles alone produced the world religion, as it would with Judaism or any religion (62-64).

Summary of translated passages
Until now, Judaism's opponents were political and religious. Kant and Fichte now added opposition on moral grounds, with that argument's element of Jew-hatred. Kant's attempt to make Christianity the religion closest to moral principles, and the exclusive religion of the age of enlightenment, was an offense against state and society. There should be tolerance, not triumphalism. Each religion should strive to bring itself closer to the principles of morality and all religions should all work together to establish the great covenant of mankind.

I would not usually expend so many words on the issue. But Kant annoyed me deeply when he based his system on the very weak assertion *that Christianity, albeit not unprepared, manifested itself suddenly.* If it is prepared it can not suddenly manifest itself in its entirety. To the extent that the preparation is related to the suddenness, the preparation should be explained and the suddenness removed. / All the hindrances which stand in the way of Christianity's aim, the evil and misery which distort rather than clarify Christianity, exist also for Judaism and its aim: One can also shout out about Judaism: "Superstition has the power to prompt such heinous acts" [Lucretius, *On the Nature of Things*, Book 1, Line 101]. / If Kant now considers contemporary times as the best times for Christianity and its special purpose, I see the same for Judaism. If Kant wants to say that Christianity's establishment was intended solely to introduce pure religious faith/belief, I can boldly assert that this intention lies also at the basis of Judaism. If Kant could prove his hypothesis with better data, if he could shed light on his proposition through the advance of enlightened dogmatic and clarified exegesis and I could not, this would not be Judaism's fault but that of its adherents.

There was a moment when war was declared against all religion. This was also the moment when my own nation produced a number of thinkers with a collective plan towards that [very] end. In the contemporary context of enlightenment, Judaism was found to be aimless, Judaism's dogma and exegesis were not reformed, as was so with Christianity, to become aligned with the requirements of the adherents of the spiritual revolution. To the contrary, dogma and exegesis were used against those requisites.

Now one sees what path the last decade of the century has taken. There is more than enough conviction for the need of religion. But which religion—which religion is appropriate to the age? Insofar as the Franconians shake off the yoke of hierarchy (whether correctly or incorrectly—I do not wish to decide) and introduce a new religion, we see peace-loving Germany inclined to fit the Christian religion to the spirit of the age. The greatest thinker—a Kant—seeks to stipulate and assert the prerogative of the Christian religion. / But must this happen at the cost of all other religions? Even at the cost of Judaism? Is the maxim of a philosopher like Kant worthy? Namely, that since Christianity is brought closer to moral principles through progress, art, scientific study and enlightenment, it is the best and holiest religion? Difficult for me to believe.

My maxim is this: The principles of morality have progressed very well through the enlightenment, while extant religions appear to be in collision with these principles. It is therefore the duty of all thinkers, of each and every religion, either to divert the public from all ideas of religion and draw its attention solely to the purely moral religion; or, if the adherents of each religion have the need (and it is up to the state to stipulate), to have them unite to bring the fixed principles of morality closer to their respective religion. / If a thinker like Kant now steps forward and uses the weapons of clever dialectic against this reasonable maxim in order to assert that Christianity alone can establish the only true church, this certainly deserves a reprimand. A rebuke, for it goes against the interest of state and society, no matter how appropriate it may be in certain limited circles.

For a flourishing state, where a dominant Church has been established, tolerance is not only morally but politically good. If a state tolerates various kindred religions, it continues to contradict itself if the maxim of members of the dominant Church is imposed upon all believers: that dominant adherents will in days to come be *triumphant*. And should this maxim rest upon a principle which directly constituted the basis of our entire morality and the dominant religion made us attentive to this morality more than any other religion, how could, and how would, this maxim [be able to] tolerate human beings who counteracted the very high purpose of humankind, or were even tempted to do so?

When I now see that through this tenet, a Christian philosopher produces this consequence [of intolerance], it becomes a primary duty to counteract this erroneous opinion, and make the non-partisan thinker aware of this hypothetical subjection. A second duty is for the thinkers of my nation to uncover the enemy who would influence the political peace of their nation detrimentally in no small measure—a peace in which the nation began to share again only a few years ago.

If until now the Jewish nation had *political* and *religious* opponents, now there are *moral* opponents positioned against it. The principle fixed by the moral opponents with respect to Judaism reads: Judaism can never accomplish enough in terms of the purpose of a religion, for its revelation did not prepare the disposition for moral religion. Judaism never raised itself to the principle of an exclusively salvific church. As adherents of their faith/belief, Jews could therefore never be good human beings. In this regard one may hear the powerful reprimand which [Fichte], the author of *Contribution to Correcting*, [addressed to] humankind.

> By what right? I will concede everything that Kant asserts: Still, it is agreed that the Christian religion itself has not yet risen to the level of a true church. What should the Jew now do? Become the sort of Christian typical of our day? Kant would not want that. Or the sort of Christian which he perhaps is or wishes to be? If I should not despair at seeing such a Christian, I would also not despair of finding such a Jew. And should I not despair, Kant would not convince me that Christianity, uniquely and alone, would establish the kingdom of God on earth. Rather, I would feel myself much more convinced that the general endeavor of all religious fraternities, that of bringing the truths veiled in their revelations ever closer to developing morality, was the one means of establishing the great covenant of humankind in its glory.

One sees from this how even critical philosophy—according to which a *Critique of All Revelation* presented the principle for criteria for all revelation, and which in respect to this principle developed Judaism-autonomy as a doctrine of religion—contributes to this: the *a priori* justification of the concept of *Jew hatred*. / In this respect we must turn again to [Fichte], the author of *Contribution to Correcting the Public's Judgment of the French Revolution*, and show to what extent his inference of the concept of *Jew-hatred* may be ascribed to the eternal battle, as to whether the Jew should be tolerated or persecuted (66-71).

4.2. DAVID EINHORN (1809-1879): CENTRALIZATION AND HISTORY

Einhorn was born in 1809 in Diespeck, Bavaria, and received yeshiva training in nearby Fürth. His main teacher was the Orthodox Jewish scholar Wolf Hamburger—who also taught Einhorn's Baltimore antagonist, Abraham Rice.[38] He took classes in philology, philosophy and theology at the universities of Würzburg and Munich—where he studied under Schelling. He received his doctorate in 1834 for a dissertation entitled "Erklärung verschiedener philosophischer Stellen im Buche

---

38   Einhorn's major works include: "Unterscheidungslehre zwischen Judentum und Christentum," *Sinai* 5, no. 7 (August 1860): 193-197 through *Sinai* 7 no. 11 (December 1862): 291-295; *Das Prinzip des Mosaismus und dessen Verhältniss zum Heidentum und rabbinischen Judentum* (Leipzig: C. L. Fritzsche, 1854); *Ner Tamid (Beständige Leuchte): Die Lehre des Judentums* (Philadelphia: n.p., 1886); "Wesen und Umfang der menschlichen Willensfreiheit," *Jewish Times*, vols. 4:1, 4:2, 4:3, 4:4, 4:5, 4:7.

On his life and thought, see Hans-Joachim Bechtoldt, "David Einhorn," in *Die jüdische Bibelkritik im 19. Jahrhundert* (Stuttgart: W. Kohlhammer, 1995), 90-194; Philip Cohen, "David Einhorn's Reading for *Tisha B'Av*: Tradition and Transformation," *CCAR Journal* 41, no. 4 (1994): 55-67; and "David Einhorn: Biblical Theology as Response and Reform" (PhD dissertation, Brandeis University, 1993); Eric Friedland, "*Olath Tamid* by David Einhorn," *Hebrew Union College Annual* 45 (1974): 307-332; Greenberg, "Mendelssohn in America: David Einhorn's Radical Reform Judaism," *LBIY* 27 (1982): 281-294; Greenberg, "The Significance of America in David Einhorn's Conception of History," *American Jewish Historical Quarterly* 63 (1973): 160-184; Greenberg, "*Religionswissenschaft* and Early Reform Jewish Thought: Samuel Hirsch and David Einhorn," in *Modern Judaism and Historical Consciousness*, eds. Andreas Gotzmann and Christian Wiese (Leiden: Brill, 2007), 106-139; Greenberg, "The Messianic Foundations of American Jewish Thought: David Einhorn and Samuel Hirsch," in *Proceedings of the Sixth World Congress of Jewish Studies, 13-19 August, 1973*, vol. 2 (Jerusalem: World Union of Jewish Studies, 1975), 215-226; and "Dialectic in Exile: Post-Emancipation Judaism's Negative Legacy to American Thought," in *Proceedings of the Eighth World Congress of Judaic Studies* (Jerusalem: World Union of Jewish Studies, 1981), 67-74; Samuel Hirsch, *Rev. Dr. David Einhorn Gedächtniss-Rede* (Philadelphia: E. Hirsch, 1879); Meyer, *Response to Modernity: A History of the Reform Movement in Judaism* (New York: Oxford University Press, 1988), 244-250; Jacob J. Petuchowski, "Abraham Geiger and Samuel Holdheim—Their Differences in Germany and Repercussions in America," *LBIY* 22 (1977): 139-159; Marc Saperstein, "David Einhorn: Two Civil War Sermons," in *Jewish Preaching in Times of War, 1800-2001* (Oxford: Littman Library of Jewish Civilization, 2008), 192-221; Wiese, "Samuel Holdheim's 'Most Powerful Comrade in Conviction': David Einhorn and the Debate Concerning Jewish Universalism in the Radical Reform Movement," in *Redefining Judaism in an Age of Emancipation: Comparative Perspectives on Samuel Holdheim (1806-1860)*, ed. Wiese (Leiden: Brill, 2007), 306-374; and Michael Zank, "Einhorn: On Sacrifice," in *The Idea of Atonement in the Philosophy of Hermann Cohen* (Providence: Brown Judaic Series, 2000), 500-505.

Moreh Nefuchim (sic!)" at the University of Erlangen.[39] His first post was to be that of rabbi of Wellhausen, beginning in 1838, but the Bavarian government withheld approval—possibly for his reformist leanings. Einhorn found private financial support to dedicate the next four years to scholarship, along with occasional synagogue sermons—including one at Kleinlanghein. He was appointed rabbi of Birkenfeld in 1842, and in 1847 succeeded Reform rabbi Samuel Holdheim in Mecklenburg-Schwerin. That appointment lasted four years, at which point he left out of frustration with the oppressive atmosphere of post-1848 German conservatism. Einhorn went to Pesth, Hungary, to head a Reform congregation there. Under pressure from the Orthodox, he resigned from the position after a year, but he stayed in Pesth and wrote the first part of *The Principle of Mosaism*. In 1855 Einhorn arrived at Baltimore's Har Sinai Congregation, where he remained for six years. He left because of personality disputes—not because of a legendary but undocumented heroic stance against slavery—and moved to Philadelphia's Keneset Israel. He was suspended in 1866 (again for undisclosed reasons), whereupon he assumed leadership of New York's Adat Jeshurun. He continued as rabbi there through the merger with Anshei Hesed and the creation of Beth-El (later Temple Emanuel) until his death in 1879.

Einhorn identified Judaism's principle as a dynamic of centralization, a theme drawn from Schelling or from Franz Joseph Molitor (1779-1860).[40] According to it, polar points of departure synthesized without losing their original identities. Thus, God was eternal and yet created a world of time which was of Him. As idealist thought had it, God retained a separation from that world. Pagan naturalism asserted that God and nature coincided. The God of Judaism synthesized His transcendental "I," *YHWH*, which freely created and entered history, with His being which epitomized cyclical nature, *Elohim*. According to the dynamics of centralization, the human being was both a spirit born

---

39   In his dissertation, Einhorn commented about Maimon's *Gibeat Ha'moreh*: "Salomon Maimoni verwirrt in seiner Erklärungsweise den richtigen Gesichtspunkt durch seine lächerliche Methode Kantische Begriffe in die Schule des Aristoteles, aus welcher Maimonides hervorgegangen, hineinzutragen." Cited by Bechtoldt, 135.
40   See Philip Cohen, "Einhorn's Theory of Centralization and its Relation to F. W. J. Schelling's Theory of Identity," in "David Einhorn: Biblical Theology as Response and Reform," 67-104; and Franz Joseph Molitor, *Philosophie der Geschichte oder über die Tradition in dem alten Bunde und ihre Beziehung zur Kirche des neuen Bundes* (FaM: Hermann, 1827), 83-91.

of God and a physical microcosm. The human being was the product of synthesis between *beriah*, creation out of nothing, and *asiyah*, production out of something already available. As *beriah*, the human received absolute spirit (*ruah Elohim*), enabling it to share in divine holiness, to be rational and to share the dynamic of centralization. The human being also received freedom, which was absolute in the sense that no evil blocked it, no outer act determined its direction, and God's control stopped at the temporal and spatial bounds to his activity. As *asiyah* the human body was produced out of available material. Spirit (*ruah*) and body were synthesized in the blood of the heart, where the *nefesh*, the original soul resided. Finally, the transcendental, revelatory dimension to God's relationship with man centralized with the human or rational factor. This was without injury to either; indeed the revealed dimension became effective in a rational context. Reason, which needed experience to develop, led Einhorn to history. History offered the time and means for reason to build its experience and collect its results. For its part, history contained the divine spirit which took form in revelational truths. History was a means for reflecting God's cosmic presence—and through it the human being as it related to divine revelation.

4.2.1. God's Light in the Individual and in History

In an early sermon Einhorn described the human being as a stranger on earth, a shadowy entity into which the fiery letters of *Torah* brought light.[41] On the individual, existential level, the light provided a way for the human being's inborn spiritual spark to escape the profane, temporal realm and to touch the brilliant, eternal paradise of God. On the collective level, the spark was transformed into the light of the universe and into the world brought into God's presence through history. For example, in one of his last sermons (*Yom Kippur*, 1868) Einhorn declared:

> What the prophets of Israel saw thousands of years ago, and what has [until now] been affirmed by the stream of history, will surely come to pass. The natural facts of mor-

---

41   Einhorn, *Predigt bei der Einweihungsfeier der Synagoge zu Kleinlangheim den 31-ten August 1838* (Kleinlangheim: Volkhart, 1838). Although the images are reminiscent of Plotinus, Einhorn did not cite him.

al and spiritual growth will [ultimately] blossom beautifully, in every single individual and every nation.... The
light of Israel will emerge and the religion of Israel will
step forth victoriously. Everyone will speak the language
of light, truth and love. Within the divine aura, the last
veils between peoples will be removed. There will be one
Adam, one God, and one knight of peace. We ourselves
will not see this beautiful time, it will shine only upon our
graves. But our lives are not in vain. God's divine breath
within us is like a spark. We will all [ultimately] join together into a single chorus and, with the sea of light in
the distance, shout out that the God of Zion rules.[42]

The path of widening light included individual freedom. Its impetus
was the synthesis of the spirit (*ruah*) and body in the *nefesh*. Freedom
implied rationality, which emerged from the synthesis between spirit
(*ruah*) and animal soul (*nefesh*), in such a way that spirit (*ruah*) was dominant. For Einhorn, rationality properly synthesized with revelation.
The human being, he wrote, should utilize his/her experience as a basis
for rational explication of revealed truths inherent to nature, history
and the human community. Within the specific context of Jewish history, the revelation of Sinai was to be brought to rational consciousness
with the aim of increasingly removing the (only subjectively) perceived
separation between rational thought and revelation. Einhorn compared
revelation to the moisture of the earth which evaporated more and more
as reason came nearer and then descended like rain. The process was,
however, endless—for revelation had a divine, eternal source, precluding total coincidence with human reason.

On a collective level, history provided the time and the stuff for reason to synthesize with revelation; historical experience was needed for
the process to take place. But in the end, history would be disposed of
like a ladder used for climbing, and reason would leave history behind as
a passing shadow for the eternal light of God's paradise. Einhorn rushed
with his reason into the future, seeking to grasp new experiences and
utilize them for coming closer to revelation and for moving beyond

---

42   Einhorn, "Des Menschen Ursprung, Laufbahn und Ziel," in *David Einhorn Memorial Volume*, ed. Kaufmann Kohler (New York: Bloch, 1911), 229-340.

history itself. He looked most of all to America, which he believed constituted the final phase of reason's pursuit. The people of Israel, for Einhorn, were the crucible for synthesizing or centralizing the temporal path of history and the eternal goal. At Sinai, Israel had coordinated reason, based upon the nation's experiences, with revelation. Thereafter, historical experience provided further basis for rationally explicating revelation. Israel was also central to world history, removing pagan obstacles to truth, and using *Torah* to turn pagan minds from shadowy sensuality towards enlightened spirituality, in order to bring the world as well into paradise. Einhorn stressed that Israel's leading role did not make it superior to other nations. To assert that Israel had superiority, by virtue of its proximity to revelation and the consequent intensity of its quest for paradise, would be similar to the absurd claim that the light of a planet belonged to the first astronomers to sight it. He also anticipated that once Israel was successful in joining pagan minds with enlightened spirituality, its ceremonies would no longer be necessary. Ceremonies, for Einhorn, were instruments for reinforcing the accomplishments of reason *vis-à-vis* revelation, symbolic means of preserving truths of reason while satisfying the needs of the senses, as well as instruments for resisting any descent into paganism. Accordingly, ceremonies had to change as the historical basis and context for reason's synthesis with revelation changed. Once Israel approached paradise, when rational truths would be universalized and paganism would no longer constitute a threat, ceremonies would no longer be needed.

IV.II.I. Selections from *The Principle of Mosaism and its Relationship to Paganism and to Rabbinical Judaism*, translated by Gershon Greenberg

Summary of translated passages
Einhorn set out to have Jewish theological study probe the primary elements of the religious system (e.g., sin-atonement and holiness) and the ceremonial expressions of religious life. He bemoaned the accomplishments of that study to date; it dwelled on what Judaism was not, instead of what it was. While this eliminated some dead material from Judaism, it also distanced Jews with a warm disposition towards religion. Life was not a matter of criticism alone, Einhorn pointed out. He proceeded to distinguish essence, which flowed from the human being's relationship with God through moral legislation, from the

forms through which religion manifests itself. His position contrasted with that of Orthodoxy, which blended form with essence. For Orthodoxy, divine revelation was entirely beyond reason, and all its elements were equally obligatory. Revealed Torah was a sacred product of God's will, parallel to the world created by Him, and rationality improperly pulled Torah into the realm of the profane. In order to scientifically probe the primary elements in terms of the essence-form distinction, Einhorn set out to identify the single principle of Scripture which governed Judaism's system of religion.

CHAPTER I: WHAT IS JUDAISM?

That age-old struggle in the Synagogue about the fathomability of the divine word is causally-connected to the *recent* struggle over the eternal binding character of ceremonial law. Is the divine law which is revealed in Scripture, as over-against the divine law which rules in *nature*, susceptible, up to its *ultimate* grounds, to research by the human mind/ spirit? If so, the first and indispensable result of such research is *the separation between essence and form*. Namely, between an *ethical law* which flows *directly* out of the human being's relationship *to God* and is therefore unchangeable and something which serves only as a medium, as a sign of remembering and awakening this ethical law. In its innermost nature, this medium falls into the sphere of changeable things. The medium lets the transformation which is actually carried out upon it by history, appear as a *natural* necessity, one able to make a claim not to self-justification but to *practical* value.

If, by contrast, the law which regulates the human being's commission and omission is a secret that cannot be fathomed, like that of *nature*, *world-creation* or *destiny*, and the duty to carry it out is based simply upon the obedience to God, whom we must in any case *blindly* obey, *whenever and wherever God demands*, then the division between essence and form in the area of religion is rightfully cast away as fully untenable. Each iota of revealed doctrine of God possesses *essential* and fundamental character. *Human* justification for religious-legislative transformation—although one always presumes the opposite—can be derived from the great historical fact of the Temple's destruction and *the religious transformation effectuated through it by God Himself* just as little as the human being is entitled by its free will to imitate ravages of blind elements of nature which are brought about by God. According to this standpoint, world and *Torah* are two external products of the divine. They run parallel to

one another. To the extent that divine will expressly allows no exception, neither world nor *Torah* tolerates intrusion by the human hand.
Although the rabbis were pressed by the influence of life to allow for very
important changes in biblical law, for the most part they held firmly to
this principle. As known, they even sought to read any of their deviations
(which for us are anyway not authoritative) into the biblical letters.

Indeed, the opposition inherent in the consequences of the two
viewpoints [one of separating essence and form, the other not] extends
much further. If the law cannot be fathomed, then any *rational* motivation for individual definition of the law could conceivably be regarded
as a desecration and misguided arrogance. Thus the rabbis teach that it
is fully justified to be silent before someone who enunciates the words
"Your compassion, O Lord, includes even the nest of the bird," because
*divine commandments should be viewed as authoritative decisions, not as
outflows of compassion (Berakhot* 33[b]). If to the contrary, the divine word
can indeed be comprehended, then the required research into that divine word must necessarily make this understanding—which undoubtedly includes a factor of veneration which is missing in the exercise of
the unknown command—into its main goal, *indeed* limit *knowledge to
the real value of the fact.*

There has been much complaint about the *precarious* and *fragmentary*
character of the efforts at Reform in the area of Judaism, about the lack
of a firm and secure foundation for preserving, supporting and instilling
trust in the minds shattered and made homeless by the development of
organic formations. This only too justified and grounded complaint can
in fact not be set aside, as long as one proceeds to represent the division
between essence and form as an obvious axiom, and with this taking a
petitio principi as the departure point when it comes to relevant efforts.
The question was enunciated from the beginning. May the Mosaic *symbol*, the *Mosaic ceremonial law*, claim eternal validity? May it make this
assertion (something opposed to the rabbinic view) without somehow
proving that symbol, that ceremonial law, was present within the Mosaic law in general? Rather than that everything belonged to the *essence*
and *core* of Mosaic law?

In no way can history provide such proof. Instead, the nature of
Mosaism itself provides an affirmative decision to the primary question
as to whether or not Mosaic law lets itself be fathomed. But how can
such an affirmative decision be reached? *Solely and only through the ac-*

tual comprehension of the Mosaic law. Only when all biblical perceptions, doctrines, ordinances and institutions are directed back to the one and same *principle* and recognized as its necessary emanations, will Judaism's designation as a *religion of knowledge, an object of scientific study*, be placed beyond all doubt. To be sure, Scripture in various places speaks about divine law in such a way as to clearly indicate the law's calling and the capability of being probed to its deepest foundations (Deuteronomy 4:6; 29:28; 30:11-12). But mere *words* never preserve real security. When distressed, the opposing opinion to that word could be invoked. The *mind/spirit* must decide to bring the relationship of the law itself to human reason into the light. A striking example may serve the many. The view about restoring the Mosaic ritual of sacrifices incontestably forms the pivotal point for the contemporary religious movement. The declarations about abolishing sacrificial prayers should be regarded as the most important act of the German rabbinical conference [in Frankfurt am Main, 1845]. Nevertheless, these articulations, which *presume* the *symbolic* character of the ritual of sacrifice, obviously have weak legs as long as Jewish-theological scientific study has scarcely begun to draw the principle of Mosaic sacrifice into the sphere of discussion, let alone placed the presumption [about its symbolic character] which will be negated by rabbinical Judaism and by a Christian-theological voice [Karl Christian Bähr] who is considered to be a very important authority in this area (1-4).

Summary of translated passages
Mendelssohn served as the foil for Einhorn's program. Einhorn credited Mendelssohn with breaking the spell of an exclusive, trans-rational Judaism. Medieval Spanish-Jewish thought had regarded Judaism as unique and objected to autonomous human thought, while Mendelssohn's self-conscious relationship with Judaism allowed him to compare it with other religions. On the other hand, he compromised autonomous thought by identifying Judaism itself in terms of revealed legislation and political institution— even though rational truths had been preserved by Scripture and realized by revealed legislation. For Einhorn, neither doctrine nor faith/belief was revealed. Religious truths were available to all men naturally and subject to rational research. Israel's uniqueness lay in its special calling to teach these truths to others.

The theory presented by *Mendelssohn* in *Jerusalem* about Judaism, its presuppositions and implications, suffers from the same insecurity [as that of Jewish-theological scientific study]. Its ephemeral, partial elucidation may no less be dealt with [now] than it was when the new religious era began concurrently with it. Incontestably, Jewish life is forever indebted to Mendelssohn for being the first to seek to determine the character of Judaism *vis-à-vis other religions*—even though he was driven to do so by external circumstances—and for the power of mind/spirit with which he took the first step [of articulating] beyond the stage of religious *immediacy* [and exclusively]. The Spanish school [of Jewish thought], by whose offspring he was reared, surely had no small share in this great accomplishment. But the Spanish school did not see Judaism as a link in the chain of [different] religious confessions, but rather—as did the *Talmud*—as *the religion*. While it made the relationship between philosophy and faith/belief in revelation an object of inquiry, the *distinctive* characteristic of Judaism *as a special form of faith/belief* never became such an object. In the writings of Maimonides, Rabbi Yehudah Halevi and others, there were initial breaches of the sphere of religious immediacy, and [these occurred] not infrequently. But overall, the Spanish school retained the perception that the results of the human power of thought—even though much room might be granted to the power of thought's *free movement* in the territory of religion—barely touched the depths of the life of the soul in its profundity. The breaches of the sphere of religious immediacy were regarded as *profane truths vis-à-vis the sacred objects*. As such, there was no way for them to be assimilated into the religious organism. Mendelssohn, by contrast, *compared* Judaism with other forms of belief. He sought to present the uniqueness of Judaism with scientific precision. By this alone, he dissolved the spell of immediacy forever and provided the most powerful impulse for transforming the entirety of Jewish-religious thought and sentiment.

But Mendelssohn was less fortunate when it came to *carrying out* the task he set. He recognized in Judaism no revealed *religion*, no revealed *doctrine*. He recognized instead a *legislation* revealed by God, as the sovereign of the Jewish state. It was to realize *rational truths* for Israel and all other human beings. According to the grounds of this view, Scripture presumed these religious truths. The knowledge of the *religious truths* designated for humankind was acquired solely through the path of rational research. Supernatural revelation was neither required for nor useful to this knowledge (*Jerusalem*, 31, 48, 112). The sacred sources never required [the people] *to believe*—they obliged *commission* and *omission* only (*Jerusalem*, 54). But these commands of commission and omission, designated only for the Jewish nation, provided constant direction to the [rational] truths. By its priestly calling, Israel was to preach and teach these truths to all nations (*Jerusalem*, 114). God revealed Himself on Sinai to the Israelite nation, not as the creator of the world but rather as the redeemer from Egypt and, as such, as having the character of a king. The entire body of legislation manifested a political character. Trespass of the law was a destructive attack upon the *political* order, upon the law of society. The legislation enabled the entire array of Mosaic punishment, something which is inadmissible *in the religious area*. It [also] had to disappear immediately upon the dissolution of the Jewish state (*Jerusalem*, 121-122).

According to this system, detailed extensively by Spinoza in his *Theological-political Tractate*, Judaism's points of departure and goals were religious thoughts.[43] Yet Judaism itself was not a religion, but an institution for education towards religion. For religion was not a matter of external manifestation, whether as customs or ceremonial law (Mendelssohn, strangely enough, did not distinguish between them), but rather *faith/belief* and tenets (4-6).

Summary of translated passages
Mendelssohn distinguished between religion and state. Religion included freedom of conscience and could, theoretically, be surrendered by contractual agreement, but religious activities required freedom and so this would never actually happen. The state acted in terms of external activity and authority. Einhorn maintained that the principles of religion and state coalesced for Judaism and that inner intention could not be severed from Jewish activity. Mendelssohn also asserted that Scripture never commanded faith/belief, such as to bring freedom of conscience and divine Scriptural authority into

---

43   On Mendelssohn's *Jerusalem* and Spinoza's *Theological-Political Tractate* see Franz Rosenzweig, "Ein ungedruckter Vortrag Hermann Cohens über Spinozas Verhältniss zum Judentum," in *Festgabe zum zehnjährigen Bestehen der Akademie für die Wissenschaft des Judentums* (Berlin: Akademie Verlag, 1919-1929), 42-68; Julius Guttmann, "Mendelssohns *Jerusalem* und Spinozas *Theologisch-Politischer Traktat*," in *Bericht: Hochschule für die Wissenschaft des Judentums* 48 (Berlin: n.p., 1931): 31-66; and Ze'ev Levy, "Shpinoza Ve'mendelson," in *Shpinoza U'musag Ha'yahadut* (Merhaviah: Sifriat Poalim, 1972), 84-95.

conflict, and punishment did not intrude into the realm of conscience. Ein-
horn countered that defiant outer expressions of faith/belief were subject
to punishment according to Scripture, meaning that conscience could be
compelled.

Given his intended purpose, Mendelssohn set out to prove too much. He
allowed himself to be swept away by assertions which, while repeated
often enough, had no basis and led to the most absurd consequences.
He wanted to show the compatibility of Mosaism with freedom of conscience, despite the disciplinary force it exercised. To do this, [for him]
it was more than enough to demonstrate the political character of the
Mosaic religious constitution, and show how it was the root and condition for the biblical law of punishment. [Over-against this], freedom
of conscience, an axiom of human reason, rejected any force generated
by *human beings* when it came to the pure relationship between God
and the human being. This was because (remaining with Mendelssohn's theory) restricting human freedom of the will was justified only
by stipulated surrender. In the religious context this was absurd, because *representative images* and *mindsets* were inseparable and *religious
activities* deteriorated into empty games unless they flowed from free
impulse (*Jerusalem*, 63). Not so the state. The state was necessarily
satisfied with pure activity, with extrinsic work. The state can allow
the individual citizen the right to *judge* the law, but cannot allow the
additional right of action according to this judgment. The existence of
a state society was thoroughly incompatible with such freedom. The individual citizen, as a member of that society, had to surrender that additional right (*Jerusalem*, 27). When state and religion did fall together,
as was the case with the Mosaic constitution, various *activities*, or more
precisely *extrinsic deeds*, could and had to be punished, in consideration
of greater or lesser danger [they posed] to the state. This involved a
complete setting aside of the powerful tutelage over conscience. None
of this made it necessary for Mendelssohn to deny what for him was
Judaism's pre-eminent, proper character, namely revealed religion. But
Mendelssohn was an enthusiastic fighter for religious freedom and it
was not enough for him to *reconcile* the divine authority of Scripture
with the doctrine of freedom of conscience [making them divisible].
For him, divine authority had to become the *herald* of freedom of conscience. The flag [of freedom] which he unfurled was not only to be

tolerated on biblical grounds and bases, it was to find a homeland, a palladium there. This bold undertaking had him overshoot the goal by far. He did not think about whether Judaism might fly in the air over the goal or—if one prefers—be suspended in the air. The relevant line of argument begins:

> Among all the prescriptions and ordinances of the Mosaic law, not a single one reads: You should believe or you should not believe. Rather all say: You should do or not do! Faith/belief is not commanded, for faith/belief accepts no other commands than those which come to faith/belief by conviction. All commands of the divine will are directed to the will, to the human being's power to act.... Where eternal truths are spoken about, it does not say *believe*, it says rather know and be aware.... Know therefore and take it to mind, that the Lord alone is God.... Never is it said, *believe* Israel, so you may be blessed; do not *doubt*, Israel, *or such and such punishment will come down upon you.* Command and prohibition, reward and punishment apply only to activities of commission and omission, *which are situated within the will of the human being....* Faith/belief and doubt, approval and contradiction are not guided by our ability to long for something. They are guided by our knowledge of truth and untruth. (*Jerusalem*, 54)

We ask: What punishment should the Bible then set for disbelief? Something similar to what the *human* judge would set? Because as long as disbelief persisted within its birth place, i.e., the world of thought, its zone remained inaccessible to the human judge. But the moment it went beyond this boundary (and manifested externally either through word or deed), from the standpoint of the Mosaic system of government it was no longer some indifferent act *vis-à-vis* political life. "Indifferent," in the sense that whether or not it was punished at the hand of judges attested as little for or against freedom of conscience as did regulations regarding other legally punishable trespasses. [In fact, applied disbelief was actionable.] For example, an attempt to move others to fall away from God drew the death penalty—whereas *at least* sins of omission were not subject to judicial punishment.

Mendelssohn had to place all weight on the fact that the Bible never threatened unbelievers' disbelief with *providential* punishment and just as little encouraged faith/belief by promising providential reward. This is the pivotal point to all the untenable portions of his system. The principle of the invalidity of any tutelage over conscience by *human beings*, which is based upon the impossibility of being forced by another into conviction through purely external, mechanical means, devoid of *inner* connection to one's thoughts and feelings, is transformed all of a sudden into the principle of a *compulsion* to believe or not believe, a compulsion which excluded all merit or justification. Religious conviction is denied the capacity to allow the agency of human will to influence it in any way to become an object of *divine* reward and punishment [instead] (6-9).

Summary of translated passages
For Einhorn, Scripture linked willing and knowing. It commanded the rational faith/belief, or religious knowledge, to our will, that knowing eternal truth involved willful involvement. He pointed out that Mendelssohn incorrectly removed tenets from Judaism, allowing any religious opinion to enter into it. In the course of Jewish history, rules were required in order to have communal standards. Mendelssohn's ambiguity about reason and legislation left Jewry with external activities which remained obligatory no matter what one thought. Mendelssohn also separated freedom of conscience from Scriptural command, but then turned around and called for inner commitment to activities and freedom in doctrines of faith/belief. In sum, Mendelssohn brought about a collapse of religious conviction. He removed the dam from the onrushing stream of scientific study, only to replace it with categorical imperatives for external behavior which were split off from inner intention.

But is it then in fact absolutely impossible for the human will to have influence on the acquisition of religious truths? In any case, the capacity of imagining cannot even slightly affect the invincible tenacity of logical conclusions, the compelling strength of the human power of thought. If, for example, I am of the [logical] conviction that the three corners of a triangle are equal to two right angles, there is no earthly or heavenly power in a position to upset this. But does it not therefore still depend upon my will to acquire or not acquire the knowledge of this truth; to obtain the means, i.e., the series of representative images which lead to these results of thought, and to order the images organically in the mind/spirit?

The logical mistake for which Mendelssohn is to be blamed is at hand: While he himself cites the biblical warning: "Know and take into your heart, that the Lord alone is God" [Exodus 16:12], he overlooks the fact that this proves precisely the opposite of what [he thinks]. [Namely, that faith/belief can be compelled.] *Knowledge in itself* can just as little be *commanded* or—what is totally the same—*recommended*, as can pure *faith/belief*. When Scripture nevertheless calls out: *Know*! it clearly demonstrates the availability of mediation between the spheres of willing and knowing. It means nothing else but this: Use your rational talents to obtain the means to divine knowledge. Guide your mind/spirit to those representative images which necessarily lead to the conviction of God's power and unity, namely to miraculously divine works and acts of providence (See Maimonides, *Hilkhot Yesodei Hatorah* 1, *Halakhah* 6). Mendelssohn confuses faith/belief and knowledge, at the same moment he sets them over-against each other [and in the process excludes the presence of human will].

Judaism views the knowledge of its eternal truths as a natural result of rational reflection, which human reason urges upon itself with the evidence which is the same as for any other external truth. Precisely because of this, Judaism is wide apart from negating the influence of human will upon the acquisition and rejection of these eternal truths. Precisely because Judaism's tenets are *rationally valid* for Judaism, denying them can by no means be a matter of the product of a conviction which is coercive and that excludes all responsibility [on the part of the individual]. To the contrary, the denial could only be a matter of *self-incriminating* lack of knowledge [and will], namely a sin in the real sense of the word: for example, when the Psalmist lets the thought "There is no God" [Psalms 14:1] enter only the heart of the criminal. Only blind, i.e., irrational faith/belief [which excludes will], cannot be commanded. Rational faith/belief [where will enters in] can be, namely, the religious knowledge which results simply from the use of talents extended by God to the human being. Scripture orders such a rational belief/faith in countless places. These include the summons *to know* God, to *fear God*, and *love God*, etc. With regard to the remaining, most problematic, omission of divine reward and punishment with regard to belief/faith and disbelief: This applies even less as soon as *thought* appears fully vital, in activities of the Biblical era.

Despite Maimonides' attempt to establish articles of faith/belief, Judaism obviously has no closed-off system. On the one hand, this absence has to do with the perception Mendelssohn adopted (which is basically Talmudic) that all Israelite obligations had their own essential character, such that any religious objects of special *fundamental* character were non-existent. On the other hand, it lies in the fact that a Church which can neither declare the taking of sacraments nor in any way ascribe to itself the right of expulsion was not pressured with the practical need for such conclusive statements. Over against this, to assert that Judaism had no precise statements of faith/belief and never *obliged* a member of its community to recognize any kinds of doctrines of knowledge was to withdraw any ground and basis, any spiritual midpoint, from the community.

Truly, Mendelssohn could not have served his cause more poorly than he did when he invoked the witness of history. Historical Judaism knows so little about freedom in terms of dogmas that in the *Talmud*, a person who denied the divine revealed-character of even a single letter of the *Torah* belonged to the class of the *Minim*—not known for being treated very considerately (*Sanhedrin* 99[a]). Even the Noahides, despite the strictest fulfillment of the obligations which applied to them, were denied eternal life if they regarded their obligations as mere outflows of reason and not of supernatural divine revelation (Maimonides, *Hilkhot Melakhim* 8:11). What gives the Jewish religion the *appearance* of freedom of faith/belief in the sense cited? Why did Mendelssohn's assertion [about Judaism's tenets] earn such a quick and willing acceptance, an assertion which sharply contradicted the entire historical perception? Incontestably, it was the illegitimacy of exclusion [of the unbeliever] from the Israelite community. But basically, this apparent freedom was based solely on the highest degree of *religious constraint* on the identification between communities of faith/belief and stock, which allowed *free-willed* separation from Jewish society as little as it did forceful separation from it.

Through this displacement of the authentic viewpoint, Mendelssohn also falls into the most striking inconsistencies. As a result of releasing doctrines of faith/belief and knowledge, only the *external act* remained a shibboleth, as a bond and manifestation of the Jewish community. Then there emerged the ethically untenable validation of the contradiction between conscience and conduct, between inner and outer religious life. That is, of the principle that whatever and however one might think about the law, one remained obligated to implement it externally. *Such obedience fully satisfied the obligations placed upon the Israelite (Jerusalem, 128ff)*. [Meanwhile], in the interest of his fiery struggle against all coercion of conscience, Mendelssohn did not hesitate to call a religious act without corresponding conviction empty child's play. He ascribed it some partial value only in the political context. In connection with the doctrine of faith/belief, he proclaimed a freedom which broke down all partitions, and one which prevented divinity itself from directing its punitive arm against the denier of divine existence. He proclaimed this extremely bold theory [about external obedience] for the mountainous heights. In practice, it became a conviction trampled to the ground, like a person chained, like a crawling worm. All at once the reason which tolerated no chains, and which was even to build the *foundation* for the divinely revealed *sanctum*, lowered itself into unreliable, despicable *sophistry*, while the external act which contradicted inner conviction ascended again to a dignity which had a restrictive, limited influence in earning divine satisfaction and eternal blessedness. On the one hand, the stream of free religious research into religious territory is unchained. On the other hand, with no internal grounding, a powerful dam is erected against that stream through a categorical imperative, and the designation to make life fruitful is denied. The religious split between conscience and act is viewed as a condition which is *appropriate to nature and normal*. The most pathetic self-deception and demoralization—certainly against the will of the noble master [i.e. God] is no less lent a helping hand.

We fully acknowledge, indeed admire, the spiritual and ethical loftiness of Mendelssohn's stance for freedom of conscience. He developed a notion of tremendous importance about the nature of the Mosaic constitution, one worthy of citing in the years to come. Nevertheless, we vehemently protest against the demand that Judaism, in contradiction to countless points in the divine sources, dispense with the character of a revealed *religion*. And that Judaism have a freedom of dogma whereby no religious idea, no matter how constituted, could [ever] annul Judaism's *internal* cohesion or rob religious activity of its value.

The rest of Mendelssohn's theory does not touch the real *essence* of Judaism at all and deals only with the *form* of Judaism, and needs no further attention. But the object of our task is to determine precisely the *essence* of Mosaic doctrine. Our task is to lay down a principle which endures as the innermost soul and main source for all formations of Mosaism, without exception. The principle reads: *Centralization of all different existences without the willful impairment of any individual existence.* This is the law which permeates all structures of Mosaism. In turn, this law appears in Mosaism itself as the basis for all *natural* formations in the material and spiritual world. Upon the standpoint of this law, these natural formations, in their totality, build an organic community. By means of their close relationship within this community, different essences merge over and over again into *special* organic formations.

In their unity, the two factors of the principle, the positive and the negative, namely directing various potencies back to a common midpoint and the exclusion of any capricious damage of the individual potency, [as it emerges] from the distinctive feature of Biblical Judaism. When understood in depth, the factors are mutually conditional. This is the distinctive feature of Biblical Judaism, and its real contrast with paganism and its emanations. Paganism takes one or the other factor, unilaterally, as guiding rule. As we shall see, it thereby necessarily deteriorates *either into raw materialism or into sick materialism* (9-14).

Summary of translated passages
Centralizing various existences without capriciously infringing upon any individual one, or steering a variety of potencies to a common midpoint while precluding any one potency from taking over, was the principle of Mosaism; Einhorn's Judaism was thus a reality-defining logical process, which was found at the core of Hebrew Scripture.

The principle manifested itself first in the relationship between God and world. In pagan naturalism, the gods blended with nature, temporally and spatially. In the process, the individual entity became abandoned to a tragic, endless war for power. As such, the universe remained decentralized. According to idealist philosophical-religious thought the world came about upon a fall from real spirit (divinity); it was deprived of reality and was evil. Here too, the world was decentralized. In Mosaic theology, God was eternal, but the world was created as good. It was of God, God cared for it, and evil remained but a construct of human delusions. Here, God and the world were central-

ized through goodness. Insofar as God was together, YHWH, *a personality completely independent of worldly existence (transcendent), and* Elohim, *the epitome of all existence (immanent), God was centralized as well.*

CHAPTER II: GOD AND THE WORLD

Reason's solution to the problem of the way in which the world came about has always been the loftiest goal. The problem confers upon reason the most powerful impulse towards a vital comprehension of the conception of God. From all sides, reason discerns an endless mass of powers and essences, partly somewhat related, partly hostile to one another. Where is reason's eternal midpoint, its inexhaustible source of nourishment to be found? To be sure, paganism has countless answers to this question. Properly understood, the answers fall into two basic views, pantheism (naturalism) and idealism. Pantheism recognizes no pre-worldly or trans-worldly entity, no *creator*. For pantheism, God and nature fall together. God and nature are concepts which fully coincide with and complete one another. The principle of movement and the principle of life is a blind soul immanent to the God of nature. But in this centralization, the individual [entity] has no protection, there is no sanctification of its existence. The trees are not seen for the forest, the divine is not seen for divinity. Blind freedom alone manages and rules. There is no other choice than to either be hurt or to hurt others. Self-preservation and despotism are one and the same. Individual existence can only maintain itself *over* the other, never merely *next* to it: The unique existence urgently strives to enslave everything, so as to be raised into a god. Finally, the activity of the [world] organism disintegrates into a war of all against all. The enormous divine body disintegrates into countless pieces of gods.

Idealism, over and against this, seeks to comprehend the divine essence as pre-worldly and trans-worldly, [an entity] which *is in itself deprived of reality* and therefore an absolute existence which is also called *non-existence*. In order to achieve reality, this non-existence/absolute existence must step forth from itself, divest itself of itself, and as a result of self-divestiture bring forth the world. Here, there certainly is direction and *subordination* of the created essence, but there is no *centralization*. For the material is *impure, fallen from God*. Only mind/spirit, by its nature, is related to God. God has broken down along with His own work. The world divides itself into two halves; the primordial principle splits itself into the two principles of good and evil, into spirit and matter. The eternal divinity, whether the Persian "time without limit" or the Egyptian "Athor," must make room for their respective disunited children, Ormuzd and Ahriman, Osiris and Typhon (See Creuzer, vol. 1, 199; vol. 2, 71).[44] In its wider ramifications, this spiritualistic system of division in Greek philosophy divides each unique entity into different concepts, as a number of *independent* essences (into stuff, form and negation of other forms). The tendency of the system finally culminates in current philosophy. Recent philosophy seeks to resolve the antithesis between absolute and real existence by raising the human "I," or the human *concept* into God, whereby the world itself is deprived of all reality.

Over-against this, how sublimely simply Mosaic theology and cosmology appear. Mosaic theology and cosmology establish God as the highest *reality* and *personality*, as a unique and eternal essence (not an abstraction which, as it were, just dissolves), who created heaven and earth with everything living and moving in it and recognized all this as *good*. Here, idealism and realism are perfectly reconciled. Creation is neither something split, nor an emanation or *self-divestiture* of God, nor *an existence of God*. It is instead a *free act* of God. In all its parts, it is an *existence in God*. This God is the *existent* in the proper sense of the word, *YHWH*. This God includes and directs all essences in their entirety, but without being bound to these essences or becoming dependent upon them. Light and darkness, good and—*naturally*—evil, nourishing dew and devastating storm—angel and insect—everything appears as the work of the One. Although invisible and without content, the One is omnipotent in heaven as on earth (Deuteronomy 4:39; 32:39; Isaiah 45:7). With His fatherly eye He protects and guards each of His countless creations (Isaiah 40:26). He is together the *primordial grounding* and *mid-point* of His work. It is not the appearance of the world, but the world's evil which is based upon the deception of our imagination. No matter how different the individual essences may be in terms of rank, nature, ability and destiny—they all stand under the same protection. They are all products of the same Omnipotence, from whose hand they emerged, good and pure. This is true centralization of

---

44 Friedrich Creuzer, *Deutsche Schriften, neue und verbesserte: Symbolik und Mythologie der alten Völker, besonders der Griechen*, vol. 1 (Leipzig and Darmstadt: 1836-1842), 531.

the whole, along with fullest justification of individual existence—up to the lowest sphere of that individual existence.

[The two realities], reality in and for itself, i.e., fully independent of creation, reality *par excellence*, as *personality*, and at the same time reality as the epitome of all existence are, in their mutuality, the *characteristic factors* of the Mosaic God. This is indicated by the two primary names of the Biblical God. *YHWH*, the existent in itself, expresses the reality of the biblical God. He neither dissolves Himself into a vaporous vision as does the idealist God of Parseeism and Buddhism, nor coincides with nature as does the pantheistic God. The biblical God as *YHWH* appears instead as the existence of existences, as personal essence before and after the world. *Elohim*, the *all-ness* of the *powers*, indicates divine epitomizing of all essences, such that nothing can be *without* or *outside* God. Reality and personality in the absolute sense, i.e., divinity, applies to *no other essence*. Nor can an existence be found outside God, be alienated from God, be something not desired by God, either directly or indirectly. Accordingly, the epitomizing allows neither for the presence of an eternally uncreated essence, nor for eternal primordial stuff, etc., next to God. Nor does it tolerate the assumption that God fixed creation by means of a self-expressive act external to Himself, i.e., in contradiction to Himself. Nor does the characterizing tolerate the assumption—as most ancient systems, even Plato's (see Creuzer, vol. 1, 558, 564) teach—that God produced various other gods out of His original unity and left the productions of creation to *those gods*. God Himself is the reality and the personality and at the same time concentrates all powers without exception into Himself. He creates, further, and also comprises all essences, He *wants* His works and *takes pleasure in them* (Psalms 104:31).

In order to comprehend *Elohim* in its totality and depth, one must think of the name *Elohim*, which the ancients, namely Bahya Ibn Asher, comprehended as the bearer of all powers (*Ba'al hakohot kulam*), in permanent connection to the name *Jehovah* or more correctly *YHWH*. That is, indicating the creative omnipotence, providence, justice and love of God. Instead of the polytheistic harmonies which are, at first glance, bound to the name *Elohim*, one must find the unity of God expressed in it in its strictest sense. The personal, real *Jehovah*—in whom all ruling powers are inherent—does not place His work of creation outside of Himself. He rather included it. He is *eo ipso* also the *Mashgiah*, the protector and guardian of the work of creation. He does not appeal to the production of other gods to mediate between Himself and creation. *YHWH* and *Elohim* simply do not let themselves become separated from each other in the presentation of Mosaic thinking of God. *YHWH* indicates God purely as *an* "I" (of eternal duration) and first receives the meaning of *the* "I" through *Elohim*. Over against this "I," all other essences are merely phantoms—although reality of itself by all means applies to them. The words "I even I am He and there is no God (*Elohim*) with me" (Deuteronomy 32:39), like the naming of God as "I" in later Judaism, are intended towards that "I." Even so, in its singularity, *Elohim* provides only a vague, elastic concept of *exuberance*. In connection with the single essence, it provides at most the concept of *supreme mastery*, while the name *Elohim* connected to *Jehovah* becomes the full expression of the essentiality of God, which encompasses all essences and power. This interpretation appears especially clearly in the confessional formula "The Lord our God the Lord is One" (Deuteronomy 6:4). Plainly, it forms a two-part sentence, where the second part contains the consequence of the first—as seen in those places in the Bible where the two names are contrasted with one another (Deuteronomy 4:39; I Kings 18:39).

Monotheism is in no way *characteristic* of the doctrine of God of Mosaism. If this were so, the Biblical writings surely would not have neglected to ascribe divine essence with a name specifically and *directly* indicating the unity of that essence. But that divine attribute (monotheism) is found not once in its substantive form (*Hid*) in Scripture. Pantheism is almost universally at the basis of polytheistic theories. Sooner or later, for reasons cited above, it leads to polytheism in popular consciousness. But considered in itself, it is also regarded strictly as [pantheistic] monotheism. The divine unity which the Bible teaches first reaches its higher meaning, as Maimonides has already presented, as a concept subsumed under *Jehovah-Elohim* (*Hilkhot Yesodei Ha'torah* 1, *Halakhah* 7). Only the two names in their mutual connection provide adequate expression of the reconciliation between the spiritualistic and naturalistic directions of thinking about God. This reconciliation alone confers the primary tone, uniqueness to and the wondrous phenomenon of the origin of Mosaic doctrine, and explains its victorious perseverance under the most adverse conditions.

Both [spiritualistic and naturalistic] directions have their indestructible point of origin in human nature, in which heaven and earth have equal share. The one-sided absorption into one at the cost of the other must inevitably lead to representative images, which either shrink God into a mathematical point or thicken Him into raw material; both results are absurd to those with healthy reason. Paganism almost always staggers between spiritualism and naturalism into one and the same system (Creuzer, vol. 2, 276). With a mysterious feeling that the two are equivalent, paganism, visibly strained, tries to ascend to that summit of religious perception, where the two become complementary and the dispute between God and world disappears. But all of paganism's efforts fail and the stone of Sisyphus must be rolled anew. Mosaism was the first to be able to effectuate a coalescence of the two perceptions. It was the first to teach human beings about a God in whose image the human being recognized itself. Overall, but primarily in the realm of the noblest of all visible creations, the God of Mosaism made the opposition [between spirituality and naturality] serve as an agent of harmony.

There is the pressing question about the connection between the divine attributes taught in Scripture and either of the two names of God. The answer to this question can first be given after presenting the *Mosaic human being* and speaking about the *doctrine of knowledge* in general. For these divine attributes relate mostly to God's relationship to the world and especially to the human being. But *one* of these attributes may not go unmentioned already at this point. This is because the doctrine about this one appears in a variety of forms, which build a new and striking proof for the accuracy of the presentation up to now. This is the attribute of divine *omnipresence*. In various biblical places (Deuteronomy 4:39; Psalms 139), it appears to be developed into the representative image of God's *unmediated* presence in all the places and extremities of the cosmos. Elsewhere, God is presented as *residing in heaven*, therefore effective on earth either through an angel or through His *descent* from *heaven* to earth, and finally *called upon with hands raised towards heaven* (Genesis 11:7; 14:22; 18:21-22; Exodus 19:20; Deuteronomy 26:15). Post-Mosaic biblical texts repeatedly emphasize this [latter] presentation and do so with decided emphasis (I Kings 8:22, 54). It is obvious that the contradiction [between the God of heaven and the God of earth] can never be set aside through sense-based interpretation. Because the appearance of angels as executors of divine commands on earth, which is irreconcilable with perfectly developed thoughts of providentially divine omnipresence, is often related in a way which disallows all allegorical meaning. Further, while the sense-based way of speaking about God residing in heaven, looking down or descending from there, surely does not necessarily empty the earth of the divine essence, it presumes to fill the earth with divine essence in a far lesser measure than the heavenly region. There is just as little space for such a *sensible image* within the representative image of uniformly God-filled regions of the world, as there is from the standpoint of today's world view where the earth itself is transferred to heaven.

Only the relationship of both names of God provides us with complete information about the variety of these representative images. The doctrine of divine omnipresence contains the full stamp of these representative images only in the name *Elohim*, where God appears as the *epitome of all powers and essences*. That stamp gains or loses in sharpness and clarity according to the extent to which the name *Elohim* steps into the foreground or background. According to the established result of biblical criticism, the phenomenon of angels, the descent of God and the raising of the hands in oath or to pray belongs not to the *Elohists* but to the *Jehovists*.[45] The diversity of the original sources in this respect is explained by the principle standing at their head. Simultaneously, it is traced to a split-off spiritualism—to which the *Jehovist*, albeit borne totally by the authentic Mosaic mind/spirit, is easily inclined. Mosaism strives in its innermost core against this spiritualism, and only partly slips back into it in its forward development. For further proof: As little as the representative image of heaven passes as a residence for God as over-against the earth for the Elohist, it is useful to observe that according to the Elohist story of creation, *the earth forms the midpoint of the universe* and accordingly appears as *better and nobler than heaven* (14-22).

CHAPTER III: GOD AND MAN

Summary of translated passages
In the sequence of God's creation, God created earth and heaven out of nothing (barah), *fire was made* (assah) *from them, and movement and time were*

---

45   Johann Gottfried Eichhorn, *Einleitung in das Alte Testament*, vol. 2, 277. I have been unable to verify the reference in the 1803, 3ʳᵈ edition (Leipzig: Weidmann, 1803).

drawn from fire's light. While the inanimate world came about through an emanative process (asiyah), God's direct intervention (creation [beriah]) was required for the animate soul to come into being. According to the Elohist, God created the human spirit directly from Himself, it was immortal and reflected Him, and He composed the human body to reflect the entire world. In the Yahwist view, the human being was originally the highest level of animal soul and then shattered this limitation to become similar to God.

We now enter the innermost sanctum of creation, where God's master hand places the crown upon His wonderful work. The creature now begins *to become mind/spirit* and a stream of light, purer and more winged than the sun, binding itself with the created dust of the ground into a *unique entity*. Given such an inception, it would not be overdoing it to glance immediately towards the glorious pedestal, which, according to Mosaic sources, the Creator established for this royal essence. And towards the splendid temple from whose cupola the infinite wisdom of the magical lamp of mind/spirit is suspended, shining into the dual quintessence of male-female—two and yet one, doing so in the higher sense of the dual essences having the same designation as that of its symbolic predecessors, as it were, the two great lights for the mastery of day and night. From this, the Mosaic history of creation sketches a picture for us. The majesty as well as the simplicity of expression of the picture's features overwhelm the thinker with admiration. Without being pedantic, one can attribute great weight to every single word of the biblical cosmology in correctly interpreting the picture in its totality. Given its characteristically precise presentation, Genesis could not have possibly unintentionally restricted the designation *barah* only to the very first act of creation, the production of the *first* living animal and finally to the production of the human being, while it expressed all other production as *asah* or with a simple description of becoming. Just as little could Genesis, without basis, let everything *between* the first and last act of creation arise upon a formal divine command, while setting down the primordial creation of heaven and earth as just some fact with no introductory command, and premising the creation of the human being with a divine self-deliberation or expression of will which was totally different than the command-emphasis. *Barah* and *Asah*, which often blend into one another, are strictly separated: *Barah* is used for creating; for the production of stuff out of nothing (*beriat yesh me'ayin*: Numbers

17:30; Jeremiah 31:22). *Asah* is used for formation or development out of what was available, for the *formation of stuff*. Likewise, despite the later synonymity of the two expressions, *human* production is always indicated by *yatsar* (building, forming) or *asah* (completing, bringing formation to completion), never by *barah*. Further, in Isaiah 43:7 the three expressions (*yatsar, asah, barah*) appear as unmistakably distinct, as *creating, forming* and *completing* things with regard to world creation.

According to Mosaic cosmology, God *created* heaven and earth at the beginning, i.e., *created* the *primordial elements* out of which, according to the subsequent story, heaven and earth were *formed*. These primordial elements, which God produced without any stuff and indeed only as *materia prima* for His *formations*, are *earth* (in the elementary sense) and *water*. Earth and heaven came about from these two primordial stuffs. The Hebrew designation for heaven, *shamayim*, discloses an inner kinship with *mayim* (water). According to Genesis 1:7-8 heaven is thought of as a watery mass raised up and borne by fixed clouds (Psalms 104:3, 7). The primordial stuff is now produced. Here, creating within a designated sphere comes to an end. The business of formation, of development, *yetsirah* or *asiyah*, begins. Precisely because of this, the *imperative form* now appears. God *commands the primordial stuff to unfold itself*. Something which has already become can be commanded to develop further, but becoming cannot be commanded to *nothing*.

And what is the *first* item in the development out of primordial elements? *The light*, the elementary fiery element which streams through all of nature, the cause of all warmth, all movement and extension.[46] Light is the first [item] to be formed out of the stuffs and forms of all things borne by the primordial material. Light appears by virtue of the attribute of the first born, as medium for all structures. With the light's emanation, primordial stuff emitted its entire inherent formative power and even transferred the formative power over to the emanated light. The light is designated to draw formations out of the womb of its own mother.

After light's appearance, God divided light from darkness. Scripture regards *this* division just as little in terms of *opposition* between sepa-

---

46 Johann Gottfried von Herder, *Ideen zur Geschichte der Menschheit. Zweiter Teil, 1785*, in *Johann Gottfried von Herder's Sämmtliche Werke zur Philosophie und Geschichte, Sechster Teil*, ed. Johann von Müller (Stuttgart und Tubingen: J. G. Cotta, 1827), 268.

rated things, as it does the division between water and water (verse 6). Rather, evening and morning form one day, a totality. To *divide* means to *limit*, to assign to each of the separated objects a special area of influence which may not be trespassed, and to protect against unruly mixture of separated objects through inviolable laws. Only Persian dualism knows of an *opposition* between light and darkness. There, light *precedes* darkness and considers darkness as a *having become*, as an *essentiality*. In the biblical position, the sequence is reversed and darkness precedes light. Light forms the *first* emanation of the primordial stuff. Darkness is nothing more than a negation, an indication of the *not-yet* become which corresponds to the *Tohu va'vohu*. In short, darkness is the yet *unveiled light*. By no means is this unveiled light anything *real* or *substantive*. In that case, it would have been available simultaneously with the primordial stuff. It would be a darkness which—like light—springs out of primordial stuff, a component of primordial stuff itself, having to be considered a *factor* of light, its very opposite.

Three further periods follow upon the first period of creation, which closes with the emergence of light: First, the separation between the higher and lower waters and the dimension of heaven. Second, the separation between sea and firm land along with vegetative fructification. Third, the light of the sun, moon and stars, which are clear *displays* of primordial stuff through the mediation of light. In the fifth period, something totally new, at least in terms of appearance, towering over everything else is created, entering the arena of becoming, *the living animal soul*. What a tremendous leap this is from dead, unmovable stone, from lifeless and unfeeling essence in motion, and even from the slumbering life of plants, to the *nefesh hayah* (living soul)! Here, light's formative-power alone is not enough. God's master hands must once again intervene *directly*, so that a new *beriat yesh me'ayin* (creation out of nothing) takes place. The *physical* product surely belongs to the primordial element and *its* production can therefore be *commanded*. But the *nefesh hayah* inherent to the physical product could be produced only through an unmediated act of creation by *Elohim*. Finally, the sixth period, that of closure, follows. Additional, partly higher animal organisms, appear. The animals in water and in the air join the animal of firm land. The sea, the air, the earth—everything swarms with living essence. Creation impatiently awaits its priests and masters.

Only one thing is still missing, *Elohim* says, for My glorious work to be crowned. *I want to make a man in My own image, similar to Me,* a master over everything living! At first glance the expression of divine utterance of will, *Na'aseh adam be'tsalmenu kidemutenu* ("Let us make man in our image, after our likeness": Genesis 1:26) is very surprising. Given the lofty and incomparable dignity of the human being, a dignity which the phrase *Na'aseh Adam be'tsalmenu kidemutenu* brings forward so impressively, we would expect direct intervention of divine potency with Adam's creation, *nivrah* (created) rather than *na'aseh* (let us bring to completion), much sooner than we would with the creation of the animal soul. But considered more closely, when the term *asah* applied to all productions up to this point, it excluded any direct intervention of God. In the present case, *asah* expresses the greatest possible divine immediacy. For that, it is precisely *asah* and not *barah*, which is the adequate designation. In divine speech, Adam is not thought of in terms of his physical or animal-soul essence, but in terms of his *spiritual, divine-like essence. God certainly did not want to produce this knowing mind/spirit similar to Him out of nothing, but out of what existed par excellence, out of Himself, as helek elohah* (part of divinity).

By contrast, the story directly following Genesis 1:27 about the *fact* of human creation, as shown by the phrase *zakhar u'nekevah barah otam* ("male and female created he them") has the human being's *physical* peculiarity in view. The expression *va'yivra,* referring to creation out of nothing as opposed to development out of primordial stuff, is therefore used again. On the one side, in terms of dignity, the human body is placed far below the *spirituality* which comes *out of God.* On the other side, it is placed above the animal body, which is derived out of primordial stuff and does not correspond to any unmediated divine act of creation. In this verse dealing with *beriah* (creation) *tselem Elohim* (image of God) is mentioned twice with exclusion of the *demut (Elohim),* likeness (of God) which appears in the divine deliberation of self. Only the *spirit/ mind* of man possesses *similarity to God.* The external form of the human being can make no claim to any *such* dignity. But that form is still incomparably higher than the animals. It is a copy of the totality of the world, a microcosm, and as such is in God's image (*be'tselem Elohim*), i.e., as though a *reflection and central point of the divine creative powers.*

Accordingly, the *Elohist* distinguishes sharply between the origin of the human *body* and the origin of the body of the animal, and places the emergence of the human being out of the earth (Genesis 2:7; 3:19), as accepted in *Jehovist* sources, into dispute. The customary derivation of the name *Adam* from *Adamah* obviously contradicts (the Elohists' distinction). The Elohist, without regard to the unsoundness of that etymological explanation, refers to a totally different origin of the name *Adam* in the phrase *Na'aseh adam be'tsalmenu kidemutenu*. Namely, to the derivation of the name Adam from *dam*, meaning *similarity*. Here, the *Alef* [*A-dam*] is to be regarded, as it is so often, and especially according to the analogy between *Adon* and *don* (to direct, master), as the *Alef prosteticum*. Outside of what has preceded [in the narrative], what speaks for this simple, unembellished meaning is the meaningful circumstances that the Hebrew language, the real speech of religion, lacks a single designation for the human being, which somehow indicates the dignity of its essence. *Nishmat hayyim* (soul of life) and *nefesh hayah* (living soul) also apply to the animal soul. Moreover, *Adam*, as *man of the earth*, lays hold of the human being in terms of its rawest, lowest side. It removes all dignity and sets the concept of *nefesh hayah*, which also includes animal life, far into the background. This phenomenon—given the high rank assigned in the Bible to the human being on the ladder of creation, as master of everything living, as the essence crowned with honor and glory (Psalms 8:6-7)—is the more inexplicable, because in the Bible the *name* generally characterized the *essence*. According to our explanation, by contrast, *Adam* means: The *similarity*, the *reflection*, the *offprint*, the *copy* and *reflex*, partly (in the spiritual sense) of *God* and (in the physical sense), partly of the *world-totality*.[47] The *man of earth* is transformed into *a man of God*, and *adam* expresses the human essence actually in its most sublime context, as, in turn, *enosh* (from *anash*, sickly, deteriorated, evil, sad) presents the shadowy side, the indigence, the ephemerality and the sinfulness of our essence. It is therefore striking how the Elohist stresses such an important point as the production of the human spirit *out of God*, merely in the relevant divine deliberation of self, and does not raise it at the same time as *fact*. But this difficulty completely disappears if one follows the path of the sources further with open eyes. The acknowledged Elohist fifth chapter of Genesis, which extends the identically named history of creation of Genesis 1:2, 4, repairs this deficiency through the *Bi'demut Elohim barah oto* ("In the image of

---

47   See Gotthilf Heinrich von Schubert, *Geschichte der Seele* (Stuttgart: J. G. Cotta, 1833), 333-351.

God created He him") and presents the higher derivation of the human mind/spirit also as a fact.

How much higher, purer and more worthy of reverence the human being appears in this light! His name—Adam, reflection of the world, reflected splendor of God; God's mind/spirit [indicates that he is not] merely a creation, but a *son* of *Elohim*. Even his body is preferable and exceptional, already at its origin above all other essences! It goes without saying that this doctrine of the immortality of the human mind/spirit, according to this interpretation, is part of Mosaism's innermost and most inalienable possession. [The possibility that] A mind/spirit born out of God can die [is] just as small as [the chance that] God Himself can die. If Scripture does not mention the doctrine of immortality in plain words, the reason lies purely in the *total* perception, in the rejection of that idealistic representative image where this world is a mere *substrate of the future* and therefore only the future world can lay claim to happiness, misery, reward and punishment. The phrase *"Vaya'ar ... ki tov"* ("And He saw ... it was good"), which appears with all other formations, is missing when it comes to the creation of human beings. Yet, from the Biblical standpoint, surely no one would consider placing human essence *below* the other essences. Anyone who knows how to dignify the Bible's eloquent silence would never take offense at such obvious deficiencies. The name for something in Hebrew antiquity is so significant that, as noted already, the same *name* and *essence* are viewed nearly as one and the same concept. In that primordial time of powerful original naturality, living feeling, more than laborious reflection, formed the medium of thinking. Things were known not so much by breaking them down into components, [but] through broadened and, so to speak, evaporated abstractions. They were known, rather, through direct observation and through the powerful draw of inner kinship. They were therefore referred to, in the proper sense of the word, with the *right name*. What one imagined to be most essential about an object was included, unfailingly, in its name. It needed no verbose mention. The human being is called *adam*. Its enduring dignity and the divine pleasure in its production was guaranteed automatically.

The Jehovist's history of creation begins with Genesis 2:4. Characteristically enough, it begins and ends with the start of the Jehovah cult (Genesis 4:26). It does not place the human beings, *from birth on*, at the same height. For the Jehovist, Adam did not come about by means of

God's direct intervening act of creation. Rather, Adam was formed according to the *body*, out of dust, by means of *yetsirah*. Even the human mind/spirit was in no way *born bi'demut Elohim* ("In the likeness of God"). It was solely a *nefesh hayah* (living soul), which is also not denied to the animal—for which Onkelos, feeling the insufficiency of the designation, substituted *ruah memalela* (speaking spirit). [The Jehovist indicated] the innermost, more direct relationship to God, with the expression *va'yipah be'apov* ("by the sweat of his brow"), basically the manifestly incomparable *higher potency of the animal soul.* The Jehovist's perception of nature, which is particularly *reflective*, does not allow any additional direct intervention by God to take place, *after* the creation of primordial stuff is complete. Everything is produced and *formed* (Genesis 2:19) out of the same earthly womb. Fructified by rain (Genesis 2:6), brought forth plants, and produced everything *living*. The progress from the lowest species of creation to the higher appears purely as a more or less orderly ascent of one and the same power of natural force. The animal became a higher plant just as the human being became the higher animal, the former making use of the surplus of vital energy for *sensation* and the latter making use of that power for *knowledge*. This knowledge proclaimed itself provisionally in the conception and therefore *naming* of living animals, and in hearing the divine command (Genesis 16:19). At the same time it is coupled with the dignity of freedom of the will presumed by this divine command.

In spite of their greatness, these good qualities appear to the Jehovist merely as manifestations of a higher animal life. The sphere of animal life retains the human being embraced tightly in its *first stage of development.* But the human being breaks through this narrow circle, acting by means of its free will against its inherent natural drive. The human being earns for itself what it first originally felt, namely *similarity to God,* the characteristic sign of which is called knowledge of good and evil (Genesis 3:22). Unlike the Elohist, for the Jehovist the human being does not *receive* the fire from heaven. It must, like Prometheus, first steal it by itself, by the sweat of its brow—as with its bread (Genesis 3:19). Thus, the human being must first *obtain with difficulty* that similarity to God denied to it as a *direct* gift from God. On the other hand, how great the human being now appears, precisely by breaking out of the enclosure of natural limits in this uphill battle towards divinity!

According to the first history of creation, human nature is *origi-*

nally separated essentially from all other natures by an enormous cleft, because human nature shares similarity to God as a *dowry*. From the beginning on, the human being just has to follow itself in order to fulfill its destiny. According to the second history of creation, to the contrary, the human being was apportioned the task of stepping forth out of the lowest animal sphere *independently* and only then earning the crown of heaven. The path is more difficult, the struggle more fiery, but the goal is equally ennobled and the victorious triumph greater (22-32).

Summary of translated passages

CHAPTER IV: BODY AND SOUL

God created a good world, and real evil did not exist over-against the good. Nor was there a natural duality between body and spirit; they were integrated in such a way that spirit was higher than body but did not oppress it. Mosaism emphasized the this-worldly life of body and spirit over any after-life condition. The nefesh *was located in the blood of the heart where all aspects of human nature were centralized.*

For Einhorn, the human being was naturally pure and disposed towards carrying out God's will. It strove spontaneously to the good, where body and spirit were united, and not towards sin, where body and spirit were split, and mutually destructive war between the polarized extremes ensued. God placed the potential for the division into human beings, but with the good intention that the human being neutralize it and thereby become holy. The germ for the separation contained both the drive to (not the actuality of) sin and the ability to become holy. For Mosaism, the human being was not sinful, naturally or by divine intervention. There was no need to escape the innate self in order to become good (32-33).

Body and mind/spirit are the two polarities of human essence. From time immemorial, non-nature on the one side and non-reason on the other have driven the two potencies into mutual wars of destruction. One wants to enrich the mind/spirit at the cost of the body and the other wants to enhance the body at the cost of mind/spirit. While the never-ending struggle between the two removed any doubt that the mind/spirit carried the *seed* of the division, the germ was nothing but the *drive* towards evil, not evil in itself. It was implanted in human beings by the beneficent hand of the Creator, with the purpose that the urge be overcome by the human being and that the victor reach the stage of *sanctification*. This is what Mosaism teaches, in that it finds the nobility of human essence in its similarity to God. [Specifically, it is] in the admirable endeavor on the part of human essence to unite body and spirit for protection and aggressive alliance *against their common enemy*, as distinct from letting body and spirit be driven into opposing, endless quarreling and dispute, where human essence subjugates itself to that old classic saying, *divide et impera*.

The covenant of God with Abraham is introduced with the command: *Hit'halekh lifanay ve'hayah tamim*: "Walk before me and be whole" (Genesis 17:1). This wholeness is the essence of the covenant, which circumcision merely acknowledges. The *ish tam* (whole man) is recognized as the most laudable characteristic of those chosen by God. The Sinai law commands: "*Tamim tehiyeh am Hashem elohekhah*" ("Thou shalt be wholehearted with the Lord thy God") (Deuteronomy 18:13). Finally, because of his energetic punishment of an Israelite who had yielded to Midianite phallus worship in the sight of the authority [i.e., Moses]—i.e., to naturalism in its most horrible perversion—Pinhas was promised *peace* as the covenant (not only as a sign of the covenant) of the eternal priesthood (Numbers 25:12-13). Why this whole demonstration? Mosaic law, in its entirety, is a living expression of the reconciliation between the antagonistic powers within the human essence. It views humanity overall as a unity and inseparable [entity]. On the one side, people are encouraged to take joy in sensible pleasure and their attention is repeatedly drawn to physical elements (Leviticus 19:27-28; Deuteronomy 16:13). On the other hand the human being is warned emphatically against "becoming fat and forgetting God." Mosaic law forbids pleasures of life without effulgent consecration to the giver of all good. It demands wise temperance and self-mastery, *mildness* towards *every* creature, and love towards God and man (Exodus 20:14; Leviticus 19:18, 34).

At the outset, nothing else could be expected from Elohist religious thought, which is the primary basis of Mosaic legislation and which forms its innermost soul. A system, whose prominent principle is that the human mind/spirit is innately similar to God, and that even the human body is a reflection of divine majesty, *must* view injury to the mind/spirit or to the body as a desecration of the holy. But the dualistic split is also far from Jehovist (thinking). Both original sources obviously place the mind/spirit higher than the body but never *opposed* to it. Rather, the most decisive protest overall is raised against killing of the flesh. *Present* life is placed in the foreground, as over-against the representative image of death as the *beginning* of life. Obedience to law is also portrayed as a factor of temporal well-being. Finally, the various factors of human nature altogether are directed back to *one* mid-point, the heart. Here too we encounter the Mosaic theme: *Centralization of all different existences without the willful impairment of any individual existence.*

The closer grounding of this assertion requires, above all, establishing the biblical concept of *nefesh.* There is no little confusion about it— in and for itself and in its relationship to the heart (*lev*). In Scripture, the *nefesh* appears in connection with both the human being and the animal and is included in the blood, or even bound to the blood. "Flesh with its *nefesh*, with its blood, you shall not eat. Yet I will require your blood for your *nefesh*" (Genesis 9:4-5). "The *nefesh* of all flesh is its blood; whoever eats it shall be destroyed" (Leviticus 17:14). In many places *nefesh* clearly refers to the *inner life.* But it appears very often as subject or object of external activities and, for example, it is *touched, offered, sworn, counted, treasured and bought* (Genesis 12:5; 46:27; Exodus 23:9). It appears on the one side as the life principle of all vital organisms, and on the other side as ascribed to the human corpse (Genesis 1:21; 2:7; Leviticus 21: 1, 11). It is held to be capable of all *sensitivities* and *activities* of the higher and lower spheres of life, and of possessing all good and evil qualities. With one single exception (Psalms 139:14), it appears nowhere as *bearer* of higher spiritual activity, of *thought, knowing and understanding* (*tevunah, da'at, mahshavah*). In view of such facts, and in spite of all artificial theories, one should no longer stamp the *nefesh* as the representative of higher human life, or even as a midpoint of the entire human being. Rather, with Josephus, Maimonides and [Abraham] Ibn Ezra (See Schubert, 431-446), one should distinguish between *soul (Seele)* (*nefesh*) and *mind/spirit*, the one bound to the blood and the other self-sufficient, derived from God. If one views the basic meaning of *nefesh* in this way, various ramifications follow.

a) *Nefesh: the animalistic life force.* Therefore, 1) The (animalistic) *life* in general (Leviticus 17:14, 29). 2) Breath.[48] 3) Sensitivities and *the ability*

---

48 See Wilhelm Gesenius, "Nefesh," in *Hebräisches und chaldäisches Handwörterbuch über das Alte Testament* (Leipzig: F.C.W. Vogel, 1828), 547-549.

to desire in the higher and lower sense, therefore *conscience, craving, wish-ing*—but not will in the higher sense (Genesis 23:8, Exodus 23:9). 4) *Raw sensuality, brutal power* (Exodus 15:9; Psalms 27:12; Proverbs 23).

b) *Nefesh: the person.* 1) The human being who steps into external appearance with its entire body and life and defined, pronounced individuality. According to this meaning, the *nefesh* is presented as visible, external. It represents the names *Adam, Ish* or the pronoun *Ani* (I), *atah* (you). 2) As *human corpse*, but *only directly after death and before burial*. The face still bears distinct recognizable outlines with which the individuality achieves external appearance. It is analogous to the Roman *persona*, which is even utilized by human-like images and idols. 3) In relation to God, as the highest personality (Leviticus 26:30; Jeremiah 51:54).

The higher activity which authentically characterizes the human being, that of the knowing mind/spirit, is therefore *absent* from the *nefesh* which resides in the blood. This higher activity is reserved for what, according to the Elohists, our essence makes into *demut Elohim* (likeness of God) in the mind/spirit which flows out of God, and resides not in the blood but in the *heart*. Wisdom, knowledge, ability to instruct, and power to judge, *free will* (or voluntary, *nedavah*) are conferred solely upon the heart (Exodus 35:22; 26:29). The intelligence which is exclusive to the human being resides solely in the heart. Because of intelligence's incomparable dignity in Scripture, it is called *ruah Elohim* (spirit of God); or, where a closer designation is provided by the context, simply as *ruah*. By virtue of the centralization theme which is characteristic of Mosaism, Mosaism also locates the proper workplace of the *nefesh*, the animal power which resides in the blood, in the *blood of the heart*. Not only does the heart's prominent position in the business of structuring the blood guide Mosaism. The endeavor to make the physical organism's midpoint into the crux of spiritual and animalistic activity, and thereby to coalesce body, soul and spirit into *one* whole, does as well. It appears to be inherently appropriate to have the body, in itself a dead mass, control from its center [which is the heart] the principles of soul and spirit which vivify the body from out of the center, and for soul and spirit to have their throne there. According to the biblical perspective, in the event that either of the two masters, body or spirit, choose a separate midpoint for its own activity, a powerful struggle between them will result, tearing the human being apart. Then, according to the Mosaic doctrine, the *heart* will become the bearer of all qualities and functions of the spirit, as well as of the *nefesh*. The heart will become the junction where all powers, without exception, are collected and developed—like the ocean into which all streams of life flow in and out in an unbroken cycle (Ecclesiastes 1:7). There, *reason and conscience, insight, ability to feel and to crave*, knowledge of good and evil and *desire* for good and evil converge as *one* (Genesis 6:5; 8:21).

In no way ... is the *nefesh* the midpoint of human collective power. It is rather merely one single factor thereof. The heart alone has this high dignity. Scripture can transfer the activity of the *nefesh* into the heart, but not the activity of the heart into the *nefesh*, not the whole into one part thereof. Moses teaches a unity (*Einheit*) but not a sameness (*Einerleiheit*). He unifies, but without identifying [the entities which] have been unified, without the willful impairment of any individual existence, without letting one factor swallow the other. This unity is a holy law of nature, and precisely because of this it is also a law of God, but only because the unity's preservation of all parts of human nature comes to good. Disturbing the unity, over-against this, brings about the greatest damage to those who disturb as well as those who are disturbed, to the tyrants as well as to the oppressed.

The human being *can*, self-willed, injure the law of God which is inherent to it. The human being has the power to tear apart, by force, the elements of *animal-soul* and *spirit* which converge into common and harmonized activity in the heart. The human being can concede overwhelming power to one or the other of these two leaders of the whole over its co-sovereign and thereby over the entire organism. But the human being *should* not use this power. God granted the power to the human being only for the combat. The human being should rather strive for the unity, the peace, the wholeness of its nature. In one word—for the *lev shalem* (whole heart) which the Bible designates as the sign of highest respectability. Biblical antiquity knows nothing about the modern opposition between *head* and *heart*. It knows nothing about the opposition between *knowledge* and *life of conscience*, between *insight* and *lust*, for it claims understanding and knowing for the *spirit*. It claims sensitivity and craving of all sorts and in all spheres for the *nefesh*, for the animalistic power of life. Insofar as biblical antiquity lets both activities rest in one and the same midpoint, and lets *thinking* and *feeling* emerge not from different organs but from one and the same organ, namely the heart, the split between the two is reconciled. It decisively rejects the perception *where reason and conscience are regarded as naturally* as hostile powers standing against one another, as elements which are brought into opposition by their innate essence, not by willfulness. As Mosaic law sharply stresses, Israel has to see its law as *its* wisdom and *its* reason. Israel should serve God with the entire heart and the entire *nefesh*, Mosaic law hereby makes it well known adequately how decisively it negates dualism. According to the doctrine of God, the human being appears as in a garden. In its midst there is the tree of *life* and the tree of *knowledge* of good and evil, rooted close to one another (32-39).[49]

IV.II.II. Selections from *Principle Points of Difference Between Old and New Judaism*, translated by Gershon Greenberg

Summary of translated passages
According to Einhorn, Biblical Judaism at times identified the means ("form") from the ends ("essence") of legislation, at other times it did not. Some laws were applicable everywhere and for all time, others were time-sensitive. In recent times a distinction developed between "old," "rabbinic" or "orthodox" Judaism and "new" or "reform" Judaism. New Judaism distinguished categorically between the essence of legislation, which was directly related to the covenantal relationship, and the form, the legal ordinances which signified the essence. It regarded divine revelation as a process. It began with the rational breath which God instilled in the human being upon creation, for reason to serve as the organ of revelation. Sinai, which further developed the Noahide laws, centralized, focused and completed the process. For "old" Judaism, revelation was an external fact which Israel encountered at Sinai, and the Torah of Sinai was new and comprehensive.

Old Judaism rejects the distinction between the essence and form of the doctrine of God
For it, all is core and essence, everything has self-sufficient, absolute value. Carrying out divine commands is never only a *means* to a higher purpose but the end itself, whereby all commands are equally holy,

---

49   Einhorn, *Das Prinzip des Mosaismus*, 1-39.

equally untouchable. Any classification of the divine commands according to their inner value appears to be fully inadmissible. The expression "ceremonial law" has, from this standpoint, no justification at all. Old Judaism knows only of a great, indivisible, cohesive law of God, whose fulfillment falls upon us because it was *given* on Sinai. The presence of a *factual* distinction between these laws cannot be denied. One portion thereof is already engraved upon us internally, another is not: The former portion is restricted neither to specific space, specific *time*, nor to specific *persons*. It *can* and *should* be carried out *always, everywhere* and by *everyone*. The latter portion is, for example, applied at one time to Israel, at another to the priestly clan, at another to Palestine during the period of the Temple. But these facts disappear before the thought of the divine origin of both portions. The value of the divine command lies exclusively in the command's *origin*. Not in its *effectiveness*, or *relationship* to *human nature*. It makes no difference how we fulfill it, what influence it exercises upon us, whether its degree of obligation extends to broad or narrow circles. They are all divine *destinies* which must be *borne*, like *fate*, no matter how, when and where it is imposed. Indeed, the rabbis observed that *ceremonial* obligation was a specifically Jewish religiosity. Its practice on the part of the non-Israelite amounted to sacrilege, a desecration of the holy (see *Sanhedrin* 58ᵇ). Only the Noahide commands, which really follow out of reason alone, are a common property common to all human beings. The higher religious status of Israel consists precisely in obligations which are not of themselves understood, whose existence is attributable to a special act of revelation, i.e., in that which we call "*ceremonial*" laws.

The polemic against Christianity appears to have contributed no little amount to the formation of this doctrine. For on the one hand Christianity adopted the Mosaic ethical law, and on the other the *Sabbath*—even if the Sabbath was adopted later with new premises and the day was changed—and also *originally* adopted several ceremonial laws. To be sure, Judaism could never tear itself free of its source of life. Directly or indirectly, the rabbis of ten enunciated a distinction between essence and form of Judaism, with essence placed higher. They responded to what was, from the rabbis' perspective, a highly enticing question: "What does it matter to God, whether the animal is slaughtered one way or the other, whether we enjoy what is pure and what is not?" with "The purpose of (ceremonial) commands is only to ennoble human beings"

(*Midrash Bereshit Rabbah, Parashah* 44, *Siman* 1 and *Midrash Tanhuma* (Buber) *ad Shemini* [*Perek* 12]). According to this interpretation, the ceremonial obligation is no longer an end in itself. It is only a *means* of perfection; and thereby *deeply undermines the entire old system of belief* (161-163).

...New Judaism distinguishes divine law, sharply and decisively, between essence and form, soul and body. It divides between commands which are axioms of the human spirit/mind as such of *absolute* and *comprehensive* validity, and commands which are to serve as a means, as mirrors and fences, for these self-grounded laws, whether these laws appear as *truths of faith/belief* or as *obligations*. The means accordingly may therefore claim only *relative* validity, restricted to specific times, spaces and persons. For the new Judaism, the knowledge of God, which is valid according to incontestable biblical witnesses, is that moral conduct *vis-à-vis* creator and creature, which is in accord with this knowledge, is the *essence* of the covenant between God and the human being. But every other religious ordinance, *without detriment to the covenant's divine character*, is only a *sign* of this *covenant* (see Genesis 18:19).

New Judaism regards divine revelation not as an *external* fact which came to light centuries ago in a specific moment of time, *perfect* and *closed*, but rather, as a process which developed in the human being gradually from out of the breath of God. It began with the primordial revelation to the first member of our species. The Sinai revelation was its most important moment in its evolution. At Sinai, divine law appeared *complete* according to the *principle*, and an entire nation assumed the mission of spreading it. We say, "according to *principle*," because, when they first shone forth, Mosaism's world-redemptive ideas did not succeed in many respects. This is demonstrated by the legally stunted position of the woman, the permissibility of slavery, polygamy and similar deeply rooted customs.

From the standpoint of the new Judaism, the obligation to Israelite *faith/belief* and life is by no means rooted in some factor which is strange to us, but in the higher nature of humanity itself. While human nature's commands and admonitions—as any natural necessity—are surely *divine decrees* which neither permit nor require any further growth, these decrees are not supposed to validate themselves as *over-against* human beings. They are not *gezerot ha'melekh* (royal decrees) in the Talmudic sense, where the reason, which should make the dispensations of divine providence known, must be silenced. If the human spirit/mind is the real ground and basis for divine commands, reason's right to probe the *ground* for these commands, i.e., to probe *their agreement with the human mind's/spirit's own laws* and whether a distinction can be stipulated between essence and form, between an ordinance's absolute or relative validity, can no longer be questioned.

Many of our readers will not be astonished to find the view of new Judaism developed here, already expressed by Abraham Ibn Ezra's clearly and conclusively written critique.

> The essential commands are the ones which are not bound to a specific place, nor a specific time, nor to anything else. They are *engraved in the hearts* of human beings. They are commands which are like a deposit, which is given to the hand of the one to whom it is entrusted. Therefore these things are called divine commands, *Pekudim (Deposita)*. Of them it is said: They are straightforward and they *"make the human heart happy"* [Psalms 19:9]. *These commands became known by means of reason, long before the Torah was given through Moses.* In their connection Scripture says (of Abraham): 'He observes My commissions, My commands, My laws and My doctrines' [Genesis 20:5. Abraham Ibn Ezra, "Hasha'ar Hahamishi," in *Yesod Mora*]. (195-197)

New Judaism is being completely consistent when it does not regard divine revelation *per se* as something external, but views God's rational breath in human reason as the organ of revelation with regard to the collective *truths* and *laws* of Judaism. Even with the prophets, this reason possessed, if not a *supernatural*, then still an *extraordinary* level of development and divine enlightenment. This level placed the prophets in a position to advance ahead of other people by centuries, indeed millennia. It is usually objected that the human power of thought is unfit to be the organ of divine revelation, because its results are often ambiguous and wind up differently with diverse peoples. Let us put aside, for example, that Pythagorean teachings use reason no less exclusively as mediator because not *every* reason stands at a level where it could develop the teaching out of itself. Let us put aside, that as the outflow of reason, even if not of legislation, the knowledge of religious truths, the grounding of legislation, is applicable even adversely. Even without these, the objection is based upon the totally false presupposition: that *external* revelation is an organ for the knowledge of divine essence and will be recognized as such by all human beings, and which must exclude every possible doubt.

Are there not countless people who deny the fact of an externally divine revelation, in part in itself, in part because of its outflow? Do not various kinds of meaning, moreover, underlie the externally revealed word itself—even in regard to the most important material? Do not the various confessions, even within one and the same religious community, read different tendencies into the Bible, made known to them partly by their reason and partly by their inherited faith/belief? Does not the human power of thought always appear exclusively as the last resort for understanding the divine word?

Indeed, one can object: at least for the direct witness to the external fact of revelation, for the insightful and perceptive prophets, and for our forefathers who surrounded Sinai, external revelation is a surety which is far beyond impeachment and skepticism. For here God speaks directly to human beings. Considered carefully, this too is based upon an empty deception. Since despite initial attempts of so-called Orthodoxy, the belief in the incorporeality of God and consequent impossibility of seeing or hearing God in any way through physical instruments, has achieved general recognition in Israel, and faith/belief in the immediacy of external divine revelation has received the death blow. Jewish dogmatics have been compelled to first make the possibility of such an external occurrence feasible. Our dogmatists [themselves] assert that God Himself, purely spiritual and world-filling, could not have put Himself down on Sinai, but only what was *produced* from Him, a glory shining out of His essence (*kavod ha'nivrah*). The *voice* which proclaimed the ten commandments on Sinai was only a *creature* which God created expressly to help Him with this revelation (*kol nivra*).

And the views about the perception of the voice are equally ambiguous. One view maintains that Israel heard all ten commandments through this voice. The other, that the nation heard only the first two words through this voice, otherwise only a sound without understanding the content, of which Moses first had to give an account. The third maintains: With the first two commands the people heard only the voice, not what was proclaimed by it. When it came to the remaining eight commandments, they heard neither voice nor content. They learned the meaning only through Moses (See Maimonides, *Moreh Nevukhim* part 2, 37; Nahmanides and Abarbanel *ad* Exodus 20:1). According to *Midrash Tanhuma, each person perceived the voice of Sinai according to the degree of his mental capacity* [*Midrash Tanhuma ad* Exodus 20:1]. One therefore *sees how it stands when it comes to the supposed immediacy* of the external divine revelation, and how the faith/belief in this divine revelation necessarily leads to faith/belief in the presence of *a divine voice which is outside God and first created by Him, and faith/belief in divine glory as mediating essence between God and the human being.* As such, it leads to a *dualism*, which damages Jewish monotheism at its very foundation and appears to be a highly dangerous advance toward Christianity.

The Korahs will never lack truth, be it inwardly or outwardly revealed. But God's existence and God's law stands in our heart, in our spirit/soul. Israel's doctrine of faith/belief and directives are thoroughly *rationally* grounded. Judaism's unshakeable ground pillar is the *humanity* which is healthy, unstunted and shining with full divine likeness. Herein lies the secret of Judaism's incomparable strength. The word has properly gotten a bad name, because it is usually bound to the concept of the idolatry of reason. But Judaism is the religion which sees the *demut Elohim* (likeness of God) in reason. It sees in reason a shining mirror in which the human being recognizes the Unfathomable and His holy will. Judaism comprehends reason as a mirror. It shines more clearly or less clearly according to the natural talent and the moral purity [of its agent], even with the prophets. But everyone is able to perceive what was envisioned by the prophets and make it his/her own (401-404).

According to the rabbinical standpoint, the revelation of Sinai was valid as a supernatural, external fact, as the creation of a *new Torah*. The *ceremonial duties* are regarded as *characteristic* of the new *Torah*. But it must also have been struck with the question, as to why, outside the distinctive solemnity of the proclamation of the Ten Commandments, which indeed mostly contained the Noahide revealed truths and commandments, there was a repetition of what was already revealed— namely the Noahide laws. One is astonished to hear the answer to this in *Sanhedrin* 59ᵃ, even if regarding a question posed about a commandment not contained in the Ten Commandments:

Every precept which was given to the sons of Noah and repeated at Sinai was meant for both heathens and Israelites; that which was given to the sons of Noah but not repeated at Sinai was meant for the Israelites but not for the heathens (*Sanhedrin* 59ª).

That is, any command which was already inculcated among the Noahides and repeated at Sinai still remained no less in force for Noahides after the Sinai revelation than it did for Israel. Over-against this, any command which presented itself to the Noahides, but was not repeated on Sinai, ceased to be binding for the Noahides upon Sinai revelation. The binding force was transferred from that point on to Israel (See *Sanhedrin* 55ª and Rashi *ad Sanhedrin* 55ª). According to this model of rabbinical sophistry, the repetition of the Noahide commandments at Sinai served the purpose of testifying to the continuance of the respective obligation—for the Noahides. This strikingly twisted assertion, to which the successors in fact attribute all sorts of meaning (See Maimonides, *Mishneh La'melekh ad Melakhim* 10, *Halakhah* 7), was opposed tacitly by the systematic Maimonides in his *Mishnah (ad Hullin* 100ᵇ), with the following words about a new solution to the relevant question:

Our contemporary preservation of all negative and positive commands is based solely on the divine command transmitted by our *teacher Moses*, not on any divine communication to *earlier* prophets. We observe, for example, how eating the limbs of a living animal was not forbidden because it was prohibited by the Noahides, but solely because the prohibition was *renewed* through the Sinai revelation. Likewise, we are obliged to perform circumcision, not because Abraham carried it out upon himself and his own children, but solely as a result of a relevant *Mosaic* command. It is the same with the prohibition of the sinew. It is in no way based on the example of the sons of Jacob, but on the *Mosaic* ordinance. (Maimonides, *Commentary to the Mishnah, ad Hullin*, 100ᵇ).

According to this remarkable principle, Maimonides views the Sinai revelation as outside all and any connection with earlier revelations. For him, Sinai revelation created a totally new human world in Israel, where not only *new* essential obligations assumed a place, but *ancient* obligations were fully annulled *as such*. According to the Talmudists (*Sanhedrin* 59ᵃ), precisely because of Israel's higher sanctity, it was impossible to allow to Israel anything which was forbidden to the Noahides.

A system with such ramifications corrects itself. It is like the case of a giant with clay feet. Neither the iron arm which embraced Israel for millennia, nor the stupor nor cloudiness of the men of the golden mean, nor the golden romanticism of the Neo-Orthodox, is positioned to conceal its weakness. Reforming Judaism, over-against this, rests upon the unshakeable pillar of a divine revelation which included all times and all generations. At Sinai, revelation produced itself only as a central point among the people of the covenant. All of its beams of light were to gather in the people in order to dispense the light and life [from them] to the one great organism of humankind (542-544).

Summary of translated passages

Einhorn listed five differences between "old" and "new" Judaism. (1) For old Judaism, all commandments belonged to Torah's *essence. Ceremonies, which characterized* Torah, *were forever. (2) For old Judaism, revelation was an external fact. The doctrine of God originated with revelation to Abraham. For new Judaism, revelation was instilled in the human being upon creation and the doctrine of God was instilled into Adam. (3) For old Judaism, the* Torah *of Sinai was complete and not subject to development. Both written and oral* Torah *were a-historical, immune to historical impact. History (including human free will) was not an arena for divine revelation, the interpretation of divine law or providential guidance towards nobler existence. For new Judaism, divine will manifested itself in history and God appeared in His sanctity in history. History was an arena for the development of revelation and divine law. History and Mosaic teaching could contradict one another, without compromising the will of God. (4) For old Judaism, the people of Israel were absolutely holy by their blood and stock and others, notably the Noahides, were less holy. For new Judaism, blood and stock were bases for difference but not for exclusive holiness. Israel was different because it was the first to be elected by God to achieve moral sanctity. The purpose of Israel's election was to work for all humankind to achieve moral sanctity. This did not mean that*

Israel was inherently moral. (5) For old Judaism, the land of Palestine was to provide isolation for Israel, in its sanctity, and a secure context for practicing the unchanging Torah. Dispersion was a punishment, subjecting Israel to a profane environment and preventing the fulfillment of Torah law until Israel atoned. For new Judaism, the land of Palestine provided temporary protection from pagan influence until Israel could be instilled with the doctrine of God. Dispersion provided the opportunity for Israel to carry out its mission of bringing moral sanctity to all humankind.

The hour of decision has been reached to settle an ancient debt—to bring the material cited in this essay to a conclusion. In the earlier discussion the following points of difference were raised. For old Judaism, all of the commandments and prohibition belong to the *essence* of *Torah*. New Judaism distinguishes between *essence* and *form*. Old Judaism teaches the eternal obligation of ceremony. New Judaism disputes this eternal obligation. Old Judaism recognizes only the *external* act of the revelation of God. New Judaism recognizes only a revelation in the human mind/spirit. Finally, old Judaism dates the origin of the doctrine of God from Abraham and Moses, new Judaism does so from Adam.

From this there emerges a further difference with regard to the essence of the *oral* doctrine and its position *vis-à-vis* written doctrine. According to the rabbinical perspective, the doctrine of God steps forth, *completed* right at the moment of its origin. This completion precludes any capacity for development. The rabbinic view sees itself required to direct laws which have not been written down and modifications of the written law back to a special orally-transmitted Sinai revelation. *Torah she'bikhtav* (written *Torah*) and *Torah shebe'al peh* (oral *Torah*) are valid in terms of being born at the same time. They are twins who grew up inseparably, but who can as little develop as diminish. By means of their divine nature, both are outside of all historical influence and therefore have *in themselves* no history.

Only the history of [the people of] Israel changes its form. It changes *apparently* as does the form of the moon, at times appearing full, at other times incomplete. The rabbis recognize no revelation of God in history [which is subject to] the free will of the human being. For the rabbis, history is a divine jurisdiction, not a divine legislature. According to their opinion, religious rules of conduct can be derived just as little from the law of destiny as they can from natural law. Direct divine communications are to be regarded as the exclusive organ of religious rules of conduct. In general, the rabbis lack the higher interpretation of history as a planned chain of events, along which providence leads humankind gradually upwards to a higher and nobler life. For the rabbis, historical occurrences are a disconnected, ever repeating fluctuation, wherein even *accident* plays a major role. To the question about how God would administer the human world the *Midrash* answers: "The All Holy leads the human being up and away on the ladder, raising one human being, lowering the other" (*Midrash Bereshit Rabbah, Parashah* 68 [*Noah*]). These words indicate the historical perspective [of the rabbis] sufficiently.

New Judaism, by contrast, interprets history as the extraordinary manifestation of the divine will. It views history, at the same time, as an organ of and commentary to legal-religious norms. For new Judaism the conduct of humankind, and Israel especially, in and with history, is valid as an authentic *Torah shebe'al peh*. History explains, restricts and expands, annuls and increases Scriptural law. New Judaism recognizes *educational institutions* of the ethically holy God both in Moses' doctrine and in history. Although doctrine and history cannot, by their nature, do so simultaneously, they can contradict one another at different times and without doing injury to the immutability of divine will. New Judaism's perception is drawn precisely from the depths of Mosaic doctrine. Mosaic doctrine takes divine manifestation in history as the starting point for history's most sublime revelation, that of the Ten Commandments. In general, the doctrine emphasizes historical manifestation much more keenly than manifestation in *nature*. This is because God appears in nature only in His omnipotence, while He does so in history in His *sanctity*. Indeed, the authentic, decisive point of Mosaic thought of God is *God in history—YHWH, Ehiyeh*. The future form exhibited exclusively in the lofty name *Ehiyeh* and exhibited as *YHWH* bound with the *Havah, the existing*, is the decisive designation of that God. God reveals the fullness of His majesty not merely as *Shaddai* (all-powerful) or *Elohim*, i.e., in eternally self-repetitive *cycles* of nature. God reveals this fullness in eternally *progressive* changes in history and thereby unfolds Himself in ever-*ascending* glory. The seemingly obscure words in the second book of Moses find their simplest and fullest expression in this characteristic designation of the Mosaic idea of God (compare Deuteronomy 4:32-40).

Wherever God's voice is heard in history in such powerful tones, the decisive influence of that voice on the religious conduct of human beings must also be conceded. Thus Moses expressly cited a command in the name of God, for which no source other than history is precisely detectable: "For as much as the Lord hath said unto you, ye shall henceforth return no more that way" (Deuteronomy 17:16). The rabbis seek in vain to resolve the question about where this command, which is otherwise never mentioned, and here presupposed, occurs. Strangely enough, the rabbis know only about the word of Moses to the people at the sight of the Egyptians pursuing them: "Fear ye not, stand still, and see the salvation of the Lord, which He will work for you today; for whereas ye have seen the Egyptians today, ye shall see them again no more forever" (Exodus 14:13. See Nahmanides and Abraham Ibn Ezra *ad* Exodus 14:13). In truth, God commanded the non-return to Egypt precisely through the fact of redemption and the guidance towards Palestine. In this great historical event, which lies at the ground of the covenant, God openly expressed His will, that in the interest of its calling, Israel should avoid descent into Egypt in the future. Obviously this command can claim no validity for later periods or for completely different historical movements. We find Jewish colonies flourishing in Egypt already during the time of the Second Temple, a fact which rabbinical Judaism has no way to explain satisfactorily. Because of this, rabbinical Judaism, in sharpest opposition to former perception, sees itself forced backwards in order to fasten itself to the purely momentary value of the command (Bahya Ibn Asher, *ad* Exodus 14:13). It is enough to call attention to the significance of this difference only in a completely similar context, to prove to its enormous importance for our entire religious life. The question as to whether Israel is destined to return to Palestine to again establish an independent political life, since God destroyed their previous political life a millennium ago and the duration of Israel's dispersion among all nations has shown itself to far exceed the duration of Israel's political existence is, as is known, most intimately tied together with the question about the significance of the ceremonial law, and in general, to Judaism's capability to develop. Yet the question can be decided exclusively according to whether or not we are to ascribe a deformed influence upon our religious will and action to historical occurrences.

A further difference concerns the relationship between Israel and the other nations. Rabbinical Judaism views Israel as having inherited nobility that is separated primarily from other stocks, which will endure even into the messianic kingdom, and which is even more strongly pronounced in that messianic kingdom. Rabbinic Judaism ascribes an *absolute* holiness, a holiness of blood, to the Jewish stock, which not even the proselyte, viewed as *new born*, achieves (See *Yebamot* 76ᵃ). In consequence of this higher sanctity, according to the rabbinic view a marriage between Jews and non-Jews *cannot take place* (*Kiddushin* 166ᵇ), and even marriage among Noahides has binding power only for them, not for Jews (*Sanhedrin* 52ᵇ and Maimonides, *Hilkhot Isurei Biah* 14, *Halakhah* 19). The Bible, meanwhile, forbids marriage with the seven nations only because of the potential seduction of the children to idolatry without ever declaring it *invalid* (Deuteronomy 7).

The rabbis obligate Noahides only to a small portion of the ethical commands and indeed only in negative terms, because of their lesser *natural* holiness, which is where the rabbis perceive the circumstances for religious obligations. Namely: not pursuing idolatry, not slandering God's name, not murdering, abstaining from incest, not robbing, not eating the flesh of living animals. The appointment of judges has no other purpose than dealing with the six prohibitions (Maimonides, *Hilkhot Melakhim* 9, *Halakhah* 1 and *Halakhah* 14). The Noahide is not obliged "To sanctify God's name, to honor father and mother, not to lie, etc." (Maimonides, *Hilkhot Melakhim* 10, *Halakhah* 2; *Kiddushin* 31ᵃ). Even the prohibition against incest is so restricted regarding Noahides, that sexual intercourse with daughters is allowed (*Sanhedrin* 85ᵇ; Maimonides, *Hilkhot Isurei Biah* 14). Opinions are divided as to whether the Noahide, along with blasphemy, is *forbidden to swear falsely* (See *Mishneh La'melekh ad* Maimonides, *Hilkhot Melakhim* 10, *Halakhah* 7 ["Ve'da"]). The fact that such ramifications of the Talmudic system now appear even to Orthodox Jews as atrocious and inconceivable, makes [the need] for its complete extinction from among us obvious, even though one still ascribes validity to the system when it comes to a thousand other matters.

When it comes to inborn, natural dignity, new Judaism recognizes no distinction between the Israelite and the non-Israelite. It decisively denies any higher blood sanctity to any stock, as incompatible with the essential Mosaic doctrine of divine likeness of all people. It knows only of a higher moral sanctity. As a vessel of divine revelation, Israel is to achieve this moral sanctity first. And Israel has in fact achieved it in many periods of its varying and painful career. The *ground* for Israel's divine election is not higher sanctity. To the contrary, Israel's election is the ground for its higher holiness, and Israel's priestly calling requires leading all rational beings to the same stage of holiness. This calling, preserved so brilliantly in world history, requires special religious signs which apply exclusively to Israel. Israel's eternal truths and ethical laws, the core of this outreach work, should and will become the common property of all peoples. Divine truth and the command of morality is the innermost, if often deeply veiled, possession of the human spirit. Whoever claims that the divine truths are in some absolute way a national patent of Israel, which Israel firstly made known, could just as well proclaim that the light of a planet belonged exclusively to the astronomer who was the first to perceive it.

In any case the ethical law, and its entire basis, were exceedingly inadequate before the Sinai revelation. Even if not nearly—as the curse of Ham on account of disrespectful behavior against the father and the covenantal oath between Abraham and Abimelekh proves—to the extent the rabbis stipulate. But ethical laws should never, in this defect, be viewed as something *closed off* from Noahide, i.e., non-Israelite, humanity. The incompleteness was due solely to the lack of religious knowledge. Like any other knowledge, it only develops gradually. It achieved a higher stage with Noah compared to Adam, with Abraham compared to Noah, and with Moses compared to Abraham. If, along with the rabbis, one wanted to reduce the *mitsvot* of the Noahides to seven categories, they are—to remain with the above parallel—like the seven planets [of] the ancient world, to which others were added much later. This was not because the [later known] planets were first *newly created*, but because the human horizon for their perception broadened. In brief: old Judaism teaches that *Torah* was given to Israel and that Israel was thereby torn away from the rest of humanity. New Judaism teaches, to the contrary, that the *Torah* was given to Israel and thereby to all humanity.

The wider gap between the two systems in regard to the motivation for the dispersion of Israel is intimately connected to this opposition. The Talmudists see the possession of Palestine, and the selection [of Israel] at Sinai, as a means for the absolute separation of Israel, holy *by nature*, from the nations. By their denial of all historical development, the Talmudists ascribe absolute, eternal validity to every iota of *Torah*, in such a way that while the conditions to fulfill individual commandments may be missing, the commands never lose force. Certain incidents could *threaten* one or another *mitsvah*, but are never in a position to *annul* any. So distant was annulment from the thought of the rabbis that they could contest whether even death—the time of resurrection—could forever free one from fulfilling the *mitsvot* (*Niddah* 61^b and *Sanhedrin* 90^b). Accordingly [for them], dispersed Israel finds itself in a doubly deficient situation. It is degraded by *local* commonality with the nations, and by the impossibility of fulfilling that portion of the law of God bound to Palestine. Such degradation can only be regarded as *punishment* for sinfulness and have the sojourn among the nations appear only as *exile*. Dispersed Israel is therefore under *banishment*. But at one point, after successful atonement through exilic suffering, Israel will and must return to the previous, normal condition, namely to the praised land. For God promised that the holy covenant was indestructible. There, Israel will live in eternal separation and enjoy all the institutions of *Torah* from beginning to end.

At the present stage of development, Judaism sees the original political separation as a momentary protective wall required for the doctrine of God, not nearly secured in the nation's heart against the paganism swirling around it. According to the divine plan, this wall was to collapse once the doctrine became the innermost life of the people. Then it was time for the children of Abraham to carry out their higher priestly role, traversing through the world, struggling and victorious. The highly significant events during the Second Temple already pointed to this task: Namely, the settlement of many Jews in foreign lands, the origin of the *Septuagint* and of Christianity. Israel's dispersion did not bring atrophy, but rather the unchaining of Judaism; not the lowering, but rather the raising of our stock. The motive of dispersion may not be sought in sinfulness, but rather in the ennobled mission of the bearer of the doctrine of God, "in the midst of many peoples [to be] as a dew from the Lord" [Micah 5:7] and to absorb into itself the cultural treasures of all the nations and to give Israel's own enlarged treasures to them in exchange. The sinner languishing in exile now becomes the *wandering messiah*. The special *national trait* has disappeared forever, and only the special *nationality*, in the narrower sense, remains. That is, the special descent, the *race*, which with its emotional and intellectual/spiritual characteristics, forms the driving impulse to each and every distinct national mission. It may disappear only after the mission is fulfilled. (Note: Even false rabbinic perceptions often have a healthy core. Thus, the exclusive capability of the Jewish *race* to fulfill the mission given to it [by the rabbis] is transformed into the Jewish blood as holiness [*Kiddushin* 70ᵇ], which is evidently about mixing blood....) In the *Talmud* itself, this messianic meaning of the dispersion is touched upon with the words "The Holy One Blessed be He dispersed Israel among the nations, only so that strangers would be added" (*Pesahim* 87ᵇ). But for rabbinic Judaism such views remain isolated and empty of impetus. They have no influence upon the rigid [legal] system and as such are sterile in terms of conscience and practical religiosity, like lightning which cannot ignite. The dominant view, which determines the entire life of spirit, [for rabbinic Judaism] remains: "On account of our sins we have been driven from the Land" ("*U'mipnei hata'einu galinu mi'artsenu*") (320-327).[50]

---

50   Einhorn, "Prinzipielle Differenzpunkte zwischen alten und neuen Judenthume," *Sinai* 1, no. 6 (July 1856): 161-163; *Sinai* 1, no. 7 (August 1856): 193-197; *Sinai* 1, no. 11 (December 1856): 333-335; *Sinai* 1, no. 12 (January 1857): 365-367; *Sinai* 2, no. 13 (February 1857): 397-404; *Sinai* 3, no. 5 (June 1857): 539-544; *Sinai* 3, no. 6 (July 1857): 571-576; *Sinai* 7, no. 12 (January 1863): 320-327.

Chapter Five

UNIVERSAL MORALITY

5.0. INTRODUCTION: ISRAEL SALANTER, SHADAL, ELIA BENAMOZEGH, HERMANN COHEN

The dissolution of the cohesive, autonomous *Kehillah* which was brought on by emancipation opened up uncharted territory in which Jewish thinkers staked out different sets of *de novo* departure points. In the first set, the dialectical principle framed the reason (philosophy)-faith (revelation) encounter. The second point involved autonomous intellection and self-consciousness. The third was that of heteronomous revelation, and the fourth, historical process and events. Collectively our thinkers shared the premises of *Wissenschaft*, and had historicist and relativist orientations. As indicated by the respective introductory materials and texts, while the thinkers developed their respective systems, they touched upon and entered into each other's primary areas. For example, Steinheim (departure point: revelation) addressed rationalism; Einhorn, Formstecher and Samuel Hirsch utilized dialectical principles; and Krokhmal dealt with historical process. While staking different departure points for their *de novo* developments, given the social and historical forces that they all shared, it was natural for them all to be concerned with the various dominant themes of the emancipation and post-emancipation universe.

There was a fifth set, one of universal ethics. Rotenstreich finds identification in modern Jewish thought between religious and moral values. Moral content had always been present in Judaism, but with modernity, religion and morality blended to a point where morality occupied the entire space of faith. The centrality of ethics played a role in the new pluralism and relativism, in which no single religion had exclusive truth. Moral commandments became universally valid, and the different religions became infused with morality.

This universalistic tendency characterized the thought of Moritz

Lazarus and Hermann Cohen. Both sought to elevate the universal foundations of Judaism-as-morality, whether in terms of the idea of messianism, the concept of holiness, or the set of commands which went beyond Judaism itself to involve all humankind. Elia Benamozegh, for his part, invoked the seven laws of Noah to demonstrate Judaism's moral universalism, and Hermann Cohen cited them as one of the proofs of the essence of Judaism as a universal religion of reason.[1]

ISRAEL SALANTER

There were moral theorists of a particularistic (as distinct from universalistic) bent in the modern period. Notably among them was Israel Salanter, founder of the *Musar* movement (1810-1883), whose work belonged to religious psychology. Salanter probed psychological and cognitive resistance to fulfilling the ethical norms of *Halakhah*, generated by the evil inclination (*yetser ha'ra*) and appetite (*ta'avah*). He sought to instill awe and fear (*yirah*), whether of divine punishment (*yirat ha'onesh*) or of sublimity (*yirat ha'romemut*), in his fellow Jews through a program of moral education of excitement (*hitpa'alut*). Although Salanter's observations related to human nature *per se*, he directed his efforts to the people of Israel alone.[2]

SHADAL

Samuel David Luzzatto ("Shadal," 1800-1865) focused Jewish belief and practice on morality, and on creating the good Jewish person. Even the prohibition against idolatry, he explained, was a means to preclude any possible sanctification of evil. Morality, for Shadal, was essentially an emotional matter, not a rational one. It revolved around feeling joy and pain with, and for, one's fellow man, and the adjustment of behavior in terms of instinctual responses to divine reward and punishment. In

---

1 Rotenstreich, *Ha'mahshavah Ha'yehudit Be'et Ha'hadashah*, vol. 2, 6-11.
2 See Imanuel Etkes, "Salanter's Mussar Doctrine—the Point of Departure and the Initial Stages," in *Rabbi Israel Salanter and the Musar Movement: Seeking the Torah of Truth*, trans. Jonathan Chipman (Philadelphia: JPS, 1993), 91-107. See also "The Vilna Writings 1843-1849," "The Kovno Writings 1850-1858," "The Early German-Period Writings 1858-1869," and "The Late German-Period Writings 1872-1881," in Hillel Goldberg, *Israel Salanter: Text, Structure, Idea: The Ethics of Theology of an Early Psychologist of the Unconscious* (New York: Ktav, 1982), 20-205; and Menahem G. Glenn, "Igeret Ha'musar: Epistle of Musar," in *Israel Salanter: Religious-Ethical Thinker. The Story of a Religious-Ethical Current in Nineteenth Century Judaism* (New York: Bloch, 1953),125-161.

the name of his principle of morality-of-compassion, Shadal attacked Maimonides for avoiding the emotional component of Judaism, such that a morally reprobate individual who was nevertheless intellectually enlightened could, because of his intellect, achieve immortality. He also attacked Spinoza, for dismissing the component of passion; because of which he led a life of personal misery (Shadal's writings on these issues have been translated for this volume).

For Shadal, monotheism provided the theological basis and framework for extending morality to all humankind—to become, ultimately, one united family. He commented on Exodus 20:2:

> Belief in many gods causes a division of heart between different nations. For the people of this nation who worship a certain god will hate another nation who worships another god. They will believe they have nothing in common with them, that it is as if they were not human like them. Only believers in monotheism know that we have one Father who created us and all men are beloved to Him.

This monotheism was to extend from Israel to all humanity. As the children of Abraham, the Jews could accept the strictest form of monotheism while other nations were polytheistic, but the goal of the Jews' revelation was for all mankind to share in the one God and the one morality.[3]

ELIA BENAMOZEGH

Elia Benamozegh (1823-1900), who received his early training from his uncle, the kabbalist Judah Coriat (author of *Ma'or Va'shemesh*, 1839), served as theology professor and rabbi in Leghorn, Italy.[4] He published

---

3 David Novak, "Rabbi Samuel David Luzzatto," in *The Image of the Non-Jew in Judaism: An Historical and Constructive Study of the Noahide Laws* (New York: Edwin Mellen, 1983), 359-360.
4 This section is based on Alessandro Guetta, "Benamozegh, Elijah ben Abraham," in *Encyclopedia Judaica*, 2nd ed., vol. 3 (Detroit: Thomson-Gale, 2007), 317-318; Guetta, *Philosophy and Kabbalah: Elijah Benamozegh and the Reconciliation of Western Thought and Jewish Esotericism*, trans. Helena Kahan (Albany: SUNY Press, 2008); Marc Gopin, "Modern Jewish Orthodox Theologies of Inter-religious Coexistence: Strengths and Weaknesses," in *Between Eden and Armageddon: The Future of World Religions, Violence and Peacemaking*

works in biblical exegesis (*Ner Le'david*, 1858; *Em La'mikra*, 1862-65), in theology (*Spinoza et la Kabbalah*, 1864; *Teologica dogmatica e apologetica*, 1877); history of religion (*Israel et l'humanité*, 1914, posthumously, and *Storia degli Esseni*, 1865); and ethics (*Morale juive et morale chrétienne*, 1867). A defender of *Kabbalah*, which he considered parallel in importance to the oral law, he refuted Shadal's discrediting of the *Zohar's* antiquity and kabbalistic theology in *Ta'am Le'shed: Bikoret sefer vikuah al hokhmat ha'kabbalah meha-R.Shadal* (Livorno, 1863).

Benamozegh spoke of the existence of a universalist, monotheist religion that implied the unity of mankind preceding the Mosaic religion. Judaism identified this religion with Noahism (*Sanhedrin* 56ᵃ). With Mosaism, the Noahide religion was channeled into a particular people. Thus, according to Benamozegh, God revealed one set of laws for all humanity, and another for His priestly people; the Jews received specialized laws for carrying out their sacred functions as a particular group.

It was natural, Benamozegh thought, for the original, universal monotheism to take time to develop. In the course of time, history synthesized the unitive conception preserved purely in Israel, with the slowly emerging awareness in the rest of the world—where multiple religions provided vague reminiscences of the original conception with their various respective duties. Judaism, the particularized inner core, inter-related with Noahism (the religions of the world) at the periphery, and moved towards the higher unity of the messianic era. As understood by Benamozegh's disciple Aimé Palliere, Judaism was not so much a discrete religion to be defended against rival forms of belief while it declared their errors, as comprising religion itself. The other approaches were special religious manifestations responding to the needs of different peoples. They gathered around Judaism, their proximity depending upon the respective deviance from the truth. From a religious perspective, mankind belonged to a real unity—which inevitably entailed diversities. Judaism remained the focal point of all religions, their different modes of worship legitimate to the degree that they were faithful to the principles contained in Judaism. The process was upset by Christianity,

(Oxford: Oxford University Press, 2000), 87-140; Gopin, "An Orthodox Embrace of Gentiles? Interfaith Tolerance in the Thought of S. D. Luzzatto and E. Benamozegh," *Modern Judaism* 18, no. 2 (May 1998): 173-196; and Novak, "Rabbi Elijah Benamozegh," in *The Image of the Non-Jew in Judaism*, 361-364.

which falsely identified Judaism as but a temporary preserver of Noahism, and claimed to assume that role for itself, permanently.[5]

As the instrument of original revelation (monotheistic and universal), Judaism also carried and represented unitive moral content. In *Jewish and Christian Ethics*, Benamozegh declared,

> In vain would Christianity lift itself into the regions of an almost mystical morality; it is on the wings of Hebraism that it soars to these heights. In vain does it assert 'God is charity.' This sublime saying that deeply stirred the whole pagan world lapped in sensuality—it got this from Judaism. (69)

For Christianity, the man to be loved was a dry abstraction. For the Jew, he was alive, with affections and wants, with a country and nationality, just as with Judaism. All were brothers, created in God's image to worship the same God—even if not as disciples of Moses. Universal charity was a doctrine unique to Judaism, where the concept of the unity of origin of all humankind precluded the subjection of one to another. In a *Gospel* story, Benamozegh recalled, a king called a solemn feast, but none of those invited (nobles, servants, anyone) ever came (Matthew 22). The Pharisees tell of a king who invited many to a great dinner; the guests arrived very late. Still the king thanked them, telling them that if they had not come, the dinner would have been wasted. So God spoke to Israel, thanking the people, for without them, the great treasure which He prepared for the future of mankind would never have been received (*Midrash Tehillim, Parashah* 25). The *Gospel* assumed that God's original intention was to exclude the human race, and then to admit it upon the accident of Israel's refusal. The Pharisees assumed God's first thought to be of justice, love and universal charity, with Israel's election serving as a temporary expedient (103).

The unity of origin, the inclusiveness, brotherhood and charity were all tied to a unity in the future. This was:

---

5   Aimé Palliere, "Preface to the First Edition (1914)," in Elia Benamozegh, *Israel and Humanity*, translated, edited and introduced by Maxwell Luria. Preface and appendix on "Kabbalah in Elijah Benamozegh's Thought" by Mosheh Idel (New York: Paulist Press, 1995), 31-38.

> The necessary supplement to *unity of origin*, destined to be one day the final terminus of this latter.... The first is natural unity, the foundation of the other; the second is free moral unity—a unity of love, faith, thought—the result at once and the crown of the former. Moses is the prophet of the first, of *man one*; Zephaniah (Sophonius) of *humanity one*, of the collective Adam. (Zephaniah 3:9)[6]

MORITZ LAZARUS

In his *Ethics of Judaism*, Moritz Lazarus (1824-1903) posited an ontological moral realm which permeated God, man and history. God and morality inter-related dialectically, with moral order emerging from the divine source, while God came to be known in and through the ethical context. Ultimately, the ethical was divine and the divine was ethical. God and man related through their mutual presence in the moral realm. Accordingly, as man transformed society into a principled arena, their relationship deepened. Judaism's own development as a scene of righteousness had a messianic, universal aim.

HERMANN COHEN

Hermann Cohen (1842-1918) defined religion as morality revealed by God. He asserted that God's nature coincided with His moral activity and that His value lay in revealing morality. The God-idea guaranteed that ethical ideals would be transmitted to culture and society, and that the moral ideal would be realized in all of human history. God and man, for Cohen, "correlated." God did not abolish the creator-creature distinction; man did not eradicate his independent, rational existence; and morality bridged over the difference. In the course of history, the ethical holiness of God (under the category of being) and the holiness of man (under the category of becoming) joined together ever more closely. In the messianic future, the trans-sensible, divine moral idea (under the category of eternity) unfolded in history (under the category of time).

Together, Lazarus and Cohen envisioned God, morality and the human being in terms of a triangular relationship of metaphysical dimen-

---

6   Benamozegh, *Jewish and Christian Ethics: With a Criticism on Mahomedism* (San Francisco: Emanuel Blochman, 1873), 77.

sions, and directed Israel's principles to a universal end. As articulated in the essay translated for this volume, Cohen agreed with Lazarus that the human spirit (or mind) was grounded in God, the essence of morality. However, he criticized Lazarus for postulating that God commanded a law because the law was (already) moral, when in fact God's essence was itself morality and the morality of the law came from God. He additionally censured him for tending towards a humanly autonomous morality, where the divine connection to morality was eclipsed.

For Lazarus, David Novak has pointed out, Noahide laws were a particularistic doctrine. They did not include the altruistic virtues of charity and love which were considered essential to the Jewish code (*Ethics of Judaism* vol.1, 221-222). For Cohen, the ethics of Judaism were universal, and the Noahide laws were their most widespread form; the laws were central to the philosophical constitution of Jewish ethical teaching. The Noahide and the Jew were correlated as the universal and the particular.[7] This difference was reflected in Cohen's criticism of Lazarus for compromising the universal dimension of ethics (see below) and for blending ethics with the collective mind (spirit) and soul of the nation of Israel. By failing to distinguish ritual and ceremonial law from ethical holiness and moral doctrine, Cohen held, Lazarus compromised the universal goal of Israel's ancient prophets and ended up confining morality to a Jewish ghetto.

---

7   Novak, "Hermann Cohen and the Jewish Neo-Kantians," in *The Image of the Non-Jew in Judaism*, 385-400.

5.1. SAMUEL DAVID LUZZATTO
("SHADAL," 1800-1865)[8]

Marc Gopin has written that Shadal assumed that the entire structure of *Torah* belief and practice was focused on creating the good person, in particular the person of compassion. Why, Shadal asked, would God care whether people believed in His unity and did not worship other gods (the second commandment)? Because idolatry was socially harmful. The belief in many gods created the possibility of worshipping evil as a separate sacred entity, conceivably encouraging people to become evil. The highest goal in the world, for Shadal, was the inculcation, not of religious dogma, but of the goodness of humanity. And the best instrument was monotheism—both because it excluded the possible evil deity and because it unified humanity into a family and generated universal love. Shadal wrote:

> The compassion that Judaism commends is universal. It is extended like God's to all of His creatures. No race is excluded from the law, because all human beings, accord-

---

8   On Luzzatto's life and thought see: Morris B. Margolies, *Samuel David Luzzatto: Traditionalist Scholar* (New York: KTAV, 1980); Luzzatto, *Autobiographie S. D. Luzzatto's, Biographie Ezechia Luzzatto's und Luigi Pasquali's*, trans. M. Grünewald (Padua: I. Luzzatto, 1882); Luzzatto, *Pirkei Hayyim*, ed. and trans. Moses Shulvass (New York: Talpiot, 1951).; Luzzatto, ed., *Catalogo regionato degli scritti sparsi di Samuele Davide Luzzatto: Con referimenti agli suoi scritti editi e inediti* (Padua: Sacchetto, 1881). See also Philipp Bloch, "Luzzatto als Religionsphilosoph," in *Samuel David Luzzatto: Ein Gedenkbuch zum hundertsten Geburtstag 22. August 1900* (Berlin: Katz, 1900), 49-71; Robert Bonfil, Isaac Gottlieb, and Hannah Kasher, eds., *Shemuel David Lutsato: Matayim Shanah Le'huladeto* (Jerusalem: Magnes, 2004); Gopin, "The Religious Ethics of Samuel David Luzzatto" (PhD diss., Brandeis University, 1993); and "An Orthodox Embrace of Gentiles? Interfaith Tolerance in the Thought of S. D. Luzzatto and E. Benamozegh," *Modern Judaism* 18, no. 2 (1998): 173-195; Monford Harris, "The Theological-Historical Thinking of Samuel David Luzzatto," *Jewish Quarterly Review* 62, no. 3 (January 1962): 216-44, 309-311; Yitshak Heinemann, "Rav Shemuel David Luzzatto," in *Ta'amei Ha'mitsvot Be'sifrut Yisrael*, vol. 2 (Jerusalem: Histadrut Tsiyonit, 1956), 61-90; Joseph Klausner, "Samuel David Luzzatto," in *Yahadut Ve'enoshut* (Warsaw: Verlagsdruckerei, 1905), 42-93; and "Sh. D. L.," in *Historiah Shel Ha'sifrut Ha'ivrit Ha'hadashah*, vol. 2 (Jerusalem: Hebrew University Press, 1935), 39-121; and Pinchas E. Rosenblüth, "Samson Raphael Hirsch: Sein Denken und Wirken," in *Das Judentum in der deutschen Umwelt 1800-1850: Studien zur Frühgeschichte der Emanzipation*, Hans Liebeschütz and Arnold Paucker, eds. (Tübingen: Mohr, 1977), 293-324.

ing to Judaism's teachings, are brothers, are children of the same Father, are created in the image of God.[9]

Abraham Geiger observed how Shadal treated language as a source for developing ethics, and that he approached Scripture, not on logical-dogmatic, but rather on human-moral terms.[10]

Despite the family's poverty, his father (a rabbinics scholar) had Samuel study *Humash*, Hebrew grammar, *Midrash* and *Talmud*, as well as the German and French languages, before he was even ten years of age. By the time he was thirteen, Shadal had translated the Italian story of Aesop's life into Hebrew, prepared a Hebrew grammar and demonstrated through linguistic analysis that Shimon bar Yohai did not compose the *Zohar*. He resisted the trade of carpentry that his father wanted him to learn. He also demurred from training for the rabbinate—given the neglect of Jewish scholarship that he observed, he committed himself to research and writing. Supporting himself by tutoring, he wrote about the relationship between philosophical reason (logic) and the truths of divine law and narrative (*Torah Interpreted*),[11] composed a prescient poem on life as a balance between joy and suffering (six of his children would die during his lifetime),[12] translated the prayer book into Italian, and prepared a critique of the wisdom of *Kabbalah*—he would eventually view *Kabbalah* as a cult that should be exposed.[13] In 1828 he introduced a theme into his writing that would become a central focus, the emotional dimension to religion. Each creature, he explained, had one dominant power created by God (e.g., the lion's strength). All these different powers were brought together and subsumed in the human being. The human also had the unique ability to choose and act freely; the rational aptitude to connect past, present and future, and a special

---

9   Luzzatto, *Il Giudaismo Ilustrate*, 11, cited in Gopin, *From Eden to Armageddon* (Oxford: Oxford University Press, 2000), 90-91.

10   Abraham Geiger, "Samuel David Luzzatto," *Jüdische Zeitschrift für Wissenschaft und Leben* 4 (1866): 1-22.

11   Luzzatto, *Torah Nidreshet* (Padua: n.p., 1878). See Luzzatto, "Tamtsit Deotov Shel Shadal [1838]," *Otsar Nehmad* 4 (1863): 237-249.

12   Luzzatto, "Helek Ke'helek Ye'akhlu," in *Kinor Na'im* (Vienna: n.p., 1825). See Luzzatto, Letter to Geiger of 27 October 1852 in *Epistolario: Italiano, Francese, Latino*, 2 vols. (Padua: Publicato da suoi figli, 1890), 64, cited in Margolies, 50.

13   Luzzatto, *Vikuah al Hokhmat Ha'kabbalah* (Gorizia: n.p., 1852).

feeling for both one's own pain and pleasure and that of the other. The divine imperatives of *Torah* were directed to these emotions.[14]

Shadal began to teach at Reggio's Collegio Rabbinico in Padua in 1829, where he would become a beloved instructor.[15] In 1832 he prepared a handbook on moral theology for the Collegio's entering students. Avoiding medieval philosophy's metaphysical basis for duty on the one hand, and responding to neglect of morality and social concerns on the part of Jewish ascetics and mystics on the other, it pointed to the ancient Israelite conception of morality as a matter of feeling rather than reason. Specifically, he wrote that the ancients sympathized with the suffering of others because of the memory of suffering in Egypt (Exodus 23:9), were sensitive to animals (Deuteronomy 22:6-7), and believed in a merciful God who acted justly with the old and the widowed and who loved strangers (Jeremiah 9:33; Deuteronomy 10:17-19). God's attributes and His administering of reward and punishment addressed the heart's moral sensibilities towards joy and pain in response to the condition of others, as well as the themes of justice, compassion, humaneness and social virtue.[16] One of his admiring students, Samson Gentilomo, wrote how Shadal's pupils honored him as a father—seeking his wisdom and personal advice.[17] Shadal also developed the reputation among colleagues for generosity with his scholarship. Leopold Zunz quoted him as saying, "If Satan himself asked me for a manuscript to publish in hell, I would kiss his hand and give him whatever he needed. Am I supposed to work for my own gain and pride?"[18]

---

14   Luzzatto, "Tselem Elohim," *Bikurei Ha'itim* (1827/28): 162ff. Cf. Avraham Sha'anan, "Hashpaot Tsarfatiot Be'mishnato Shel Shemuel David Luzzatto," *Molad* 5 (1950): 314-21.
15   Luzzatto, Letter of 17 July 1868 in *Epistolario*, cited in Margolies, 35-36. On the college, see Maddalena Del Bianco Cotrozzi, *Il Collegio Rabbinico Di Padova* (Florence: Leo S. Olschki, 1995) and Gustavo Castelbolognesi, "Il Collegio-rabbinico di Padova al tempo di Samuel David Luzzatto," *Rassegna Mensile Di Israel* no. 11 (1966): 205-211.
16   Luzzatto, *Lezioni di Teologia Morale* (Padua: n.p., 1862). German translation: Luzzatto, *Israelitische Moral-theologie von Samuel David Luzzatto*, trans. Lazar Elias Igel (Czernowitz: Rudolf Eckardt, 1864). English translation: Luzzatto, "Lessons in Jewish Moral Theology," *Jewish Index*, trans. Sabato Morais (16 October 1872 and ?). Hebrew translation: *Tsedakah U'mishpat: Kolel Musar Ha'dat Ha'yisraelit*, trans. Eliezer Dov Lieberman (Vilna: 1866). The first 47 paragraphs appeared originally in *Revista Israelitica* (1846).
17   Ignaz Blumenfeld, ed., "Schreiben des Herrn Samson Gentilomo in Venedig an Herrn Ignaz Blumenfeld in Brody. Nisan 5594," *Otsar Nehmad* 1 (1856): 56-65, cited in Margolies, 37.
18   Cited in Bernfeld, *Kämpfende Geister im Judentum* (Berlin: L. Lamm, 1907), 135-136.

In 1833, already besieged by illness, he collected his writings (poems, history of literature, linguistic analysis), he said, for posterity.[19] Nor did his illness prevent him from continuing to write. In subsequently published correspondence with Reggio of 1838, Shadal attacked Maimonides for stressing laws of belief rather than deeds, and for making intellectual knowledge the grounds for immortality—such that even a robber who happened to be enlightened would be eligible (text included in following). The attack affected his relationship with Nahman Krokhmal. He had written Krokhmal a year before, reaching out, telling Krokhmal that he was right about the dangers he, Shadal, was creating for himself by his writing. It could not be avoided, he explained, given the deplorable nature of Jewish thinking of the day. Were God to come to Sinai at the present time, he claimed, it would be doubtful that He could penetrate Jewish hearts. His voice would first have to shatter those hearts—and then Jews would need to repent for forty days to get rid of their errors before He could actually enter them. And it would not matter what Shadal said about faith; somebody would be offended. In Rambam's day, all the mistakes and disagreements aside, not even philosophers denied God's reality, revealed *Torah* or prophecy. Now, it was otherwise. With Shadal's attack, the friendly relationship between himself and Krokhmal ended.[20]

In his 1839 correspondence with Reggio, he discussed revelation and the emotion of compassion. "Autonomous" revelation, he observed, consisted of natural moral consciousness (exemplified by Abraham). It was manipulated (in a positive sense) by divine reward for compassion, and divine punishment for egoistic self-interest. The "heteronomous" type consisted of the divine imperatives of *Torah*, exemplified by Mosaic laws against abusing slaves. Both types functioned according to instinct and feeling—not abstract philosophical motives such as adhering to the premise that one's actions would become universal law.[21]

---

19   Luzzatto, *Mehkerei Shadal* [An acronym for *Mikra, Hakirat Kadmoniot, Refaim Yakumo, Shirim* and *Darkhei Lashon*] (Warsaw: n.p., 1913). Luzzatto, Letter of 18 February 1839 to M. I. Landau, *Igerot Shadal*, ed. E. Graeber, 2 vols. (Przemysl and Cracow: Zupnick and Knoller, 1882-1894): 590 as cited by Margolies, 39.

20   See Krokhmal, "Likhvod Ha'maskil...," in *Kitvei Rabi Nahman Krokhmal*, 432-443 and Guttmann, *Philosophies of Judaism* (New York: Holt, Rinehart, 1964), 327-328. Luzzatto, "Mikhtav Me'et Ha'hakham Shadal [to Osias Hirsh Schorr]," *Otsar Nehmad* 4 (1863): 108-131.

21   Luzzatto, "Briefwechsel über religiöse Zustände," *Israelitische Annalen* 29 (19 July

In 1840, after publishing the manuscript of Yehudah Halevi's poetry during his journey to Palestine,[22] he expanded his 1839 discussion of revelation and compassion to include a distinction between patriarchal (Abrahamitic) and Mosaic revelation. With the former, human moral feelings were projected onto God to become reward-punishment imperatives which steered the human being towards compassion and away from self-interest. Mosaic revelation, on the other hand, addressed morality according to three lines of legislative defense. The first line legislated instincts and feelings of compassion. The requirement to respect one's neighbor, for example, included the obligation to consider any plight in which a neighbor who had to repay a loan might find himself (Deuteronomy 24:10-14). The second line of defense legislated the potential conflict between the instinct for compassion and the instinct for self-love. The laws turned actions on behalf of others into a matter of self interest, by administering reward and punishment. The chastisement of the Egyptians, for example, illustrated the consequence of wickedness. The third line enhanced feelings of compassion between individuals of the elected national group by instilling themes of peoplehood, chosenness and ethnic pride. The laws for food, festivals and sexual relationships belonged in this category.[23]

In 1847 Shadal criticized Spinoza for identifying humankind with intellectualism, and discounting feelings (especially compassion); he likewise disparaged him for denying the creator God who rewarded and punished. Spinoza ended up with a miserable life, Shadal alleged, left only with the necessities of natural law and human capriciousness. Following the 1848 revolution against Italian rule, anticipating new equality for Italian Jews, Shadal wrote of the universalistic (but not missionary) dimension to Jewish prophecy and ethics. He spoke of return to the Holy Land as a path towards the universal peace of the messianic age. It was not, he explained to Abraham Geiger, a matter of some pagan-like desire to return to a womb-like land under some particular deity's reign.

1839): 227-228; 30 (26 July 1839): 235-237. See also the Shadal-Reggio correspondence, *Annalen* (1839), 99-373, *passim*.

22   Luzzatto, *Betulat Bat Yehudah* (Prague: n.p., 1840).

23   Noah H. Rosenbloom, *Luzzatto's Ethico-Psychological Interpretation of Judaism: A Study in the Religious Philosophy of Samuel David Luzzatto* (New York: Yeshivah University Press, 1965). This volume includes *The Foundations of the Torah*, the translation of *Yesodei Ha'torah* (Przemysl: Graeber, 1880).

It was rather part of Israel's ultimate goal, for which it was chosen, to propagate the unity of God and mankind.[24]

In the 1850's, despite losing sight in his left eye and the death of his son Filosseno (a Semitics scholar), he published a commentary to Isaiah, an introduction to the *Mahzor*, and an Italian translation of the weekly *Torah* portions and respective *Haftarot*.[25] In the 1860's, after his last surviving daughter Miriam and second wife Leah died, he wrote about how personal tragedy would not cause him to lose a day of scholarship. There was no room left in his heart for joy, he felt, and he could lose himself either in reflection or writing.[26] His *Diwan* of Yehudah Halevi appeared.[27] He also turned out a distillation of his views (1863), included below, in which he spoke of the uselessness of philosophy (referencing Maimonides) and charted the differences between the Atticist force of civilization, which promoted reason and love of beauty, and the Jewish force, which promoted morality of heart and soul, and love for the good (included below). He died on the eve of *Yom Kippur*, 1865.

V.I.I. Selections from *Criticism of Maimonides* (1838), translated by Gershon Greenberg

Summary of translated passages
In his published correspondence with Reggio, Luzzatto attacked those who adored Maimonides to the point of having him eclipse the rabbinic sages themselves. In fact, he claimed, Maimonides' philosophizing damaged Judaism. Instead of the rabbinic sages' proper emphasis on deed rather than idea, Maimonides stressed laws of belief. He adopted Aristotle's view that immortality of the soul depended upon intellectual knowledge, such that

---

24   Luzzatto, Letter to David Schwarz of 13 April 1848 in *Igerot Shadal*, 1051, cited in Margolies, 43. Luzzatto, *Il Giudaismo Illustrato* (Padua: n.p., 1848). Salo Baron, "Shadal Veha'mahapekhah Bi'shenot 1848-1849," in *Sefer Asaf*, ed. Umberto Cassuto (Jerusalem: n.p., 1952/53): 40-63. Luzzatto, Letter to Geiger, *Ha'magid* 2, no. 30 (4 August 1858) cited in Margolies, 14.

25   Luzzatto, *Il Profeta Isaia: Volgarizzutto e commentato ad uso degl Israeliti* (Padua: n.p., 1855, 1867). Luzzatto, *Mavoh Le'mahzor Ke'minhag Benei Romi* (Livorno: n.p., 1856). Luzzatto, *Il Pentateuco colle Haftarot volgarizzato* (Trieste: n.p., 1858-1860).

26   Luzzatto, Letter of 1 April 1863 to S. Olper in *Epistolario*, 1017, cited in Margolies, 54.

27   Luzzatto, *Diwan Le'rabi Yehudah Halevi* (Lyck: n.p., 1865). See Irene Kajon, "The Problem of Divine Justice in Samuel David Luzzatto's Commentary on the *Diwan* of Jehuda Halevi" in *Jewish Studies at the Turn of the Century*, vol. 2 (Leiden: Brill, 1999), 48-53.

even an enlightened robber was eligible for immortality. Ignoring Scrip-
ture's account of bodily resurrection, Maimonides spoke of the intellectual
soul's coincidence with God, ending individual memory or consciousness,
and precluding final judgment.

In 1857 Shadal would characterize Maimonides as a student of Greece
and Araby, whose writings only demonstrate something obvious—that
Jews could master the sciences like other mortals. It would have been better
had he dedicated himself to showing how the Torah, prophets, and rabbinic
sages stood apart when it came to educating men to be righteous (the pre-
requisite for society), through sensitivity to compassion and belief in reward
and punishment.[28]

Maimonides thinks his words are "fastened nails" [Ecclesiastes 12:11]
which cannot be budged. His allegedly definitive *halakhot* are supposed
to remove all doubts and disagreements. They are to bring all of Israel,
with its sages of all generations, under the yoke of conclusions which
are correct according to Talmudic scholars, which is to say Maimonides
himself. But the *Mishnah* cites words of individuals. This is in order that
future generations know the variety of views, and would research them
and define the *Halakhah* according to that view which satisfies contemporary needs. Had Rabbi Abraham ben David of Posquieres not resisted
Maimonides and "repaired the damage" [Isaiah 58:17], the *Mishnah* and
Talmud might have been lost forever. We, our sons and grandsons, would
then be enslaved to Maimonides and Aristotle. We could not search for
the source of the issues or know the subjects authentically.

I said "and to Aristotle." There are many subjects in Maimonides'
Mishneh Torah which do not come from the rabbinic sages. They come
from Aristotle and his Arabic interpreters—which is the case with Maimonides' *Hilkhot Yesodei Torah* and in *Hilkhot De'ot*. I cannot resist citing
a belief which Maimonides took from Aristotle and his interpreters, one
which did injury to our people. He believes that the substances (*mahut*)
of the soul is solely its potential for perfection (*hakhanah*). The entity
(*davar*) [i.e., the potentially perfect soul] separates out after death and
achieves actuality (*Guide for the Perplexed*, Part 1, ch. 70). The soul is an
idea (*deah*) with the strength to grasp the creator Himself. It is definable
in terms of distinct ideas (Maimonides, *Hilkhot Teshuvah*, ch. 8). The soul

---

28   Luzzatto, ed., "Schreiben des Herrn Prof. S. D. Luzzatto an Herrn Ignaz Blumenfeld in
Wien," *Otsar Nehmad* 2 (1857): 173-174, cited in Margolies, 8.

is immortal if one has wisdom about the supernatural and acquires correct ideas about knowing (*yediah*) the creator and separate intelligences (*ha'sikhlim ha'nivdalim*). Without these ideas (*yediot*) the person dies and disappears like a beast. As the scholar Bibago [Abraham ben Shemtov of Saragossa, fifteenth century] explained,

> The reward of true faith is faith itself. The reward of false faith is the faith itself.... For the evil spoils itself and does not last. This is so with heretics with damaged beliefs. These believers will not endure. They are absolutely damaged. (*Derekh Emunah* 59:4 column 4)[29]

...In *Guide for the Perplexed*, Part 3, ch. 27, Maimonides maintains that perfection of the soul (which is to say the acquisition of true ideas) is the grounds for eternal life,which is impossible without it/this acquisition. In his *Commentary to the Mishnah* (*Baba Kamma* 4:3) he maintains:

> Do not be surprised at this. Do not make it any more difficult in your eyes than the slaughter of innocent animals. Even if someone does not sin, without perfect human attributes [in terms of the ideas] one is not authentically a man....

Anyone whose faith (*emunah*) is not upright, that is different than our own [i.e., Israel's] (of course any individual considers his or her own faith upright) is not [truly] human. We are not commanded to love him. Maimonides wrote in his interpretation of *Mishnah Sanhedrin* 10, *Perek Helek* ["Each Israelite has a portion in the world to come"]:

> A person's deepest foundations are destroyed when he is aberrant, when he denies the principle of religion. He is called a *Min* and *Apikores* and mutilator of young plants

---

29   Abraham Bibago, *Derekh Emunah*, ed, and introduction by Chava Fränkel-Goldschmidt (Jerusalem: Bialik, 1978), 240-42. Luzzatto attacked Bibago's reliance on Aristotle and Maimonides. See Allan Lazaroff, *The Theology of Abraham Bibago* (Tuscaloosa, AL: University of Alabama, 1980), 64.

[of the garden of religion; *Hagigah* 14^b]. It is a commandment to hate him and destroy him.

Instead of sweetening the bitterness contained in what the *Talmud* says
about non-Jews, the wise Maimonides makes it worse. He makes us the
scarecrow of all the nations of the earth, and "not for any injustice on
our part" [Job 16:17]. No. [Contrary to what he says], it is not part of
Israel's faith to believe that God punishes all nations on account of their
belief or idolatry. Rather, He punishes for injustice and matters concerning human relations. All the words of the prophets bear this out.
The few Talmudic Sages with animosity towards Gentiles do not hate
their religion but their corruption, their immorality, their violent oppression of Israel. In the written and oral *Torah* there are many statements which teach the ways of peace, judgment and righteousness with
regard to those outside the house of Israel. Outside his false belief about
the substance of the soul, Maimonides was careful not to establish his
points as unshakable dogmas, as allegedly divine commandments. They
are presented in the context of contemporary crises.

Maimonides' belief about the substance of the soul brought on two
evils. From the ethical perspective, there are those in our community [of
Israel] who hate religions and non-religions which differ from our own.
This is not something we inherited from our forefathers. From the perspective of temporal well-being, Maimonides' belief has tarnished our
image in the eyes of the world. Another damage [it has incurred] relates
to his denial of resurrection of the dead. In Maimonides' opinion, only
wise and pious [individuals] qualify for resurrection, not those who are
evil and commit [intellectual] errors. And resurrection does not apply
to body and soul but to the soul alone. Many contemporaries knew he
annulled belief in [physical] resurrection, as he himself acknowledged
in his *Letter on the Resurrection of the Dead* (*Igeret Ma'amar Al Tehiyat
Ha'metim*, 1191). Meir Abulafia [1170-1244] complained about this
phenomenon (cited in *Igerot Ha'rambam*).[30] See also Rabbi Shemtov ben

---

30   Meir Abulafia, *Kitab al Rasa'il*, ed. Y. Brill (Paris: n.p., 1871), 14 as cited by D. J. Silver,
Maimonidean Criticism and the Maimonidean Controversy, 1180-1240 (Leiden: E. J. Brill, 1965).
On the description of Maimonides' *Ma'amar Al Tehiyat Ha'metim* in Abulafia's commentary
to *Sanhedrin: Perek Helek* see Yitshak Shilat, *Igerot Ha'rambam*, vol. 1 (Jerusalem: Ma'aliyot,
1987), 316. I have been unable to find Maimonides' reference to Abulafia in his letters.

Shemtov in [*Sefer Ha'emunot*, 1556, 6]. In his *Letter on the Resurrection of the Dead*, Maimonides claims that anyone who suspects him is liable to judgment. Luzzatto addresses him:

> Is "the eye of perfect man gouged out" [as in Judges 16:21]? Should one not respond to him, saying, We know you acknowledge the resurrection of the dead. But it is of Aristotle and his interpreters, not our fathers. Yours is of the soul. Ours is of body and soul. Yours relates to scholars and good people. Ours relates to good and bad scholars and stupid people. How would you deny this serious division between your belief and our belief? You may say that the division between you and us is not serious. In your view, there is neither judgment nor any accounting at all after death. Rather, an evil person is utterly wiped out like a beast. But if nothing remains, how can the person be judged? Moreover, the resurrection you promise pious scholars is not our resurrection. Your soul is so closely associated with that which is intellectualized by it, namely God, that they become one. Even if this dream would come true, we would never hope for such a reward. It eliminates the individuality of the soul. The pious one no longer exists as an individual. He does not remember his deeds, and could not enjoy any reward. He becomes part of divinity. / We simple people are not sophisticated about philosophy's manipulations. We have accepted your thirteen principles, which you ordered us to believe for several generations. This is because we did not probe your intentions and discover the twisted implications. When you interpret *Perek Helek* [containing your thirteen principles of faith], you claim that even someone who reads you ten times is mistaken to think he understands you. Your words hide secrets. We simple people did not try to understand them. / You implied that your thirteen principles explained resurrection of the dead. This is not so. You say only that reward in the world to come has to do with the soul's enduring intel-

lectual existence (*kiyum*). This would mean as the blessed creator, for the creator and enduring soul become one entity. You describe the words of [rabbinic] scholars as allegories and puzzles, which guide the infant to learn in terms of rewards which it can depict and desire. Since we cannot depict the soul's pleasure, our rabbis allegorize the revival of Ezekiel. [...] Eventually, God made us understand your secrets. We saw how, in your *Essay on Resurrection of the Dead*, you also hint at something which negates resurrection. You say resurrection of the dead is a wonder and a miraculous act. But it is impossible for the wonder to last. The staff which changes into a snake must change back into a staff. Thus, even if the dead are resurrected, it is not possible for them to stay alive and they die immediately. [...] You make us into men standing in the shadow of a mountain. According to your opinion and that of your friends and philosophical teachers, life of the soul is not for the pious but for intellectuals. In the *Guide for the Perplexed*, Part 3, ch. 27, you say that final perfection is not for acts or qualities but for ideas alone. You say final perfection is honorable, indeed the exclusive ground for life eternal. What you apparently mean is that an intellectual philosopher can acquire life in the world to come—be he thief, killer or prostitute. Nothing depends on merit. Everything depends upon knowing truths [*Guide for the Perplexed*, Part 3, ch. 27]. What a difference between your world to come and our world to come!

...Maimonides incurs further damage with the principles he establishes as foundations for our faith in his interpretation of *Perek Helek*. It is all a contrivance, and neither intended nor expressed by our predecessors. Prophets, *Tannaim*, *Amoraim* and *Geonim* delineated no criteria of belief. They did not say that someone who believes such and such or who does not believe such and such may or may not be aberrant in Israel. They did not place the ideas of our rabbinic sages in chains, preventing people from making their own observations. If the actions and intentions were good, their ideas were respected. They were not despised because their beliefs differed. Rabbi Shemuel Ha'nagid expresses this so sweetly at the end of his *Mavo Li'gemara*: Differences of opinion which are not practically binding, but only theoretical, are not construed as Halakhic decrees.[31] But Maimonides determines which *halakhot* we are obliged to believe and which we are not. This damages the faith of Israel. This stems from Maimonides' belief in the substance of the soul, and that its well-being and ultimate perfection depend upon intellectual knowledge. Recognizing that not everyone can probe supernatural truths intellectually, he prepares a table of correct beliefs. The intention may be truly good, but he is taking an awful risk.

To rationalize his own permanent structure, Maimonides contends that our Rabbenu Hakadosh [Yehudah Ha'nasi] wrote the *Mishnah*, and that *Rav* Ashi wrote the *Talmud*. He claims that heads of yeshivas, eminent in *Torah*, established legal limits for later generations, such that one must not raise hand or foot except according to their ordinances and inferences. This is all false! Rabbenu Ha'kadosh did not write the *Mishnah*. *Rav* Ashi did not write the *Talmud*. They taught their students, respectively, *Mishnah* and *Talmud*, as did their contemporary Sages and their predecessors. They gave their own views. It never occurred to them that their words should be taken as "fastened nails" [Ecclesiastes 12:11], permanent laws forever....[32]

V.I.II. Selections from *Against Spinoza* (1847-1865), translated by Gershon Greenberg

Summary of translated passages
In these essays Luzzatto spoke of natural thoughts which unfolded with history and were used to improve earthly existence; and emotions, which were present at the beginning of history and were employed in order to help others. He alleged that Spinoza identified man solely with intellectualism, discounting feelings in general and compassion in particular. Spinoza tried in vain to understand creation through metaphysical philosophy, denying the reality of a creator God, divine providence and reward and punishment. He ended up

---

31   Jeshua ben Joseph Halevi, "Mavoh Li'gemara," in *Halikhot Olam Im Mevo Ha'gemara Le'rabi Shemuel Ha'nagid* (Leiden: n.p., 1634), 230.
32   Luzzatto, "Mikhtav 5 [to Reggio]," *Kerem Hemed* 3 (1838): 61-76.

an atheist, in a world left to necessities of natural law and human caprice. His own miserable life and death illustrated the consequences.

[Thought and Passion]

Man is endowed by nature with thought. He also has many emotions [Isaiah 63:15]. The power of thought enables him to understand an object on its own terms, to proceed intellectually and reveal wisdom's secrets. It gives him strength, as he rationally advances step-by-step. He does wonderful things, subdues and governs everything on earth. Furthermore, the power of emotions means that he is pained when a neighbor is pained. One sorrows at another's troubles and rejoices when one's neighbor is relieved of his afflictions. It makes one love righteousness. One is concerned if someone causes trouble for one's neighbor—steals from him or is violent towards him. This reveals the soul's attachment to what is beneficial for it. To love a person is to help that person. Emotions are strong at the beginning of human and national history. Thought is weak at the beginning, but waxes stronger in the course of [the individual's] years and the ages [of mankind]. Emotions do not grow but rather decrease, because intelligence prevails and weakens the emotions.

The power of thought invents things daily. It is constantly renewable. Therefore, it is favored. It makes a person despise emotions, which do not refresh reality or increase benefits; they do nothing wondrous. Because of this, it is said that thought constitutes the person. This is not true; it represents only half of the person. Judging a person in terms of the power of thought alone throws people into a pit of false hypotheses. Such are the corrupt opinions in the *Ethics* of that famous philosopher Spinoza.

Spinoza unabashedly says that compassion and mercy are the legacy of simpletons and of feminine weakness (*Ethics* II, proposition 49, note: point 3). The wise person conducts him/herself only intellectually and does not try to be compassionate, pitiful or consoling (*Ethics* IV, proposition 50). Righteousness towards poor people is a duty in which only the community is obliged. It was not proper for the individual to oversee the poor at all (*Ethics* IV, appendix 17). The person should rather seek only to protect him/herself and his/her own interests. This is all of wisdom (*Ethics* IV, proposition 22, corollary and *Ethics* V, proposition 41). Spinoza maintains that the power of thought comprises the whole person. He dismisses feelings of the heart as unnatural or as responsible for human decline. It is improper to praise or denigrate righteous or wicked acts. The just one is similar to the wicked:

> The person who has properly understood that every-
> thing follows from the necessity of the divine nature, and
> comes to pass according to the eternal laws and rules of
> Nature, will in truth discover nothing which is worthy of
> hatred, laughter or contempt (*Ethics* IV, proposition 50).

If this philosopher were honest, he would conclude that all this might
be so from the point of view of reason, but man insofar as he is human
loves good deeds and those who do them. He hates violence and injustice and abhors those who perpetrate them. If he becomes so wise that
he overcomes his nature and neither loves nor hates, he is no longer a
man but a flint-stone.

The habit of seeing things solely in terms of the power of thought
and perceiving natural necessity in everything leads the philosopher Spinoza to deny the creator's reality. Natural things exist by mandate, he
contended. The eye sees, the ear hears. This or that was created by necessity; it was implicit in a father or mother. Worlds revolve by the necessity
of central revolutions. This is false. Our God creates with His wonderful
wisdom in order to carry out His intended purposes. Spinoza's world,
on the other hand, exists and acts by necessity. What is this necessity?
Anyone with a sensitive heart, i.e., who has not murdered half his soul,
refers mandate to the supreme will which causes it. Necessity testifies to
the creator's essential power. Elements of nature reflect wondrous wisdom and lead to knowledge of the greatness of the creator who produced
them. Anyone with emotions is grateful for the creator's deeds of lovingkindness. Anyone with a heart hardened like stone finds only necessity
in nature's wonders. Spinoza says: "It is scarcely necessary that I should
show that nature has no fixed aim in view, and that all final causes are
merely fabrications of men" [*Ethics* I, appendix].

[*Spinoza's Characteristic Death*]

Spinoza's name used to be a curse word. In our generation, he is glorified
and praised. His books, once banned from the public, are now reprinted
and spread around—even translated into German and French. The sanctity of the Hebrew language did not allow my friend [Meir Halevi Letter-
is], the interpreter and famous poet, to present a clear commentary on

the philosopher's thought. Therefore, he dressed him in holy vestments and made him into a *Hasid*.[33] He claims that Spinoza stopped going to synagogue only because he was afraid of zealots, and that he continued to praise God secretly at home.

I do not like this at all. Letteris fails to mention that Spinoza, of the seed of Israel, distanced himself from the people. He did not live with them and did not die among them. For the full story, Letteris should have told us how he died. When Spinoza became sick, his trustworthy doctor [Ludwig Mayer] came from [Amsterdam]. He had members of Spinoza's household make soup from an old rooster and give it to the sick man at noon. They did. After the philosopher ate and drank [Genesis 25:34], they went to the house of prayer while the sick man remained alone with the doctor. When they returned from the [afternoon] sermon they found the philosopher dead. They could not find the little money left on Spinoza's table because the doctor had stolen it; he hid it in his instrument bag and sped back to [Amsterdam] that night.

The celebrated interpreter [Letteris], my friend the philosopher's biographer, would have enhanced his reputation, demonstrated his own strength and that of the Hebrew language, had he shown how [Spinoza's] reliance on reason turned his heart from God and how he died in mid-life. Spinoza was sick for twenty years. No one came to his bedside. No wife, children, brothers, relatives, nor even the people of the house he lived in, but only a treacherous doctor who took spoils and booty and who might even have precipitated Spinoza's death. This is the doctor whom the philosopher, in his wisdom, chose and trusted and called from another city to cure him. This is what philosophizing, which makes intellectual power into human principle, is all about. It degrades feelings of the heart. It gets around by speech and writing. It conquers by contrivance, schemes and diminishes compassion, mercy, love and lovingkindness. [...]

[Philosophy and denial of the transcendent God]

Cleverly, Spinoza never denies God explicitly, but rather speaks of God with glory and awe. But his God is not the creator, he is, rather, the totality of the created. Nothing at all is engendered with intention.

---

33   Meir Halevi Letteris, "Toledot Ha'hakham Ha'hoker Barukh di Shpinoza," *Bikurei Ha'itim Ha'hadashim* 1 (1845): 27-32.

All substance was, is and will be, by eternal necessity. This substance is original, eternal; it is called "God." [Look at what this leads to.] Our contemporaries are stupid and impertinent enough to make the Tetragrammaton into substance (ha'metsiut), the totality of existence (kelalut ha'nimtsa'im). The leprosy of God-denial may not be widespread in Israel, but its close sister, providence-denial, is.... [Following the denial of providence, comes] "Our strength has brought success. We act on our own strength. With our wisdom and insight we shall succeed. With wisdom, cunning and fraud, we will fight. We shall oppress the indigent, whose words are ignored. We will promise but not deliver ... we will rob the orphan, since no one helps him. We will do violence to the widow, because she has no one to assist her. We will boast about that which is not ours, gouge the eyes out of the people, steal, swindle and lie." Why not? People anyway operate in terms of appearance [I Samuel 16:7]. Who looks inside [Jeremiah 17:10]?

The Hebrew language is different. It is based on Holy Scripture. Its cornerstones are compassion and heavenly reward—i.e., lovingkindness, pity, and the belief that man gets the fate he deserves. [...]

[Philosophy and egoism]

The theoretical portion of Spinoza's philosophy denies the creator. The practical section teaches man to love himself and seek only his own peace and good. Spinoza states explicitly that the person acting according to his intellect tries to avoid feelings of compassion and pity (Ethics IV, proposition 50). [...] Spinoza abandons the upright path for one of darkness. He stands for atheism in the theoretical dimension and egoism in the practical. The true, lasting philosopher [by contrast,] bases the theoretical upon God's reality, and the practical on compassion and pity. He would not take evidence from beyond nature (metaphysics) to prove God's reality, but from within observable nature. [...] He would delight in what has been given to him for seeing and understanding. The fool walks in darkness. He closes his eyes to what is revealed, unable to see what is hidden. The essence (mahut) of creation will never be understood. But signs of wisdom and intention in creation are open to all. It is enough for man to recognize that he, and all creation, are works of wisdom and the act of God. Why inquire about how it was created? Whatever the path, be it creation from nothing or existence of primordial matter, this subject will never be comprehended.

I never had the urge to write philosophical books. True philosophy cannot be spread among human beings. I laugh at how philosophers indulge in dreams and vanities, and how stupid people respect them. I discount those who mock me, and place me beneath the philosophers. It is they who walk on their bellies, [like snakes], never lifting their heads above the dust of the earth, their hearts above material consumption. Still, it is my duty to raise my voice like a ram's horn against Spinoza and his despicable thoughts, and to separate myself from all those who honor and disseminate them. [...][34]

V.I.III. Selections from *Epitome of Luzzatto's Views* (1863), translated by Gershon Greenberg

Summary of translated passages

Shadal asserted that Maimonides' reliance on Greek and Muslim scholarship disrupted the cohesion of the Jewish community. Maimonides wrongly devalued Biblical anthropomorphisms, which actually provided useful models for behavior and a means to recognize Divine providence. As far as Luzzatto was concerned, philosophy in general was a useless exercise. Otherwise, philosophers would have agreed by now on at least some things. Worse, Greek philosophy fostered moral depravity and suicidal depression. The common man was best off recognizing the limits to his knowledge.

Luzzatto distinguished two forces of civilization. Atticism promoted philosophy, reason, and love of beauty. New forms were ever being developed as man progressed towards perfection. Judaism promoted religion, morality of heart and soul, love for the good. Human nature was static. It originated in God and was not changed by history. Goodness and perfection were inborn and evil need only be rejected. Ultimately Judaism, not Atticism, would attract mankind, because of its unquenchable thirst for goodness. Until then civilization would move in cycles, combining Atticism's progressiveness and Judaism's anti-progressiveness.

---

34   Luzzatto, "Neged Shpinoza" in *Mehkerei Ha'yahadut* 2 vols. (Warsaw: n.p., 1912-1913), 198-221. See Aryeh Leo Motzkin, "Spinoza and Luzzatto: Philosophy and Religion," *Journal of the History of Philosophy* 17 (January 1979): 43-50; Rivkah Horvits, "Shadal Ve'shpinoza" in *Barukh Shpinoza: 300 Shanah Le'moto*, ed. Ze'ev Levy (Haifa: University of Haifa, 1978), 167-186 and "Motivim Haskalati'im Ve'anti-haskalati'im Be'mishnato Shel Shadal" in *Eshel Beersheva: Perakim Be'mahshavah Ha'yehudit Le'dorotehah* 2 (1980), 287-310.

[Philosopher vs. Jew]

I criticize Maimonides, no matter his truly good intention of showing the philosophical community that anyone who forsakes the wisdom of Israel to rely on Greece and Ishmael would become confused.[35] This upsets the community, more than all that confusion which, in Maimonides' opinion, we inherited from our fathers. [...] Maimonides was worried about ancient perversities like anthropomorphism, the feast of Leviathan [see *Baba Batra* 75a], amulets. What is the damage? Jews who believe ancient descriptions about a God who sees and hears, also believe that God oversees the whole universe, and that providence applies universally. They fear God, and are therefore compassionate to men, even animals who are His works. Meanwhile, the philosopher says (*Guide for the Perplexed*, Part 3, ch.18), man has a special providence. It is not [a democratic matter]. It depends upon intelligence. Others are left to circumstances and accident. The simple-minded have no guardian. There is no one to punish the rebel.

The Jew [who is] true to his God and his elders believes that action, not learning, comes first. Someone [who] engaged only in *Torah* and not in good deeds, is like someone with a God. For the philosopher, the ultimate, essential, and highest perfection is the man with [Aristotle's] Active Intellect who knows everything he can (*Guide for the Perplexed*, Part 3, ch. 27). Contrast [him with] the honest French Jew (whom Maimonides mocks in his letter [i.e., his will] to his son)[36] who ate boiled bull meat dipped in vinegar and spices, and thought God was near during prayer. Contrast the one who studies *Talmud* with the philosopher who tries to acquire ultimate, perfect knowledge of everything possible. To which of these would you turn if you needed help?

You ask why I get into a fight with the philosophy of Maimonides, since by now the issue is dead? Because it reappears in different forms. [...] Any philosophy rooted in Greek wisdom will sprout poison hemlock

---

35   On Luzzatto's critique of Maimonides see Tsevi Hirsh Chajes, "Ma'amar Tiferet Le'mosheh" in *Kal Sifrei Maharits Hayot*, vol. 1 (Jerusalem: n.p., 1958), 397-433; Motzkin, "On the Interpretation of Maimonides," *Independent Journal of Philosophy* 2 (1978): 39-46; Sarah Rustovsky-Halperin, "Shadal Ve'hitnagduto Le'rambam," in *Mehkarim Be'toledot Ha'sifrut Ha'ivrit* (Tel Aviv: Dvir, 1954), 2: 1-55.

36   See "Musar Na'eh Me'od Meha'rambam z"l Le'harav Ha'hakham R. Avraham Beno z"l," in *Kovets Teshuvot Ha'rambam Ve'igerotav: Igerot*, ed. Abraham Lichtenberg (Leipzig: n.p., 1859), 38-40.

and wormwood. Greek wisdom and ethics are oriented towards egoistic pleasure, towards this-worldly success, love of false honor, pursuit of anything beautiful, towards saying much and doing little.

[The Crisis in Judaism]

For twenty-four years I studied philosophers in various languages. I longed to find materials of value, truth and uprightness. Most of them just wander around a pathless wilderness. One builds, the other destroys. They lead their students into chaos. They let them dive into mighty waters, only to come up with clay. If only the exit would be [as easy as the entry]. Students not only do not learn anything good, they lose their inherently good dispositions—in terms of morality, intelligence and insight (binah). I have seen natural intelligence rescue common men, ignorant of philosophy and logical knowledge, from the errors in philosophy. The common man knows by himself that he will not know. The philosopher thinks he knows what he does not know. In most matters, he confuses his audience. He captivates them, so they think nothing is hidden from them. Often all this talk adds up to zero. Otherwise, how to explain that all the thousands of books of philosophy agree on nothing? Darkness continues to grow in their dwellings [Exodus 10:23]. [...] The heritage of Greek philosophy, particularly in our epoch, not only does not make students wise and better than before. It transforms their natural happiness into sadness, their good-heartedness into grief and depression. How many of today's beautiful youth become bitter, sullen, hateful of themselves and others, because of their studies, to the point of suicide?

[On 18 January 1838] one such youth came to me with tears on his cheeks [Lamentations 1:2]. He was not my student and did not know me directly. He heard about me from someone who did. He trusted me and opened his heart. I walked with him through the markets and streets at twilight, while the day faded [Proverbs 7:9]. I probed his mind. From the depths of his sorrow, and with confidence in me, he revealed all his secrets. I listened carefully to all the ideas frightening him, and about the grave danger he was in. His sickness was Greek philosophy [hokhmah]. I decided to alert his heart gently to the characteristics (tekhunot) of Israel. He improved from day to day. Before long he recovered in heart and body. God found me worthy to raise one soul of Israel [Mishnah Sanhedrin 4:4]. He loved me more than a brother.

[I controlled my sorrow about what Greek philosophy was doing to our children for years, until I established my reputation as a
scholar]. If I rushed to open my mouth against philosophy, people
would say I was a simpleton who automatically believed that older
was better and therefore followed our fathers. Or that I ignored the
benefits of foreign wisdom for unfortunate Jews. I waited until last
year, and even then only implied what I felt. I explained the qualities of Israel *vis-à-vis* Hellenism....[37]

Addendum: Atticism and Judaism

Civilization of the actual world is the product of two heterogeneous
elements—Atticism and Judaism. We are indebted to Athens for philosophy, art, science, the development of reason, symmetry, love for the
beautiful and sublime, for rational and intellectual morality. We are indebted to Judaism for religion, morality of the heart, selflessness, and
love for the good.

Atticism is progressive, since understanding can continually develop
itself further and make new discoveries. Judaism is static, its doctrines
immutable. The heart is corruptible, but not perfectible: Good is inborn,
while evil is acquired. Judaism can purify itself from accretions alien to
it. It can re-establish itself in its original condition. It can, however, not
make itself more perfect.

Atticism, as demonstrably progressive, always assumes novel forms.
Through them, it can please, charm and attract. Judaism, ever immutable, seems always to grow older and more crippled every day. Consequently it bores, shocks and repels; thus the apparent preponderance
and triumph of the former over the latter.

However, there is an unquenchable need for the good in human nature. Nor do beauty and sublimity replace the good. Society needs soul
and understanding and Atticism does not inspire soul. Rather, it weakens or extinguishes it. That is why human nature reacts and will forever

---

37   Luzzatto, "Tamtsit Deotov Shel Shadal [1838]," *Otsar Nehmad* 4 (1863): 237-249.
Luzzatto blessed Schorr for wanting to respond to Goldenthal's insult of Reggio. Reggio,
he wrote, had instilled Luzzatto with a desire to study Hebrew morphology and motivated
him to raise his voice like a *shofar* in battle, for God's name and for *Torah* among the Jews.
See J. Goldenthal, "Beiträge zur Literatur der jüdischen Religionsphilosophie: *Ha'torah
Veha'filosofiah,*" *Allgemeine Zeitung des Judentums: Literarisches und Homiletisches Beiblatt* 33-
36 (17 November – 27 December 1838): 131-166 *passim*.

react, in favor of the heart, of goodness—of Judaism.

If Atticism is ever overcome and vanquished, human nature will also react on itself. For intellectual development also has its requirements. Atticism could re-establish itself, but it will never be able to enjoy enduring preponderance, free of opposition or counter-reaction.

Civilization therefore necessarily moves according to cycles. It does not progress in [a] straight forward fashion. Nor is there any point where it stops. Such a point of cessation would require complete harmony between Atticism and Judaism. This could only take place with tremendous sacrifice on the part of the progressive element. That element would have to seriously restrain its *elan* without rationale. The static element, as essentially immutable, is incapable of offering sacrifice.

The static element, it is true, could rid itself of those elements which are alien to its morality. That is, it can renounce its quality of supernatural revelation, and rid itself of its entire theological and historical component. It could probably, without losing its divine dimension, also rid itself of all or some of the ceremoniality irrelevant to morality. But in either case, Judaism would lose all or some of its influence on the heart of man. This influence depends totally on Judaism's belief in its divine origins and its own immutability. Besides, in spite of any sacrifice, the struggle with Atticism would continue, for Atticism is essentially progressive, while Judaism is anti-progressive.[38]

---

38   Luzzatto wrote the statement after walking together in the snow with the troubled student and returning home at midnight. See Luzzatto, "Mikhtav Me'et Shadal [to Osias Hirsh Schorr], *Otsar Nehmad* 4 (1863): 108-132. Luzzatto, "Atticisme et Judaisme," *Otsar Nehmad* 4 (1863): 131-132. Originally published as "Derekh Erets O Atitsizmus: Shirat Shadal Le'doro," in *Tsiyon: Vehu Otsar Hadash Le'hakhmei Benei Yisrael*, ed. Creizenach and Jost (FaM: J. J. Adler, 1840-41), 81-93.

5.2. HERMANN COHEN (1842-1918)

Born in Coswig, two hundred miles southwest of Berlin, Hermann Cohen studied traditional Jewish texts with his father Gerson (from whom he also inherited a taste for cantorial music) and attended the Dessau *Gymnasium*, the Breslau Theological Seminary (beginning at age fifteen) and then the University of Berlin—where his instructors included the ethnic psychologist Heymann Steinthal and the historian of philosophy Friedrich Adolf Trendelenburg.[39] He chose a career in philosophy over

---

39   On Cohen's life see Cohen, "Vita" in *Hermann Cohens Schriften zur Philosophie und Zeitgeschichte* (Berlin: Akademie, 1928), 28-29. Rosenzweig recalled how Cohen substituted for his sick father as cantor on *Yom Kippur*. See *Kleinere Schriften* (Berlin: Schocken Books, 1937), 327. His father-in-law was the cantor Louis Lewandowski. Cohen's teachers at Breslau included Zechariah Frankel, Jakob Bernays and Heinrich Graetz. See Cohen, "Grätzens Philosophie der jüdischen Geschichte," in *Jüdische Schriften*, vol. 3, ed. Bruno Strauss (Berlin: C. A. Schwetschke und Sohn, 1924), 203-212.

On Cohen's ethics see Altmann, "Hermann Cohens Begriff der Korrelation," in *In zwei Welten: Siegfried Moses zum fünfundsiebzigsten Geburtstag*, ed. Hans Tramer (Tel Aviv: Bitaon, 1962), 377-399; Samuel Hugo Bergman, "Sefer Ha'zekunim Shel Cohen," in *Hogei Ha'dor* (Tel Aviv: Metsapeh, 1934/35), 219-243; and "Hermann Cohen: The Religion of Reason from the sources of Judaism," in *Faith and Reason* (Washington, D.C.: B'nai B'rit Hillel Foundation, 1961), 27-54; Meyer, "Ha'sinodim Ha'yehudi'im Bi'germanyah Be'mahatsit Ha'sheniah Shel Ha'meah Ha'tesha Esrei," in *Mehkarim Be'toledot Am Yisrael Ve'erets Yisrael*, ed. A. Gilboa (Haifa: University of Haifa Press, 1978), 239-274; Jehudah Melber, "The Autonomy of the Individual" and "Morality in Judaism," in *Hermann Cohen's Philosophy of Judaism* (New York: Jonathan David, 1968), 252-318; Reiner Munk, "The Self and the Other in Cohen's Ethics and Works on Religion," in *Hermann Cohen's Philosophy of Religion*, ed. Stephane Moses and Hartwig Wiedebach (Hildesheim: Olms, 1997), 161-182; and "On the Idea of God in Cohen's 'Ethik'," *Journal of Jewish Thought and Philosophy* 13, nos. 1-3 (2004): 105-114; Novak, "Universal Law in the Theology of Hermann Cohen," *Modern Judaism* 1 (1981): 101-117; and "Hermann Cohen and the Neo-Kantians," in *The Image of the Non-Jew in Judaism* (New York: E. Mellen, 1983), 385-413; Kenneth Reinhard, "The Ethics of the Neighbor: Universalism, Particularism, Exceptionalism," *Journal of Textual Reasoning* 4, no. 1 (2005): n.p.; Rotenstreich, "Religion Within Limits of Reason Alone and Religion of Reason," *LBIY* 17 (1972): 179-190; Sinai Ucko, *Der Gottesbegriff in der Philosophie H. Cohens* (Königsberg: Reuther und Reichard, 1927); Reiner Wiehl, "Das Prinzip Treue in Hermann Cohens Ethik und Religionsphilosophie," in *Hermann Cohen's Philosophy of Religion*, 245-262; Michael Zank, "Atonement in Hermann Cohen's Project of Renewing Jewish Philosophy of Religion and Ethics," in *The Idea of Atonement in the Philosophy of Hermann Cohen* (Providence: Brown University Press, 2000), 45-206; and "The Ethics in Hermann Cohen's Philosophical System," *Journal of Jewish Thought and Philosophy* 13, nos. 1-3 (2004): 1-15. In addition to the partial translation of *Die Religion der Vernunft aus den Quellen des Judentums* by Mordecai M. Kaplan in *The Purpose and Meaning of Jewish Existence* (Philadephia: Jewish Publication Society, 1964), 42-252, and

the rabbinate, and in 1865 received a doctorate from the University of Halle for a dissertation (written in Latin) on autonomy in Aristotle's doctrine of necessity and contingency. Over the next years he wrote on Jewish subjects—including Spinoza, Kant and Judaism, Heine, Christian prejudice, and the cultural and historical significance both of the Sabbath and of the issue of Sunday observance.[40]

In 1873 Cohen was appointed to teach philosophy at the University of Marburg—where he developed his own philosophical system and what came to be known as the Marburg School of neo-Kantian philosophy.[41] His Jewish identity *vis-à-vis* German Christianity became an arena of tension. On the one hand, he told Friedrich A. Lange, who was instrumental in bringing him to Marburg, "What you call Christianity, I call prophetic Judaism," praised Luther for engaging the deep-seated recesses of the German mind and soul, and hoped that philosophical idealism could now reinvigorate Luther's efforts.[42] On the other, the com-

the complete translation by Simon Kaplan, *Religion Out of the Sources of Judaism* (New York: Ungar, 1972), two essays have been translated by Alan L. Mittleman from Cohen's *Jüdische Schriften*: "The Jew in Christian Culture," *Modern Judaism* 23, no. 1 (2003): 51-73; and "The Significance of Judaism for the Religious Progress of Humanity," *Modern Judaism* 24, no. 1 (2004): 36-58. Tsevi Wislawsky translated *Die Religion* into Hebrew: *Dat Ha'tevunah Mi'mekorot Ha'yahadut*. Notes by Bergman and Rotenstreich. Introduction by Sinai (Siegfried) Ucko and Yosef Ben-Shelomoh (Jerusalem: Mosad Bialik, 1971).
40   Cohen, "Heinrich Heine und das Judentum [1867]," in *Jüdische Schriften*, vol. 2, 2-44; "Spinoza über Staat und Religion, Judentum und Christentum [1915]," in *Jüdische Schriften*, vol. 3, 270-372; "Der Sabbat in seiner Kulturgeschichtliche Bedeutung," in *Jüdische Schriften*, vol. 2, 45-65; "Innere Beziehungen der Kantischen Philosophie zum Judentum [1910]," in *Jüdische Schriften*, vol. 1, 284-305; "Virchow und die Juden," in *Jüdische Schriften*, vol. 2, 457-462; "Ein ungedruckter Vortrag Hermann Cohens über Spinozas Verhältnis zum Judentum. Eingeleitet von Franz Rosenzweig," in *Festgabe zum 10 jährigen Bestehen der Akademie für die Wissenschaft des Judentums, 1919-1929* (Berlin: Akademie, 1929): 42-68. Rosenzweig, "Über den Vortrag Hermann Cohens 'Das Verhältnis Spinozas zum Judentum,'" in *Kleinere Schriften*, 351-353. See Leo Strauss, *Spinoza's Critique of Religion* (New York: Schocken Books, 1965), 23-24.
41   On the Marburg neo-Kantian school see Paul Natorp, *Hermann Cohens philosophische Leistung unter dem Gesichtspunkte des Systems* (Berlin: Reuther and Reichard, 1918) and *Kant und die Marburger Schule* (Berlin: Reuther and Reichard, 1912). Cohen wrote on Kant's theory of experience (Berlin: Ferd.Dümmler, 1871), grounding of ethics (Berlin: Ferd. Dümmler, 1877), impact on German culture (Berlin: Ferd.Dümmler, 1883) and foundations of aesthetics (Berlin: Ferd.Dümmler, 1889). His 1873 *Habilitationsschrift* dealt with Kant's pre-critical writings. Cohen's own system of philosophy is contained in *Logik der reinen Erkenntnis* (Berlin: Bruno Cassirer, 1902); *Ethik des reinen Willens* (Berlin: Bruno Cassirer, 1904) and *Die Aesthetik des reinen Gefühls* (Berlin: Bruno Cassirer, 1912).
42   Cohen, "Der Jude in der christlichen Kultur," in *Jüdische Schriften*, vol. 2, (Berlin: C.A.

mittee for his promotion to full professor balked at the thought of a Jew holding a chair at a Hessian university (he did become a full professor in 1876); he was not invited to other universities, not appointed *rector magnificus* as befit his scholarly status, and was excluded from Wilhelm Dilthey's publication of Kant's works. He had to hold his lectures on Judaism outside the university, he failed in his attempt to have his Jewish student Ernst Cassirer succeed him, and local philosophers did not attend his funeral.[43]

In 1912 he moved to Berlin, where he taught at the *Hochschule für die Wissenschaft des Judentums*. Rosenzweig thought that Berlin, a center of concern for Jewish identity, gave Cohen the opportunity to satisfy his core desire to serve "his Jews."[44] Cohen's lectures (the basis for the posthumous *Religion of Reason Out of the Sources of Judaism*), which Rosenzweig characterized as the road of a *ba'al teshuvah*, were directed to intellectually-intense Russian Jewish students; it held no interest for the assimilated majority of the Hochschule.

5.2.1. Nationalism

In 1880, in response to University of Berlin historian Heinrich von Treitschke's opposition to Jewish participation in German culture on the ground that Judaism was a national religion of foreign origin, Cohen contended that religion *per se* was essentially universal. First, the two scholars differed in terms of their historical vehicles. Second, Germany identified with Christianity and Christianity itself had its roots in Judaism. Specifically, the humanizing of God in history was drawn from Judaism's ideas of divine spiritual essence and the messianic promise of

---

Schwetschke, 1924), 73-94. When asked by a Marburg colleague about attending the Luther festival Cohen responded: 'If I did not attend, who should?" See Fackenheim, *Encounters Between Judaism and Modern Philosophy* (New York: Basic Books, 1973), 248. See Ya'akov Fleischmann, *Be'ayat Ha'natsrut*, 31-146; Robert R. Geis, "Hermann Cohen und die deutsche Reformation," *LBIY* 4 (1959): 81-91; and George L. Mosse, "The Influence of the Völkisch Idea on German Jews," in *Studies of the Leo Baeck Institute*, ed. Max Kreutzberger (New York: Leo Baeck Institute, 1967), 81-114.

43   Liebeschütz, "Hermann Cohen and his Historical Background"; "Hermann Cohen: seine Philosophie und die Zeitgeschichte," in *Von Georg Simmel zu Franz Rosenzweig* (Tübingen: Mohr, 1970), 7-54. Fackenheim, *Encounters*, 248. Cohen's student Ernst Cassirer arranged for a separate edition of Kant's work through his cousin Bruno Cassirer. Immanuel Kant, *Werke*, in *Gemeinschaft mit Hermann Cohen [et al.]*, ed. Ernst Cassirer, 11 vols. (Berlin: B. Cassirer, 1912-1923).

44   Rosenzweig, *Kleinere Schriften*, 236.

realizing the ethical ideal through history.[45]

Cohen also criticized Moritz Lazarus' response to Treitschke. Lazarus, from the town of Filehne, had learned *Talmud* with his father Aron Levin (a student of Akiva Eger, 1761-1837), studied Greek, Jewish and German philosophy at the Braunschweig *Gymnasium*, then at the University of Berlin and finally at the University of Halle, where he received his doctorate for a dissertation on the aesthetic dimension to education. He committed himself to helping Jews integrate into the national education [system] in Germany, that they might share the post-Luther atmosphere of liberated human spirit and individual responsibility. His teaching career took him from the University of Bern to the *Hochschule für die Wissenschaft des Judentums in Berlin*, and finally to the University of Berlin.[46] In response to Treitschke, he maintained that Jewish immersion into German national culture was not at odds with Jewish tradition or Judaism's universal ethical principles.[47] To the contrary,

---

45   Cohen, "Ein Bekenntnis in der Judenfrage [1880]," in *Jüdische Schriften*, vol. 2, 73-94.
46   On Lazarus' life and thought see Kaufmann Kohler, "Lazarus' Ethics of Judaism, 1898," and *"Loyal and Free*: Addresses and Lectures by Prof. M. Lazarus," in *A Living Faith: Selected Sermons and Addresses from the Literary Remains of Kaufmann Kohler*, ed. Samuel S. Cohon (Cincinnati: Hebrew Union College, 1942), 212-221; and Michael A. Meyer, "Ha'sinodim Ha'yehudi'im Bi'germanyah Be'mahatsit Ha'sheniah Shel Ha'meah Ha'tesha Esrei," in *Mehkarim Be'toledot Am Yisrael Ve'erets Yisrael*, ed. A. Gilboa (Haifa: University of Haifa Press, 1978), 239-274. See also Ingrid Belke, ed., *Moritz Lazarus und Heymann Steinthal: Die Begründer der Völkerpsychologie in ihren Briefen* (Tübingen: Mohr, 1971), xiii-lxxx; Moritz Lazarus, *Aus meiner Jugend*, ed. Nahida Ruth Lazarus (FaM: J. Kaufmann, 1913); David Baumgardt, "The Ethics of Lazarus and Steinthal," *LBIY* 2 (1957): 205-217; Hans Liebeschütz, "Hermann Cohen and His Historical Background," *LBIY* 13 (1968): 3-33; Franz Rosenzweig, *Kleinere Schriften* (Berlin: Schocken Books, 1937), 299-349; and Lazarus, "Zwei Reden auf Moses Mendelssohn zur Gedenkfeier seine hundert-jährigen Todestages, I. Am 4, Januar 1886, in Friedericianum, zu Dessau, II, Am 11 Januar 1886, in 'Gesellschaft der Freunde' zu Berlin gehalten," in *Treu und Frei* (Leipzig: C. F. Winter, 1887), 200 and *Aus meiner Jugend* (FaM: J. Kauffman, 1913), 113-114.
47   Lazarus, "Was heisst national?"; "Unser Standpunkt: Zwei Reden an seine Religionsgenossen am 1. und 16. December 1880"; and "An die deutschen Juden," in *Treu und Frei*, 53-113, 117-155 and 157-180. See Michael A. Meyer, "Great Debate on Antisemitism: Jewish Reaction to New Hostility in Germany, 1879-1881," *LBIY* 11 (1966): 137-170; Walter Boehlich, ed., *Der Berliner Antisemitismusstreit* (FaM: Insel Verlag, 1965); Sanford Ragins, *Jewish Responses to Antisemitism in Germany, 1870-1914* (Cincinnati: Hebrew Union College, 1980); Seligmann Meyer, *Ein Wort an Herrn Heinrich von Treitschke* (Berlin: Jüdischer Presse, 1880); and Jacob J. Petuchowski, "On the Validity of German-Jewish Self-Definitions," *Shofar* 6, no. 1 (1987): 7-19.

> We are Jews no less than we are fully Germans. The
> German language is without qualification our mother
> tongue. The German land is our fatherland. We speak
> and think in German. Our soul is filled and grows with
> German poetry and scientific study. We labor on behalf
> of German endeavors with all the power of our spirit and
> heart. Our conscience longs for the greatness, loftiness
> and power of the German nation.[48]

Cohen believed that Lazarus wanted to simultaneously immerse Judaism into German culture and to maintain distinctions between Jewish and German tradition, while Cohen wanted Jews to subscribe to German national self-consciousness and adapt Jewish traditions to German culture. He also rejected what he thought was Lazarus' conditional love for the fatherland on prior demonstration by Germany that it deserved such love. Cohen's approach was unconditional:

> We love our fatherland because it is our mother earth,
> because we love our homeland, because Palestine to us
> is but a travel option. Because the German tongue is our
> mother language, and it is sounded in our fatherland—it
> was the first sound I uttered as a child, the first sweet
> motherly word. Because we are but children of human-
> kind, and every human being wants to have a father-
> land.[49]

For his part, Cohen did not regard such commitment and adaptation to Germany as being a surrender of Jewish identity. For example, when Cohen was honored in 1914 for his journey to Russia, he declared that he had become a *ba'al teshuvah* (one who returned to Judaism) thirty-four years earlier. Franz Rosenzweig wrote that

> Cohen dated his return home to 1880, which is when he
> sent his *A Confession Regarding the Jewish Question* into

---

48   Lazarus, "Unser Standpunkt," in *Treu und Frei*, 93. See Lazarus, "An die deutschen Juden," in *Treu und Frei*, 157-180.
49   Cohen, "Ein Bekenntnis in der Judenfrage [1880]," in *Jüdische Schriften*, vol. 2, 73-94.

the fray. It attacked on two fronts, Treitschke on one side and [Heinrich] Graetz and Lazarus on the other. He undoubtedly infuriated his own group more than his antisemitic opponents. He was well aware of where he was going, and thought he traveled a single path. We agree.[50]

Cohen took his response to Treitschke and Lazarus further in 1915/16, when he maintained that Judaism could progress from the medieval ghetto into modernity by sharing Martin Luther's struggle for the freedom of inner conscience and universal ethical ideas—which in turn renewed the messianism of the Biblical prophets.[51] For Cohen, adaptation to German culture and *ba'al teshuvah*-identity combined in symbiotic fashion: "As Germans we want to be Jews, and as Jews, Germans."[52] Specifically:

> As concerns our own soul-life, we have established the innermost religious commonality in a contemporary harmony between Jewish messianism and German humanism. Our feeling for the German state and nation glorifies and reinforces us religiously. Our soul flourishes evenly and harmoniously in our German patriotism and in our religious consciousness. This consciousness is rooted in and crests into the single God of one mankind.[53]

---

50   See Belke, xvii. Rosenzweig, "Hermann Cohens *Jüdische Schriften*," in *Kleinere Schriften*, 307.
51   Cohen, *Deutschtum und Judentum* (Giessen: A. Töpelmann, 1915); also "Deutschtum und Judentum" in *Vom inneren Frieden des deutschen Volkes*, ed. Friedrich Thimme (Leipzig: S. Hirzel, 1916), 541-562.
52   Cohen, "Deutschtum und Judentum [1915]," in *Jüdische Schriften*, vol. 2, 280.
53   Cohen, "Deutschtum und Judentum [1916]," in *Jüdische Schriften*, vol. 2, 316. Cohen's student Jakob Klatzkin said that "This *Tendenzschrift* ultimately backfired. The risk of presenting Germanism and Judaism as essentially similar or related could not succeed without detracting from German and Jewish cultural spirits together. Cohen thereby did injury to both." See Klatzkin, *Hermann Cohen* (Berlin: Jüdischer Verlag, 1921),125-126. Emil Fackenheim, who studied at the Hochschule in 1939, observed:

> Not even Moses Mendelssohn (who ushered in the era of German Judaism), came anywhere close to Hermann Cohen (who stood at its end), in the degree to which he lived up to Mendelssohn's own advice of

V.II. Selections from *The Problem of Jewish Ethical Doctrine. A Critique of Lazarus' 'The Ethics of Judaism,'* translated by Gershon Greenberg[54]

Translator's preface

Lazarus wrote The Ethics of Judaism *upon the initiative of Wilhelm von Gutmann, who convened European Jewish leaders in Koblenz in the fall of 1882 to formulate a response to growing antisemitism. The group decided to do so by demonstrating the centrality of ethics and Judaism and thereby create common ground between Jews and German Protestants. In volume 1, Lazarus described morality as having its end in itself, while it simultaneously provided purpose for human effort—intellectual, artistic and practical spheres. Ultimately the moral realm assumed ontological dimensions, pervading God, man and history. For Lazarus, God and morality interrelated dialectically. Moral order emerged from the revelatory divine source, while God emerged from hiddenness to be known in the ethical context and was subject to ethical imperatives. The two also related as endless concentric circles: Morality was absolute because it rested in God. However, God had an infinitely moral nature and the reality of morality existed in itself. Ultimately the sequence of priority dissolved into a point where the ethical was divine and the divine was ethical. In a characteristic formulation, Lazarus wrote that "Not because the principle is in God is it the moral principle; but because it is the moral principle, in itself and absolutely, therefore it is necessarily in God" (Section 98). Man and God, he explained, related to one another by their mutual presence in the ethical realm—God was absolutely good, while man was filled with the idea of God's goodness and driven to transform so-*

---

living at once in both worlds. And such was Cohen's trust in both worlds, and in their inherent affinity, that he had no inkling of or premonition that disaster was imminent.

Hermann Cohen: After Fifty Years. Leo Baeck Institute Memorial Lecture 12 (New York: Leo Baeck Institute, 1969): 4. See Steven S. Schwarzschild, "Germanism and Judaism—Hermann Cohen's Normative Paradigm of the German-Jewish Symbiosis," in *Jews and Germans from 1860 to 1933: The Problematic Symbiosis*, ed. David Bronsen (Heidelberg: Winter, 1979), 129-172 and Hans Alfred Grunsky, *Der Einbruch des Judentums in die Philosophie* (Berlin: Junker und Dünnhaupt, 1937).

54 Lazarus, *Die Ethik des Judentums*, 2 vols. (FaM: J. Kauffmann, 1898, 1911). Citations are from the translation by Henrietta Szold, *The Ethics of Judaism*, 2 vols. (Philadelphia: JPS, 1900/1901).

ciety and nature into moral entities. As man strove to transform society and nature, he progressively unveiled absolute, ethical reality; he thus came closer to God and deepened the channel of their relationship. Jewish laws were instruments for enhancing the relationship, and were to be followed because of their internal ethics: "The moral law is a categorical imperative, which has its basis not in the lawgiver but in the significance and dignity of the law itself" (Section 101). Judaism's national process of ethical development was tied to universal morality and had messianic implications. Throughout his work, Lazarus acknowledged his indebtedness to the views of Kant—although he considered them to belong to the larger Jewish tradition. Specifically, the categorical imperative was implicit to Deuteronomy 22:3; and the conception of autonomous, moral spirit was stipulated in Yoma 7^b.[55]

Summary of translated passages
Cohen began his critique by distinguishing Christian moral doctrine, based upon closed Scriptural revelation, from ethics, which involved the philosophical conceptualization of a system. In Judaism the sources for moral doctrine were ever-developing and subject to scientific study; moral doctrine intermingled with doctrines of faith.

An ethics of Judaism is a grand, noble undertaking, but a difficult problem methodologically. In Christian scientific study, the analogous title "Christian ethics" rather than "ethics of Christianity" is used. This distinction is worth considering. Christian ethics distinguishes itself from philosophical ethics. It therefore prefers to call itself not ethics but ethical doctrine, or if need be morals, because ethics involves the philosophical conception of a system.[56] This philosophical conception probably cannot be considered without the correlative concept of logic, which in turn refers to physics. In that Christian ethical doctrine is delineated from the philosophical, its designated basis is the revelation in the Old and New Testaments. These define Christian ethical doctrine's historical sources and positive literary records.

It is otherwise in Judaism. The Biblical sources extend over a range of

---

55   Cohen, "Das Problem der jüdischen Sittenlehre: Eine Kritik von Lazarus' *Ethik des Judentums* [1899]," in *Jüdische Schriften*, vol. 3, 1-35.
56   I have translated *die Ethik* as "ethics" and *die Sittenlehre* as "ethical doctrine." As David Novak observes, *die Ethik* refers to ethics as a religious philosophy; *die Sittenlehre* to the material content of the Jewish ethical tradition.

centuries. Oral law further disperses the unity of time and thereby the unity of basis. But finally, it is implicit to the concept of oral law that it does not reach any conclusion; and when it wants to impose a conclusion by force, it always ends up restlessly beginning over again. This is the light of tradition thrown over the shadow. It is not only oral doctrine that has no dead point when it comes to customs and traditions. The same is so with religious and moral thought as well. When reformed Jewish theology promotes the concept of development and enthusiastically employs the scientific study of Jewish antiquity and Jewish history under its banner, it is not being impelled by something superficial or just fashionable, but rather by the vital interest and fruitful insight of historical thinking. Judaism does not terminate internally with the onset of Christianity. What comes later to Judaism does not emerge under the spell of reaction or restoration on the external level. Rather, the life which comes later develops out of Judaism's original life, ever rejuvenating itself. At the same time, as difficult as this may be to accept. In this way Judaism actually forms an undeniable type of unity over many thousands of years of history. But on account of this, the difficulty facing ethical doctrine is severe to the point of appearing insurmountable.

First of all, this observation necessarily implies that inquiry into Jewish ethical doctrine is a task for historical research. The presentation of Jewish ethical teaching has the unequivocal requirement of a basis in historical research. It raises itself from a secured and securing foundation and must control itself at the level of historical research. Otherwise, the presentation would have neither stability nor composure. The historical principle of development must direct the exploration. If not, one surrenders to the caprice of homiletic fantasy. Exploration and research both belong to the language of Jewish scientific study. The provided description related to scientific study should result only from that.

Immediately, Jewish ethical doctrine, and even methodical treatment of Jewish moral doctrine, is a problem for the scientific study of antiquity and history. The presupposition of, and connection with, Biblical exegesis and Christian history of literature and dogma are indispensable to Christian ethical doctrine. Similarly, if not additionally, the more extensive the historical basis for Jewish ethical doctrine, the more Jewish ethical doctrine must rest upon Biblical research, and along with this, upon the Jewish scientific study of antiquity as related to the broad territory of Talmudic and Midrashic literature. There is also the inevitable supplement of later development, whereby the historical problem becomes increasingly intensified and hardened.

Another observation brings up a new sort of difficulty for the problem of Jewish ethical doctrine. In terms of ethical content, the primary material for Judaism's development is constituted by its *doctrines of faith/belief*. The morality of Judaism is contained in its religion. In Biblical sources, as is known, doctrines of faith/belief and ethical doctrine are intermingled not only with prescriptions for worship, but with political, civil and public law, not to mention the complex ingredient of legendary narrative and poetry. For oral doctrine, this complex ingredient is both a vital benefit and a methodological obstacle. The onset and development of *midrash*, as a special literary *genre*, should be understood in terms of informal dogma. Scarcely did this literature reach some sort of conclusion, than its contact with philosophy, which was deeper and livelier—because more concrete and self-sufficient than was so earlier in Alexandria—led to a new composition of doctrines of faith/belief. Jewish religious philosophy emerged this way after the tenth century. In its dominant, uplifting, and stimulating meaning for all life of Judaism—if at times interrupted or oppressed—it has never been totally extinguished from among us.

Summary of translated passages
Cohen considered Lazarus' claim that his was the first (philosophical) ethics of Judaism to be false. While Christian belief was dogmatic, such that faith and moral doctrine conflicted with philosophy, Jewish belief was not opposed to philosophy. Not even immortality, revelation or the idea of God were dogmatic; and while ceremonial law was, conceivably, opposed to philosophy, it was no more than a "hedge" around religion. Medieval and modern philosophical systems of doctrines of faith automatically involved doctrines of morality—although they did not develop any system of moral doctrine, lest opposition to ethical dogma be incited. Cohen also regarded Lazarus' attempt to universalize ethics and lift morality out of the respective contexts of doctrines of faith to be illusory. To the extent that he wished to develop moral principles out of specific foundations of faith-doctrines, Lazarus should have carefully explored historical sources. This he did not do.

[THE MORAL DOCTRINE AND JEWISH BELIEF]

The book to which these observations are devoted claims to offer the ethics of Judaism *for the first time*. Thoughtless reviewers have merely assented. By doing so, they have reinforced the author's grave assault upon our intellectual history. Without intending any personal reproach, it must be said that such a claim contains the gravest and bitterest insult that could possibly befall us in these bad times. What? Has the entire grand, rich and deep history of our scientific study of religion provided no such testimony? Have we prepared the table but spurned the teaching of wisdom? Are we entangled and imprisoned in so-called law to the point that we allow morality to lie around [unattended] like some accessory?

Why have we not had or, more precisely, why would we not have had, a special Jewish ethics? In the first place, no complex proof is required to delimit the literary fact. There always were "books of ethical doctrine" among us. These books do not lack titles about the virtues, ethical concepts and "duties of the heart." We need not even cite the fine example of the departed [Hirsch Baer] *Fassel.*[57] But why have epoch-making works of the medieval period and recent religious philosophy made the system of doctrine of belief/faith an issue for study, but not the system of ethical doctrine?

The answer lies in the definition of the Jewish religion's essence as distinct from the Christian. With Christianity, the special content of belief/faith unavoidably leads to the difficult, controversial concept of dogma. As much as the ancient Church's Greek Fathers aspired to reach an understanding with philosophy, an aspiration revived in the blossoming of the Middle Ages, dogmatic content has remained opposed to, and in contradiction with, reason's different methods and premises. There is a conflict between Christian faith/belief and human, scientific reason. *The problem of Christian ethical doctrine* follows for Christianity, not only regarding its culture and scientific study, but for its theology. To the opponents of belief/faith, Christian ethical doctrine constitutes not only a hostile arena but replaces [what is authentic]. For the staunchest dogmatist it remains a living source, enlivening and fructifying the confused maze of doctrines of belief/faith. In Christianity, the severing of

---

57 For example, Hirsch Baer Fassel, *Die mosäisch-rabbinische Tugend-und Rechtslehre* (Aalen: Scientia, 1981 [1862]).

all connections between a Christian ethics and dogmatism is thoroughly understandable. The situation is totally different in Judaism.

Which content of Jewish doctrine of belief/faith could constitute a rebuke to skepticism, such that the fixation of dogma would have to stick obstinately to it? Which element of Jewish doctrine of belief/faith tolerates, let alone requires, the separation between ethical doctrine and the antithesis to ethical doctrine? One could think of the *ceremonial law*. But after sacrifice disappeared, ceremonial law could no longer constitute a real problem, one from which the opposite to an ethical doctrine could grow. Indeed the *Sayings of the Fathers* already indicated that the ceremonial law was the "hedge" for doctrine. A hedge is not a garden. The incomparable value of the life-sources of religion remains clear everywhere. No matter the enthusiasm about maintaining and securing the hedge, no one could be misled into thinking that it was not the protection but the treasure itself. Deep learning and philosophy are not required to prevent the hedge from growing up inwardly over the head.

Does this mean that one should object to the many mythological motives of the doctrines of belief, such as resurrection? Even questions of this type cannot err about the purely ethical character of the doctrine of belief/faith. Even the basic concept of this class of motives, [namely] *immortality*, in no way remained the focus for questions of belief/faith. This basic concept is first appropriated, and then dug up from its own soil and developed. Also the question of *revelation* is capable of effectuating obduracy against revelation's principle (*Prinzip*) of reason, because revelation delineates between content and form from the onset. For those who are most ill-disposed, only the single God was left, in whom opposition between ethics and dogmatism could achieve powerful expression. But one has to lack even superficial knowledge of the meaning of the Jewish idea of God to allow space for this thought. Certainly our medieval dogmatists, that is, our philosophers, let it be known clearly enough in their aggressive polemics against Islam and Christianity that they recognized their own God as the God of morality. They contested any other knowledge of God, and any kind of attribute other than His ethical path. *The God of our philosophers' faith/belief is the God of their doctrine of ethics.*

This is why the philosophers composed no special ethics. They not only did not want to allow the antithesis to their dogmatics to manifest itself. They had absolutely no feeling that there would be any opposition, nor could they have. The thought of any such antithesis first presented itself to these philosophers from the outside, not from they themselves. Anyone who thought of some antithesis to the doctrine of belief/faith would have been counted among "the perplexed," and in need of a "guide."

We must therefore designate it a confusion, for an ethics of Judaism to be brought forth as a new task, as some heretofore unheard-of accomplishment. The Jewish ethical doctrine is the inner source, more precisely the substantial principle, of the Jewish doctrine of belief/faith. Jewish ethics is the standard of the Jewish religion. *It is the principle and not the consequence.* It can be derived from Jewish religion only in the sense that axioms (*Axiome*) are derived from the instructional content of mathematical theorems (*Sätze*). The ethical doctrine is not the consequence of the principle of divinity for the human being. Rather, the principle of divinity cannot evolve in any way other than through ethical doctrine. There is an indissoluble unity between Jewish ethical doctrine and the Jewish doctrine of God.

Such considerations depict the problem of a Jewish ethics from a new side: Jewish ethical doctrine is nothing other than the Jewish doctrine of faith/belief. Therefore, there never could have been a special Jewish ethical doctrine in the thought and intention of the distinction. *And there may not be any from now on.* Thought of a Jewish ethical doctrine is a fateful error; it is a factual as well as historical error. At the same time, one might think that extracting ethical themes out of the self-evident core of the doctrine of belief, despite these considerations, is a valid and worthwhile undertaking. The most authentic and indisputable content of faith/belief would thereby be moved over into general scientific study with its interest in culture. Moreover, this content of belief/faith constitutes an object for the most difficult world-historical conflict. Should it not be most instructive and telling, then, that apart from the controversial principles of belief all parties appear to be in agreement in terms of the unity of morality? Sharp dogmatic opposites are unthinkable without ethical differences. One might think that the plan which aims towards harmony in *ethics*, where even dogmatic opposites reach accommodation or moderation, is the more desirable. We must insist: In this thought of well-intentioned tolerance, there is a fundamental illusion. We will have no part of it. For the moment, let us assume that an ethics of Judaism is worth striving for in the sense under consideration—that ethical principles can be worked out of the formations of the doctrine of faith/belief. At that point the problem of such an ethics would encounter a new difficulty.

One may concede to the author of such a work as much unrestricted independence as possible. We do not blame anyone for being unable to bring the responsibility of one's personal style of philosophizing into harmony with the closed system of Jewish doctrine of belief/faith. One may fully concede that the author disclosed Jewish ethical doctrine from out of Jewish doctrine of belief/faith by himself. But one essential requirement must remain, the one dealing with the scientific content of the theme of his concept of Judaism. Namely, that the author of such a Jewish ethics draws the content and history of Jewish dogmatics from within the range of his sources. Let us say a new Jewish ethics arose which cited all possible statements dispersed in the Bible, *Talmud* and *Midrash*. Let us say that even the "two collection boxes" of some beneficent Berlin organization were introduced as being equally productive as literary sources. If the sources set before us in *books of our religious philosophers* in consistent scientific form are neglected, then the sources which are most important, because they are most vibrant, remain suppressed. *The most fateful error in the book before us* is that the concept of the sources used for the book's problem completely ignores and neglects the sources scientifically and methodologically closest, and does so capriciously and unmethodically.

This rebuke applies to the entire *scientific character of the book* in terms of its own territory. One could not assume from the work that the author has professional competence in Biblical research or in the wide field of *Talmud*. He should not have found it necessary to excuse himself by distinguishing between "philological criticism" and "historical conscience." There is no "historical conscience" without thorough philological knowledge, any more than moral conscience would be beneficial without knowledge of the law. Moral conscience offers no protection against clever capriciousness in terms of strained *aggadic* explanation. But let us put all this aside. Let us not go into the authority which the author [Lazarus] attributes to the variegated multitude of his other sources. The author still has the unconditional duty of professional knowledge of the subject. He allows for the terrible suspicion that the most important and appropriate sources of Jewish philosophy are being skipped over [in this work] and that not much more is dealt with. We need to examine whether allusions to Maimonides are based upon philosophical knowledge. Among other philosophers, *Aristotle*, *Spinoza* and *Kant* are more than just cited as Lazarus distinguishes himself from Mr. [Nicolai] von Hartmann , [who] belongs to the field of *belletristic*. Aristotle is someone behind Maimonides, who is shoved aside. Spinoza is exhumed as a disciple of *Talmud* in a way that can hardly be taken seriously. Regrettably, it could hardly neutralize Kuno Fischer's malicious word about the splendid work of [Manuel] Joel: That Joel did not succeed in bringing Spinoza back among the Jews. When it comes to Kant, we will deal with this as a major theme, since the essential thought of the entire book is—in order not to use a harsher expression—"borrowed" from Kant.

Summary of translated passages

Lazarus wanted to deal only with thoughts which stemmed from the collective mind of Judaism. In fact, there never was such a "ghetto," Cohen averred; it was psychologically impossible. To contend that there was would be factually wrong and morally questionable. The Jewish mind sought, rather, to absorb the intellectual environment, especially in contemporary Germany. Lazarus wanted Jewish ethics to be systematic. But systematic concepts—as distinct from scientific study per se—were inapplicable to religion. Religion produced a philosophy of religion, one of a religious philosophy of morality. The ethics of Judaism was the religious philosophy of the Jewish doctrine of morality, which was not systematic. "Systematic" ethics also gave a false impression of self-sufficiency. For Cohen, the culture of the Jewish religion deepened when it dispensed with self-sufficiency, enriched itself through philosophy, rejected any "collective mind" and tried to reconcile the truths of Judaism with scientific study.

[THE COLLECTIVE MIND OF JUDAISM]

All these special questions about professional erudition pale before the author's self-consciousness about relating his work to his sources. At the conclusion of the presentation Lazarus makes the ceremonious declaration before God and all the world that he did not want to bring forth any thoughts not "stemming from the collective mind/spirit of Judaism." What is this collective mind? Who could define it, so that the ceremonious affirmation could satisfy the definition? Was there ever such a collective mind of Judaism, as distinct from the minds of world culture? Praise God, there never was any such ghetto. [But Lazarus states:]

What I have learned from the Greeks and Romans, and
from philosophical as well as other literature of modern
nations, helps shape my presentation: [But] to the best
of my knowledge and conscience I have drawn the content from Judaism [alone] and from the Jewish collective mind. (82)

This ceremonious declaration is worthy of standing alongside the declaration about the book's being the first [statement of] Jewish ethics.

First, it is false in psychological terms. Even if a scholar were convinced that there was such an isolated collective mind/spirit to a nation,
doubt must arise about the psychological possibility of such isolation.
Doubt increases if the possible isolation refers to a *religious* collective
mind/spirit, the reality of which is put forward primarily by, and has
duration in, literary testimony. Second, it is factually incorrect, because
the collective mind/spirit of Judaism never fell victim to such particularism, not even in the medieval period. Our dogmatists precipitate suspicion by the boldness of their absorbing the teachings of Aristotle and
the Arabs, as if they were internally dependent upon them. Thirdly, it
is morally deceptive, because it shows the crudest possible ingratitude
of which Jewish particularism could be accused. "We accept the truth,
from whoever has spoken it." Our collective mind has always proceeded
according to this doctrine. Philo thought and felt like a Greek, and our
philosophers in the medieval period wrote their holy books in Arabic.
How could we moderns, let alone a German person, want to establish
our [own] religious collective mind, even as we would like to recognize
the world of the German mind alone as the source for our [own] style?
And if we think as Germans in all our intellectual questions, as we have
generally done since Moses Mendelssohn, should and must we not recognize the German mind as having a voice in the content of our faith/
belief? Christian thinking appears differently among the German people
than among the Roman. And the minds of Lessing and Herder, of Leibniz and Kant, of Schiller and Goethe, are supposed to have no influence
upon our Judaism? No. Hopefully, the case is [in fact] no differently for
the author. We shall see. But that he does not recognize this and will not
speak of it, is a personal aberration, a methodological error. It has to do
with how the book *relates to philosophy in general*.

This book purports to be a "systematic ethics." Supposedly there has been none until now. "System" is [properly] used to express any ordering of concepts, especially the classification of forms of nature, a task which is the content of descriptive natural sciences. Very generally, one can also call a system any ordering of thoughts which is derived from a definite principle of classification. But this is not the technical, world-historical meaning of philosophical system. According to such a designation, ethics is systematic insofar as it is linked to a system of philosophy. To which system of philosophy does the systematic ethics of Judaism belong? Judaism is no system of philosophy, it does not intend to be and it cannot be. As its first term, a system of philosophy requires logic, i.e., the logic of scientific study. Judaism has no natural science. From this alone it follows that it has no systematic ethics in the philosophical sense. It is instructive that the Bible does not constitute such a system. The author himself says that the *Talmud* "can dispense with the form of scientific system" (67). One may argue about the virtue of this claim, which the author makes out of necessity. The fact itself, however, he has already conceded.

The application of the concept of system to religion at all is a methodological confusion. The notion of a system is the life-concept of philosophy. Religion wishes to be ethical doctrine. It cannot be a philosophy of ethical doctrine, which is to say ethics. Because of this difference the scientific character of religion is withdrawn, and the possible knowledge available from its scientific character is consequently curtailed. Since religion itself cannot be philosophy, out of craving for knowledge religion endeavors to establish a connection with philosophy. This is how the philosophy of religion arises. But what is the special content towards which this philosophy of religion strives, from beginning to end, in all its questions and interests? Nothing other than morality. *The philosophy of religion is the religious philosophy of morality.* Thus, the ethics of Judaism is not a systematic ethics, but rather *the religious philosophy of Jewish ethical doctrine.*

This is not merely the appropriate title for the problem. The title [also] indicates the appropriate *method.* This is not just some kind of battle of words. It is, rather, a sign at the crossroads. This directional sign averts confusion in scientific study as well as in religion. Systematic ethics bestows upon religion a false appearance of self-sufficiency. Religion pursues the cultural path only when it does not believe in its self-sufficiency. It does so rather by endeavoring to add human scientific study to its divine wisdom. Fortunately, our dogmatists have not isolated religion within some alleged collective mind of Judaism. They have rather sought the most thorough, intimate and thereby critical agreement with Hellenism, Islam and Christianity. They did not want to create any self-sufficient ethics, but instead a philosophy of Jewish faith/belief. Insofar as they set the correct object for themselves and found the right focus for their inquiry, through philosophy they could succeed in enriching their faith/belief and deepening its grounds. Our dogmatists were far away from any superficial, arrogant delusion that this was liable to damage the collective mind of Judaism. To them, the collective mind had the ideal task of relentlessly developing their faith/belief until the end of days. With their philosophical honesty they contributed greatly to the world, to the philosophy of the world, and not only to their own religion. This is something not appreciated enough, in general or in particular. When Leibniz caught sight of [Henry] More, he was gripped with admiration. What Leibniz derived from this [experience] holds much interest. This is, then, the natural task, religious as well as scientific: To compare, and as much as possible to reconcile, the truths of Judaism with every type of scientific study.

Summary of translated passages

[LAZARUS' PRINCIPLES OF SCIENTIFIC STUDY]
Lazarus, Cohen continued, confined the scientific study of ethics to the "soul of the nation," while its authentic task was to secure the certitude of moral knowledge. What were the principles of Lazarus' scientific study? 1) God? This was impossible, because Lazarus' ethics were opposed to religious philosophy. 2) Autonomy? This was impossible, because it was a Kantian idea and therefore did not belong to the collective mind-spirit of Judaism. 3) The equivalence of God and autonomy? This was also impossible. As autonomy was Lazarus' principle of mankind, it would mean that the concept of God was equivalent to the concept of man. This would surrender the Jewish doctrine of God and blend the collective mind of Judaism with that of Christianity.

What is *the author's concept of ethical scientific study?* [Lazarus states:]

The proper assignment and purpose of the scientific study of ethics must be so designated: to keep the living

source of ethical judgment pure, fresh and fluent, etc.
in the picture. But to carry out this assignment, it must
sink into the soul of the nation so that it may hold its
own clear mirror before it. (73).

However, this attention to the source cannot be recognized as the proper assignment for the scientific study of ethics. In terms of scientific study, ethics is not to concern itself with the so-called soul of the nation. Otherwise, other people could say that it was too narrowly grounded. It would be just as well to turn to the Hottentots. In terms of scientific study, ethics seeks no fresh river. It seeks rather to secure *the reliability* of ethical judgment and *the manner of certainty of ethical knowledge*. This is its appropriate and authentic assignment. This requires a principle. All scientific knowledge is based upon principles and conditioned by them. The presupposition of ethical scientific study is the ethical principle. What, then, is the author's *principle of the Jewish ethical doctrine*?

One would think that because Jewish ethics is not Jewish religious philosophy, that God cannot be posited as the principle of Jewish ethics. On the other hand, one is anxious to ascertain what principle, which is distinct from God, could be accepted by the author—having dammed off any outside influence upon these ethics and surely upon the principle of ethics as well. The author surprises us from two sides: On the one side *he makes God into the principle of Jewish ethics*. [This is the first difficulty.] Anyone else might have the right to do this, but not him, for he has written his ethics in opposition to religious philosophy.

On the other side, he makes *autonomy into the principle* of Jewish ethics. But autonomy is the principle of *Kantian* ethics. Thus, Lazarus falls into the same error—to speak in his language, if the comparison may be permitted—which, according to him, Maimonides committed by making himself dependent upon Aristotle. We will need to set this right later. But it is incontestable that autonomy, as the principle of ethics, was Kant's discovery. *A Kantian principle thereby becomes the principle of the ethics of Judaism*. By itself this may be quite possible, since the Old Testament had a powerful influence on Kant. But for a systematic ethics which ceremoniously closes itself off from all philosophy and culture and endeavors to construct itself exclusively out of the collective mind of Judaism, this is a contradiction. And because this contradiction had to occur—for how should Judaism be able to contain a *scientific prin-*

ciple?—it is no wonder that a *third* [surprise] enters in. Namely, that God and autonomy become *equivalent*. But autonomy [for Lazarus], as we will see, is the principle of mankind. Thereby, through this confusion, Lazarus' *concept of God is made equivalent to the concept of man. The ethics of Judaism* thereby surrenders the principle of the Jewish doctrine of God. And the collective mind/spirit of Judaism flees into an expanse where its distinction from Christianity disappears. We now want to portray the *three stages of this error*, whereby it will be shown how a *fourth* [erroneous] significance of [Lazarus'] principle [of Jewish ethics] is tied to the three. [Lazarus'] allegedly unified collective mind enacts obviously peculiar growths.

Summary of translated passages
Cohen agreed with Lazarus that human mind/spirit was grounded in God as the essence of morality. Cohen's own moral law was founded directly in divine essence; the concept of God's essence was identical to the concept of morality or moral law. But Lazarus was wrong to maintain that God commanded a law, because it was (already) moral, tying morality to law and law to command. Rather, morality referred to God's essence, and any command was secondary. The morality of the law came from God. If ethics was tied to command and law, as Lazarus would have it, what was God's essence prior to the command?

[GOD AND MORAL LAW]
1.[The first stage of error.] "Jewish ethics is originally theological" (85). Why only originally? Does this mean it does not remain so? [According to Lazarus]:

> Ethical law and divine prescription, we said, are insepa-
> rable concepts.... Inseparable but not identical. / If the
> human mind/spirit delves into the question about the
> essence of the ethical and its ground, then... [85-86]

—We must continue (paraphrasing Lazarus): the human mind/spirit first correctly recognizes the ground of the ethical in God. For the more the human mind/spirit delves into the foundation of the ethical, the more it delves into the essence of God; for God means nothing else for religion than the essence of the ethical. Every other opinion is mythological illusion and theological aberration. So Maimonides would teach. But the author proceeds:

> Then there confronts us everywhere in Judaism this clear thought: a law is not ethical because God commanded it. Rather because it is ethical, therefore God commanded it. [86]

While by no means clear, this thought is not totally ambiguous. Inexcusably, it plays around with the deepest human problem. If the author had not taught the strange historical view that while Socrates was vanquished by Sophists, Judaism had no Sophists (79), we could have tried to transfer this thought into the clarity of Socrates' wind-direction.

We have two questions. First, why is the law ethical? That was indeed the question: The ground of the ethical. Secondly, the whole formulation of the question is false because it refers solely to the *command* of God; and not to the essence of God. The command has secondary importance: "You were God, even when You were alone." But the *essence of God is morality*, it is the ethical law. These concepts are not only inseparable but identical. Admittedly, the author says something similar. But the thought is not acknowledged or fixed as a principle. Everything is deferred. While Lazarus allows the ethical law to flow out of the "inherent essence of God Himself," (87)—nevertheless without strictly identifying ethical law with the inherent essence of God—on the other hand he denotes God as the "archetype" of all morality" (89). This archetype indicates the *fourth* sort of error. If God were a type (*Gestalt*) He would not be the archetype, but rather the type for the ethical. So thoroughly is His essence identical with the essence of the ethical. [Lazarus continues to say:]

> Therefore, ethical law is not based upon any dogmatic representative image of God, but rather upon thoughts about His morality. That is, the ethical law is grounded upon the essence of morality itself (89).

We would hope the latter for the ethical law, namely for it to be grounded upon the essence of morality. But if the ethical law is grounded upon thoughts about God's morality, is it not then grounded upon "some dogmatic representative image of God?" What a strange representative image the author must have of theological dogmatism, to believe that this sort of grounding is philosophically opposed to it. But we see again: The idea of God should be the principle of morality, and [at the same time] should not be. The substitution of divine command for the divine essence takes care of resolving the contradiction.

> God, not as commander but as paradigm of all morality,
> is conjointly the aboriginal source of all human ethical
> doctrine (90).

Now the source is not merely the archetype but rather, as original source, the paradigm as well. We have happily arrived at Plato and Philo.

Since the matter is not put to rest with God as sole principle of morality, human reason rightly makes the fitting transition: "Abraham already observed all ethical law.... His own reason was the source of all ethical teaching" (91). Incidentally, this explanation is insufficient; it depends upon discovery. But even this constitutes no contradiction for the dogmatists. As is ethical law, ethical reason is equally identical with God— the two are the same. For Abraham also, God is the author of morality. But here the connection of the ethical with God means: *The connection to God does not belong to the grounding of the ethical, but to curtailing the ethical.* [58] In turn, therefore, for Lazarus, God does not constitute the ground of the ethical. Connection to God [for him] is not the grounding and never belonged to the grounding. The value and advantage of the ethics of Judaism now supposedly consists solely in its having revealed Kantian ethics prior to Kant (Cf. 95). In view of the ceremonial affirmation, one might have expected some acknowledgement that rediscovery through Kant could have received some recognition by the author. We are obliged to insert a brief exposition of the importance of the principle of autonomy within Kantian ethics. Through this clarification, we hope to protect the ethical principle of Judaism as well as the principle of its dogmatics from distortion.

Summary of translated passages
In the scientific study of ethics, a principle without historical bias was re-

---

58 Lazarus' text has *Einschärfung* (inculcation or impression). Cohen has *Einschränkung* (curtailing).

quired for cultural data to be discovered. Such a principle was the autonomous concept of moral law. Kantian autonomy conceived of the moral individual as a partial manifestation of the principle of unified humankind. This entailed moral legislation that extended over all humankind. Kant's god was the sovereign of the kingdom of morals, who guaranteed the full future realization of law discoverable by moral reason.

[KANTIAN AUTONOMY]

Autonomy is the methodological principle of ethics, as scientific study. In natural science, for example mathematical natural science, a principle of knowledge is indispensable. As a matter of course, there are no objects of nature, let alone natural powers, for scientific study. Rather, powers and bodies have first to be discovered through law. It is implicit to the concept of law that these powers and bodies are not by themselves available, but first must be discovered. They require a principle, or a plurality of principles. Such principles are the principles of natural law.

Most important for *ethical* knowledge is the insight that it must be based upon such a principle. In nature, bodies and powers constitute a forum beyond which there is no appeal. In the ethical realm cultural values, manifestations of morality and so-called psychological experience, comprise such a forum. The principle of autonomy creates the *first* condition for ethical knowledge. It liberates rich historical cultures of nations from prejudice. *Nomos* is not the law, for it is a spokesman for historical prejudice. Who or what is now that "itself" (*Selbst*) which replaces *Nomos*? One does not say reason, for controversy surrounds it. Not the human being or the essence of human beings. All these are expressions of the same problem. The only concept capable of eliminating false law can be the true *concept of law itself.* Autonomy means that the principle of morality is to be the principle of ethical *knowledge*, which is to say the *concept of ethical law.* As the problem of ethics is the problem of ethical law, so the principle of autonomy means the *principle*, the *basic law* of *ethical knowledge.* Ethical laws may not be derived from historical prejudices, nor from disclosures by genies, out of psychological prejudices or out of alleged anthropological discoveries. Rather, ethical laws are to be derived ultimately and exclusively from a principle of knowledge, one which has the power of a principle: namely, to make laws derivative out of it. *The meaning of the principle of autonomy is, accordingly, first of all exclusively methodological: to make the knowledge of ethical law, and thereby of ethics, possible as scientific study.*

Fundamental determinations about concepts are directly connected to this methodological value. These concepts are themselves only expressions for the problem of morality. Accordingly, they achieve a new determination through the new principle. The new concept of law, as the principle for the law, produces a *new concept of ethical reason*. But ethical reason indicates, primarily, the essence of the human being. Therefore, the principle of autonomy results in a *new concept of the human being*. This newness consists in the fact that the human being as bearer of this newly determined practical reason, is recognized more precisely than previously in terms of the creative self-sufficiency of its essence for the benefit of its scientific studies. It also consists of the fact that the human being's objective content is also changed by the concept of this law. Of course, one always must recognize that the human being is not to be alone. The prophets transformed the plurality of human beings into the unity of humankind. But the human being, itself the ethical individual, would be a partial manifestation of this humankind; this insight—thought of not allegorically but strictly conceptually—results from the principle of autonomy. *The concept of the human being becomes the idea of humankind.*

The human being appears to be a natural essence, and as such has the special existence of an individual. That may be the theoretical concept, the natural concept of the human. But the ethical concept of the human being, that it becomes an ethical individual only insofar as the human being is derived from the principle of mankind, would be appropriate to the principle and consistent with it. In this strict sense, the principle of autonomy means the *form of a universal legislation*. The form constitutes the opposite to the *stuff of prejudice*, natural as well as historical. The *legislation* represents the scientific and methodological basic concept of knowledge. No knowledge without law. No law without principle. Therefore, ethical law, as the law of an ethics, as scientific study, must be based upon its *own, pure legislation*.

In terms of content, this pure, general legislation means and vouches for the unlimited validity of the law, the unlimited range of its application; that is, the law is universally applicable. In objective terms this means that humankind constitutes *the range of its application*. The human individual is an ethical individual, only insofar as the human being is derived from the principle of humankind. Humankind is the "kingdom of purpose." For human beings should be the final purpose or their own purpose. Autonomy is conceptually interchangeable with perfection (*Autotelie*). Humankind is the "community of moral essences," and ethical law constitutes the community's system of government in terms of autonomy. *Thus, autonomy determines the concept of the human individual out of the concept of human community.* The human being of ethical autonomy is the individual of humankind.

Does the concept of the human being exhaust and bring to completion the entire concept and problem of the ethical? The relationship of the scientific study of ethics to the *idea of God* depends upon the answer. The acknowledged answer, if not literally in Kant's words then in the spirit/mind and context of his basic concepts, is that the concept of God constitutes a supplement to the scientific study of the ethical. God is *not the principle* of morality. For the principle of any knowledge can only be a principle. As such, it can be, strictly, only a thought which is thought. In religion, it is recognized that God should be more. But even if the God of scientific ethics cannot signify any principle, He does not therefore have to be degraded into a postulate for the benefit of the obstacles of moral-theological casuistry. God is the "sovereign in the kingdom of ethics." As such, however, He not only has something to say but—and which is more—something to accomplish. And not just something, but everything. *The sovereign in the kingdom of ethics means a guarantee: that the laws*, which ethical reason discovers in ethical scientific study and prescribes, *will achieve full reality in the distant future*, and that no opposing skepticism may be allowed to arise to contest them. "As truly as God lives," say the prophets. "As certain as the idea of God is my truth," says the idea of scientific study. Without the idea of God, ethics has no guarantee that its laws are any more than chimeras of methodological knowledge. With the idea of God, ethics provides certainty to itself that ethical law advances reality until the end of days.

This is the significance of the Kantian principle of autonomy. It discovers the human being within humankind. But it does not debase the concept of God. The concept of God is rejected only as the principle, in ethics just as in natural science. Nevertheless, the concept of natural law has by no means taken care of the idea of creation. With the creation of the ethical law, the idea of God may not be excluded from any sort of relation due to the fact that for scientific study of ethics autonomy is fixed as a methodological principle.

Summary of translated passages
Lazarus, Cohen maintained, was unclear about whether autonomous mo-
rality created the moral law, found the law in itself or produced it. Lazarus'
morality was found within the human being, albeit not created by it, and
consecrated as such. Lazarus incorrectly maintained that moral law was au-
tonomous, as it stemmed from the human mind-spirit and was grounded in
man's nature (and as feeling rather than reason). The ethically holy had val-
ue without realization in God, and in fact God became holy through human
beings. Divinity, and the essential connection between morality and God,
thus was eclipsed and compromised. At best, Lazarus' confusion about prin-
ciples of God and the human ended up in a mysticism, where they submerged
into one another. Cohen emphasized that the human was to be viewed as
making itself and becoming holy.

[LAZARUS' ANTHROPOLOGICAL MORALITY]

We now see what the author does to the Kantian principle of autonomy, when he makes autonomy into a thought which is original to the collective mind of Judaism. We cannot enter into the particular distortions, only provide one example. Not once is the categorical imperative cited correctly. Instead of the "universal law," the law "for all" is cited. But we understand what is being corrupted. For Lazarus the "all" means the compilation of individuals. Instead, [for Kant] the individual only emerges out of the collective, out of the community. [For Kant] the community is represented by universal law.

We are concerned here with what the *contradiction between God* and the *human being, as the principle of morality, unveils*:

> Even fully autonomous morality does not create the eth-
> ical law, it does not produce it out of its own freedom or
> even out of its own will. Rather, autonomous morality
> finds the ethical law in itself and recognizes it with in-
> ternal and inflexible necessity. (98)

In the strict sense, autonomy would then be annulled [for Lazarus]. It produces nothing but only finds. And where does it find? In itself. If this means [finding] in the concept of autonomy, then it would rather mean producing.

> The true meaning of the autonomy of ethical law is not
> that man gives it to himself. Rather, that the ethical man
> or the morality in him, and it alone, provides the law. (98)

Even in such ambiguous phrases, it is not the human being itself but the
morality-yet-to-be-produced, which provides the law. But [this is] still,
indeed, "in him." Who is he? The difference between Jewish and Kantian
autonomy [according to Lazarus], is that for Kant the status of the ethical principle persists in autonomy. "In the Jewish mind, consecration is
also suitable to this status" (101). I cannot say "Amen" to this because
the divine principle does not mean merely additional consecration. The
divine principle means total determination by a methodological principle to the extent that such a principle is attributable to religion as distinct from scientific study. The expression "God is the archetype (*Urbild*)
and prototype (*Vorbild*) of all morality" (102) is ambiguous. It would be
correct to say that God means essence and therefore must be valid as the
originator of morality. The innocuous-sounding question: "May a man
not follow a noble prototype?" (102), taken strictly, is not something
one can ask on the grounds of Judaism. In Judaism, God is not the "noble prototype" or "sublime model." This diminishing of the essence and
of the [divine] originator into prototype and paradigm clearly presents
the author's vacillations, whereby he strives to roll the principle of God
over to the human being.

The undefined concept of human spirit indicates another deviation.
"Ethical law is autonomous, because it stems from the essence of the
human spirit/mind and *from it alone*" (104). Therefore, in no way [is this
law] anymore from God.

> All that is relevant here, is that through autonomy, every
> alien will is distanced from the creation of morality. This
> sublime purity and dignity of the ethical is independent
> *of any theistic representative image*. (104)

This is what the collective mind of Judaism is supposed to say?!

The author continues, "Because it stems from the essence of the human spirit itself" (104). What is, then, the essence of the human spirit?
Is it the essence of the individual spirit or the essence of the spirit of

mankind? Does it indicate the psychological nature of the human individual? Or the ethical idea of the human community? *"The ground of the ethical, as said, lies in the nature of man* and in the essence of morality itself"* (115). That the root of the ethical is supposed to lie in the essence of morality is one of many tautologies drifting around in the book's rhetorical dialectic. Be that as it may, the ground of the ethical is expressly placed [by Lazarus] in the nature of the human being. This nature is even thought of, and indicated as, psychologically sensitive: "As the human being distinguishes light and darkness with unavoidable necessity, it also distinguishes between good and evil" (115). The nature of the human being as origin of the ethical, is not only equated with the visual faculty. Rather, autonomy is consigned to general *feeling*, to the sensible expression of what is opposed to the principle of reason. "The feeling of duty is therefore the autonomous source of the ethical overall" (116). The difference between reason, feeling and even impetus—[Gustav] Rümelin [1815-1889] is now elevated to Kant's level—"constitutes a psychological and not an ethical difference" (117). "Regarding the final ground of the principle of morality, one or the other form is suitable to ethical status" (117). Should one not at least be allowed to be concerned with ethical consecration? Is making God into an impetus a matter of indifference? But now the author is the exclusive advocate of the human being. Caught up in the enthusiasm, he even has the *midrash* say: "The human being, as a moral essence, is its own self-creator ("*Ki Tavo*" in *Tanhuma Va'yikra*, ch. 35)" (124). Later, in the context of distinguishing the religiously-holy from the ethically-holy, Lazarus states:

> But the ethically holy can also be thought of as independent of the religious. It has its value and rank in itself, and *therefore without the connection to God* as legislator of morality. The ethical idea lives and is active in itself, *even without the simultaneous insight that it is realized in God*." (196).

The relationship between God and autonomous morality could not be more conclusively dissolved. But is this Judaism?

This corresponds only superficially to Kantian autonomy. "The idea of morality itself is the ground of all good. But the person is its cause" (216). Which person? The person or the personality? The psychological person or the ethical? The ethical community or the sensible individual?

> *Egoism* is necessary, and *not merely a necessary evil but a constituent element*; ... in order to have it, one must acquire it. The same applies to the opposition between individuality and the universality. (343)

Thus in the end, the ethical spirit/mind shrinks by means of feeling and impetus into egoism. But this selfish man is the strict antithesis to the humanistic human being as autonomous inventor of its morality.

We have acknowledged the destructive ramifications of having vague vacillations between God and man serve as a principle for the problem of a Jewish ethical doctrine. At the same time, we must see that the confusion between God and man promotes a mysticism which has never been more than a side road for the collective mind/spirit of Judaism, recognized by leading minds as deviant. Out of the fasting sermon of Isaiah [58:4-12] Lazarus concludes "that even all ethical conduct becomes in turn a symbol, a symbol for surrender to God and submersion into God" (277). Is this Judaism? Is the surrender to God in Judaism the same thing as submersion into God? The interpretation of a *midrash* [cited by Lazarus] in which the main point is pushed into its opposite is explained by the eclectic error of such mysticism: "If you make yourselves holy, so I will reckon it for you" (more correctly, "I will bring it upon you"), "as if you had made Me holy" ("*Im mekadeshim atem atsmehem ma'aleh ani aleikhem ke'ilu kidashtem oti,*" *Torat Kohanim: Kedoshim, Parashah* 1). This sends the author into an authentic paroxysm:

> One can without further ado designate as the boldest, noblest, most blissful and graceful thought, that God who is completely holy is supposedly made holy through men. The *ve-nikdashti* ["I made myself holy"] (Leviticus 22:32, Ezekiel 20:41 and elsewhere) is the highest concept contemplated by the human mind. It is the noblest word spoken by the human tongue. (197-198)

I take exception to the author's style. He manages to blend the grandest expression of religious wonder with the promenade expression of "without further ado." But to the point. The "I have made myself holy" (*ve'nikdashti*) is not the highest concept. Rather the "If you make your-selves holy" (*vehit'kadashtem*) is. This is where the *midrash* places the emphasis, and this is the autonomy according to the *midrash*. In order to elicit the primary condition of morality as such, the *midrash* plays with the essence of God. Mysticism takes this play seriously. Rabbi Aki-va, on the other hand, represents the collective mind/spirit of Judaism with his great statement."Sanctify yourselves, Israel, you who purify yourselves and *before whom you purify yourselves*" ("*Heil Euch Israel, wer reinigt Euch, und vor wem reinigt ihr selbst Euch*") (*Mishnah Yoma* 8:9). That is the autonomy in Judaism. And the reference to "upon the Fa-ther in Heaven" is strictly maintained with this sort of autonomy. God remains in the distance and He does not become an object for [human] submersion. But obviously, this is approximately what Maimonides al-ready said. We shall see what role the author assigns to this systematiz-er of our dogmatics, and thereby to our ethics, in the collective mind/ spirit of Judaism.

Summary of translated passages

Regarding Lazarus' phrase "morals as lawfulness," Cohen distinguished be-tween lawfulness as legality (self-lawfulness) in ethics as scientific study, and lawfulness as divine morality in religion. How the essence of religion related to historical phenomena in the course of time would determine the extent to which the two coincided. Lazarus, Cohen wrote, sacrificed the prin-ciple of developing knowledge to the unified collective mind which continued in terms of stable principles. Cohen's continuity involved distinctions rather than identity, and as such could be comprehensive of a dialectical process.

[LAWFULNESS AND CONTINUITY]

... We would have expected chapter [five, "Moral Improvement is Law-fulness"] earlier. For lawfulness is indeed the concept of ethical law, the concept of autonomy. But obviously, like law, lawfulness constitutes the real difficulty, the real problem. Autonomous lawfulness is *self-legisla-tion*. Judaism, as a religion, does not require this methodological con-cept of ethics as scientific study. Let me offer an analogy. God is mo-rality. Therefore morality, because [it is] equivalent to God, is equiva-lent to lawfulness. Of decisive importance for the ethical estimation of Judaism, in terms of both its historical development and in terms of the relationship of Judaism's essence, as religion, to the appendages to its historical appearances [is]: *the degree and range to which Judaism has located lawfulness near God* as the representative of *self-legislation*. It is precisely according to this standard that lawfulness is to be recognized as morality. But lawfulness as *legality* must be *distinguished* from *morality* precisely according to the degree and range to which Judaism, on the other hand, is supposed to distance itself, or deviate from this leitmotif of self-legislation; and to the extent to which this leitmotif is accessible to Judaism in the vicissitudes of its historical reality, the *most other* fateful error of this book is that it has, in a fawning manner, obliterated this distinction, a distinction crucial for estimating Judaism in terms of the history of general culture.

Perhaps the concept of collective mind/spirit was presented to set this distinction aside. In any case, one of the most important, and relatively most difficult, fundamental concepts of scientific study, the principle of continuity, is usurped for the benefit of the unity of this collective mind/spirit. The principle of continuity thereby becomes victim to the most unintelligible opinion. *The principle of continuity* was considered the ground idea of existence already in ancient philosophy. But ever since Leibniz it has become the tenet of current *mathematics and physics*. Such a ground concept of scientific study obviously passes over into the daily language of general education; it already served especially as a principle of *biology* with Aristotle. It has also done so in contemporary times. From this point on the concept was made into a tenet of *history*. But history is based primarily upon the *principle of development*, which is a valid synonym for continuity both in antiquity and in contemporary times. Without development there is no continuity. Rather, continuity should serve as a *leitmotif* for the sake of growth alone. An advancement should run its course not in terms of chance leaps, but be carried out according to an inner lawfulness: this should bring the continuity to knowledge so that one should not be deceived about the range and depth of development. Development does not remain on the surface area. It rather extends to the deepest grounding of the cultural layer. Without metaphors: Progress does not ultimately refer to nonessential appendages of historical phenomenon; to external forms of presentation. Rather, it primarily denotes essential historical powers. In terms of scientific study, [that means] to principles; in terms of religion, no less than to its ethical bases, to religion's type of principles.

With the "Principle of Continuity," the author wishes to outline "a complete and self-enclosed system of the ethical doctrine of morality of Judaism" (8).

> The unity consists, horizontally, in the continuity of all contemporaries, vertically, through the continuity of the mind, in successive living generations (319).

In spite of the geometrical distinction, the continuity remains in reference to men.

> One may perhaps say without any exaggeration, that the solution to the enigma that the small tribe of Jews has remained alive lies [in] the continuity of the mind/ spirit (22).

That is the continuity of the nation. In what, then, does the continuity of the mind/spirit in the nation consist?

> The weighty significance of the continuity of the mind/ spirit in the activity of the collectivity itself need hardly be referred to, because the entire creative existence of the collectivity is based clearly upon that continuity (329).

But this is indeed the main thing, the real problem: The *continuity of the ground concepts which make up the mind of religion*. But here again, only the "true memory" of the destinies and experiences of the nation is considered to be continuity. Over against this, it should be asked: Do the ethical principles exhibit continuity in the historical development of the religion of Judaism? This question is the best way to bring the principle of continuity to substantive and productive effect, but the book does not pose it. In the book there is no development when it comes to the principles, and therefore no continuity for them. "The principles themselves persevere with equanimity and stability" (49). The author therefore stipulates identity for the principles. He appears to think of continuity in general as identity; in fact, it is a principle which supplements identity. Identity excludes distinction. Continuity, on the other hand, proceeds from variety and seeks to bring the variety under the aspect of lawfulness. If the mind/spirit of Judaism needs something other than historical and substantive knowledge of the principle of continuity, then this presupposition lies at the basis: *That this mind/spirit comes to pass in terms of antitheses.* The extent to which these antitheses remain opposed to one another, or that they harmonize all differences [is unclear]: this question applies to the principle of continuity. The degree to which there ensues a sharpening of antitheses into contradictions on the one hand, and the balancing out of various principles on the other, is determined by the degree and the direction of the application of continuity.

Summary of untranslated passages

Cohen concluded by saying that Judaism distinguished between sacrificial laws/rituals and doctrine. The "hedge" around the law did not determine the "earth" at its center. Although Judaism was an intellectual force in contemporary political struggle, there was still hatred of the Jews. Until the messianic age, the "hedge" had protective value—without having to squelch the aesthetic vitality within it or access to philosophical interpretation. Judaism's intellectual vigor was traceable to the prophets. Their goals were universalistic, rather than particularistic. In their spirit, the "ghetto" of ceremonial law should not be allowed to compromise moral feeling. Customs had to remain subject to doctrine. Lazarus mistakenly claimed that ethical holiness and religious duties and rituals were not distinguishable in Judaism. He was wrong. The pious act of love had always been definable apart from legal usage and ceremony.

Further, while Lazarus distinguished national/particular from human/universal in psychological terms, he was not interested in the ethical/doctrinal difference. And he overlooked the crucial distinction between the priestly and prophetic motifs in Judaism, which extended even into messianic expectations. Finally, he blurred the difference between the Noachide concept of ideal morality, upon which universal justice was based, and the confessional bias to be found in Christianity.

Lazarus, Cohen averred, showed little respect for Socratic-Hellenistic culture. He centered Aristotelian ethics on virtue to human decorum, and claimed that Aristotle's god has none of these assets. In fact, eudaemonia (happiness) was Aristotle's central theme, and his god was raised to a level of sublimity beyond the highest human virtues. Lazarus thought that systematic philosophical thinking was absent from Judaism. The advantage of the Talmud was allegedly its lack of system and logical concepts. Maimonides— for Lazarus little more than an Aristotelian disciple—followed in this vein. But Maimonides rejected the center of Aristotelian ethics, eudaemonia, and

*replaced it with justice as the principle of self-perfection. In any event, Mai-
monides would not have qualified for Lazarus' collective mind of Judaism,
since Maimonides dealt seriously with external thought.*

*Cohen concluded with a hope. While the book sought mass appeal, it arro-
gantly injured the pious feelings toward the greats of Jewish intellectual history
held by the masses. Cohen hoped that the unfavorable consequences of the book
would be limited and passing. But he also hoped that its negative impact would
be overcome by something better and something more correct. Namely, "that
a scientific presentation of our religion would be again ultimately possible for
us; one based on historical research into the sources including 'dogma,' one with
vital and unifying connections with our scientific philosophy."*

Lazarus was offended by the attack. He confided to his friend Sigmund
Maybaum how Cohen had already criticized his *What is the Meaning of
National* while defending Treitschke and his antisemitic *Our Viewpoints*.
Fortunately, the Jews were smart enough and the Christians dignified
enough to remain silent about Cohen's "reckless behavior."[59] Could he
now respond to Cohen's latest assault? He was seventy years old, *The Ethics of Judaism* had received many positive responses, and [he reasoned,]
"who cares if some malicious fool thinks otherwise?" The book could
defend itself—assuming the reader was reasonable, knowledgeable and
in possession of pious discernment. Cohen, judging by the form and
tone of his criticism, lacked the latter attribute. "Were his objection[s]
accurate, and they are not, he would not be speaking in such a common,
sneering manner, devoid of seriousness and dignity. My opponents,
even the most antisemitic ones, have conducted themselves appropriately. They were not out to humiliate me personally. That was left for Cohen," he declared.[60] When Lazarus published the second volume of *The
Ethics of Judaism* in 1911, he alleged that Cohen's criticism, like that of
the Christian [Walter] Bensemer in the *Antisemitic Annual* (1900), was

---

59   Cohen, "Das Problem der jüdischen Sittenlehre: Eine Kritik von Lazarus' *Ethik des
Judentums* [1899]," in *Jüdische Schriften*, vol. 3, 1-35. Originally published in *MGWJ*
43 (1899): 385-400 and 433-449. See also Treitschke, "Unsere Aussichten," *Preussiche
Jahrbücher* 44, no. 5 (1879): 559-576; Lazarus, "Was heisst national" and Cohen, "Ein
Bekenntnis in der Judenfrage [1880]," in *Jüdische Schriften*, vol. 2, 73-100.
60   Lazarus to Sigmund Maybaum, 19 December 1899 and 22 December 1899, with
explanatory notes by Ernst Simon, in Ingrid Belke, ed., *Moritz Lazarus und Heymann Steinthal*,
vol. 1 (Tübingen: J. C. B. Mohr, 1971), 228-232. See Rosenzweig "Hermann Cohens *Jüdische
Schriften*," in *Kleinere Schriften*, 324.

prejudicial in character. Whatever their differences, when it came to *The Ethics*, Cohen and Bensemer were "a pair of faithful brothers" (Horace, *Satires*, vol. II, no. 3, line 243).[61]

Translator's afterword

Cohen's own philosophy of Judaism and ethics emerged over the next twenty years. In "Autonomy and Freedom" he defined religion as the morality which God revealed. Morality which originated in man would eventually lose its value, while God would lose His value unless He was exclusively involved with revealing morality. The pursuit of the divine ideal of ethics/morality made it possible to transcend the limitation of the individual—and also to create a messianic community.[62] In Ethics of Pure Will *(1904) Cohen explored man's liberation from nature through the process which religion provided of transmitting ethical ideals into culture and society. The God-idea guaranteed that the process would be fulfilled.[63] In* Religion and Morality *Cohen spoke of the proph-*

---

61 Lazarus, *Die Ethik des Judentums*, vol. 1, xxxix. I have been unable to verify Bensemer's critique in *Antisemitisches Jahrbuch* (1900). Walter Bensemer was the author of "Beiträge zu einer Geschichte des Blühens und des Niederganges der Juden in Königreich Polen," in *Antisemitischen Jahrbuch* (Berlin: Giese, 1898) and *Beiträge zu einer Geschichte der Juden in Spanien und Portugal* (Berlin: Giese, 1898). Baumgardt observed that in view of the Holocaust, it turns out that it was Cohen, who accused Lazarus of a ghetto approach to Judaism, and not Lazarus, who had the narrow view. David Baumgardt, "The Ethics of Lazarus and Steinthal."

62 Cohen, "Autonomie und Freiheit" in *Gedenkbuch zur Erinnerung David Kaufmann*, ed. M. Brann and F. Rosenthal (Breslau: Schles. Verlags Anstalt, 1900), 675-682. Meanwhile, Cohen's God of belief, the God of *Rosh Hashanah*, remained. See his 1872 letter to Hermann Lewandowski in *Briefe*, ed. Bertha and Bruno Strauss (Berlin: Schocken Books, 1939), 42, as cited by Liebeschütz, "Hermann Cohen and his Historical Background." Leo Strauss related that when a certain Orthodox Jew objected to Cohen's theologizing and asked about his world-creator, Cohen cried—overcome by the unbridgeable cleft between his thought and traditional belief. See *Philosophie und Gesetz* (Berlin: Schocken Books, 1935), 39-40.

63 Cohen, *Ethik des reinen Willens* (Berlin: Bruno Cassirer, 1904), 554-556. Fackenheim referred to this work's radical messianic dimension. Before Cohen, he wrote, Jewish thinkers projected into the future what for Hegel was already implicitly present. For Cohen the future was radicalized, and not a mere reformed version of the present. The future was messianic, and its ultimate ground was to be found not in aspects of the modern world (secular morality, the Protestant spirit, or even philosophical reason), but rather in an explicitly Jewish article of faith See *Ethik des reinen Willens* (Berlin: Bruno Cassirer, 1907 second edition), 407. With this messianism, Fackenheim continued, Cohen dealt aggressively with the relationship of modern Jewish thought to modern thought. Modern philosophy required a foundation which was originally Jewish. Cohen assailed Hegel's maximal self-understanding of the modern world on behalf of the very Jewish messianism which Hegel ignored. See *Hermann Cohen: After Fifty Years* (New York: Leo Baeck Institute, 1969).

ets' moral view, according to which the human being liberated itself from sin through actions. God—whose nature coincided with His moral activity—was the archetype.[64] In The Concept of Reason Out of the Sources of Judaism (1915) Cohen presented the theme that a loving relationship with God is what enabled the sinner to forgive himself and become moral.[65] Finally, in The Religion of Reason Out of the Sources of Judaism Cohen met the challenge of his 1899 critique and presented Judaism in terms of scientific study—basing himself on research into the historical forces. God and man were connected by "correlation," such that God did not abolish the distinction between Himself as creator and His creation, man did not abdicate his independence as a rationally creative being, and morality bridged the points of separation. God guaranteed the realization of His moral ideal in human history, relating to the individual as a point on the path towards the universal goodness of humankind, and to humanity as it proceeded through time towards the messianic future. God's holiness (in the category of being) and man's holiness (in the category of becoming) came closer together in the course of history and ultimately joined in the messianic future—where the trans-sensible moral idea (of eternity) unfolded in history (of time). Cohen pointed to Yom Kippur as an annual moment of this future. Within it, the individual (of time) was purified as all humankind would ultimately be purified (in and of eternity); the day after, history reopened for a year's path into the messianic future.[66]

---

64   Cohen, "Religion und Sittlichkeit: Eine Betrachtung zur Grundlegung der Religionsphilosophie," *Jahrbuch in für jüdische Geschichte und Literatur* 10 (1907): 98-171.
65   Cohen, *Der Begriff der Religion im System der Philosophie* (Giessen: Alfred Töpelmann, 1915).
66   Cohen, *Die Religion der Vernunft aus den Quellen des Judentums* (Leipzig: Falk, 1919). A second edition was published in Frankfurt am Main in 1929.

Chapter Six

THROUGH THE TWENTIETH CENTURY

6.1. THE IMPACT OF EMANCIPATION

With emancipation, territory opened up in between the previously de-marcated autonomous, Halakhically structured Jewish society and the exclusive Christian world. This territory was uncharted, but its fertile, changing ground allowed for the development of *Wissenschaft*, histori-cism, and new points of departure for Jewish thought. They related to the previous mutually exclusive realms, the line between them now hav-ing become hyphenated or even invisible, as they dissolved into neutral territory. The expanding space and the flux within it allowed for a va-riety of different ideological starting points. Modern Jewish thinkers were in agreement about the relative, comparative value of religion (as distinct from construing Judaism as exclusive and absolute), and the existence of historical development and change. They differed about the foundations and optimal starting points of this process, however—al-though the "branches" of their respective "trees" touched one another, and so the thinkers referenced or included differing starting points in the course of developing their respective bodies of thought.

Five sets of points of departure took root. The first sought to rec-oncile revelation (belief) and reason (rationality), by assuming that the dialectical principle was true. The second option, of a humanistic char-acter, based itself in autonomous intellection (Maimon) and self-con-sciousness (Samuel Hirsch, Formstecher). The third grounded itself in heteronomous revelation while addressing the roles of reason and histo-ry. For Steinheim, reason was mutually exclusive with reason (except for critical reason's self-surrender to reason), and history adapted to revela-tion. Samson Raphael Hirsch relegated reason to a service role at the periphery of revelation, and removed it from any potential impact that might emanate from historical progress. Rosenzweig looked upon history as the arena for Christianity to bring the world into the redemption of Israel. The fourth area was that of historical progress. Saul Ascher, on his part, viewed post-Napoleonic history as the determinative ingredient in Judaism's new self-definition, while David Einhorn understood historical progress as the vehicle of reason's access to revelation. Zechariah Frankel spoke of accessing revelation through the historical nation of Israel, while Abraham Geiger referred to Israel's genius for tradition (as the "daughter of revelation"), a concept that re-worked Judaism in terms of building the present from the past, and keeping any specific era from becoming normative. For Graetz, collective history, which defined Jewish identity, was the actualization of the political, religious and reflective parts of an *a priori* idea. Moses Hess moved Jewish history from the ideational realm to focus on the organic development of the Jewish people. In the fifth realm, universal morality, Shadal focused on Judaism as morality rooted in emotion, intended for all mankind. Benamozegh highlighted morality as a unitive force in the world, coinciding with universal revelation and monotheism. Lazarus and Cohen, for their part, conceptualized morality in metaphysical terms, as the key to man's relationship with God, and as having universal, messianic implications—although Cohen held that Lazarus succumbed to ghettoizing Israel's ethical behavior.

6.2. RAV KOOK

For the practical reason of lack of space, I have not included Hasidism and *Kabbalah* in this volume; certainly a comprehensive representation of modern Jewish thought would need to do so. At the very least, however, the renowned *Rav* Kook should be cited. Avraham Yitshak Ha'kohen Kook (1865-1935) was known in his native Latvia for having an exceptional religious mind. He moved to Smargon, Byelorussia at the age of eighteen to join up with *Musar* adherents, and then to the Volozhin yeshiva (Byelorussia) led by Naftali Tsevi Yehudah Berlin. He served as rabbi in Zaumel (Lithuania) and Bauske (Latvia), and in 1904 in Jaffa, Palestine. Caught in Europe when World War I broke out, he served as rabbi in London before returning to Palestine in 1919 to become the Chief Rabbi of Jerusalem. He was appointed Chief Ashkenazi Rabbi of the Land of Israel in 1921.

Kook stipulated a division between the natural and ideal conditions of the human being, frameworks set by God to enable man to strive towards Him. That striving included both ascent and descent (and distance). But this did not discourage the enlightened spirit, who was aware that the universe pulsated with divine energy and who could discern how each retreat included potential for forward movement. Every individual had the capacity to disclose the light of holiness and become aware of the illumination which filled the world. Once this took place, attempts could be made to overcome the deficiencies of profane existence, discern ideals inscribed upon the soul by higher illumination—expressed as moral imperatives—and strive towards moral perfection. Reaction to deficiency and commitment to perfection framed *teshuvah*, which was a penitential act, overcoming alienation from God and returning the Jew to Him as the source of the world. It began with flashes of light which revealed the holiness of a universal soul, diminishing the inherent flaws. The process of removing profane layers of the self was painful, and there were feelings of inadequacy to perform the *teshuvah*. Distance remained, even as holiness flowed into the soul, bringing the moral ideal closer. Through it all, as the human being acted from below, God operated upon the human being from above.

Once *teshuvah* was underway, the individual recognized himself as joined to all humankind in an ocean of sanctified light, each individual contributing a unique identity to a comprehensive harmony. Self-love gave way to participating with unitive existence. Once unified, existence moved towards redemption. For *Rav* Kook, such a movement was in fact beginning to take place in his own time, through settlement in the Land of Israel. There, a holy spirit was bursting forth through those who studied *Torah*. By living in the Land, the impure thoughts of exile were removed and holiness became accessible.[1]

---

1   Avraham Yitshak Kook, *Orot* (Jerusalem: Mosad Ha'rav Kook, 1961), 62, 119-137, 152, 160; "Avodat Elohim," in *Ikvei Ha'tson* (Jerusalem: n.p., 1905/6), 48-69; *Orot Ha'teshuvah* (Jerusalem: Or Etsion, 1970), 19-20, 24-26; "Nafshi Sho'efet," *Sinai* 9 vol. 17, nos. 1-4 (May-August 1945): 8-19; *Orot Ha'kodesh* (Jerusalem: Mosad Ha'rav Kook, 1962/63), vol. 1, 28, 120, vol 2, 568-569, vol. 3, 314-322; *Olat Re'iyah* (Jerusalem: Mosad Ha'rav Kook, 1939), 588; *Arfilei Tohar* (Jerusalem: Ha'makhon Al Shem Ha'rav Tsevi Yehudah Kook, 1982/83), 31-32; *Orot Ha'kodesh*, vol. 3 (Jerusalem: Mosad Ha'rav Kook, 1962/63), 314-322; *Igerot Ha'reiyah* (Jerusalem: Mosad Ha'rav Kook, 1961), vol. 1, 111-114; vol. 2, 292-293.

6.3. METAHISTORY AND HISTORY

6.3.1. *Orthodox Religious Thought and the Holocaust*

The Holocaust transformed the emancipation-world's assumptions of historicism, rationalism and universalism into questions. Indeed, *Wissenschaft* and *Haskalah* were attacked as bearing responsibility for the catastrophe. Hayyim Ozer Grodzinski (Vilnius) and Elhanan Wasserman (Baranowitch), observing how the troubles began in western Europe and moved eastward, cast blame upon the likes of Heinrich Graetz. Mosheh Avigdor Amiel (Tel Aviv) cited Moses Mendelssohn and his successors for obscuring the division between Israel and the nations, thereby precipitating the transformation of latent into actual and implemented hatred. Agudat Yisrael and Mizrahi thinkers held that emancipation-born assimilation evoked divine intervention to have Israel suffer and thereby withdraw from the secular world and back to its *Torah*-true self. Instead of revelation, moral universalism and religious pluralism, they invoked a metaphysical division between holy Israel and profane nations. The emancipation, they contended, had backfired completely, and the deeper Jews penetrated into non-Jewish society, the harsher and more severe the repulsion. For Orthodox Jewish thinkers, the salient departure points that had emerged with the emancipation lost meaning. The humanistic endeavor of probing a dialectical relationship between reason and revelation, or approaching God through intellection or self-consciousness, were eclipsed by the chaos. Any positive role for history in explicating revelation was doubtful. The idea that history (event, process) could be definitive for Judaism was incomprehensible, and that Israel's morality would or could be universalized was an absurdity.

With regard to rationalism, for example, Elhanan Wasserman wrote that any attempt to understand the troubles related to the Holocaust through natural reason would only drive a person insane. Yehezkel Sarna (Jerusalem) and Reuven Katz (Petah Tikvah) could cite no empirical precedents for a rationally comprehensible explanation. Logical attempts in the area of theology were caught up in contradiction. God was transcendent and free, yet necessarily reacted to Israel's sins with punishment. If the people responded to punishment with transformation, Israel's history would not return to the *status quo ante*, before the troubles, but be transformed into redemption. The Nazis were absolutely evil, but the absolutely good God employed them as an instrument.

The catastrophe was a divine response to *Torah*-loss, yet the primary victims were those who were true to *Torah*. God was omnipotent, but once He delegated the power of punishment to Esau, Esau had total control and made no distinction between good and bad Jews.

The world of emancipation with its *Wissenschaft* and historicism, assimilation and rationalism was set aside. So were the philosophical themes which emerged from the process: the dialectical relationship between reason and revelation; intellection and self-consciousness; revelation, to which historical events adapted; universal morality; Holocaust-era thinkers fell silent. But they circumscribed the silence, and entered into metahistorically-grounded religious reflection. The themes included divine presence, secularization, Amalek, *teshuvah*, the suffering of the pious, and the path to redemption. In their search for explanations, and for spiritual vitality itself, the thinkers drew from rabbinic and mystical tradition. Given the extraction of much religious and religious-philosophical thought from the philosophical framework during the Holocaust, the outlines of Orthodox thinking that emerged require our attention.

In Jerusalem, Sarna identified a metaphysical triad of *hurban* (Holocaust), *teshuvah* and *geulah* (redemption), and uncovered its reflection in Israel's metahistory (i.e., the direct relationship between Israel and God according to divine law—as over-against the nation's existence solely according to the laws of nature). The Temple's destruction implanted the potential for redemption, to be actualized with the Holocaust's evocation of *teshuvah*. In Brooklyn, Yosef Yitshak Schneersohn, pairing metahistory with metaphysics, explained that after Israel failed to use the opportunity provided by the exile to repent as God intended, God imposed the choice of *teshuvah* or death through the Holocaust (metahistory). Along with this, the entities of *hurban* and *geulah* interrelated dialectically through *teshuvah*, and *teshuvah* connected one with the other (metaphysics). Israel's atonement on the existential and anthropological (lower) plane reflected the higher reality. Should the lower not be aligned with the higher in time, at the last chaotic moment God Himself would force the alignment to take place.

On some level, the religious thinkers felt assured of God's presence. In Budapest, Aharon Rokeah was convinced that God was manifesting Himself in his own imminent escape in early 1944 to the Land of Israel, and that God's *sefirot* (attributes) would bond with earthly reality in his very person after he arrived there. Sarna asserted that the notion that God's face was hidden (*hester panim*) was but a subjective perception, not an objective fact. God removed Himself only after, and to the extent that man removed himself from God. The (subjective) hiddenness of God's face, it followed, could be overcome only by man himself. God remained present in the sorrow of those who did not turn from Him, weeping and helping them to perform *teshuvah*.

Often, the thinkers blamed other Jews for the disaster. Elhanan Wasserman wrote that the simultaneity of oppression of *Torah*, from within by the Jews themselves through their secularism and from without by the persecutors, was divinely arranged. Israel's religion had deteriorated with the decline of *Torah*-scholarship and assimilation to foreign cultures, and God responded to the decline by thwarting assimilation and punishing the people so as to cause them to change their minds. For example, Shelomoh Zalman Unsdorfer (Bratislava) maintained that during World War II the greatest distress was from heaven. The Jews' troubles were intended to force them to confess their sins and straighten their ways. God brought suffering through the nations, he claims, to evoke *teshuvah*, remove trespasses, and improve the Jewish nation. Once the return was complete, God would renew His protection against suffering. Whatever the level of Esau's animosity, Esau attacked Ya'akov only when *Torah*'s voice diminished—and then only under divine *aegis*. In January 1942, Unsdorfer enumerated the measure-for-measure punishments that had been imposed, which were specific and balanced to a degree possibly only for God to design. Jews were confined to their homes during Christmas, after they had participated in the Gentile Christmas celebrations in former years. They were forced to wear the *Magen David* patch, after they stopped dressing as traditional Jews. They had to mark their stores as Jewish-owned, after they stopped posting *mezuzot* on the doorposts of their enterprises. Even following massive deportations to Poland in the spring of 1942, Unsdorfer spoke of catastrophe in terms of divine response to religious failure. Jews, particularly in Germany, had been intruding into Gentile culture. They incited Esau, and God let the incitement turn into assault. Meanwhile, having left the fold, Jews were no longer protected by the *shekhinah*.

The suffering could be relieved only be restoring *Torah* authority—but it also belonged to a metahistorical process of redemption. If *Torah* was not to be restored, the punishment would turn extreme—whereupon it would be replaced by redemption. The figure of Amalek, Israel's ancient and paradigmatic persecutor with whom God was forever at war (Exodus 17:14-16), was regularly invoked. Earlier thinkers had stressed Amalek's role in the course of divine action in history. God used him to turn the people of Israel back to their authentic *Torah*-selves. As the war progressed this association was overtaken by a stark dualism, whereby the only connection between Israel and Amalek was the latter's homicidal assault upon Israel and subsequent self-destruction while Israel became redeemed.

Teshuvah was identified by the writers of this period as a key to alleviating Israel's plight. In Gateshead, England, Eliyahu Dessler explained that when Jews did *teshuvah* they remained part of God's own moral realm, and thereby blended with the objectively real universe. When they did not, and instead turned away and towards the nations of the world, they descended into disastrous chaos. That was the Holocaust— which for Dessler was a subjective reality. It followed from this logic that the thorough restoration of *teshuvah* would stop the Holocaust. Schneersohn and Sarna, for their part, understood *teshuvah* as a two-tracked dynamic, which unfolded below and above simultaneously. It belonged to a metaphysical triad, along with catastrophe and redemption, but was also enacted on existential and metahistorical levels. As the catastrophic conditions of the Holocaust removed the very ability to perform *teshuvah*, God entered human presence to inspire and enable it. Schneersohn was convinced that existential *teshuvah* would affect historical reality and displace catastrophe with redemption. As to the suffering of the righteous, many believed that God shared in human suffering. In the Warsaw ghetto, Kalonymous Kalman Shapira, overwhelmed by his realization of God's torment, sought to transcend his own agony, which belonged to finitude, in order to touch God's infinite pain. As he achieved this, his physical suffering became absorbed by God. Others identified the suffering with the binding of Isaac (*Akedah*), or with the pains which will precede the birth of the messiah. With regard to redemption, where the thinker's experience of tragedy was direct and the catastrophe was both subjective and objective, the attempt to verbalize the path to salvation was abandoned and in its place silence mediated between present and future. Those distanced by place and/or time were able to articulate the content of the path, some in terms of *Torah* knowledge, others in terms of the Land of Israel.

For these religious thinkers reality was grounded outside history, which had become hopelessly profaned. Religious thought belonged to a-temporal, a-spatial metahistory. There, Hitler became transformed into the metaphysical Amalek. Restoration to *Torah* sanctified Israel's existence and assured life. Suffering, on the other hand, belonged to the *Akedah*. God suffered with Israel, and catastrophe implied redemption.[2]

6.3.2. Historical Civilization: Mordecai M. Kaplan

At the other extreme, the philosopher Mordecai M. Kaplan (1881-1983) rejected the metahistorical framework for a radically historical view of Judaism as an evolving civilization. Born in Svencian, Lithuania, Kaplan was brought to America in 1888, received ordination from the Jewish Theological Seminary, and served as a rabbi until his appointment to the Jewish Theological Seminary in 1909. The religious thinkers in Europe, Palestine and America described above surrendered natural history to Hitler. They turned for grounding and context to the vital sources of their spiritual tradition in order to endure the catastrophe in continued faith and to the metahistorical and metaphysical layers beyond immediate time and space. In America, Kaplan turned away from metaphysics and revelation to the socio-cultural framework and remained within its boundaries throughout the war years and for decades thereafter. His was a philosophy of historical optimism, with little room for Israel's anguish or tragedy, whether psychological, personal or national, or for self-transcendence towards an infinite, wholly other God outside the bounds of reason.

Kaplan identified Judaism as a civilization, a socio-cultural organism, composed of ethnic factors, *Torah* and faith. Ethnicity for him included language, communal institutions and attachment to the Land of Israel. Religious ideas were articulated by, and subject to, these aspects. The *Torah* was not a revealed reality ("*Torah min ha'shamayim*"); the written *Torah* was, rather, a natural creation on the part of prophets, poets and men of wisdom, and the oral *Torah*, also a natural creation, was developed over the generations in concert with the needs of each respective era. Together, they serve as a repository for Israel's

---

2   On Jewish religious thought through the Holocaust see *Wrestling with God: Jewish Theological Responses During and After the Holocaust*, eds. Steven T. Katz, Shelomoh Biderman and Greenberg (Oxford: Oxford University Press, 2007).

law, customs, historical memory, and unifying symbols. In this capacity they direct Israel's economic, political and communal life. Together, they were at once a component of Israel's civilization and the ongoing bearer of its imprint.

For Kaplan, religion was the primary creative power of culture. It centered on faith in God within a naturalistic, functional context. Faced by a world at times inert and liable to disintegration, God provided man with a natural power to overcome the obstacles and develop a full and healthy existence. The emotions (rather than the rational capacities) of faith and trust enabled man to overcome distress and suffering and work towards redemption. God provided the natural power, supporting and strengthening the human quest for life and happiness. He was also the touchstone for the faith and trust that redemption was real and accessible. Kaplan's God was not ontological or metaphysical, He did not create or issue commandments, nor was He providential. He was, rather, the objectification of redemptive power, to which man's purposeful choices were subjective counterparts. The redemption and the happiness it incurred, both of which were assured by God, provided motivation for realizing the moral values upon which civilization rested.

Kaplan's God was a cosmic process—rather than a personal being. He functioned as a power which impelled man to make the best use of life. Faith in God was faith in the existence of a power which furthered human redemption, and faith in a universe so constituted as to urge and help man to reach salvation. These ideas about God related organically to man's self-understanding, and in turn viewed the experience of redemption as the flow of God's strength into man.

Kaplan rejected supernatural elements—such as miracles, reward and punishment, and supernatural revelation. These had proved broken and false, he declared, and also were harmful, because they diverted the people of Israel from heightening their national life—and in addition shut Israel off from potentially positive influences from other cultures.

While the majority of religiously oriented thinkers throughout the Holocaust era rooted themselves in metaphysical realities, surrendered natural human explanation to silence or revealed sources, and then removed Israel from the (profane) nations, Kaplan naturalized theology and confined religious experience within the parameter of evolving historical civilization. There, culture dominated idea, and human values and development controlled the God-man dialectic. Kaplan's thought was not a return to the *status quo ante*, namely of Jewish thought of the nineteenth century. His God was neither a source for revelation nor for absolute morality. Nor the infinite intellect nor the higher ground for freedom. Rather, Kaplan's God belonged to a process which enabled man to make the best of life. Accordingly, a century and a half after its inception he returned to the original landscape of the emancipation, to define a new point of departure for Judaism, one of absolute humanism and functional divinity.[3]

6.3.3. Metahistory-History
Leo Baeck

There were figures who integrated metahistorical grounding with historical reality, or alternately moved from one to the other. Leo Baeck (1873-1959), who received rabbinical ordination at the *Hochschule für Wissenschaft des Judentums* in Berlin and studied philosophy at Breslau and Berlin universities, was the leading rabbinical figure in Germany until the Second World War. He was interned in Theresienstadt from1943 until 1945. Upon liberation he served in London as president of the Council of Jews in Germany (1945-1948) and then as professor at Hebrew Union College in Cincinnati. Baeck subscribed to the ethical monotheism of Hermann Cohen—who considered Baeck his greatest disciple. He posited that the essence of Judaism was morality (marked by justice, humaneness and peace), and that insofar as it was revealed by the one deity, the universal and absolute character of the essence was assured. The people of Israel, deeply committed to God's moral law by reason of their having been elected to receive divine (moral) revelation, accepted the mission to mediate between unity, infinite and eternal and the finite and transient, and to spread the moral ideal throughout society. God remained the source of the ethical command, as well as of Israel's faith as it led the advance towards redemption. Indeed, Baeck declared, God was

---

3   On Kaplan, see Schweid, "Levatim Shel Emunah U'kefirah," in *Toledot Ha'hagut Ha'yehudit Ba'meah Ha'esrim* (Tel Aviv: Dvir, 1990), 259-266; "Ha'yahadut Ke'tsivilizatsiah Veha'dat Ke'ehad Mi'markivenah: Ha'filosofiah Ha'rikonstruktsiyonistit-Ha'tsiyonit Shel Mordekhai Kaplan," in *Toledot Filosofiyat Ha'dat Ha'yehudit Bi'zeman Ha'hadash* (Tel Aviv: Am Oved, 2006), 363-367; and "The Restoration of Judaism out of Secular Culture," in *The American Judaism of Mordecai Kaplan*, eds. Emanuel S. Goldsmith, Mel Scult and Robert M. Seltzer (New York: New York University Press, 1990), 35-52; Ira Eisenstein, "Kaplan as Liturgist," in *The American Judaism of Mordecai Kaplan*, 324-325.

present in the world as the source for the spirit of holiness with which His absolute moral commandment was received.

Baeck identified the prophet as key to this process. The prophet experienced God's presence, apprehended reality as unitive, and received the moral commandments as flashes of lightning which broke through clouds surrounding a divine mystery. The experience was mystical, yet without breaking away from earthly life. Once it took place, Baeck avowed, the prophet understood the world from the perspective of divine eternity, yet in the here and now. The prophet was then to emanate the intimacy with God towards others, and shed his own inspiration upon them. Each Jewish individual should feel as though he stood at Sinai, sharing the direct experience of the prophet, and the prophet's destiny of ethical-religious divine service, to the extent of his own power. The prophet also encapsulated the special Jewish genius, a creative power which renewed Jewish history. Jewish history was one of organic life cycles wherein, empowered by God's grace, the single deed was ever reborn anew. It was the prophet who provided the break that allowed a new point of view to emerge. Through the prophet, each age of Jewish history interwove its heritage with what was most relevant to itself, self-conscious yet remaining within a continuum—albeit with the inner limit of *Torah* revelation, given once and remaining stationary amidst the change.

As the people of Israel mediated between revelation and society, and the prophet mediated between God's eternity and Jewish history, Jewish history itself was a form of mediation. Dispersed Israel integrated into cultures and isolated itself, moved into society, contributed to the world and returned within itself, absorbing the best of other cultures, on an ongoing basis. Baeck remained committed to this process throughout the catastrophe of World War II. To him, the emancipation was a success—assimilation being a necessary first step to counter particularism, which would be balanced out by new creativity from within. Such integration was indispensable to Israel's universal mission of advancing ethical monotheism throughout the world—a mission destined to succeed, given its absolute character. By distinguishing Nazi anti-Semites from the majority of German society, Baeck was able to affirm the theme of Israel's mediating relationship to the world as a means towards universal morality.

For Baeck, the Holocaust was a *caesura* in human progress towards the messianic redemption. It belonged, however, to the episodes of suffering which marked Israel's history. The Jewish soul inevitably confronted a choice between political-earthly realities and divine, eternal presence, and the choice for the eternal meant suffering and sanctification of God's name in death. Episodic suffering and sanctified death were constants in Israel's history, but so was survival. Israel ever vanished and reappeared, following its line towards the divinely directed end, he professed. The ethical imperative involved suffering and martyrdom, and the Jew had to be prepared to fulfill his moral responsibility, to surrender will and life for God's command. With sanctification of God's name, the Jew testified against antisemitism and for the truth of human redemption.

Throughout the Holocaust, Baeck shed light on the role of the cyclical and mediating nature of Jewish history, and the role of episodic suffering in Israel's mission. By doing so, he assumed this role for himself. As he shed the light of hope amidst the suffering, he enacted the faith provided by God's presence, and became an impetus to Israel's renewal. Baeck did not retreat from history to metahistory. He was convinced that post-emancipation history remained the arena for the advance of the world under Israel's leadership. Just as the mystical experience of the prophet was bounded by earthly life, the Hermann Cohen-defined metahistorical drama of divinely-revealed morality remained immanent to history.[4]

Eliezer Berkovits

Eliezer Berkovits (1908 Romania – 1993) studied at the Hildesheimer

---

4   My summary is based primarily on Eliezer Schweid, "*The Essence of Judaism* to *This People Israel*: Leo Baeck's Theological Confrontation with the Period of Nazism and the Holocaust," in *Wrestling Until Day-Break: Searching for Meaning in the Thinking on the Holocaust* (Lanham, MD: University Press of America, 1994), 3-84. See also Leo Baeck, *Der Sinn der Geschichte* (Berlin: Carl Habel, 1946). I am grateful to Albert H. Friedlander (a disciple of Baeck) for the gift of this rare pamphlet. See also Meyer, "The Thought of Leo Baeck: A Religious Philosophy for a Time of Adversity," *Modern Judaism* 29 no. 249 (1999): 107-117; Friedlander, *Leo Baeck: Teacher of Theresienstandt* (New York: Holt, Rinehart and Winston, 1968); Hans Liebeschütz, "Judaism and the History of Religion in Leo Baeck's Work," *LBIY* 2 (1957): 8-20; Altmann, "Theology in Twentieth Century German Jewry," *LBIY* 1 (1956): 193-216; and Fackenheim, "In Memory of Leo Baeck and Other Jewish Thinkers in 'Dark Times': Once More, After Auschwitz, Jerusalem" in *The Philosopher as Witness: Fackenheim and Responses to the Holocaust*, eds. Michael L. Morgan and Benjamin Pollock (Albany: SUNY Press, 2008), 3-14.

Rabbinical Seminary in Berlin and the University of Berlin, escaped Germany in 1938, served as communal rabbi in Leeds, Sydney and Boston, and from 1958-1975 taught philosophy at the Hebrew Theological College in Chicago. In 1975 he moved to Jerusalem. Over the course of the Holocaust, he wrote, God's relationship to Israel within history moved to the metahistorical boundary at history's edge. In response to God's hiddenness, Jews of the catastrophe emulated the pure faith of Abraham (*emunah*), who obeyed the command of *Akedah* and prepared Isaac for sacrifice—despite the covenantal promise that his seed would grow into a great nation. The *emunah* of Jews of the Holocaust, enacted as *mitsvah*, took place despite the absence of any assurance that a Jewish community would survive, to bring vitality to the *mitsvot* offered to it. Through and in *emunah* and *mitsvah*, the people of Israel remained suspended in metahistory. With the creation of the state of Israel, history was retrieved out of the depths for Israel, and raised up to the very level of metahistory.[5]

Emil Fackenheim

The philosopher Emil Fackenheim (1916-2003) attended the *Hochschule für Wissenschaft des Judentums* to prepare for the rabbinate, and studied philosophy at the University of Halle. His study was cut short in 1939, when he was taken to Sachsenhausen. But he was able to leave Germany, and he found a home in Toronto, Canada. He received a degree in philosophy from the University of Toronto in 1945, and served as professor until the early 1980's, when he moved to the Land of Israel. Fackenheim held that the Jewish people were the first to affirm the God of history—whereupon they bound their collective survival to Him. Jewish faith meant affirming God's connection to history and remaining with God, who maintained the people of Israel throughout exile and into redemption (the covenant).

God's presence at Auschwitz was not fathomable theologically, and the covenant was inaccessible. But God was not, not there. From above, His voice commanded Jews to survive. From below there were those

---

5   Eliezer Berkovits, *Faith After the Holocaust* (New York: Ktav, 1973); *Crisis and Faith* (New York: Sanhedrin, 1976); *With God in Hell: Judaism in the Ghettos and Death Camps* (New York: Sanhedrin, 1979); David Hazony, "Introduction," in Berkovits, *Essential Essays on Judaism*, ed. David Hazony (Jerusalem: Shalem, 2002): ix-xxxvi.

who comprehended the Nazi logic-of-destruction, their attempt to erase all sanity, Jewishness, life and reason. It was a comprehension at once outside all relation (for all relation had turned destructive) and receptive to the imperative from above to resist the Nazi logic. The voice from above and the transcending comprehension from below met, realizing absolute transcendence in the midst of time as *tikunim* (literally, "mendings")—metahistorical signs including vestiges of Jewish observance, the *tekiah* of a *shofar* at Hasag-Skarysko, and the Warsaw ghetto revolt.

Tikunim continued in the years following the catastrophe. The Jewish survivors remained alive, because after the Nazi celebration of death, life itself acquired sanctity. They remained Jewish, because after Auschwitz Jewish survival became sacred testimony on behalf of life and love. Because the voice was heard in Auschwitz, it could be heard again and obeyed later. The traces of God's presence which had touched the eyes of the Auschwitz realm as *tikunim* found collective expression in political sovereignty. The God of history began His full return. This opened a threshold to metahistory, and its redemption. The voice of the redeemer was not, and would not ever be, heard from Auschwitz. But now perhaps it could be heard in the Land of Israel. Having identified points of divine presence at the edges of the death camp and having found instances where these points touched historical reality thereafter (*tikunim*), Fackenheim perceived an opening for the covenant and for messianic hope.[6]

---

6   Greenberg, "Metahistory, Redemption, and the *Shofar* of Emil Fackenheim," in *The Philosopher as Witness: Fackenheim and Responses to the Holocaust,* eds. Morgan and Benjamin Pollock (Albany: SUNY Press, 2008), 207-223; Morgan, "The Central Problem of Fackenheim's *To Mend the World," Journal of Jewish Thought and Philosophy* 5, no. 2 (1996): 297-312; *The Jewish Thought of Emil Fackenheim: A Reader*, intro. by Morgan (Detroit: Wayne State, 1987); *Emil L. Fackenheim: Philosopher, Theologian, Jew* eds. Sharon Portnoff, James A. Diamond and Martin D. Jaffe, foreword by Elie Wiesel (Leiden: Brill, 2008).

Fackenheim was intent upon recapturing the Jewish thought of the nineteenth century for the English readership, and asked me to provide lengthy translations for publication in the Behrman House series in Jewish studies (following volumes by Isador Twersky, Yosef Dan, Ruth Wisse, Meyer, and Marshall Sklare). It took longer than anticipated—and by the time the work was ready, Behrman House had terminated the series. A new publisher could not be found. Voicing his frustration at the summer 1989 workshop in the study of Jewish philosophy at Moshe Davis' International Center for the Study of Jewish Civilization, Fackenheim spoke of an absurd situation. American publishers and Jewish studies instructors responded, that as the texts were hardly known (those who cited them often never read them), there was no need to know them! Nor would the book sell. Thus the world of these

6.4. EXISTENTIALIST THOUGHT

6.4.1. Martin Buber

Buber (1878 Lvov – 1965 Jerusalem) studied under his grandfather Shelomoh Buber, the rabbinics scholar, at the universities of Vienna and Berlin, and immigrated to Palestine in 1938. Buber did not seek to construct a philosophical system, but to draw from the prophets in order to articulate a dialogical philosophy in the context of existential reality. Rather than starting from Plato, with his abstract, general and timeless concept of the truth, he looked to the prophets, who had received messages for particular historical situations that could be re-created and applied over history (see Kaplan). Buber's philosophical concern was not for any systematic body of thought, but with mediating between "I-It" knowledge and "I-Thou" knowledge (see Fackenheim). He viewed himself not as a professional philosopher but as a prophetic educator (see Schweid).[7]

As portrayed by Eliezer Schweid, Buber looked to the prophets' testimony for the authentic presence of a transcendent divine personality. They were certain that the voices they heard and their visions came not from themselves but from another living being—God Himself. The intensity of the experience transformed their lives from egoistic concern to devotion to the mission placed upon them by the Almighty. A love for God awakened within them, greater than their love for themselves, and they could not resist the influence that flowed into them. The experience was dialogical, between the self-conscious subject (the prophet)

---

thinkers, already eclipsed, was poised to enter oblivion for the English-speaking academic establishment. The sources for changing a cyclical confinement to well-known twentieth-century thinkers would be gone and the history of modern Jewish thought left with a black hole (His taped remarks are held at the Center's office at Hebrew University). Fackenheim would not live to see whether the entrenchment of currently dominant scholarship in this field was too deep for the publication of the sources in this present volume to have any real impact. See *Jewish Philosophy and The Academy*, eds. Fackenheim and Jospe (Cranbury, NJ: Associated University Presses, 1996).

7   Kaplan, "Buber's Evaluation of Philosophical Thought and Religious Tradition," and Fackenheim, "Martin Buber's Concept of Revelation," in *The Philosophy of Martin Buber*, eds. Paul Arthur Schilpp and Maurice Friedman (LaSalle, IL.: Open Court, 1967), 249-272, 273-296. See also Schweid, "Ha'shivah El Ha'shitim Ha'nitshiyim: Ha'mifgash Bein Ha'am Le'elohav: Ha'filosofiah Ha'datit Shel Martin Buber," in *Toledot Filosofiyat Ha'dat Ha'yehudit Bi'zeman Ha'hadash, Helek* 3 (Tel Aviv: Am Oved, 2005), 60-95.

and the divine subject who emerged from hiddenness in expectation of a human response. It was meta-psychological (not to be explained in terms of the soul's activity) and meta-philosophical (not of man's rational initiative). But it was not mystical, for it entailed the practical reality of doing God's will on earth. The experience was free: The transcendental "I" turned freely to the human "Thou," and the individual "I" responded freely to the divine "Thou." This inter-subjective event was one of direct encounter (not a matter of objective knowledge), and it was to be available to all.

Buber distinguished two aspects of human experience, the "I-Thou" and the "I-It" relations. With the former, the self and the other were for each other (subject-subject). With the latter, the other was for the self but the self was not for the other (subject-object). Human consciousness was dual, and the two were complementary, each the butterfly to its own chrysalis. It was not possible to live always in the I-Thou; the two would inter-relate, with a remnant ever unreachable by unifying consciousness.

There was, however, an antecedent dialogue, one between the man who came into existence and longed to realize his temporal being (in terms of "butterfly" and "chrysalis") and the eternal God who created him. In the depths of consciousness lay a fixed dialogue between creature and creator, for an eternal attachment to the transcendental being lay within the depth of man. The dialogue between man and man, between man and nature, and the dual aspects of consciousness could provide a "skylight" to this connection. But to access that deeper dialogue, divine *hesed* was needed. *Hesed* was the "ladder" set on earth from above for man to ascend, from mediated encounters to the immediate meeting with God. There was a hidden source within man, enabling him to reach the transcendent, a subconscious point of absolute experience of mutuality—symbolized by God.

Man, unconscious of what was hidden, could not initiate this deeper dialogue. God, however, did turn to man at times to shake up the subconscious and raise the creature-creator bond out of the depths and into consciousness. This meeting, a moment of prophetic-like revelation, took the form of becoming conscious of a demand of absolute trust in the presence of the being which made the demand. Every person was born with the possibility for such a demand—indeed, none was ever free from it.[8] Fackenheim explained that the revelatory dialogue opened by God did not communicate any content, but rather God's presence. God was within what He revealed and communicated, translated into the (humanly articulated) commandment. The God who commanded was given to man with the commandment. Each such revelation was unique to the situation, momentary and new; God's self-disclosure could not be anticipated by any universal criteria.[9]

Mindful of the eternal dialogue between God and man, how was any Holocaust possible? For Buber, whereas in the realm of nature divine revelation was constant, there were times in history when God became eclipsed because of human failure. This was so in modern times, when man lost the ability to relate to or seek God. But there were times when God also hid His face. There was silence from the perspective of Being itself, an absence of direct divine revelation in history. Nevertheless, the divine Thou was not to be deduced from nature or history, and the antecedent, primordial relation with the absolute other, the dialogical constitution within man, endured. Buber called for trust in God and His companionship despite the insecurity about the metaphysical bonding. One must confront God's silence and yearn for His voice, remain (however pained and doubting) within the bounds of faith; keep the channel to God open and be ready for possible revelation (even one of hiddenness or silence). That is to say: The God of dialogue was within the man who related to God, and one could and must burst forth from the eclipse and the hiddenness of God, to the extent of reflecting the metaphysical bonding existentially, unclear as the reflection may be. One must continue to live as if the bond with the transcendental God endured—if only because nothing was to be gained by not doing so. To the contrary, to lose faith was to lose one's humanity, and thereby surrender to anti-humanity.[10]

---

8   My description of Buber's thought in this section is drawn from Schweid, "Ha'shivah El Ha'shitim Ha'nitshiyim."
9   See Fackenheim, "Martin Buber's Concept of Revelation," in *The Philosophy of Martin Buber*.
10   David Forman-Barzilai, "Agonism in Faith," *Modern Judaism* 23, no. 2 (May 2003): 156-179. See also Berkovits, "God's Silence in the Dialogue According to Martin Buber," *Tradition* 11, no. 2 (1970): 17-24; and Berkovits, *A Jewish Critique of the Philosophy of Martin Buber* (New York: Yeshivah University Press, 1962).

6.4.2. Abraham Joshua Heschel

Abraham J. Heschel (1907 Warsaw – 1972 New York), a descendant of Hasidic masters, studied at the *Hochschule für Wissenschaft des Judentums* (Leo Baeck was one of his teachers) and received a doctorate at the University of Berlin for a dissertation on prophecy. He was appointed to succeed Martin Buber to direct the *Jüdische Lehrhaus* (FaM) in 1938, but in October of that year he was deported to Poland. He taught at the Warsaw Institute of Jewish Studies until six weeks before the Nazi onslaught (September 1939). He then found refuge at the Hebrew Union College in Cincinnati, from where he went to the Jewish Theological Seminary in 1945.

The essence of Heschel's religious (philosophical) thought was the existential, psychological relationship between God and man. God was a living reality, passionately interested in His creatures; man was challenged to transcend egoistic interests and respond to His imperatives. God's existence could not be proven scientifically, and the encounter was not a subject for *Wissenschaft* or for (solipsistic) human reason. God was not the object of human understanding; God was rather the subject of which man was the object. Thinking of God was to think from within Him, analogous to how a thought in man's mind would feel if it had self-consciousness. For any encounter with God to take place, the soul had to be aware that divine reality was not grounded in the human mind, but open to the ineffable. Furthermore, one must be conscious that the human mind was itself a mystery, and that the conscious self was an expression of something never fully expressed.

Such an encounter could be found in Hebrew Scripture, where God revealed Himself to the prophet. The prophet knew God directly and intimately, and so disclosed His relatedness to Israel, sharing an inner identity with God's *pathos* with others. That is, the God who was emotionally affected by man, moved by what happened in the world, who transcended the gulf separating Himself from man through His emotion. The prophet was aware that man could not escape the field of God's concern, and was forever sheltered within God's care. For his own part the prophet, aware of God's stake in the human condition, made God's concern his own.

This encounter also comes to light in accounts of Rabbi Akiva. In *Heavenly Torah as Refracted Through the Generations*, Heschel offered a typology of religious experience, contrasting Rabbi Ishmael with Rabbi Akiva. For Ishmael, the *Torah* was a source of wisdom, centered on insight about God's will. Ishmael did not overcome the separation between God and man, which was created by limiting God to the boundaries of the human mind. And Ishmael's *Torah* was earth-bound; the righteous were rewarded and the wicked were punished in this world—such that sin was expiated through suffering, while suffering without sin led to protest against God. For Akiva, the *Torah* was a source for forging a direct relationship between God and man. His encounter with God was spiritual and passionate, beyond the intellect; it was intimate, even mystical. He intuited the merciful God, who participated in, and was affected by, Israel's suffering. Reward and punishment extended beyond this world; when the righteous suffered, there was assurance of greater reward in the world to come. At the same time, God suffered with the sufferer, so that suffering was a channel for intimacy with God, and martyrdom to loving God.

Heschel began with God, who needed man for dialogue in order to participate together in activities of creation. He needed man to perform His *mitsvot* so that He could lead history. God needed man, that is, in order to be God. The need placed a heavy burden upon man—who wished to be independent but was now responsible for satisfying God's needs. To avoid responsibility, to rationalize resistance to serving God, man would sometimes fall back on the complaint that God failed to respond to prayer, or claim that there was no evidence of God's leadership in the world. Yet this left him lonely, devoid of purpose, and discontented, with a pseudo-independence. Seeking refuge, man then looked to faith, and sought consolation for the suffering and evil which surrounded him. But to turn to God in this way, which meant to serve one's own needs, only undermined faith. Faith was a matter of assuming responsibility in terms of serving God. Faith required a turn from interest in self-development to a commitment to fulfill the Almighty's needs. In turn, for that to happen one had to recognize those moments when one hid within one's ego from God, guilty at the failure to serve Him. Through faith, however, it was possible to transcend the self as well as its search for assistance from above, and to accept both moral responsibility for one's actions and the task of participating with God in creation. Then God's voice, searching for man, would be heard, the presence of God known. Consequently, one would understand that the search for God was a response to God's search for the one. Through this, man would come to testify to God's presence within the human heart, and to His leadership of history.

The Holocaust was at once a challenge to, and affirmation of, Heschel's probe into the God-man encounter. That encounter was grounded in God's ongoing presence in human experience, in the presence of man within the field of divine perception, and in God's stake in humanity through Israel. But for Heschel, the attempts to challenge these realities, to ask how God could have allowed the Holocaust, was a symptom of the catastrophe's very cause. There was a Holocaust, he believed, because mankind turned from God, because western civilization had become morally callous and spiritually vacuous. God was to be seen as the subject, searching for man, so that man would be inspired to live up to God's expectations. Instead, He had been objectified to the ego-centered human subject. When man fled from God, God abandoned man. To persist in repudiating God, in effect to exile Him, prolonged the catastrophe. Instead, having been responsible for the tragedy, man was also responsible for turning to God—a God whose essence had never been absent and who longed for man's return. For Heschel, this had already happened within the Holocaust itself. As Israel died at Auschwitz, as Isaac's blood was being shed, the faith of collective Israel survived—as with Rabbi Akiva, finding loving intimacy with God through suffering and death.[11]

---

11 Heschel, *Man is Not Alone. A Philosophy of Religion* (New York: Farrar, Straus and Giroux, 1951); *God in Search of Man: A Philosophy of Judaism* (New York: Farrar, Straus and Cudahy, 1955); *Israel: An Echo of Eternity* (New York: Farrar, Straus and Giroux,1969); *Heavenly Torah as Refracted Through the Generations*, trans. Gordon Tucker and Leonard Levin (New York: Continuum International Publishing, 2005). On Heschel see Berkovits, "Dr. A. J. Heschel's Theology of Pathos," *Tradition* 6, no. 2 (1969): 67-104; Eliezer Schweid, "Teologiah Shel Shiva," in *Toledot Ha'hagut Ha'yehudit Ba'meah Ha'esrim* (Tel Aviv: Dvir, 1990): 365-367; and "Netivat Moreshet Merkezei Ayropa Ha'nehravim Be'artsot Ha'berit: Hitpathut Mishnat Leo Strauss U'fetihat Ha'mishnot Shel Yosef Dov Soloveitchik Ve'avraham Yehoshua Heshel," in *Toledot Filosofiyat Ha'dat Ha'yehudit Bi'zeman Ha'hadash* (Tel Aviv: Am Oved, 2006), 421-429; Edward K. Kaplan, "Confronting the Holocaust: God in Exile," in *Holiness in Words: Abraham Joshua Heschel's Poetics of Piety* (Albany: SUNY, 1996), 115-131; Robert Eisen, "A. J. Heschel's Rabbinic Theology as a Response to the Holocaust," *Modern Judaism* 23, no. 3 (October 2003): 211-225; Fackenheim, "Review of God in Search of Man," *Conservative Judaism* 15, no. 1 (1960): 50-53; Morris M. Faierstein, "Heschel and the Holocaust," *Modern Judaism* 19, no. 3 (1999): 255-261.

6.4.3. Joseph Dov Soloveitchik

Joseph Dov Soloveitchik (1903 Pruzhany, Belarus – 1993 Boston) studied *Talmud* with his father Mosheh, graduated from the Dubno *Gymnasium*, and studied at the Free University of Warsaw (1924) and the University of Berlin. He received his doctorate for a dissertation in the epistemology and metaphysics of Hermann Cohen in 1932. Arriving in America that same year, he served as rabbi in Boston and, beginning in 1941, as professor of *Talmud* at Yeshiva University. The instruction of *Halakhah* as a pure discipline was his primary concern, but he also prepared a series of texts for the wider audience—albeit without composing a full philosophical system: *Halakhic Man (Ish Ha'halakhah*, 1944 and 1983), *The Halakhic Mind* (1944 and 1986), *Kol Dodi Dofek* (1961) and *The Lonely Man of Faith* (1965).

Soloveitchik delineated two sides to the human personality, identified in Genesis 1 as the majestic man and the man of faith. The first was the Adam created in God's image, man and woman together, to be fruitful, to subdue the earth and have dominion over all living beings ("Adam the first"). This Adam was a creator within the world, the user and controller of the earth. He was result-oriented, interested in practical success, his dignity came from taming the environment and he was intent on showing his (outer) accomplishments to the community. His personality was aggressive, bold and social. Faith entered in, but only when he encountered limits in the scientific laboratory. When in need of something more, he looked to God—not on God's terms but on his own. He fit God in, on the Sabbath, and expected something in exchange for his prayer. Faith, that is, was a matter of manipulation.

"Adam the second" was formed of the dust of the ground by God, who breathed life into his nostrils to become a living soul. God placed man into the garden of Eden to serve and keep it. This Adam was enveloped by the mystery of existence, concerned not about the "How?" and the function, but about the "Why?" and the essence. ("Why did the world come into existence? What was its purpose?") God followed him, uninvited, and vanished into the transcendent realm as soon as he turned around to look at Him. He saw God's commandment in every aspect of life and wanted only to serve Him, trusting that by observing the *mitsvot* he would have all he needed for life. He belonged to a covenantal community, together with others dedicated to serving God. Receptive in personality, he perceived the world in its own terms, respecting nature and cultivating it. Faith for this second Adam was an explosive experience, all-encompassing and expressive of all his hopes, fears and desires. It was a matter of eternity's intrusion into time and the natural order, and was drawn from the absolute, redeeming one from time and historical change. The man of faith confronted God in his own uniqueness, a singularity which could not be shared with or expressed to others. The assertion of one's full individuality enabled one to know God, while the confrontation with God was possible only through one's uniqueness.

The two Adams were essential to God's creation, but in the modern world the dual personality relationship was perverted because the role of the man of faith was smothered. The covenantal community was suppressed and the second Adam thrown into isolation, marginality and loneliness. In the modern world, only the majestic man had credence. The man of faith had nothing to say in a society which was technical, self-centered, narcissistic, materialistic and of the "here and now" only. While Adam the second had become irrelevant, however, Adam the first was left frustrated. For majesty and dignity extended to the spiritual world, and moral and aesthetic success required reaching into the beyond. To become complete, majestic man required experience of transcendental reality.

There were ways to restore and maintain the balance. This was the way of "Halakhic man." *Halakhah* for Soloveichik was concerned with resolving theoretical problems which arose from daily experience, and applying the solutions to life—although the process belonged essentially to following *Halakhah* for its own sake. *Halakhah* resolved practical problems from the perspective of *Torah* revelation, which was the ideal plan from the perspective of the creator—and daily life was to be viewed in terms of that ideal. The halakhic man approached realities in terms of the higher, objective truths. He sought to actualize what was potentially desirable in available experience according to the creator's plan as articulated in *Torah* and *Halakhah*. While utilizing the wisdom offered by science, the halakhic man drew that wisdom into the range of revelation—thereby rising above limited, subjective human reason, towards transcending wisdom, to the objective truth with which the world was created. In the process of applying the ideal to the real, in actualizing the potential, the halakhic man channeled inner belief into real time-space events and objectified subjective faith with deeds. He directed himself to the same earthly reality as the majestic man, but did so to raise human behavior towards ideal moral standards. He applied the *a priori*, divinely given *Halakhah* to concrete reality, objectifying activities by raising them to principles and patterns belonging to objective cognition—ultimately grasping human reality in terms of the thoughts of creation. The halakhic man belonged to both the covenantal and majestic communities, uniting them without annulling their natural tension. They unified through him to serve God, to participate with God in completing his creation.

Recognizing the tenuous character of the halakhic man's synthetic effort, Soloveitchik also spoke of a source to strengthen it: *Teshuvah* (repentance). Out of Adam the first and Adam the second, the *Ish Ha'teshuvah* forged the highest unity, the most perfect individual. *Teshuvah* provided the man of faith and halakhic man with the strength to endure; it bridged the two tracks of life on the existential level, and was able to bring a mending to life, internal and external, which even the halakhic man could not reach.[12]

---

12   Schweid, "Netivat Moreshet Merkezei Ayropah Ha'nehravim Be'artsot Ha'berit: Hitpathut Mishnat Leo Strauss, U'fetihat Ha'mishnot Shel Yosef Dov Soloveitchik Ve'avraham Yehoshua Heshel," in *Toledot Filosofiyat Ha'dat Ha'yehudit Bi'zemen Ha'hadash, Helek 4: Ha'hitmodedut Im Hithavut Merkezei Yahadut Hadashim Be'erets Yisrael Ube'artsot Ha'berit* (Tel Aviv: Am Oved, 2006), 412-421; and "Teologiah Shel Shiva," in *Toledot Ha'hagut Ha'yehudit Ba'meah Ha'esrim* (Tel Aviv: Dvir, 1990), 373-380. See also Eugene Borowitz, "The Typological Theology of Rabbi J. B. Soloveitchik," *Judaism*, vol. 15 (1966): 203-210; Lawrence Kaplan, "Rabbi Joseph Soloveitchik's Philosophy of Halakhah," *Jewish Law Annual* 7 (1988): 134-197; "Hermann Cohen and Rabbi Joseph Soloveitchik on Repentance," *Journal of Jewish Thought and Philosophy* 13, no. 1 (2004): 213-258; and "The Religious Philosophy of Rabbi Joseph Soloveitchik," *Tradition* 14, no. 2 (1974): 43-64; Dov Schwartz, *Haguto Ha'filosofit Shel Ha'rav Soloveitchik* (Alon Shvut: Tevunot, 2003); Pinhas Peli, "Repentant Man—A High Level in Rabbi Soloveitchik's Typology of Man," *Tradition* 18, no. 2 (1980): 135-159; David Hartman, *A Living Covenant: The Innovative Spirit in Traditional Judaism* (New York: The Free Press, 1985); and Aviezer Ravitzky, "Hakarah Mada'it U'devekut Datit Be'haguto Shel Ha'rav Soloveitchik: Bein Ha'rambam Le'neo-Kantianim," in *Herut Al Ha'luhot: Kolot Aherim Shel Ha'mahshavah Ha'datit* (Tel Aviv: Am Oved, 1999), 178-206.

6.5. TOWARDS THE FUTURE: ELIEZER SCHWEID

The emancipation opened an arena for Jewish thinkers to begin *de novo*, grounding themselves in different premises: dialectical truth, intellection and self-consciousness, revelation to which history adapted, and universal morality. With the unfolding of the twentieth century, the pattern and structure changed. The Holocaust moved thought away from the rationalistic process utilized or integrated by thinkers from Mendelssohn through Cohen and Rosenzweig, as well as from the open reliance on historical events. Reason proved itself impotent for many thinkers, and they relocated into an a-philosophical mode of religious thought grounded in revealed texts and metahistory.

Among these philosophers, Mordecai Kaplan, who did not include the Holocaust in his published thought, made a radical return to rationalism and historicism—even beyond that of emancipation-era thinkers. Others (Baeck, Berkovits, and Fackenheim) sought some form of resolution with history without diminishing their metahistorical grounding.

Parallel to the development of thought framed by metahistory and history, there was development of existentialist character. Martin Buber drew from the prophets to speak of a hidden and enduring inter-subjective relationship between God and man, which remained present in all of Israel. All subject-object relationships, as well as the event of the Holocaust (when man allowed God to be eclipsed and God hid His face), were secondary to this ultimate reality. Abraham Heschel spoke of God's yearning for dialogue with man, and the human failure to transcend ego so as to serve God. Even the Holocaust could be traced to the egoistic flight from God in the form of human self-aggrandizement—while it could be overcome if man would allow himself to reside within the field of God's perception, in the way of the prophets and Rabbi Akiva. Joseph Dov Soloveitchik was concerned with the marginalizing in modern times of the man of faith to the point of his devaluation, in a world in which the aggressive, majestic side of the human personality as created by God, was taking precedence. But there was a means of resolving the tension between the faithful and majestic man, that of *teshuvah*-instilled *Halakhah*, and he devoted himself to educating his students towards it.

I have suggested that a coherent, over-arching structure emerged with the emancipation, touching the formerly autonomous Jewish community at one end and the formerly exclusive Christian world on the other, with five different departure points in between. With the Holocaust, the coherence collapsed. That catastrophe engendered a shift to metahistorical considerations, which began at the edge of history and reason. Existential thinkers moved to the inner self's encounter with God (Buber's "Thou," Heschel's revealed deity beyond the border of the self, Soloveitchik's God encountered in the loneliness of the unique self). The work of Eliezer Schweid integrates post-emancipation sets of departure points, the religious philosophical responses of the Holocaust, and existentialism, into the context of the overall history of Jewish thought and into grander Jewish historical consciousness, setting the stage for the future.

INDEX OF NAMES

CPSIA information can be obtained at www.ICGtesting.com
Printed in the USA
LVOW101326090112

263030LV00003B/3/P